# DOING EDUCATIONAL RESEARCH

D1374259

# BOLD VISIONS IN EDUCATIONAL RESEARCH

## Series Editors

**Kenneth Tobin**
*The Graduate Center, City University of New York, USA*

**Joe Kincheloe**
*McGill University, Montreal, Canada*

### Editorial Board

**Heinz Sunker**, *Universität Wuppertal, Germany*
**Peter McLaren**, *University of California at Los Angeles, USA*
**Kiwan Sung**, *Woosong University, South Korea*
**Angela Calabrese Barton**, *Teachers College, New York, USA*
**Margery Osborne**, *Centre for Research on Pedagogy and Practice Nanyang Technical University, Singapore*
**Wolff-Michael Roth**, *University of Victoria, Canada*

## Scope

*Bold Visions in Educational Research* is international in scope and includes books from two areas: *teaching and learning to teach* and *research methods in education.* Each area contains multi-authored handbooks of approximately 200,000 words and monographs (authored and edited collections) of approximately 130,000 words. All books are scholarly, written to engage specified readers and catalyze changes in policies and practices.

Defining characteristics of books in the series are their explicit uses of theory and associated methodologies to address important problems. We invite books from across a theoretical and methodological spectrum from scholars employing quantitative, statistical, experimental, ethnographic, semiotic, hermeneutic, historical, ethnomethodological, phenomenological, case studies, action, cultural studies, content analysis, rhetorical, deconstructive, critical, literary, aesthetic and other research methods.

Books on *teaching and learning to teach* focus on any of the curriculum areas (e.g., literacy, science, mathematics, social science), in and out of school settings, and points along the age continuum (pre K to adult). The purpose of books on *research methods in education* is **not** to present generalized and abstract procedures but to show how research is undertaken, highlighting the particulars that pertain to a study. Each book brings to the foreground those details that must be considered at every step on the way to doing a good study. The goal is **not** to show how generalizable methods are but to present rich descriptions to show how research is enacted. The books focus on methodology, within a context of substantive results so that methods, theory, and the processes leading to empirical analyses and outcomes are juxtaposed. In this way method is not reified, but is explored within well-described contexts and the emergent research outcomes. Three illustrative examples of books are those that allow proponents of particular perspectives to interact and debate, comprehensive handbooks where leading scholars explore particular genres of inquiry in detail, and introductory texts to particular educational research methods/issues of interest. to novice researchers.

# DOING EDUCATIONAL RESEARCH

**Kenneth Tobin**

*The Graduate Center, City University of New York, USA*

**Joe L. Kincheloe**

*McGill University, Montreal, Canada*

SENSE PUBLISHERS
ROTTERDAM / TAIPEI

A C.I.P. record for this book is available from the Library of Congress.


Paperback   ISBN 90-77874-48-8
Hardback    ISBN 90-77874-01-1


Published by: Sense Publishers,
P.O. Box 21858, 3001 AW Rotterdam, The Netherlands

WWW.SENSEPUBLISHERS.COM


*Printed on acid-free paper*

# CONTENTS

**I**    **Introduction**    1

1    Doing Educational Research in a Complex World: Preface    3
*Joe L. Kincheloe and Kenneth Tobin*

2    Qualitative Research in Classrooms: Pushing the Boundaries of Theory and Methodology    15
*Kenneth Tobin*

3    We Make Our Road by Talking: Preparing to Do Dissertation Research    59
*Pam Joyce and Joelle Tutela*

**II**    **Ways of Doing Educational Research**    85

4    Research as Bricolage: Embracing Relationality, Multiplicity and Complexity    87
*Kathleen Berry*

5    Critical Cultural Studies Research: Bricolage in Action    117
*Shirley R. Steinberg*

6    Philosophical and Historical Research    139
*Barbara Thayer-Bacon and Diana Moyer*

7    Participatory Activist Research (Teams)/Action Research    157
*Greg Martin, lisahunter, and Peter McLaren*

8    Doing Critical Research in Mainstream Disciplines: Reflections on a Study of Black Female Individuation    191
*Aaron David Gresson III*

9    Criticality in Education Research    211
*Christine A. Lemesianou and Jaime Grinberg*

10    Conversation Analysis: Deconstructing Social Relations in the Making    235
*Wolff-Michael Roth*

11    On Hermeneutics: "Over and Above Our Wanting and Doing"    269
*David W. Jardine*

12    Motion-Sensitive Phenomenology    289
*Rebecca J. Lloyd and Stephen J. Smith*

13    Historical Research in Education    311
*Leila A. Villaverde, Joe L. Kincheloe, and Frances Helyar*

14    Literary Study as Educational Research: "More than a Pungent
and Corrosive School Story"    347
*William F. Pinar*

15    Speculations on Qualities of Difficult Knowledge in Teaching and
Learning: An Experiment in Psychoanalytic Research    379
*Alice J. Pitt and Deborah P. Britzman*

**III    Reflections: After Doing the Research**    403

16    Limits of Knowledge in the Physical Sciences    405
*Phil Frances Carspecken*

17    When the Research's Over, Don't Turn Out the Lights    439
*John Willinsky*

**Contributors**    457

**Index**    461

# I. INTRODUCTION

JOE L. KINCHELOE AND KENNETH TOBIN

# 1. DOING EDUCATIONAL RESEARCH IN A COMPLEX WORLD

*Preface*

The last half of the first decade of the twenty-first century is a strange time for educators. Many of the gains many of us thought we had made twenty years ago are under assault and many of the epistemological fights for the benefits of multiple ways of doing educational research in which we were forced to engage in the 1980s are breaking out again. The right-wing recovery movement—a reeducation of the public to accept Eurocentric and often male ways of both being and seeing—has shaped everything from the corporatization of the public space, the social positioning of poor people and people of color, the politics of public knowledge to the ways we conceptualize and validate research about education.

Indeed, it is a strange and challenging time. It is in such a Zeitgeist that we have put together *Doing Educational Research*. After having lived through this last 25 years, we have come to believe that a book dealing with diverse, innovative, challenging, and rigorous ways of conducting educational research that is both thought-provoking and practical is sorely needed. To accomplish this task, we have brought together some of the most innovative minds in contemporary educational research. We believe that the combined efforts of these scholars have produced a unique and highly usable text that will work to engage new generations of scholars while reinvigorating mature researchers in the complications and vagaries of doing educational research.

We find educational research intrinsically exciting and even mysterious. No matter how much the mavens of evidence-based inquiry in right-wing movements may insist that there is one right way to produce educational research, we are convinced of the power of multiple ways of seeing the world—the educational world in particular.

We believe that there are yet unexplored domains of human consciousness, cognition, teaching and learning. While we make no claim that we have achieved some transcendent way of approaching knowledge—not by a long shot—we do believe that some of the ideas and concepts explored here may lead the wisest among us to new domains of human thinking, exploring, being, and doing.

*K. Tobin & J. Kincheloe, (eds.), Doing Educational Research—A Handbook, 3–13.*
© 2006 Sense Publishers. All rights reserved.

A STARTING POINT FOR RECONCEPTUALIZING EDUCATIONAL RESEARCH

We construct *Doing Educational Research*, thus, as a starting point for something much greater than what is produced here. In the finest critical tradition the authors writing here initiate an exploration of what could be: new exciting ways of understanding educational phenomena, being students of the world, and changing those aspects of education that bring about injustice, pain, and suffering. Indeed, we believe in the power of the ideas the authors of this book delineate in their chapters, and in this context, we sense we are still in the early stages of a journey that will eventually change the basic ways we conceptualize both the act of knowledge production and the process of teaching and learning.

Employing these diverse ways of seeing and making meaning delineated in the following chapters, educational researchers begin to discern interconnections between ideas, physical objects, political decisions, social circumstances, and the teaching and learning process that have been previously ignored. A complex critical mode of educational research is aware of many different perspectives, the vantage points of diverse disciplines of knowledge (e.g., history, philosophy, economics, psychology, literary criticism, sociology, etc.) and transdisciplinary ways of seeing such as cultural studies. Educational researchers informed by these multiple perspectives understand relations between values and different interpretations of the world in general and education in particular. They understand the way one's location in the world or position in the web of reality (e.g., one's race, class, gender, sexuality, religion, ideology, epistemology, etc.) helps shape how one sees self and world. Educational researchers who do not understand these dynamics of positionality (the way one is situated in the world) and their impact on the questions we ask of education, schooling, politics, etc. are babes in the research woods. Their claims of objectivity fall on fallow ground.

The researchers who have written the following chapters understand these issues and work to follow them to new research spaces and intellectual places. With this in mind we want our readers to accompany our authors on these journeys. Indeed, we want them to recognize and understand the benefits of diverse ways of thinking and understanding the world and the cosmos of education. While we deeply respect those who have come before us and have helped us get where we are, we are ambitious—we want to go farther into the epistemological and ontological fog. While important benefits have historically come from educational research, past practice in the domain and the contemporary regressive efforts to reclaim the worst of such ways of researching are insufficient to the task of improving education.

Not only is there more to learn, more to be addressed, more to do, contemporary educational researchers must have the skill and will to fend off the regressive purveyors of one-truth, monological, and reductionistic ways of viewing education. In this context the researchers who crafted this book provide alternatives to the arrogance of positivist reductionism with a radical humility, a fallibilism, an awareness of the complexity of our task. We are aware of how little we know about the immensity of it all, but we push on. We view ourselves and our ways of seeing in the light of new horizons and new contexts, in the process recognizing previously unnoticed connections. Such connections alert us to new dimensions of what we are capable of engaging—the ones we previously missed. Critical, yet humble, we push for something better.

## BEYOND HYPERRATIONALITY: INTO A NEW DOMAIN OF CRITICALITY AND COMPLEXITY

Obviously, one of our most important concerns in this volume is to avoid the surge of hyperrationality and the instrumental rationality that characterizes it. Such a rationality involves an obsession with means rather than ends, method, procedure, and efficiency rather than an effort to understand the world so we can better serve the needs of human beings. As this hyperrationality limits questions to "how to" rather than "why should," we are reminded of the meticulous Nazi medical researcher obsessed with recording and analyzing the "cephalic index" (the shape of one's head) of those entering Hitler's death camps while ignoring the moral implications of genocide. Concurrently, we understand that resistance to such hyperrationalism does not necessitate the embrace of an irrationality characterized by a nihilism and relativism that offer no hope for scholarly growth or ethical action. In *Doing Educational Research* we avoid these untenable extremes and search for new and more compelling modes of reason—in other words, new forms of knowledge production that allow us to understand more so that we can engage in empowered action for our individual and social good.

As you read the following chapters, one begins to understand that all of the authors in this volume are searching for something better, are attempting to move into a new domain of educational research. All of them are concerned with the role of the self in research, the role of relationship(s) and multiple contexts in understanding pedagogical phenomena. With these concerns at the front burner of our consciousness, we attempt to blaze new trails into the epistemological (the branch of philosophy that deals with knowledge) and ontological domains (the branch of philosophy that deals with the nature of being in the world). In the epistemological domain we begin to realize that knowledge is stripped of its meaning when it stands alone. This holds profound implications in education and research because more positivistic forms of educational science have studied the world in a way that isolates the object of study, abstracts it from the contexts and interrelationships that give it meaning. Thus, to be a critical researcher that takes the complexity of the lived world into account, we have to study the world "in context." All of the authors here agree that we have to search for the interrelationships and contexts that give knowledge meaning while avoiding reliance upon decontextualized study.

Operating in the ontological realm educational researchers understand that to be in the world is to operate in context, in relation to other entities. Western Cartesian (coming from the tradition of the scientific method delineated by Rene Descartes in the 1600s) science has traditionally seen the basic building blocks of the universe as things-in-themselves. What much recent research in physics, biology, social science, the humanities, and cognitive science has posited involves the idea that relationships not things-in-themselves are the most basic properties of things in the world. In the ontological realm this would include human beings themselves. To *be* in the world is to be in relationship. People are not abstract individuals who live as fragments, in isolation from one another.

Humans come to be who they are and change who they are as a result of their interrelationships, their connections to the social sphere. They learn to think and talk via the socially constructed languages, deport themselves via cultural norms in their communities, and take care of themselves by imitating significant others in their immediate environment. Race, class, gender, sexual, religious, geographical place affiliations exert powerful influences on how they see themselves and their relation to the world. To be human is to be in relation to…. And, importantly, for those engaging in educational research, we understand that to be human is to possess the power to change, to be smarter than we now are, to engage in praxis—transformative action informed by the insights gained from our inquiry.

As most of us know by now, many observers have come to the conclusion that the simplicity of Cartesian rationalism and mainstream forms of educational knowledge production has not meet our needs. This is the realization that is being challenged by those who would attempt to recover the infallibility of Western traditions. The web of reality is composed of too many variables to be taken into account and controlled. Scientist Illya Prigogene (Prigogene & Stengers, 1984) labels this multitude of variables, "extraneous perturbations," meaning that one extraneous variable in an educational experiment can produce an expanding, exponential effect. So-called inconsequential entities can have a profound effect in a complex nonlinear universe. The shape of the physical and social world depends on the smallest part. The part, in a sense, is the whole, for via the action of any particular part, the whole in the form of transformative change may be seen. To exclude such considerations is to miss the nature of the interactions that constitute reality. The development of a reconceptualization of educational research does not mean that we simplistically reject all empirical science. It does mean, however, that we conceive of such scientific ways of seeing as one perspective in the complex web we refer to as reality.

ACCOUNTING FOR THE COMPLEXITY OF THE EDUCATIONAL COSMOS

All of the authors of *Doing Educational Research* attempt in their own way to account for this complexity and develop ways of seeing and being that avoid reductionism. As educational research comes to recognize the complexity of the lived world with its maze of uncontrollable variables, irrationality, non-linearity, and unpredictable interaction of wholes and parts, they begin to also see the interpretative dimension of reality. Educators have been "scammed" by a science that offers a monological process of making sense of the world. Critical researchers who appreciate the depth of this complexity maintain that we must possess and be able to deploy multiple methods of producing knowledge of the world. I (Joe Kincheloe)—borrowing from Norman Denzin and Yvonna Lincoln, Claude Levi-Strauss and Jacques Derrida—have referred to this elsewhere as the bricolage (Kincheloe, 2001, 2005; Kincheloe & Berry, 2004). Kathleen Berry and Shirley

Steinberg extend our understanding of the bricolage in their chapters in this volume.

Such methods provide us diverse perspectives on similar events and alert us to various relationships between events. In this complex context we understand that even when we use diverse methods to produce multiple perspectives on the world, different observers will produce different interpretations of what they perceive. Given different values, different ideologies, and different positions in the web of reality, different individuals will interpret what is happening differently. We never stand alone in the world, especially when we produce knowledge. We are connected and constantly affected by such connections in every step of the research act. Understanding these aspects of the connections between the knower and the known modifies the very way we approach knowledge, research design, research method, and interpretation.

When inquiry is conceptualized as a complex process we begin to understand that research is not something employed by solitary negotiators operating on their own. Educational researchers use language developed by others, live in specific contexts with particular ways of being and ways of thinking about thinking, have access to some knowledges and not others, and live and operate in a circumstance shaped by particular dominant ideological perspectives. In its effort to deal with previously neglected complexity, the view of research offered here appreciates the need to understand these contextual factors and account for them. Connected, critical research sensitive to the complexity of the lived world are not isolated individuals but people who understand the nature of their socio-cultural context as well as their overt and occluded relationships with others. Without such understandings of their own contextual embeddedness, individuals are not capable of understanding from where the prejudices and predispositions they bring to the research act originate. Any educational research that attempts to deal with the complexity of the lived world must address these contextual dynamics.

The editors and authors of *Doing Educational Research* maintain that these, social, philosophical, political and pedagogical theoretical knowledges are essential to the development of a rigorous and complex mode of educational research capable of lifting us to a new intellectual, agency-enhancing, action-based domain. In the social theoretical domain, for example, we might ask how does the existence of socio-economic inequality along the axes of race, class, gender, sexuality, physical ability, religion, and language influence the way we approach research. What happens to our research when we bring an understanding of power and justice to our analytical table? What is the effect of social theoretical insight on the subjectivity and context-dependency of knowledge production? Might, for example, the knowledge emerging here help shape the way we answer questions about the curriculum? About school purpose? About strategies for reform? About the control of knowledge? About the disturbing covert political agendas that motivate the research and research policies of particular political and educational leaders?

So-called evidence- based research and hyperrationalistic modes of positivist inquiry do not help us answer such questions. How does evidence-based research help us answer questions, about the purpose of schools? Social theory viewed in relation to pedagogical theory in this context profoundly enhances the ability of educators as critical thinkers to evaluate the worth of particular educational purposes, public knowledge policies, articulations of curriculum, and evaluation practices. Indeed, as you read the various chapters of *Doing Educational Research*, it becomes increasingly obvious the importance each of the authors places on such social theoretical insights. The editors and authors believe that these theoretical modes help educational researchers—as well as teachers and students—escape the well regulated and administered world that unbridled rationalism works to construct. Critical, connected researchers sensitive to the complexity of socio-educational reality use these theoretical tools to sidestep new models of social control that put a chokehold on individual and social freedom. They use these tools to enhance their own and other individuals' agency.

As we engage in research to enhance our agency to fight the power of oppression in its contemporary Hydra-headed forms, the researchers operating here draw upon a critical complex theory of epistemology to provide insight into the nature of pedagogical knowledge. Rejecting hyperrationalistic notions that there is a monolithic knowable world explained by positivist science, an epistemology of complexity views the cosmos as a human construction—a social creation. The world is "officially" what dominant groups of humans perceive it to be. This complicates our notion of theory. Positivistic/rationalistic theories were simple to the extent that they claimed truth-value on the basis of how they corresponded to *true* reality. More complex, counter-positivistic theories study the various philosophical and social groundings of diverse theories, learn from them, and understand the social construction of them all. In the theoretical speculations grounding our research, we take this understanding of social construction and add the critical theoretical, hermeneutical, feminist, and fallibilist dimensions. Our pluralistic and multiperspectival orientation is omnipresent, as we seek benefits from a variety of social, cultural, philosophical, theoretical positions.

In other work I (Joe Kincheloe) have used the term critical constructivism (2005) to denote my epistemological perspective and postformalism (Kincheloe & Steinberg, 1993) to denote my cognitive theoretical orientation. A short description of critical constructivism might be helpful at this point to ground the theoretical maneuvers operating in this reconceptualization of critical thinking. An epistemology of constructivism has maintained that nothing represents a neutral perspective, in the process shaking the epistemological foundations of modernist Cartesian grand narratives. Indeed, no truly objective way of seeing exists. Nothing exists before consciousness shapes it into something we can perceive.

What appears as objective reality is merely what our mind constructs, what we are accustomed to seeing. The knowledge that the world yields has to be interpreted by men and women who are part of that world. Whether we are attempting to understand the music of West Africa, the art of Marcel Duchamp, the social theory of Max Horkheimer, the epistles on indigenous knowledge of George Dei, the curriculum theory of William Pinar, or the insights into hermeneutics of David Jardine, the constructivist principle tacitly remains. For example, most analysts don't realize that the theory of perspective developed by fifteenth-century artists constituted a scientific convention. It was simply one way of portraying space and held no *absolute* validity. Thus, the structures and phenomena we observe in the physical world are nothing more than creations of our measuring and categorizing mind.

A critical constructivist epistemology forces educational researchers to ask:

- Does much of the research conducted in the field of education simply reflect the context, values, and assumptions of researchers?
- In light of such constructions, what is really meant by the term objectivity?
- By what processes are our constructions of the world shaped?
- Are our psychosocial dispositions beyond our conscious control?
- Do we simply surrender our perceptions to the determinations of our environment, and our social, cultural context?
- What does this process of construction have to do with the education of pedagogical researchers

## DIVERSITY AND EDUCATIONAL RESEARCH: THE POWER OF CONTEXTUALIZATION

Researchers who understand complexity understand why we ask these questions; they understand that knowledge producers, teachers, and students perceive the world from a center located within themselves, shaped by the social and cultural context in which they operate, and framed by languages that contain within them tacit views of the world. As they dig deeper into the contexts surrounding the construction of self and the lived world of education broadly defined as well as schooling, research sensitive to complexity find that students from different racial, ethnic, and class locations will relate to education in different ways. They learn from their studies that if students who fall far from the middle class, white, English speaking mainstream are not provided assistance by insightful teachers, they will often become the victims of decontextualized ways of producing knowledge about education. Critical researchers aware of these complex dynamics understand that such students will not fail because of some inability or lack of intelligence but because of a set of forces unleashed by their relation to what is often labeled the "common culture." Indeed, we learn that the more educators use the term, common culture, in an unexamined way, the more those students who fall outside of its boundaries will fail.

Researchers who understand this contextual complexity appreciate the notion that Western culture and Western colonized cultures do not present a homogeneous way of life but a domain of difference shaped by unequal power relations. They understand that they must act on an appreciation of the way these differences shape people's relationships to various institutions. If everyone is seen as a part of some narrow articulation of a common culture, then those who don't fit the mainstream criteria will find themselves looking into the society's institution as unworthy outsiders. Critical complex researchers work to understand these important social tendencies, make sure that steps are taken to include everyone in a high quality education, and avoid the deficitism that emerges when such ways of seeing are disregarded.

The way these factors play out in the everyday life of school is multidimensional, complex, and always significant. When classroom instruction is driven by technical standards with their fragmented factoids, the same pedagogical actions take place repeatedly without regard for who succeeds and who fails—in particular, what social groups succeed or fail over time. A creative way of merely delivering content, no matter how ingenious it may be, still works to produce much the same results as long as the epistemological assumptions are the same. Thus, to avoid falling into these age-old traps, researchers must help educational leaders, politicians, and teachers understand both the social context that shapes learners and the epistemological context that molds the way knowledge is viewed and thus educational goals are forged in the classroom. Such contextual awarenesses provide teachers with a monitoring system that allows them a cognizance of the multidimensional effects of their pedagogy.

The ability to employ contextualization in the pursuit of multiple perspectives is an important skill promoted by the researchers the editors and authors of *Doing Educational Research*. As researchers begin to discern the multiple perspectives that always surround any topic, they examine such viewpoints in relation to one another. The insights derived from such an activity lead directly to new ways of seeing and appreciating the complexity of the cosmos. In this context we believe that our approaches to research are particularly important in this disturbing era where standardized curricula are being implemented in numerous national and local educational systems.

When such policies are pursued—on the basis of reductionistic, decontextualized, epistemologically naïve research—the ability of teachers to develop pedagogies for their unique students is subverted. In such decontextualized situations teachers are disempowered—teaching itself is deprofessionalized. The prerogative of master teachers to act on their knowledge of and participation in critical and complex research in a way that accounts for the multiple contexts of schooling and its students is undermined. Their capacity to study the contexts in which knowledge is produced and validated is subverted. In such simplified standards-based, test-driven classrooms, it doesn't matter who students are or what their specific needs may be—the curriculum has already been mandated on the basis of pseudo-rigorous research. The views of research presented in this volume can help researchers, teachers, and other individuals begin to free us from this ever-worsening pedagogical/epistemological crisis.

In this contemporary quagmire of regressive knowledge production, teaching and learning are becoming less immediate, less connected to the conditions of the community, less involved with what motivates students, less concerned with moral and ethical issues in the life of the school, less connected with other bodies of knowledge produced in different situations, less aware of the ideological motivations that drive educational and political leaders. Moreover, the rationalistic policies emerging from this decontextualized and misleading research about education remove schooling even further from the socio-economic and cultural changes surrounding it. As the capital driven, global information society changes the nature of jobs and the tools required for them—not to mention the need for new citizenship skills in a new transnational knowledge order—teachers and students drift along in low-level memory work far removed from the commerce of everyday life. The educational researchers writing in *Doing Educational Research* understand the context of socio-economic, political, and cultural change, so that teachers and students can keep ahead of it and help direct it in positive, democratic, and just ways.

Educational reforms based on decontextualized, rationalistic research remove teachers and students from an understanding of the compelling intellectual and political issues of the day. This is a fatal pedagogical mistake as it sets up a dichotomy between school and the "real world." Such a division will always undermine motivation, as teachers and students come to see the mandated activities of school as trivial and irrelevant. Critical complex researchers understand that to be able to integrate these understandings into their pedagogies, all educators must appreciate the way the world has changed in the last few decades. The rate of socio-economic, political, and cultural change has accelerated and in this process identities are no longer as stable as individuals are bombarded with information to the point of incomprehensibility. Traditional forms of problem solving where variables are limited and are assumed to act in predictable ways are less useful in an era marked by the complexity of multiple causality and as many have termed it, chaos. With globalization and new forms of information production and communication individuals in various fields have been confronted with more ill structured and divergent problems, cultural misunderstandings and value conflicts, and problems of power inequities. It is apparent that rigorous educational research would include an understanding of this new context and the forms of knowledge, skills, and cognitive abilities needed to deal with it successfully.

Critical research aware of the complexity of these new contexts understand that even the era of images and pictorial representations ushered in by television has never been adequately addressed—if addressed at all—by mainstream educational research and integrated into schooling. Media literacy, a set of skills so central to citizenship and an understanding of the contemporary world, is provided little respect in the mainstream educational knowledge climate of the last half of the first decade of the twenty-first century. When such imagery is not integrated with hypertext and cyberspace schools fall even further behind cultural and informational change. Those students who are conversant with such dynamics learn about them on their non-school time. While their insights and abilities often border on genius, there are still many aspects of the contemporary techno-electronic landscape that are missed by such students.

Nevertheless, the technological abilities obtained by such students exacerbates the gulf between the haves and have nots in alarming ways. Technical rationalistic educational policies that emphasize memorization of data are devised as if we are still living in an oral culture. The cognitive and pedagogical processes required by such decontextualized policies hearken back to medieval schooling where students memorized texts because there was so little literature in print. The editors and authors of *Doing Educational Research* understand both the importance of these new

11

developments in communications and the necessity of devising new methods of researching their complex roles in the contemporary education and schooling.

In the context of cyberspace we possess less and less knowledge of the cultural location, the human contributions, the socio-political and economic interests that shape information. In those few classrooms where students are asked who produced the data they downloaded off the Internet the night before, they are often at a loss to answer such a query. They have never considered such a question or its multi-dimensional implications. Information in such situations has lost its borders, it moves and flows in the non-linear and instantaneous ways that human thought operates. Traditional forms of knowledge as it is researched in reductionistic designs and as it is organized in books and official interpretations are undermined in this new context. A subversive element implicitly operates that challenges the informational status quo but at the same time allows power wielders who control informational pipelines to covertly promote data that serves their economic, social, and political interests. Obviously, such a dangerous reality demands new forms of knowledge work and educational inquiry. In an era where the power of economic institutions—especially in relation to control of information—has risen to unprecedented heights the development of our ability to delineate the hidden interests of the knowledge cyber-technology provides us so abundantly is crucial to the future of democratic education. The need for innovative and rigorous forms of educational research has never been greater.

## EDUCATION RESEARCH AS COURSE REQUIREMENTS

Traditionally graduate studies have involved research and were regarded as research degrees. Indeed, when I (Ken) was involved in higher education in Australia, advanced degrees that involved coursework (such as honors and masters degrees) were regarded as inferior to those that were research-only degrees. Of course many students who started out on research-only degrees floundered at the beginning, especially if they were not connected to a research group to provide scaffolding associated with how to do and learn from research, what to read, and how to present what you learn from research. Research groups also provided for participation in various forms of peer review and dissemination at brown bag seminars and more formal colloquia. In the sciences research groups have a long history that continues to the present time. In contrast, this was not such a tradition in education where individual researchers often worked independently throughout their career. Perhaps in education it was easier to see a rationale for two trends that have profound impacts on graduate degrees in education—the mergence of coursework as a partial fulfillment of degree requirements and the creation of methods courses designed to teach the foundations of educational research.

In particular circumstances both of these trends make sense—especially if degree candidates cannot participate conveniently in appropriate research groups. However, as is often the case with institutionalization of such trends, rules are created to specify the authorized pathways for obtaining a degree and standards come to be defined in terms of adherence to the rules. Hence, in doctoral and masters degrees students may be required to take courses in specified areas irrespective of the knowledge they need to attain their scholarly goals and undertake research in a chosen area. Also, method is separated from the substantive research focus and many universities embrace a bankrupt dichotomy of qualitative and quantitative research methods, stipulating that all students should take at least one course in each area.

In compiling this Handbook we did not envision it only as a textbook in qualitative methods courses—though it may find uses in research methods courses. The chapter authors raise issues of epistemology and ontology that are germane to the doing of educational research by individual researchers and research groups. Every chapter serves as an introduction to learn more about the issues it raises and thereby is a foundation for deeper learning to support inquiry in education. For many educational researchers it makes more sense to pursue deeper studies through focused reading in the areas we explore in the Handbook rather than stipulating that graduate students take a time out to study methods that are not relevant to their scholarly interests. Ironically, the tendency to specify particular methods in educational research is not found in the same way in the sciences where it would be unthinkable that, for example, the mass spectrometry group would become adept at electro fluorescent spectroscopy or that theoretical physicists would do any required laboratory methods.

The issues raised in the chapters of the Handbook are germane to the practice of educational research wherever it is undertaken and, in the spirit of bricolage, complementary methods are explored that have the potential to add value to ongoing investigations as well as to serve as an aid to planning research. Furthermore, the issues addressed in the Handbook can comprise a critical framework for review of research and the associated claims; including policies and practices that truncate the agency of scholars in the name of higher standards. Not the least of these is the regression toward prescribed standards for educational research—standards that embrace an oversimplified grasp of the natural sciences and adherence to positivism and causal relationships between over-reduced social systems defined in terms of variables.

## REFERENCES

Kincheloe, J. (2001). Describing the bricolage: Conceptualizing a new rigor in qualitative research. *Qualitative Inquiry, 7,* 679-92.
Kincheloe, J. (2005a). On to the next level: Continuing the conceptualization of the bricolage. *Qualitative Inquiry, 11,* 323-350.
Kincheloe, J. (2005b). *Critical constructivism.* New York: Peter Lang.
Kincheloe J., & Berry K. (2004). *Rigor and complexity in educational research: Conceptualizing the bricolage.* London: Open University Press.
Kincheloe, J. & Steinberg S. (1993). A tentative description of post-formal thinking: The critical confrontation with cognitive theory. *Harvard Educational Review, 63,* 296-320.
Prigogene, I. & Stengers I. (1984). *Order out of chaos.* New York: Basic Books.

KENNETH TOBIN

# 2. QUALITATIVE RESEARCH IN CLASSROOMS

*Pushing the Boundaries of Theory and Methodology*

My first studies of science classrooms, undertaken in Australia and the United States were quasi-experiments and involved investigations of the relationships between teaching and science achievement. For more than a decade I participated in a program of research that explored verbal interactions, teacher and student participation in science classes, and achievement. I was also interested in learning environments and issues such as formal reasoning ability and locus of control[1]. Although I felt that I was learning a great deal from this research, I experienced several sources of frustration. First, making sense of teaching and learning in terms of variables was extremely reductionist and my research involved large sets of variables and complex statistical algorithms (unconvincing processes of breaking down and packing together—never quite capturing an elusive whole). In many instances the most salient features of classroom life seemed to be outside of the statistical model and I found myself writing more and more about what I referred to in those days as context—the factors I had not identified a priori; that were surely shaping what happened in the classes in which I was an observer. Second, macroscopic social forces, such as race, social class, equity and policy mandates were not represented convincingly as quantified variables, even when multivariate approaches allowed me to represent such factors with clusters of variables. Furthermore, macro social forces, such as poverty and stipulations for high stakes tests, seemed to be overwhelmingly important in comparison to within-school and -classroom variables (e.g., how questions were posed and answered). I sought an approach that was amenable to understanding how learning in science classes occurred within a complex social system in which what happened within schools and classrooms was saturated by macroscopic forces such as race, social class and state and national level policies. Third, I wanted to employ a methodology that was more closely aligned with the ways in which scientists do science, when they are involved in explorations of new areas in which there is much to be learned. I wanted to explore and probe macro social forces that could be described and interpreted without a need to reduce and quantify. My search for a new approach was deeply theoretical and the transformations from quasi experiments to interpretive forms of inquiry were not revolutionary in the sense that there was an abrupt shift. Instead, over a 10-year period my methodology evolved to be consistent with sociocultural theory, using collective forms of qualitative inquiry to build understandings of social life; informed by multiple voices, diverse participants, and dialectical relationships that seek to transcend part-whole dichotomies.

*K. Tobin & J. Kincheloe, (eds.), Doing Educational Research—A Handbook, 15–58.*

## ABOUT THIS CHAPTER

Research in classrooms focuses on better understanding teaching and learning, using what is learned to create and sustain improved learning environments. The methodology I present in this chapter is grounded in sociocultural theory and an ethical stance that obligates me to adhere to criteria that acknowledge that, while education research is central to effective practice, it is a privilege and must be undertaken in ways that meet four authenticity criteria, which I describe later in the chapter. The remainder of this chapter contains seven sections. First, I address the necessity for research with human subjects to be ethically sound, undertaken with the informed consent of all participants. In subsequent sections I review participant observer forms of research, how to make sense of data resources, involving students as researchers, undertaking auto/ethnography and auto/biography, and incorporating microanalyses into critical ethnography. Finally, I conclude the chapter with discussions about judging whether or not a study meets the criteria for high quality, authenticity and credibility, doing research at different grain sizes, and generalizability.

## RESEARCH WITH HUMAN SUBJECTS

When I commenced education research in 1973 there was no necessity to obtain approval from an Institutional Review Board (IRB) or its equivalent for research with human subjects. However, because of many high profile ethical problems with research involving human subjects (mainly in the sciences), peer review processes have been established in most countries to protect the rights of human subjects involved in research. Here I address the central issues associated with obtaining and maintaining informed consent of participants in a study and enacting ethical research practices.

### Negotiating Entry

My first step in getting involved in research is to talk to teachers about the possibilities before I have worked out all the details. Initial contacts are oral and open ended, allowing the participants opportunities to make suggestions. My purposes in doing this are to ascertain whether the teacher is comfortable with what I have in mind and to provide opportunities for her[2] to make suggestions about possible foci, likely participants, and the duration of the study. For example, Donovan, a first year science teacher from an inner city high school, frequently complained to me about his students and the school. He and I were serving together on an advisory group assembled by the regional coordinator from an urban school district. Based on numerous conversations in and out of the group Donovan and I agreed to co-teach his science classes. Since the regional coordinator was present during many of our conversations she encouraged our collaboration and facilitated the necessary permissions from the school district.

Donovan and I made an appointment with his principal and requested her consent for us to coteach Donovan's classes and approach the school district and the university IRBs for permission to undertake a longitudinal study of the teaching and learning of science. The principal was highly enthusiastic, gave her approval, and came with us to discuss our proposal with the coordinator of the *Incentive* small learning community, one of 10 small schools within a larger school of about 2,000 students. I took notes and promised that prior to seeking formal approval to undertake the project I'd write a draft incorporating their suggestions and get further input from them. Subsequently, the classroom teacher, principal, and small learning community coordinator all agreed to a multi-phase project involving coteaching and then, subject to the research being formally approved, coteaching with research.

*Getting Started*

Although we had agreed to coteach, Donovan preferred to enact a peripheral role, observing my teaching and struggles to succeed. Even though it did not work out as intended, coteaching was important because it allowed me to begin teaching, get to know students, co-plan lessons with Donovan, and videotape lessons so that we could critically examine our teaching and the students' learning, and identify changes we'd like to make. The videotaping and associated analyses were not done for research purposes, but with the goal of improving learning environments. Even so, the students and their parents or guardians had to give their permission to be videotaped, using the standard permission forms employed by the school district when the purposes of videotaping are for instructional improvement. Approvals to videotape for the purposes of instructional improvement and professional development allowed us to focus on the priority of student learning, afforded me gaining valuable experience of this classroom and school, and provided all of us with experiences and time to become comfortable with our interactions being videotaped. Coteaching and videotaping became a part of what was regarded as normal practice in Donovan's science class, a fact that was highlighted in the proposal to the IRB—since the research did not require a significant change to the practices already approved by parents/guardians, school, and district.

During this period of about six weeks the IRB approvals needed to do research were being prepared by us and reviewed by panels in the university and school district. These were submitted simultaneously despite the contradiction that the approval of each was contingent on approval of the other.

A critical issue was when to commence videotaping and how to deal with the situation of students not returning parental consent forms. We discussed the issue with the principal and agreed to a procedure that allowed us to start once a reasonable proportion of the consent forms were returned. In this instance, one student did not assent to being videotaped and the parent/guardian consent forms were returned over a period of two weeks. Once we had received more than a third of the signed consent forms we started videotaping, taking precautions not to inadvertently capture images of students for whom consent had not been obtained. We

17

asked students to assist us by avoiding movement into the line of the camera. Even though we were videotaping we did not change other aspects of what might be regarded as normal classroom practice. For example, seating arrangements were not changed to make it easier to avoid videotaping particular students. Our primary goal was to ensure that no students were disadvantaged by our decision to use video resources to improve our teaching and the benefits of videotaping interactions were shared among all participants.

Initially we placed the camera at the side of the classroom, focusing on the coteachers and only zooming in on students whose consent forms were returned. However, when all consent forms were on file the coteachers hand-held a small digital camera or positioned it on a desk to capture different forms of interaction as they unfolded.

*From Instructional Improvement to Research*

My perspectives on obtaining approval for undertaking research with human subjects are guided by the Belmont Report (1979), which addressed three general principles: respect, beneficence, and justice. Proposals to the IRB should show clearly how the research respects human participants by maximizing their autonomy to make choices about their participation, that there is a balance favoring the benefits associated with being involved in research compared to the harms from being involved, and that the practices involved in doing the research and distributing the benefits and harms are equitable.

The proposal to the IRB should address the ways in which human subjects will be recruited to participate in the study, what they will be told as part of the informed consent process, how they can exercise their autonomy during the conduct of the study, and the benefits and harms associated with being involved, withdrawing, and staying involved. Details should be provided on the scope of the study, defining the boundaries of what the study is about and being precise about where the study will take place and its duration. Assurances also should be given about anonymity and confidentiality and the ways in which data will be stored, used, made available to others, and protected from tampering. If the data are to become part of a database this should be made clear and if data will be destroyed at a particular time the dates should be specified.

Once our proposal was written, and Donovan agreed to it, we obtained letters of support from the regional coordinator, school principal, and small learning community coordinator. I then prepared informed consent protocols to be signed by the people we would invite to be involved. In this study the primary participants were high school students who were less than 18 years of age, and therefore could not consent. Accordingly, we produced two forms, one to obtain consent from parents/guardians and the other for students to assent to be involved in the study. Only students who signed an assent form were given a consent form to take to their parents/guardians.

Good morning. I am Dr. Ken Tobin from the Graduate Center of the City University of New York. I am a researcher who focuses on improving the quality of learning and teaching science and mathematics in urban schools.

Today I'd like to invite you to get involved in a study that will involve me, your teacher, and three other teachers and their classes. Being involved in the research will involve me coming to your class about once a week and carefully watching what happens, taking videotape of what happens, and using audiotapes to record what is said in whole class and small group settings. I will do my best to assist your teacher to teach you science and when I can I will help your teacher to respond to questions and assist with teaching the lesson.

In addition to watching science lessons your teacher and I will study the work you produce in class and we may ask you questions about what happens and why certain things happen the way they do. We may invite you to be interviewed and you can fill out a short form to request an interview with your teacher or me. Anything you say will be kept confidential and we will never use your actual name in anything you write. You will be asked to let us have a name we would use in our writing about what we learn.

I will watch the videotapes and select parts that interest me. I will then analyze these tapes. Usually I will write my impressions of what happens, and analyze how the teacher interacts with students and how the students interact with one another. I will study how the teacher and students talk to one another. I will examine the loudness and pitch of sentences and words and I will see how pauses are used in the talk of the teacher and students.

I will discuss what I learn from the research with students in interviews and in small groups that I call cogenerative dialogues. During interviews I may use video clips, which will vary in length from 30 seconds to 2 minutes in length. If your images are in the video clip I will ask your permission to use the video clip.

About once a month I will select short video clips to show to the whole class so that I can discuss what I see together and work out how to improve the quality of teaching and learning science. I want these discussions to be serious and we should all show respect for one another and not make fun of anyone who is shown in the video clip. If your image is in the video clip I plan to use I will ask your permission.

As part of this study I will look at your performance on quizzes and tests so that I can see how your involvement and work relates to your achievement in science.

If you agree to be involved in the study you should sign the assent form and then take a consent form for a parent or guardian to sign. When I have both forms signed I will copy them and give you a copy of each. The forms have a place for you to show whether or not you agree to have what you say recorded and for me to videotape you during the class.

You can decide at any time not to be involved in the study. To indicate your decision to withdraw you would let your teacher or me know and at that time I would not audiotape you, interview you, or use any video images of you in the research.

*Figure 2.1. Sample recruitment script to be presented orally (not read).*

Because coteaching, videotaping, and conversations about instructional practice were part of the normal day in Donovan's classes there were no additional burdens placed on participants as a result of this study. Accordingly, we were able to apply for what is referred to as expedited review from the IRB—a request that was approved by the IRB Chair, allowing the proposal to be reviewed by two members of the IRB and the committee chair. Because of Donovan's official relationship with the students I was designated to collect the assent and consent forms to minimize feelings of coercion for people to be involved in the study.

---

CONSENT FOR MINOR TO PARTICIPATE IN RESEARCH

**Title of the Study:** Use of research to improve the quality of science education in an urban high school.
**Invitation to Participate:** Your child is being asked to participate in this research because he/she is a student in a school that has agreed to participate in a study of the teaching and learning of science in an urban high school.
**Purpose:** This study seeks to enhance science education in urban schools. The study will explore how students' learning of science is affected by teaching and the ways in which your child and other students participate in the class.
**Procedures:** During this study your child may be videotaped or audiotaped. He/she may be asked to take part in interviews. In addition, test scores and school records may be accessed. Selected excerpts from the videotapes will be used in the dissemination of what is learned from this study.
**Risks:** Except for the embarrassment of seeing him- or herself on videotape segments shown to the class there are no potentially harmful risks related to participating in this study. Your child's images will not be shown to the whole class without first obtaining his or her permission.
**Benefits:** As a result of participation, your child's awareness about school and learning may be increased, particularly in science. The study provides students with valuable insights into different approaches and practices in teaching and learning science.
**Withdrawal:** Participation in the study is voluntary and if your child decides to participate, he or she can withdraw without any penalty at any time. Participation in the study is not a factor in determining your child's grade or standing in any course.
**Alternatives:** You may choose not to allow your child to participate in this study. If so, he/she will not be videotaped, audiotaped, or interviewed, and no references to him/her will be made in the reporting of this study.
**Compensation:** Your child receives no financial compensation for his/her participation.
**Confidentiality:** All information collected in this study will be kept private and your child will not be identified by name. The researcher will keep the audio- and videotapes from this study in a locked filing cabinet. Only the researchers will have access to these tapes.
**Subject Rights:** If you have questions about your child's rights as a participant in this study, you can contact the IRB Administrator, Gotham City University, (367) 373-2724, IRB@gcu.edu.
**Conclusion:** You have been given the opportunity to ask questions and have had them answered to your satisfaction. You have read and understand the consent form. You agree to allow _____ to participate in this research. Upon signing below, you will receive a copy of the consent form.

| | | |
|---|---|---|
| I agree for my child to be videotaped | Yes | No |
| _____ (Initial) | | |
| I agree for my child to be audiotaped | Yes | No |
| _____ (Initial) | | |

| Name Parent/Guardian | Signature | Date |
|---|---|---|

---

*Figure 2.2. Sample consent form for the participation of minors.*

The IRB required an example of the script I would use to recruit participants in the study. Although I did not intend to read to students and other potential participants I informed the IRB that the text of the script contained below in Figure 1 contained the essence of what I would say to possible participants.

After a statement like the one in the script is presented orally to students they would be advised about how to get involved in the research should they have an interest in participation. Involvement requires understanding fully what is involved, that is informed consent, and a signed willingness to participate. If the participants are less than 18 years of age they are not able to consent to be involved and a two stage process is needed—assent from the student and consent from the parent/guardian.

---

### CONSENT OF PARENT OR GUARDIAN

I am Ken Tobin, a professor in Urban Education at the Graduate Center of the City University of New York. I am doing research in New York City public schools in an effort to learn more about how to improve the quality of teaching and learning science. I can be reached at (737) 327-3437. Alternatively you can email me at ktobin@gcu.edu.

You have previously consented for your child to be involved in a study of the teaching and learning of science at his or her school. As part of this research I have used videotape to explore how learning happens as the teacher and students interact with one another and materials from the classroom. I want to use short segments of the video to educate others about what I have learned from the research. Your child's image is included in one or more of the short excerpts I want to use in meetings with science teachers and with researchers at professional meetings throughout the world.

I am requesting permission to use your child's image for the purposes of professional development for teachers and disseminating what I have learned from the research. You can view the videotape at the school or request a compact disk or digital videodisk containing the images for which I am requesting your permission.

If you have questions about your about your rights as a participant in this study, you can contact IRB Administrator, Gotham City University, (737) 327-3437, IRB@gcu.edu.

Please read the following, select Yes or No to indicate your preferences, and sign below.

Circle Yes or No as appropriate:
I allow you to use the video segments that contain my child's images: Yes     No
I would like to view the video segments at school:                    Yes    No
I would like a CD or DVD containing the video segments:               Yes    No

I give permission for you to use video clips that include the image of _____
(insert child's name) in professional development activities with teachers and meetings of researchers to let others know what has been learned from the research.
Print name: _____ Date: _____
Signature: _____

---

*Figure 2.3. Informed consent protocol for additional uses of videotape.*

There are numerous ways in which potential participants can be informed about the purposes of a study. The process starts with an explanation like the one provided in Figure 2.1. The next step can involve distributing assent forms to an entire class, explaining what the various sections mean and allowing those who are willing to participate to complete them. A potential problem is that some students might feel coerced into participation by peer pressure—the classroom providing a context in which students might be influenced one way or the other by the presence of peers and perhaps the teacher. For this reason I prefer to meet with students one-on-one in an office away from the classroom. I can then speak to them about the study, answer questions, assure them that participation is voluntary, and distribute the consent forms to students who assent. Figure 2.2 contains an example of an informed consent protocol to be signed by a parent/guardian.

Additional informed consent protocols were needed for the adults participating in the study, in this case other teachers who were colleagues of Donovan's, school and small learning community administrators, parents and guardians, non-teaching assistants, and school police. Also, because I would use videotape for a variety of purposes I prepared an additional consent form for these purposes. It is provided above in Figure 2.3.

*Sharing Opportunities to Participate*

---

Name: _____    Email address: _____

Please check any that apply and put your request for an interview in the box at the back of the room.

I would like to be interviewed about the science class from _____ (write the day or date).
I would like to be interviewed about what generally happens in my science classroom.
I would like to be interviewed about my participation in science.
I would like to be interviewed about the teaching of science.
I would like to be interviewed about why we do science and what science might be like.

---

*Figure 2.4. Protocol to request an interview.*

In interpretive research it is customary to speak to students informally about what they are doing and why they are doing it. Informal interviews take the form of conversations and can occur as a lesson unfolds. Usually, the conversations are quiet and relatively short. Efforts are made not to disadvantage any students by taking too much of the time of the person being interviewed or by distracting others. Informal interviews are augmented by formal interviews with students selected to provide insights into what is happening and why it is happening. Interviews might also be set up for students to check on what is being learned from a study and to get participants' perspectives on the patterns of coherence and the contradictions that have been noted. In the selection of participants from a stakeholder group (e.g., students), I use a process that involves the use of opposites. I never use random selection. The participants are chosen because their perspectives are judged to be worth knowing and of value to the research. I select someone who has something to contribute to the study. Having selected a first person to interview, I then select a second who is as different from the first as possible. In this way participants are selected serially based on their differences from one another and contingently—based on what I'd like to learn next. However, there may be participants who want to be interviewed and do not get selected. Accordingly, to be fair, I use a process to allow students to request to be interviewed by filling out a form (Figure 2.4) that is available at the back of the classroom. In this way participants are not prevented from experiencing the benefits of being interviewed in a study (and if there is harm from being interviewed it is shared out).

*Negotiation of Approval*

I ran into difficulties with the IRB when I moved to a new institution and did not understand the culture of the peer group at my new university. Whereas there was a special IRB panel to review education research at my previous university, here there was just one panel for all research in the social sciences. Two issues caused me most concern, essentially because I did not understand the difference between writing a proposal for a funding agency and writing one for IRB approval. An initial stumbling block concerned an IRB request for research questions and hypotheses. My knee-jerk reaction was that the request reflected an epistemological position that I rejected because in ethnography the questions are broad and only narrow down as the study progresses. Usually I do not write hypotheses and focus on identifying patterns and associated contradictions that relate to what is happening and why it is happening. However it is clear that my knee-jerk thoughts are wrong. The IRB wants to know what a researcher will study and what she expects to learn from the research. Their request makes sense if the IRB is to do its work of peer review. Providing the information also makes sense from the perspective of good ethnography since it provides a baseline for what Guba and Lincoln refer to as ontological authenticity (discussed in the next section of this chapter), whereby a researcher is obliged to show that her initial constructions change as a result of doing the research (Guba & Lincoln, 1989). Hence, providing the IRB with hypotheses is a first step in establishing that a qualitative study has ontological authenticity.

The questions you provide to the IRB should be broad and cover the domain of your research interests. For each broad question also provide five more specific questions to explicate the likely areas in which the study will be undertaken. Hypothesize on the likely answers to these specific questions—based on what you know now. Nobody will hold you accountable for these answers. By responding in this way I define the scope of my study and the boundaries for which I am seeking approval. If, in the course of doing the research, I stray from within those boundaries, I need to seek additional approval from the IRB. This can prove to be extremely important in the event that a participant or her guardian complains about some aspect of the research. You want to be sure that what you do has been approved by the IRB—so your predictions are important. For example, one of my graduate students recently undertook research with middle school students in inner city schools. One of the students she interviewed raised the question of sexual harassment and the researcher decided to ask other participants about sexual harassment in her interviews. Almost immediately there was a protest from a concerned parent, pointing out that she had not been informed that questions about sex were part of the research. The topic was beyond the scope of the informed consent and had not been approved by the IRB.

Thanks for taking the time to speak to me this afternoon. I now have a clear idea of some of the concerns you have about my proposed research "Use of research to improve the quality of urban science education."

The ethnography planned for each of the four case studies is longitudinal and researchers will examine the ways in which the teachers and students interact when science is taught in regular classroom settings and when the teacher and students interact in cogenerative dialogues. Past research in urban high schools, in Philadelphia, suggests that the students learn to interact with one another and the teacher in cogenerative dialogues and build new procedures for interacting with peers and the teacher. Similarly, the teacher learns to successfully interact with students, listen and learn from them, and effectively deal with their ways of interacting. Cogenerative dialogues are safe spaces in which to learn new ways of interacting across differences in age, ethnicity, social class, and gender. Key to previous research and this proposed study is that once these new ways of interacting are learned the teacher and students are then able to enact what they have been learned in actual lessons. Not only that, the students can become leaders in initiating interactions with peers and the teacher.

We regard cogenerative dialogues as a professional development activity in which teachers and students can accept shared responsibility of the quality of teaching and learning, and by regularly meeting they can learn to interact successfully with one another. We will study what happens in the cogenerative dialogues intensively. As I explain in the materials I sent you we will use a variety of qualitative data sources to ascertain what is happening in the cogenerative dialogues and why that is happening. By undertaking analyses on a weekly basis through until the end of the year we will be able to identify patterns of change in the ways in which the teacher and students interact. We will explore patterns and associated contradictions using ethnography and then we will examine interactions using microanalysis. The microanalysis will enable us to explore the ways in which the teacher and students use their voice, gesture and body movement and orientation. We will explore which interactions have successful outcomes and which do not. Evidence of improvement will be sought in longitudinal studies that are undertaken weekly.

In parallel we will explore the ways in which the same students involved in the cogenerative dialogues participate in regular science classrooms. We will look to see if patterns from the cogenerative dialogue are evident in the classroom and vice versa. We will also ascertain the extent to which new interaction styles developed in cogenerative dialogues transfer to the classroom.

A question we discussed on the telephone is how will we know if we are successful. The criteria for success will emerge from discussion between all the teacher researchers. We will meet at least once a week as a group and will discuss what is happening in the classroom and design procedures to be used in the forthcoming week to test how robust our claims for success are. We will also search strenuously for contradictions to any claim that is made. Some of the criteria for deciding whether positive environments are occurring will include criteria such as the following:

Higher levels of student engagement. Higher levels of attendance. Higher levels of synchrony in the interactions involving student<-> student and student<->teacher. Higher quality of teacher and student discourse as evident in solicitations, responses, reactions, and structuring.

Standard procedures of discourse analysis will be used and advanced technological tools, such as PRAAT, will allow us to measure such characteristics of speech as pauses, frequency of utterances and the amplitude of utterances.

There are many more examples of what would constitute higher quality teaching and learning. I am very experienced in such analyses and since 1973 have been involved continuously in qualitative and quantitative studies of teaching and learning. The bottom line is in higher quality learning environments and higher achievement in science-- including high stakes tests like the Regents' exams. I also expect more students to go on to college and expand their career options as a result of being involved in the study.

The four case studies in the first year involve a middle school, a new high school, a high school for relatively high performing students, and a school for students who have been expelled from their previous school because of violence to a teacher (i.e., a last chance school).

I hope I have addressed all of the points you raised in the telephone conversation. If you have further questions I will be happy to respond to them.

*Figure 2.5. An email response to questions raised by a school district IRB.*

The above incident was quickly resolved, but served as a wake up call for me. It is important in seeking IRB approval that careful attention is given to identifying the likely areas of interest that will arise and to identify the places in which the research will be undertaken. If changes happen as a study unfolds then the IRB should be informed and a decision should be taken about whether or not the informed consent protocols need to be changed.

After I had obtained the official approval from the university IRB, the school district IRB asked me additional questions to clarify the scope of the study. These requests occurred in a telephone conversation with the committee chair and a follow-up email message confirmed what we agreed to in writing. With the common use of email I regard it as important to consolidate into one document the original proposal together with subsequent questions and answers, so that IRBs, researchers, and participants are clear on what has been agreed. The letter in Figure 2.5 provides an example of my responses to queries raised by the school district IRB coordinator during a telephone conversation.

## AUTHENTICITY CRITERIA

What criteria can be used to judge whether or not high quality ethnography has been planned and undertaken? Different researchers will adopt different stances, however, I use the four criteria advocated by Guba and Lincoln—recognizing that education research with human subjects must benefit those who are involved in the study and that researchers have a responsibility to those who agree to be involved that benefits will not be realized only in the future, but will also lead to improvements as the research is enacted.

### Criterion 1: Learning from a Study

Although it is customary for researchers to engage in programmatic research in which each successive study builds on what was learned previously, it is important that they do not commence a study with preconceived ideas about what will be learned. The danger is that such ideas can serve as templates that filter data and confirm a priori expectations. To guard against this occurring researchers can document the progressive changes in their understandings and the foci of their research. The intention is that researchers learn from the data and associated analyses. Evidence of learning from the study would include a changing trajectory of answers to a research question, possibly through the inclusion of nuances and the identification of contradictions to patterns of coherence. Of course the patterns themselves could change over time and the initial constructions could become contradictions to those patterns. While learning from a study it is important to obtain and retain diverse perspectives of participants who are located in different social spaces by virtue of such factors as race, social class, gender and first language. In the remainder of this chapter I refer to participants in these different social spaces as stakeholder groups. Hence in meeting criterion 1 it is important for researchers to show how research questions are answered for different stakeholder groups—

how the answers evolve over time, are nuanced for different participants, and incorporate contradictions.

Ontological authenticity relates to the ways in which participants in the study alter their perceptions of the nature of social life, as it pertains to the research foci. The role of the researcher is to document these changing perceptions. Traditionally researchers, including those within my group, have focused on documenting their own changing ontologies. One important way to do this is to undertake auto/ethnography and dedicate a significant part of the writing of a study to the documentation of changing ontologies and making sense of such changes in relation to what is learned from a study.

An important part of the analysis of a researcher's changing ontology is an examination of the changes that occur in the theoretical underpinnings of a study and the associated changes in the methodologies employed. It can then be shown how changes in the frameworks alter the ways in which social life is illuminated and represented in descriptions and explorations. In this way, changes in the theoretical underpinnings of a study can be linked to the realities presented as outcomes of a study. Perhaps, as a further emphasis on the relationships between theoretical frames, research questions, and methodology it can be shown that decisions to employ one set of theoretical constructs rather than another not only illuminates social life differently by highlighting certain features, but also obscures others. For example, in research on teaching and learning a decision to theorize learning as cultural production brings into focus such issues as cultural reproduction (of the canon), cultural transformation, and cultural fluency, including conscious and unconscious ways of knowing. At the same time issues associated with conceptual change may be shaded from view. Also, opting to use Sewell and Bourdieu as starting points for conceptualizing culture led us to adapt our methodology to search for patterns in social life that have thin coherence and are interconnected with contradictions. The purpose of our research then was not to explain away the contradictions, but to understand them as an expected part of social life that together with the patterns of thin coherence were central in what we could learn from a study and perhaps would have to address in efforts to improve the quality of learning environments.

Concerns about ontological authenticity should extend beyond university-based researchers to include each of the salient stakeholder groups. To what extent do stakeholders construct their lived lives in the fields of study in ontologically changed ways? If ethnography is to be critical in ways that catalyze and sustain desirable changes, from the perspectives of stakeholders, then the ways in which stakeholders enact and perceive social life ought to change as a result of the research. Enduring transformation, for the better, might be sustained if fresh theoretical and empirical lenses are acquired for making sense of teaching and learning and the ways in which participants successfully interact to produce learning[3].

## *Criterion 2: Educating Stakeholders about the Unfolding Outcomes*

In a process of informing stakeholders about what is learned from a study it is important to educate each stakeholder group about the nuances of a study, what is learned from the different stakeholder groups, assisting them to understand the patterns of coherence and contradictions. This criterion can be addressed in a number of ways and the process can be continuous. Within the framework of negotiated agreements, anonymity, and confidentiality, the unfolding outcomes of a study can be made available to participants on a website that can be accessed at their personal convenience. Depending on how public these findings should be, the website could be password protected with access limited to researchers and participants.

Clearly, educative authenticity is at the heart of ontological authenticity and is seen as an essential step in sustaining beneficial changes due to research in classrooms. Not only is it important to obtain rich descriptions of what is happening and why it is happening, but also to ensure that all stakeholder groups understand how others experience and make sense of reality. If issues of equity and oppression in classrooms are to be addressed effectively through research an effective program of educating all stakeholder groups about the constructions of others seems central.

## *Criterion 3: Research Should Catalyze Improvements*

Researchers have an obligation to educate all participants in ways that afford improvements in regard to what is learned from a study. Accordingly, to the extent possible, situations of disadvantage, inequity, and oppression are addressed in ways that expand the collective agency of stakeholder groups. Hence, the results of a study are expected to change over time as adjustments are made by stakeholders to create and sustain environments in which all stakeholder groups can meet their goals. If this is to occur it might be necessary for representatives of each stakeholder group to meet to discuss the unfolding results of a study and negotiate changes to produce desirable goals and outcomes. Ideally, the participants in such discussions would assume a shared responsibility for enacting agreed to changes.

Just as criterion 2 (i.e., educative authenticity) was related to authenticity criteria 1 and 3, so is this criterion related to the others. Research is not a privilege to benefit researchers alone. Instead there is a tax to be paid for the privilege of doing research and that is to act in ways that catalyze desirable changes, not just for the well positioned within the fields of study; but also for all participants. Scholars such as Lather (1993) and Kincheloe and McLaren (1994) refer to the centrality of research catalyzing positive changes for the participants involved in a study. As a quality criterion, researchers should structure a study so that all participants are educated by what is learned in a study and can then use what they learn agentically; to improve the quality of their social lives in the fields in which they participate.

*Criterion 4: Assist all Individuals to Benefit from the Research*

Even though the steps taken to educate stakeholder groups and catalyze positive changes to the learning environments will expand the agency of most participants there will be some who cannot make the changes needed to reduce their disadvantage. Accordingly, researchers have an obligation to help those participants who are unable to help themselves or whose disadvantage continues as the study proceeds. That is, the researchers provide additional structures for those individuals for whom the efforts to educate them and catalyze worthwhile changes were not enough.

For example, a pattern that we observed was that African American males were underachieving in science compared to their female counterparts. This was partly due to the sporadic attendance of some youth who were suspended from class and school for a variety of reasons. Despite the principal, coordinators of schools within a school, and teachers knowing about this trend, when Shakeem was suspended from school and had to transfer to another school because of his high frequency of suspension I intervened with the principal; making a case for allowing him to continue at the school because he did not want to go to a new school and a change of schools would further disadvantage him. Fortunately the principal agreed to my request and Shakeem was permitted to stay at the school. In this instance the principal, a Black female, recognized that the enforcement of the rule would needlessly disadvantage Shakeem. Similarly, when Tyrone was suspended for 5 days, essentially because his mother could not come to the school for a compulsory conference, I asked the principal if she would waive the rules for Tyrone and consider changing a school policy that was keeping urban youth out of the school.

*The Bottom Line on Authenticity*

Although I dealt with the four authenticity criteria in a linear way, it is apparent to me that this is yet another example of factors that constitute a whole—they are dialectically related. I do not envision a researcher claiming that classroom research is authentic or credible based on just one or two of the authenticity criteria. Because each is constituted in a whole, the quality of a study can be judged in terms of the ways in which each of the four criteria is addressed and accomplished.

DATA RESOURCES

Interpretive research is a form of participant observation that has the goal of ascertaining what is happening and why it is happening from the perspectives of the participants in the fields of study. Hence, as culture is enacted within fields, the researcher describes what happens in terms of the emergent patterns and associated contradictions. To do this, the researcher visits the field regularly, becomes a participant observer, a visitor to the field with a set of roles that other participants need to understand and accept. The presence of the researcher (as a participant observer) changes what happens because his or her presence, and associated practices and schema, alter the structure of the field and hence the agency of all participants. Accordingly, as participants appropriate the dynamic structures introduced by the researcher, different forms of culture are produced and enacted than would be the case if the researcher were not present. Although the roles of the researcher inevitably change as she becomes more familiar with the fields of study and is known by the participants, it is important that all participants are aware of the roles to be enacted, accept them, and are apprised of changes as they occur.

In my research described earlier, I negotiated with the school principal, the coordinator of the small learning community in which the study was to occur, and the science teacher that I would coteach with Donovan. The students understood that I was a professor from the university and that I would serve as a coteacher when I came to their class to do research. Enacting the role of coteacher gives me close access to the students' praxis as learners and also to the teaching praxis of my fellow coteacher. I am also able to access multiple data resources, an important criterion in ethnographic research. Accordingly, students knew that I would observe, take notes, videotape what happened, photograph their work, speak to them about their work during the class and, as necessary, teach individuals, small groups and, if called upon by the teacher, the whole class. Students did not hesitate to ask me for assistance. In this way I was a coteacher, usually involved in peripheral roles that occasionally became more central. By having a form of participation that was active I had access to the unfolding production of teaching and learning. My practices and associated schema were part of the dynamic structure of the classroom and were structured by it as well.

A problem associated with me being a "coteacher as researcher" is my inability to create field notes as the lesson progresses. I use two approaches to address this limitation. One is to speak into the microphone of the camera, which I hold in my hand as I move around the classroom, thereby catching what happens (in the direction of the lens) in terms of video and audio. The second is to speak my descriptions and interpretations—things to pay attention to—into a hand held digital recorder, in my case iTalk connected to an iPod. Rather than reading back over field notes written during a lesson I can play back my recorded comments and, as I watch the video replay, I can take those comments into account as I make sense of the data.

During a lesson I routinely speak to students, usually recording what they have to say through the microphone on the camera. Often this is accomplished as the camera points elsewhere, making the speakers less conscious of being recorded. If I feel the necessity to have video and audio I usually ask permission of the student to shoot the video as well as have a short conversation. When I talk to students, either informally or formally I make a point of trying to structure the interactions such that students speak for longer than me. To the extent possible I want to capture their perspectives on teaching and learning and the many relationships that are central in my research—such as agency|structure, individual|collective, and practices|schema. When I first introduce the study I let them know that when I interact with them I want them to speak until they "run out of gas."

The other piece of technology I carry with me as part of my ethnographer's toolkit is a Nikon Coolpix 4600, a digital camera with a 512 MB memory card that can be used to take high quality pictures of artifacts used during teaching and learning. In effect this replaces a photocopier in that I can photograph student work, chalkboard inscriptions, the layout of the class, the uses of equipment and materials and capture the ways in which particular resources are used during the lesson. These digital images are of high quality and, as a slide show, are a way for me to quickly reconstruct the key features of a lesson. When I use the digital camera I usually set the videocamera on a desk or table, leaving it to record events as I capture specific high quality images.

## Analytic Memoranda

As soon as possible after coteaching a lesson I endeavor to write analytic memoranda, with and without the assistance of video replay. An example of an analytic memorandum is provided in Figure 2.6.

Analytic memoranda are used as data resources and can be used as evidence to support patterns of coherence or contradictions to those patterns. Another use of analytic memoranda is to give a copy to participants to see whether they correct and elaborate on the text and to highlight areas of agreement and disagreement. Hence, analytic memoranda are generative and interpretive resources.

## MAKING SENSE OF THE DATA RESOURCES

A critical part of interpretive research, as I do it, is to stay on top of the data analysis. Hence, as soon after being in the field as possible, it is important to answer the two main questions of interpretive research, namely, what is going on here?—and why is that happening? In formulating responses my methodology guides me to search for patterns of coherence in the data and associated contradictions. Once I identify patterns and contradictions I want to be able to describe both in terms of examples, what I refer to as vignettes, or little stories. I do not expect the patterns of coherence to be thick, just systems of practices and schema that tend to cohere and always contradictions, or inconsistencies with those patterns. Accordingly, I do not try to explain away the contradictions as error, but seek to understand them along with the patterns of coherence. I am guided theoretically by William Sewell's ideas on culture, whereby culture is enacted as patterns of practices and schema that have thin coherence; dialectically interconnected with contradictions (Sewell, 1999). Hence, in an important sense, the patterns of coherence and the contradictions represent a whole, or to think of it another way, when culture is enacted, patterns of coherence and contradictions are mutually constitutive—that is, each mediates the other.

the periodic table or to its probable valence. She asked many questions about why the correct formula for magnesium bromide contained two atoms of bromine. In my efforts to explain how she could write chemical formulae for each of the reactants and products as a first step into the given problems Kamica became frustrated and began to write a letter about how much she disliked chemistry. With 20 minutes still to go it was a struggle for me to connect with Kamica.

Several of the students had their heads on the desk. Aaron could be aroused and he told me that he did not know what to do. Once I had taught him what to do he stayed on task for most of the rest of the lesson. Another African American male looked menacingly at me when I aroused him. "I have a headache man. Don't mess with me," he snarled. Remembering Tyrone's advice of not messing with students who did not want to be taught I quickly moved away to deal with other students who were interested in receiving assistance. The male sitting near to Kamica was rarely at school. When he too complained about not being taught the material I asked him why he was absent so much. His response was not at all rational and he then indicated that he did not like chemistry and since failure was no stranger to him he was not concerned at the thought of failing the course. Throughout the 75 minutes he toyed with the problems but made no serious commitment either to learn or work his way through any of the problems. I had a sense that he would have engaged if I could have given him a set of problems that he could be successful at.

The lesson reinforced how the students can manage book-focused activities. It was relatively easy to move from student to student and to keep them quiet and moderately active. However, connecting to what the students could do was a challenge in this activity. At any time that I tried to teach to the whole class the students switched off and hardly paid attention at all. When I worked with them one on one they appreciated the effort usually and were prepared to work in this way for as long as I was prepared to teach them.

The students were unable to navigate a textbook and searched through their notes to find what they needed to solve the problems. If they did not have notes on a given topic they were of the opinion that we had not covered it in class. To avoid the problem of having them spend so much time on writing notes I had been giving them handout sheets from the first day I taught them. I did not see any of these notes being used as a resource. For me this raises the question of what students regard as resources to support their own learning. Although I invited students to work together to solve the problems there was no apparent take up of this offer. The students seemed to want to work alone and any conversations were social rather than substantive.

The lesson ended with an invitation for the students to complete up to number 11 for homework. From my standpoint this was a compromise. I had initially set a target of 50 problems to be completed. The rationale offered by Donovan for the reduced target was that the first 11 problems provided both the reactants and the products whereas the final 39 only provided the reactants, leaving students to work out the products as well as to balance the equation. Reluctantly I agreed with this reduced assignment even though I felt privately that in 75 minutes of class time it ought to have been possible to complete the entire 50 problems and do other work as well. I am greatly disturbed that students can accomplish so little in a double period of chemistry and then we adjust our expectations downward with an inevitable outcome being the addition of fuel to the cycle of social reproduction.

As I walked down the hallway to exit the building I encountered at least five students from my class who were absent from the first period. The issue of truancy and absence from class is a major problem that influences the extent to which a coherent program can be planned and enacted. How is it possible to plan for instruction when on the average a student will only attend for three-fifths of the classes in a given week?

*Figure 2.6. An example of an analytic memorandum.*

So, where to start? If I have digital audio messages I begin there, by playing them through, so that I can pick up my memory joggers, recorded while I was in the field. Usually my recorded comments impel me toward particular tasks and perhaps lead me to focus on specific events and examine the evidence for identified patterns or contradictions. Once I have dealt with my oral remarks I like to review the videotape. I find it best to watch the tape having first imported it into iMovie. Once it has been imported and saved, as an iMovie file on a 500 GB external hard drive, I watch it in real time and use my computer to make notes. If something catches my interest or if complex interactions occur, I play the tape back, over and over if necessary and when salient vignettes occur I clip them, so that they exist as discrete entities. On the first pass through I do not delete any of the images—I simply break down the file into smaller segments and write notes about the patterns and contradictions I notice.

As I identify patterns of coherence (often called assertions) and associated contradictions I make a note of the evidence to go with each. At this time I make decisions about whether or not to show particular clips to the participants either as a whole class, in cogenerative dialogues, or to individuals such as selected students and the teacher. Usually the clips I select range in duration from 30 seconds to 3 minutes. If I decide to show selected clips to the participants I save them as Quick-Time files and store them on a DVD or CD ROM. To the extent possible I like to write interpretive memoranda based on my initial review of the tape. The interpretive memoranda will connect what I am learning to what I have learned previously from the study, to the theoretical framework, and to what others have learned. Usually the others will be from my research group and close associates.

These initial analyses and interpretations help to focus what happens next in my research and also provide a basis for me to get feedback on my tentative findings from participants and peers who are not directly involved in the research. The process of discussing what I have learned with participants and asking for their input on my interpretations is called member checking. I do not privilege the interpretations of any particular participant, but want to get input from a range of them as additional data to provide nuances to what I have learned. Member checking might lead me to change my mind, or more often, to elaborate what I have learned from a study to include additional patterns of coherence and contradictions, or to consider alternative interpretations as contradictions to my claims. Whatever happens I keep a record so that over time I can explore the trajectory of my changing understandings—a key authenticity criterion.

Once a week I schedule a meeting of my research group. Usually each person in the group is involved in his or her own research and we come together to discuss what we are learning and thereby learn from one another's ongoing research. Also we share our foci and methodologies. For example, at the present time my research group is tiered, the base group consisting of four colleagues who are doing research in their own classes and me. Each month the base group meets for three consecutive weeks on Wednesday evening for two hours. Each person in this group takes a turn at leading the research group until, over a five meeting cycle, all researchers have had an opportunity to lead and get focused feedback on their research. This is called peer debriefing and its purpose is to enrich a study through the critical insights of peers.

A second tier consists of the base group plus two other research groups, which undertake research in New York City. The first and second tiers meet on Friday once a month and each month we rotate the meeting venue—the host researchers leading the conversation about our research. This meeting of the larger group is also a form of peer debriefing allowing for even more disparate perspectives to inform our studies.

A third tier is distributed nationally and internationally and consists of colleagues who are undertaking similar research to that being undertaken in the first and second tiers. Some scholars in this network participate in many of the tier 1 and 2 meetings, either by traveling to New York City or by videoconferencing using iChat. In this way valued perspectives enrich our research on a regular basis. In fact, the uses of videoconferencing afford important conversations within and across the tiers.

As I learn from my study I make sure that I have sufficiently compelling data to support the patterns of coherence and the associated contradictions. I want all claims to be nuanced and illustrated with vignettes, narratives of what I experienced as a researcher. For any pattern of coherence, or claim I want to make about the study, I expect to have multiple data sources. That is, I do not want to make a claim that is based only on interview, or just on my impressions of one short excerpt from videotape. Hence, as a pattern and its associated contradictions begin to emerge I examine the design of the study to ensure that I get more data resources to address the pattern and associated contradictions. When I call for multiple data resources I mean that the data assembled to support coherence and contradictions should be compelling, supported by evidence that is appropriate for the claim.

## INVOLVING STUDENTS AS RESEARCHERS

The use of students as researchers provides a way to obtain their perspectives on what is salient in terms of school, teaching, learning and myriad other issues. Having identified foci for research they can provide insights into what is happening and why it is happening, in terms of patterns of coherence and contradictions. Especially since we began doing research in urban high schools we have utilized numerous student researchers and their expertise has benefited the research. Elsewhere Rowhea Elmesky and I provided a detailed account of the ways in which we have expanded the roles of students in our research (Elmesky & Tobin, 2005). Here I provide some windows into their roles, how they enacted them, and what use we made of their intellectual work.

Initially the key idea in using student researchers was to obtain their answer to the question of how to better teach kids like me on a lesson-by-lesson basis. This role then expanded to allow student researchers to interview their peers. I was astonished by the work of Tyrone in this regard. He took the task very seriously and prepared for his interviews by coming to my methods classes to hear what issues we spoke about and browsing through the bookshelves in my office to get insights into issues that were central to urban education. For example, without prompting from me he perused a book that addressed Fordham and Ogbu's ideas about acting white and then proceeded to interview a number of his peers about the construct (Fordham & Ogbu, 1986).

The battle for me has been to include the student researchers as researchers and not regard them as data resources enacting different roles. Accordingly, we schedule research meetings with the student researchers to discuss our research in relation to theory and methodology. As the student researchers begin to understand the theoretical underpinnings they can connect with the research and identify and produce resources that would not otherwise inform the research. Their development as scholars is no different than any other researcher—that is university and teacher researchers. What tends to hold them back is a tendency for some of us to reify traditional student-adult power differences. For example, some of our most successful teacher-researchers, such as Alex, had difficulty in dealing with the expanded roles of student researchers, such as Shakeem. As researchers we welcomed Shakeem's perspectives on teaching and learning; however, as a teacher Alex regarded some of them as brash and disrespectful. Also, when Shakeem returned to his classroom his critical discourse about what was happening was sometimes regarded as "out of line." Being a student researcher allows students to produce new culture that can transform their identities and roles in many facets of their lifeworlds. As student researchers learn to use their voices to identify new sources of inequity and to advocate new roles and activities it is not surprising that the traditional power brokers might resist these new forms of culture. The potential for student researchers to encounter difficulties because of their changed agency and identity ought to be closely monitored to ensure they do not encounter serious problems.

*Interviewing Peers*

When student researchers interview their peers the peer-to-peer talk seems to be distinctively different than occurs when an adult, like me, conducts an interview. My approach has been to talk to the student researchers about conducting interviews and let them decide how many students to interview, whom to interview, and what to ask. Whether or not follow up interviews are desirable also is left to the student researcher to decide. I encourage student researchers to write a brief analytic memorandum about each interview, focusing on what was done and what was learned. The student researcher then transcribes the interview, which is recorded on a small hand held digital recorder.

In terms of the mechanics of doing an interview I usually discuss the place of the interview with the student researcher, the optimal length, and the ways to avoid interrupting responses with questions. The heuristic we use and advise student researchers to use is to let the persons being interviewed know that they should consider questions as invitations to discuss issues that are important to them, especially things that happen commonly in their class and contradictions. The persons being interviewed should talk for as long as they want to, until they run out of gas. When they let the student researcher know they are out of gas (using the timeout signal from sports) the turn at talk can transfer to the student researcher who can then ask for clarification, elaboration, or pose a fresh question.

The following transcript is from an audiotape made by Tyrone as he listened to the playback of an interview with Amirah. Tyrone was fluent orally and we obtained much richer interpretations when he audiotaped his interpretations. In Tyrone's case we did not consider it good use of his time to transcribe interviews. Accordingly, we oriented his researcher roles to his interests and capabilities. Of course when we needed his assistance to decipher parts of an interview his insider knowledge was invaluable.

All in all, I think that was a good interview I had with Amirah because she stated a lot of good points. And she had a lot of things to get off of her head. I think it's good that a lot of....I think a lot of people should be talking to Amirah. Not actually interviewing, not actually talking about school, but actually trying to get her to express her feelings on certain things because she has good feelings and good ideas and good thoughts. Plus she has a lot in her head. And I think some of the things need to be let off of her head, and maybe she'll be able to calm down and act like a child again . Because even though she's a teenager, and she's almost grown, she's acting a little older than she is. And she feel as though that's the right way to be. I feel as though it's good to act a little older than your age, but you're still supposed to act your age and have fun. You're not supposed to just be a 16-year-old acting like you're a 34-year-old like you've got to maintain two jobs and ten kids. She has to be able to lay back and relax sometimes. And I feel as though she feel as though she can't do it that way.

Tyrone's insights into Amirah incorporate an insider perspective that nobody else on our research team had. As an African American youth who is growing up in poverty, he recognized Amirah's necessity to fend for herself because at the age of 3, within a few months her single supporting mother died and then just a few months later, her guardian grandmother also died. Now raised by her cousin, Amirah has the responsibilities of home duties, and providing food and clothing for herself and others in the home. At home and in her neighborhood Amirah has the responsibilities of an adult and yet at school she is required to be compliant and is treated as a child. Not surprisingly, Amirah is very resistant to efforts of teachers to control her and suspicious of efforts to create collaborative activities in which she can coparticipate. Tyrone's interpretation of his interview with Amirah contained perspectives that have significant implications for the ways in which we structure classes in urban schools, interact with urban youth, and make sense of what we regard as their resistance to enacted curricula.

*Doing Urban Ethnography*

One of the early ways we involved student researchers was to ask them to undertake ethnography of sounds of the city. We provided them with audio and video recording equipment and invited them to record sounds in different parts of the city, such as on busy street corners, in fast flowing traffic, in parks, in stores, on a building site, and on bustling sidewalks. After a discussion about what was happening and why, the students used iMovie and QuickTime Pro as tools to produce a movie, to capture what they learned from their ethnography. To us, their movie and the processes that led to its production were salient windows into their perspectives on science and its intersections with an aspect of urban life. Foci for other video ethnographies undertaken by student researchers included the shopping mall, rapping in the 'hood, going to church, my family, and homework.

In a similar vein we have taught high school youth an elective course on public interest anthropology, whereby they learned how to do ethnography and then undertook a study of their neighborhoods, exploring issues of salience to the residents. These ethnographies provide compelling insights into the neighborhoods in which urban schools are situated and can inform the foci and interpretations of ongoing research that focuses primarily on what is happening in classrooms.

*Video Vignettes*

As an alternative to one of the coteachers identifying video vignettes for analysis and discussion we regularly asked students to identify and analyze clips that were salient to our research. The video vignette and associated analyses then were discussed critically during a research meeting. The following is an example of a written critique of a video vignette identified by student researchers from Ms. Bonds' science class.

Ms. Bonds Boring (January 16, 2003)

The way she was teaching was appalling. She just sat on the table and lectured the students. As you can see the students are very uninterested and are not listening. As a student I know that that isn't an effective way to teach the class. Ms. Bonds was also lacking power. I say this because earlier in the clip the students were out of control and very rambunctious and when she said stop they ignored her. There was only one student who was actually paying attention. Later on in the clip she started yelling and shouting commands and instructions at the class. Yelling to your class isn't effective because it will just be an invitation for that student to be impertinent to you and to be resistant towards you. A student may also sense that the teacher doesn't care if she/he yells at the student.

Although the above interpretations are harsh for Ms. Bonds to read she welcomed the feedback, along with some earlier comments from student researchers that she was "stiff, white, standin'." In effect the student researchers identified a potential connection between a teacher's verve and the interest and focus of students. Students tended to shut down whether Ms. Bonds stood straight and talked at them or sat on her desk and talked at them. Consistently the student researchers selected examples of ineffective teaching as those in which the teacher was relatively immobile. In contrast, examples of good teaching were those in which the teacher showed oral fluency and moved her body energetically. Another key point in this analysis of the vignette is the senselessness of a teacher's efforts to establish control over students (rather than creating collaborative rituals) and especially acting in ways that are disrespectful and likely to catalyze forms of resistance.

The student researchers are wonderful storytellers and can produce auto ethnographies and autobiographies—especially using video and audio media. We also had a great deal of success in asking student researchers to document their autobiographies, for example, as science learners, in written form. The following is an example from Natasia.

As the years go by it seems that I have done worst in sciences, the reason being my attention span and tolerance for being ideal. When I say "my attention span" I mean that when I get bored I acquire a short attention span. When this occurs I tend to sleep, disrupt the class, talk to the other students and other things of that nature, therefore my work doesn't get completed. When I say my "tolerance for being ideal" I mean my zero tolerance for having nothing to do. This only happens when I finish my work before the rest of the class and then I have nothing to do. I absolutely dislike to have nothing to do, in this case my work would sometimes get misplaced or destroyed or very seldom turned in. It is in this case, that the only work that would get turned in is the work turned in as soon as it is completed. The other work get lost because it is mixed up in all of the junk that I have, by this point, taken out trying to find something to occupy myself with. These, in the long run, cause my grade to fall to a near failing grade. Not the best reasons, but the reasons nonetheless.

I not bored in all of my science class, just chemistry and physics. Chemistry bores me be cause I had had it after I had had biochemistry which is much more in-depth than chemistry. To me chemistry is more bookwork than anything. Where as biochemistry is more lab work to me, it was fun. Physics is boring to me because all it is just a group of measurements that you will never in life use again in life. Physics is one of theses class that you really don't needs but you have to take it because they said so.

The only two challenges that I have in my science class now is drawing the pictures for the magnitude and displacement, and stay awake in class.

In my science class no one helps me well other then to tell me to stay awake in class. But my friends help me to stay on task as far as homework, now. Other than the usual, there's nothing much to say about homework. We don't really get much of if it, but we do get homework, and sometimes it useful and sometimes it not.

Natasia's narrative raises some crucial points that also arose in other parts of our research. As a grade nine youth Natasia was clearly the leader in her class and had quick insights into the biological sciences, especially genetics. In the four years of high school Natasia struggled to succeed despite the fact that she wanted to be a doctor, had a strong interest in science and studied at least one and often two science courses a year. Issues addressed in her narrative include the lack of challenge in school science, catering for talented students, connecting studies to the interests and perceived relevance of students, sequencing science courses, the role of homework, and ways in which teachers and other students can provide support for learning.

## Making PowerPoint Presentations

Student researchers are routinely asked to prepare PowerPoint presentations to support oral presentations they will make at research meetings and to stakeholder groups like peers and teachers. The students create presentations that include text, graphics, illustrations, digital images, and short video clips. Such presentations serve multiple purposes such as viably presenting student researchers' perspectives, allowing student researchers to become technologically fluent, and providing a context for interactive exchanges about research.

## Students as Teachers and Teacher Educators

As we undertook research in urban classrooms we have been responsive to requests by school administrators and teachers to offer a variety of options to benefit the students and hence the school. For example, we have provided elective credit for student researchers to teach science to children in a nearby middle school. We worked out a plan with the principals and other administrators and the science teachers from the two schools. According to the plan a group of high school students would meet with our researchers on Mon, Tues to plan what they would teach on Wed and Thurs and then on Fri the group would meet to review what they had learned from their experiences and how to make improvements for next week. We divided the middle school class of about 30 students into five groups, each taught by two high school student researchers. In a semester we typically taught two five-week units to the middle school students. This activity created many foci for intensive research, including our teaching of the student researchers on Monday and Tues, the students' coteaching on Wed and Thurs and the critical analyses and research undertaken on Friday. In addition, we were most interested to see how the experiences of teaching others afforded the learning of science and the emergence of new roles as learners in the student researchers' other classes.

Obviously there are many potential foci for research in just the peer teaching activity described above. In this example, the school requested the activity and as a research team we did not have the resources to study it to fully realize the potential of the data resources that were accessible to us. Importantly we had to limit the scope of what we researched and focus our efforts on doing the activity successfully, being sure to answer the broad questions of what is happening and why is it happening. However, it is also important not to privilege the sort of research I do over the sorts undertaken by the teacher and student researchers. Although I was not collecting data resources at the micro level to support my research agenda, the students and teachers undertook research to improve the quality of the activity and to learn what might be retained from this study for enactment in the forthcoming semesters and years. In terms of the authenticity criteria all participants in the peer teaching activity were guided by and achieved all four of them. Students, teachers, administrators and university researchers learned enough from the study to be able to describe what happens and make suggestions on what should happen in the future. Furthermore, if challenged in any point there were compelling data to support claims.

On a regular basis we arrange for the student researchers to interact one-on-one with small groups of prospective teachers in their methods classes and as an expert panel. In this way they disseminate what has been learned from our research in ways that can potentially impact practice. Even though student researchers have coauthored papers and book chapters with other researchers, their roles as teacher educators and when they use PowerPoint presentations (as described above) are the most authentic ways we have used to allow them to present their voices in credible and authentic ways. Obviously, such presentations also serve as data resources for ongoing analyses and interpretations. In addition, the following testimony from a candidate science teacher suggests she found the information provided by the panel of urban youth to be of considerable value.

You were all great! I know I, personally, learned a lot (probably more than you think we all did). I am new to the Philly public school system, and I just want to say that you have helped to alter my perspective on the school system. All of you were articulate, candid, and well spoken. You also helped me to see some of the things that can make me a better teacher (being caring, but not overbearing; or to be sure to approach the students before calling the parents; and many other things).

Just as we have expanded the roles of students to allow them to contribute to key aspects of education, it is feasible to expand the roles of parents, school administrators, and members of the community. Appealing pathways for getting them involved as coresearchers are coteaching and cogenerative dialogues.

## AUTO/ETHNOGRAPHY AND AUTO/BIOGRAPHY

It seemed to me that much of the research in urban education was premised on deficit perspectives of the school systems, the teachers and the students. While I acknowledge that unbridled optimism is unlikely to catalyze the improvements in urban education that we all would like to see, I am equally sure that describing a flawed landscape and producing policies to hold participants accountable for the flaws will not produce improvements of the required magnitude. Accordingly, when I faced mounting contradictions about urban science education I resolved to undertake auto/ethnography—to learn from ethnography of my own efforts to teach science in inner city schools. These initial efforts were followed up by studies of others' teaching, however in a context in which I cotaught with regular urban science teachers.

When I began my research in urban schools in 1998 I didn't set out to do auto/ethnography—but with hindsight it was exactly the right thing to do. The problem for me was that I had just moved to Philadelphia and the schools in the inner city were unlike any I had ever experienced in my lengthy career as a teacher and researcher. The first hint that there was something wrong came in the form of complaints from my science methods students who felt that what I was teaching them "didn't work." I felt that what I was teaching was solid and that they were just not up to the task of teaching in urban schools. When I observed Donovan teach at City High—the supervisor of one of my student teachers—I did not regard him as effective. My perspectives were external, distant, and laden with deficits. As I previously described, Donovan agreed to coteach with me—however, he did not do that, leaving me instead to go it alone. I did not mind since I was confident of success. What a shock to me when I found that I was unsuccessful.

Autobiographies and the stories about how I taught and why I did what I did flowed in narrative form. Naturally the stories incorporated an historical perspective that brought the different cultures of suburban and rural students in Australian schools in the 1960s and 1970s into juxtaposition with urban youth in the 1990s and 2000s. Through a variety of theoretical lenses the research showed that my teaching, which I felt to be effective in Australian high schools several decades earlier, could not adapt to the culture of the students and provide the structures needed to expand their agency and afford their learning of science. When this study began my research group was relatively small, consisting of a doctoral student, a student teacher, and several high school students who served as researchers. Donovan was a researcher too, but it took him some time to assume that role. So, making sense of the data resources was very difficult in the first six weeks or so. I had field notes, videotape, many formal and informal interviews, and regular conversations with Donovan. I was puzzled by the way in which the students refused to show me respect and virtually ignored me when I spoke to them. They would not cooperate with me and often put their heads down as if to sleep in my class. If I pushed too hard they responded aggressively and I was clearly out of my depth. To make matters worse, they had difficulty understanding my Australian accent and I found it impossible to understand their dialect. The learning environments in the class were dysfunctional from my perspective and I did not have the tools to create and sustain productive learning environments.

I was emotionally involved in ways I did not think possible. I had trouble sleeping and often felt so frustrated that I became angry with myself. I prepared for many hours each night and purchased materials to enrich the learning environment and build the curriculum around lab activities. To no avail—each day brought its new wave of failures to report to my close colleague Wolff-Michael Roth. Having a critical colleague to shed light on what was happening was fruitful. In those days we interacted many times a day using email—now we use iChat[4]. Even though Michael had not at that time been a researcher in urban schools of Philadelphia, he had deep theoretical insights that greatly shaped my ways of making sense of what was happening. He was sympathetic, but also a critical friend—exactly what Guba and Lincoln meant by peer debriefing. As I offered my accounts of what was happening he mentioned alternative theoretical ways to think about my experiences. I am sure that I was not as open to his suggestions as I should have been. However, two comments he made were highly influential in shaping my research and providing a foundation for much of the work we did in our urban education research. These pertained to focusing the curriculum on students' interests rather than my perceptions of what students would be interested in, and my failures to succeed being an example of a breach of habitus.

*Students' Interests as a Focus for Curriculum*

I was convinced that I would succeed as a teacher if the students were interested in science. Like most teachers I felt that I had to cover the state and school district standards and so I worked from them to plan a lab centered approach in which students also talked and read a lot about science. I found myself relying heavily on what and how I taught in Australia up until 1974 when I became a university teacher educator. I was confident that, as David Hawkins had noted in his classic paper *Messing about in Science* (Hawkins, 1965), the students would be curious about science and use inquiry as a basis for learning. Michael pointed out to me that each of the units I designed was built around my sense of what the students were interested in rather than what they said they were interested in. Although this is quite a difference in orientation I did not see the difference initially. I felt that if I designed labs that were interesting students would create interests in new aspects of science, and learn. The following is an excerpt from an autobiography, one of many written in conjunction with this study.

> I was determined to enact a science curriculum that was libratory and poten-
> tially transformative in the sense that, by virtue of their participation and
> learning, students would have a better appreciation of their world, enhanced
> opportunities for advanced study in science, and increased choices for career
> placement and training (Barton, 1997). I wanted to enact a curriculum that
> the students would perceive as interesting, relevant to their lives, and useful.
> To the extent possible I wanted the students to have choices in what they
> would study and where they would study it. I predicted that they would enjoy
> doing science if the program was based on investigations and I had a prefer-
> ence for the activities to involve real world problem solving. Although I
> would focus on inquiry as a means to develop deep understandings of science
> subject matter the critical defining characteristic of my approach to the sci-
> ence curriculum would be deep learning whereby students would pursue ar-
> eas of interest in detail and, in so doing, employ a multitude of resources to
> support their learning.
>
> Even though I began to teach with a transformative/libratory agenda I was
> by no means sure of how to proceed with the teaching of consecutive units on
> chemistry and physics. I intended to use a multi-faceted approach. For exam-
> ple, I wanted students to read about contemporary science and thought they
> could access science from journals, newspapers, magazines, and the Internet.
> To accommodate my initial thoughts on what the enacted curriculum might
> be like I requested that my class be scheduled for two days in a computer lab

and three in a science room that would support a range of activity types, including investigations.

I planned to begin with an activity sequence on chromatography, examining the dyes from M & Ms and Skittles because those items of candy were potentially interesting to students, involved simple materials with which they were familiar, and could easily connect to a unit on food and nutrition. While studying food coloring and the relative safety of different dyes I believed we also could study the chemical constituents of the foods consumed by students in various meals. As part of a unit on food and nutrition I considered that students might grow sprouts, radishes, and other edible plants. Also, within the chemistry course, I thought they might grow fast plants, study life cycles, and learn how to grow nutritious plants, such as corn, in relatively quick time. I did not expect that these activities would replace chemistry but set a context in which concepts of chemistry could be explicated.

Narrative accounts like this can be used in a publication as a vignette—thick descriptions that provide detailed accounts of my experiences in a holistic, unfolding sense that is well-captured by narratives.

## Peer Debriefing

I wrote several papers that were published and in the process applied sociocultural theory to make sense of my experience. By publishing with a student teacher, doctoral student and one of the high school students I was learning from their perspectives and in the papers made sure that their perspectives were retained. However it was in my first autobiographical piece from this study that Michael, as a peer reviewer, made the comment that my habitus was being breached. I did not like to read that at first because it seemed to impugn my teaching—yet in hindsight it was a critical review that allowed the research to progress in leaps and bounds. Once I realized that my teaching, as praxis, was not working as I intended I began to see that, in becoming conscious of what was happening, my teaching lacked fluency and was not timely, anticipatory or appropriate. This realization drew attention to the ontological characteristics of teaching and focused attention back on how I was implementing my methods course. Clearly there were major contradictions between my experiences in teaching at City High and how I was expecting my student teachers to learn to teach.

Writing papers and presenting them at national meetings opened the door for peer debriefing and when I returned from the April meetings I was determined to coteach with Donovan, rather than always be the central teacher. From that point onward the classes were much more productive and the doctoral student also got involved in coteaching. With more teachers the students were able to expand their agencies and learn more science and the coteachers were able to experience more teaching and learn to teach by being at one another's elbows. As coteachers we also were coresearchers and had direct access to important experiences associated with learning to teach, teaching science, and learning science. From this point onwards all of my research in urban science classes employed a methodology of co-teaching.

*Learning from the Literature*

A key resource at any stage of research is the research and theorizing of others. In my urban research there are three good examples of the ways in which others' scholarship made a profound difference to the focus and practice of my research. The first example of a central resource was a pair of publications by a colleague of mine from the sociology department at the University of Pennsylvania. Elijah Anderson had written two books, *Streetwise* (Anderson, 1990) and *Code of the Street* (Anderson, 1999). In these books he wrote about the culture of African American youth in West Philadelphia. In particular, he wrote about the poverty extant in this part of the city and the ways in which respect assumes the place of a currency. Respect had to be shown and it had to be earned. I read with great fervor and built new lenses for making sense of my autobiography and making sense of what people were telling me about my teaching and their learning. The students were earning respect among themselves by showing their disrespect for me. Anderson laid out a culture that was foreign to me and as I gleaned insights into it, I was able to make sense of what had happened in my class and then to educate others about what I was learning and even to catalyze changes in the learning environments of the classes I taught.

My involvement in sociocultural theory was somewhat ad hoc, often related to the citations of colleagues and their recommendations about which scholars and works were germane to my research. Of course, doctoral students were a wonderful source of new ideas and resources to study. However, in the early 1990s I realized my reading needed to be much more systematic and I decided to study a course in African American psychology and then two doctoral-level courses in theoretical sociology. These courses allowed me to identify new ways of looking at my research, which was deeply influenced by Wade Boykin's ideas about African American dispositions and the triple quandary faced by participants from minority ethnic and racial groups (Boykin, 1986). An even greater emphasis was due to William Sewell's perspectives on culture, structure and agency (Sewell, 1992, 1999). Direct outcomes of my re-education were dramatic changes in focus and methodology, especially in my uses of microanalysis to augment what I referred to then as critical ethnography.

My entrée into microanalysis placed a strong focus on interactions of participants with structures (i.e., resources). My theoretical framework, which was essentially post-Bourdieusian, did not successfully connect interactions with the creation of productive learning environments. Regina Smardon, and later Stacy Olitsky, took courses from Randall Collins, who was completing a book on *Interaction Ritual Chains* (Collins, 2004). They introduced me to his theoretical framework and immediately we saw applications in our research. Over a period of years we incorporated Collins's sociology of emotions into our theoretical framework to produce a coherent theory that afforded research across the micro, meso, and macro levels of social life.

## Incorporating Microanalysis into Critical Ethnography

During my studies of others' teaching and the associated learning environments I incorporated critical ethnography as I described earlier and microanalysis, based on the uses of videotape. In the next section I focus on the methodology employed in microanalysis using two studies undertaken by Alex (Tobin, 2006a) and Victoria (Tobin, 2006b) respectively. As I have done previously, I use excerpts from a paper written about this research to make salient points.

Microanalysis involves the use of videotape to examine practices in detail by replaying excerpts and manipulating the replay speed to search for patterns and associated contradictions. I use the iMovie application to produce and analyze videoclips. For users of the Windows Operating system the applications I have found most useful are QuickTime Pro and Studio Mediasuite (version 10 by Pinnacle). Transana is a cross-platform application that many researchers use[5].

## What's Happening?

When I do microanalyses I explore agency|structure relationships in detail. First, I address the general question of "what is happening?" and then undertake a detailed analysis of "why is that happening?". In the following example, the answer to what is happening is referenced to the practices of key participants during a selected vignette. How do you decide whether or not a vignette is salient? I watch videotape and identify episodes that are relevant to the research questions. The episode should depict either a good example of what tends to happen or a contradiction to what usually happens. The first thing I do is to write a short description of what the episode represents—for example, in this episode a female shows unusually intense engagement in a dissection lab. It is unusual in that most students participate in sporadic ways and are easily distracted. Also, it is often the case that males are more often engaged than females. The amount and quality of the engagement make this episode quite salient to the roles of urban youth in lab activities that connect directly to their interests and in which they have the autonomy to choose what, how, when and with whom. Also salient in this episode is the central role of Alex, the science teacher. In contrast to what is often advocated vis a vis the role of a teacher in a lab, Alex enacts his roles in a very central way, exhibiting his competence in science fluently and showing students what and how to participate. When he joins students he does so with purpose and structures their experiences so that they can participate autonomously in his absence.

The selection of an episode is followed by detailed analysis that focuses on the unfolding agency|structure relationships in terms of verbal and non-verbal interactions among selected participants. The analyses involve the production of a transcript that includes details of the words spoken as a function of time, body movements and the appropriation of resources.

Science in the *Science Education and Technology* small learning community was taught in a former shop room—a large room in the basement of City High. My initial impression, based on entry to the classroom, was how different the classroom felt and looked. There were no students seated in the desks where whole class interactions usually occurred and Alex was nowhere to be seen. Clusters of students were interacting at workbenches dispersed throughout the large classroom. At the dissection table four students were examining the latex gloves, dissection kits, and aprons. As they got themselves ready to start their dissections Alex emerged from the storeroom with a frog, still in a plastic bag. As Kareem, one of the students, placed the frog on the dissecting tray, Alex began to interact with the students about their roles and the resources they could use to support their learning. In addition to the lab equipment and materials the resources available to support the students' learning included manuals for the organisms they were to dissect, a computer connected to the Internet with a high-speed T1 line, reference books, peers, and Alex.

During an eight-minute vignette selected from the beginning of a lesson Alex came to the dissection group on four occasions. His first visit to the group was brisk, lasting less than a minute. While he was with the group he explained what equipment was available for them to use and reviewed the division of labor that the group might adopt. He negotiated with Katrina who had dissected a frog yesterday and discussed what she needed to include in a report on the dissection of a starfish. He suggested to her that she dissect a grasshopper today, adjacent to the other three students in the group, who would dissect a frog. Alex listened attentively to Katrina and requests for equipment from the others in the group. Then he explained to them the value of doing their dissections close to one another, thereby affording comparisons of the structures of the two organisms that were very different from one another. He then left the group purposefully, to get what they needed from the storeroom. Immediately, the group commenced various forms of participation.

Within a minute Alex returned to the group with a grasshopper to be dissected. As he arrived the two females requested gloves, since Katrina did not yet have any and Samantha's gloves were too small. Alex affirmed that he would get them and, noticing Katrina pull back the frog's outer skin with her fingers, discussed safety and explained that students should treat the animal with respect, using a probe to hold back the skin, lift organs and so forth. As Alex spoke to the students they stopped what they were doing and oriented their heads to listen to him. After explaining to them how to use the probe he volunteered to give them his dissection kit, which contained a greater array of scalpels and dissection tools. After 50 seconds with the group Alex left with the comment "go to work!"

From the moment Alex arrived at the group he was an active participant. He interacted with Katrina and Darnell and challenged what they were doing and why they were doing it. Based on his experience he knew they would want to cut and

45

remove the organs without a plan and so he asked questions that would pique their curiosity, directing them to other resources so that they would know what to look for, in determining the sex of their frog for example. Alex showed his knowledge of the anatomy of the frog and at the same time made it clear to the students that they would decide what to do and when and how to do it. That is, through his verbal and non-verbal practices Alex expanded the agency of all three students who remained in the group during the above interactions. Figure 2.7 shows the orientation of the four participants in this episode.

*Figure 2.7. The participants lean forward to interact about dissecting a frog.*

*Utterances and Time as Resources*

As an example of how verbal interactions are used as a resource, I provide a transcript of a segment of a frog dissection in which Alex interacts with Katrina and Darnell. The conventions I use are similar to those employed by Roth (2005) and are printed using Courier font, because each character is assigned equal spacing, making it possible to vertically align speech utterances that occur at the same time.

The following transcript[6] depicts fast talk and fluent action as participants use gestures, tool manipulation, and body sways to interact successfully with one another and material resources. Chains of verbal and non-verbal interactions are in synchrony and produce successful outcomes and obvious signs of enjoyment, interest and sustained involvement from all participants.

```
1. Katrina: These two things
2. Darnell: =Well what about it?
(1.4)
3. Katrina: Let's find out where it's going
(0.6)
4. Alex: See but that's why you cut things. Well. You, make a deci-
sion.
```

5. Katrina: =It's coming. It's got. It's got. I think it's coming this way.
6. Darnell: =It's the smaller thing. It's right there.
7. Alex: =Where?
8. Darnell: =This.
9. Alex: =Yeah. The end of it is called the cloaca. That's probably gonna be the gall bladder. But you figure that out.
(0.8)
10. Alex: Take. Start taking organs off from the top end then. Right?
11. Darnell: =Are you serious?
12. Katrina: =Can we cut it here? (0.4) Can we cut it here?
13. Darnell: =No. No. You're going to cut its gender loops
14. Alex: =Awright. Let me tell you.
15. Katrina: =I'm cutting it.
16. Darnell: =No. You're not.
17. Alex: =First of all, do you know if it's a female or a male?
(0.5)
18. Darnell: Yep.
(0.8)
19. Alex: That's a question for you
20. Darnell: =I don't see nuthin' there so I guess ((points to the groin))
21. Alex: =Well if it's in there on the bottom there. If it's a fe-male you know (1.1) actually on the end of that website it'll tell you what to do to figure out if it's a male or a female. I think it's a male to tell you the truth.
(0.6)
22. Alex: I need to go fro:m
23. Katrina: =Can I cut it around here?
(0.3)
24. Alex: I I don't know.
(0.8)
25. Eventually you might want to cut here but I don't know if you want to cut here yet.
(0.8)
26. Right. (0.2) See. (0.3) Do the organs first and then find out
(1.3)
27. Darnell: Why for?
28. Alex: =Because the opening for the anus is going to be different for from everybody. Right?
29. Darnell: =Awright.
30. Alex: =Now what are you doing with your hand?
(0.5)
31. Katrina: Me?
(0.4)
32. Alex: Yeah.
(0.5)
33. Katrina: I'm doing what I can.
(1.2)
34. Alex: Okay. What's your plan? What are you guys gonna do? What and why are you doing what you're doing? Right now you're just ex-ploring and just poking around?
35. Darnell: =Yeah. [I'm not. I'm not
36. Katrina:       [I'm finding that You see this rough thing attach with this?
37. Alex: =Hm. Hm.

38. Katrina: =allow me to see if this one prefer that it makes it um um
(1.2)
39. Alex: You wanna see how the opening goes from the mouth to over there. Right?
40. Katrina: =Hm. Hm.
41. Alex: =Right?
(0.9)
42. Darnell: Awright. I take this out from right here?
(0.7)
43. Katrina: Oh. It's [the heart?
44. Darnell:        [I can dig deeper down in there?
(0.2)
45. Alex: Yeah. (0.4) Did you want to remove the liver?
46. Darnell: =Yeah.
47. Alex: =So what I'd say before you do that, go on the website and see if it suggests a cut because they'll suggest to you how to cut and where to cut to get the liver out easily and not destroy anything else. Okay?
((Darnell leaves to access the website))
(0.6)
48. Alex: Put your aprons on, both of you. Put aprons on you won't stink. (0.5) ((Alex strides away from the group)) Aprons are over there. So you won't stink when you go home. ((Both girls move to get aprons and Alex leaves to interact with another group))

Alex spoke for 22 of the 48 moves and in so doing provided suggestions for dissecting the frog (moves 10, 25, 26, 39, 45), asked questions to create a focus (moves 21, 47), showed evidence of interest and curiosity (moves 7, 28), suggested resources for the students to access (moves 21, 47), affirmed the autonomy of students (move 4), used canonical knowledge (move 9), challenged students (move 34), showed uncertainty (move 24), and emphasized safety (move 48). Only 1 of the 22 verbal moves focused on what not to do and was likely to create negative emotional energy (move 48). On this occasion Alex waited until there was a transition and Darnell had moved off before he spoke firmly, briskly stressing what had to be done and alluding to an earlier joke about avoiding the "stinking up" of clothing due to splashing of the formaldehyde used to preserve the frog.

Katrina was central in the dissection because of her prior experience, knowledge, and where she sat—directly in front of the dissecting tray with the others on either side of her. Since Katrina had the dissecting tools throughout the interaction it is no surprise that 9 of her 12 verbal moves consisted of talk about the organism. Of the other 3 verbal moves, one was clarifying, one was explaining, and the third affirmed an agreement. Hence Katrina's talk was an extension of her manipulation of the dissecting tools and her gestures, many of which pointed to specific organs.

Darnell was between Katrina and Alex and interacted with both of them, often providing short verbal affirmations to acknowledge what they had said. Sometimes these took the form of acknowledgement (move 18), agreement (moves 29, 46) and disagreement (moves 13, 16). Also, because he had dissection tools in his hand, many of his verbal moves were about the frog (moves 6, 8, 20, 42, 44). Other verbal moves involved challenging Katrina (move 2), expressing surprise (move 11), raising a query (move 27), and explaining (move 35). None of his turns at talk were especially long, the longest being six to eight words about the organism being dissected.

Pam was silent and attentive throughout the interaction, observing how to use the dissection tools and listening to Katrina and Alex. Her attention was intensive and at times she leant forward to observe closely. Pam's head moves and body orientation and sways were in synchrony with the dynamic structure of the frog dissection. Her participation appeared to be an active form of observation. As soon as Pam collected her apron she was ready to assume Katrina's place as the central person involved in dissecting the frog.

The pauses in the transcribed episode ranged from immeasurable to 1.4 seconds. Few pauses exceeded 1 second. In fact, the transcript shows many instances of overlapping speech and speaker exchanges that were not separated by a discernible pause. Twenty-seven of the 48 moves were separated by immeasurable pauses of 0.1 seconds or less. My interpretation is that the participants were coparticipating and maintained brisk interchanges that added to rather than detracted from making sense of the task at hand—to dissect the frog and learn about its anatomy. The longer pauses occur between and within moves. The distinction is somewhat arbitrary since I could have created a new move whenever a pause of more than 0.2 seconds occurred. I did not, however, preferring to change moves with speaker or when the semantic focus changed. Fourteen pauses separated different speakers. That is, pauses were resources for changing speaker, affording the agency of speakers and presumably the listeners as well. I analyzed these interactions to see if there were patterns. Five of the 14 pauses followed an utterance from Alex, three to Darnell (0.5, 1.3, 0.9) and two to Katrina (0.5, 0.5). Four of the speaker exchanges involved Darnell, transferring twice to Katrina (1.4, 0.7) and twice to Alex (0.8, 0.2). The remaining five transfers were from Katrina to Alex (0.6, 0.3, 0.4, 1.2, 1.2). This trend more than likely reflects Alex's central role in creating structures to allow students to be autonomous in proceeding with the dissection in his absence. Katrina spoke about the frog and when she paused for a sufficient time Alex followed up with the verbal moves previously described. The transfers associated with pauses of 1.2 seconds were salient in the interaction in that in each case Alex spoke for longer, the first calling for a group plan and the second suggesting a procedure they might follow in their dissection of the frog. Even though these verbal moves followed Katrina's comments, they were directed at Darnell and Pam who would have to create the plan and in a short time assume full responsibility for dissecting the frog[7].

Eleven discernible pauses were not associated with a change of speaker. These pauses ranged from a low of 0.2 to a high of 1.1. With one exception all of these discernible pauses occurred in Alex's speech. Katrina showed the group where to cut, paused for 0.4 seconds, and then asked if she could cut an organ in a particular spot. In all other instances, it was Alex who used discernible pauses and retained a turn at talk. On most occasions, and for all speakers other than Alex, discernible pauses signaled the end of a turn at talk.

There is a high degree of synchrony among the participants as Katrina, Darnell and Alex interact and Pam leans forward to observe. Katrina and Darnell continue to use the dissecting tools as they verbally interact with Alex and ascertain how to structure the dissection of the frog. Figure 2.8 shows the coordination of Katrina's and Darnell's hands as they examine various organs and discuss how to proceed. The ungloved hand of Alex points to the cloaca (move 9) as he identifies what is possibly the gall bladder. Interaction chains involving Alex, Katrina and Darnell are in synchrony, mutually constituting a dynamic structure that affords individual and collective agency of all participants.

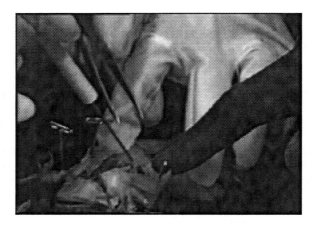

*Figure 2.8. As Alex points, Katrina and Darnell use a probe and forceps to explore the frog's organs synchronously.*

The analyses suggest that sense making during interactions about a material object, this time a frog's organs, extend far beyond talk, and that the meaning arises from more than the spoken words; requiring (in this case) a frog and the tools, gestures and body orientations used to create and sustain focus among participants. The transcript shows that the talk flows quickly from speaker to speaker, with short turns at talk, and some overlapping speech. The speech structures the interactions, contributing to meaning making in many ways as the purposes of dissecting the frog become clearer and emerge from the unfolding experiences. These interactions are not rehearsed or a result of careful planning by any of the participants. Alex has experience of teaching dissection to other classes and students within this class and in previous years he has enacted dissection activities in his classes. However, what happens in this vignette is similar to what has happened before and unique in the ways in which participants interact with one another and appropriate structures to meet their goals—which change from the first to the 47th turn at talk.

## Pitch and Amplitude of Utterances

In the above analysis I did not explore the intonation of the voice or variations in the amplitude within and between speakers. PRAAT is a cross-platform tool that can be used to analyze audio files to provide measures of variables such as time, pitch and amplitude of utterances (Boersma & Weenink, 2006). I usually export the sound from iMovie or QuickTime Pro, as an AIF file, which can be read into PRAAT and is ready for analysis. Because PRAAT provides plots of pitch and amplitude against time (for example) we can examine variations in pitch and amplitude as a function of time.

In a study of the ways in which teachers were able to adapt their culture to align with that of the students, Victoria (teacher) and Mirabelle (student) were involved in a series of interactions in which emotions were salient. Victoria was showing the class how to obtain information about chemical valence from the periodic table. Mirabelle listened to Victoria and then attempted to provide an alternative model for valence. Victoria did not accept the model as viable and the exchange between Victoria, Mirabelle and several of her classmates involved many examples of cultural alignment and misalignment. Data resources include a transcript, analyses of the audio file to obtain measures of time, pitch and amplitude, and analyses of a video to obtain descriptions of gestures and body movements.

```
Victoria:      Look at the placement on (83 dB, 294 Hz) the table
               (0.3) of the element. So that's the trick for figur-
               ing out the valence electrons. ((Mirabelle raises her
               hand.)) Yes Mirabelle.
               (0.1)
Mirabelle: I figured out (79 dB, 233 Hz) a system way you can remem-
               ber. (0.8) [How many val- valence electrons?
Victoria                       [yeah. So this is the trick. The
               placement on the table↑ is how you can remember how
               many electrons there are. (1.2) So now it's two boxes
               over?
               (0.7)
Mirabelle:     I'm not talkin' about that.
               (0.6)
Victoria:      What are you talking about? (77 dB, 227 Hz)
               (0.9)
Mirabelle:     Arright. (75 dB, 213 Hz)
               (0.6)
Victoria:      You just said placement for valence electrons
               [so that's the trick.
Mirabelle:     [Yeah, there's another way you can figure it out.
               (1.2)
Victoria:      This is (79 dB, 321 Hz) the way to do this.
```

Victoria reviews valence of elements in terms of electron configuration and the placement of elements on the periodic table. She wants students to be able to look at the group in which the element is placed and predict its valence. She refers to this as a "trick for figuring out valence electrons." Mirabelle, seated at the end of the second of three rows, raises her hand and volunteers that she has "figured out a way you can remember how many valence electrons." However, before she can complete her sentence, Victoria speaks in overlapping speech that "Yeah. This is the trick."

As Victoria continues to explain how to figure out valence from the periodic table Mirabelle interrupts her to emphasize that she is speaking about something different. Numerous non-verbal interactions between students communicate solidarity among them. At 30 seconds, as Victoria says, "This *is* the way to do this." Tasha, the student sitting adjacent to Mirabelle, turns her head toward her, smiling broadly as she makes eye contact. Victoria's statement is a challenge to Mirabelle and the way she says it, raising intensity and pitch, may have created a resonant structure for Mirabelle and other students in the class. Heads turn, attention is focused on Mirabelle, and there is anticipation about what is to follow. Mirabelle inclines her head to one side, makes eye contact with Tasha, and smiles. As others in the class turn their heads they too have supportive expressions on their faces, although they do not appear to make direct eye contact with Mirabelle. The head turns and eye gaze of many students suggest that Mirabelle's explanation is a mutual focus for them. Mirabelle's explanation is loud, expressive and rhythmic and she uses her right arm to gesture toward the periodic table and the teacher, pointing at times with her index finger and at other times spreading her fingers for emphasis (Figure 2.9). The student researchers recognize this as typical of how Mirabelle interacts when challenged in out-of-school settings, one of them characterizing it as bullying.

The following excerpt from my analytic notes provides a glimpse into the interactions featuring Tasha, Mirabelle and Stacy (seated in the front row) in the first five seconds of the episode.

> Tasha was in synch with Mirabelle in several ways. The two females turned their heads toward each other and smiled broadly at one another. Also as Mirabelle gestured toward the periodic table Tasha gestured at about the same frequency and each held a focus that was evident in eye gaze and head tilt. Stacy turned to look at Mirabelle and as she made eye contact with her, Tasha smiled and also turned to look at Mirabelle. The look on Stacy's face is one of empathy.
>
> In the first five seconds there is other non-verbal evidence of mutual focus. Students in the front row orient themselves either to look at Mirabelle or to watch the periodic table as they listen to her oral presentation.

The interaction sequence is characterized by several breaches when Victoria and Mirabelle speak at the same time and in opposition to one another. The intensity and pitch analyses show that Victoria speaks loudly and at a fairly high pitch as she explains about valence electrons to the whole class. When called upon Mirabelle speaks discernibly softer, 4 dB less intense and at a slightly lower frequency. Nonetheless, for a student speaking to a teacher the initial statement is relatively loud. After she completes her first explanation of what she wants to say she pauses for 0.8 seconds. This pause then becomes a resource for Victoria to take back the turn at talk. However, it is also a resource for Mirabelle to continue with her turn at talk. Accordingly, there is overlapping speech as Victoria reiterates her trick for calculating valence. Her turn at talk contains a relatively long pause of more than a second and even though Mirabelle attempts to interrupt, her effort is not loud and her hand partly covers her mouth. Victoria continues and after a pause of 0.7 seconds Mirabelle steps in, and informs the teacher that she is not talking about that. A rapid exchange occurs until Mirabelle makes it clear that she is proposing an alternative model. Mirabelle's assertion is followed by a pause of more than a second, after which Victoria is emphatic, raising her voice to 79 dB, noticeably above Mirabelle's previous turns at talk, which peak at approximately 75 dB.

*Figure 2.9. The spatial orientation of the students.*

Both speakers showed signs of frustration and there is a hint of anger from both of them. Mirabelle cannot locate spaces to explain her model for valence in Victoria's stream of talk. At the same time Victoria is focused on explaining to all students a way to quickly find out the valence, especially if they need to know to respond to a test question. Whereas Victoria has the symbolic capital of being the teacher, Mirabelle is supported by structures associated with solidarity among at least several peers. Hence, even though Victoria is emphatic that her way is the right way, Mirabelle uses her agency to make a case for an alternative model for valence.

## DOING HIGH QUALITY RESEARCH IN CLASSROOMS

Qualitative research is an investigation of cultural enactment that describes what happens in terms of patterns that have thin coherence and contradictions to those patterns. These patterns are pieces of evidence that "hang together" and are deemed to have salience to the research. Some of the places in which patterns can be seen

QUALITATIVE RESEARCH IN CLASSROOMS

are in interactions among participants, schema of a field, and the participants' practices. My preference is to describe an identified pattern, and provide evidence for the pattern in the form of thick description, included in a vignette. To the extent possible multiple data resources should support each claim. It is not sufficient to identify and describe the patterns of coherence and ignore the contradictions. Special efforts should be made to identify contradictions, understand what they represent, and illustrate them with vignettes.

At a very basic level the patterns of coherence and contradictions are regarded as assertions about social life in the fields involved in a study. Similarly, they might be regarded as answers to research questions. Intellectual efforts to explain why patterns of coherence and contradictions occur should connect to the theoretical framework that underpins a study and to the empirical and theoretical works undertaken by a researcher and others. Explanations of why phenomena occur are theoretical and should elaborate on what was known prior to the study. Citations to other studies and scholarly works should be substantive and not symbolic. That is, a citation should include an explicit connection of what is learned in a study to salient aspects of the cited works. What should be clear is what has been learned from a particular study, its implications, and what needs to be done next.

Obtaining evidence for claims necessitates prolonged engagement and the use of multiple grain sizes for analyses. Roth uses a zoom lens as a metaphor for thinking about the process. For me the key to effective classroom research is learning from coparticipation in the classroom as curricula are enacted. Making sense of these experiences is the initial step in a process that employs mesoscopic analyses in which time is not manipulated. The data resources for such analyses include field notes, analytic memoranda, video replay, transcripts of conversations, including interviews, and digital photos of artifacts such as students' work, blackboard inscriptions and wall charts. My interest, in teaching and learning, focuses on the ways in which teachers and students access and appropriate, that is interact, with classroom structures. Hence, as I intensively analyze the all data resources my interest is in interactions of selected participants with social, material and symbolic resources. On the basis of these intensive analyses patterns and associated contradictions emerge. The point to emphasize here is that the patterns and contradictions are based on mesoscopic analyses.

Theoretically, evidence for any claims at the mesoscopic level should be available at the microscopic level. Of course, such evidence would be confirming and disconfirming, with the confirming instances constituting a pattern that has thin coherence. Based on my theoretical framework for cultural enactment, any pattern of thin coherence would be dialectically related to contradictions and my search would involve the identification of evidence for coherence and contradictions at the microscopic level. In this context the question of what would be a salient video clip is referenced to the mesoscopic claim. A useful episode to analyze microscopically would be one that depicts a particular instance of a pattern I have identified or contradictions to that pattern.

Returning to the metaphor of zooming, it is also possible to zoom out, which, in this case suggests a macroscopic or multi-field analysis. The macroscopic issue, in this instance, is whether or not claims made based on mesoscopic analyses are evident in other fields—that is at other times, in other types of activities associated with this class (e.g., whole class interactive; small group; individualized; labs; field trips), and in classes with different participants (e.g., same teacher with different students; same students with different teacher; different teacher and different students). In making macroscopic claims it is useful not only to project forward, but also to look backwards and situate claims historically. Also, by looking at other classes and, if relevant, other parts of the school (e.g., hallways, lunchroom, entrance foyer), claims can be made about the extent to which patterns apply in other fields. Over time it is useful to examine how culture associated with fields outside of the school permeate the porous boundaries of the school fields (e.g., such as a science classroom). It goes without saying that macroscopic analyses would explore the extent to which culture produced in a classroom permeates fields outside of the classroom, since it is assumed that education will make a positive difference on social life writ large. Hence it is within the ambit of classroom researchers to undertake studies that span the micro-, meso- and macroscopic levels of social life, building understandings of cultural production, as reproduction and transformation.

Having laid out the terrain I conclude with a cautionary note. It is always best to focus on quality and the scope of a study must be referenced to the resources available to support high quality scholarship. Whatever is planned and done should be done well, quality is a first criterion, and it has been my experience that researchers (even senior researchers) err on the side of attempting to do too much. Hence, at the planning stage of a study, identify the boundaries and, as the study unfolds, re-examine earlier decisions to ensure that what is done meets the authenticity criteria and that all claims are nuanced—paying attention to contradictions and supporting claims with compelling evidence, describing how much of it there is, and providing salient examples with thick descriptions. When I have clearly described what I have learned in a study it is for readers to decide if they are convinced and whether any of what I have learned is applicable to and has implications for their professional activities.

ACKNOWLEDGEMENTS

The research in this book is supported in part by the National Science Foundation under Grant Nos. REC-0107022 and DUE-0427570. Any opinions, findings, and conclusions or recommendations expressed in this chapter are those of the authors and do not necessarily reflect the views of the National Science Foundation.

# NOTES

[1] The extent to which participants assume control for what happens or attribute control to others
[2] Female pronouns are used when male or female forms could be used.
[3] Based on questions and comments by Joe Kincheloe at a recent doctoral defense I decided to add to what I had originally written in this section.
[4] iChat is a videoconferencing application that runs on Macintosh computers
[5] http://www.transana.org/
[6] I use transcription conventions employed by Roth (2005).

| | |
|---|---|
| [ | beginning of overlapping talk or gesture; |
| = | equal sign at the beginning of turn indicates no gap between two speakers; |
| (2.1) | elapsed time in tenths of a second; sound intensity (dB) and pitch (Hz) also are in parentheses. |
| :: | colons indicate lengthening of the preceding phoneme, approximately one tenth of a second for each colon used; |
| – | a dash indicates sudden stop in talk; |
| ↑↓ | arrows indicate shifts to higher or lower pitch in the immediately following utterance part; |
| °uh hu° | utterances surrounded by degree signs are less loud than the surrounding talk; |
| (()) | double parentheses (italicized) are used to enclose comments and descriptions. |

[7] Katrina would soon leave to dissect a grasshopper.

# REFERENCES

Anderson, E. (1990). *Streetwise: Race, class, and change in an urban community.* Chicago: University of Chicago Press.

Anderson, E. (1999). *Code of the street: Decency, violence and the moral life of the inner city.* New York: W.W. Norton.

Belmont Report. (1978). *Ethical principles and guidelines for the protection of human subjects of research.* Washington, DC: The National Commission for the Protection of Human Subjects of Biomedical and Behavioral Research. Retrieved March 4, 2006, from http://ohsr.od.nih.gov/guidelines/belmont.html

Boersma, P., & Weenink, D. (2006). *Praat: Doing phonetics by computer* (Version 4.3.27) [Computer program]. Retrieved March 4, 2006, from http://www.praat.org/

Boykin, A. W. (1986). The triple quandary and the schooling of Afro-American Children. In U. Neisser (Ed.), *The school achievement of minority children: New perspectives* (pp. 57-92). Hillsdale, NJ: Erlbaum.

Collins, R. (2004). *Interaction ritual chains.* Princeton, NJ: Princeton University Press.

Elmesky, R., & Tobin, K. (2005). Expanding our understandings of urban science education by expanding the roles of students as researchers. *Journal of Research in Science Teaching, 42,* 807-828.

Fordham, S., & Ogbu, J. U. (1986). Black students' school success: Coping with the "burden of 'acting White.'" *The Urban Review, 18,* 176-206.

Guba, E., & Lincoln, Y. S. (1989). *Fourth generation evaluation.* Beverly Hills, CA: Sage.

Hawkins, D. (1965). Messing about in science." *Science and Children 2*(5), 5-9.

Kincheloe, J. L., & McLaren, P. L. (1994). Rethinking critical theory and qualitative research. In N. K. Denzin & Y. S. Lincoln (Eds.), *Handbook of qualitative research* (pp. 138-157). Thousand Oaks, CA: Sage.

Lather, P. A. (1993). Fertile obsession—validity after poststructuralism. *Sociological Quarterly, 34,* 673-693

Roth, W-M. (2005). *Doing qualitative research: Praxis of method.* Rotterdam: Sense Publishers.

Sewell, W. H. (1992). A theory of structure: Duality, agency and transformation. *American Journal of Sociology, 98*, 1-29.

Sewell, W. H. (1999). The concept(s) of culture. In V. E. Bonell & L. Hunt (Eds.), *Beyond the cultural turn* (pp. 35-61). Berkeley: University of California Press.

Tobin, K. (2006a, January). *Structuring success in science labs.* Paper presented at the annual Hawaii International Conference on Education, Honolulu, HI.

Tobin, K. (2006b). Aligning the cultures of teaching and learning science in urban high schools. *Cultural Studies of Science Education, 1*, (DOI: 10.1007/s11422-005-9008-3).

PAM JOYCE AND JOELLE TUTELA

# 3. WE MAKE OUR ROAD BY TALKING

*Preparing to do Educational Research*

POSITIONING OURSELVES

Similar to the book, *We Make the Road by Walking* by Paulo Freire and Myles Horton, we (Pam and Joelle) are two social activists who emphasize the importance of critical pedagogy, social justice, equity as well as the use of revolutionary teaching practices for democratic education. In this chapter we discuss our journey from teaching in a urban-suburban high school, thirty minutes outside New York City, to entering a doctoral program in urban education, to researching and writing our dissertations; we make our road by talking. This chapter is written to help novice doctoral students examine their own lives, so that their life experiences can be incorporated into the process of educational research. In effect, it presents the dissertation process as an opportunity to open a wide array of spaces that can lead to transformative action. Like, Freire and Horton, we have an educational conversation about how we moved from teacher-practitioners to teacher-researchers. We write this chapter on doctoral research as a conversation because it captures three key aspects in producing doctoral research: the development of a theoretical framework, the employment of dialogue as a methodology and the use of personal narratives as a way of transformation. In this chapter, we use the theoretical perspectives of critical pedagogy and feminism to help guide our conversation, focus our dialogue, and understand our personal narratives. Through our educational conversation, we tell how our personal histories have informed our vision for democratic teaching and ultimately, led us to pursue our doctorates. In this context, our womyn's ways of knowing are validated, as we come to understand how teaching is political and how schools deskill teachers. With these insights in place we discuss the value of personal narrative in doctoral research.

*The Womyn: Joelle and Pam in Third Person*

Joelle Tutela is an Italian-American female who was raised in the affluent community of Short Hills, New Jersey. Like most teenager, Growing up was complicated for Joelle. On the outside, her appearance was the typical wealthy white privileged teenager, but being raised by a large extended, Italian, Roman Catholic family; a mother who immigrated from Italy and a first generation father, fitting in was not always easy. She lived on a block where most of her friends were latch key kids while she was always under the supervision of an extended family.

*K. Tobin & J. Kincheloe, (eds.), Doing Educational Research—A Handbook, 59–84.*

Joelle developed an early awareness of cultural difference and an interest in social justice and equity as a result of growing up with her parents, three brothers, one sister and her grandmother and frequent visits made from her aunts, uncles and cousins who lived near by. She, also regularly visited her relatives in Piedimonte Matese, a small town in the foothills of the Appennini Mountains in Italy. It was there that she became fascinated by differences between American and Italian customs, forms of governments, governmental participation, and way of life. In particular, she was impressed by the active involvement and political awareness of Italians of all ages and always wondered why predominately so many Americans did not actively and critically participate in our democracy.

The idea of promoting cultural pluralism and improving Americans' active governmental involvement were not the only reasons, Joelle wished to pursue a career in education. She was also influenced by the inequity of education that her mother, Francesca, received at an urban high school in New Jersey. In the fall of 1957, Francesca registered for classes as the first Italian immigrant and was excited to start her new life as a student in the United States. She learned English very quickly and excelled in all of her classes, even making the honor roll. She became actively involved in the school's drama club and student government. Due to financial constraints, Francesca had to get a job. New to the country and eager to work, she decided to meet with her guidance counselor for advice on available jobs for teenagers on the honor roll and actively involved in the extracurricular activities at the local high school. Without examining Francesca's school records or asking her why she was interested in attending college, the counselor recommended that since she was an immigrant she should apply for a job at the local raincoat factory. Again, in Francesca's senior year, she met with her guidance counselor; this time to discuss her life plans after high school. Francesca asked her counselor, about the process of attending college and her counselor suggested that she get a job because "college was not for her kind." These two examples of discrimination in Francesca's life reflect how the educational system in the United States lacks equity as it prepares children from different social backgrounds for different roles within the economic division of labor. More importantly, these examples represent the need for culturally responsive teaching and research.

Joelle's interest in contrasting lifestyles and cultural differences within her widespread family as well as trying to eradicate the injustice her mother received in school, led her to pursue her education in higher education and ultimately, start a small learning community at Steele Divide Division High School, called Social Justice. In the planning of Social Justice, Joelle drew from her interdisciplinary graduate studies at Columbia University and New York University. Her time at Columbia University gave her a thorough grounding in women's history, African-American history and Native-American history; her three years at New York University taught her to use the arts to complement historical research and pedagogy. Thus, the small learning community that she designed combined history, English, and the arts in an investigation of the contradictions between democratic ideals and the realities of American life. She designed Social Justice to motivate students to develop their own voices and to provide creative outlets of expression in concert with their diverse learning styles and sociocultural backgrounds. Her overall rationale for the design of Social Justice stemmed from her belief that exposure to a more expansive version of American history and involvement in the community would foster student empowerment and equity.

Pam Joyce is an Afro-Caribbean female born in America and raised in a strict West Indian household by parents who emigrated from Jamaica to start a new life in New York. During the 1960s and 1970s, Pam lived in St. Albans, which was at that time a predominately white middle class neighborhood in Queens, New York. In the 60s, a small group of West Indians and African Americans began to buy homes in the area, which inevitably led to a drastic and sudden change in the demographics. Upon the arrival of these minority groups, there was a mass exodus of white homeowners causing the real estate market to plummet. Eventually, this led to a drastic decline in the quality of the public schools. It was in St. Albans that Pam first experienced the sad reality of the racist geographic demarcations of society. Since Pam's parents were new to the country and unfamiliar with the American school system, navigating the academic system proved to be a challenge. In order for Pam to receive a good education, her parents decided to send her to Catholic School.

Although, Pam's parents were not Catholics, they enrolled Pam in a Catholic in order for her to receive a "good" education. During this time, many black families believed that their children would get a better education in a religious school rather than in a predominantly minority public school. Since education was ranked as a priority by her parents, they opted for the quality education—a decision that assured a racially mixed student body. Both of her parents spoke with West Indian accents known as patois. Her dad had an added twist to his accent because he was born in Costa Rica and raised in Jamaica leaving him with a West Indian accent that sped rapidly off his tongue due to the influence of the Spanish language.

Coupled with this multifaceted array of rich ancestral roots was embedded a traditional and straight-laced outlook on life. Surprisingly, with such a restrictive background, Pam was gradually propelled over the years to seek out and fight for more democratic ways of being. In her effort to shed her internalized "stay to the norm" mentality, Pam left the safe zone of the "norm" and eventually settled into a more progressive way of thought.

Her college years reflect her dedication to personal and intellectual growth. She attended Queens College for a Bachelor's Degree in Early Childhood and Elementary Education, Montclair State University for a Masters Degree in Reading, and currently the City University of New York's Graduate Center for a PhD in Urban Education. Pam's experience ranges from developing transdisciplinary literacy curriculum, support programs for parents and students, supervising new teachers, and writing for educational publications. As a result, years of schooling have kept her on the cutting edge of educational research and have continued to ignite her passion for teaching as well as learning.

Pam's dissertation is a personal labor of love designed to help shatter the bonds of injustice in the educational system that she experienced in both private and public schools. Her hope is to abort those feelings of inadequacy that numerous minority students continue to endure on a daily basis often throughout a lifetime not only in school but also in adult life. She uses a reflective journal text as a vehicle to make that possible.

Old traditions make it difficult to deviate from the "norm" especially for womyn. Pam and Joelle experienced rather similar family backgrounds, growing up with first generation parents, which involved deep-rooted family traditions. In addition, both were daughters of immigrants and whose families stressed education as a vehicle for change. They have also shared a thirst for knowledge, which is apparent from their extensive schooling and desire to create new possibilities. Taking these similarities into consideration it is important to understand the historically and culturally engrained definitions of femininity and womanhood and acknowledge how individuals such as Pam and Joelle came to write this chapter and start the process of making a difference.

## The Setting of Storm Steel Divide High School

We met during orientation for new teachers at Storm Steel Divide Division High School, SSDD, and have been best friends and colleagues ever since. SSDD is a suburban high school in Highlander, New Jersey. The city of Highlander represents socioeconomic and racial diversity, yet a well-known railroad track divides its population. On one side of the tracks reside predominantly middle-class to upperclass white, or European, residents; on the other side, lies Lowlander, populated by lower-income residents, many of them of color. The Highlander public school district, nationally recognized as a model for a racially integrated district, had ensured that racial balance was achieved and maintained in all of its schools. Nevertheless, there is a persistent academic achievement and opportunity gap – along racial lines. SSDD is 40 percent white and 60 percent nonwhite, no less than 78 percent of the students who are classified as Special Education are nonwhite, and 79 percent of the students who fail one or more classes are African-American.

## The Need for Change

We both came to SSDD from large, dysfunctional urban high schools and were eager to begin our first year at the school. During that first year, we spent countless hours on the phone and much of the conversation involved improving the achievement and opportunity gap at the school. Since that first year of teaching at SSDD, we have been committed to move beyond a celebration of cultural diversity to a systematic scrutiny of historical systems of power, privilege and authority through various new courses we created. During these personal innovative times we were met with covert and overt sabotaging responses. Consequently, we attribute much of our growth spurts in critical consciousness to these deskilling moments. Through these debilitating encounters, we were able "to name [our] discontent and act on such an articulation" (Kincheloe, 2003, p. 2). In effect, we found a voice, continued to fight for our beliefs, and came to terms with the "what is" at SSDD.

These transformative experiences helped us to realize the potential damage of a restrictive environment to the human potential of teachers as well as students.

As advocates of a more democratic reconceptualization of education, we were aware of the demoralizing effects of teacher and student deskilling practices and in response sought multiple ways to address that situation. In addition to creating new courses and moving away from prepackaged curricular material, we became actively involved in our community, going beyond school walls in our teaching practices, discovering critical voice, and eventually coming to terms with the need for furthering our studies.

"Teachers are 'studied down' in the sense that those who control the research use their inquiry to inform themselves about their subordinates (mere practitioners), later using their information to manipulate and control them" (Kincheloe, 2003, p. 35). As teacher researchers, we go against the grain and dispel the myth that teachers are only qualified to "follow the leader". As demonstrated in this chapter, we creatively use text which represents our passion for "what can be". In dialogue, we become involved in collapsing the traditional approach to educational research. In actuality, we jump out of the box and dare to conceptualize and interpret our own experiences. Ultimately, contrary to Taylorist efficiency that involved the "reduction of the role of the laborer," we enhance the role of the laborer—which in this case was our roles as teachers (Kincheloe, 2003, p. 119).

Research is central to enhancing the role of the teacher. It is complicated because it involves change in the "self" which often requires divorcing traditional perspectives as well as changes outside of "self" such as educational institutions. Thinking of research as a tri-level cognitive act as Kincheloe suggests, helps to appreciate the complexity of the feat. In summarizing the three level cognitive act of research: *Level 1* represents puzzle-solving, *Level 2* represents self-monitoring, reflection, and meta cognition, and *Level 3* involves questioning the process as well as making sense of it and contextualizing the work itself (2003, p. 153-154). The cognitive research act in its entirety epitomizes teachers as change agents and as educators. As educators, we feel we have a "moral obligation to be agents of change" (Villegas & Lucas, 2002 p. 64). We adhere to Villegas's suggested list for teacher preparation, which can be both applicable to new and veteran teachers. In order for teachers to be change agents Villegas proposes that they:

- Emphasize the moral dimension of education.
- Guide prospective teachers in developing their own personal vision of education and teaching.
- Promote the development of empathy for students of diverse backgrounds.
- Nurture passion and idealism as well as a realistic understanding of obstacles to change, provide evidence that schools can become more equitable, teach about change process, and promote activism outside as well as inside the classroom.
- Emphasize the importance of and the development of skills for collective action and collaboration (2002, p. 59).

This list is by no means exhaustive in an ever-changing society but provides a starting point and acts as a guide for all teachers. In addition, it provides an informed framework for teachers to promote democratic practices in the educational system.

## Womyn's Way of Knowing

In a field, which is dominated by white males, it is important to examine how womyn and students of color prevail through this process. This chapter examines how two female doctoral students, one Jamaican-American and one Italian-American, identify themselves, validate their modes of knowing and learning and most importantly, talk about how they do their research. Over the past several decades, scholars have made many strides in uncovering the diverse roles of womyn in society as well as validating and promoting what some call womyn's ways of knowing (as diverse as they may be when class, culture, and race are considered), although much more needs to be done.

Since the 1970s much work has acknowledged how womyn's voice has been missing from research as well as research subjects. Carol Gilligan in her book, *In Different Voice Psychological Theory and Women's Development*, reveals the importance of searching for, hearing and understanding womyn's voices. She argues that due to fundamental and physiological differences, womyn see the world differently from men; they interpret it through their own perceptions. She asserts that when we acknowledge and promote these differences, the understanding of human development can finally become complete. According to Gilligan, "women . . . define themselves in a context of human relationships" and have "sensitivity to the needs of others . . . [which leads] women to attend to their voices other than their own and to include in their judgment other points of view" (Gilligan, 1994, pp. 16-17). By using this expansive perspective, issues of race and class can also be included, and are central topics in our educational research agenda.

By using the model of conversation, which is considered by many as a feminine way of understanding, we are able to validate our ways of knowing and include marginalized voices as part of our research agenda. "To have voice is to be human, to have something to say is to be a person. But speaking depends on listening and being heard; it is a relational act" (Gilligan, 1994. p. xvi). By validating conversation as a way of understanding, womyn begin to define themselves on their own terms. Conversation is a dialectical act and provides for a connection between the people talking because it "requires careful listening; it implies a mutually shared agreement that together you are creating the optimum setting so that . . . ideas can grow and . . . reaches deep into the experience of each participant; it also draws on the analytical abilities of each" (Belenky, Clinchy, Goldberger & Tarule, 1986, p. 144). Thus, conversation includes "discourse and exploration, talking and listening, questioning, argument, speculation and sharing" and ultimately allows womyn to hear their own voices, connect to others, acquire and communicate new knowledge and most importantly, know the world from others peoples' point of view (Belenky et al., 1986, p. 144). As a result of the flow of conversation between us, we are able to establish our own point of view and through these experiences we feel strongly about the need for the exploration and validation of feminist ways of knowing.

Using a feminist paradigm as an archetype begins to break the typical sexist stereotypes that prevail in our society. Such a model develops a more accurate portrayal of womyn and provides representations of female accomplishment. This chapter explores our research, as we use conversation to frame how we came to write our dissertations.

In the search for finding the womyn's voice in research, it is important to recognize historical and cultural influences on womyn's ways of knowing. Throughout history, white womyn have been disadvantaged by gender but empowered by race while black womyn had to face the double discrimination of sexism and racism. This reality prompted black womyn to set a personal agenda. They took feminism one-step further defining it as womanism, which affirmed that the fight for womyn's rights includes both race and class, issues (Gordon, 1994, p. 113). We speak about both race and class issues from personal perspectives and incorporate this information into our scholarly conversation.

Paulo Freire in *Pedagogy of the Oppressed* asserts the importance of dialogue. For him, it is a rebirth and a necessary step for transformation and ultimately, liberation (Freire, 1990, pp. 47, 52). Freire believes that dialogue is central to human life and combines both reflection and action leading to praxis. Emancipatory dialogue, Freire maintained, has six central characteristics:

- Love, a commitment to others;
- Humility, learning and acting together without arrogance;
- Critical faith in man, the ability to reinvent one's self;
- Hope, for action and change;
- Critical thinking, reality is a transformative process; and
- Trust, a bond (Freire, 1990, p. 75-81).

Freire speaks about the importance of transforming education from a passive act to an active act and affirms the importance of dialogue as this vehicle for change. To avoid education as a banking system where students are empty vessels who record, memorize and repeat what the teachers says, dialogue breaks the chains of the banking system and allows for both the teacher and student to become jointly responsible for learning (Freire, 1990, p. 58-66). Dialogue is an act of creation and helps humans understand and investigate the world from their own web of reality while concurrently working to awaken them as conscious beings (Freire, 1990, p. 89). Freire's analysis of dialogue helps prove the importance of conversation as a way of knowing, ultimately, validating womyn's ways of knowing. Interestingly enough, Horton and Freire in their book (Horton & Freire, 1990), *We Make the Road by Walking* record their conversation on justice and equity, using what many might call a feminine way of communicating. In this chapter, we engage in dialogue, in Freirean style as a means of creatively approaching the dissertation process.

THE CONVERSATION BEGINS: JOELLE ASKS PAM NINETEEN QUESTIONS ABOUT RESEARCH AND HOW LIFE EVENTS SHAPE ACADEMIC AND RE-SEARCH INTERESTS

*Teaching Practice and Philosophy*

Pam: As I have been doing my preliminary research for my dissertation, I have been thinking about the various theoretical frameworks that would guide my dissertation. In my findings, I started to examine how many of our conversations revolved around the problems we encountered at SSDD and now, how we solve many of our issues in our doctoral studies through our weekly meetings and conversations on the phone. By using our conversations as ways of understanding, we then further validate the feminine way of knowing. It is through discussion of our personal experiences, that we make a true connection to our research and are able to represent diverse ways of knowing and doing research. I thought it would be interesting for us to have a conversation in this chapter about how our teaching experiences led us to apply to a doctoral program as well as helped to inform our research.

*Question #1: So, how would you characterize your teaching practices and philosophy and how has it informed your research?*

Pam: Based on my thirty years of experience, I would say that my teaching practices and philosophy have evolved over time. It progressed incrementally at different levels in my career from preschool to college level teaching. In that progression, I have been teaching in the area of urban education for fifteen years and with that experience I have come to acknowledge the worth of each student and the complexity of each individual. I know that is why I am so passionate about all students reaching their highest potential.

I remember in one of my undergrad education courses, a professor gave my class a mnemonic, P.I.E.S. (physical, intellectual, emotional, and social) and indicated that all of these factors relate to the understanding of the total child. P.I.E.S. keeps me focused and cognizant of the reality that when dealing with young people their education goes far beyond school walls. I never forgot P.I.E.S., and still today it informs my teaching practices, philosophy, and now my research focus.

Joelle: I agree with you in the importance of tapping into students' lives and making them feel like school is a place for them to learn and grow. By using student's personal experiences, we build on their prior knowledge and allow them to begin to actively participate in their construction of knowledge. My pedagogical approaches are rooted in constructivism and remind me of the work of educational theorist, James Gabriano. He believes that there are four components to students' lives: their friends, their family, their school and their community and when we combine all four elements in our teaching practices and research, we make students feel invested and provide useful and practical scholarship for educators, administrators and policy makers. Communities of learners are quite important to me and are why I developed the small learning community at SSDD and presently devote much of my research to learning beyond the four walls of the classroom.

*Question #2: How do you see your role as an educator and how does that influence your research?*

Pam: I see my role as an educator in the form of a motivator, role model, and an "out of the box" representative for innovative alternatives in the field of education that will promote life-long learning. I interact with students and essentially tap into their world, through whatever means necessary, in order to have the tools necessary to stimulate their minds. In thirty years of teaching, I have observed many children but sadly in the twenty-first century I have noticed a dramatic change in the energy level and motivation of the students I teach. I have watched students sitting in class unmotivated and lethargic. It's as if the thirst for discovery has been sucked out of them and because of that debilitating energy, efforts to ignite their imaginations and rekindle their spirits have become increasingly difficult. In response to this dilemma, I am determined to uncover societal as well as human influences connected to this problem that work to incapacitate my students.

The need for relationships both in education and in various aspects of inquiry has evolved from my research. I have seen that building relationships with parents and students can help to motivate students who have lost their zeal for learning. My research explores the need for teacher/parent relationships to ignite the spirits of unresponsive students. As a result of the research, teacher relationships with students as well as parents should be deemed mandatory groundwork when addressing student self-motivation. Consequently, with an effort to nurture relationships as a priority in education the whole child is taken into consideration and more individual progress, both in academics as well as with "self," becomes visible over time.

Joelle: As an educator, I believe my role is to provide my students with opportunities to become proactive, effective citizens who appreciate the importance of social responsibility to the greater community and who are motivated to engage in activities that build self-confidence and competency. In order to accomplish these goals, we need to provide students with critical approaches to learning, in which they learn about, and question, interrelationships between culture, power, and subjugated voices. By providing students with opportunities that allow them to question and inquire about how our society operates then we allow our students to become researchers, and ultimately build a community of life long learners.

My role as an educator is rooted in Freire's educational scholarship. No longer, are teachers gatekeepers of knowledge, but facilitators of learning experiences. The teacher's role changes to a coach that creates a variety of ways for students to learn content information and to develop varied ways of instruction and assessment.

One way I accomplished this goal was to alter the traditional forms of assessment. No longer would students just write essays and take multiple choice tests but create a museum exhibition with a catalogue, design a war game, create a newspaper, write letters to the editor, write a eulogy, create a brochure and present a radio broadcast. By deconstructing the typical pedagogical approach to education, we invigorate students, and encourage them to participate in their learning, allowing us to put our theories into practice.

Using a constructivist approach to teaching helped inform my role as a researcher. By using the students' lived experiences, I started to see the many intersections between theory and practice and ultimately synthesize both.

Pam: Like you, I also adhere to a Freirean mindset and promote transgressive teaching. I feel that we are all interconnected and basically shrouded by a multitude of diverse surroundings not simply entombed within us. In effect, I believe everything I do has a ripple effect, which makes me constantly aware that my actions in the classroom have a resounding influence and therefore, warrant the need for critical thought to precede action. I incorporate this level of awareness and inclusive philosophy in my teaching practices and in my research. In my research as in teaching there has been evidence of my life experiences as well as in social situations that have melded together overtime and has trickled down to profoundly influence the direction of my research.

I believe that the various interconnected relationships of life helped me to formulate a firmly grounded educational vision. A part of this vision, which is dealt with in my dissertation, is to teach students and their parents how to navigate the system and be in relationship with it by first modeling "how to" and then gradually demonstrating the benefits of being among the power holders.

*Question #3: We have been discussing the importance of building a community at the high school level; do you think that building relationships with peers and professors as well as a community is necessary at the university level?*

Pam: Based on my experiences in the doctoral program, I would say yes, the university experience requires navigating the system "know how" and constructing relationships. Much needs to be learned and relationships have to be built along the way to assist with the learning process. Ultimately, in order to circumvent the dreaded All But Dissertation (ABD status) in the doctoral program, survive the coursework requirements, and eventually earn a PhD degree, we have to be able to nurture a variety of relationships and critically negotiate through the system.

Joelle: In looking back over the past two years that I have been at the City University of New York (CUNY) Graduate Center, building relationships with my colleagues and professors has been essential. Actually, I am quite impressed with the relationships I have been able to forge with my professors. They have considered me a colleague and helped me to grow and take risks with my educational scholarship.

*Entering the CUNY Graduate Center*

*Question #4: What motivated you to enter the Urban Education doctoral program at the CUNY Graduate Center?*

Pam: A strong desire to be heard motivated me to continue my education, and the Ph.D degree appeared to have the potential for creating a more credible voice for me. At SSDD, *outside* Ph.D voices were always heard as opposed to *inside* teacher voices. The belief at SSDD was that a Ph.D degree meant people would listen to you as well as value what you had to say. I thought if that was truly the case, I needed to earn a Ph.D because I had something to say about urban education and I needed to be heard.

Observing administrators and educators who were not willing to go the necessary extra mile to understand the underlying issues that shape minority underachievement was another motivating force for me. In response to this disservice to minority students and in an effort to address teacher deskilling, I enrolled in a doctoral program with the hope of enhancing the volume of my voice as an advocate for students who often demand unprecedented levels of understanding.

Joelle: There were several reasons that I applied for my doctorate. Similar to your reasons, I had a difficult time accepting the fact that administers were not supporting student-based learning and not providing equal education for all its students. It amazed me that SSDD, a school so rich with diversity of all kinds, the only students that received a great education were the students tracked in the Advanced Placements classes and had parents who were overt advocates for them. I had a difficult time understanding that a good education at our high school was for the few. For me, I believed that we were not serving all of our students and I wanted to provide qualitative research models that would help educators reach all of their students. By using a constructivist pedagogical paradigm I started to see the change in my classroom where all of a sudden the shy students began to speak out in class and reflect on the lessons. I wanted to share these successes and build on this type of inquiry.

I was also motivated by my mother's educational experience. I wanted to become the first Italian-American womyn in my family to hold a doctorate.

*Question #5: Did you face any challenges in the process of applying to the Graduate Center?*

Pam: My biggest concern, which also became my personal obstacle, was being a woman of color entering an environment that was traditionally not welcoming to minorities and reserved for "whites only." What about you?

Joelle: I was nervous about the workload and whether or not I could meet the challenge. What did you do to overcome that challenge?

Pam: I had to make sure that I was mentally and physically ready for the challenge. I had help from family and friends, which became my support network, but I had to grapple with my inner psyche in order to set out on this demanding venture.

I also decided to trust the intuition of two professors that had faith in my ability to succeed. They mentored me through the enrollment process and have faithfully continued support throughout the program. In the months prior to the first day of class, I sought reinforcement and spoke with professors of color from my undergrad college. They were inspirational and helped me to feel even more secure with my decision to enter into a doctoral program.

After completing the registration procedure, paperwork, and entrance interview, I immediately began to meet other encouraging doctoral students who helped to relieve my lingering anticipation.

Joelle: Pam, I feel very fortunate to have you as my mentor. Watching you develop from a classroom teacher to a teacher researcher really inspired me to become a part of the process. And, of course, hearing your words of encouragement motivated me to take the next step in my career.

Since you are a year ahead of me, you gave me important insights and techniques to becoming a good doctoral student. I could not believe the intricate concepts I needed to understand in order to become a successful doctoral student. I think one of the first classes for a doctoral program should deal with the change from a master's student to a doctoral student. Since the first semester comes and goes so quickly, it is difficult to master everything in 16 weeks.

Finally, my parents were an encouraging factor and support with me going back to school. They stressed that the type of change I wanted to see in schools would take more schooling and with that I could be more productive and reach more students by training teachers and engaging in research that would promote the type of education I believed in.

*Confronting the Dissertation*

*Question #6: I know you are interested in change in the educational system. Now that you're almost finished with your doctorate, can you summarize your dissertation topic and explain how your personal experiences led you to your dissertation topic?*

Pam: My study documents five years of experiences in SSDD through journal entries that reflect the teaching experiences of a teacher in an urban/suburban high school in the northeastern part of New Jersey. The journal text situates the study in the context of SSDD and in "my own evolving research agenda" (Roth, 2005, p. 13). The agenda, though in a school context, also spills outside the walls of the school during the course of the five-year time frame. As the research agenda evolves both inside and outside the school walls, a history gradually unfolds within the walls and subsequently serves to direct the research.

I am studying how a teacher uses an evolving critical consciousness through the lens of a researcher as a focal point for change in an academic context. As the teacher, I observe through reflective journaling how my world within school walls tends to encompass the world of students, parents, administrators, and other faculty members. It also goes beyond school walls and entangles outside influences such as popular culture and the media, just to name a few.

In the past as well as the present, the "achievement gap" has embedded itself within schools and society without the emergence of any effective pathways for closing it. As a result of my research, through the use of teacher voice, the hope of releasing underachieving minority students from the negative entrapments of the phenomenon of the "achievement gap" becomes a possibility for transformative change. In essence, the study proposes that first, we must be conscious of the "what is," and then we can move on to action by creating possibilities for the "what can be".

*Question #7: Is there a specific reason why you chose journaling as a research method and what did you uncover through journaling?*

Pam: The initial rationale for the teacher journal was to make room for personal improvement within the educational realm by reflecting on my teaching practices. However, after journaling for five years, the initial rationale expanded and the idea of a research project evolved from glaring and disturbing racial discrepancies that progressively became apparent in my daily work. This recognition helped to nurture the idea for a more extensive study.

Describing and exploring the ever-expanding situation of minority underachievement through journaling created the possibility for enhanced critical consciousness. Immersed in the unfolding events, I was moved to question, "Why are minority students over-represented in lower tracked classes in a racially diverse school?" So puzzling was the "gap" phenomenon that I chose to document my observations and ponder them reflectively in the hope of gaining some insights. Hence, through critical consciousness, I gradually realized that specific themes as well as openings for human agency were emerging from the journal. The magnitude of these circumstances compelled me to further explore the inequities undermining the educational process at SSDD. Consequently, documented lived experiences coupled with my thoughts converged to inadvertently create a text that had the possibility to enact transformational change within the educational realm.

The experience seemed natural for me because I documented my lived experiences, therefore becoming extremely close to the text. The writing was based on my role as a teacher recording lived experiences over a five-year period from 1998/1999 - 2002/2003. Collectively, ingrained racial inequalities, socially accepted traditional positioning of students and teachers, and the institutionalized mechanisms that keep injustices alive were revealed through the text generated in the journal. During this time period, I took daily notes as well as some random notes and filed all faculty memos and newsletters. I worked with a number of students outside of the classroom in social situations around the school as well as over one hundred students that were assigned to me in classroom settings. I interacted with approximately one hundred faculty and staff members in multiple capacities and disciplines, including guidance counselors, administrators, student teachers, security guards, secretaries, and other staff members for a myriad of reasons in various contexts. I observed the attitudes and reactions of my students in relation to their designated "achievement gap" label. I listened to faculty express attitudes, as they pertained to underachieving minority students during lunchroom chatter or brief hallway encounters. Journal entries were thus acquired from discussions in the teacher's room, classroom activities, varied student interactions, the cafeteria, faculty meetings, and professional development workshops. As a result of my role as teacher/researcher in the journaling process, my awareness level was raised and I became more conscious about my life, the people surrounding me, and the lives of students. First, interactions inside the encapsulated environment of SSDD provided text for entries in the journal. In the latter years of my journaling the outside community and even the larger society became a source for my journal entries. The culminating result was that a text was created that housed my lived world experiences while documenting the lives of a diverse population of individuals at the high school.

*Question #8: How did you come up with your initial research techniques?*

Pam: Initially, I drew on past knowledge from my master's level coursework because at that time I only knew the general area of my doctoral research—minority underachievement. I was unsure how I was going to proceed theoretically and methodologically in that context. The research techniques simply evolved from my lived world experiences, such as teaching, coursework, and everyday life. Even with these experiences, I was not certain what procedures to follow but quickly gained direction from synthesizing my experiences from the doctoral course work. I realized much of the course work pertained to my research topic. I was fortunate because I zeroed in on my research topic early on, making it possible to relate my readings and papers directly to it. Situating course work around your dissertation topic during the beginning stages of your doctoral work is a valuable tip for students who want to avoid a ten-year doctoral program.

Joelle: So as you took your classes you were able to further develop your research ideas by linking the course readings with your research topic. This is an important connection allowing your research interest to be enhanced by the courses and the readings.

Pam: Exactly, and while reading the assigned books, I made notes that pertained to my areas of interest, minority underachievement and/or the "achievement gap" phenomenon. Eventually, through trial and error, I discovered a "best practice," which was a user-friendly coding system.

*Question #9: Can you describe that coding system?*

Pam: Yes, it was a simple system and easy to implement. The coding system involved using sticky notes to earmark various sections, pages, quotes, or excerpts from required course readings that were pertinent to my research topic. Sticky notes with information that was useful for the dissertation I labeled "diss"—an abbreviation for dissertation. The note meant that this particular text was to be revisited at an appropriate time in the future. At first, it seemed as if the date for revisiting would never come because there was so much to learn in order to be ready to revisit the "diss" sticky notes but gradually as you can see the date finally came.

Joelle: Pam, I have to say, I'm so happy you shared the coding tip with me in the beginning of my first year because it allowed me to guide my course readings with my research interests. It really helped to keep me organized and focused in my readings.

Pam: I'm excited that I was able to offer something useful to you by sharing what worked for me. I believe that sharing what works is one of the ways doctoral students can all learn to become professional researchers and to make it successfully through a Ph.D program.

Joelle: Another useful research tip I learned from you was to become a more reflective note-taker. Instead of just outlining the chapters in the books, I started to question the text I was reading. I think by questioning the text you are forced to see what works in the author's arguments and what does not. It also allows you to see how the text is related to your research topic.

Pam: I agree. It is a process and you learn as you go along. For example, I also learned in my second semester to annotate every book and article read during the program. Remembering to jot down summative information about each book makes the process easier whenever you are ready to write your dissertation. I would develop a system for annotating books, summarizing pertinent information for example, the copyright date, the title, the authors, and any other relevant information.

As with everything in life, we have to choose what is most appropriate for us. Therefore, these ideas and study tips will vary and students will continue to formulate what works best for them.

*Question #10: Are there any other tips that come to mind, Pam?*

Pam: Yes, there is one, I set up an index card system in which I would take notes after each chapter or subheading of a book. The index card notations helped me to keep focused on the most important aspects of the book as well as be prepared for "in-class" book discussions. In addition to chapter notes, if

I had questions on the information in the book, I would note them on the index cards or directly in the book and pose them at appropriate times during class discussions. I would also use the word "life" on sticky notes to indicate anecdotes that helped me make connections while reading.

This information sorting system was used as a way of handling the large amount of reading material we were given. Looking back, I would say by the end of the doctoral program, a conservative estimate for required reading was approximately 200 books and 150 articles. The personal system helped to keep the information straight in my head as well as maintain my sanity. In the final months of the doctoral program, which were devoted simultaneously to my last courses and writing the dissertation, all information sorting, storing, and categorizing techniques were revisited.

Lastly, I would say another tip involves the need for researchers to be able to explain their research—this became another important requirement later in the program. The art of presenting research involved an acquired expertise. It involved practice in oral delivery of information and proved to be valuable for the dissertation defense as well as a prerequisite to publishing and presenting at conferences. Needless to say, I soon discovered it was beneficial to verbally clarify my research to anybody who would listen. A good rule of thumb would be to give mini presentations whenever the opportunity comes up!

Another observation that seemed to surface at the end of the program was that many professors, in class or outside of class, often neglect to share "insider" information about research with their students. Under these circumstances the student needs to become an investigator and pursue an unbeaten path, if necessary, to retrieve as much "insider" information as possible in order to master being a doctoral student.

Joelle: I think because we are at the doctoral level, it is important that professors share their little anecdotes for doing research. I remember one of my professors shared with me his inside way of coding and it helped me think of how to organize my work in themes.

Pam: Yes, they assume that doctoral students have mastered how they learn and should know the tricks of the trade. I think however, that some students might be shocked early in the program when given an assignment of 15 books, plus a number of articles, a presentation, and multiple papers as an assignment all to be completed in a 16-week period. The shock might also intensify if students are returning to school after a lengthy hiatus. This is when the professor's "insider" information could help.

Joelle: And, I was one of those shocked students. Ha-ha. But in looking back, your tips and guidance really helped me stay focused and re-tune my organizational skills.

*Question #11: Since, we first met nine years ago, we have been through many edu-*
*cational cycles—ones of hope for change, ones of defeat and deskilling and now*
*writing our dissertations. You are on the home stretch and getting ready to defend*
*your dissertation. How do you recommend I proceed on making the transition from*
*ABD to a Ph.D.?*

Pam: I would suggest first looking at the three primary parts of the dissertation, the literature review, the methodology, and the theoretical framework.

The literature review is a survey of the research relevant to the dissertation—a doctoral student can use a lot of the research she does in the coursework of her program and material she has read in her area of interest. It is
important to keep in mind that your dissertation must be designed to generate
new knowledge in your field and in order to accomplish this goal, you must
know the field, know the concerns and interests and what is the known and
unknown in your domain. You must make theoretical decisions, which involve coming to understand what theories will guide your research and then
relate them to the research methods—how you are going to do your research
and what techniques you will implement—you choose.

The literature review should be a priority because it helps you focus your
research topic. Therefore, in the beginning you should be like a gatherer and
simply obtain general information about your topic. Later you will need to be
more and more specific when sorting out the literature related to your study.

Joelle: Based on your advice I am envisioning a funnel. I must start out
with understanding all the research in my field and then pick and choose
themes that directly relate to my research interest. So it is important to gather
general information in the field and then specific details that directly relate to
your research topic and finally report on the aspects that are missing in the
field.

Pam: I would say, yes, based on my experiences in the program. The dual
perspective, involving a general as well as specific outlook, is aligned with
critical consciousness because it allows the researcher to approach the study
from a more expanded critical lens. All the while you are gathering information, you are using your theoretical lenses to sort it, understand its assumptions, its biases, and its unstated views of human beings and how to conduct
research about them.

*Question #12: The literature review seems to be an important part of the disserta-*
*tion. Can you tell me about your literature review and how you did it?*

Pam: My literature review represents a broad spectrum of significant literature connected to the notion of the "achievement gap" between African-
American and white students. I brought together a body of literature to answer the question: What are the inherent dynamics within a school context
that influence the continuity of minority underachievement? A review of the
literature has provided an introduction to key factors emphasizing the exposure of the deficit realties surrounding the achievement gap phenomenon.

The literature covers educational, psychological, historical, political, and philosophical domains and exposes the power dimensions involved in the education of minorities of African descent, namely, Black Americans, Afro Caribbean Americans, and students living in America that were born in Africa or various Caribbean islands. These domains propagate through the student web of reality, set the stage for life performances, and interestingly commingle with the teacher's web of reality.

I argue that literature that covers diverse domains provides a broader perspective. It highlights the "what is" by examining realities within the school walls, the role of teachers, aspects of power, and racism, as well as societal influences, as having an influence in the underlying causes for the achievement gap. At times the literature is conflicting and fragmented which only serves to further concretizes the continuation of the "what is" in the world of minority underachievers and promote the need to sort and merge the more effective information. What is not discernible from the literature in its fragmented representation of the problem is an explanation of why the problem still persists in the twenty-first century. Essentially, given that the purpose of this dissertation is to present an interconnected merging of the literature reviewed, I attempt to do that in order to provide viable alternatives to the continuing problem of minority underachievement.

When faced with an overload of information, it is difficult to restrain oneself to not include unnecessary information in the literature review—a dissertation writer has to recognize that one cannot include everything. There is much to consider in this context. We need to weed through the literature and determine what should and should not be included as well as make sure that whoever is on your dissertation committee acknowledges your choice of authors. Basically, it would be wise to have the blessing of your dissertation committee on the matter of acceptable authors. Of course, this will vary from committee to committee, which then brings us to the many considerations connected with the dissertation committee itself.

*Question #13: I was just going to ask you; how did you go about picking your committee and what would you say could be criteria for choosing a dissertation committee?*

Pam: I chose my committee based on three criteria. First, I took classes with a number of professors and in this way I was able to determine which professors were aligned with or were open to my educational philosophy as well as my research topic. Secondly, I chose professors who could gently guide me to my highest intellectual potential and thirdly, I searched for professors who could respect my expertise and believe that I had something worthwhile to offer to the field of education.

I would also emphasize that your committee members must be in sync with your ideas. It is wise to consult with your dissertation committee concerning all areas of your research and whenever possible seek like-minded ideas. That does not mean that you cannot have your own ideas, but rather that your committee members should be aware of the direction of your research at all times especially if you take any unprecedented turns away from the "norm" or traditional ways.

Lastly, but most importantly committee members should be in sync with each other!

*Question #14: Pam, you gave a brief overview about what I need for the beginning of my dissertation: Can you talk a little bit more about how you picked the theory that guided your research?*

Pam: My theory emerged from various texts, as well as doctoral course work, which was progressively instrumental in guiding the direction of the theory. I started to see reoccurring themes and connections with my journal, which led to an overall formula that I was then able to document and use.

*Question #15: What specific theory did you choose to guide your work?*

Pam: I chose critical theory to guide my work because it required going deeper, peeling the many layers of the social, cultural, political, and pedagogical onion. My research required exploration of the underlying reasons why minority underachievement still existed after such a turbulent history concerning issues of racial injustice and the lack of power directly relating to the "gap" phenomenon. The five core doctoral level courses required by the CUNY doctoral program in Urban Education imparted a wealth of information and established my theory-research focus. After completing the core courses, I understood the worth of the work because it gave me background information and a more defined focus. Overall, the core courses put me on a path that heightened my critical consciousness and with this new awareness; I began to question everything with which I was not satisfied. I brought this criticality into my teaching practices and subsequently, began to realize the tacit as well as apparent meanings of the undemocratic practices of SSDD. I began to realize minute-by-minute world changes and their effects on humanity. My new awareness culminated in the understanding that nothing is fixed and that we should be mindful of the potential flexibility and fluidity in experiences.

My dissertation is based on a critical theoretical framework, which encompasses aspects of socio-political theory, pedagogy, ontology, and cognition. The research data are introduced through the lens of critical consciousness, which is the primary overarching theoretical framework of the study. The critical thread circulates through my teacher web of reality revealing from this critical perspective the experiences of all those who enter my world and touch the lives of underachieving minority students.

Joelle: How interesting, what you were learning from your course work was directly influencing your teaching practice. And in essence, you started to become more aware of how the sociopolitical aspects of life affect your students' lived worlds. The theory that you use in your dissertation now informs your practice and allows you to reconstruct your old views and question your approach to teaching. It seems like you are able to really connect to students' webs of reality. Critical theory acts as an umbrella to all of the wonderful experiences you provide for your students and more importantly has allowed you to include issues of race, class and gender in your class discussions.

Pam: Yes, and I also think that it allows me to see the "what is" more clearly, through this expanded critical lens. With this lens, I can include the future and project the "what can be"—this is the "immanent critique" of critical theory. Essentially, I gain the ability to see beyond the destruction of underachieving minority students and envision the possibilities—I can see what such students are capable of doing with their lives and for the world. Such a vision of immanence is a priceless gift in the field of education.

Critical theory grounds my dissertation. Criticality in the present state of urban education demands an understanding of the type of level of complexity involved in relation to underachieving minority students trapped in the "achievement gap" and their subsequent marginalized placement in the world. Hence, "a critical social theory is concerned in particular with issues of power and justice and the ways that the economy, matters of race, class, and gender, ideologies, discourses, education, religion and other social institutions, and cultural dynamics interact to construct a social system" (Kincheloe & McLaren, 2005, p. 281). Critical theory allows for an examination of the power factors that evolve from self, school, and society, which all join together to exacerbate the conditions that cause the minority underachievement or the "achievement gap."

Critical theory challenges the traditional binary perspectives of positivistic science such as "the knower and the known, the researcher and the researched, the scientific expert and the practitioner" (Kincheloe & McLaren, 1994, p. 150) and asserts that "the notion of self-reflection is central to the understanding of the nature of critically grounded qualitative research" (p. 147). In my dissertation, self-reflection is required in order to situate the teacher as well as the student, to begin to see from a critical consciousness what innate dynamics and repetitious influences affect minority underachievement within school walls. In sum, from this critical stance an introspective expansion of the "selfhood" of teachers as well as students emerges in transformative proportions. Here is where teacher and student agency to change the self and the world is enhanced.

Joelle: It seems one of the important aspects of being a teacher-researcher is having the ability to understand who you are and understand your web of reality as well as knowing your students and their lifeworlds.

Pam: I think you are correct because with a heightened critical consciousness about my web of reality, I naturally—as if on automatic pilot—was led to a phenomenological methodology for my research. I became focused on lived experiences.

Joelle: I have a firm understanding of how you picked your theoretical framework. I think it might be safer to say how it picked you. What scares me the most about my dissertation is coming up with the methodology. But, I feel like once I have the methodology my nerves will be at ease.

*Question #16: How did you come up with your methodology?*

Pam: The methodology for my research evolved from critical theory. The idea of going deeper prompted me to consider the bricolage qualitative approach. Bricolage involves taking research strategies from a variety of disciplines and traditions as they are needed in the unfolding context of the research situation (e.g., Kincheloe, 2005). The bricolage method is a good fit for my study because it allows for a broader critical vision and the merging of complex splintered pieces of information related to minority underachievement. It captures the multiple sides of the underachievement issue as well as grasps the complexities of the individuals involved through the layering of the methodologies.

The bricolage qualitative approach is open-ended and when combined with a layering of methods, it expands the overall breadth and value of the research. In my research, an open-ended approach is needed in order to capture the behind the scenes, hidden nuances that occur unnoticed or that are suppressed in a regular school day. Due to the opening and exploration of these additional avenues of expression, the result is more comprehensive research and subsequently, the opportunity for more inclusive information about minority students from a multilayered bricolage perspective.

Critical phenomenology—one layer of the methodology—is demonstrated through teacher journaling in an attempt to replicate a portion of minority school life from a teacher perspective. Critical hermeneutics, through textual analysis of the journals, weaves together unfolding themes and patterns within an overarching framework of critical theory. Together, these methodologies reconstruct minority life experiences at SSDD. These methodologies specifically examine the "within school walls" environment as it interacts in a circulatory pattern influenced by "self" as well as "other" dynamics. Ultimately, it is my hope to witness unexpected and unpredicted results from this research that will contribute viable alternatives to counter the present "norm" of minority underachievement.

Joelle: So the journaling method, first allowed you to observe and reflect on what you were seeing, then it allowed you to interpret. It allowed you to put a practice into an action. And, now you are using a critical lens to deal with the problems you see.

Pam: Yes, for me everything boils down to action—the purpose of critical theory and critical theoretically informed research. The worth of the research involves the new information it produces and the action that emerges from data. In my research, my action, passion, and dedication to finding alternatives to minority underachievement are visible through teacher advocacy and emancipatory activity.

*Question #17: How did you choose what to include in your journal entries?*

Pam: Fundamentally, being mindful of life's unpredictable connections is a step toward the complexity of criticality, which paces itself and eventually envelops the research in multiple ways. My choices demonstrate an awareness of power in diverse manifestations, a rejection of oppressive social and educational structures, and a support for emancipatory efforts in the interest of change. I simply wrote about observations and did not tamper with the naturally unfolding drama of life. I made journal entries on what affected me and what activated my sensibilities about undemocratic practices toward minorities in the context of school.

This all encompassing circular thought process aptly points to the hermeneutic circle. It appears that "the part can only be understood from the whole, and the whole only from the parts." (Alvesson & Skoldberg, 2000 p. 53). Thus, analyzing the multiple sides of minority underachievement, which comprise the "parts," combined with the complexities that slowly come to light in the interpretive phase and comprise the "whole," inevitably provides a constantly changing, expanded context as well as a broader perspective about the phenomenon of underachieving minority students. Understanding these part-whole relationships, I entered into the hermeneutic circle of interpretation.

An example of an all encompassing circular thought process involving "parts" and "whole" and the interrelated relationships they create is demonstrated by underachieving minority high school students is a journal text excerpt below dated 10/2/98:

*Journal Text Entry—October 2, 1998*

Today my students finally settled into the learning process and I was greeted with a surprising wave of protest. They complained about the work. They wanted to know why they had to do so much work and asked if they could go back to dittos like they used to do in the previous basic skills classes. "Isn't this a basic skill class," they questioned? "Why do we have to do so much work?" "It's only a basic skill class."
I was disturbed by their thoughts and their questions. They begged me to go back to a non-thinking approach of teaching where their brains could experience the least amount of use and they could be fed dittoed information.
Based on these student protests, my conclusion was that basic skills students needed work that was more challenging rather than skill and drill assignments, which made them content to accept less. The disturbing student stance against using their brains insinuated that they were not used to being pushed to their ultimate potential and that they had been allowed to get lazy in the past. It prompted me to question how teachers in other disciplines

treated the basic skills students in their classes. Were the demands different for the basic skills students vs. the non-basic skill students? Did teachers misinterpret and allow low visibility and non-academic behavior as the accepted and voluntary direction chosen by some students?

*Internalized Oppression (Tatum, 1997)*

A "part" of the web of reality for the underachieving minority students is the acceptance of negative attributes about themselves. Through years of being in a basic skills program these students are slowly robbed of their self-worth and potential for higher growth. They are repeatedly positioned in a way that forces them to accept their lower tracked status as the "norm" and gradually internalize the self-fulfilling prophesy of the underachiever, who is unchallenged and basically invisible. The result is the devaluing of the "whole" child and an example of the relationship of the part to the whole. The negative "parts" fed into the "whole" child and in the process influenced the outcome.

*Question #18: Pam, it seem like you are able to use your research as a transformative action plan, one that allows change to occur. Could you talk a little bit about moving from research to action?*

Pam: Keeping in mind the idea that history, ontological perspectives, and everyone we come in contact with influences our actions, that is all the more reason to be critical when the role of researcher is assumed. I believe the critical researcher role has a responsibility to act on information uncovered in the research. In reality, everything comes full circle, the historicity of the teacher/researcher, participants in the study, as well as the complexity of society and from that interconnected circle openings for agency appear. In effect, being mindful of the comprehensive nature of the lived world through my research moved me to action. Within the five-year journaling period, I created innovative curriculum for underachieving minority students, established a parent/student support group run by teachers, began advocating for students and parents who kept a low profile at the school, and mentored other teachers by modeling how to reject deskilling precedents set by the school. My research was the catalyst for these actions and such actions helped to keep my spirit renewed in the understanding that incessant effort could make a noticeable difference in the lives of underachieving students.

*Question #19: In a nutshell, what would you say is an overall personal gain from the journaling experience?*

Pam: Noting lived experiences in a journaling format enabled me to better understand the present state of minority education in America and thus, create the possibility for a broader spectrum of experiences to be included when exploring the minority underachievement phenomenon. My assumed role as a phenomenologist provided me the analytical power not only to tap into the lived world experiences of minority students but to also use my intuitive ability to go below the surface. Thus, I entered the teacher's web of reality with the intention of not only understanding "what is" but also understanding "why it came to be that way." Such knowledge led directly to critical immanence—insight into the possibility of "what can be." In this sense, the use of phenomenology in research taught me that we cannot understand an educational act without understanding the framework, and the context within which teachers, students, and administrators make sense of their thoughts, feelings, and actions (Kincheloe, 2001, p. 222). Furthermore, if we are to uncover the intricate complexities of individual lives as they relate to educational and societal life, we must be ready to implement meaningful change and if necessary embark in transgressive, unorthodox research strategies, social and pedagogical theories, and ways of teaching and learning.

### WRITING THE CRITICAL DISSERTATION

Our main concerns have been how to democratize urban schools and the need for culturally responsive teaching and research. In our journey from teacher-practitioner to teacher-researcher, we realized the importance of diversifying the research process. By using critical inquiry, we can improve educational research and incorporate various ways of knowing. For us, education is political and embedded in it are particular values of the dominant culture and as teacher-researchers we must promote ideas of social justice through our research. Especially today when, current federal policy initiatives are largely driven by quantitative results, our charge is to demonstrate the importance of qualitative research. By using experience to construct meaning as well as narrative inquiry, the researcher becomes situated in the lived experience and gains a greater sense of intersection between her beliefs, motives, practices, and the world she is studying. Our approach to research is framed around the importance of understanding student and teacher lived experiences and how research can empower and transform experiences for those involved.

It is our hope that after reading this chapter, doctoral students and other researchers will take away a number of insightful tips and useful strategies that make the journey easier and bring them closer to producing informative research and earning a PhD. Given the epistemological threats to critical and even qualitative research in the last half of the twenty-first century, we must continue our conversation about research and practice in order to keep the lines of communication open and remain in the flow of a constantly changing world.

### REFERENCES

Alvesson, M., & Skoldberg, M. (2000). *Reflexive methodology: New vistas for qualitative research.* Thousand Oaks, CA: Sage Publication.

Belenky, M., Clinchy, B., Goldberger, N. & Tarule, J. (1986). *Women's ways of knowing: The development of self, voice, and mind.* New York, NY: Basic Books.

Freire, P. (1990). *Pedagogy of the oppressed* (Raos, M. B. Trans.). New York, NY: The Continuum International Publishing Group.

Gilligan,C. (1994). *In a different voice: Psychological theory and women's development.* Cambridge, MA: Harvard University Press.

Gordon, L. (1994). *Pitied not entitled.* Cambridge, MA: Harvard University Press.

Horton, M. & Freire, P. (1990). *We make the road by walking: Conversations on education and social change.* Edited by Bell, B. Gaventa, J. and Peters, J. Philadelphia: Temple University Press.

Kincheloe, J. L. (2001) *Getting beyond the facts: Teaching social studies/social sciences in the twenty-first century.* New York, NY: Peter Lang.

Kincheloe, J. L. (2003). *Teachers as researchers: Qualitative inquiry as a path to empowerment.* (2nd ed.). London: RoutledgeFalmer.

Kincheloe, J. L. (2005). On to the next level: Continuing the conceptualization of the bricolage. *Qualitative Inquiry, 11*, 323-350.

Kincheloe, J. L. & McLaren P. (1994). Rethinking critical theory and qualitative research. In Denzin N. & Lincoln Y. (Eds.), *Handbook of qualitative research.* (pp. 138-157). Thousand Oakes, CA: Sage.

Kincheloe, J. L. & McLaren P. (2005). Rethinking critical theory and qualitative research. In N. Denzin and Y. Lincoln (Eds.), *Handbook of qualitative research.* Vol. 3. (pp. 303-42). Thousand Oakes, CA: Sage.

Tatum, B. D. (1997)."*Why are all the black kids sitting together in the cafeteria?*" *And other conversations about ra*ce. NY: Basic Books.

Villegas, A & Lucas T. (2002). *Educating culturally responsive teachers: A coherent approach.* Albany: SUNY.

**II    WAYS OF DOING EDUCATIONAL RESEARCH**

KATHLEEN S. BERRY

# 4. RESEARCH AS BRICOLAGE

*Embracing Relationality, Multiplicity and Complexity*


Bricolage: The processes by which ... societies construct language and myth

Claude Levis-Strauss (1966)

The activity of borrowing from one's own textual heritage whatever is needed to produce new and different texts, with an emphasis on intertextual borrowing for the purposes of textual construction

Derrida (in McLerran & Patin, 1997)

## PROLOGUE TO RESEARCH AS BRICOLAGE

As the use of traditional dominant quantitative and qualitative methodologies comes into question, a framework is needed so novice and seasoned researchers can manage the complexities of doing research in the postmodern era. With this in mind, I would like to elaborate on the concept of *bricolage* as a way of researching human activities, relationships and cultures. Bricolage is fast becoming a key way of rethinking what counts as research and how to conduct research. My intention in this chapter is to supply an introductory stance to a changing body of knowledge and methodologies about research. Further discussions on possible ways to begin and continue through the complexity of a research process using bricolage are included. To complete the research cycle of employing bricolage, possible innovations on recording and reporting will be shared towards the end of this chapter. Words that appear in the glossary are **bolded**. Clarification of some terms is kept in the context of the text in [squared brackets].

My French Acadian neighbors know what bricolage means when I ask them. "Oh yes", they reply, "It's like when the carpenter who builds a house and *uses anything he (she) has handy to get the job done*". Another neighbor builds bird-houses as a hobby and calls himself (in French), un bricoleur. He *uses scraps* of leftover wood from large scale projects to create the most unique and charming birdhouses and *notes that no two ever look the same*. I watch Monsieur Gallant *collect scraps of metal, wood, tossed out chairs and other furniture*; extract *assorted* nails from moldings; *gather* nuts, bolts and screws *of all shapes and sizes* from the ground around construction sites and drive around in his pickup on garbage days to select *odds and ends* of 'the other person's junk'. I ask him what he is

*K. Tobin & J. Kincheloe, (eds.), Doing Educational Research—A Handbook, 87–115.*

going to do with all these materials. *"Buildin'* a cabin on my little private island", he giggles. "But M. Gallant", I observe, "nothing matches and how do you know what you need or what it's going to look like? Do you have a plan? Do you use everything? What do you do with the leftovers?" He shrugs his shoulders, "Uh? *I don't use everything, just what I need. No plan, I just get started and then depending on what I've got available decides what way I'm going to build it, what shape it will take. And the leftovers?— I just use them for the next job, ya' never know what I'll use them for the next time"*. Daringly, as the academic, I ask, "Es tu un bricoleur?" "Mais oui – of course!"

These anecdotes help me to understand what is meant by bricolage when applied to the field of research and what is meant when researchers are called bricoleurs. Several key features of bricolage include: "using the tools at hand"; "many different tools"; "collecting different parts from different sources"; creative, unique and no two look the same"; "no blueprint on how to build/construct the object (*the knowledge* - my italics)"; "don't know in advance what shape the building (*text/knowledge/research*) will take"; and "you don't use all the parts".

Introduced into the field of research by the French anthropologist Levis- Strauss in *The Savage Mind (*1966)*, adopted by Denzin and Lincoln (1994) in T*he Handbook for Qualitative Research* and developed further by Kincheloe and Berry (2004) in their book *Rigour and Complexity in Educational Research*, bricolage is gradually addressing a growing concern about what counts as and how to do research in an age of postmodernism, other postdiscourses and digital technologies. At a time when the discourses of emancipation, inclusiveness, social justice, plurality, multiplicity, diversity, complexity and chaos are entering academic circles and mainstream communication media, a way of incorporating these discourses and their complimentary practices requires new research questions, tools, processes and ways of reporting. Bricolage offers the potential to do so.

Some of the common questions asked by both novice and seasoned researchers unfamiliar with bricolage are:

- What is it?
- Where does it fit in the field of research?
- Why use it instead of other types of research?
- How do you get started?
- How do I know what to do if there are no explicit directions?
- How do you know what 'tool' to use/select from all that information?
- How do you write it up?
- How do you report it?
- How do I know if it will be an acceptable way of researching?

Many, but not all, of these questions and concerns are addressed throughout the chapter. Here are some of the concerns when there is a degree of familiarity:

- Too much for beginning researchers
- Too messy
- No depth
- No focus

- Lacking logic and evidence/proof
- Too bulky/lengthy to include everything

THE HISTORICAL AND POLITICAL CONTEXT OF BRICOLAGE

While Kuhn (1970) led the way for thinking about research and scientific break-throughs as a sociological process of normal and revolutionary sciences respectively, what has emerged over the past two decades still tends to support a **monological** process of conducting research in the arts, humanities, social sciences and, specifically in the context of my world, education. Contemporary research theorists and practitioners alike have developed a host of new research methodologies but still tend to think in terms of **totalizing frameworks.** Research processes and methodologies seem self contained, individualistic, singularly applied, isolated from one another or merely laid out in a block pattern similar to that suggested by Denzin and Lincoln (1994, 2000, 2005) in their introductory chapter under the heading *Qualitative Research as Bricoleur and Quilt Maker.* Researchers as quilters may become astute at doing one or a few types of research but use the principles and practices in a manner that strongly hints at authority and objectivity, neither of which are conditions for postmodern sensibilities or bricolage.

It might be a human trait to want manageable, workable, familiar structures and guidelines to frame the research process and product. So most researchers, needless to say, grasp at different metaphors such as quilt maker, collage artist, film montage, and potpourri to help conceptualize what bricolage means as a way of researching. In chapter five of Kincheloe and Berry (2004), to image the process of research as bricolage, I used several metaphoric and mapping devices such as trees and forest [foregrounding-backgrounding]; transparent overheads [each layer contains multiple theoretical, methodological , interpretive, political and narrative discourses, styles and perspectives]; DVD menu selections and hypertexting. In the end, the image that worked best for me was the map of Lorenz's butterfly effect (p. 112) borrowed from theories of chaos and complexity (Prigogine & Stengers, 1984).

Positivistic and other traditional research designs tend to work with a singular, linear, step-by-step structure with certain features such as rationality [critical bricoleurs ask whose rationality and what counts as rationality?]; significance, limitations, literature review/background to the study [not usually a discussion of the theories employed in the study as bricolage demands]; one kind of design and methodology [thus one kind of research and analysis]. Bricolage, however, works with elements of randomness, spontaneity, self-organization, far-from-equilibrium conditions, feedback looping, and bifurcations, all features of the world of chaos and complexity. In addition, poststructuralists, feminist perspectives, and researchers working with other post-multiple discourses, and a host of various narrative structures, create and borrow features from multiple sites befitting bricolage; in a manner similar to *intertextuality.* Bricoleurs struggle to avoid a monological, single path or method. This is where novice and seasoned researchers need to unlearn as much as learn about research when engaging bricolage.

Much of the discussion and many of the examples in this chapter are drawn from my work with MEd and PhD graduate students over the past few years in our attempt to make sense of why bricolage, what and when to use bricolage, and how to do bricolage yet maintain the expectations and quality of academic and scholarly work. My work as a professor of multiple literacies with both undergraduate and graduate students also adds to my understanding of how to do bricolage as a means of research. Overriding all this knowledge gained from experience is my forty years of teaching, twenty-five of those at the university level. With this background, I feel I have lived through a historical account of changing theories and practices of what counts as research in the social sciences, arts and humanities including education. A personal contextualization of that history might clarify how I came to be located in the field of research as a bricoleur [one who uses bricolage]—a use of *narrative* bricolage, so to speak.

For contemporary research content and processes such as bricolage, identifying how and why the researcher is positioned in the study is a must. Shifting positionalities [based on place, time, gender, race, class, sexuality etc.] from which a researcher reads, writes, analyzes, indicate a recognition of the part played by the socializing texts of scholarly discourses, academic expectations and contexts throughout time and space. I have listed my personal research history by dates to coincide with that of Denzin and Lincoln (2000, 2005). They are calling the dominant research periods historical 'moments' of research and claim the different moments overlap and operate simultaneously. It is noted that even from the second edition published in 2000 to the third edition in 2005, the authors have added four historical moments, which reflect the fast-paced changes occurring in the field of educational research. In addition to the extra moments, fourteen new topics have been added to the 2005 edition, which are reflective of the changing landscape of what counts as research and the increase in research 'tools' available for a bricoleur.

I tell this story as a narrative account of not only how I came to be positioned as a bricoleur in the historical and political contexts of doing research but as an individual subjected to the contexts of societal, institutional and Western civilizational notions of what counts as research. Furthermore, using bricolage to do research requires a wide and deep knowledge of multiple *theories* and *methodologies*; multiple ways to collect, describe, construct, analyze, and *interpret* the object of the research study; and finally multiple ways to *narrate* (tell the story about) the relationships, struggles, conflicts, and complex world of the study that maintains the integrity and reality of the subjects. The purpose of research as bricolage involves providing new knowledge, insights, ideas, practices, structures that move towards social justice, inclusiveness, diversity, plurality and so forth. And all of these elements of the bricolage need to be connected and interconnected to the historical, intellectual and political landscape in which the research occurs. Relationality instigates social action at more than just the personal level.

## THE MAKING OF A BRICOLEUR

Denzin and Lincoln (2000, 2005) call the first historical moment of research *the traditional* which covers a period from approximately 1900 to 1950. I feel that period of logical positivism, objectivity and scientific rationality still exists today (remember they claim these moments overlap). I was introduced to research through this traditional moment. In the 1960s, while studying for a BA in sociology with minors in psychology and geography, I had to take courses in both quantitative and qualitative research methodologies. I remember the lab experiments in psychology and the isolation of variables that might contaminate the findings. There was the perennial case study methodology about how to interview research subjects and how to remain objective throughout the interview and in the interpretation of the data. I obviously remember the discourse that shaped what counted as research; variables, standard deviation, contamination, control and experimental group and placebo. I will never forget standing on a street corner of Toronto fulfilling a research mini-assignment in sociology. Dressed one day in hippie garb and looking quite disheveled, I asked directions to a local bookstore and a colleague recorded passer-by's reaction and responses – everything from ignoring me to 'get a job slob'. A few days later, dressed in a three-piece pantsuit and with a manicured appearance, I made the same request for directions while the same colleague recorded the responses. The passer-bys seemed more helpful with even offers to escort me to the bookstore. The purpose was to answer the research question, *Do people stereotype based on a person's appearance*? The professor's feedback to the mini-research mentioned problems about researcher's bias, lack of control of the variables and how my descriptive passages were interesting but too subjective and irrelevant to the findings.

The second historical moment that Denzin and Lincoln (2000, 2005) identify is *the modern* ranging from the 1950s to the 1970s. In the 1970s, while taking honors courses in marine ecology, synergy (I still don't know what it means), microbiology, Canadian history, drama and various other disciplines (my entry into blurred genres and interdisciplinary studies but the academy still wanted to know "what the h…" my major was) and continuing to teach in elementary schools (where blurred disciplinary borders tried to exist), I was required to approach my studies with a broader lens than just that of clinical, laboratory type research. Although scientific objectivity and other traditional research methods were still expected in some courses, I was introduced to modern research fields such as descriptive observation [borrowed from anthropology] and naturalistic settings (even in observing swamp life as ecological) where subjectivity and narrative records counted. Professors versed in research approaches of the time, emphasized the interrelationships between knowledge of one phenomenon/object/subject of the study and another. In marine ecology courses two different professors taught research about marine life in two different ways. One professor insisted that quantitative measurements of insect life, bird life, plant life, fish life and the levels of oxygen in the water gave a picture of the swamp. He had us reduce the complexity, interactive relationships, and the shifting dynamics at the micro and macro levels to isolated batches of numbers and averages [the traditionalist approach]. Another professor had each student go into the swamp with hip waders and stand in the water for approximately 10 minutes, slowly rotating and making observations about what we observed from the different viewpoints. We had been informed beforehand about what possibilities to look for but he left us enough space to bring in our own observations. After 10 minutes, the students reported their observations from each individual standpoint. It was impossible to reduce the complexity of swamp life to mere numbers, averages and isolated, decontextualized knowledge. Perhaps my propensity towards personal, subjective, descriptive storytelling biases my observations; however, I still carry the ecological knowledge produced in the latter approach with me today as a favored way to do research. It is not that one way is better than the other one, it is just that each research approach produces different knowledge, tells a different story and in different ways.

My work as a teacher was beginning to show signs of modern research techniques in schools through focus groups, action research and shared narratives. These activities plus asking classroom teachers to share their everyday observations and anecdotal documentation of the theory (literacy) and how it was enacted in actual practice and, in turn, informed the theoreticians [praxis] was given credence and legitimized by both school administrators and university professors. Although Denzin and Lincoln (2000, 2005) call the third historical moment from 1970 to 1986 the time of **blurred genres**, I was not at the university level so I wasn't aware of the formalized field of research during this stretch of time.

From 1980 to 1987, I pursued a MEd and PhD in education. This time period crosses over the third and fourth designation of Denzin and Lincoln's (2000, 2005) historical moments, blurred genres (1970-1986) and **crisis of representation.** Graduate students were expected to include two mandatory generalist courses in research which included mainly a study of quantitative methodologies with the usual qualitative uses of case study, ethnography, in-depth interviews and anecdotal questionnaires. But with a visionary advisor able to convince a Dean's committee otherwise, I was able to substitute the two mandatory courses for one in the anthropology department [study of the patterns/everyday rituals of a culture in naturalistic settings, everything from the cultures of 'Other', wolf culture to classroom culture]. The other substituted research course was hermeneutic **phenomenology** with Max van Manen and many of his colleagues including those using a Marxist or Existentialist or Psychological approach to phenomenology.

Introduced to new research methodologies, I felt equipped to begin my graduate research studies. A major obstacle, however, presented itself. The politics of what counted as research at that time (1980 - 1987) made it difficult to proceed without further barriers including thesis committee membership, institutional history and funding agencies. Firstly, committee members versed in anthropological and phenomenological methodologies were sparse or, in many cases, resistant to these approaches. Secondly, the history of research in the institution of higher learning and research policy guidelines had, over time, secured and legitimized certain kinds of research, mainly quantitative, while pooh-poohing or rejecting others. Writing research proposals that used phenomenology were met, except for a few leaders in the field such as van Manen (1990), with resistance and skepticism. Thirdly, as an example that confirms the politics of research, representatives from the major Canadian funding agency for research in the social sciences and humanities (which included educational research) told graduate students they had limited to nil chance of being funded if their research was ethnographic. In fact, they clearly stated that national funding committees and government agencies looked mainly for quantitative and objective methodologies and were hesitant to fund proposals using qualitative methodologies—something about "too subjective" and "not measurable" rang throughout the room. Not only does this demonstrate the politics of research but also clearly suggests that the traditional notions of what counts as research are still prevalent throughout all historical moments and exist at all cultural, societal and institutional levels of research. An indication that the politics of research are constantly shifting is exemplified in a recent (2005) policy statement by the same national funding agency that frowned on qualitative research twenty years earlier. The agency's focus has shifted from a Funding Council to a Knowledge Council and it seeks innovative approaches to research. Perhaps bricolage will fit that demand?

Throughout the late 1980s to 2005, as a university professor and researcher, I read widely in several theories and research methodologies and, along with colleagues, introduced graduate students to the same. In the late 1980s, ethnographic research gradually became more acceptable and predominate at both the institutional and national levels and, for many researchers, funded. Personal narratives, focus groups and action research started to enter research discourses and practices. I remember my first conscious introduction to the word **postmodernism** in 1991 at the home of Joe Kincheloe and Shirley Steinberg. I had picked up two books from their shelves; one academic (Lash, 1989) and one fictional (Carter, 1990). Both were gateways into postmodernism and revisionist writing for me [Carter rewrote the Red Riding fairy tale from a feminist perspective, although there are many critiques of her work as feminist writing]. Entry into the multiple theories, discourses and practices that a bricoleur can use to construct the research is different each time and for each person.

From approximately 1991 to the present I have been introduced to, introduced students to, taught and written about several ways to do research. From the late 1980s to 2006, my knowledge and practice (and the issues and conflicts) about doing research include: Feminist research [from first wave to Marxist and poststructural feminism]; poststructuralism [claims language is an unstable system of referents; the slippery slope of language and signifiers]; postcolonialism [challenges research as Euro-American imperialism and the inherited power and crisis of representing the Other from a colonialist perspective]; semiotics [a study of the signs, symbols, signifiers and what meanings are attached to them – in critical studies as signs of power]; poststructuralist semiotics [how the meanings of symbols and signifiers shift in different historical and political contexts] and Foucault's archeological genealogy [digging through the layers of discourses that shape knowledge and gain power; how they connect to the historical, intellectual, cultural contexts of the time that construct certain practices and not others]. Researchers like myself (because of years in the field of research and experience) have available a host of tools and several other ways of thinking about research especially as a critical theorist and pedagogue [a person who studies, teaches and practices about power relations, social justice, inclusiveness, plurality, diversity and so forth]. I have dabbled with phenomenography when graduate students ask what it is because a colleague asked them to do this kind of research. I explore other fields and regions of research depending on the questions asked of the research object and what 'research tools' will be needed to construct knowledge for social justice. I challenge what counts as research at any given time and place; whose research counts and gets funded and why.

It appears that from the late 1980s to the time of writing this chapter in 2006 that I passed through several historical moments of what counts as research. According to Denzin and Lincoln's (2005) recent edition of their handbook on qualitative research, those moments are: the fifth moment – *postmodern*, 1990-1995 [a period of experimentation and challenge to modern research methodologies in particular logical positivism, objectivity and scientific rationality; new forms of text building such as hypertext that provide a possible formatting for writing research as bricolage; texts/research becomes writerly, in other words, the reader writes back to the author to challenge or change the text]; the sixth moment – *post-experimental inquiry*, 1995-2000; and the seventh moment from 2000 to 2004 – the *methodologically contested* present. Since I formally and institutionally donned the mantle of bricoleur in 2002, there are many times when I feel I am reliving the traditional and methodologically contested moments again in what is known as the eighth moment and identified as the *fractured future* 2005 – a period that "confronts the methodological backlash of evidence-based social movements, moral discourses and the development of sacred textualities" (3). For example, when one of my students employed the bricolage for his study, between his struggle to find a form that was creative yet scholarly and colleagues complaints about the student not using a singular methodology to report his work, and the questions about proof [evidence-based], and no literature review of his field of study (there was but it appeared as a theoretical bricolage as a review of the theories he used to interpret his research), he and I experienced the phenomenological [experience as lived] and political backlash described above as the fractured future.

What has this lengthy, personal journey through the fields of research to do with bricolage? I would characterize the ninth moment of research as belonging to bricolage. This moment for me is a gathering of all the past moments and has been fluttering (*the butterfly effect*) for the past three decades to create chaos in the field of research. It is my way of leading you through some of the multiple tools [theories, histories, methodologies, stories and politics] that a researcher can access when using bricolage. Granted I have a forty-year span to draw from but as novice bricoleurs know, the repertoire builds from day to day and year to year. This is where rigor comes into play when doing research as bricolage instead of following a prescribed format and step-by-step single methodology. Bricoleurs read a lot of theories and methodologies that will be added to their research toolbox when needed. They read a lot of academic materials in their field but as disciplinary boundaries blur and interdisciplinary studies seep into each other, bricoleurs read in and are familiar with many fields; from high to popular culture; from the sciences to the arts and humanities; from academic journals and reports to film, theater, Internet and other digital technologies.

The most difficult aspect of doing research as bricolage is the writing; that is, how to shape and format a text that avoids the linear, reductionist structure of traditional research thesis or report. I encourage students to read poststructuralist, revisionist, postcolonial and postmodern fiction in addition to watching films that might help fracture traditional research reporting structures and dissemination processes. From these forms, bricoleurs can borrow a host of both traditional narrative conventions such as irony, parody, foreshadowing, split text, overlapping narratives and unfamiliar ways of storytelling such as those in postmodern fiction and films.

## HOW DOES A NOVICE BRICOLEUR GET STARTED?

It seems when university students and professors embark on a research journey through the complexity and multiplicity of doing bricolage; the major concerns are where and how do we start? With no familiar structure, with no explicit directions as were available in traditional and modern research processes and practices, bricoleurs need a starting point. And, like bricolage, there are many. In keeping with the possible ninth moment of research, the plurality and diversity of starting points in bricolage must remain forefront. But given this statement, novice bricoleurs and even seasoned researchers ask; "How do I get started". The following activities and discussions are only suggestions but at the same time drawn from experience and possibilities. As bricoleurs become more articulate about their work, I assume there will be volumes just on 'getting started'.

### 1. Research Background

Start from what you know and where you are. Students and researchers, even novice ones, do not come to the research process without some knowledge, formally or informally, of what counts as research. Researchers are not blank slates and have been asking questions and doing research since birth. The research may not have been named or institutionalized as is the case with academic research but was done as curiosity and wonderment. The trick is to keep **rhapsodic intellect** alive and not feel bogged down with intellectual paralysis throughout the research. If you do, take it as a stumbling block that all researchers and writers are confronted with constantly. Let passion for new knowledge and insights keep you focused. Let compassion for others drive you forward.

To practice what I've just preached, I suggest that professors and students brainstorm what they already know about research and put headings such as in Figure 4.1 (Please note this is not an actual example but a composite taken from a beginning research course).

| Name | Already Knows This About Research | What Conventions | What Historical Moment | Why So | What Questions Does It Ask | What Results |
|---|---|---|---|---|---|---|
| Bill | quantitative | Statistics Mean Deviation T-Scores | Traditional Modern | Scientific Objectivity | How Much? Norms | Measurement percentage numbers rating |
| Linda | Feminist Research | Discourse Analysis of Texts | Crisis of Representation | Problematic how Women are Represented | Ones that challenge dominant patriarchal worlds, practices | Transformation of society's knowledge about women, valuing women's worlds |
| Joy | Race Studies | Deconstructs texts as racialized, colonialized, whiteness | Postmodernism, Crisis of Representation | Challenges authority and shaping devices of whiteness and euro-colonialism | Ones that challenge the invisible powers of colonial ideas and practices that marginalize colonized peoples | Insights about marginalization of people based on race |
| Mike | ethnography | Observation key informant | Modern | studies other cultures | What are the Patterns of Behavior? Rituals of this culture? Mythology? Social Structures? | Knowledge about other cultures |

*Figure 4.1 - Brainstorming Chart*

From this chart (and there are other ways to construct it) come a variety of possible discussions, pedagogical practices, and paths to follow when doing research as bricolage. A picture of the research profile from the course members makes 'the getting started' transparent in addition to constructing a contingent, big picture of where we are coming from (as if gathering the historical moments from 1900 to 1995 in one chart). As you can see from only five members in a class of twenty or more there is already a variety of research backgrounds that are available from the bricolage toolbox. The task for the professor and other students is to discuss the limitations, similarities and conflicts between the different areas of the profile. The discussions are not meant as a debate about which research period or practice is best—they are intended to initiate dialogue to show differences between and within each research moment. In this way, budding bricoleurs come to understand how each research approach or period constructs certain knowledge [epistemology], about being human and relationships [ontology], self, society, values, practices and social action. Furthermore, the discussions should expose the assumptions in each area of the grid. Each area trains the researcher to see, read and interpret in certain ways yet neglects many other ways of seeing the world being researched. Opening the fields of research for discussion such as in figure 1, evoke dialogue as a stepping-stone for moving into bricolage.

In addition to charts and other formatting, I have used large different colored file cards for each different activity/discussion previously mentioned and that follows. As the students' knowledge and practices about doing bricolage expand though participation in each of the activities, the colored-coded file cards produce a visual map of the multiplicity and complexity of doing research as bricolage - a non-computerized hypertext, so to speak. I also find the file cards help the novice learn what's involved (and me too!) in research as bricolage when they come to do their own individual research. The cards can be shuffled, moved around, laid on top of one another (blurred genres perhaps?), packed up at the end of class and brought out before beginning the next activity. Unlike an actual computer hypertext model, the students get to see the process and history of research as bricolage.

Each time I do this, it evokes different ways to proceed, different use of 'tools', different ways to start, and different reasons for using certain 'tools' and not others. In addition, playing with the ideas, knowledge, questions etc. on the file cards prepares the novice bricoleurs for using features of complexity and multiplicity which research as bricolage demands. The features of complexity (in italicized words) unfold when students can: 1) mix and match cards at different moments (*randomness* but with purpose); 2) come to a point where they have to decide which route to follow next (*bifurcations*); 3) take advantage of serendipitous moments when someone has a modest or major epiphany (*spontaneity*); 4) from the group discussions, use someone else's comments, questions, conflicts and suggestions to change or modify or rethink their thinking and in turn have those people rethink (*feedback looping*); and 5) challenge, disrupt, and interrupt when consensus sets in, rock the boat and upset familiar thinking, preconceived ideas and categories, don't take for granted ideas, knowledge that is espoused as common sense, natural, and normal (practice creating *far-from-equilibrium* conditions). And there is no step-by step procedures or methods to follow, no preconceived format, no familiar structure but only the respect for difference and the desire to continue constructing new knowledge and possibilities, to pull from other places and times when needed (*self-organization*). The flexibility and structuring devices of the file cards or hypertext programming allow many students and even seasoned researchers to shift from a positivist world of research to the unfamiliar territory of using bricolage to do research. Novice bricoleurs relearn how to play and live in a ludic, postmodern world, not as shallow intellectualism but as intelligent, differently informed social theorists and activists.

## 2. Expanding the Bricolage Toolbox

From these dialogic discussions, it seems fitting that the tools for doing bricolage need to be expanded to a point of exhaustion (dependent on time, space and institutional expectations) when heading for the ninth historical moment of research. Added to their background knowledge, novice bricoleurs need to access multiple theories [theoretical bricolage], research genres and conventions [methodological bricolage], ways to interpret [interpretive bricolage] and ways of reporting/telling the story [narrative bricolage]. Kincheloe and Berry (2004) list a plethora of possible regions to explore with multiple sub-areas included. The regions (115-127), to name a few, include:

- multiple critical socio-theoretical discourses
- traditional and contemporary research genres/methodologies and their analytical tools
- cultural/social positionalities
- disciplinary/interdisciplinary departmentalization of knowledge
- philosophical domains
- modes of power
- narratological strategies
- dismantling western grand narratives
- contexts of human activity
- accessing different sources of knowledge
- archeological genealogy
- axiology
- semiotic readings
- a brief encyclopedia of discourses
- othering

Many other books and Internet sources list similar and additional regions such as Denzin and Lincoln's 5th edition (2005) of The Sage Handbook of Qualitative Research. As mentioned previously in this chapter, they have added "*fourteen totally new topics between 2000 and 2005, including, among others, indigenous research, ... critical and performance ethnography, arts-based inquiry, narrative inquiry, Foucault, the ethics and strategies of on-line research, cultural and investigative poetics and the politics of evaluation*" (amazon.com—accessed 9/20/05). A bricoleur's toolbox is starting to spill over with choices.

One glance at this list of potential regions tends to turn many future bricoleurs away from entering the multiple doors of doing bricolage. One way to revive confidence is to have each novice take on an area and/or sub-area not part of anybody's background discussed in #1 (Research Background) and report back to the others. Each novice takes on 'the mantle of an expert' in a particular area. This mantle is not 'an expert' but beginning an apprenticeship into becoming a bricoleur. Nobody at this point in the initiation can claim actual expertise in an area so they can be rough around the edges hopefully not imprisoned by grades but learning in the spirit of collegiality and play.

At some universities in Europe, both at the undergraduate and graduate level, a student is considered a reader in an area or areas. Instead of course work, the student is given an extensive book list (nowadays other sources of knowledge such as the Internet would be part of the list) by one professor in the area/s; reads them, writes a paper to present at a seminar, and presents at the seminar with several professors and students of differing theoretical and disciplinary backgrounds. At the seminar, attendees make suggestions and critique the individual's work. Then the 'reader' gets another list of books, reads and rereads, writes and rewrites, presents and continues this process several times before completion of that area. Overlapping this process, the student receives feedback from a supervising professor and from colleagues on an individual basis. For the purpose of nurturing bricoleurs, perhaps thinking of them as 'readers' and using this process of seminars is similar to what is meant by each student responsible for a specific theory, methodology and such. As I reflect on this idea, however, I realize that I have appropriated a colonial model that is exclusive of different ways of increasing the tools for apprentice bricoleurs. Here's where one 'reader' might be asked to read Smith's *Decolonizing Methodologies* (2001), and challenge my notions of research as well as my idea of the teaching and learning process. Bricolage is as much about conflict of ideologies, theories, methodologies, discourses and practices as it is about multiplicity of those areas.

When the novices report back to each other, it is not a case, however, of just reporting the knowledge and practices for their region/sub-area. Bricolage is not about amassing a host of tools. It's about using the available tools as bits and pieces to construct new knowledge; but as knowledge that exposes complicity, contradiction and conflict about the world under scrutiny. Added to the critique of knowledge and the regions reported are sets of questions and issues that build on the background knowledge produced by discussions such as in figure #1. Further discussions should include:

a) how each region/sub-area (including the multiplicity of the bricolage) claims authority to speak as knowledge, as legitimized research

b) what discourse, assumptions, practices, strategies are generated by each area

c) what those discourses, assumptions, practices, etc. claim counts as research

d) what promises each region makes about why and how it serves the individual, society, institutions and the micro and macro world that does or does not construct knowledge for inclusiveness, diversity, plurality and social justice

e) a critique of how each theory, methodology, region etc. problematizes or makes claims that: *generalize* [knowledge of this study can be transferred to other situations and cultures etc. and the results will be the same]; *universalize* [we all are the same, we belong to the human race]; *naturalize* [it's natural to be like that; i.e. boys will be boys as legitimizing certain behaviors]; *pathologize* [people living in poverty don't want to get off welfare]; *essentialize* [a research study and discourse that makes claims that speak for all – women, middle classed, aboriginals etc.]; *neutralize* [differences based on class, race, gender, religion are not made problematic, left out to be politically safe]; *normalize* [there is something, someone gets to be defined as normal and against which others are considered abnormal, initiates research that takes action to make others like those who count as normal]; *reduce* [eliminates the complexity, fluctuations, variables and dynamics of human activity for purposes of objectivity and 'hard science'], *assimilate* [where difference is blended into the mainstream because they want to be like the mainstream]; and *erase* [eliminates certain truths and knowledge by romanticizing or not talking about the complexity of human activities, agency and relationships by not telling the unromantic, horrid, actual aspects of humanity, like Disney's take on fairy tales]

f) challenges/questions/resistances to any theory, methodology, interpretations, narratives [grand and petite, local and global, national and international], research and researchers etc. to claims of absolute truth, meaning, and knowledge [for example, I was raised on the totalizing knowledge of the King James Bible, the way I must live and accept as absolute truth. But when I challenged the grand narrative of patriarchy in that text with feminist discourse I had to leave the church]

g) personal responses to the research genre/area, to its assumptions, claims, discourses, etc. based on your positionality in relation to the region being discussed. For example, when Diane who is multi-racial (of African, White European, Chinese and Caribbean descent) and I, mono-racial (of white European descent), discuss a film or book, we are located as racially different and see/read the text differently. Constructs/representations of race that I take for granted, she notices as misrepresentations and contradictions and as erasure and essentializing the Other

h) a brief discussion of the terminology in your own words with actual personal and local examples specific to each of the different areas. (Kincheloe

(2002) did this with a graduate research class and they found it to be a very useful exercise for understanding the multiplicity and chaos of bricolage)

i) a writing process workshop approach which, similar to what was mentioned previously when a 'reader' presents in a seminar, includes writing draft essays (not the typical reduced five paragraph type but 'real' essays like those in *Harpers*, *The Atlantic* and *New Yorker* for example). When each student presents his/her area of the bricolage, including further readings in the area, a draft essay is distributed to the other members of the seminar in paper, CD or on-line format. Each member then responds to the draft essay by writing back; that is, from his/her positionality, using the specific area in which he/she read. For example, if the draft essay were in semiotics; the responses to the draft are from all the other areas in which each student was a reader. Again, it is not writing back to the author to report the information of the specific fields but to set up challenges, contradictions, conflicts, purposes, concrete examples, questions that, for example, ethnography/ethnographers might have for a semiotician about the different theories, methodologies, strategies, interpretations, and ways of reporting the knowledge work as research. In addition, if research using bricolage is about researching for inclusion, diversity, plurality, complexity, multiplicity and social justice, then the responses from colleagues must also reflect these purposes. The original draft is handed back to the author with notes in the margins, in the empty spaces and so forth.

The processes mentioned above in a) to i) are excellent opportunities for rehearsing the thinking, reading and writing processes and practices that a bricoleur will meet when engaged in using bricolage as research. These are also opportunities to introduce novices to the ideas and discourse of the hermeneutic circle of interpretation; another tool for bricoleurs to include in their repertoire. Other discussions and ways of introducing novices to the principles and processes of bricolage are also possible. One book I use in teaching bricolage and in my critical literacies classes is Tyson's (1999) *Critical Theory Today*. In it, there are multiple readings of *The Great Gatsby* (Fitzgerald) based on several theoretical discourses such as: Psychoanalytic Criticism, Marxist Criticism, Feminist Criticism, Reader – Response Criticism, Lesbian, Gay, and Queer Criticism and Postcolonial and African American Criticism. Novice bricoleurs find the different readings of the same text are very helpful especially the questions presented at the end of each theory.

When Denzin and Lincoln (2000) and Kincheloe and Berry (2004) presented possible arrangements for research as bricolage, they collapsed the multiplicity under five areas: the *theoretical* bricolage; the *methodological* bricolage, the *interpretative* bricolage, the *narrative* bricolage and the *political* bricolage. I'm assuming this is done so for the purposes of academic criteria of what counts as research and as a way of organizing the complexity and huge amounts of content available for doing this kind of research. The danger in these categorizations might defeat the purposes of engaging some of the major principles of bricolage, such as profiling the interconnectivity, conflicts, resistances, silences, complexity, the political and historical conditions between new knowledge and insights to human activities, relationships of power and conditions of exclusions, inequities and social injustices. One student, for example, used these five areas for his thesis formatting and to fulfill the academy's criteria for what counts as research. What happened seemed to crush the purpose of the multiplicity and complexity in bricolage. His thesis read like a typical empirical study, linear in structure and redundant in content as it was a mere summary of some of the 'tools', such as postmodernism and poststructuralism that he tried to apply to his research. In fact, he simply applied several post-discourses in addition to four other theoretical and methodological areas to his text being researched. It read like an encyclopedic rehash of the areas he selected instead of creating new knowledge for inclusion and social justice. Please let it be known, however, that he was not responsible for this situation but his supervisor – me. In trying to meet traditional academic criteria and introduce research as bricolage, I was caught between two moments of research –the modern and bricolage. The student became caught also. This represents a good example of the politics of research in the academy.

From the discussions, beginning researchers may wish to chart out or create visual images/metaphors (such as the butterfly effect in Kincheloe and Berry, 2004, p. 112) or create a DVD hypertext as a means to show the interrelationships, multiplicity, complexity, conflicts and contradictions between and within a region/area. Whatever means are used to image the various fields, keep in mind the purpose is to expand the bricoleur's knowledge [epistemology] for later use when constructing new knowledge through research. An understanding of the history and content of multiple theories, methods and techniques, their overlaps and limitations, their similarities and conflicting discourses should help the bricoleur to see how each region creates its own set of questions, focuses, processes and practices.

In traditional and modern research moments, researchers use paradigms and conceptual frameworks to guide their research process. Paradigms represent a fixed body of knowledge and a particular belief system, a way to view the world such as Newton's theory of gravity. Einstein challenged that system and using metaphors drawn from images and perceptions outside of Newton's world and the scientific rationality of the time to create a scientific revolution and a paradigmatic shift in knowledge about the world. Bricolage works with 'bits and pieces' of theoretical, methodological and interpretive paradigms. It works with scattered parts, overlaps and conflicts between paradigms. In other words, the novice learns what each 'tool' does and can do thus creating a host of possibilities (not mere facts and information) to select from when conducting his/her individual research as bricolage. The researcher practices bricolaging with guidance and feedback about how and when to use the different aspects of the field when needed.

## 3. Learning to Problematize

When novice researchers have an initial understanding of the complexity and multiplicity of using bricolage, they can use the various parts to apply to any **text** to be researched. But to move beyond simply cutting and pasting the parts together in a collage-like manner, bricoleurs must know why and how to problematize the details of the research text including all the relational elements. Since a major principle of bricolage and of other more recent historical research moments is the shift from problem-based/problem-solving research to problematizing/social action research, students need to recognize the difference between the two and the implications for using bricolage.

McLerran and Patin (1997) define the term problematic as "derived from the writings of Marxist theorist Louis Althusser and used to designate theoretical and/or ideological formations. It can also be used to refer to rather large and wide-ranging belief systems". As Fedory (2005) notes, problem is a noun and problematizing is a verb; the former suggests object, the latter motion (6). Problematizing seems to have entered the discourse of research as a response to the thinking and practices of the **scientific method**. The term problematizing certainly is important to several research moments since blurred genres and especially important to social action research and thus bricolage. It means the bricoleur faces the challenge of problematizing every detail before, during and after the completion of the research process.

In problem-based research, assumptions about knowledge, truth and meaning are **aporia**, what already counts prior to conducting the research. Problem-based/solving research finds out if something exists or doesn't exist, whether someone is abled or disabled and how to solve the problem. Problem based research isolates the object of the study from the multiplicity and complexity in which the object of study is situated. It treats the object of study, whether an issue, question, group of people, testing techniques, knowledge or community development as a fixed entity. Thus the end result is data that has answers or conclusions for problem solving; features of research belonging to the scientific method. Granted there are problems that need to be solved immediately, for a long time or forever. The leaky roof presents a problem. Repair it and fix the problem. Having one arm is a problem but isn't solved by assuming or taking-for-granted the world that one armed people live in.

Having one arm is *problematic* when that person faces a world planned, designed, and meant for two armed people. That's me. I belong to the culture of one armed people. To problematize our world doesn't mean it will solve the problems of being one armed. What problematizing asks is for the world to be transformed in many different ways, at many different levels, and in the many different situations and times we encounter everyday, as do two armed people. The subjects of the research are not seen as problems to be fixed but the world they live in is problematized. Why? To transform the world so we can live with equity, inclusion, agency, plurality, and social justice at all levels of society, institutions as do two armed people. Substitute any difference in the place of the world of one-armed people and you have the shift to problematizing.

In the process of becoming a bricoleur, novices begin to recognize that problematizing includes the complexity and multiplicity, to name a few, of human relationships, of discourses that shape relationships of knowledge and power, of structuring the world at the individual, societal, institutional and civilizational levels, of the shifting individual, historical, intellectual, social, economic and political experiences at local and global levels. Problematizing is done in order to rethink and re-see not solve. To rethink and re-see the world leads to transforming the policies, discourses and practices of exclusion, inequities and social injustices – research for Social Action. Actually, for bricoleurs, everything and everyone in the world is problematized. Once introduced to the term, many novices think this means a negative stance in the world ("You're always soooooo negative Kathy and you're trying to teach us to be the same"). Immediately that tends to suggest they are still working with the binarism of positive/negative. When I work with novices to problematize the binarism itself, the gradual realization of the difference between problem and problematizing becomes 'slightly' understood with granules of resistance (perhaps from a novice's long term familiarity and unexamined working relationship with logical positivism and its production of binarisms?). But discussions about binary opposition are, for me, a **segue** from problem-based research to problematizing.

Learning to problematize the world follows on the previous activities in #1 and #2.Assuming apprentice bricoleurs have accessed a wealth of research tools to use, and have delineated the premises, purposes and practices for contradictions, conflicts and so forth, the practice of problematizing moves them further into the cracks and gaps in knowledge produced by research throughout all historical moments including bricolage. The following, in no specific order, are suggestions for learning to problematize the worlds to be researched.

a)    Bring a poster or magazine/photograph/picture/classic piece of art (the types of texts are unlimited but I find a visual text is easiest to start with). Ask what each student's specific bricolage 'tool' would say is problematic about the text. Some students will say what is right/wrong, good/bad, positive/negative about the text according to their individual region of the bricolage they are applying. Then mention that these are **binarisms** and will be discussed later as problematic in and of themselves. One way I charted this activity of learning to problematize is have each student write on a large colored file card what each particular bricolage theory, method, interpretation etc. would say is problematic and post it around the visual text. A variety of points will emerge but the focus remains on problematizing the text as the purpose of the activity.

b)    The previous activity in (a) usually generates a plethora of binarisms. Novice bricoleurs need to problematize the use of these words when they appear at any time before and during the research process. Have one or two people record words that arise from the problematizing of the text such as right/wrong, good/bad, male/female, us/them, positive/negative and the many other words that can be paired with an oppositional word. For example, students may say: the house in the picture is middle classed; poor people in the picture deserve to be poor; the picture depicts a man and a woman in a loving relationship—that's normal; the children are acting bad; and that's natural for boys to play sports. These are perhaps obvious and weak examples but it is not hard to find texts where the binarisms can be spotted and problematized. Newspapers, curriculum guides, conversations, television shows and the world are packed with binarisms. The task for the bricoleur is to problematize them. They set up unequal representations and relationships and privilege one side of the binarism as being normal, natural, right, true and so forth and the other side abnormal, unnatural, wrong or disabled. They describe social situations. They govern social policies, testing practices, job employment, evaluation criteria, and actions. They shape who gets to be called a reader and who doesn't. I have even worked on the binarisms in fairy tales with elementary and secondary students. Bricoleurs are continuously problematizing binary oppositions that appear in research texts as if normalized and legitimized categorizations of the human condition, relationships, practices and agency. Practice in problematizing binarisms is part of the learning process for novice bricoleurs.

c)     What to problematize? – everything and everybody. Why problematize? – to avoid reducing the complexity of the world for the sake of control, management, objectivity, classification, and the production, maintenance and circulation of inequities, exclusions, and social injustices based on difference in gender, race, class, age, body, religion, education, sexuality and so forth. How to problematize more than the surface and obvious levels of the text and recognition of the invisible agendas of power is just a small part of the knowledge a bricoleur uses when doing research. They also learn to recognize that at different historical, intellectual, cultural, and political times and places, what is identified as problematic is constantly shifting and undulating. In addition, problematizing what's not part of the text and what is invisible in the text is as important as what is there.

That's why problematizing adds to the rigor of doing bricolage. Each historical, intellectual, social, and political period has specific needs for problematizing the research text and its constituents. Thus, problematizing the worlds/texts/issues /events etc. to be researched requires an additional recognition of connectivity with the world of the text with the world outside the text. The students could bring to the class a variety of texts and practice problematizing them and the world in which they are located. Ask not just what is problematic but also why it is problematic for inclusion, social justice and agency. Students might find this activity exhaustive and endless but certainly can sense the complexity and multiplicity of doing research as bricolage. I find problematizing is the ground from which the research text grows in purpose and directs the bricoleur to what tools to use and when.

## 4. Learning to Contextualize, Situate and Decentre

Contextualization is another major aspect of doing bricolage. Whereas traditional and modern research used only the research text itself as the context, bricoleurs expand the research beyond itself to a multitude of contexts. Because bricolage considers research to be a complex act embedded in and contested by a host of social, intellectual, historical, economic, institutional, local, global and political beliefs, values and relationships, it is imperative that contextualization plays a major part in the bricoleur's construction of knowledge through research. A bricoleur asks how the world being researched is connected to the policies, structures, discourses, and practices of the dominant political, economic, institutional, intellectual and other powers that govern social activity. Even the responses, for example, of subjects talking about the topic being researched have to be taken outside the interview context and analysis.

In bricolage, the responses can not be reduced to categories, classifications, numbers or themes in the manner that most research using interviews does. Bricoleurs frame their questions not just to evoke conversation but to push the topic under scrutiny beyond the immediate context and link the responses to other contexts which visibly or invisibly shaped or influenced the interviewee's knowledge, beliefs and actions. The links are reminiscent of a hypertext image in which, as one response is elicited, the bricoleur 'clicks' on the response and moves it to another context. The bricoleur might be asking a single mother living in conditions of poverty how she teaches her child at home to read. She responds that she doesn't have the time or money to do so. The bricoleur hears her response as blaming herself, blaming the individual, pathologizing the realities of mothers living in conditions of poverty. Sensitive to the limits of a single and individual context and recognition that the individual is embedded in several other larger and more powerful contexts, the bricoleur begins to frame questions that move the interviewee to think beyond the boundaries of the individual context. Linking the individual's experiences and understandings to, for example, the historical, societal, institutional, religious, economic, and political contexts and re-linking each of these with each other; linking this mother's context with the contexts of her neighborhood, surrounding neighborhoods and with the neighborhood schools reveals the relationships and interrelationships that exist for single mothers living in conditions of poverty. What is missed by reporting just the context of the individual interviewees—*reducing* their world to categories, themes, generalizations and problem—is problematic for a bricoleur. Problematic because it leaves the responsibility for transformation and struggle in the hands of the individuals instead of society, institutions and other contexts in which the women live their lives. Keeping responsibility at the individual level also removes hope for change. A different kind of knowledge than individual knowledge alone could do is obtained by showing how the conditions of poverty are linked to the policies and practices of society and institutions in historical, economic and political contexts of time and space.

Simultaneously as relationality, multiplicity and complexity are unfolding through the connectivity by the bricoleur of the interviewee's responses, the personal can not be lost to the abstractness of academic discourse and so forth. This is a situation where the bricoleur turns to another tool to keep the personal vibrantly present. The bricoleur might, for example, feel that when showing the relationality between the interviewee's life and, let's say, an institutional policy, he/she inserts, as a phenomenologist would, an eidetic [vivid] description or variation from the interviews.

Furthermore, a bricoleur might use the 'tools' of Foucault's archeological genealogy and critical discourse analysis to get the job done'. Granted this pulling in of a new tool from the theoretical and methodological bricolage adds to the complexity of knowledge and interpretation of the initial interviews but also adds new knowledge and insights to the research study that might be overlooked or erased by decontextualization or reduced contextualization. The spontaneous insight to use Foucault's theory and the methodologies of critical discourse analysis of the initial interviews is just one of many possibilities the bricoleur could use but could not have planned ahead of time that this would occur.

Contextualizing in the manner described above also requires a situating and decentering on the part of the researcher. While contextualizing is about connecting and contesting the different contexts relevant to the research, situating is about presenting the autobiographical aspects (what I call the critical ethnobiographical bricolage) that indicate how the bricoleur came to be situated in the research study and influences the process of selecting, choosing, speaking, interviewing, observing, interpreting and telling the story. Situating is not about remaining objective or isolating one's biases, a trait of logical positivism, but identifying what the socializing texts of the bricoleur's life are that locates her/him in the research in a particular way with certain knowledge, beliefs, and values related to the research.

If we use the example above of the interviews with single mothers living in conditions of poverty, there is no question that a researcher enters the interviews with previous knowledge and beliefs that shaped what he/she already thinks/knows about the topic. Situating examines not only the bricoleur's taken-for-granted assumptions about the topic but the established and unexamined 'common sense' knowledge and beliefs of the society, institutions, media and cultural artifacts related to the topic. The countless number of socializing texts (tools) and processes ranging from oral to printed; family to media, from birth to date and multiple other texts adds another dimension to the knowledge, interpretation and understanding of the research as bricolage. Also a bricoleur must consider how the research is written and read in relation to the constructs of gender, race, class, sexuality, religion and other constructs of culture. In other words, how the bricoleur and the research subjects are situated in the research by gender, race, class and other different cultural constructs shapes the knowledge produced.

Identification of how the researcher is situated in the study requires a decentering on the part of the researcher especially during the interpretive and narrative processes of bricolage. Decentering from the research subjectively situates the researcher in the research but allows a distancing for objective observations and perspectives. On the one hand, bricolage allows subjective input to the research with such conventions as first person, multivocal perspectives, and non-reduced personal narratives. In fact, similar to The Orchid Thief by Susan Orlean or the more recent version of the film Moulin Rouge, authors using bricolage write themselves into the text as active participants in the construction of knowledge, allowing personal opinion and reflective moments to interrupt the objective flow of the text (writing, viewing, reading). Here is a good example of bricolage borrowing conventions from other sources and disrupting the text to have the readers challenge their own thinking and the topic being examined. On the other hand, decentering forces the bricoleur to be sensitive to the research subjects' position in the research and not misrepresent them as, for example, inactive, disenfranchised, lazy, or apathetic. A researcher who is privileged by class and/or gender, race (a concern of postcolonial, race and whiteness studies) needs to decenter from those positions especially when researching subjects who are not privileged by dominant cultural constructs.

Further complexity is added when the bricoleur also situates the study in related fields and other research studies (called background literature or review of the literature in traditional and modern research). However, instead of listing the studies and their findings to prove they have read in the field, bricoleurs situate where their study stands in relation to the other studies. The main purpose of situating instead of reviewing the literature is to uncover the historical and political agendas of the background literature as research legitimized by logical positivism and scientific rationality. If indeed, the research and literature of related studies is found to be located in traditional and modern research moments, without question, bricolage problematizes these studies and the knowledge they produced. To reiterate, the point is that bricoleurs tell a different, not necessarily better, story than traditional and modern research literature.

As novice bricoleurs practice contextualizing, situating and decentering as dynamic parts of the research process, they build a knowledge base for and understanding of what is meant by engaging complexity and multiplicity. When a research class as a group applies bricolage to a single text (such as a poster, a visual/artwork, a familiar book, a film, a TV show, newscast or other media text), the principles and processes discussed to this point in the chapter act as a rehearsal for when each bricoleur conducts his/her own research. To practice problematizing, contextualizing, situating, and decentering, there are many great examples in postcolonial fiction and revisionist writing such as Angela Carter's *Bloody Chamber* mentioned earlier. I have suggested that novice bricoleurs read the traditional canonized *Robinson Crusoe* by Daniel Dafoe as an example of a text that privileges and legitimizes European knowledge, history, values and practices. Then I have them read *Friday* by Michael Tournier, a revisionist writing of Robinson Crusoe. In Tournier's text, without direct reference he problematizes, re-situates and decenters the position of Crusoe in Dafoe's book as representative of European powers. The emerging bricoleurs search the pages for examples of the premises listed previously in #4 in addition to asking what their respective theoretical, methodological and interpretive areas of bricolage would problematize and/or say about the books. In a manner of speaking, others may want or need to introduce novices to bricolage in different ways and for different reasons. These suggestions are only a few of many possible ways. And yes, there is more.

## 5. Learning About Intertextuality

To create a research text, bricoleurs borrow from other texts. Thus it seems wise for bricoleurs to learn about intertextuality, a literary idea "coined by Julie Kristeva ... and employed in structuralist, poststructuralist, semiotic, deconstructive, postcolonial, Marxist, feminist and psychoanalytical theories" (Allen, 2000), as just some of the regions employed in the theoretical bricolage. Although the term has many different meanings, it is useful to employ some of its major principles and practices for the purposes of doing bricolage. Since bricolage borrows from many theories, methodologies, interpretive practices and narrative conventions, an under-standing of intertextuality is considered helpful.

At this point in the discussion on doing research as bricolage, a delineation of some of the major principles of intertextuality should demonstrate for the novice the connections to doing bricolage as multiplicity and complexity. Some of the premises (taken from Allen, 2000 and with modifications to connect to bricolage) include the assertions that texts in an intertextual context

a) lack any kind of independent meaning (thus contextualizing etc. in brico-lage)

b) create [research] which plunges us into a network of textual relations (in bricolage,
 theoretical, methodological, societal, institutional, local, global relationships)

c) are part of a process of moving between a variety of texts (in bricolage, borrowing and using when needed)

d) practice theoretical [and methodological] intervention and debate (prob-lematizes in bricolage).

e) replace assertions of objectivity, scientific rigor, methodological stability and positivistic rationality (monologism) with an emphasis on uncertainty, indeterminacy, non-communicability, subjectivity, desire, pleasure and play

f) disrupt notions of stable meaning and objective interpretations

g) challenge long-held assumptions concerning the role of the author in the production of meaning (bricolage problematizes researcher, literature re-views, common sense, normalizations, etc.)

h) lead [researchers] and readers on to new textual relations (a purpose of bricolage)

i) help authors create and readers discover multiple meanings in the research text (the attempt of bricolage to avoid positivistic reductionism)

j) celebrate plurality (Barthes); others see this as problematic and not neces-sarily liberatory

k) are concerned with marginalized and oppressed communities

l) are used to reflect and transform [knowledge, beliefs, values, practices] of society and human relations

m) mix already established styles and practices (bricoleurs mix theories, methodologies, narrative styles etc. to get the job done)

n) foreground notions of relationality, interconnectedness, and interdepend-ence

o) promote a relationality that may involve the radical plurality of the sign; the relation between signs and texts and cultural [historical, political, intellec-tual, theoretical, discourse] texts; and, extremely important to research as bri-colage, the transformative relation between the final research text and another text [practices of society, institutionsl, policy, curriculum, testing, inclusion, equity and social justice

p) support a new vision of society, authorship and reading, researching and research

q) resist ingrained notions of originality, uniqueness, singularity, and autonomy.

This is by no means the only available or exhaustive list of premises on intertextuality and their relationship to doing research as bricolage. The list serves as another way of introducing future bricoleurs to the multiple principles and practices
(tools) available to use when enacting research as bricolage.

To practice intertextuality, I use films, especially those drawn from popular culture (as most people in a class have seen them) as they can be shared easily in a
class and, in a shorter period of time, cover several of the premises of intertextuality. The Shrek 1 and 2 films both provide very simple and basic examples of texts
within texts or texts that cross over into other texts. To understand most of the hu-
mor in the two Shrek films, the viewer has to recognize texts that lie outside the
movie itself; a premise that texts have no independent meaning (see (a) above). To
obtain meaning out of Shrek, the viewer has to know several European nursery
rhymes (problematic for culturally different students), watch/read other texts such
as the TV game show *The Price is Right* to get what Donkey (Donk-a , important
here to know whose voice it is -Eddie Murphy's - and why it is pronounced this
way ) meant by "giving the cat the Bob Barker Treatment" (Bob Barker, the host
always ends the show with "Remember to help control the pet population, have
your pet spayed or neutered"). One viewer, who is homosexual, pointed out several
examples of homophobia and signifiers of homosexuality which several heterosexual viewers could not assign meaning to in their first viewing of the movie. A
poster in the film (which is set a long time ago in Far Far Away Land) is of Stone-
henge Night Club - a gay night club in London, England. There is one scene in
which the three main characters are driving down the main street of Far Far Away
Land; a street filled with shops from days of yore but with Arthurian twists on
names from Hollywood's Rodeo Drive. In that scene alone, viewers would have to
know past and present times in addition to Arthurian legends, European fairy tales,
the names of modern day stores but with names merged with medieval shops. This
is a very small sample of how many texts from outside the film are important to the
film's success. More importantly for bricoleurs is how the film's intertextuality
"plunges us into a network of textual relations", and "moves us between texts" in
different times and places.

Intertextuality exists in newspapers, television newscasts, religious texts, magazines, school disciplinary textbooks, history books, photographs, academic journals, personal experiences, autobiographies, fiction and non-fiction books. In one
university class I taught intertextuality using texts about Iraq and American relations. Each student was to bring in any five texts they thought relevant to this topic
but none produced after 9/11. They went on a one week scavenger hunt for materials. Each student could not bring in any two texts of the five that were of the same
media or date. One week later, the classroom was filled with boxes of materials
and every one of us was surprised at the variety. The sources of materials above
were collected plus a father's war medals; books on oil production and trading; an
interview with a Canadian peace keeper; maps on the shifting borders of the Mid-

dle East with colored - coded explanations; editorials from magazines as far back as 1930s; a Koran; a Christian bible; clippings from different political journals and banking newsletters.

Then there were discussions on why the selection and how connected to Iraqian - American relations. Then we referred to different lists of premises and questions asked by different theories and methodologies in the bricolage toolbox, problematizing, contextualizing and those of intertextuality. Then all the tables in the classroom are placed together to provide a space to begin mapping out the bricolage. In the center of the table is a huge poster with the words [A Map of Iraqian- American Relations]. This becomes our point of entry text (POET) from which all other texts are connected and hypertexted. Each time we refer to a premise or question, we also returned to one of the texts collected and place it on our huge bricolage map using different color-coded file cards, different colors of string, post-em stickers, overheads and a wad of other materials that can be written on, moved, organized differently, stretched, connected and layered. As we discuss the texts, the relationships, premises and questions the map unfolds in a fashion similar to a Jackson Pollock painting and reminiscent of the model of complexity in Lorenz's Butterfly Effect.

Bricoleurs, both novice and seasoned, gradually see the emergence of new knowledge, insights and connections. Eventually we become overwhelmed by the complexity and multiplicity as the connections grow and continue to grow. In order to organize but not totalize the complexity and multiplicity we decide on a stopping point. Then decisions are made, to name a few, about: what to keep in the map or toss aside for the moment; how to organize the map for meaning; how to recognize what counts as new knowledge or conflict and contradictions in ideologies and practices; if we actually have a variety of perspectives, opinions, references, conflicting and complicit ideologies; what connections we made that would perhaps speak to different audience/readers and evoke rethinking their thinking and changing practices; and what political actions and discourses could be challenged and used to " make a difference" in the world (one student's comment). This activity is an accumulation of what novice researchers have learned to this point about research as bricolage.

Just getting started, practicing the thinking and the processes of complexity, including multiplicity and making hypertext connections and relationships between texts and discourses is a vast undertaking. The practice of building the 'tools' as a group/class, applying them to first a single texts and then multiple texts seems a good way of introducing beginners to doing research as bricolage – a preparation for the ninth moment of research history. From here they can go to their individual research projects with some sense of what it means to engage relationality, complexity and multiplicity through bricolage. But the most difficult questions remain – How do I format this complexity so it can be 'read' by others? How do I organize the messiness and process of bricolage into a final product for dissemination?

## 6. Learning to Self-Organize The Messiness

If there is a point in which I myself almost give up on bricolage is when it comes to organizing the messiness into a 'readable' but writerly text. I wonder how I can move the novices beyond the formulas of positivism, scientific rationality and methodology; beyond traditional and modern ways of constructing texts; and de-centering the dominance of printed text especially with academic criteria, expecta-tions and structures looming over both the head of myself and the students doing research. After finishing the Iraqian- American activity, several students answered, in part, those questions for me; they were not, however, graduate students bound by thesis expectations (again the politics of research). When at least ten out of thirty students submitted their final assignment on a CD ROM as hypertext, I knew they were of a different generation than I. The CDs were laden with the content, connections, and multiplicity we had practiced in class. I was able to click on dif-ferent texts, print excerpts from magazines, newspapers, academic journals, music, visuals, interviews, polls, quotes, and go from each of them to theoretical discus-sions that problematized, interconnected, challenged, and contextualized. One stu-dent used split screen conventions to show the conflict between two reports on Iraqian-American relations with her own interpretations and analysis of the dis-course in each.

Another student used his life as the son of Canadian military parents as his point of entry text and used the digital technology of a DVD. From there he developed a hypertext narrative that used the personal but connected it to historical and political texts. He very clearly showed how the personal is political; how he was socialized by the military contexts and texts in which he was exposed to certain knowledge and beliefs about Iraqian- American relations. He inserted memories from child-hood conversations (more like lectures he noted) he had with parents and other military personnel. He disrupted these texts with newspaper clippings written at approximately the same time of his memories. He included vivid descriptions (the phenomenological strategy of eidetic description, reduction, and variation of the lived experience) of the physical abuse from his father overlaid with transparent magazine photos of Iraqian and American military scenes concurrent with his memories of personal abuse. This student was very well read and a student of his-tory. He accessed passages on the topic from textbooks he was asked to read in history courses at both the secondary and university levels of education. It was frightening how one-sided and objective the knowledge was which he remembered as having to regurgitate in assignments and exams. He pointed out the lack of mul-tiple perspectives and sources; the same and only textbook for all students and usu-ally written by one or two authors. I still carry the work of this student with me today. As I write this example of bricolage, in no way it is as important as the stu-dent himself and his impact on my life. I only hope I can honor him as a person by using his work to inform my work as a bricoleur.

Many other sources (narrative tools) are available that might help the novice and seasoned researcher organize the *narrative* bricolage; help him/her use different tools to self-organize the messiness of bricolage into a final text for readers/viewers/listeners without resorting to traditional academic structures of reporting. Another example and one that was very useful for many students learning to do research was using Kincheloe's book *The Sign of the Burger* (2002). He used bricolage to research MacDonald's as a culture of power. After reading the book, students and I use it to scrutinize for content and form. We ask how does he include, theories, methodologies and interpretations that maintain research integrity through using bricolage? Does he avoid positivism, scientific methodology and rationality, and objective reductionism? How did he or did he remain truthful to the promises of bricolage as engaging relationality, complexity and multiplicity? And finally how did he tell the story as narrative bricolage? There are other examples of bricolage texts but using a single text such as Kincheloe's helps to clarify how to organize the messiness of bricolage.

I have mentioned before how I use postmodern, poststructural and postcolonial writers of fiction to help students organize the messiness. Students and I have examined films on DVD's such as, to name a few, Pulp Fiction, Run Lola Run, Memento, Like Water For Chocolate, The Hours, Shrek, Adaptation and many others that disrupt traditional, linear monological narratives. We have read scripts for plays that incorporate multi-voiced, multi-perspective conventions such as those written by Anna Deavere Smith. Students will sometimes combine medias that range from reading texts, to television clips to live performances and photographs.

## IN CLOSING

As I share discussions about bricolage with colleagues, undergraduate and graduate students, I still sense the nervousness and hesitancy to use bricolage to do research. I am amazed, however, that those same colleagues and students are very comfortable using Web, Internet and different hypertext programs. They can access and produce more texts in an hour than traditional research technologies could in a lifetime. Mind you, accessing and producing texts is not necessarily doing research as bricolage. Bricoleurs keep in mind major principles of relationality, multiplicity, complexity and, most importantly, criticality for social action and justice. I have alluded to the politics of doing research as bricolage especially in academia. Hopefully, however, academia begins to look differently at what counts as research. Bricolage offers that potential.

## GLOSSARY OF TERMS

**aporia** – impassable path, a contradiction of the logic or sense and the rhetoric in a text
**blurred genres** – where the distinct borders between research methods, disciplines, and strategies fade into and over one another
**butterfly effect** – Lorenz's theory of chaos and complexity which he metaphorically frames as the butterfly effect; that is if a butterfly flaps it wings in Brazil, it causes a tornado in Kansas (and I thought it was Dorothy's shoes!)

**crisis of representation** – 1986 -1990, research more reflexive, called into question issues of gender race etc. and challenged older models of truth and meaning

**intertextuality** – a relation between two or more texts in which one text is echoed or included in another (McLerran & Patin, 1997). Allen (2000) defines the term to mean a text that does not lack any kind of independent meaning but borrows from previous systems, codes and traditions of other texts and cultures thus moving from the independent text into a network of textual relations (1). In bricolage, the research text borrows from many other texts (see glossary for the meaning of **texts).**

**monological** – one way only of thinking about the research, one logic; but whose counts?

**phenomenology** – studies the pre-conceptual, pre-linguistic experiences of life as lived; hermeneutics is used to bring the experience to language while still maintaining the experience 'as lived'

**postmodernism** – privileges no single authority/grand narrative such as patriarchy, middle class values, Euro-American white race, Christianity, Colonialism, capitalism and others especially those constructed during modernist era

 **rhapsodic intellect** – the joy, excitement of working serendipitously and towards epiphanies

**segue** – a transition from one way of thinking/doing to another way

**scientific method** – a way of researching that dominates the natural and physical sciences and includes the principles of logical positivism, objectivity, reductionism and scientific rationality

**text** – a system that produces meaning, beliefs, values and knowledge such as an oral text, a printed or visual text, a research study, a classroom, a policy document, a theory, a culture, an institution and so on. Original meaning, a tissue, a woven fabric

**totalizing framework** – a right way to do a particular kind of research; i.e. ethnography

**variables** – the exceptions, other perspectives, polyphonic, polylogical, and polyoptic approaches that are eliminated in traditional and modern research because they interfere with or contaminate objectivity, the truth, the data

REFERENCES

Allen, G. (2000). *Intertextuality.* New York, NY: Routledge.
Carter, A. (1990). *The bloody chamber.* England: Penguin.
Denzin N.K. & Lincoln Y.S. (Eds). 1994. 2000. 2005. (1ˢᵗ, 2ⁿᵈ, 3ʳᵈ editions respectively). *The handbook of qualitative research.* Thousand Oaks, CA: Sage.
Fedory, Z. (2005). *Dismantling the Grade nine Visual Arts Curriculum using Bricolage.* Unpublished MEd thesis. University of New Brunswick, Canada.
Kincheloe, J. L. & Berry, K.S. (2004). *Rigour and complexity in educational research: Conceptualizing the bricolage.* London: Open University Press.
Kincheloe, J. L. (2002). *The Sign of the Burger: McDonald's and the culture of power.* Philadelphia: Temple University Press.
Kuhn, T. S. (1970). *The structure of scientific revolutions.* Chicago: University of Chicago.
Press Lash, S. (1989). *Sociology of postmodernism.* New York: Routledge.
Levi-Strauss, C. (1966). *The savage mind.* Chicago: University of Chicago Press.

Manen, M., van (1990). *Researching lived experience: Human science for an action sensitive pedagogy.* London: Althouse Press.

McLerran, J. & Patin, T. (1997). *Artwords: A glossary of contemporary art theory.* Westport, CT: Greenwood.

Prigogine, I. & Stengers, I. (1984). *Order out of chaos: Man's new dialogue with nature.* New York: Bantam Books.

Smith, L.T. (2001). *Decolonizing methodologies: Research and indigenous peoples.* New York: Zed Books.

SSHRC (Social Sciences and Humanities Research Council of Canada) (2005). *Knowledge council: SSHRC 2006-2011.* web/about/publications/strategic_plan_e.pdf.

Tyson, L. (1999). *Critical theory today: A user-friendly guide.* New York, NY: Garland.

SHIRLEY R. STEINBERG

# 5. CRITICAL CULTURAL STUDIES RESEARCH

*Bricolage in Action*

In the contemporary information environment of the twenty-first century-so aptly named hyperreality by Jean Baudrillard, knowledge takes on a different shape and quality. What appears to be commonsense dissipates slowly into the ether, as electronic media refract the world in ways that benefit the purveyors of power. We have never seen anything like this before, a new world—new forms of social regulation, new forms of disinformation, and new modes of hegemony and ideology. In such a cyber/mediated jungle new modes of research are absolutely necessary. This chapter proposes a form of critical cultural studies research that explores what I refer to as cultural pedagogy. Cultural pedagogy is the educational dimension of hyperreality, as learning migrates into new socio-cultural and political spaces. In these pages, I will focus my attention on my research with film, specifically on *doing educational research* with a bricolage of methods leading to tentative interpretations.

## CULTURAL STUDIES

Observing that the study of culture can be fragmented between the disciplines, those who advocate cultural studies look at an interdisciplinary approach, that which transcends any one field. Additionally, a critical cultural studies does not commit a qualitative evaluation of culture by a definition of "high" or "low" culture, and culture may be the most ambiguous and complex term to define in the domain of the social sciences and humanities. Arthur Asa Berger (1995) estimates that anthropologists alone have offered more than one hundred definitions of culture. At the risk of great reductionism, I use the term in this chapter to signify behavior patterns socially acquired and transmitted by the use of social symbols such as language, art, science, morals, values, belief systems, politics, and many more. Educators are directly implicated in the analysis of culture (or should be) in that culture is transmitted by processes of teaching and learning, whether formally (schools) or informally (by wider social processes, e.g., popular culture). This pedagogical dynamic within all culture is a central concern of this chapter. Indeed, culture is inseparable from the human ability to be acculturated, to learn, to employ language and symbols.

*K. Tobin & J. Kincheloe, (eds.), Doing Educational Research—A Handbook, 117–137.*

Culture, in this chapter, involves specifically its deployment in connection with the arts. This is where we move into the social territory traditionally referred to as elite or high culture, and popular culture. Individuals who attend symphonies, read the "great books," enjoy the ballet, are steeped in elite culture--or as it is often phrased, "are cultured." Referring to "low" culture, many scholars assert that the artifacts that grew within a local or regional movement are indeed low. Fitting neither into a category of low or high culture is mass culture. Cultural theorists do not agree on any one definition for each type of culture. However, Dwight MacDonald summarizes the difference between the three, and the propensity of all types of culture to become political:

Folk art grew from below. It was a spontaneous, autochthonous expression of the people, shaped by themselves, pretty much without the benefit of High Culture, to suit their own needs. Mass Culture is imposed from above. It is fabricated by technicians hired by businessmen; its audiences are passive consumers, their participation limited to the choice between buying and not buying. . . .Folk Art was the people's own institution, their private little garden walled off from the great formal park of their master's High Culture. But Mass Culture breaks down the wall, integrating the masses into a debased form of High Culture and thus becoming an instrument of political domination (MacDonald, 1957, p. 60).

Within critical cultural studies it is maintained that the boundary between elite/high culture and popular/low culture is blurring. Such occurrence holds important ramifications for those interested in pedagogy (Berger, 1995). The study of culture, for the purpose of this chapter, is not to delineate the "level" or "type" of culture invoked by popular films, but to discuss the pedagogical, sociological and political themes within the films. Consequently, a debate as to the "quality" of popular culture or its place in the light of elite culture will not be undertaken. I will use the term popular culture to define that which is readily available to the American public as a form of enjoyment and consumption.

Popular culture defies easy definition. It can be defined as the culture of ordinary people--TV shows, movies, records, radio, foods, fashions, magazines, and other artifacts that figure in our everyday lives (Berger, 1995). Often analysts maintain that such artifacts are mass-mediated and consumed by large numbers of individuals on a continuing basis. Such phenomena are often viewed condescendingly by academicians as unworthy of scholarly analysis. As addressed in this chapter, the aesthetic dynamics of popular culture are not the focus; rather the social, political, and pedagogical messages contained in popular culture and their effects are viewed as some of the most important influences in the contemporary era. In this context the study of popular culture is connected with the sociology of everyday life and the interaction and interconnection of this micro-domain with macro-socio-political and structural forces. Thus, the popular domain--as ambiguous and ever-shifting as it may be--takes on unprecedented importance in the electronically-saturated contemporary era.

118

## CULTURAL STUDIES AND PEDAGOGY

Cultural studies and pedagogy involves education and acculturation that takes place at a variety of cultural locations including but not limited to formal educational institutions. Cultural studies scholars extend our notion of cultural pedagogy, focusing their attention on the complex interactions of power, knowledge, identity, and politics. Issues of cultural pedagogy that arise in this context include:

1) the complex relationship between power and knowledge.

2) the ways knowledge is produced, accepted, and rejected.

3) what individuals claim to know and the process by which they come to know it.

4) the nature of cultural/political authority and its relation to the dialectic of empowerment and domination.

5) the way individuals receive dominant representations and encodings of the world--are they assimilated, internalized, resisted, or transformed?

6) the manner in which individuals negotiate their relationship with the "official story," the legitimate canon.

7) the means by which the official and legitimated narrative positions students and citizens to make sense of their personal experience.

8) the process by which pleasure is derived from engagement with the dominant culture--an investment that produces meaning and formulates affect.

9) the methods by which cultural differences along lines of race, class, gender, national origin, religion, and geographical place are encoded in consciousness and processed by individuals.

10) the ways scientific rationality shapes consciousness in schools and the culture at large.

It is with the above issues in mind that I create my bricolage.

The attempt to delineate a universal research method for the study of the cultural curriculum and cultural pedagogy is a futile quest. The critical research of cultural studies and cultural pedagogy can make no guarantee about what questions will be important in different contexts; thus, no one method should be promoted over others--at the same time, none can be eliminated without examination. Ethnography, textual analysis, semiotics, deconstruction, critical hermeneutics, interviews, psychoanalysis, content analysis, survey research, and phenomenology simply initiate a list of research methods an educational scholar might bring to the table. Such an eclectic view of research has been labeled bricolage by several scholars. A term attributed to Claude Levi-Strauss (1966), bricolage (use of a tool box) bricolage involves taking research strategies from a variety of scholarly disciplines and traditions as they are needed in the unfolding context of the research situation. Such an action is pragmatic and strategic, demanding self-consciousness and awareness of context from the researcher. The bricoleur, the researcher who employs bricolage, must be able to orchestrate a plethora of diverse tasks including interviewing and observing, to historiographical analysis, to self-monitoring and intrapersonal understanding.

The text produced by this research process of bricolage should be a complex collage, as it weaves together the scholar's images, insights, and interpretations of the relationship between the popular cultural text, critical questions of justice, the social context that produced it, and its effect on youth and the cultural curriculum (Kincheloe & Berry, 2004). Using theoretical and conceptual frames drawn from critical theory, poststructuralism, postmodern epistemologies, feminism, psychoanalysis, hermeneutics, recovery theory and other traditions, bricolage interprets, critiques, and deconstructs the text in question. Because scientific research has traditionally offered only a partial vision of the reality it seeks to explore, pedagogical bricoleurs attempt to widen their perspectives through methodological diversity. In no way, however, do they claim that as the result of the multiperspective bricolage they have gained "the grand view"--from their poststructuralist perspective they understand that all inquiry is limited and incomplete. Humble in this knowledge, the bricoleur attempts to gain expanded insight via historical contextualization, multiple theoretical groundings, and a diversity of knowledge by collecting and interpreting methodologies (Kincheloe 2005).

Theoretical bricolage compensates for the blindness of relying on one model of reading a cultural text. Bricolage does not draw upon diverse theoretical /methodological traditions simply for the sake of diversity. Rather, it uses the different approaches to inform and critique each other. A critical theoretical analysis of popular culture, for example, that is informed by psychoanalysis will be different than one that relies only on the sociological dimension of the text under analysis. Such an interpretive process subverts the tendency of knowledge producers to slip into the position that their interpretation is the "right one" (Kincheloe, 2005). As we study the pedagogy of film, we are able to position it not only in historical, socio-political, and economic context but in relation to other films on a particular topic, with similar themes, or identified with a particular genre--for example, the films of John Hughes concerning middle-class male misbehavior. Expanding our ways of seeing with diverse perspectives we begin to grasp the ideological dimensions of films that often fall through the cracks. A more specific focus on how particular methodologies may be used in this popular cultural/film context may be in order.

## CRITICAL ETHNOGRAPHY

Critical ethnography is an example of a critical research methodology that can be used within the bricolage. Ethnography is often described as the most basic form of social research: the analysis of events as they evolve in their natural setting. While ethnographers disagree about the relative importance of each purpose, ethnography attempts to gain knowledge about a cultural setting, to identify patterns of social interaction, and to develop holistic interpretations of societies and social institutions. Thus, typical educational ethnographies attempt to understand the nature of schools and other educational agencies in these ways, seeking to appreciate the social processes that move educational events. Ethnography attempts to make explicit the social processes one takes for granted as a culture member. The culture could be as broad as the study of an ethnic culture or as narrow as the middle-class white male culture of misbehavior. The critical ethnographer of education seeks to describe the concrete experiences of everyday school/educational life and the social patterns, the deep structures that support it (Hammersley & Atkinson, 1983). In a bricolage, ethnography can be used in a variety of ways to gain insight into film. The most traditional involves audience studies where ethnographers observe and interview film audiences. John Fiske (1993) began his book, *Power Works, Power Plays,* using such a methodology, as he observed and interviewed a group of homeless men in a shelter as they watched the movie, *Die Hard.* What was the nature of the interrelationship between the viewers and the text? What did the men's responses to the film tell us about their self images? What did the men's responses tell us about film viewing in general and its ideological effects? Fiske's effort to answer these questions--to interpret his data--constitutes much of the content of the book.

In addition to such "audiencing" ethnographies, scholars can use ethnographic methods to explore the characters and cultures portrayed within the film and their relation to social dynamics outside the texts. Gaining knowledge about the "film culture" provides insight into the ideological orientations of film makers and entertainment corporations. Through the identification of patterns of cultural expression and social interaction, researchers can begin to specify the ideological dynamics at work. As socio-political processes are exposed, hidden agendas and tacit assumptions can be highlighted so as to provide new appreciations of the power of film to both reflect and shape culture. Poststructuralist forms of ethnography have focused on the discontinuities, contradictions, and inconsistencies of cultural expression and human action. As opposed to more modernist forms of ethnography, poststructuralist methods refuse to reconcile the asymmetries once and for all. The poststructuralist dimension of ethnography highlights the tendency of classical ethnography to privilege a dominant narrative and a unitary, privileged vantage point. In the effort to connect knower and known, the poststructuralist ethnographer proposes a dialogue between researcher and researched that attempts to smash traditional hierarchical relations between them (Atkinson & Hammersley, 1994).

In this critical process the modernist notion of ethnography as an instrument of enlightenment and civilization of the "native" *objects* of study is overthrown. Poststructuralist ethnographies are texts to be argued over, texts whose meaning is never "natural" but are constructed by circumstance and inscribed by context (Aronowitz, 1993). Thus, a film never stands alone as an object of study in poststructuralist ethnography. Seen as a living part of culture and history, the film takes on new meaning and circumstances and contexts change. How different the movie, *The Green Berets* (1968) looked to the young audience that viewed it in the late 1960s and early 1970s than it does to young people viewing it in the post-Gulf War 1990s. More young people of the present era may positively resonate with the ideological intentions of the film makers than did young, anti-war viewers of the era in which it was produced. Circumstance and context must always be accounted

121

for in critical poststructuralist ethnography. In this context poststructuralist ethnography informs and is informed by feminist and minority researchers concerned with the status quo of apologetics of film and traditional ethnography itself.

## CONTENT ANALYSIS

Traditionally a content analysis could be considered methodical and quantitative in nature. The important issue about literally analyzing text is to allow the text to open and present themes for the researcher. Following is a method I have used with success in first, analyzing text, and second, in letting the textual analysis speak to me and suggest the themes that can be included. The content analysis then becomes an authentic interpretive analysis that precludes preliminary hypotheses, and instead waits to allow the data to speak for themselves in muli-layered ways. The analysis especially lends itself to research in film, written text, visual text (comics, photography, etc.). It then becomes ready for the critical hermeneutic interpretation which is my tentative research goal.

In addition to such ethnographic analysis critical educational scholars use other methods of studying the social dynamics and effects of film. Douglas Kellner (1995) performs content analyses of film reviews and criticisms in the process gaining new vantage points out the ways that film texts become embedded in popular discourses. This "mode of reception" study was promoted by the Frankfurt School critical theorist, Walter Benjamin (Kellner, 1995). Appropriating Benjamin's methodology, literary critics and theorists developed literary reception research that continues to contribute innovative ways of exploring textual effects. Distributed throughout Aaron Gresson's analysis of *Forrest Gump* is the discussion of the film by various critics and the news media. Beginning with the traditional "thumbs up" or "thumbs down" types of articles and moving to more esoteric and scholarly discussion, Gresson is able to trace themes relating back to his original suggestion of the recovery of whiteness and maleness in film (Gresson, 1996). In this context, various research methodologies can be added to the bricolage, in the process providing ever more nuanced forms of insight into popular cultural texts.

Semiotics plays an invaluable role in the methodological pantheon with its focus on codes and signs that contribute to individuals' attempts to derive meaning from their surroundings. Educational researchers can use semiotic methods to gain insights into the social dynamics moving classroom events. Classrooms are full of codes calling out for semiotic analysis. Not only are classrooms saturated with codes and signs but are characterized by rituals and conventions that are rarely questioned. The ways teachers, students, and administrators dress; pupils' language when speaking to teachers as compared to conversations with classmates; graffiti in a middle school restroom; systems of rules of behavior; the uses of bells and the intercom in schools; memos sent to parents; and the nature of the local community's conversation about school athletics are only a few of the topics an educational semiotician could study.

## OBSERVATION METHODS

Contrary to notions that qualitative research dealing with popular culture is vacuous and without rigor, I submit my methodology in the spirit of academic scholarship and indeed, a poststructuralist, feminist, pedagogical research in which I am not seeking answers, but seeking questions, questions and more questions in which to make sense of the world of youth and of education. In their *Handbook of Qualitative Research,* Norm Denzin and Yvonna Lincoln (2005) discuss their union of poststructural/postmodernist cultural research (Denzin) and constructivist /pedagogical research (Lincoln). They contend that traditional research stops short of boundary crossing within interpretation. Observing that "over the past two decades, a quiet methodological revolution has been taking place in the social sciences" (p. ix, 1994 ) Denzin and Lincoln define this revolution as the "blurring" of the boundaries within disciplinary research. As I discuss my methods and objectives in my research, keep in mind that I want to make "noise" in this so-called "quiet" revolution. In fact, I question whether or not it has ever been quiet. Certainly there have been attempts to silence the noise caused by radical qualitative research-- silence in the denial of the politicization of the research of pedagogy; however, my qualitative predecessors have worked long and hard in the legitimization of the discipline. The word *rigor* seems to rear its ugly head at methodological junctures. I assert here that my research is indeed rigorous, challenging and constantly changing. Unlike a statistical formula, an organized hypothesis and a proven theorem, I am not beginning with any assumptions other than the one that popular culture must be studied. My thoughts about my subjects and my expectations in my observations changed each time I analyzed and recorded (for lack of a better word) *data.* It was within this discovery and rediscovery that I found rigor and challenge. It is within this context that I present my *literal method of interpretation.* I assert that rigorous scripting, recording and viewing/re-viewing (or consuming/re-consuming) is essential for critical hermeneutical research, and it is this process I delineate here.

The postmodern condition has also re-determined and re-defined the actual research methods and practices that we use. No longer, as in earlier cultural research, do we view a film at the theater, go to the typewriter and write a response and review. We have the tools of hyperreality, through portability, films are readily available in VHS, DVD, and iMovie, consequently, we are able to view, then script, interpret, re-interpret, then problematize our interpretations as we attempt to make meaning from the text. Unlike viewer/ historians of the past, we are able to re-visit an event, a text, and look for the tacit assumptions that reside within each signifier, floating signifier, code and ideology presented within the film.

## MATERIALS AND PROCESS

In order to be able to re-visit and re-view text, I found it essential to have access to videotapes of the films I wished to discuss. Wherever possible, I have avoided even alluding to films still in the theater as I feel they are available for a shallow interpretation at best (unless, of course, one owns his or her own theater). Along with the video tapes, I needed a video recorder, television and a good remote control. Other "equipment" I needed was an unlimited amount of colored pencils, ruled notebooks and a pen. However, on review of these methods, I feel that the use of a laptop computer while viewing could have or would have enhanced and possibly quickened the recording method.

In the manner of traditional ethnography, I used scripting as my form of recording. I wrote constantly through each film, usually filling up my notebooks after two films. I wrote quickly, and intuitively. I cannot delineate *what* to record. I can only describe that I recorded *everything* that made me think, consequently I relied on my own pedagogical intuition in my records. The use of the remote was essential in being able to rewind and record exact dialogue or to view a scene closely. In some films, I recorded no dialogue, only impressions of the scenery or music or cinematography. In most films I did record dialogue, discerning it as the salient data that would eventually be entered into my hermeneutical interpretations and discussions.

Each film took many hours to watch and re-watch. When I felt comfortable that I had scripted enough to begin my transcriptions, I transcribed the notebooks into word processed form. Using phrases, I typed my entries going down each page as I had originally written them. After completing the transcription of all of the films, I read through the entire set of data. As I examined this completed set of scripting, themes and motifs started to emerge. As they began to repeat themselves, I wrote down my impressions of their emergence, *named* them as separate entities. After my first reading of the data, I used the colored pencils to code each theme/motif that I wanted to pursue. Underlining each item with a different color, macro-themes began to emerge, as the micro-themes seemed coalesced under the auspices of larger themes. Analyzing all the pages of scripting, I discovered additional themes each times. In many instances there would be three or four different colors under a certain situation or dialogue indicating an overlap among the themes.

*A note:* Not appear a "Luddite," I want to clarify that I chose to use both video and DVD to use in my work. I feel organically connected to the materials in this way, as a audience participant. This is my quirk. However, those with the technical abilities and equipment will find this method quite easy to do digitally using iMovie and competent software.

Both visually and intuitively, I began the task of arranging micro-themes and placing them within the macro-themes. Given the thematic crossover, it was important to not essentialize any situation or dialogue and limit it to only one "category." I kept in mind that through my choice of bricolage, that I was not adhering to one method of interpretation, consequently it was important to record and underline each micro-theme every time it emerged in all macro-categories.

## VIEWING AND NAMING FILMS

As this is a chapter discussing critical pedagogical research methods, I chose to not use traditional methods of film theory and criticism. I will delineate three terms that I used within my bricolage. As a bricoleur, I cut and pasted what I felt was significant and examined the multiple meanings that emerged. Traditional film criticism, as in any form of sociological research, has categories and philosophies attached to methods of interpretation of audiences and of text. And, as in traditional research, this criticism essentializes and closes itself off to the boundary crossing to which Denzin and Lincoln have chosen to blur. By taking each interpretative method and applying it to a film bricolage, I was able to use film criticism and theory to my advantage in my critical hermeneutical readings.

Traditional film criticism "reads" film in many ways. The most compelling methods and classifications involves concepts such as 1) *auteurism* 2) *montage* and 3) *genre*. Each term has value in critical hermeneutics, however, using them in a unilateral deconstruction would limit interpretation to a dogmatic ideological framework established by the original researcher.

*Auteurism*

As the name suggests, auteurism refers to the authorship of the text. As in a Derridian deconstruction, the text becomes the only artifact examined, and unlike a Derridian deconstruction, the text in relationship to the author/creator is the essential interpretation. The entire act of meaning making in auteurism is restricted to who the author is, his or her positionality, and tacit and overt agendas in regard to the text. While I would be unable to discount the inclusion of auteurism in interpreting film text, in no way would I be comfortable limiting the interpretation to this narrow theory. In the case of the writer/director, John Hughes--on whose films I rely heavily in my research--I cannot discount the fact that he is a white, middle-class male, and a baby boomer from Chicago. Further discovery of his own background and education *can* inform me about him and "where he comes from." However, to allow auteurism to define the purpose of his films, for example: Ferris Bueller *is* John Hughes or Hughes's plotlines revolve around his own personal agenda for humiliating adults would direct and possibly limit my interpretation(s). Robin Wood (1995) insists that limiting film theory to auteurism adds to the propensity of inconclusive, inaccurate research that insists "on its own particular polarization" (p. 59).

*Montage*

Like auteurism, montage relies on one lens through which to view a text. Unlike auteurism, montage examines the intent of the editor in the analysis of the "essential creative act" of film making (Wood, 1995). While auteur theory exclusively read the act of the author as the textual interpretation, montage theory introduces the notion that the cutting room floor becomes the site for the decisive interpretative act. Once again, one cannot ignore the possible intent of the film editor and/or cinematographer, however, to limit interpretation to montage at the expense of any other aspect of film criticism and theory would once again limit the thickness of the interpretation.

*Genre*

In the traditional literary manner, the concept of genre is used to define and classify texts into manageable categories which immediately allow the interpreter to draw conclusions and make expected observations. For instance, when we refer to the Western as a genre, it is easy to imagine horses, Indians, pioneers and a white cowboy on a majestic horse. Within genre theory we are able to find familiar Western themes of patriarchy, white supremacy and colonialism without much effort. If we refer to *film noir*, we easily picture the frames of shadowy figures, a femme fatale and a Bogartesque antihero engaged in questionable activities. Once again, a prevailing theme of patriarchy emerges without question. Consider the l950s sci-fi genre--a white, middle-upper-class scientist who goes against the odds to defeat an alien invader--back to patriarchy, colonialism, and so forth. Exclusive reliance on genre theory determines in advance which themes will be analyzed and which will not--again the possibility of new interpretations is truncated. Categorizing texts aids us in the ability to place films on the shelf, to place books in the library and to choose different genres in which to research. However, the discussion of genre should be used only to name in a general sense, the macro-category of film that the researcher chooses to interpret. The catch, is that the genre must be determined and defined by each researcher in the context of his or her own research. Consequently, what I view as a western, may indeed be viewed as a political satire to one researcher and a classic to another.

With the use of auteurism, montage and genre, I have combined the qualitative method of bricolage using critical ethnography, semiotics, feminist theory and critical hermeneutics to interpret my research

## FEMINIST RESEARCH

Another important aspect of the bricolage involves feminist research with its subversion of the principle of neutral, hierarchical, and estranged interaction between researcher and researched (Clough,1992). It is important that no one body of feminist theory exists. Three forms of feminist analysis have dominated the feminist critique:

1) liberal feminism has focused on gender stereotyping and bias. While such analyses have provided valuable insights, liberal feminism in general has failed to engage issues of power. As a result the position has been hard pressed to make sense of social reality with its subtle interactions of power, ideology, and culture--an interaction that needs to be analyzed in the larger effort to understand both the oppression of women and male privilege (Rosneau, 1992);

2) radical feminism has maintained that the subjugation of women is the most important form of oppression in that it is grounded on specific biological differences between men and women. In radical feminism concerns with race and class are more rejected than ignored, as radical feminists maintain the irrelevance of such categories in the study of women's oppression;

3) the form of feminist theory privileged in my research is critical poststructuralist feminism. This articulation of feminism asserts that feminism is the quintessential postmodern discourse. As feminists focus on and affirm that which is absent and/or peripheral in modernist ways of seeing, they ground the poststructuralist critique in lived reality, in the material world (Kipnis, 1988). As critical poststructuralist feminists challenge modernist patriarchal exclusions, they analyze the connections between an unjust class structure and the oppression of women (Rosneau, 1992). Often, they contend, male domination of women is concretized on the terrain of class--e.g., the feminization of poverty and the growth in the number of women who are homeless over the last fifteen years (Kincheloe & Steinberg, 1997).

In this poststructuralist feminist context research can no longer be seen as a cold, rational process. Feminist research injects feeling, empathy, and the body into the act of inquiry, blurring the distinction between knower and known, viewer and viewed--looking at truth as a process of construction in which knowers and viewers play an active role, and embedding passion into the bricolage. Researchers in this context see themselves as passionate scholars who connect themselves emotionally to what they are seeking to know and understand. Modernist researchers often weeded out the self, denying their intuitions and inner voices, in the process producing restricted and object-like interpretations of socio-educational events. Using the traditional definitions, these object-like interpretations were certain and scientific; feminist self-grounded inquiries were inferior, merely impressionistic, and journalistic (Reinharz, 1992). Rejecting the authority of the certainty of science, feminist researchers charged that the so-called objectivity of modernist science was nothing more than a signifier for the denial of social and ethical responsibility, ideological passivity, and the acceptance of privileged socio-political position of the researcher. Thus, feminist theorists argued that modernist pseudo-objectivity demands the separation of thought and feeling, the devaluation of any perspective maintained with emotional conviction. Feeling is designated as an inferior form of human consciousness--those who rely on thought or logic operating within this framework can justify their repression of those associated with emotion or feeling. Feminist theorists have pointed out that the thought-feeling hierarchy is one of the structures historically used by men to oppress women (Walby, 1990). In intimate heterosexual relationships if a man is able to present his position in an argument as the rational viewpoint and the woman's position as an emotional perspective, then he has won the argument--his is the voice worth hearing.

Drawing from feminist researchers, critical poststructuralists have learned that inquiry should be informed by our "humanness," that we can use the human as a research instrument. From this perspective inquiry begins with researchers drawing upon their own experience. Such an educational researcher is a human being studying other human beings focusing on their inner world of experience. Utilizing his or her own empathetic understandings, the observer can watch educational phenomena from within--that is, the observer can know directly, he or she can watch and experience. In the process the private is made public. Not only do we get closer to the private experience of students, teachers, and administrators and the effect of these experiences on the public domain, but we also gain access to the private experience of the researcher and the effect of that experience on the public description the researcher presents of the phenomena observed (Reinharz, 1992). Thus not only do we learn about the educational world that surrounds us, but we gain new insights into the private world within us--the world of our constructed subjectivity. By revealing what can be learned from the every-day, the mundane, feminist scholars have opened a whole new area of inquiry and insight. They have uncovered the existence of silences and absences where traditional scholars had seen only "what was there." When the feminist critique is deployed within the methodological diversity of the bricolage, new forms of insight into educational and social affairs as well as the cultural curriculum emerge.

## CONNECTING TO SOCIAL THEORY

In examining social dynamics of media/popular culture via the research methodologies of ethnography and semiotics and the political and epistemological concerns of poststructuralist feminism, an effort is made to connect research to the domain of social theory. Indeed, theory is very important in the bricolage of critical poststructuralist research. Theory involves the conceptual matrix analysts use to make sense of the world. Theory, whether it is held consciously or unconsciously, works as a filter through which researchers approach information, designate facts, identify problems, and devise solutions to their problems. Different theoretical frameworks, therefore, privilege different ways of seeing the world in general or the domain of popular culture in particular (Kincheloe, 2001). The theory behind a critical poststructuralist way of seeing recognizes these theoretical dynamics, especially the potential tyranny that accompanies theoretical speculation. The problem that has undermined the traditional critical project of understanding and changing the inequality plaguing modernist societies has involved the production of a theory that was too totalizing (all encompassing) and rigid to grasp the complexity described here. Critical poststructuralist theory is committed to a theoretical stance that guarantees the individual or community the capacity to make meaning and to act independently. Any theory acceptable to critical poststructuralists, thus, must take into account local divergence. This is not to adopt a position that insists researchers allow phenomena to speak for themselves. Theory in this context is a resource that can be used to generate a dialogue with a phenomenon; it is always contingent and it never whispers the answers to the researcher in advance (Grossberg, 1995). Theory does not travel well from one context to another. Indeed theory's usefulness is always mitigated by context.

Such a locally sensitive theoretical position allows bricolage research a space from which to view movies and popular cultural phenomena that maintains an oppositional but not a totalizing and deterministic interpretive strategy (Smith, 1989). Such a strategy searches for manifestations of domination and resistance in popular texts in light of larger questions of democracy (Kellner, 1995). Drawing upon the theoretical work of the Frankfurt School of Critical Theory, the concept of immanent critique helps us understand this oppositional dynamic. Critical theory, according to Max Horkheimer, attempts to expose and assess the breach between reality and ideas or "what is" and "what could be." Within capitalist society, Horkheimer maintained, there is an inherent contradiction between the bourgeois order's words and deeds. The more the power bloc speaks of justice, equality, and freedom, the more it fails under its own standards. Immanent critique, therefore, attempts to evaluate cultural production "from within," on the basis of the standards of its producers. In this way it hopes to avoid the accusation that its concepts inflict superfluous criteria of evaluation on those it investigates. Employing such a theoretical critique, critical theorists hope to generate a new understanding of the cultural phenomenon in question--an understanding that is able to articulate both the contradictions and possibilities contained with it (Held, 1980).

CRITICAL HERMENEUTICS AND THE PROCESS OF INTERPRETATION

I ground my research in the hermeneutical tradition and its concern with both the process of understanding the meaning of various texts and the production of strategies for textual interpretation. Traditionally concerned with the interpretation of religious texts and canonical scriptures within their social and historical context, hermeneutics, after the scientific revolution of the European Enlightenment, emerged as the tradition that challenged the increasingly powerful shibboleths of the empirical scientific tradition. One of the central assertions of hermeneutics is that research and analysis of any variety involves an awareness of one's own consciousness and the values residing tacitly within it. Such values and the predispositions they support, hermeneuts maintained, unconsciously shape the nature of any project of inquiry. Such profound arguments, unfortunately, exerted little influence on their scientific contemporaries, as they held fast to their science of verification, the notion of objectivity, and the absurdity of the need for self-analysis on the part of the researcher (Kincheloe, 2005).

Central to the hermeneutic method is an appreciation of the complexity and ambiguity of human life in general and the pedagogical process in particular. Hermeneutics attempts to return lived experience and meaning making to their original difficulty. In this context, words and images are relegated to the realm of the living with all the possibility for change such a state implies. Words and images to the hermeneutical analyst are not dead and static but alive and dynamic. Such a reality, of course, complicates the process of interpretation but concurrently provides a far more textured picture of human experience. The Greek root of hermeneutics, *hermeneuenin,* refers to the messenger god Hermes. Such an etymology well fits hermeneutics' ambiguous inscription, as Hermes was often a trickster in his official role of translator of divine messages to human beings. Interpretation is never simple and straight-forward—humans in the Greek myths learned this lesson frequently at the hands of their deceptive messenger. This lesson is not lost in twentieth century hermeneutics, as analysts focus their attention on the sediments of meaning and the variety of intentions that surround social, political, and educational artifacts. Transcending the scientific empirical need for final proof and certainty, hermeneuts celebrate the irony of interpretation in the ambiguous lived world. Framing the methods of such interpretation as both analytic and intuitive, hermeneutics pushes the boundaries of human understanding in a manner more consonant with the contradictory nature of the world around us.

## The Nature of Hermeneutic Interpretation

Hermeneutics insists that in social/educational science there is only interpretation, no matter how vociferously empirical scientists may argue that the facts speak for themselves. The hermeneutic act of interpretation involves in its most elemental articulation making sense of what has been observed in a way that communicates understanding. Not only is human science merely an act of interpretation, but hermeneutics contends that perception itself is an act of interpretation. Thus, the quest for understanding is a fundamental feature of human existence, as encounter with the unfamiliar always demands the attempt to make meaning, to make sense--but such is also the case with the familiar. Indeed, as in the study of commonly known popular movies, we come to find that sometimes the familiar may be seen as the most strange. Thus, it should not be surprising that even the so-called objective writings of qualitative research are interpretations, not value-free descriptions (Denzin, 1994).

Learning from the hermeneutic tradition and the postmodern critique, critical researchers have begun to re-examine textual claims to authority. No pristine interpretation exists--indeed, no methodology, social or educational theory, and discursive form can claim a privileged position that enables the production of authoritative knowledge. Researchers must always speak/write about the world in terms of something else in the world. As creatures of the world, we are oriented to it in a way that prevents us from grounding our theories and perspectives outside of it. Thus, whether we like it or not we are all destined as interpreters to analyze from within its boundaries and blinders. Within these limitations, however, the interpretations emerging from the hermeneutic process can still move us to new levels of understanding, appreciations that allow us to "live our way" into an experience described to us. Despite the impediments of context hermeneutical researchers can transcend the inadequacies of thin descriptions of decontextualized facts and produce thick descriptions of social/pedagogical texts characterized by the context of its production, the intentions of its producers, and the meanings mobilized in the process of its construction. The production of such thick descriptions /interpretations follows no step-by-step blueprint or mechanical formula. As with any art form, hermeneutical analysis can be learned only in the Deweyan sense--by doing it. Researchers in this context practice the art by grappling with the text to be understood, telling its story in relation to its contextual dynamics and other texts first to themselves and then to a public audience (Kincheloe, 2005).

## Thoughts About Hermeneutical Methods of Interpretation

These concerns with the nature of hermeneutical interpretation come under the category of philosophical hermeneutics. Working in this domain scholars attempt to think through and clarify the conditions under which interpretation and understanding take place. The following analysis moves more in the direction of normative hermeneutics in that it raises questions about the purposes and procedures of interpretation. In its critical theory-driven cultural studies context the purpose of hermeneutical analysis employed in this research is to provide understanding of particular cultural and educational phenomena of contemporary American life. Drawing upon the Frankfurt School's goal of theorizing the driving forces of the present moment, critical hermeneutics is used to develop a form of cultural criticism that sets the stage for a future politics/pedagogy of emancipation. Hermeneutical researchers operating with these objectives build bridges between reader and text, text and its producer, historical context and present, and one particular social circumstance and another. Accomplishing such interpretive tasks is a difficult endeavor, and scholars interested in normative hermeneutics push aspiring hermeneuts to trace the bridge-building process employed by successful interpreters of culture and pedagogy (Kincheloe, 2005).

Grounded by this hermeneutical bridge-building, critical social analysts in a hermeneutical circle (a process of analysis where interpreters seek the historical and social dynamics that shape textual interpretation) engage in the back and forth of studying parts in relation to the whole and the whole in relation to parts. No final interpretation is sought in this context, as the activity of the circle proceeds with no need for closure (Kincheloe, 2005). This movement of whole to parts is combined with an analytical flow between abstract and concrete. Such dynamics often tie interpretation to the interplay of larger social forces (the general) to the everyday lives of individuals (the particular). A critical hermeneutics brings the concrete, the parts, the particular into focus, but in a manner that grounds it (them) contextually in a larger understanding of the social forces, the whole, the abstract (the general) that grounds it (them). Focus on the parts is the dynamic that brings the particular into focus, sharpening our understanding of the individual in light of the social and psychological forces that shape him or her. The parts and the unique places they occupy ground hermeneutical ways of seeing by providing the contextualization of the particular—a perspective often erased in modernist science's search for abstract generalizations (Kincheloe, 2005).

The give and take of the hermeneutical circle induces analysts to review existing conceptual matrixes in light of new understandings. Here preconceptions are reconsidered and reconceptualized so as to provide a new way of exploring a particular text. Making use of an author's insights hermeneutically does not mean replicating his or her response to the original question. In the hermeneutical process the author's answer is valuable only if it catalyzes the production of a new question for our consideration in the effort to make sense of a particular textual phenomenon (Gallagher, 1992). In this context participants in the hermeneutical circle must be wary of critical techniques of textual defamiliarization that have become cliched. For example, feminist criticisms of Barbie's figure and its construction of the image of ideal woman became such conventions in popular cultural analysis that other readings of Barbie were suppressed (Steinberg, 2004). Critical hermeneutical analysts in this and many other cases have to introduce new forms of analysis to the hermeneutical circle--to defamiliarize conventional defamiliarizations--in order to achieve deeper levels of understanding (Berger, 1995).

Within the hermeneutical circle we many develop new metaphors to shape our analysis in ways that break us out of familiar modes. For example, thinking of movies as mass-mediated dreams may help us reconceptualize the interpretive act as a psychoanalytic form of dream study. In this way, educational scholars could examine psychoanalytical work in the analysis of dream symbolization for insights into their studies of the pedagogy of popular culture and the meanings it helps individuals make via its visual images and narratives. As researchers apply these new metaphors in the hermeneutic circle, they must be aware of the implicit metaphors analysts continuously bring to the interpretive process (Berger, 1995). Such metaphors are shaped by the socio-historical era, the culture, and the linguistic context in which the interpreter operates. Such awareness is an important feature that must be introduced into the give and take of the hermeneutical circle. As John Dewey wrote almost a century ago, individuals adopt the values and perspectives of their social groups in a manner that such factors come to shape their views of the world. Indeed, the values and perspectives of the group help determine what is deemed important and what is not, what is granted attention and what is ignored. Hermeneutical analysts are aware of such interpretational dynamics and make sure they are included in the search for understanding (Berger, 1995).

*Situating Interpretation*

Researchers who fail to take Dewey's point into account operate at the mercy of unexamined assumptions. Since all interpretation is historically and culturally situated, it befalls the lot of hermeneutical analysts to study the ways both interpreters (often the analysts themselves) and the object of interpretation are constructed by their time and place. In this context the importance of social theory emerges. In this research critical social theory is injected into the hermeneutic circle to facilitate an understanding of the hidden structures and tacit cultural dynamics that insidiously inscribe social meanings and values (Kellner, 1995). This social and historical situating of interpreter and text is an extremely complex enterprise that demands a nuanced analysis of the impact of hegemonic and ideological forces that connect the micro-dynamics of everyday life with the macro-dynamics of structures of white supremacy, patriarchy, and class elitism. The central hermeneutic aspect of this work will involve the interaction between the cultural curriculum and these situating socio-historical structures.

When these aspects of the interpretation process are taken into account, analysts begin to understand Hans-Georg Gadamer's contention that social frames of reference influence researchers' questions which, in turn, shape the nature of interpretation itself. In light of this situating process the modernist notion that a social text has one valid interpretation evaporates into thin air. Researchers, whether they admit it or not, always have a point of view, a disciplinary orientation, a social or political group with which they identify (Kincheloe, 2005). Thus, the point, critical hermeneuts argue, is not for researchers to shed all worldly affiliations but to identify them and understand their impact on the ways they approach social and educational phenomena. Gadamer labels these world affiliations of researchers their "horizons" and deems the hermeneutic act of interpretation the "fusion of horizons." When researchers engage in the fusion of horizons they enter the tradition of the text. Here they study the conditions of its production and the circle of previous interpretations. In this manner they begin to uncover the ways the text has attempted to represent truth (Berger, 1995).

In the critical hermeneutical tradition these analyses of the ways interpretation is situated are considered central to the critical project. Researchers like all human beings, critical analysts argue, make history and live their lives within structures of meaning they have not necessarily chosen for themselves. Understanding this, critical hermeneuts realize that a central aspect of their cultural pedagogical analysis involves dissecting the ways people connect their everyday experiences to the cultural representations of such experiences. Such work involves the unraveling of the ideological codings embedded in these cultural representations. This unraveling is complicated by the taken-for-grantedness of the meanings promoted in these representations and the typically undetected ways these meanings are circulated into everyday life (Denzin, 1992). The better the analyst, the better he or she can expose these meanings in the domain of the "what-goes-without-saying"--in this research those features of the media curriculum that are not addressed, that don't elicit comment.

At this historical juncture--the postmodern condition or hyperreality, as it has been labeled--electronic modes of communication become extremely important to the production of meanings and representations that culturally situate human beings in general and textual interpretations in particular. In many ways it can be argued that the postmodern condition produces a second hand culture, filtered and pre-formed in the marketplace and constantly communicated via popular cultural and mass media. Critical analysts understand that the pedagogical effects of such a *media*ted culture can range from the political/ideological to the cognitive/epistemological. For example, the situating effects of print media tend to promote a form of linearity that encourages rationality, continuity, and uniformity, on the other hand, electronic media promote a non-linear immediacy that may encourage more emotional responses that lead individuals in very different directions. Thus, the situating influence and pedagogical impact of electronic media of the postmodern condition must be assessed by those who study the pedagogical process and, most importantly in this context, the research process itself (Kincheloe, 2005).

## CRITICAL HERMENEUTICS

Understanding the forces that situate interpretation, critical hermeneutics is suspicious of any model of interpretation that claims to reveal the final truth, the essence of a text or any form of experience. Critical hermeneutics is more comfortable with interpretive approaches that assume that the meaning of human experience can never be fully disclosed—neither to the researcher nor even to the human that experienced it. Since language is always slippery with its meanings ever "in process," critical hermeneuts understand that interpretations will never be linguistically unproblematic, will never be direct representations, critical hermeneutics seeks to understand how textual practices such as scientific research and classical theory work to maintain existing power relations and to support extant power structures (Denzin, 1992). This research draws, of course, on the latter model of interpretation with its treatment of the personal as political. Critical hermeneutics grounds a critical pedagogy that attempts to connect the everyday troubles individuals face to public issues of power, justice, and democracy. Typically, within the realm of the cultural curriculum critical hermeneutics has deconstructed popular cultural texts that promote demeaning stereotypes of the disempowered (Denzin, 1992). In this research, critical hermeneutics will be deployed differently in relation to popular cultural texts, as it examines popular movies that reinforce an ideology of privilege and entitlement for empowered members of the society—in this case, white, middle/upper-class males.

In its ability to render the personal political, critical hermeneutics provides a methodology for arousing a critical consciousness through the analysis of the generative themes of the present era. Such generative themes form the basis of the cultural curriculum of popular culture (Peters & Lankshear, 1994). Within the academy there is still resistance to the idea that movies, TV, and popular music are intricately involved in the most important political, economic, and cultural battles of the contemporary epoch. Critical hermeneutics recognizes this centrality of popular culture in the postmodern condition and seeks to uncover the ways it impedes and advances the struggle for a democratic society (Kincheloe, 2005). Appreciating the material effects of media culture, critical hermeneutics trace the ways movies position audiences politically in ways that not only shape their political beliefs but also formulate their identities. In this context, Paulo Freire's contribution to the development of a critical hermeneutics is especially valuable. Understanding that the generative themes of a culture are central features in a critical social analysis, Freire assumes that the interpretive process is both an ontological and an epistemological act. It is ontological on the level that our vocation as humans, the foundation of our being, is grounded on the hermeneutical task of interpreting the world so we can become more fully human. It is epistemological in the sense that critical hermeneutics offers us a method for investigating the conditions of our existence and the generative themes that shape it. In this context we gain the prowess to both live with a purpose and operate with the ability to perform evaluative acts in naming the culture around us. In the postmodern condition the pedagogical effects of popular culture have often been left unnamed, allowing our exploration of the shaping of our own humanness to go unexplored in this strange new social context. Critical hermeneutics address this vacuum (Kincheloe, 2005).

Critical hermeneutics names the world as a part of a larger effort to evaluate it and make it better. Knowing this, it is easy to understand why critical hermeneutics focuses on domination and its negation, emancipation. Domination limits self-direction and democratic community building while emancipation enables it. Domination, legitimated as it is by ideology, is decoded by critical hermeneuts who help individuals discover the ways they have been entangled in the ideological process. The exposé and critique of ideology is one of critical hermeneutics' main objectives in its effort to make the world better. As long as the various purveyors of ideology obstruct our vision, our effort to live in democratic communities will be thwarted (Gallagher, 1992). Power wielders with race, class, and gender privilege have access to the resources that allow them to promote ideologies and representations in ways individuals without such privilege cannot. Resources such as entertainment and communication industries are used to shape consciousness and construct subjectivity (Kincheloe, 2005).

## CRITICAL HERMENEUTICS, THE PRODUCTION OF SUBJECTIVITY AND CULTURAL PEDAGOGY

Those who operate outside the critical tradition often fail to understand that the critical hermeneutical concern with popular culture in the postmodern condition is not a matter of aesthetics but an issue of socio-political impact. In light of the focus of this research on the cultural curriculum and cultural pedagogy, a key aspect of this socio-political impact involves the socialization of youth. Those same outsiders sometimes look down their noses at the popular texts chosen for interpretation in the critical context, arguing that cultural productions such as *Fast Times at Ridgemont High,* for example, doesn't deserve the attention critical scholarship might devote to it. Critical hermeneuts maintain that all popular culture that is consumed and makes an impact on an audience is worthy of study regardless of the aesthetic judgments elite cultural scholars might offer (Berger, 1995). In the case of a movie like *Fast Times at Ridgemont High,* it is important to critical analysts because it is both inscribed with profound cultural meanings and so many people have watched it. In its interest in oppression and emancipation, self-direction, personal freedom, and democratic community building, critical hermeneutics knows that popular texts such as movies shape the production of subjectivity; it also understands that such a process can be understood only with an appreciation of the socio-historical and political context that supports it (Ellis & Flaherty, 1992).

Norm Denzin (1992) is extremely helpful in developing this articulation of critical hermeneutics, drawing on the sociological genius of C. Wright Mills and his "sociological imagination." A key interest of this tradition, which Denzin carries into the contemporary era, involves unearthing the connections among material existence, communications processes, cultural patterns, and the formation of human consciousness. This articulation of a critical hermeneutics has much to learn from Denzin and Mills and their concern with subjectivity/consciousness, their understanding that cultural productions of various types hold compelling consequences for humans. Denzin is obsessed with the way individuals make sense of their everyday lives in particular cultural contexts by constructing stories (narratives) that, in turn, help define their identities. Employing a careful reading of Denzin, a critical hermeneut can gain insight into how cultural texts help create a human subject. How, Denzin wants to know, do individuals connect their lived

135

experiences to the cultural representations of these same experiences (Denzin, 1992)?

Following this line of thought a critical hermeneutics concerned with the pedagogical issue of identity formation seeks cultural experiences that induce crises of consciousness when an individual's identity is profoundly challenged. Such moments are extremely important to any pedagogy, for it is in such instants of urgency that dramatic transformations occur (Denzin, 1992). In this research it is argued that such moments are not uncommon in individual interactions with popular texts and that the results of such experiences can be either oppressive or liberatory in nature. Indeed, some pedagogical experiences may be characterized as rational processes but they almost always involve a strong emotional component. Too often in mainstream research this emotional dynamic has been to some degree neglected by logocentric social science (Ellis & Flaherty, 1992). A critical hermeneutics aware of such cultural pedagogical dynamics will empower individuals to make sense of their popular cultural experiences and provide them with specific tools of social interpretation. Such abilities will allow them to avoid the manipulative ideologies of popular cultural texts in an emancipatory manner that helps them consciously construct their own identities. Critical social and educational analysis demands such abilities in its efforts to provide transformative insights into the many meanings produced and deployed in the media-saturated postmodern landscape (Kellner, 1995).

## CONCLUSION

This chapter describes the way that cultural studies can be used with a bricolaged approach; combining critical research methods in order to critically interpret film, in this case, for a cultural pedagogical reading. As one who self-defines herself as abstract random, with a strange penchant for organization, I believe that cultural studies is best read through an approach that does not limit itself to one research method.

## REFERENCES

Aronowitz, S. (1993). *Roll over Beethoven: The return of cultural strife.* Hanover, New Hampshire, NH: Wesleyan University Press.

Atkinson, P. & Hammersley, M. (1994). Ethnography and participant observation. In N. Denzin and Lincoln, Y. (eds.), *Handbook of qualitative research.* (pp. 83-97). Thousand Oaks, CA: Sage.

Berger, A. (1995). *Cultural criticism: A primer of key concepts.* Thousand Oaks, CA: Sage.

Clough, P. (1992). *The end(s) of ethnography: From realism to social criticism.* Newbury Park, CA: Sage.

Collins, J. (1990). *Architectures of excess: Cultural life in the information age.* New York: Routledge.

Denzin, N. (1992). *Symbolic interactionism and cultural studies: The politics of interpretation.* Cambridge, MA: Blackwell.

Denzin, N. (1994). The art and politics of interpretation. In N. Denzin and Y. Lincoln, (eds.), *Handbook of qualitative research.* (pp. 500-515). Thousand Oaks, CA: Sage.

Denzin, N. & Lincoln, Y. (2005). The *Sage Handbook of Qualitative Research.* 3rd edition. Thousand Oaks, CA: Sages

Ellis, C. & Flaherty, M. (1992). An agenda for the interpretation of lived experience. In C. Ellis and Flaherty, M. (eds.), *Investigating subjectivity: Research on lived experience.* (pp. 1-16). Newbury Park, CA: Sage.

Fiske, J. (1993). *Power plays, power works.* New York, NY: Verso.

Gallagher, S. (1992). *Hermeneutics and education.* Albany, NY: SUNY Press.

Gresson, A. (1996). Postmodern America and the multicultural crisis: Reading *Forrest Gump* as the call back to whiteness. *Taboo: The Journal of Culture and Education:* Spring, pp. 11-34.

Grossberg, L. (1995). What's in a name (one more time)? *Taboo: The Journal of Culture and Education,* Spring, 1-37.

Hammersley, M. & Atkinson, P. (1983). *Ethnography: Principles in practice.* New York, NY: Tavistock.

Held, D. (1980). *Introduction to critical theory.* Berkeley, CA: University of California Press.

Kellner, D. (1995). *Media culture: Cultural studies, identity and politics between the modern and the postmodern.* New York, NY: Routledge.

Kincheloe, J. (2001). Describing the bricolage: Conceptualizing a new rigour in qualitative research. In *Qualitative Inquiry, 7,* 679-692.

Kincheloe, J. (2005). On to the next level: Continuing the conceptualization of the bricolage. In *Qualitative Inquiry, 11,* 323-50.

Kincheloe, J. & Berry, K. (2004). *Rigour and complexity in educational research: Conceptualizing the bricolage.* London: Open University Press.

Kincheloe, J. & Steinberg, S. (1997). *Changing multiculturalism.* London: Open University Press.

Kipnis, L. (1992). Feminism: The political conscience of postmodernism. In A. Ross (ed.), *Universal abandon? The politics of postmodernism.* (pp. 149-166) Minneapolis: University of Minnesota Press.

Levi-Strauss, C. (1966). *The savage mind.* Chicago: University of Chicago Press.

MacDonald, D. (1957). A theory of mass culture. In B. Rosenberg and White, D. (eds.), *Mass Culture.* (pp. 59-73). Glencoe: Free Press.

Peters, M. & Lankshear, C. (1994). Education and hermenetics: A Freirean interpretation. In P. McLaren and Lankshear, C. (eds.), *Politics of liberation: Paths from Freire.* (pp.173-192). New York, NY: Routledge.

Reinharz, S. (1992). *Feminist methods in social research.* New York: Oxford University Press.

Rosneau, P. (1992). *Postmodernism and the social sciences: Insights, inroads, and intrusion.* Princeton: Princeton University Press.

Smith, P. (1989). Pedagogy and the popular-cultural-commodity text. In H. Giroux an R. Simon (eds.), *Popular culture: Schooling and everyday life.* (pp. 31-46). Granby, MA: Bergin and Garvey.

Steinberg, S. (2004, 1997). The bitch who has everything. In S. Steinberg and Kincheloe, J. (eds.), *Kinderculture: The corporate construction of childhood.* (pp. 207-218). Boulder, CO: Westview Press.

Walby, S. (1990). *Theorizing patriarchy. Utne Reader, 64,* 63-66, July/August.

Wood, R. (1995). Ideology, genre, auteur. In B. Grant (ed.), *Film genre reader II.* (pp. 59-73). Austin, TX: University of Texas Press.

## FILMOGRAPHY

*Die Hard,* 1988. John McTiernan, Director.

*Fast Times at Ridgemont High,* 1982. Amy Heckerling, Director.

*Forrest Gump,* 1994. Robert Zemeckis, Director.

*Ferris Bueller's Day Off,* 1986. John Hughes, Director.

*The Green Berets,* 1968, Ray Kellogg and John Wayne, Directors.

BARBARA THAYER-BACON AND DIANA MOYER

# 6. PHILOSOPHICAL AND HISTORICAL RESEARCH

## INTRODUCTION

We write this essay as colleagues who work in the same program, Cultural Studies of Education, that is located in a department that is home to a very eclectic group of scholars, including people in instructional technology, health and safety, curriculum, research and assessment. We all participate in a seminar for our department where we come together and meet the new PhD student cohort and we try to explain to them what our programs entail and the kinds of research we do. As can be imagined, with such a diverse group of scholars, there is a variety of forms of research going on in our department, including filmmaking, program assessment, learning motivation, technology implementation, theory writing, and public health promotion.

Such a diverse array of programs brings logistical and conceptual challenges to the students and faculty. But it also offers our students a unique opportunity to see different research traditions presented in relation to one another. We attempt to use philosophy and history of education to broaden students' knowledge of educational research and theory. Most of our students are familiar with the quantitative /qualitative distinction and some of the methods associated with each. They have seen examples in journals, talked to peers who are planning to an ethnography or survey, and can visualize themselves within a narrowly defined quantitative or qualitative tradition. In contrast, students' connection with philosophical and historical research is rare or marked by misperceptions. In the absence of more familiar and tangible products such as taped interviews, field sites, or chi-squares, alternative forms of research can appear abstract and disconnected from educational practice.

As might be expected, our filmmaker in the department has to make the case that what he does counts as research, that making a film is a creative endeavor that produces a product (a film), and it is just as difficult, time consuming, and of possible scholarly significance as the writing of a book, report, or article, or the publishing of a how-to manual. That our filmmaker has to make the case for his artistic work to be recognized as a form of research is a sign of a problem we want to discuss in relation to our own research work. The problem is that science holds sway in academia presently and scientific research is the norm used to define educational research. Science has the highest status and other forms of scholarly endeavors such as artistic work are viewed as the exceptions that prove the norm is scientific scholarship.

*K. Tobin & J. Kincheloe, (eds.), Doing Educational Research—A Handbook, 139–156.*

In cultural studies the concept hegemony, originally developed by Antonio Gramsci (1971), is used to explain what happens when one group of people or one way of thinking is so powerful that it is considered "natural" and "normal" and what others may do or think that is contrary or different is considered "unnatural" or "abnormal," if it is even recognized at all. Included in the concept of hegemony is the idea that when something is considered the norm, it holds powerful sway on all people's lives, such that people who don't meet the standard of the norm will view themselves as lacking, or inferior, or deviant, and they will discipline themselves to try to fit the norm. Gramsci noticed that in his country, Italy, people were often voting for policies or politicians who actually represented policy positions that were harmful to the people voting. Gramsci tried to understand why people would vote for something or someone that is harmful to them (such as regressive sale tax laws). He developed the concept of hegemony to explain this phenomenon. People will vote for policies that actually only help the rich and powerful, but they do so with the hope that it might help them as well, and because they accept the norms of the rich and powerful as their own. Not only will they vote for policies that are harmful to them, they will police what others do and pressure them to vote the same way.

We want to argue that science and scientific forms of argumentation are considered the norm in research, and other forms of arguments that are not scientific are considered inferior forms of research, if they are even recognized as research at all. Policing action is taking place regularly to make sure faculty are doing scientific research and those who aren't don't get published, funded, tenured, or promoted. This hegemonic situation applies to educational research as well. Students are taught in educational research courses on how to do quantitative and qualitative research, both of which are scientific forms of research, but philosophical arguments often are not even considered a form of research and are not included in their course curriculum. Historical research does get recognition as a form of research, under the broad umbrella of qualitative research, but is often seen as a humanities discipline with little to offer students in the social sciences. Students are required to learn statistics to graduate, so that they can make sense of a quantitative study and determine if it is sound or not, but they are not required to learn logic, so they can make a well reasoned argument and critique others' arguments for their soundness and fruitfulness.

We will discuss our various fields of study below as we explain what historical and philosophical research is, against the norm of scientific research. But it is important to notice right from the beginning that we are working in a situation where we are not the norm, and often feel like we must defend our very existence, given the current conditions within which we work. One of the things that makes both of our fields of study so interesting to examine, in contrast to work in film for example, is that history and philosophy are two fields of study that have been around a long time. They are not new to the academy, like instructional technology is. In colleges of arts and sciences, history and philosophy are two departments that are mainstays and have been visible in universities from their very beginnings. Philosophers and historians enjoyed prestige and status for their scholarship at one point in time. Yet today they are barely visible, and find themselves having to survive on starvation diets, while their colleagues over in the sciences receive tremendous support in a variety of ways. It is the hard sciences that receive grants that help them buy new equipment and hire graduate assistants, as well as more faculty. The sciences are located in the nicest buildings, and the scientists receive the highest salaries and teach the least number of courses. They are the ones in the news and the ones whose names are mentioned when university presidents talk about their faculty's research work.

Philosophical and historical scholarship had status that has been lost to science. Along with that status, they had hegemonic power as well in their heyday. Even today, without the status that science enjoys, we can still see examples of hegemony within our fields of study. Both historians and philosophers of education work to advance educational practice and thereby reject the model of research for its own sake. This practitioner-orientated work is not held in as high regard as "pure" philosophy or history, which is viewed as unencumbered by the need for applicability. We can see the evidence of these claims by how seldom "pure" philosophers cite philosophers of education's scholarship in their own work, whereas philosophers of education regularly cite "pure" philosopher's work. Similarly, historians located in history departments sometimes dismiss educational history as "presentist" in its use of history to address current educational issues. Historians of education attempt to speak to both the past and present while satisfying the disciplinary expectations of history and education (Donato & Lazerson, 2000).

We write this essay in an effort to help others understand that the scholarly work we do represents various forms of research. Research is a concept that is continually in need of reexamining, for it is a growing, changing concept in a constant state of flux. What we would like to write about is the kind of research we do within our specific fields of study within the cultural studies program. We both do different kinds of research, yet we find that our paths often cross, not only because we are sometimes interested in similar topics and issues, but we also find we often cite the same sources and apply similar forms of analysis with our work. We understand what each other does much better than our colleagues in our department or college understand what we do, let alone their students. We hope this effort will help to make our work "visible" and have it "count" as research, and maybe we will even succeed in convincing some budding scholars of the exciting possibilities within our fields of study, and they will come and join forces with us, over on the outskirts of educational research.

## PHILOSOPHICAL ARGUMENTS

I (Barbara Thayer-Bacon) teach a course titled, Philosophy of Education, CS 526, that is a nuts-and-bolts, how-to course on theory writing.[1] We learn how to read a theoretical argument, describe it, interpret it, and evaluate it. We practice the steps on how to do this with six essays over the course of the semester. In the end the students have learned how to write what philosophers call an "epistemic commentary" or what conferences will present as "replies" to a conference paper. I am very proud to be able to say that at the University of Tennessee this course counts as a research course that graduate students can take. That was not the case at my previous university. Before I arrived at UT another colleague of mine in philosophy of sport, Bill Morgan, had already made the case that a course he taught for sports studies students on philosophical argumentation should count as a research course. I was able to have my course easily added to the list of possibilities. I also teach a second level theory writing course for doctoral students who want to write a philosophical dissertation. But my focus here will be on the first level course that students from all over our college now take. The last several times I have taught the course, it has been full. The students are spreading the word, "This course counts for the research requirement, and it will help you be a better reader, writer, and thinker." I am so glad the word is out! I want to argue that it will also help the students be better *researchers*, even if they do not write a philosophical argument for a thesis or dissertation.

*Arguments*

The first thing I have to address in CS 526 is what a philosophical argument is, in contrast to scientific arguments, and other types of arguments such as testimonial arguments. Each time I watch the students struggle with trying to understand what a philosophical argument is, I am reminded how powerfully strong the hegemony is that science holds over what counts as research today. Philosophical arguments sound to students like hearsay, or what some have labeled "b.s." or "crap," just an author's opinion on the topic. If it is not trying to establish a fact and it is not warranted by verifiable, observable data, it must not be research, or at best, it is bad research. I share with my students a true story: a friend of mine was taking a research course somewhere in Ohio toward earning her masters degree, not where I worked. I believe the focus of the course was on quantitative research, but it could have included qualitative research. Either way, it was definitely a scientific research course. My friend's professor used out-of-context pieces of a published essay by me to show his students an example of "bad research." The professor was making the case that my discussion of another philosopher's ideas was an example of an appeal to authority. My friend was shocked, first to discover that she knew the author of the example her professor was using, but also to find that he was using my work as an example of what not to do, when she had taken courses with me and held a different opinion of my work. I asked my friend if her professor had acknowledged to his students that my work was philosophical, not scientific. She said no. And then I explained to her why what he did is not only unfair, in terms of pulling out pieces of an argument rather than looking at the entire argument, but also because it is unfair to judge a philosophical argument based on scientific standards, and vice versa.

Philosophical arguments do not try to accomplish the same goal as scientific arguments, and they are not warranted in the same manner. Scientific arguments try to establish facts. They are warranted by verifiable, observable data. We judge whether or not it is good science by looking at the quality of the data collected and the methods used for collecting the data. Philosophical arguments try to establish norms and standards. They don't try to make the case for what is (that's science); they try to make the case for *what should be ideally*. Philosophical arguments try to make the case for what is the best, the right, the good, the beautiful, the fair and just, the true. These are arguments that are warranted by reasons, using logic to make their case. We judge whether or not it is good philosophy by looking at the soundness of the logic and the fruitfulness of the argument. I have argued elsewhere that philosophers don't just rely on reason, as their essential tool for making an argument, but that they use other tools that are just as important: intuition, emotions, imagination, and their communicating and relating skills (Thayer-Bacon, 2000). However, it is still the case that philosophers use all of these tools to help them develop reasons to make the case for what should be ideally. We may use a variety of styles of arguments, where some of us use formal logic to establish our claims, and others use a narrative style of argument, for example, but all of us warrant our arguments with reasons. Reasons are the "data" for a philosophical argument.

When philosophers try to make the case for what should be, what's called a normative argument, we aren't trying to say, "This is what I think should be." That would be an argument based on personal opinion that others may take or leave as valuable or b.s. The response to such an argument is likely, "Well you may believe that, and you're entitled to your opinion, but that's not what I believe, and I don't have to listen to you." Or, "so what?" Instead, philosophers are trying to say, "This is what we all should agree to, not because it is what I think, but because it is right, or good, or just." When philosophers say, "we all should agree to this," they mean "all people throughout time," not just Americans, or people from the 21st century, but all of us, across time and across our various cultures and settings. For example, philosophers have argued that all people should be treated with dignity and respect (Locke) and that women are equal to men and are equally capable of leading a country/state (Plato). If a philosopher is trying to make a normative argument that is universal, it only takes one counterexample to prove them wrong. That is a very tough standard for a philosophical argument to have to hold up to. In science, if the data I collect is verifiable and repeatable, if others can do the same experiment and get the same results, then I can begin to consider that I have managed to establish a fact. The more tests I make that return with the same results, the better. But, I don't have to keep testing my data until the end of time. Philosophical arguments are open to continual reexamination and continual amending and extending, they do not go out of date. This is why people still consider today what Plato and Aristotle argued, and we still find their ideas worthy of reconsideration.

As soon as I attempt to try to define what a philosophical argument is, which by the way is something philosophers do—try to define key concepts and look at basic assumptions embedded within those definitions—I am vulnerable to criticisms by other philosophers. We don't all agree on what philosophy's role is, and the kind of arguments philosophers can make. We don't all agree on what the limits are for philosophical arguments. And, we certainly don't agree on how to go about making a good philosophical argument. Some philosophers argue that the problems of the world have been solved, but our problems today are really due to misunderstandings and miscommunications with each other due to the ambiguity of language. They describe the role of philosophers as one of clarifying our obtuse language and they apply a method for doing this that has been labeled "language analysis." Analytic philosophers use logic to clarify the meaning of terms. Other philosophers, such as pragmatists, argue that philosophers' roles are to be prophets, poets, and soothsayers, helping us solve human problems that exist through a greater understanding of our social context, and helping us imagine new possibilities. Pragmatists seek to heal the dualisms we have created over time. They may use an historical approach, as Dewey did, and compare the development of ideas over time as a way of exposing the splits that have developed, between theory and practice or the mind and the body, for example, to help us heal them. Still others, postmodernists, argue that the role of the philosopher is dangerously similar to legislative and police work, where what are established as the rules and standards for a good philosophical arguments are then used to police people's thoughts and keep out unwanted views, which become labeled as "irrational" or "illogical."

Given all the ways we disagree with each other and the varieties of ways we approach our task, we still agree that philosophers work with ideas and that they seek to establish normative claims. And, we also agree that this is important work that is different from science. Scientists try to establish what is. Philosophers try to get us to think about what would be the ideal way to be. Philosophical arguments are not bound by what is, for example, how much time is available and how much money. Theirs is the world of possibilities, what could be, and they are only limited by their imaginations, emotions, intuitions, and reasoning to help them consider what those possibilities are. Philosophers don't go out and interview people and collect samples of their writings. They don't need to apply for research funding to send out survey mailings or to visit an archival collection at a particular site. Philosophers need time to think about ideas. They gather their own experiences, read what others have argued about those ideas, discuss their thoughts with others who are currently working on similar ideas, and write down their ideas, all as ways to help them clarify their own thinking. What could be more fun?

When I worked at my first university, there were research funds available for faculty to apply for, but I could never figure out how to get those funds. This was because what I did was not recognized as research. My colleagues applied for the funds to help pay for things such as mailings, but I didn't need funds to collect data as scientists do, I needed the research funds to help me travel to conferences where I could discuss my ideas with others and I needed the funds to give me more time to think. I applied for these funds annually to no avail. I even requested meeting with the college committee to try to make the case for what I needed, under the category of research funds. They didn't change their minds. One of my colleagues who served on the research funds committee started teasing me by asking me if I was doing research when he would see me standing at the elevator waiting for it to arrive. I would laugh and say, "You bet. I'm thinking about the ideas I'm working on."

When I went to apply for a sabbatical at this same university, I was advised by my college-level colleagues who had served on the university-wide committee not to write up my sabbatical as a desire to do research, but as a request for faculty development. My colleagues read my proposal and knew that it would not be recognized as research across the campus. This is because what I wanted to do was go to Teachers College at Columbia University and read and discuss my ideas with other philosophers of education located there. For a philosopher, that is what we do as researchers. But for scholars who only define research as quantitative or qualitative collection of data that is observable and verifiable, as science, working with ideas is not recognized as data collection. Because I wanted the sabbatical, I swallowed my pride and asked for a faculty development leave, which I was granted, but once again I was forced to face the hegemony of a scientific definition of research. I wondered, how can I be hired to be a researcher, even tenured and promoted, and not have the work I do be recognized as research? What a strange world we live in! Hegemony is not rational though, as Gramsci realized, it does not make sense.

*Reasons*

When philosophers try to explain their ideas to others, they use all sorts of examples to help illustrate what they mean. They may turn to nature and compare their ideas to bees (Plato), or to farming (Dewey). They may turn to fictional stories (Plato's "ring story" in the *Republic,* 1979) and literature (Nussbaum's use of Greek tragedies and other classic Euro-western literature in her narrative arguments, 1992) to help them, or today you might find them turning to film (Blum, 2000), rock 'n roll lyrics (Thayer-Bacon, 1998), and even television shows such as "The Simpsons" and "South Park" (Hostetler, 2005). Philosophers have the freedom to use anything to help explain their ideas, for what matters are the ideas, and the examples are meant to serve as illustration to help explain the ideas. Again, what could be more fun? This is the poetic side of philosophy.

One of the ways to criticize a philosophical argument is to look at the examples used and determine if they work well or not. Do they add clarity (exactness) and help explain the ideas or do they make things more confusing? Do they include more than what the key idea includes (exclusivity) or are they too limiting (extendabilty)? While we evaluate each other's examples in terms of whether or not they work well, we do not try to place limits on what can be used for examples, for what is important to consider are the ideas. For philosophers, our focus is: What is the central claim the scholar is trying to make and has s/he supported that claim with good reasons?

While philosophers may use anything for examples, we are limited only by our experiences and our abilities to use our imagination, intuition, emotions, and reason, still, we do use certain kinds of reasons to structure our arguments. Reasons play different kinds of roles in an argument. *Need reasons* usually come at the beginning of a philosophical argument as their job is to establish that there is a problem in need of solving. Need reasons try to get us to see that there is a need to look at an issue, and think about it. The philosopher's first task is to convince us that we need to think about such-and-such. "Why should I even bother to think about this?" Need reasons answer that question.

Once the philosopher has established a need, her next task is to justify what s/he intends to argue. S/he has to make the case that what s/he will claim is the solution, the answer, the way things should be. The argument is not meant to establish, this is how things are (once again, that's science), the argument is meant to establish, this is how things should be ideally. How things are right now is often described as a way to make the case that there is a problem we need to address. And, how things are can be used to justify how things should be.

For example, suppose I want to look at how we define democracy in the USA as a way of trying to address the educational problem in our schools of exclusion and/or lack of success of children who come from collective, communitarian cultures, such as Native Americans, Mexican Americans, and African Americans. This is my current research project, which I call the C.A.R.E. Project (culturally aware, anti-racist, relationally focused, educational communities) (Thayer-Bacon, in process). First I need to establish that there is a problem, and I can do that by giving drop out rates, test scores, number of students attending and graduating from college, for example. Then I need to look at the history of how democracy has been defined, trace its roots as a concept, and look at its underlying assumptions. Then I need to show how this conception of democracy is expressed in our schools. And, I need to examine the three collective cultures I named and determine if they share the same underlying assumptions, or others, and what these are. What I have discovered is that democracy in the USA is based on Locke's (1960/1823) and Rousseau's (1968/1762) concepts of democracy and both of them start with an assumption of individualism. Classical liberal democracy assumes individualism and this assumption is expressed in the USA's public school design. Yet, individualism is logically contrary to collective cultures that start with an assumption of group identity. A student who comes from a collective culture and attends a school based on individualism is put in the position of having to choose between either losing their family values in order to be successful in school or giving up on being successful in school in order to maintain her family values. It is an either/or logical problem. I want to argue for a pluralistic, relational democracy that begins with an assumption of transactional relationships, that I influence the group and the group influences me and we both are affected and changed by each other. It is a both/and logical approach to democracy. The reasons I give to justify my claims are what I call *justifying reasons*.

Philosophers don't limit themselves to how things are or have been in their reasoning. They also try to think about what would be the consequences of changing how we describe things, or changing our ways of doing things. They offer us warnings about how things are going to get worse if we don't change and embrace their central claim and follow their recommendations and they offer us predictions of what will be the benefits of embracing their argument and following their advice. These are *consequential reasons*. They are not as strong in supporting the central claims as need reasons and justifying reasons because they are not based on the past or what is, but are based on the future and what could be. The future is a prediction, we don't know for sure if what we predict will come to past. Our predicted consequences might happen, but then again they might not. There could be unforeseen variables that we can't account for that change what occurs. This is the soothsaying side of philosophy, the prophesizing. Consequential reasons help us anticipate the results of reaching our ideals, and think deeply about whether or not we really want those results. These kinds of reasons serve an important role in helping us determine if this argument is fruitful or not. But there is no way to test them out for certainty, as the future is not here yet.

*Evaluation*

How do we evaluate philosophical arguments? We said science was warranted by verifiable, observable data and we know that the way to check scientific arguments is to look at the data. This should tip us off that since philosophical arguments are warranted by reasons and logic, the way to evaluate them is by going back and looking at the reasons given, and the way they are put together. Are there any gaps in the reasoning? How is the argument arranged and connected together? If there are problems with the chaining of the ideas, how well they connect together, then there is a syntax problem that will affect the soundness of the logic. *Syntactic evaluation* has to do with judging the form (structure) of the argument.

What about the terms that are used? Are they well defined and is their meaning clear? Do they meet the criteria of exactness, exclusivity, exhaustiveness, external coherence, and extendability? If the terms are used in ways that are problematic this will effect the semantics of the argument, the meaning. Semantic problems lead to an argument that is not logically sound too. Sometimes the problems can be minor and easily fixed. However, sometimes they can be significant and they will affect the validity of the argument. *Semantic evaluation* judges the meaning of the argument.

Philosophical arguments are also judged on pragmatic grounds. *Pragmatic evaluation* judges how well is the central claim supported? How well do the reasons work (operative soundness)? Does the author give enough need reasons and justifying reasons to support the central claim, or could the argument use more? Does the author rely mainly on consequential reasons, which are weaker, or does the author offer enough need and justifying reasons along with consequential reasons? Maybe the author offers only need and justifying reasons, does this limit the range of the argument and its fruitfulness? Not only do we insist that philosophical arguments are logically sound, but we also judge them on their *fruitfulness*, if they are valuable and beneficial or not. A philosopher can offer an argument that is logically sound but has no impact on our lives. Then we will all feel disappointed and wonder, "So what? What this author has to offer does not contribute in any way to improving the human condition." Philosophical arguments are normative arguments that hope to contribute to a better world. They are arguments that hope to establish ideals that can guide us and help us make decisions today to help us reach our aims. They help us understand changes we need to make to reach our goals.

Have I convinced you yet that philosophical arguments are not just b.s. or crap? That they are held to rigorous standards and are not easily defended? Are you beginning to understand that they are important and have something significant to offer to research, even though they are not scientific arguments? I hope so! I hope for even more though, that you may be intrigued and actually want to further explore the possibilities of philosophical research. Come on over and join us on the outskirts of educational research! Whether you do so or not, at least now you know that there are other kinds of arguments besides scientific ones and they have a different role to play in educational research. This does not mean scientific work is not valuable or important as a form of research, but that scientific work is not the only kind of research there is. My argument is that philosophical work is also a form of research that has a valuable and important contribution to make. When I apply for grants, which I do so regularly without much success, my hope is that I can now refer reviewers to this essay to help them avoid imposing scientific criteria on a philosophical argument and instead judge the proposal for research using philosophical criteria. Maybe then, the next time I apply for a sabbatical I can ask for it on research grounds, and say that I want to go talk to some key scholars in New Zealand about New Zealand's concept of bi-cultural democracy and compare it to my idea of relational, pluralistic democracies-always-in-the-making, as well as read what others have to say on the topic, to help me clarify my own thinking, and my request will be granted because my work is valued for its possible significant contribution to educational research.

## HISTORICAL RESEARCH

The natural sciences continue to serve as the exemplar of legitimate research. Barbara Thayer-Bacon's experiences powerfully illustrate the difficulties of pursuing research that diverges from the norm of science. As an educational historian, I (Diana Moyer) have faced fewer of these challenges. The scientific model heavily influenced the development of historical research and education historians benefit from the discipline's long alliance with science. Traditionally, grant reviewers and peers in other fields rarely questioned that historical inquiry was a valid form of research. But debates over history as science or art and the proliferation of nonrepresentational historical approaches challenge historical writing as a form of research.

History and philosophy of education employ very different research methods. Despite these differences, both fields fit uneasily within the norms of educational research. The direction of current research policy further marginalizes historical and philosophical inquiry as outside the norms of legitimate inquiry. I anticipate a move toward using narrowly defined norms of scientific research to evaluate historical projects. If that occurs, historians will face very similar barriers to those philosophers have encountered for years.

We hope this combined discussion will explain the methods of our research and add to the visibility of historical and philosophical research within education. We also aim to challenge the scientific hegemony that constricts what counts as legitimate educational research. My discussion addresses procedures that ground historical inquiry, history's contributions to qualitative research, and its divided status as both science and art. Some would argue that questioning the appropriateness of the scientific model undermines history's legitimacy. I see the debates over written history's ability to represent the past as strengthening, rather than diminishing, historical inquiry's value as a form of research.

*Perceptions of History*

Students enter my graduate History of American Education course with a variety of experiences with studying the past. Some praise high school teachers who dressed in period clothing or used role-play to make history exciting and relevant. Others equate history with memorized dates and names disconnected from social and cultural practices. Some students enroll in the course looking for historical insight into ongoing problems such as racial segregation in schools and the slow pace of educational change.

On the first day of class, I give my student several pages of quotes on the topic of history. Some of the quotations are familiar, others humorous or provocative. Regardless of tone or author, I select quotes that touch on larger questions about the writing and purpose of history. As illustrated below, people have debated the meaning of history for centuries.

"History is written by the victors." Source Unknown

"Those who cannot remember the past are condemned to repeat it." George Santayana

"History is the best medicine for a sick mind, for in history you have a record of the infinite variety of human experience plainly set out for all to see, and in that record you can find for yourself and your country both examples and warnings: fine things to take as models, base things rotten through and through to avoid." Livy

"History is but a pack of tricks we play on the dead." Voltaire

"History, real solemn history, I cannot be interested in.... I read it a little as a duty; but it tells me nothing that does not either vex or weary me. The quarrels of popes and kings, with wars and pestilences in every page; the men all so good for nothing, and hardly any women at all - it is very tiresome." Catherine Morland in *Northanger Abbey* by Jane Austen

"Historical evidence has special functions. It lends weight and depth to evidence which, if culled only from contemporary life, might seem frail. And, by portraying the movements of men over time, it shows the possibility of change." Howard Zinn

I use these contrasting quotes to encourage students to reflect on their own assumptions about the meaning and significance of history. Beginning the course in this way underscores the importance of reading history critically. I want students to learn about the historical development of schooling while also reflecting on the types of questions implied in the quotes above. Should the goal of history be to guide action? Should history be used to address contemporary political concerns? Does history reinforce the views of those in power? All these questions speak to larger issues of historical research.

*Researching History*

Most people see history as a window to the past. We pick up a history book or turn on educational programming to learn more about the what, where, and why of past events. The finished products of historical research, however, tend to obscure the subjective choices that led to the final conclusions. A well-written history can lull us into thinking that it is the only possible story. The goal of the following discussion is to help nonhistorians understand two aspects of the process of historical research: 1) the sources that serve as evidence and 2) the relationship between what occurred in the past and what historians write about the past.

Historical research can conjure up the figure of a lone scholar poring over faded papers. Given the importance of archival research in historical study, this popular image of the historian is not without merit. The historian's main concern is locating primary sources--texts produced during the time period under study.[2] The number and type of sources can vary depending on the topic, source availability, and consistency with existing research. Sources might be numerical, narrative, graphic, or auditory. Quantitative historians might use labor patterns, census records, or literacy rates. Other common sources include letters, oral histories, speeches, institutional records, diaries, newspapers, and photographs. Given the sheer volume of information, historians rely heavily on the archivists and librarians who preserve and catalogue primary source materials. These are the individuals who organize primary sources into collections housed by libraries, universities, museums, and historical associations.

For example, some of the primary sources I used in researching the 1930s educator and administrator Elsie Ripley Clapp, I obtained easily. My university library owned copies of her book, *Community Schools in Action*, and her articles in the journal *Progressive Education*. Other sources required trips to the repositories where they were housed. I viewed materials such as her unpublished manuscripts, letters she wrote to John Dewey, and her scrapbook of newspaper clippings on site at the Special Collections of Southern Illinois University.

If history were simply the accumulation of facts concerning dates, events, and people of the past, it stands to reason that each new source would bring us closer to the truth. But as with other forms of qualitative research, historical methods include both empirical data and researcher perspective. Despite 19th century historian Leopold von Ranke's urging for a scientific history that simply "showed how it really was," writing about the past always involves interpretation. Historical projects may vary by type (e.g. social, cultural, intellectual, political, military, etc.), theoretical orientation, guiding questions, and goals. Even the seemingly transparent issue of historical "fact" is fraught with difficulty. Evidence may offer conflicting perspectives and sources such as letters and oral histories may be difficult to authenticate.[3]

The subjectivity of historical sources extends beyond individual judgment. Larger social and political norms influence what is documented, what is preserved and the topics deemed worthy of study. Without external verification to adjudicate among multiple perspectives, it may seem that history is an art of persuasion rather than evidence. If historians are not neutral gatherers of fact are they, as quoted above, merely authors of "tricks...on the dead?"

Most historians reject having to choose between fiction and fact in describing historical research. Carr, for example, described historical research as embedded in the time and place of its creation. He wrote:

> The facts of history never come to us 'pure,' since they do not and cannot exist in a pure form: they are always refracted through the mind of the recorder - Study the historian before you begin to study the facts - When you read a work of history, always listen out for the buzzing. If you can detect none, either you are tone deaf or your historian is a dull dog. (1961, pp. 25-26)

Readers used to more transparent forms of qualitative research may quickly despair of tone deafness when encountering history. Compared to many other fields, historians have largely neglected issues of methodological reflexivity (McDonald, 1996). Readers accustomed to authors' self-disclosure about their identity, connections with participants, and research mistakes may find it difficult to distinguish the "buzzing" of interpretation that reveals the historian behind the narrative curtain.

The field of historiography, the study of the methods and theory of writing history, is one avenue for learning the characteristics that define different approaches to history.[4] Books that provide an overview of different traditions combined with examples help illustrate the connection between historians' theoretical frameworks and their research assumptions.[5] A quick scan of the historiography literature reveals the implications of postmodernism for historical practice continues to inspire controversy. A central issue of the debate is whether historical writing corresponds to a real past or is the historian's construction (Iggers, 1997).

Joan Scott and Gertrude Himmelfarb, for example, approach history with radically different assumptions about objectivity and the impact of postmodernism on the discipline. Scott sees traditional historical narratives as imposing false coherence on the past to legitimize power differences. For Scott, historians have the dual responsibility of providing knowledge about the past and revealing the processes of historical construction (1988). Historical narratives should acknowledge the role of power, bias, and suppression in their creation. (Abelson, Abraham & Murphy, 1989).

Gertrude Himmelfarb, in contrast, writes extensively on postmodernism's damage to the historical profession (2004). She also reminds advocates of the "linguistic turn" that historians questioned the fallibility of representing the past long before Foucault and Derrida. Himmelfarb parts paths with Scott most dramatically on the use of race, class, and gender as interpretative frames. For Himmelfarb, these categories politicize history and distort the past with the ideologies of the present.

I think it is important to understanding the points of contention between Scott and Himmelfarb. The danger is that students will see historical scholarship as comprising only two incompatible approaches from which they must choose. There are numerous epistemological and methodological perspectives that inform history. Despite the tendency of books on historiography to divide historical frameworks into rigid categories, approaches often defy easy classification.

My research reflects Scott much more than Himmelfarb. Her emphasis on power in shaping historical knowledge is consistent with my integration of cultural studies and history of education. I see history as vital to understanding issues such as why the vast majority of teachers are white women and how gender influences educational theory and practice. One of the ways I do this is by analyzing the categories and interpretations historians use to make sense of the past. For example, in researching progressive education of the 1930, I was particularly interested in the role of gender in classifications of educators as "child-centered" or "social reconstructionist" (Moyer, 2001). Historians' descriptions (or lack of mention) of the work of Elsie Ripley Clapp highlighted the role of historical writing in reinforcing gender norms.

## History and Educational Research

Knowledge of the past contributes to a variety of forms of educational research. Rousmaniere (2004) asks all educational researchers to reflect on how a historical perspective might contribute to their work. Whether one is doing an ethnography of a single school or analyzing national policy, historical context provides insight into institutional cultures and offers a long-term view of school/community relations. Recognizing qualitative researchers' justifiable reluctance to add to their project with a historical "detour," Placier makes a persuasive case for the value of historical context in understanding the present (1998, p. 320). Reviewing several qualitative junior high/middle school studies, she explains the role of historical research in understanding how a school arrived at its present circumstances, the school's link to broader educational trends, and its past experiences with reform.

Researchers today have far more options for incorporating history than in 1998 when Placier published on the value of history. The rapid move to digitizing materials for online access and increasingly sophisticated search engines has greatly expanded the accessibility of primary sources. Nonhistorians in particular have new opportunities for incorporating a range of historical materials into their teaching and research. For example, websites such as the Library of Congress American Memory collection (http://memory.loc.gov/ammem/index.html) offers over nine millions items documenting American history and culture.

The breadth of online searches can range from a single website or institution to international access. Harvard University's OASIS (Online Archival Search Information System) is a finding aid for the University's nineteen different repositories. ArchivesUSA encompasses over 5,500 repositories and more than 154,000 collections of primary source material across the United States. A search in ArchivesUSA for Elsie Ripley Clapp, for example, shows one collection bearing her name located in the Special Collection of Morris Library at Southern Illinois University at Carbondale. The search result includes a brief description of the collection, the dates that the materials in the collection span, and the size of the collection.

Print and online source directories, like any finding aid, have their limitations. They don't include all collections and one may not be able to find relevant materials depending on the match between the indexing and the search terms. Many databases also restrict access to those affiliated with institutions that have paid the subscription cost. Even more significantly, online directories such as ArchivesUSA continue to follow the norms of print materials and have not kept pace with the move toward digitization. The directories are online and searchable but are defined by traditional archival practices. ArchivesUSA assumes materials are indexed and stored as boxed folders and housed in traditional repositories such as universities, museums, and historical societies.

Digitization and online access of historical sources brings previously unknown opportunities and responsibilities (Giakoumatou, 2005). Formerly the province of large manuscript repositories, housing and sharing sources can be done by individuals and small groups via the internet. But accompanying this expanded accessibility are new issues of preservation, authentification, and the limitations of online search technology. Efforts such as the 2002 Workshop on Research Challenges in Digital Archiving and Long-term Preservation, are working for more flexible, reliable digital preservation and less labor-intensive methods of organizing and evaluating digital collections (NSF, 2003).

### Can History Guide Future Action?

One of the quotes that began this discussion was Santayana's warning about repeating the past mistakes. His cyclical view of history mirrors the pendulum swings of educational reform. Educators stand witness to the numerous fluctuations between traditional versus progressive methods, high standards versus accessibility, and local versus national control. Educational "reform" often seems like recycling rather than innovation. Was Hegel correct that "We learn from history that we never learn anything from history?"

Studies of educational reform offer a more complex picture than repetition of the same approaches and debates. Each time has its own unique circumstances that alter the cycle. The success of educational practices is contextual and responsive to specific circumstances (Kliebard, 2002). Contrary to the current emphasis on scientifically tested, generalizable "best practices," the lessons of history are that one cannot transcend the specifics of time and place. The history of education tells us much, though, about the enduring faith in the power of education to change society. Historical perspectives on educational reform teach us that reform movements are much larger than what happens in schools (Tyack & Cuban, 1995). Domestic and international circumstances such as unemployment and trade deficits trigger talk of educational crises regardless of stable test scores and graduation rates. History teaches us that educational change and demands for reform are intertwined with broader economic and social interests.

## CONCLUSION

History and philosophy cannot meet the standards of a science based in models of prediction and control. The push for a narrowly defined research base for educational practice, threatens the future of both philosophy and history of education.[6] The National Research Council publication, *Scientific Research in Education* (2001), categorizes our fields as the "other" that solidifies the dominance of experimental science. Historical, philosophical, and literary studies are mentioned on one page as the "other approaches" that might serve as supplements to scientific research (p. 26). The pairing with literature is significant, for it underscores the dismissal of all three areas as restricted to the realm of values and ideologies. We hope our joint venture challenges such dismissals and the shortsightedness of collapsing the categories of valid educational research.

As can be seen in our above discussions, we do not do the same work, nor do we write in the same manner, and yet we both recognize the value and importance of each other's field of study, and how our work contributes significantly to each other's individual research projects. History helps us understand our current educational research within a larger context, and protects us from repeating ourselves, so that the work we do really is original research. Philosophy helps us analyze the basic categories we use to define our research as ontological categories that are never truly value free. Both fields of study insist that we carefully scrutinize researchers and the work they do, as we are always situated knowers embedded within a larger context. We can never claim to have a God's eye view of Truth, a view from everywhere, as science wants to claim (and traditional philosophy has wanted to claim as well); our views are always limited, from somewhere, thus underscoring the need for multiple perspectives, and for others to be included in the conversation. It is very dangerous indeed, for scientific research to deceive itself into thinking it doesn't need history and philosophy to help it critique itself. Without history and philosophy, scientific research risks arrogance and deception, which will lead not to possible truths and better understanding, but instead to its own demise.

## NOTES

[1] I want to give credit to Professor Emeritus George Maccia, one of my major professors in the philosophy of education program at Indiana University, for what I describe as CS 526. George taught me a philosophy of education course on theory writing that has served as my inspiration and model, and I am very much indebted to him for the description of philosophical arguments that follows.

[2] For an introduction to identifying primary sources and finding them online see http://www.lib.washington.edu/subject/History/RUSA/

[3] There are numerous guides on locating and evaluating sources. See, for example, Howell, M. and Prevenier, W. (2001). *From reliable sources: An introduction to historical methods.* Ithaca, NY: Cornell University Press. An example of a guide for students in disciplines other than history is Startt, J.D and Sloan, W.D. (2003). *Historical methods in mass communication, (Rev. Ed.)* Northport, Al: Vision Press.

[4] A useful introduction to historiography that explores the implications of postmodernism is Appleby, J., Hunt, L. & Jacob, M. *Telling the truth about history.*

[5] See Green, A. & Troup, K. (Eds.). (1999). *The houses of history: A critical reader in twentieth-century history and theory.* New York: New York University Press and Tosh, J. (Ed.). (2000). *Historians on history.* Harlow, England: Longman.

[6] For a discussion of the political implications of the NRC reports on research see P. Lather's This *IS* Your Father's Paradigm: Government Intrusion and the Case of Qualitative Research in Education. Guba Lecture, sponsored by AERA Special Interest Group: Qualitative Research Chicago, April 2003. Paper accessed at www.coe.ohio-state.edu/plather/ and Scientism and Scientificity in the Rage for Accountability: A Feminist Deconstruction. Paper presented at the American Educational Research Association annual convention, April 11-15, 2005, Montreal, Canada.

## REFERENCES

Abelson, E., Abraham, D. & Murphy, M. (1989). Interview with Joan Scott, *Radical History Review, 45,* 41-59.

Appleby, J., Hunt, J., & Jacob, M. (1994). *Telling the truth about history.* New York: W. W. Norton & Company.

Becker, C. (1931). Everyman his own historian. *American Historical Review, 37,* 221-236.

Blum, L. (2000). Universal values and particular identities in anti-racist education. In R. Curren (Ed.), *Philosophy of education 1999* (pp. 70-77). Urbana, IL: Philosophy of Education Society.

Carr, E.H. (1961). *What is history?* New York: Vintage Books.

Center for Education. (2001). *Scientific research in education.* Accessed at http://www.nap.edu/books/0309082919/html/R1.html

Donato, R. & Lazerson, M. (2000). New directions in American educational history: Problems and prospects. *Educational Researcher 29,* 4-15.

Giakoumatou, T. (2005). When history becomes digitalized. Elearn ingeropa.info. http://www.elearningeuropa.info/index.php?page=doc&doc_id=6793&doclng=6&menuzone=2. Accessed December 12, 2005.

Gramsci, A. (1971). *Selections from the prison notebooks* (Q. Hoare and G. Nowell Smith, Trans. and Eds.). London: Lawrence & Wishart.

Green, A. & Troup, K. (Eds.). (1999). *The houses of history: A critical reader in twentieth-century history and theory.* New York: New York University Press.

Himmelfarb, G. (2004) *The new history and the old: Critical essays and reappraisals* (Revised ed). Cambridge, MA: Harvard University Press.

Hostetler, K. (August/September, 2005). What is "good" educational research? *Educational Researcher, 34,* 16-21.

Howell, M. & Prevenier, W. (2001). *From reliable sources: An introduction to historical methods.* Ithaca, NY: Cornell University Press.

Iggers, G. (1997). *Historiography in the 20$^{th}$ century: From scientific objectivity to the postmodern challenge.* Hanover, NH: Wesleyen University Press.

Kliebard, H.M. (2002). *Changing course: American curriculum reform in the 20$^{th}$ century.* New York: Teachers College Press.

Lather, P. (2005, April). *Scientism and scientificity in the rage for accountability: A feminist deconstruction.* Paper presented at the American Educational Research Association annual convention, Montreal, Canada.

Lather, P. (2003, April). *This IS your father's paradigm: Government intrusion and the case of qualitative research in education.* Guba Lecture, sponsored by AERA Special Interest Group: Qualitative Research Chicago, IL.
Lerner, G. (1997). *Why history matters.* New York: Oxford University Press.
Locke, J. (1960). *The second treatise on government.* Cambridge: Cambridge University Press. (Original work published 1823).
MacDonald, T.J. (1996). Introduction. In T.J. MacDonald, (Ed.), *The historic turn in the human sciences.* Ann Arbor: University of Michigan Press.
Moyer, D. (2001). 'Sentimentalists and radicals': The role of gender in the construction of progressive education in the 1930s. Unpublished doctoral dissertation, Ohio State University.
National Science Foundation. (2003). *It's about time: Research challenges in digital archiving and long-term preservation.* (Nowell Smith, Trans. and Eds.). London: Lawrence & Wishart.
Nussbaum, M. (1992). *Love's knowledge.* New York: Oxford University Press.
Placier, M. (1998). Uses of history in present-day qualitative studies of schools: The case of the junior high school. *Qualitative Studies in Education, 11,* 303-322.
Plato. (1979). *Republic* (R. Larson, Ed. and Trans.). Arlington Heights, IL: Harlan Davidson.
Rousmaniere, K. (2004). Historical research. In K. deMarrais & S.D. Lapan, (Eds.), *Foundations for research: Methods of inquiry in education and the social sciences* (pp. 31-50). Mahwah, NJ: Lawrence Erlbaum Associates.
Rousseau, J. J. (1968). *The social contract* (M. Cranston,Trans.). Harmondsworth: Penguin Books. (Original work published 1762).
Scott, J. (1988). *Gender and the politics of history.* New York: Columbia University Press.
Startt, J.D. & Sloan, W.D. (2003). *Historical methods in mass communication (Rev. ed.).* Northport, AL: Vision Press.
Thayer-Bacon, B. (1998). The power of caring. *Philosophical Studies in Education,* 1-32.
Thayer-Bacon, B. (2000). *Transforming critical thinking: Thinking constructively.* New York: Teachers College Press.
Thayer-Bacon, B. (In process). *Beyond liberal democracy: Diverse educational relations in democracies-always-in-the-making.*
Tosh, J. (Ed.). (2000). *Historians on history.* Harlow, England: Longman.
Tyack, D. & Cuban, L. (1995). *Tinkering toward utopia: A century of public school reform.* Cambridge, MA: Harvard University Press.

GREGORY MARTIN, lisahunter AND PETER MCLAREN

# 7. PARTICIPATORY ACTIVIST RESEARCH (TEAMS)/ ACTION RESEARCH

"Doing justice" notes Pat Thomson (2002), is forever a daunting task. The very idea seems to require extraordinary tenacity and capabilities, to demand efforts beyond the possible. Yet despite what appear to be insurmountable difficulties and obstacles, Thomson's conviction that social justice reflects both the means and the outcome for each and every act of learning remains unassailable. Expanding on her concept of social justice, she writes that:

> realism should not translate into lowered expectations for individual children and young people. Teachers and schools must act as if every [student] can learn what matters for them to have equal life chances, as well as take up the things that interest them. And while teachers and schools might be disappointed when this does not miraculously occur within the time frame of the annual or three-year plan, they should not be regarded or regard themselves as failing–they are engaged in an ongoing intellectual and emotional struggle against the odds. Nor should realism equate with the abandonment of the imaginary of a just and caring society. It is these dreams that provide us with hope and with ways of being (ontologies) and ways of understanding the world (epistemologies) and how it might be (axiologies): it is with and from this standpoint that we interrogate and make judgments about our everyday practices as well as that of the school system. (p. 182-183)

Participatory Activist Research, most often in collectives or Teams (PART) works axiologically with this notion of "doing justice" by and for those oppressed by the practices that need changing. This chapter intends to introduce you to action research (AR) broadly and then PART to take up Pat Thomson's suggestion of "doing justice." Firstly we describe two projects (Vignette 1 and 2) where action research informed the methodology so that readers have a context for our subsequent description of action research and PART. Through Pat Thomson's statement you may have already picked up that this work is fraught with difficulties, as well as rewards, so we also discuss some of the limitations and cautions associated with AR/PART. As you read through the vignettes you may begin to develop a picture for some of these limitations and cautions. To close we will highlight method, theory, limitations and cautions in the vignette examples for you to check for understanding.

*K. Tobin & J. Kincheloe, (eds.), Doing Educational Research—A Handbook, 157–190.*

VIGNETTE 1: GREG'S EXPERIENCE: DON'T LEAP INTO THIS

In the late 1990s, I was employed as a Formal Training Presenter by a community-based youth agency as part of their Landcare and Environmental Action Plan (LEAP). The LEAP was a nation-wide labour market initiative funded by the former Australian Federal Labour government in response to persistently high rates of youth unemployment. Under these conditions, the LEAPs were deployed to assist unemployed youth (aged 16–21) identified as "at risk" with the skills, education and experience required to either enter the labour market or to pursue further education/training. Each plan or project had an environmental theme and the one in which I was employed was aimed at providing the young people with skills in making recycled paper products. The site of the LEAP was a youth centre located in a working class semi-rural/urban community, a short distance from Perth, the capital city of Western Australia. The project included a Coordinator, Youth Support Worker and 15 young people. My role was to facilitate an accredited Technical and Further Education (TAFE) course called *Work and Personal Effectiveness*, approximately 4 hours a week over a 17-week period. The young people were referred to the LEAP by the former Commonwealth Employment Service (CES), a Federal government agency, responsible for providing free labour market assistance to all Australians registered as unemployed. The CES, and other government and non-government agencies actively sought to recruit volunteers. Contra to these protocols of identification and solicitation (as foregrounded in policy statements and public relation materials), I learned that some of the young people felt they had been pressured to participate. Certainly, under the direction of CES staff, the young people were concerned that a refusal to participate would result in suspension of their unemployment benefits. Given this situation, these "conscripts" were resentful of having to complete the course and expressed their anger and frustration in different forms of "active" and "passive" resistance (McLaren, 1986). In the following I provide a brief account of an action research cycle as I sought to engage the LEAP students as part of a Bachelor of Education action research unit I completed at Murdoch University in Western Australia (Martin, 2000).

*Background*

Memory has a habit of retouching the past rendering it suspect in the present. For example, sometimes there are gaps in our memory that can evoke an idealised or romantised past. Although one of the functions of memory is to forget, one memory that I am unable to hit the delete key is when a student stood up in my first class, kicked over a chair and yelled "this is fucked" (Craig, LEAP participant). This was definitely not the way it was meant to be. Despite or perhaps even as a result of my initial shock, I proceeded by ignoring the student's disruptive behaviour, at which he rather angrily returned to his chair. It was only after the class had formally ended that I asked the student to explain what was wrong. Regarding his outburst, the student told me that he was infuriated about a situation in his personal life and the constraint of the LEAP classroom had only added to his frustration and despair. Taking seriously into account his views and opinions, I engaged in a number of informal conversations with staff and students. What emerged most clearly, to my disappointment, was that LEAPs were often characterised by acts of what Peter McLaren (1986) terms "active" and "passive" resistance. In this respect, my previous experience working with adult learners in literacy and numeracy did not prepare me for the LEAP classroom. Generally speaking the majority of the students in this teaching/learning environment were enthusiastic learners, who at least superficially appeared to accept my location in the classroom and the objectives of the course.

Having been personally acquainted with the alienation and despair associated with long-term unemployment, my initial recognition of the existence of oppression within the LEAP ignited my desire to understand and change my practice within these "unjust and unsatisfying social relations" (Kemmis & Wilkinson, 1998, p. 35). Although the intensity of negative feedback from participants animated a commitment to social justice, my initial focus was on developing my "technical" expertise as a way of improving the problematic situation for my students. Less interested in creating the conditions for substantial social change than in establishing a dialogue that would make it possible to improve my teaching practice in a neat and practical way, I was seduced by the need to be an accepted "professional." Whether intended or not, this value stance always threatens to fossilize reform efforts within the "political contested spaces" of the classroom (Kincheloe, 2003, p. 5). Looking at the project in retrospect, it is important to avoid this pitfall as it undercuts critique (which can be painful for everyone involved) and in turns produces narrow and predictable forms of action. Despite my naïve stance, however, the project did not produce such a personal or structural outcome. It is very difficult to get people to critically reflect on their values and practices in relation to their work. What emerged, however, is that the recursive and participatory dimensions of the research process brought the underlying value conflicts evident in current practices to the ugly fore.

### Clearing House: Power and Resistance

Despite being told that the LEAP was for their benefit, a recurring complaint amongst the young people was that they did not have any control over the program's activities or content, which formed the official curriculum. It was this contradiction that provided the basis of my action research project. With a focus on professional development, my original intent was to theorize contradictory practices in the programme in ways that provided students with a greater sense of agency. During my reconnaissance in the first week of class, the young people readily informed me that LEAP staff treated them like children by constantly telling them what to do and when to be quiet. As one student stated: "this course is shit, they treat us like kids and like where at school" (Daniel, LEAP participant). While I continued to collect and file critical incidents into my diary to confirm what I suspected was happening in the LEAP, I intensified my analysis by completing an "ideology critique" on a taken-for-granted practice in the program called

Clearing House. What captured my notice about Clearing House is that the students' attitudes and behaviours in my classroom were much worse before and after it. In a chapter that discusses some of the processes of socially reflexive action research and identifies my LEAP project as an example of it, David Tripp (1998) describes "ideology critique" as "an analysis and critical evaluation of assumptions, rationales and actual practices" (p. 43). Here, ideology critique is not merely negative but rather a way of focusing theory and action. With the assistance of my critical friend (David Tripp), I used this research method as outlined in Tripp (1993, p. 59) to help me plan new action in the research cycle.

## Clearing House: Ideology Critique

### What is meant to happen?

Clearing House was generally accepted to be a part of the LEAP programme valuable for resolving conflict. Clearing House was posited as a structured time/space when students, the Coordinator and the Youth Support Worker gathered on a regular basis to discuss any issues of concern to the group. The LEAP participants sat in a semi-circle with the Coordinator at the front in the centre of the classroom with the Youth Support Worker to her side. The process of Clearing House began with the Coordinator asking the participants if there were any issues or problems they wished to discuss. Students or staff then raised individual or collective concerns about the LEAP and their place within it. The discussion usually centred on and around issues of concern such as the "docking" of wages (reductions in welfare payments made by LEAP staff for infractions such as lateness, absences, misbehaviour and so on), damage to LEAP property including graffiti or other similar complaints from LEAP staff or the young people. It was perceived as a time/space in which everyone could argue, take risks and speak and be heard without fear of intimidation from either staff or students. It was a time for honesty, critique, participation and rethinking the way things were in order to improve the working environment.

### What does happen?

First, I think it is important to note that I grounded my observations and reflections in the shared understandings of the young people. I found that this approach enabled me to transcend the individual pathologies fostered by the LEAP staff who knowingly or not used this structured space to enforce their own authority, values, rules and regulations. For example, staff imposed their own authority by silencing students through their own interpretation of events, which did not acknowledge the lived experiences and locations of students. Students were encouraged to share their opinions, but the ultimate authority resided with staff who made final decisions with little consideration (and often in contradiction) to the accepted views of the students. While some students felt that Clearing House was useful for solving conflict, it was still a frustrating experience:

Clearing House is good. It helps to sort any problems between the participants and coordinators. The only problem is that people go defensive and
there is a yelling contest. In Clearing House you need to be able to look at a
situation from both sides and listen to each other. I think there is probably a
lot of participants that are annoyed, but are to scared to say something because they are worried that they are going to get yelled at and the problems
gets worse eg the amount of damage done to the centre. Certain participants
are not respecting the property. You don't say anything because they don't
care or listen and they continue to run the course for the other participants.
(Anne, LEAP participant)

On the other hand, a student who felt Clearing House was "a waste of time"
responded with the following:

Clearing House is basically rubbish because while we get to say what we
think the decision has already been made by the counsellors who very rarely
compromise and reverse their decisions even less, no matter how the entire
group feels or however good our argument is. (Andrew, LEAP participant)

Put simply by one student:

Its good to get our problems heard, but they always have the last word. (Alan,
LEAP participant)

As a result of this, students became frustrated and angry about the way disputes
were handled:

If you know you should get paid and you don't you just get hell pissed off
and start yelling and then you get paid and go home. If you get docked for
1/2 hour for being 5 minutes late, that fucked, and getting kicked our for a
week for 5 minutes, that's absolutely fucked. (Nigel, LEAP participant)

*Why the difference?*
Clearing House is a practice tied to the maintenance of vested interests and structures of power in capitalist society. In particular, the course is intended to socialise
students into the dominant ideology to produce a disciplined and flexible labour
force for employers. The successful completion of the course indicates that a certain kind of learning has taken place and relevant competencies achieved, e.g., deference to authority and abuse without complaint (Tripp, 1998). Clearly, while these
labour market programs are construed as meeting the needs of job seekers, employers and the state these needs and interests are divergent. On the negative side,
these conflicts in interests and contradictions of process in Clearing House produced a brooding atmosphere of 'them and us" that inculcated a deep sense of
alienation and despair among the students.

Although Clearing House was designated as a democratic environment, the reality was that the dominant and parental discourse of the staff represented a form of
exclusionary discourse, which designated some participants as deviant and lacking
in rationality (Mitchell, 1991). This approach was often successful for the staff

161

who seemingly justified it by pointing out their accountability to a higher departmental authority. The result was that students expressed their frustration and anger with the "system" by shouting, leaving the room, ignoring what was happening or remaining silent. The effect was to divert attention away from the problems of students to problems to do with students themselves. In keeping with this agenda, while staff informally acknowledged problems such as inappropriate referrals, interactively they distanced themselves from the young people, if anything tending to blame them for many of their problems. In short, I found that the staff subordinated the wishes of students to the requirements of employers and the government because they were employed to deliver these labor market programs and wished to achieve their aims to ensure further funding (Martin, 2000).

As my review of the research literature made abundantly clear, the existing social order is never indifferent to ideology (values, ideas and beliefs), which in its negative form invariably serves the interests of dominant groups and classes in capitalist society (Aronowitz & Giroux, 1985; McLaren, 1995a). Exemplary of this, Clearing House served as a device of social control by reaffirming the authority and values of the staff and inducing conformity amongst students. These were attributes much valued in an employee by an employer. They were achieved through Clearing House because "it is a way of bringing out the students' anger and frustration so it can be dealt with in such a way that the students either take themselves out of the course (and so further lessen their chances of employment) or they remain in it (becoming more passive and accepting and therefore more suitable as employees" (Tripp, 1998, p. 45). My argument, therefore, was that by regulating and containing the noisy and disruptive discourses of the young people, LEAP staff made the insertion of "docile bodies" into capitalist relations of exploitation not only possible but also even *desirable* (Foucault, 1977).

*Plan*

As I engaged LEAP students and staff in a search for an alternative institutional structure, I decided that my first action step would be to reframe the narrative by providing each team or group with opportunities to articulate their positions in order to determine what was known or not recognized (L. Rogers, personal communication). In conjunction with my critical friend, I chose to use a form of triangulation interview with focus groups to obtain a "fairer" picture of what was happening in the classroom (Tripp, 1996, p. 48).

*Act*

Making myself not only open but also vulnerable, I began by explaining my intentions to all the participants and invited them to break into teams or groups so that they could respond to a series of written questions about their perceptions of Clearing House, myself, LEAP staff and students. Initially, the students divided themselves into three teams. However, these teams soon disbanded with students consolidating themselves into two larger teams or groups: A and B. To deepen the students' involvement in the inquiry process and to ensure that I was not imposing an authoritative claim on what was written, in the second cycle of interviews, the two groups of students and LEAP staff were provided with the opportunity to read and to reply to each other's responses.

The responses I received from each group were informative and useful. Tripp (1996) argues that it is impossible to obtain an "objective" or "true" account of what is happening in the classroom (p. 48). For example, I wondered if students would feel that their views would not be valued or be careful with their responses, fearing reprisal from LEAP staff or even myself in this institutional context. In pursuing a participatory approach that is emancipatory, Tripp (1996, p. 48) observes that triangulation is useful in providing an understanding of each of the group's positions. In this respect, by reviewing the data obtained from the triangulated interviews, it was evident that there were differences of opinion amongst each of the student groups and LEAP staff. Despite these differences, however, Group A and Group B identified the LEAP staff as their primary source of conflict. Group A, when asked about Clearing House and their perceptions of LEAP staff, replied that they "... over react about the simplest things. Bitches!" while Group B stated that LEAP staff, were "always docking us," "changing rules" and "take jokes too seriously." At times angry and defiant, both of the student groups were frustrated about the ability of LEAP staff to make and change decisions with little or no regard to students. Group A felt powerless to express their concerns in Clearing House:

These discussions are just plea-bargins to get a better deal. The decision has been made prior to discussion with little chance of reversing decision ever with group unity.

In general, I found that the feedback on my practice from the student groups was positive and encouraging. However, I acknowledged that the students might have been hesitant to share their "true" feelings, even though I encouraged them to engage in a critique of my own position as teacher/researcher. For example, Group B stated that the teacher "sees things from both sides" and "suggests ideas to resolve conflict."

Unfortunately, I was unable to continue with the triangulation process because LEAP staff took offence to comments made by a student in Clearing House and temporarily banned this component of the course. At the end of my employment contract, I asked for some formal feedback from LEAP staff, which I explained would be used in a self-evaluation of my action research project. Janice, the LEAP Coordinator wrote, "Listening to the young person's point of view is an important aspect of conflict resolution and you put this into practice on many occasions." Bracketing this, a more critical appraisal of my practice was contained in the following:

I found that you were reluctant to enforce the rules of the project, especially if it meant having to 'dock' someone's wage. Unfortunately, this meant the participants knew they could push you and get away with it. The rules (and consequences to breaking the rules) were initially produced by the young people themselves and were therefore not unrealistic. As such, it is important that leaders ensure the rules and consequences are adhered to. (Janice, LEAP Cooridinator).

In this instance, it seems that my failure was to adequately ensure the self-regulation of the students by getting them to be complicit in their own oppression.

*Reflect*

An inherent difficulty of the action research process was that it politicised the contradictions embodied in the relationships of the participants, who did not share identical interests or agendas. In spite of the collaboration between the two groups of students I was unable to negotiate anymore time because the research generated such anger, hostility and conflict that LEAP staff no longer wanted to participate.

To this end, the ideology critique and triangulated interviews provided me with an understanding of how LEAP experiences were structured within specific relations of power and authority (McLaren, 1986). While the praxis of the research project was to open up spaces of dialogue and participation in order to change the working environment for all the stakeholders, the question of student choice and agency ran up against the reality of administrative authority. Lagging behind the students' knowledge and understanding, I became aware of how the different locations of LEAP staff enabled them to control important sites of cultural production that shaped the students' identities and actions in relation to their class, gender, ethnicity and age. It was within this oppressive context that students continued to engage in forms of resistance such as shouting, kicking chairs, punching holes in walls, or remaining silent. These acts of resistance were in response to their sense of oppression and despair and represented an attempt to reaffirm their dignity and the validity of their lived experiences (McLaren, 1986). Clearly, the young peoples' behaviour was regulated through the discourse of the staff who had the final say in determining whether a student completed the course. In fact, almost half of the participants were eventually removed from the course for breaking the rules and regulations.

*Understand*

If nothing else, my analysis of Clearing House enabled me to re-evaluate the taken-for-granted assumptions and expectations guiding my actions (a liberal belief in freedom of choice and social mobility) and to identify the problems I faced in realising my values in practice. By selecting which action steps I would take as a means of realising my newly redefined commitment to social justice, I understood action research to constitute a form of critical rather than technical inquiry. Without altering the underlying relations of production, I realised that my original focus on "technical" expertise was a misguided form of individual inquiry, which implied a "top-down" approach. Obviously, in light of my commitment to issues of social and economic justice, my understanding of unequal power relations within the LEAP dramatically shifted the focus of my inquiry toward an "emancipatory" approach which sought instead to "empower" the young people (Kincheloe, 1995).

*Plan*

Moving away from a mythic conception of liberalism (full rights of political participation, access to social choices and social control over the curriculum, workplace and living places), I decided to try to shift power from "the system" to the participants because I wanted to provide more opportunities for student agency in order to help the learning environment become more alive with possibilities for growth and substantial change. To do this, I planned to:

- be less exclusionary and provide everyone with the opportunity to speak and be heard (Giroux, 1994);
- make my class into a space place where students could engage in a genuine dialogue with me and the other students (Freire, 1972); and
- enable students to rethink the ways things were to develop a sense of self and their connection to the world in which they lived.

After I delved back into the literature on critical pedagogy and consulted with the students and my critical friend, my next action step was to begin this process through:

- acknowledging the different histories, locations and experiences of students (McLaren, 1994);
- recognising that the social use of language incorporates many discourses and consequently acknowledging the different terms of reference and narrative styles used by the students to enable everyone to be heard (Mitchell, 1991);
- repositioning the students as "makers of meaning";
- encouraging the students to subject this approach to continuous critique through shared conversations, written assignments and teacher evaluations

To monitor the process of implementation and the outcomes of this strategy (whether intended or not), I then:

- made a point of recording anything I saw as a critical incident;
- worked with the above approaches, inviting the students to discuss anything I saw as a critical incident with me;
- wrote up their responses and, still with the above approaches, checked with them that I had understood and accurately reported their points of view;
- then used this information to plan my next action step (see also Tripp, 1998)

Compelled to take sides, in this way, I was still able to proceed with a typical action research cycle and navigate my way through the program until the end of my contract.

VIGNETTE 2: LISA'S EXPERIENCE: TRANSITION PROJECT

As the class space teacher involved with student transitioning from primary to secondary school I noticed the pleasures and pains of transition in my students. I had worked with the primary schools whose students would be coming to my secondary school the following year. I had many, many hours of conversation with mum, a year 7 (final year) primary teacher when I was a year 8 coordinator, conversations about the inconsistent messages and positioning of students in the different schooling contests. I had been going to meetings between schools in the same locality to think about how we could organize some of our processes to ensure more effective and efficient resource allocation and practices around transition. I had studied students' experiences of transition with the intention of making the experience more productive for students and teachers. However, none of these actions felt like they really made any noticeable difference to either the young people I worked directly with or the young people in general who had to deal with transition.

I was intent on using my privileged position as an adult to make changes, with and for the students, in considering how we organize our schools, knowledge and learning, and therefore "what [we are] saying to students about how seriously we take them, their opinions, abilities and learning" (Holdsworth, 2005, p. 140). I wanted to create a more socially just and engaged class space for the young people in my class, one that would be part of the transition process where transition becomes the curriculum, as understood and experienced by those in the process. With my knowledge of critical theory, feminist theory, middle schooling and action research I tried to put into practice these ways of knowing as action, with interesting results.

It was a warm sunny day and I was ready to get stuck into the day with my class, a vibrant but "difficult" class in their last term of elementary school. As many teachers who go through this know it is a time of excitement and angst for the students, but also for yourself who, after spending such quality time with 30+ personalities for a year, you are attempting to make the transition to secondary or middle school as positive and effective as possible. Knowing that for some of my students this transfer would be quite traumatic and for others a very welcome change (to start a new leaf or to branch out into unknown territory) I was determined to make it a useful learning experience rather than just a "right of passage" that they experience as a homogenized group where we all hold our breaths and hope for the best.

Instead of spending the term doing a multitude of numeracy and literacy tests, spending weeks of my time marking and reporting for the teachers' information in the new school (most which is never used), our class decided to negotiate our final term curriculum as a class so that our "product" was not a report card and lots of empty "facts" but a set of portfolios that demonstrated individual and group knowledges within the class. These alternative "products" would be used to introduce the new year 8 teachers to my students so that they would know the range and

166

depth of abilities these students had; so they could meet them as capable people dealing with a new context collectively but with different individual needs.

The first step was to outline to the students what I thought the issue/s was/were and facilitate discussions and activities to get a better understanding of what transition was and how the different people involved perceived it. This meant doing small focus group discussions between those in our class, designing a survey for other year 7's and for those who had been in year 8 for nearly a year, as well as a few interview questions for the year 8's and their teachers and parents. Some students digested a few newspaper articles and a couple of journal articles and book chapters I had collected about transition. We also linked with another school in China via the web, a school with which we had already done some online conversations previously, and asked them questions about what transition meant to them and what sorts of things they did as part of transition. This was the reconnaissance phase of the project and the idea was to include all participants in the process.

Individuals and groups of students had produced various "data sets" of information about transition, some about us specifically and some with a broader focus from the literature and sources outside our class. Many of the literacy, numeracy, group work, research and reporting knowledges that had been practiced throughout the year were put into relevant practice. Along the way there were also other knowledges developed including ways of thinking using philosophy and sociology and ways of acting, like in activism and collective decision-making. Using James Beane and Barbara Brodhagen's model (1995) of negotiating the curriculum we planned a curriculum for the final term that would take into account everyone's feelings about transition, what they wanted to know more about, and how we might represent what the students were capable of. We also planned a possible term 1 curriculum for when we went to secondary school. This was with the help of some of the new teachers the students would have in year 8 and after talking more with the year 8's and their parents.

That was the planning phase so now we would move into "action." Through our work we had realized some of the differences between students and how different students were already experiencing transition differently. Some had brothers or sisters in the secondary school while others had never set foot outside our primary school. Some who had often been marginalized by their primary colleagues were looking forward to a different set of potential friends while others felt this would just increase their marginalization. Some were looking forward to the new subjects that would be available to them while others talked of missing the smallness and familiarity of the primary school. Through our research it became clear that these were not unusual feelings and that our year 8 colleagues had similar issues the year before. It also became apparent that for some they were in constant transition, within their family, in where they lived, in who was part of that family, and the roles they played within it. Some of the issues related to what transition meant for girls or boys, what it meant in terms of their relationships with each other, what it meant for the two newcomers from Japan, and what it meant for one student who never had money to go on school trips or to socialize with his friends on the weekends.

167

Our actions included ways of making school a nicer place for the students and ensuring they were learning and knew what and how they were learning. They also involved lots of activities around relationships, feelings, passions, support, and seeing our own worlds from others' perspectives. We developed skills in problem solving as we role played some of the situations of angst that the year 8 students had described. We put together reports of our data and a small guide for other year 7's about the stories of year 8's experiences of transition. We organized talks by year 8's and 9's and developed relationships and strategies for getting the most out of high school with them. We documented the skills and knowledges that individuals and different groups demonstrated and constructed three possible year 8 term 1 curricula units for the year 8 teachers to think about. We created a small website to store all of this information and make it available to others and then made individual portfolios that highlighted what each student had accomplished.

One of the points that became quite clear when we reflected on the process so far was that our school, like many schools, made learning fairly abstract, monotonous, fragmented and narrow in the sorts of knowledges we drew on. The richness of students' lives became apparent when we gave the time and focus to their lives, to their issues, and to their dreams. This was not without challenge and much of my work was in facilitating group dynamics and to work with those students who were exclusionary, dominant and privileged in many ways that others were not. As teachers we realized that most learning activities provided purposes for students that are deferred rather than present. They had been positioned within the primary school as decision-makers but had a very passive role in secondary school, shielded from responsibility. We also realized how tokenistic some of the roles they had in primary school despite teachers attributing these roles as responsible. Many of the values around transition were those that we as adults valued but did not match the students' collectively or given the heterogeneous nature of the individuals in the class. While we had been organizing high school orientation visits, common reporting frameworks between the primary schools, and preparatory classes in primary school for the new secondary school subjects, on reflection many of these were largely a waste of teacher time and students learned very little from them. In the past we had listened to what students had to say about transition but we had never created the space for that to result in action or agency where decision-making was supported and shared and action was implemented and reflected upon WITH the students.

As we reflected on the project so far, like moving through the first large cycle of the project we began to understand the complexity and pluralism within the group, that which would be totally interrupted and reformed in many varied ways in the new school year as the students moved to high school. In planning the next cycle of the project teachers and students had a greater appreciation of each other, of the dynamics of groups of people, of the transitions within one person's life and some of the strategies for understanding how one is positioned by others and how one can try to reposition oneself and that which might be valued within groups. We understood that transition was not a static and homogeneously experienced event but part of an ongoing process that we made together. Our suggested planning for the next cycle had started with the year 8 teachers agreeing to trial one of our suggested curricula and we started to plan how the students would be a part of that in the first few weeks of secondary school. The students practiced group building activities, challenge activities, debating techniques and PowerPoint presentations in order to facilitate the first few weeks of secondary school, leading activities to include the new students and teachers. But there was still much work to be done in the form of what their data collection would look like in the following year and who would keep the project going. But we had made a start.

## CONTEXT OF PAR(T)

At a time when our social institutions such as public schools, day-care centers and hospitals are marked by a catalogue of ineptness and cruel indifference due to restrictions in government expenditure and shameful tax cuts for the rich, struggles for social justice are, or ought to be, as urgent today as they ever were in the past. Unfortunately, in public discourse the horrors and crises associated with the plight of the ever growing ranks of the poor, the hungry and the homeless are tucked neatly away behind the politically paralyzing media stoked fears and paranoia of random weather, flu pandemics and terrorism. Utopian rhetoric aside, we know that social change is not a spontaneous gift of good fortune. In this regard, as teachers are stripped of their social roles and reduced to mere technicians and supervisors in the educational assembly line, we argue that social life ought not to be presumed to be static and eternal but rather the product of struggle and history. Likewise, as students continue to be forgotten as participants in social issues it is important to also be mindful of the positioning of those in loco parentis and their young people in the struggle and history; legally required to spend a substantial part of their lives in the institution of school. Within the framework of PAR(T) the construction of socially useful knowledge is based upon action, where individuals and groups of people come together in community groups to work on real issues and problems. As critical researchers we propose that a move towards a deeper engagement of the political within these issues and problems, referring to the intentions advocated by action researchers such as Wilfred Carr and Stephen Kemmis (1986), might be achieved by the idea of "activism." This form of action differs from the structure and boundaries of activity in general because it is also mediated by theory, which directs its means and end.

Throughout this chapter, we take an oppositional view of theory, which understands it to be critical (not simply affirmative) and capable of producing knowledges that provide subjects with an understanding of their situatedness/positionality within emerging social relations (McLaren, Martin, Farahmandpur & Jaramillo, 2004). At root, critical theory is not neutral and identifies itself with specific and concrete interests that are based in material struggles for survival and justice of the people we are involved with as educators. Much of the work in this critical tradition is preoccupied with uncovering the ways in which social reality is variously negotiated and resisted "from below" within established networks of power and authority. In sharing the vitality, strength and life of people engaged in emancipatory and school reform movements, one criterion for critical theory is the degree to which analysis uncovers the practical "unactualized potential" for transcendence, social change and human liberation "inherent in any social institution" (Kirkpatrick, Katsiaficas & Emery, 1978). In challenging the current social order that systematically negates the full potential of human knowledge, creativity and solidarity, the philosophical ambition of activist scholars goes beyond social theory. As a guide to action, a criterion for judging the soundness or truth of critical theory "is praxis, or the degree to which sociological analysis is responsive to human values" (Kirkpatrick, et al., 1978). Rather than embark on a random foray into research, the type of methodology we are advocating provides an interactive architecture for critical awareness and operation in the world.

This chapter is written for students, teachers, academics and administrators who are actively involved in promoting social change in immediate social situations such as school and community contexts. By active, we mean collectives who are involved at the point of knowledge production in the often less-than-glamorous political struggles to "make a difference" in their everyday labor practices. Under difficult and trying conditions the difference these critical and self-reflexive agents for social change aim to make on the ground (amidst constraints) implies an intentional act of consciousness. Regardless of the topic or methodological approach, the purpose of all research is ultimately to extend our understanding of the world and to influence ideas and action through the generation and application of new concepts and practices. Despite the human potential to change everyday life, it is important to remember (if one allows the analogy) that the road to hell is paved with good intentions. To say this is to recognize that research is not a neutral process but is always informed by the theories, values and intentions people bring to it. This is the understanding brought to us by Marxist, feminist, queer, critical race and postcolonial scholars who point out that research is inherently a value-laden practice (judgments and decisions about what to research and how to do it), even if we are unaware of the philosophical traditions of knowledge that inform it.

Unwittingly, perhaps, it is precisely for this reason that most researchers tend to overlook the epistemological assumptions that guide their social practice and research agendas. In its institutional guise, epistemology is concerned with the study of knowledge, how it is acquired and the external criteria used to verify and justify truth claims, i.e., to distinguish between "true" knowledge and "false" knowledge. Closely related to this is ontology, which like many rich and complex philosophical disciplines, is not easily defined. Marked by a range of different philosophical projects, ontology in general is the application of methods that may have a formal theoretical foundation to solve classical philosophical problems relating to the notions of being or existence. What remains to be indicated, is that at its core:

> Ontology is therefore concerned with the level of reality present in certain events and objects, but more importantly with the systems which shape our perceptions of these events and objects. These perceptual systems are important because they apply values that attribute meaning to such objects and events. (Jackson, 1998)

This highlights the fact that the definition of ontology we decide to use has consequences at a concrete level, which can place limits on human agency and research. As distinct from a metaphysical and idealist ontology that inspires personal reflections and idle speculation, the materialist ontology of Karl Marx has an active subject and is grounded in the material. Against the impotence of a metaphysical ontology, with its voyeuristic detachment from the social world, materialist ontology takes on a gritty and radical dimension. Certainly, from the standpoint of socialist feminists such as Nancy Hartsock (1998), Marx's materialist ontology is important in the sense that he "escaped the duality of observation and action by beginning from a worldview founded on acting and feeling human beings" (p. 87). Without dispensing of idealism, the subject is an active participant in the process of knowledge production, with an emphasis on understanding and transforming the actual everyday conditions that are the effect of the relationship between the economic base of society and its institutions. In action driven ontologies idealism and materialism are clicked together like Lego and emphasis is placed upon the "dialectical relationship between the improvement of understanding and the improvement of action" (Kemmis & McTaggart, 1988, p. 6). The formation of this dialectical ontology serves to justify social change as a process whose outcome is determined by the value orientation and value criteria that inform the subject's research and social practice (Callinicos, 1983, pp. 62-63). Animated by a variety of commitments (feminism, Marxism, lesbian and gay activism, anti-colonialism), radical ontology is "something made" through praxis as subjects engage in social interaction to identify and change the historically specific conditions underlying observable social and economic inequalities (Martin, 2005).

Although eighty percent of the world's population lives in poverty (less than two dollars a day), we live in a period when most people who live under stable "democratic" regimes accept the ideology of capitalism and believe that it is the best possible system. At the same time, the demands of the global market on national governments (e.g., downward wage pressure on local employers from slave labor-style wages in China) have brought the underlying contradictions of capitalism surging to the surface (a reduction of wages, social benefits and "security"). Given that these social inequalities and social antagonisms pose a very real threat to the state's legitimacy, the treadmill of research and theoretical analysis is focused on practices and prospects of participation and promotion within the "Security State," which supports institutions that preserve the ideological and material interests of dominant classes, groups and strata (Martin, 2005). Written into institutional relations, the crisis of the state and the crisis of politics have given rise to a new form of "pragmatism that serves in this crisis moment…as an apparatus of crisis management" (Zavarzadeh & Morton, 1994, p. 3).

To resolve the underlying class, gender and ethnic tensions that always threaten to spontaneously erupt (riots in Paris, Los Angeles and Sydney), the regulatory state has acted to cut itself off from an ethical relationship with community by exporting this crisis "outside of itself" (Zavarzadeh & Morton, 1994, p. 3). Here, the downward recycling of blame is achieved through the deployment of "self-management" and "improvement" discourses, strategies and structures, e.g., decentralization and devolution. Under neo-liberal rhetoric of greater individual choice and market freedom, local actors and authorities such as principals, parents and teachers in newly decentralized schools are "empowered" through these reform efforts to make decisions (hiring) within certain parameters such as global budgetary constraints. However, in actuality, real power is (insidiously) exported to higher administrative tiers of the state bureaucracy through national forms of curricula, standards and assessment. Too often we hardly notice but the ideology of efficiency and control finds expression in these accountability discourses and practices (often punitive), which serve to enhance administrative rationality. What matters here, as Gerard Delanty (2003) notes, is that "Legitimacy is achieved through efficiency" (p. 75).

Researchers/educators need to critically examine the development of these discourses and practices because as a form of performance management, the self-improvement discourse is not value-free. In its erasure of conflict and struggle, it points to the limits of the dominant ideology and boundaries of allowable meaning. While certain administrative responsibilities are devolved to the local level, as a technology of surveillance and control, the forcible articulation of the improvement discourse functions as a never-ending cycle of target setting monitoring and reviewing designed to increase the productive efficiency of teachers and potential workers (students) (Hill, 2005; Rikowski, 2000). Instead of preparing innovative programs that promote an understanding of issues and democratic practice, teachers are required to perform to targets and manage the performance of learners, e.g., standardized test results. In turn, analogous to Erving Goffman's (1968) study of regulatory life in asylums, the "inmates" that inhabit the public education system are forced to enter into a degrading arrangement (social contract) within this "total institution," which finds concrete expression in the institutional fetishisation of performance appraisals (teaching) and so on.

In short, the pragmatic model of traditional research associated with professional development supports the ideology of capitalism in the workplace by producing compliant dispositions and shutting down critical thought. Despite expressions of discontent over the speed up of work, overwork, and burnout, subjects are sucked into the logic of self-propelled capitalism, which is elevated as a principle of social life. Make no mistake about its origins: the pragmatism of managerial capitalism is nothing short of a management of its crisis. Mas'ud Zavarzadeh and Donald Morton (1994) write:

> This pragmatism teaches the subject of late capitalism how to "survive" (get through) the contradictions of their "daily" life by ignoring the "big picture"...and by dwelling instead on the actual, empirical aspects of "community" life. This pragmatism therefore rejects "theory" (the knowledge of totality) and focuses instead on the "dailiness" of life, taking the various facets of life as separate, discrete and utterly disparate entities. (p. 3)

Foreclosing the possibility of solutions from the "outside," most research operates as a sophisticated instrument of social control (pragmatic problem solving) to create new types of subjects and objects that are subordinated to capitalist accumulation, e.g., regulating knowledge, values and bodies to ensure "standards" and maximize work performance. Tied directly to the interests of transnational capitalism or other collectives of privilege such as race, gender, ethnicity or sexuality, in its most popular form this kind of value-added research distorts social practice and is almost entirely disconnected from the life circumstances and interests of ordinary individuals and groups.

## A HISTORY OF ACTION RESEARCH

Let us now proceed with a brief overview of action research's salient features, forces and moments that contribute to a genealogical understanding of its commitments and possibilities. From its earliest stages of development, the story path of action research is complex, labyrinthine and still emergent. Since the social psychologist Kurt Lewin, a Jewish refugee from Nazi Germany, coined the term "action research," it has emerged as an established research method in teacher professional education, education management and organizational development (Kincheloe, 2003). Driven by a concern for the democratization of the workplace and the reduction of prejudice, the intellectual impulse inspiring Lewin's pioneering work was an optimistic view of action research as a tool for reducing prejudice and improving inter-group dynamics and social relations (Lewin, 1998). Using real life situations and problems "as the locus of social science research," Lewin's conception of action research was grounded in experiential learning or "learning by doing," which was understood to be specific to each situation (McKernan, 1991, p. 9). To achieve this goal, Lewin's well-defined spiral process was based on repeated cycles of planning, action and evaluation. Breaking down the hierarchical (traditional) relationship between the researcher and researched, Lewin argued that in order to "understand and change certain social practices, social scientists have to include practitioners from the real social work in all phases of inquiry" (McKernan, 1991, p. 10).

Certainly, Lewin's work was the benchmark, the point of reference for Stephen Corey at Columbia University's Teachers College, who introduced the term action research to the educational community in 1949 (Kincheloe, 1995). From professional development to curriculum reform and school restructuring, Corey defined action research as the process through which teachers, working together in groups, solved problems specific to their own schools and classrooms. It is by no means insignificant that Corey was strangely ambivalent toward Lewin's principled commitment to democratic ideals in the workplace. Swaying slightly from Lewin's formula, Corey was primarily interested in action research for narrow instrumental purposes related to professional development and educational improvement (Noffke, 1997). It must be pointed out that Corey was influenced by the logic of positivism and in his efforts to secure the acceptance of action research as a legitimate research form used it to resolve social problems "scientifically." Thus freighted, the relationship between theory and practice was understood to be largely technical and despite his best intentions action research was increasingly carried out by outside researchers with the cooperation of schools and teachers. Whether we agree with this approach or not, this positivist framework made it difficult to imagine that action research be used for political purposes, especially in the conservative climate of 1950s (Noffke, 1997).

To his credit, Corey did launch the "teacher as researcher movement" that flourished in schools during this period. Despite a promising start, however, action research quickly fell on hard times in the 1960s. Few would disagree, we think, that the theory used to guide the research process has a profound effect on its outcomes. What bothered the false objectivity of traditionalists, however, was the formation of a linkage between the language of critical theory and left-wing political activism (Smith, 2001; Stringer, 1999). This radical strand of participatory action research (PAR), which did not hide its political project, had its roots in the critical theory of the Frankfurt School, feminism, Third World socialism, Latin American research traditions based on indigenous knowledge, the movement for popular education as expressed for example at the Highlander Centre and Paulo Freire's well-elaborated notions of education for "critical consciousness" (conscientization) and "cultural action for freedom" (Carr & Kemmis, 1986; Freire, 1972). In fleshing out a practice that gave salience to the often silenced struggles of oppressed and exploited individuals and groups, participatory action research gained a significant foothold as a grassroots movement both within the realm of community-based participatory approaches to research and action (CBPR); and as a form of political mobilization and research oriented to the recuperation and enrichment of educative encounters, organizational change and social transformation (Carr & Kemmis, 1986). Addressing the reality of power and authority, its commitment to shared problem-solving, distributed decision-making and local activism distinguished it from styles of management and administration common in many highly centralised, autocratic and unresponsive institutions such as schools. Unlike the kind of detached research that is so often undertaken by outside experts, the amount of life and energy that is projected into this collaborative educative process (through repeated face-to-face interactions) creates a rather specific value commitment (Martin, 2005). Here, action research is not a means to an end but an end it itself.

Unfortunately, the critical focus on questions regarding power and authority largely fell off the agenda of action research after it was embraced by educators influenced by Lawrence Stenhouse's view of "teacher as researcher." No wide-eyed radical, Stenhouse revived the teacher-as-researcher movement in the 1970s. He achieved this by hailing the practicing classroom teacher as the most effective person in the research process to identify and prioritize problems and to develop and evaluate solutions, whether it be to improve their own reflective teaching practices in the classroom, for teacher preparation in pre-service and graduate education programs, as school-based curriculum development, or in the formulation of education policy (Johnson, 1993). During this catalyzing period, action research evolved as a specialist area of research under the direction of John Elliot and Clem Adelman in the UK, as exemplified by the work of the Ford Teaching Project between 1973 and 1976 (Holly, 1991). Unlike its previous incarnation in the United States, the teacher as a researcher movement that gained new life in the UK as well as throughout the Western world resisted its previous pragmatic addiction to "science" and "technical control"-and sometimes even with an edge. Placing teachers at the centre of theorizing about their own practice, it experienced exponential growth in the school system as it boosted professional identity, autonomy and status (Winch & Foreman-Peck, 2000).

However, there was a downside to the increased acceptance and visibility of action research, for example, through its connection to labour and social reproduction. Contrary to loose claims of political status and efficacy, Chris Winch and Lorraine Foreman-Peck (2000) observed that most teacher-led action research "is much more prosaic and practical, and always was." Its prevailing disposition is the result of an optimistic belief in the individual as a free and creative participant in the social and political life of the community, where teachers nonetheless are "are torn between believing in the school's goals and frustrated with carrying them out" (p. 97). Viewed in such administrative and ideological contexts, action research can become just another normalising practice if its quiet acquiesce with the status quo is not challenged (Martin, 2000). Far removed from Lewin's group method of creating change, in the late 1970s and early 1980s, Kemmis (1991) argued that action research had become "too individualized" and tied to the pragmatic realities of particular classrooms and schools, whether undertaken by teachers for their own intrinsic purposes or externally motivated, e.g., institutional rewards in the form of wage income or accredited expertise (p. 70).

To help combat this tendency, in its next phase of development, action research became more subversive. Despite appearances, the radical formulations of action research such as those grounded in the work of Freire did not collapse in the 1960s but rather became actively pursed by a widening community of action researchers and action research facilitators around the world (Kemmis, 1991, p. 70). Clashing over the most basic issues of theory and practice, Kemmis had a bone to pick with the latent pragmatism of the UK strand of action research. To this end, in the 1980s, he led an academic group of "barefoot educators" at Deakin University (which became a haven for academics interested in critical theory and action research) out of this pragmatic thicket (Kemmis, 1991). The quest to move beyond professional pragmatism and institutional patronage ignited a debate between the two schools of thought in the UK and Australia, and signaled the beginning of substantial radical scholarship, rooted in critical theory. There is a powerful popularism that resists critical theory and indeed, there has been a certain amount of hostility between these two camps (Elliot, 2005; Carr & Kemmis, 2005). Embracing the notion that the contradictions of capitalism will find resolution only through social struggle and change, the response of the Australian group was to argue that older models of action research were uncritically aligned with conservative economic interests and the maintenance of the status quo. According to the Australian group, "as action research becomes more methodologically sophisticated and technically proficient, it will lose its critical edge" (Anderson, Herr & Nihlen cited in Diniz-Pereira, 2002, p. 388). Mapping these territorial struggles, Kemmis and Shirley Grundy (1997) distinguished the unique features of Australian action research from its counterparts in Britain, continental Europe and the United States:

It is important to note that Australian educational action research emerged as distinct from its counterparts in Britain, continental Europe and the United States of America. British action research in the 1970s shared with Australian action research the participatory and collaborative style of work, but was less strategically-oriented and probably less politically aware. It emphasized interpretative inquiry where Australian action research was more critical. Continental European action research shared a similar critical perspective with Australian action research, but did not appear to have developed the same practical thrust of the Australian work, and American action research developed as more teacher-oriented and teacher-controlled. (cited in Diniz-Pereira, 2002, p. 388)

Against the dominance of "teacher-as-researcher" forms of action research, critical frames (Lather, 1992) have also looked to include participants other than teachers, calling for research as radical pedagogy in order to locate students' voices (e.g., McLaren, 1998; McLaren & Pinkney-Pastrana, 2000) or more broadly those of the oppressed (Freire, 1972). While notions of "voice" or representation are problematic (Holdsworth, 2005) it is the intention of PAR(T) to explicitly deal with this to ensure agency, as participants act in the framing and intervention practices of the issue.

## WHY "TEAMS" AND "PARTICIPATORY"?

In integrating the personal as, and with, political change, indigenous, feminist and socialist feminist researchers such as Sandy Grande (2004), Morwenna Griffiths (2003) and Nancy Hartsock (1998) have been primarily concerned with the relationship between epistemology and power, particularly in terms of knowledge relations (Coalition politics, allowing others to tell own stories). To ensure knowledge relations are worked through as part of the method it becomes important to involve as many of the participants as possible to reduce yet another form of oppression instigated by limiting who has agency within the research. While some research collectives use action research principles as a form of participant agency and empowerment, others argue that it is not so much about empowerment as it is power. As such it becomes important to understand, and possibly shift, the power relations that exist between the participants and their conceptualizations of the issue at hand, ensuring it is not just another interpretive research project driven from only one portion of the collective. As such, "team" suggests a form of cohesion between participants, this cohesion not necessarily inferring a reduction of pluralism but rather a shared issue of concern. Clearly reflexivity is essential in this process. The researcher participants must constantly be aware of how their values, attitudes, perceptions, practices and therefore positioning within the "team" are influencing the research process, from the formation of research questions, through data collection state, to ways in which data are analyzed and theoretically explained.

Whereas traditional research is based on implicit norms and values (dominated by white/male/capitalist ideology) that shape our understanding of education and regulate society by integrating individuals into the logic of the system and bringing conformity to it, researchers in the critical tradition are concerned with the relationship between power and knowledge and changing the underlying relational basis of exploitation and oppression that constitutes this historical set of social relations (Kincheloe & McLaren, 2000). The production and transmission of knowledge is intimately connected to the way society organises itself, particularly as it relates to the systematic marginalization of knowledge of the Other (McLaren, 1995c). Here, at the level of consciousness, knowledge operates as a mechanism of social control and is inseparable from its process of production, reproduction, legitimation and representation. Grappling with these issues, action research offers a way out of this quagmire because it is a type of non-linear inquiry that opens up a field of questions, challenges and possibilities including interaction with participants. Here, it is not controversial for the often conventional methods (modified to avoid racism, sexism, homophobia) that it uses (quantitative or qualitative) but for the areas that it focuses on and the manner in which it employs its findings (Elliot, 1997).

The question of human agency and social change is central to action research. Rory O'Brien (2001) writes, "It is often the case that those who apply this approach are practitioners who wish to improve understanding of their practice, social change activists trying to mount an action campaign, or, more likely, academics who have been invited into an organization (or other domain) by decision-makers aware of a problem requiring action research, but lacking the requisite methodological knowledge to deal with it." Unlike the stratifying ontology of traditional forms of research that concentrate power in the hands of experts, the kind of action research we are advocating is socially enabled by a commitment to shared participation in problem identification, problem solving processes and social change. This causes the configuration, the power relation between the researcher and researched, to change, initiating a new structure of knowledge which generates insights and thoughts, that are transposed into action.

Explicating the political bias in socially critical participatory action research runs counter to the stereotypical view of research as pure and objective. Given the ideological dominance of scientific inquiry or positivism this skewed understanding, particularly amongst preservice teachers, is understandable. Positivist researchers maintain that the relation between the researcher and subject should be a distant one in order to minimize response bias due to interviewer effect and interpretation bias due to excessive empathy with the world of the respondent. This approach discounts the degree to which social and political commitments "are built into the technical details of scientific practice as well as their subsequent use in the public sphere" (Demeritt, 1998, p. 187).

While the logic surrounding this traditional scientific paradigm appears fairly innocent and direct, feminists have called this regulatory method into question over the past thirty years. Contrary to the claims of positivists, researcher bias and subjectivity play an inevitable and invaluable role in the way meaningful knowledge is created. More often than not, though, the epistemological or philosophical approach that forms the basis of research is "missing in action." It is a classic case of the divorce of thought from action in that particular lineage of drive-through (in-and-out) research, which ends up collecting dust in cardboard boxes. By contrast, feminist engagement with epistemology has demonstrated that all measurements involve values and scientific "facts" are not "out there" waiting to be discovered, obtained independent of human social interactions (Hartsock, 1998). Facts are not discovered but are rather made, through praxis, and therefore it is critical that all who are positioned within the issue or problem have access to the definition, clarification, understanding and practices in making change (Hartsock, 1998).

METHOD

Action research is often described as a complex set of spirals that make a larger spiral of understanding, planning, acting and reflecting, each stage informed by theory (see figure 7.1). As previously mentioned it is vital for there to be a critical awareness of the discourses informing the process (see figure 7.2). Questions that ask "who gains by how we understand the issue?" and "who does not?," or even "who gains/loses as a result of the issue/problem?" become important drivers of the research. Other questions might include:

- "what are the power relations inherent in the issue?"
- "who is privileged in the planning?"
- "who gets to act and who does not?"
- "how do particular actions benefit some while disadvantaging others?"
- "how are participants encouraged to reflect and whose reflections count?"
- "how do we come up with the research question initially?"

*Figure 7.1: Action research cycles*

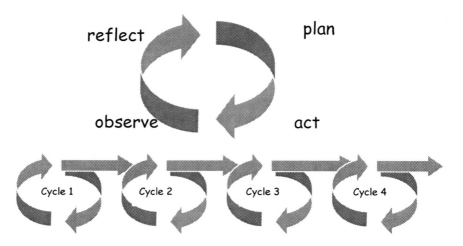

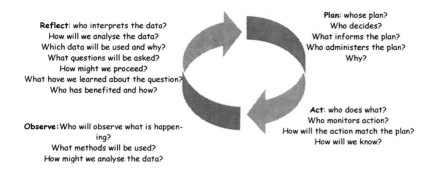

*Figure 7 2: Some of the discourses informing the phases*

The practical approach to this form of research is to determine the initial idea for change, that is identify a theme or concern and then observe the context and anything that informs your knowledge of the concern. This is done as a reconnaissance and leads into planning for the change. Once you have implemented the initial ideas it is important to evaluate the action through systematically collecting data including observation and other forms of evidence. Using this information you may amend the plan and continue the cycle. Kemmis and Robin McTaggart (1988) use the steps indicated above, that is Plan, Act, Observe, and Reflect while others use differing degrees of detail to work through this process. An example of this is Elliot's use of 5 phases:

1.  Identify initial idea
2.  Find out facts and analyse
3.  General plan with action steps
4.  Monitor implementation and effects
5.  Reconnaissance

Some of the key points to note about this type of work is that it is participatory and collaborative, it is focused on change and improvement; it is based on self-critical communities; it develops and includes a self-critical community, and embodies praxis – critically informed committed action, that is action informed by literature and theories beyond that of the group. This also includes the group theorizing its own practice through the data collection and testing assumptions. It is also important to note that it is explicitly political in nature, a point that is sometimes ignored by all research but upfront in PART and AR.

It is often difficult to initially frame the process of change so we have found it very helpful to focus on a particular issue, problem, question, or issue. If working from the idea of an issue you might target sexism, transphobia, racism, diversity, teacher-student relationships for example. Particular problems such as incomplete homework, only having a single text for a range of learners, poor communication processes in the classroom, or some students not engaging with group work. It is often useful to have a question that drives the action, for example what are the challenges in using digital texts? Or how do we assess learning? You might also want to work through an idea as your organizing framework driver. Examples might include teaching math through physical activity; integrating the Health and Physical Education curriculum; addressing middle schooling in a traditional school, or enacting a democratic classroom. Clearly there are overlaps in each strategy that might initially frame the process so it will be less about which to use and more about starting somewhere to begin.

Finally, there are core values of this way of researching, that of the pursuit of social justice, deliberative activism, collective practice and reflective practice. Social justice has multiple definitions (see McLaren, 1995b) but it does indicate that you are attempting to reduce oppression for a collective of people who are coming together to implement the change). Thus the action is informed by careful and strategic planning based on what you understand about the issue and those involved in it, but drawing on what is also known about the issue beyond that of the participants' experiences. It is deliberate in that it involves "doing" and not just intending to "do" and not just becoming aware of the issue but the importance of reflecting on actions and asking some purposeful political questions such as "who benefits?" and "what power mechanisms are occurring?" The process is always evolving and is therefore represented as a spiral or a series of cycles.

As the mechanics of the process are outlined briefly above to give you an introduction to the process you might find that PART is a very useful tool, method, and philosophy in your work and want to learn more. There are numerous "how to" sources in texts and on the web so rather than going into more detail here we will now alert you to some of the limitations and cautions before returning to the vignettes to illustrate PART.

## RETURNING TO THE VIGNETTES

To help you make a connection between the "real life" examples of two attempts to 'do' action research we revisit them to make more explicit the methods, theory, outcomes and limitations of actual practice. Clearly the process is neither straightforward, uncontentious, unproblematic, unidirectional nor singular given the range of theory and method that informs and is informed by practice. However, we will make some of these stand out as we now refer to both the sites of practice and the theory that informs it.

*Methodological illustrations*

In "Transition" vignette the various phases of the first cycle might be described in Table 7.1:

*Table 7.1.*

| Understand | Researching the problem or issue of transition broadly from the literature |
|---|---|
| Reconnaissance | Year 7 and year 8 interviews |
| | Surveys of parents and teachers |
| | Talk with Chinese colleagues |
| Plan | Negotiate what we need to know and how we might know it, e.g. further interviews, |
| Act | Skills around group work, ways of understanding people through philosophy, cultural studies, psychology and sociology |
| | Construct year 8 curriculum |
| | Create reports of findings |
| Reflect | Read and discuss findings |
| | Compare with other contexts |
| | Ask who was included and who was left out, how and why? |
| | Were there other questions we should ask? |
| | What worked for who and what didn't? |
| | How could it be done next time to be more helpful to all? |
| | What does this mean for the next stage or cycle for year 8? |
| Understand | Use reflections and build understanding of new context |
| Reconnaissance | Use meetings and focus groups in year 8 of newly formed classes to develop an understanding of the issues important to the new students and those important to the students who were there previously |

In "LEAP" vignette the first phase of the cycle written up for this chapter might be described in Table 7.2:

*Table 7. 2.*

| Entry | Initial contact as Formal Training Facilitator and Bachelor of Education student at Murdoch University |
|---|---|
| | Explanation of research process |
| | Negotiate participation/co-operation within a mutually accepted framework |
| Reconnaissance | Orientate myself to the particularities of the LEAP program and how I feel about it |
| | Use journal to begin writing up observations and reflections immediately |
| | Write up critical incidents and critiqued incidents (Clearing House) and share with critical friends (see Tripp, 1993) |
| | Draw picture of the classroom to establish the structure of teaching/learning environment |
| | Establish a dialogue with LEAP staff and students through shared/informal conversations in order to engage the participants in "their own knowledge (understandings, skills and |

values)" and stay in touch with what is happening in the classroom (Kemmis & McTaggart, 2000)

Operating from a standpoint of social justice in a way that values the young peoples' interpretations and actions in the program, I identify student resistance as a "thematic concern" for the project

Contribute to process of resolving practical problems and concerns raised by LEAP participants by targeting a social practice that is susceptible to improvement, i.e., Clearing House (Kemmis & Wilkinson, 1998)

| | |
|---|---|
| Understand | Critically reflect on prior learning experiences including earlier LEAP |
| | Research the issue or topic area of student resistance (McLaren, 1995d) |
| | Develop theoretical orientation by reviewing a large body of literature on critical social theory and critical pedagogy |
| | Write up research proposal and reflect on constructive feedback provided |
| Plan | Set aside time to write and reflect as I attempt to balance work and study |
| | Plan first action step in detail |
| | How does the project aim to improve practice? |
| | How can the project be participatory? |
| | How can students be involved in finding solutions to their problems? |
| | Decide what action to take initiate a formal dialogue and to "capture" data, e.g,, methods such as focus groups |
| Act | Implement focus groups to ascertain what is happening from as many different perspectives as possible (triangulation) |
| | Record observations and reflections in journal |
| | Ensure LEAP participants are not "disadvantaged" or put "at risk" |
| Reflect | Critically analyse and discuss initial data and experiences of facilitator and group to evaluate past actions |
| Understand | How can project be understood as emancipatory? |
| | Revisit the literature and make an interpretation |

Where one stage finishes and the next stage starts is sometimes not clear or clean cut and smaller cycles within one stage might be occurring as you reflect on what is going on and make changes according to where things have moved to rather than sticking to a rigid plan.

*Theoretical illustrations*

As well as the cycles, some of the qualities of PART that were informed through theory in Transitions are highlighted in Table 7.3:

*Table 7.3.*

| | |
|---|---|
| Social justice | There were various points in the project where it was important to acknowledge everyone's feelings and experiences, perceptions and imaginations so we used methods such as surveys or small friendship focus groups and reported on the differences as well as similarities within the group. We endeavored to understand the plurality of the group when it came to negotiating what the curriculum would look like particularly when most wanted to go one way but some others wanted to go another way. In cases such as this we talked about the process of democracy but also the violence that it creates and explored ways of meeting everyone's needs at some point, even though it might not always be everyone's needs and all at the same time. |
| Activism | Students were very much a part of the process but it was not in the form of just participating, although this was important that they all participated, but also in the form of political action; an understanding of the power plays at work and strategies to destabilize some of the taken-for-granted ways that power played out in the group, between people, and in decisions made. |
| Participatory | All students were involved in different ways but there were points where it was important that each person was "heard" and had an opportunity to "act" as well as claim responsibility for "products" that could be included in their portfolios |
| Team | We would work between the individual and the group or the individual and smaller groups within the group and then the larger group to develop the notion of "team" as being all who are involved in the same project. We worked very strongly around the notion of teaming to include practices such as informed debate, problem solving, cooperative learning, collaboration and collective outcomes |
| Reflexivity | At the end of the first cycle we were able to draw on many of the smaller events where we developed skills of reflection, critical thinking, application of critical theory, and reflexivity. Not only did they develop conceptually in these notions but expanded metacognitive skills to a greater number in the group and as part of the process that informs the next |

*Limitations and Cautions*

Far from representing clinical case studies, the LEAP and Transition vignettes contain cogent and convincing warnings about the limits and challenges of "doing" PART. It is important not to romanticize (or pathologise) PART as it requires a significant investment in both time and energy (intellectual, emotional and political) and is difficult to do (Moore, 2004). Tripp (1996) writes that the action research sequence should be carefully thought out and planned. It ought "not be rushed" as changes in practice take time (p. 90). To add to this, questions of validity are habitually raised by traditional researchers about "openly ideological research" (Lather, 1986) and the action potential of subjects are often constrained within the current conservative environment in which teachers must justify their understandings and actions to authorities at a higher administrative scale (Kemmis, 1991).

Challenging and changing exploitative and oppressive practices at the level of everyday life (face-to-face) also requires critique, which is often thankless task. In the face of capitalist authority, the effort to democratize knowledge and power through an emancipatory research framework can result in damage for the local participants (e.g., in the form of retaliations and reprisals). This is why it is vitally important for the committed researcher to understand the issues and the local power structure from the perspective of the participants, e.g., in terms of framing the problem, discussing solutions, and interpreting findings. Using critical theory as a guide, McLaren (1995c) maintains that educational research "must be organic to and not administered upon" (p. 291). Clearly it is of vital importance to understand not only how the situated understandings that make up the participants' own beliefs influence what counts as valid and relevant knowledge in the classroom, it is also important to understand how the researcher's own political, theoretical and methodological biases influence the process of analysis. Not only must researchers have a strong transdisciplinary grasp of the capitalist totality within which research is refracted through institutional, academic, cultural, political and economic systems of mediation in class society, they must understand how hegemonic pedagogical practices created at the micropolitical level are dialectically related to these systems.

*Limitation Illustrations*

*Blind or manipulative power dressed up as emancipation or empowerment*
There is an argument that in order for PART to fulfill its claims of participation, activism, critical inquiry and team there should be a process of democratic decision making throughout the project. Within the transition project the issue was framed by the researcher initially, rather than one raised by the students so it could be argued that it was not the other participants' issue but rather one that someone already privileged perceived incorrectly. One of the cautions in attempting to make spaces for agency available to those seen as passive (in this case the students) is that the missionary zeal of the privileged does not just become another way of colonizing others' experiences. This limitation was also evident in the LEAP where decisions about the production of the curriculum constituted sites of struggle, which ultimately determined what was learned. Here, the credibility of the data gathered influenced the research process as Greg attempted to decentre power in

the classroom to reconstruct the relationship between LEAP staff and students. Forced to operate within the margins of his own area of teaching responsibility (*Work and Personal Effectiveness*), Greg strived throughout the remainder of his employment contract to put into effect a curriculum that acknowledged the notion of different curricula, and the different histories, experiences and locations of students (Martin, 2000). Greg's relationship with the young people was inherently problematic since his dominance was not only sanctioned by the institutional structures in which the students lived and worked but constantly re-inscribed through the advantages conferred upon him at every turn as he "negotiated" with the youth people. As Greg reflected on his practice, he discovered that he would seemingly defer to the young people and solicit their ideas and opinions as he sought to have them comply with the requirements of the course. On his part, this was a genuine effort at "empowering" the young people. However, Greg realised that he was simply fostering the illusion of choice and that, in being mindful of how he enacted his power in the classroom, he was "negotiating" a more powerful position for himself (Mills, 1997).

*Partiality, fluidity and complexity*
As with any research certain politics or epistemological positions are foregrounded and backgrounded. Regardless of which theoretical positions and methods used there will always only be a partial representation of reality and so it is vital that we constantly ask "from which position do we speak?" and how can we work reflexively to ensure a less oppressive reading of, and participation in, our world as a result of the research. This "reality" is also contextualized and so may be fluid, or constantly changing therefore recognizing the complexity and fluidity of the context and perhaps even the question/s acts as a reminder to the research process and its participants to be open for multiple and sometimes even contradictory outcomes. One characteristic of this type of research is that it is often difficult to make fixed, simplistic and unitary statements about project outcomes without asking another barrage of questions. Like the example in the LEAP vignette, in Transitions the position taken was rooted in critical theory, feminist theory and the work of transgressive educators as we attempted to shift the balance of power and curriculum construction from a few adults (year 7 and 8 teachers) to the students about to experience school transition. We did not foreground the experiences of teachers or parents in this instance but in recognizing this perhaps one of the changes we would make for the following cohort would be to include these people a lot more. It was also important for us to realize that the experiences of this cohort, and how they were positioned within the school, how they positioned each other, was dynamic and potentially very different to the cohorts they would become a part of in year 8. So too would the following year 7 cohort be equally complex and different although they were all experiencing transition. It was an important reminder to us that these "events" were very complex and although we could not fully capture and represent everyone's experiences we could, through the PART process, begin to have a more clear understanding of the process and a more

relevant and inclusive attempt to learn through transition rather than just have it "done" to the students.

*Focus*
Methods of inquiry that do not foreclose findings as being "in support of" or "providing evidence against," as may be found within the positivist tradition, have the potential to grow beyond a form that is both manageable or focused enough to be able to say anything. In order to "keep on track" without becoming so fixed in the process that reflexivity cannot occur it is important to return to the question/s (issue/problem) that generated the research action and ensure that micro and macro phases of the cycles act to help answer the question/s. That is not to say that other questions will not be generated and that part of the project's reflexivity is to ignore other possibilities but this situation might call for a redesigning of the question/s based upon the outcomes of the previous cycle, so that it is informed through practice and theory. This new question then acts to generate a new cycle but systematic data collection, theory, and rigorous planning should still inform action if anything substantial can be added to how the question is understood and answered. For example, in Transition many subsidiary questions and opportunities for action were raised and it felt quite overwhelming in how we might manage this, particularly given the diversity within the class. By returning to our original question "how can transition become a more productive learning experience for students and teachers" we could return to the research process that helped us answer this question while at the same time keeping a list of subsidiary questions for possible attention in the next cycle or as a possible question for another group to take up, or after we were happy that we had answered our first question.

*Winners and losers*
At the outset we tried to make it clear that this form of research was to recognize oppressive situations within education and attempt to change the context to ensure more socially just outcomes for those participating in the project. It is important to note though, that where some participants may have been positioned very powerfully and being very privileged, it might be necessary for that positioning to be changed to allow for a more equitable space for those oppressed by the current practices. In Transition the "popular" students who also had many positive connections with the secondary school could not see the value in much of what we were doing and took an individualistic approach to what their learning should be. They could not see the value of working with others or learning about others' lives, perceptions or perspectives. Likewise, very technically oriented teachers obstructed some of the processes that we attempted to put in place, particularly for the year 8 curriculum planning believing that they knew what was best for the primary students, students who were essentially the little fish in the big pond, beginners in the knowledge stakes, and characterized by many deficits. As these teachers came from a dominant position of subject experts and secondary (as opposed to primary) school there was much to be lost by agreeing to a curriculum that did not introduce the new year 8 students to the basics of their subject areas. What is important to

186

note is that with change in practice there will also be a change or redirection of power for some individuals or collectives. It therefore becomes necessary to be aware or ready for the resultant implications while working to subvert current positions and argue for a more equitable positioning of participants with a more positive eventual outcome or cultural wealth for all involved.

## CONCLUSION

Visions of a democratic life with a generation of public spaces and where sustained communication would critically interrogate distortions of democracy caused by various forms of oppression including racism, patriarchy, colonialism and transphobia have important implications for education "as they generated a re-envisioning of the function of schools and the media as places where social, economic, and cultural power could be confronted and, in some ways, transformed" (Shapiro, 2002, p. 2). As part of this vision we have attempted to provide you, the reader and new researcher, with some background literature and field stories to illustrate how and why you might "do" PART within your work. By now you will be aware of some of the relationships with other forms of research paradigms, such as positivism and action research, as well as some of the ontological and epistemological differences between some methods. There is still much to learn—from the literature in terms of the "how" and "why," and from the stories of those who have participated in this type of research in differing contexts. Again, it is in the dialogic relationship between theory and practice, each informing the other as praxis that you will enact PART and take it beyond these printed words, an adventure in which we invite you to participate so as to interrupt some of the oppressive practices in which we are ourselves involved, instead working towards a more socially just society for all. There are pragmatic considerations in research and foolish to ignore them, however, also ethical and political questions that ought to be addressed.

## REFERENCES

Anderson, G., Herr, K., & Nihlen, A. (1994). *Studying your own school: An educator's guide to qualitative practitioner research.* Thousand Oaks, CA: Corwin Press.
Aronowitz, S., & Giroux, H. (1985). *Education under siege: The conservative, liberal, and radical debate over schooling.* South Hadley, MA: Bergin & Garvey.
Beane, J., & Brodhagen, B. (1995). 'Strategies for improving the schools', Exploring middle school curriculum options: Part 2 (workshop). On *The middle years kit.* Ryde, NSW: National Schools Network.
Callinicos, A. (1983). *The revolutionary road to socialism.* London: Socialist Workers Party.
Carr, W., & Kemmis, S. (1986). *Becoming critical: Education, knowledge and action research* (Rev. ed.). Geelong, Victoria: Deakin University.
Carr, W., & Kemmis, S. (2005). Staying critical. *Educational Action Research,* 13, 347-358.
Delanty, G. (2003). Ideologies of the knowledge society and the cultural contradictions of higher education, *Policy Futures in Education, 1,* 71-82.
Demeritt, D. (1998). Science, social constructivism and nature (pp. 173-193). In B. Braun & N. Castree (Eds.), Remaking reality. London and New York: Routledge.

Diniz-Pereira, J. (2002). "Globalisations": Is the teacher research movement a critical and emancipatory response? *Educational Action Research, 10*, 373-389.

Elliot, J. (1997). School based curriculum development and action research in the United Kingdom (pp. 17-28). In S. Hollingsworth (Ed.), *International action research: A casebook for educational reform*. London: Falmer Press.

Elliot, J. (2005). Becoming critical: The failure to connect. *Educational Action Research, 13*, 359-374.

Foucault, M. (1977). *Discipline and punish: The birth of the prison*. New York: Vintage Books.

Freire, P. (1972). *Cultural action for freedom*. Harmondsworth: Penguin.

Giroux, H. (1994) *Disturbing pleasures: Learning popular culture*. London: Routledge

Goffman, I. (1968). *Asylums: Essays on the social situation of mental patients and other inmates*. Harmondsworth: Penguin Books.

Grande, S. (2004). *Red pedagogy: Native American social and political thought*. Lanham, MA: Rowman & Littlefield Publishers.

Griffiths, M. (2003). *Action for social justice in education: Fairly different*. Maidenhead, Philadelphia: Open University Press.

Hartsock, N. (1998). Objectivity and revolution: The unity of observation and outrage in Marxist theory (pp. 85-104). In N. Hartsock (Ed.), *The feminist standpoint revisited and other essays*. Boulder, CO: Westview Press.

Hill, D. (2005). Globalisation and its educational discontents: Neoliberalisation and its impacts on education workers' rights, pay, and conditions, *International Studies in Sociology of Education, 15*, 257-288.

Holdsworth, R. (2005). Taking young people seriously means giving them serious things to do (pp. 139-150). In J. Mason & T. Fattore (Eds.), *Children taken seriously: in theory, policy and practice*. London: Jessica Kingsley Publishers.

Holly, P. (1991). From action research to collaborative enquiry: The processing of an innovation (pp. 36-56). In O. Zuber-Skerritt (Ed.), *Action research for change and development*. Aldershot, England: Gower Publishing Company.

Jackson, T. (1998, March). A prisoner of hope in cyberspace: The ontological nature of new media technology is in process and will remain so for generations. *BadSubjects*, 37, Retrieved October 1, 2005, from http://bad.eserver.org/issues/1998/37/jackson.html

Johnson, B. (1993). Teacher-as-researcher. Retrieved December 5, 2005, from http://www.ericdigests.org/1993/research.htm

Kemmis, S. (1991). Improving education through action research (pp. 57-75). In O. Zuber-Skerritt (Ed.), *Action research for change and development*. Aldershot, England: Gower Publishing Company.

Kemmis, S., & Grundy, S. (1997). Educational action research in Australia: Organization and practice (pp. 40-48). In S. Hollingsworth (Ed), *International action research: A casebook for educational reform*. London: Falmer Press.

Kemmis, S., & McTaggart, R. (1988). *The action research planner* (3rd rev. ed.). Waurn Ponds, Vic.: Deakin University.

Kemmis, S., & McTaggart, R. (2000). Participatory action research (pp. 567-605). In N. Denzin & Y. Lincoln (Eds.), *Handbook of qualitative research* (2nd ed.). Thousand Oakes, CA: Sage Publications, Inc.

Kemmis, S., & Wilkinson, M. (1998). Participatory action research and the study of practice (pp. 21-36). In B. Atweh, S. Kemmis & P. Weeks (Eds.), *Action research in practice: Partnerships for social justice in education*. London: Routledge.

Kincheloe, J. (1995). Meet me behind iron curtain: The struggle for a critical postmodern action research (pp. 71-87). In. P. McLaren & J. Giarelli (Eds.), Critical theory and educational research. Albany, New York: State University of New York Press.

Kincheloe, J. (2003). *Teachers as researchers: Qualitative inquiry as a path to empowerment* (2nd ed.). New York: Routledge Farmer.

Kincheloe, J., & McLaren, P. (2000). Rethinking critical theory and qualitative research (pp. 279-313). In N. Denzin & Y. Lincoln (Eds.), *Handbook of qualitative research* (2nd ed.). Thousand Oakes, CA: Sage Publications, Inc.

Kirkpatrick, G., Katsiaficas, G., & Emery, M. (1978). Critical theory and the limits of sociological positivism. Retrieved September 28, 2005, from http://www.tryoung.com/archives/176krkpt.htm

Lather, P. (1986). Issues of validity in openly ideological research: Between a rock and a soft place. *Interchange, 17*, 63-84.

Lather, P. (1992). Critical frames in educational research: Feminist and post-structural perspectives. *Theory Into Practice, 31*, 87-99.

Lewin, K. (1998). Action research and minority problems (pp. 41-46). In S. Kemmis & R. McTaggart (Eds.), *The action research reader*. Deakin University, VIC.: Deakin University Press.

Martin, G. (2000). Don't LEAP into this: Student resistance in labour market programmes. *Educational Action Research Journal, 8*, 533-548.

Martin, G. (2005). You can't be neutral on a moving bus: Critical pedagogy as community praxis. Journal for Critical Education Policy Studies, 3(2). Retrieved November 11, 2005, from http://www.jceps.com/index.php?pageID=article&articleID=47

McKernan, J. (1991). *Curriculum action research: A handbook of methods and resources for the re flective practitioner*. London: Kogan Page.

McLaren, P. (1986). *Schooling as a ritual performance: Toward a political economy of educational symbols and gestures*. London: Routledge.

McLaren, P. (1998). Afterword: Ya Basta! (pp. 411-431). In Y. Zou & E. Trueba (Eds.), *Ethnic identity and power: Cultural contexts of political action in school and society*. Albany, New York: State University of New York.

McLaren, P. (1994). *Life in schools: An Introduction to critical pedagogy in the foundations of education*. (2nd ed.). New York: Longman.

McLaren, P. (1995a). *Critical pedagogy and predatory culture: Oppositional politics in a postmodern era*. New York: Routledge.

McLaren, P. (1995b). White terror and oppositional agency: Towards a critical multiculturalism (pp. 33-70). In C. Sleeter & P. McLaren (Eds.), *Multicultural education, critical pedagogy, and the politics of difference*. Albany, NY: State University of New York Press.

Mclaren, P. (1995c). Collisions with otherness: "Traveling" theory, postcolonial criticism, and the politics of ethnographic practice (pp. 271-300). In. P. McLaren & J. Giarelli (Eds.), *Critical theory and educational research*. Albany, New York: State University of New York Press.

McLaren, P. (1995d). Critical pedagogy in the age of global capitalism: Some challenges for the educational left, *Australian Journal of Education, 39*, 5-21.

McLaren, P. (2003). *Life in schools: An Introduction to critical pedagogy in the foundations of education*. (4th ed.). New York: Longman.

McLaren, P., Martin, G., Farahmandpur, R., & Jaramillo, N. (2004, Winter). Teaching in and against the empire: Critical pedagogy as revolutionary praxis. *Teacher Education Quarterly, 31*, 131-153.

McLaren, P., & Pinkney-Pastrana, J. (2000). The search for the complicit native. *International Journal of Qualitative Studies in Education, 13*, 163-184.

Mills, S. (1997). *Discourse*. London: Routledge.

Mitchell, C. (1991). Preface. In C. Mitchell & K. Weiler (Eds.), *Rewriting Literacy: culture and the discourse of the other*. New York: Bergin and Garvey.

Moore, J. (2004). Living in the basement of the ivory tower: A graduate student's perspective of participatory action research within academic institutions. *Educational Action Research, 12*, 145-162.

Noffke, S. (1997). Themes and tension in US action research: Towards historical analysis. In S. Hollingsworth (Ed.), *International action research: A casebook for educational reform*. (pp. 2-16). London: Falmer Press.

O'Brien, R. (2001). Um exame da abordagem metodológica da pesquisa ação [An Overview of the Methodological Approach of Action Research]. In Roberto Richardson (Ed.), *Teoria e Prática da Pesquisa Ação [Theory and Practice of Action Research]*. João Pessoa, Brazil: Universidade Federal da Paraíba. (English version). Retrieved November 11, 2005, from http://www.web.ca/~robrien/papers/arfinal.html (Accessed 20/1/2002)

Rikowski, G. (2000). *Messing with the explosive commodity: School improvement, educational research, and labour power in the era of global capitalism. If we aren't pursuing improvement, what are we doing?* A paper presented at the British Educational Research Association Conference, Cardiff University, Wales, September 7-9. Retrieved November 11, 2005, from http://www.libr.org/ISC/articles/14-Glenn_Rikowski.htm

Shapiro, S. (2002). Introduction. In S. Shapiro & S. Shapiro (Eds.), *Body movements: pedagogy, politics and social change* (pp. 1-24). Cresskill, NJ: Hampton Press.

Smith, E. (2001). Student voice, student agency, student research. *Connect*, 132, 20-24.

Stringer, E. (1999). *Action research: A handbook for practitioners.* Newbury Park, CA.: Sage.

Thomson, P. (2002). *Schooling the rustbelt kids: Making the difference in changing times.* Crows Nest NSW: Allen & Unwin.

Tripp, D. (1993). *Critical incidents in teaching: The development of professional judgement.* London: Routledge.

Tripp, D. (1996). *E471 Action research for professional development: Unit reader.* Perth, WA: Murdoch University.

Tripp, D. (1998). Critical incidents in action inquiry. In G. Schacklock & J. Smyth (Eds.), Being reflexive in critical educational and social research. (pp. 36-49). London: Falmer Press.

Winch, C. & Foreman-Peck, L. (2000). Teacher professionalism, educational aims and action research: The evolution of policy in the United Kingdom, *Teacher Development, 4*, 165-176.

Zavarzadeh, M., & Morton. D. (1994). *Theory as resistance: Politics and culture after (Post)structuralism.* New York: The Guilford Press.

AARON DAVID GRESSON III

# 8. DOING CRITICAL RESEARCH IN MAINSTREAM DISCIPLINES

*Reflections on a Study of Black Female Individuation*

Joyce Ladner, an African American sociologist, introduced a tension in qualitative work in the early 1970s. In her ethnography of young Black girls living in the inner-city, *Tomorrow's Tomorrow* (1971), and an edited volume on theory and methodology, *The Death of White Sociology* (1973, 1998), Ladner excited a new generation of minority and majority group social scientists when she insisted that "value-neutrality" was neither practiced by mainstream sociology nor should it be a tenet of activist minority social science. This orientation broke with the traditional insistence that researchers achieved "objectivity" and "validity" through being removed from their own influence or impact on the research act and context. The boundaries between self and other, researcher and researched, were seen to be significantly less rigid or pure than imagined or desired. In more recent years, other critical research traditions have taken up this theme (Kincheloe & McLaren, 2005). Charles Menzies (2001), reviewing this critical literature, identified one rationale for this radical critique of mainstream social science as its share in the maintenance of social inequality.

Critical scholars working as "insider" researchers—bound to the researched by shared identifications—have added "reflexivity" as a core quality informing critical research (Alridge, 2003; Chaudhry, 2001). Reflexivity is broadly defined as reflection on one's own share in the construction of knowledge, particularly how and why and with what consequences this knowledge has been produced (Johnson & Duberley, 2003).

In this essay, I elaborate upon these elements in my own work. My goal is to illustrate the kinds of reflexivity called forth when one seeks to "study" a phenomenon using mainstream social science but remain alert to the limitations of that scholarship for articulating the lived-experience of the studied. First, I will describe the context and process of the 1985 study. Second, I will address the methodological issues raised by the extant literature on commitment behavior. Finally, I consider some of the strategic maneuvers qualitative research allowed me in this thorny inquiry into the contradictions and casualties of racial, gender and class oppression against the backdrop of individual agency and voice.

*K. Tobin & J. Kincheloe, (eds.), Doing Educational Research—A Handbook, 191–209.*

## THE STUDY

The 1985 inquiry was a qualitative study of fifty African American women's individuation behaviors in relation to race. As a study in psychology, it was conceived under certain disciplinary assumptions regarding both theory and method. At the time, experimental and quasi-experimental designs dominated the field; and research questions, unfortunately, sometimes were guided by methodology rather the reverse. The first research issue I faced pertained to how I would frame the inquiry. This was an especially important step in a study proposing to examine psychology and Black women. The historical denigration of racial minorities in social science research has cautioned both minorities and minority scholars in this regard (Engram, 1980; Guthrie, 1998). I did not want to implement the study from within the prominent deficit and pathology models that dominated the early decades of the twentieth century (Guthrie, 1998). Thus, I needed to frame the inquiry as a critical project.

The study was entitled: "Towards a Dialectical Psychology of Commitment: Black Women, Individuation and Cultural Contradiction." The concepts "dialectics" and "cultural contradictions" were strategic additions to the mainstream psychological perspectives on commitment and individuation. As critical concepts, they announced my intention, which could be a tricky proposition for a dissertation supervised by sympathetic but mainstream faculty, to take a radical or critical stance on positivist methodologies and epistemologies.

### Preliminary Work: Theorizing the Study

Framing the inquiry within the critical perspective I adopted in the early 1980s, meant that I had to deal with the core issues of racial oppression and the oppressiveness of the social sciences traditionally employed to study African Americans and other disenfranchised groups. The mandate/mission identified by Ladner, among others, required me to take an ideological, partisan position on the sociohistorical contexts informing the study itself and the phenomenon—Black women's racial commitment—I proposed to define, construct, and study. For me, a heuristic model of commitment among the oppressed under conditions of cultural contradiction was the answer. Designating them as collaborators was yet another critical act and ideological decision. Although the psychological literature had only partially began to consider "experimenter's bias" as a countertransference issue (Baehr, 2004), I partly recognized that I was going to be a participant in the construction or creation of "Black female commitment" by the very nature of the questions and interactions I proposed to introduce into the lives of these women. (Only later did I begin to see just how much I was a part of the process under study.) By naming Black women's commitment-related behavior as individuation, I was also shaping the way in which I proposed to access the *epistemology* (knowledge creation) and *ethical* (relational and moral) dimensions of inquiry. Epistemology in this instance pertained to what is or can be known and how this knowledge is achieved or constructed.

With respect to African Americans, this was an issue of *agency* (Alridge, 2003; Gresson, 1995; 2004). It was, moreover, a matter of Black female voice and agency (Gresson, 1982; Hull, Scott, & Smith, 1982). Both race and gender were factors driving my decision to pursue a course sanguine to critical feminist research (Hutchinson, 1988). Treating the Black women as collaborators in the study acknowledged the epistemological issue as one concerned with whose knowledge for whom? Women who participated as well as those who refused to participate in the study often addressed this aspect of the knowledge-producing role of research (Gresson, 1995). This concern with the ethics and morality of the study also pointed to other philosophical or theoretical aspects of knowledge: subjectivism and constructivism.

Individuation, as a guiding conceptual dimension of the study of racial commitment, started from the assumption of subject primacy: the women as agents on their own business as well as that of others were the active part of this project. Related to their being active was their own *lived experience* as the basis for understanding choices, including commitments. The kinds of choices open to them as women and African-American were grounded in real day-to-day experiences. Sexuality, religion, class, and other multiple identities (Merchant & Willis, 2001) also figured in their lives.

Subjectivity and constructivism also introduced another philosophical concern, one pertinent to the methodology with which I was constructing the design. I refer here to the social construction of reality. Reality, an ontological and epistemological matter, had been popularly recognized as socially constructed in the social sciences, if not psychology per se, since the seminal essay by Berger and Luckmann (1966). Recognizing that individuals purposefully put forth realities for others about both themselves and their relations with others had been popularly described in Erving Goffman's classics, *The Presentation of Self in Everyday Life* (1959) and *Stigma: Notes on the Management of Spoiled Identity* (1963). These works helped create a scholarly atmosphere responsive to the discussion of purposeful activity even among the socially oppressed. Applied to African American women, these ideas—subjectivity and constructivism—pointed to the next questions about the theoretical and methodological design of the inquiry.

### The Literature Review: Individuation and Black Women's Commitment

Only after addressing these broadly philosophical issues was I ready to delve into the mainstream literature on individuation and try to relate its core and pertinent aspects to the question of Black female individuation as a racial commitment issue. From this view, how these women differentiated or separated from former or assumed group identities and then reintegrated with or against them were the issues under study. In psychology, "separation individuation" is the concept used to describe the dialectical processes of separation and reintegration. Little research or theorizing had been done on this topic using non-White, middle-class subjects (Akhtar & Kramer, 1998; Gresson, 1995; Pena, 2003; Pinderhughes, 1995). Thus, hypothesis-testing the relations of individuation and minority identity and commitment, generally, and Black women, in particular, was not a meaningful way of accessing my interests in racial commitment as an issue in individuation. My goal was not to prove something; rather, I wanted to understand something more fully. I wanted to get beyond some of the more partisan aspects of the so-called "Black male/female sexism" and "betrayal" debates of the late 1970s (Gresson, 1982).

Previous inquiry on Black female attitudes and personal growth had yielded dialectical and incomplete descriptions (e.g., Gilkes, 1982; Myers, 1980; Rogers-Rose, 1980). Gilkes' ethnography of Black female leaders in a southern town led her to posit important enhancements of aspects of Rosabeth Moss Kanter's (1972) commitment study of communes. Gilkes found that Black women made important decisions about family and community that were complicated by their assessment of their lives at specific times in the life span. She additionally found that although class, education and various life events might take them down different initial paths, these women often ended up sharing related roles as community leaders.

Qualitative studies by Cheryl Gilkes and theoretical work by Audre Lorde and other Black feminists (Gresson, 1995) guided my thinking about the importance of agency and voice in the lives of Black women and their ongoing dialogue with Black men around each others' "racial uplift" obligations. Narratives were assuming an increasingly strong relevance in the lives and communicative initiatives of Black women activists. Mary Helen Washington, Alice Walker, Maya Angelou, Toni Morrison, and bell hooks were at the forefront of a cascade of Black female storytellers. Narrative had come to have some currency in psychology as well with the influence of Jerome Bruner, Kenneth Gergen, and others. The convergence of both grassroots and academic interest in narrative method was fortuitous in this regard; it proved relatively easy to get my committee to let me attempt to work with narrative methods although this was fairly new to Counseling Psychology research, especially minority focused and conducted inquiry.

At the time of my study, very little scholarship existed on minority individuation processes. But a major new area of research was under way at the University of Michigan where Patricia and Gerald Gurin and James Jackson (Gurin, 1975; Jackson, McCullough, & Gurin, 1988) headed up research teams looking at various aspects of African American mental health and identity. James Jackson and Gerald Gurin, in particular, shared their findings with me regarding the role of reference and friendship groups on the differences in Black identity dynamics. They had begun to find, through multiple regression analysis, that African Americans revealed heterogeneous and sometimes contrasting patterns of identity. This was crucial when thinking through some of the coding analysis discussed below under methodology.

Commitment theory and certain principles from ego developmental psychology, family theory and individuation psychology were only helpful in formulating a broad backdrop to the study. The dearth of solid research on racial commitment meant that a different set of theoretical ideas was needed to guide the study design and research proper. For example, the notion of culture, from a radical and Afrocentric perspective, meant alertness to the *cultural contradictions* (Bell, 1978)

194

shaping or driving individual and group agency in ways that forefront confusion, ambivalence, even helplessness (Pinderhughes, 1982).

While psychological theorizing often neglects these structural and cultural forces, their importance was evident in Black feminist (e.g., Engram, 1982) and Afrocentric (e.g., Nobles, 1986; Stewart, 2004) scholarship. For example, methodologist Eleanor Engram (1982) wrote a path-breaking critique of the literature on the Black family, exposing the "mythic" underpinnings of alleged scholarly works. Like Ladner's earlier studies, Engram's work pointed to the significantly ideological underpinnings of social science scholarship, especially which focused on African Americans.

Multiculturalism educator-researcher James Banks (2002) pinpointed the sociological or ideological roots of the various scholarly works on racial and ethnic education. Banks argued, in the sociology of knowledge tradition, that various scholars largely approached their research through lens very much tainted by the dominant values and ideas of their period. Like Engram, Banks saw the values orientation of this scholarship. These philosophical orientations informed my method in important ways. In particular, they encouraged me to empower the collaborators over and against traditional ways of separating self as researcher from other as researched. They also led me to seek to identify dominant cultural values being renegotiated to accommodate the lived realities of the women. Michele Fine (1994) crafted a useful essay on this dynamic and challenge using the metaphor of the hyphen. For me, like other "native" researchers (e.g., Chaudhry, 2001; Mehra, 2001; Menzies, 2001), the hyphen also entailed resisting the potential of over-identification and fusion with the collaborators. Methodology was useful in this regard as well as the primary function of guiding data-collection, analysis, and interpretation.

## THE METHODOLOGY

Given the paucity of research and theory on minority separation-individuation, an exploratory approach seemed the best strategy. This approach required a minimum of intrusiveness from a theoretical perspective. I could let the women, their thoughts, sharing, and actions guide both theory and interpretation or understanding. Thus, the inquiry sought to develop a theoretical framework capable of explaining aspects of the observed shifts in some aspects of Black female behavior around issues such as education, marriage, sexuality, and politics. Because I was concerned with understanding a phenomenon—racial commitment as core actions, themes and concerns—I considered grounded theory, phenomenology, narrative, ethnography, and the case study as ways of approaching the research design (Merriam, 1998).

Grounded theory development was especially attractive to me because of my own clinical and theoretical interests: I wanted to do effective interventions in the minority community, but I realized too little theory was related directly to the minority communities and circumstances I wanted to engage. A major limitation of the field was the assumption regarding the relationship between psychological healthiness and the dynamics undergirding individuation in the United States. M.D. Fishbane has noted in this regard: "… cognitive processes of differentiation take place for everyone everywhere, since every person is aware of being a separate entity. However, [the] 'individuation-separation hypothesis' goes beyond that into the psychological construal of self-other relations, defining healthy and pathological functioning" (2001, p. 1).

Because individuation theorizing had taken place within a class and culture bound context, it was not readily apparent to me how to frame a set of hypotheses that captured what Black women perceived their behaviors to mean. The ideas they gave for what they were trying to manage around traditional racial matters were therefore important clues to understanding the processes and dynamics involved in separation and integration behavior. The method that seemed most useful for me was one that allowed me to access their worlds with a minimum of preconceived assumptions.

Grounded theory, focusing on inductive methods of theory development, called "theoretical sampling," allowed me to enter the realm of Black female cognitions about self-other relations and conceptualize commitment in terms of their culturally derived evaluations. Their acceptance, rejection and renegotiation of these cultural-contrived values pertain to individuation. These processes and the meanings placed on them became the focus of the study.

In addition to grounded theory, other methodologies I used included ethnography, object relations theory, Afrocentric and Black identity theory, symbolic interactionism, Black feminist theory, and radical feminist theory. I also relied on a knowledge orientation I called "minority epistemology" (Gresson, 1977) which emphasized the lived experiences and shared fate realities of the oppressed. Specific methods were guided by assumptions associated with these theoretical and political writings.

*Methods: Sampling, Interviews, and Participant Observation*

The data-gathering techniques reflected the over-all methodological stance: collaboration with purposeful, self-other oriented women operating within conditions of cultural contradiction. Four methods were central in this phase of the study: sampling; interviews/narrative histories; ethnographic participation; and critical interpretation.

*Sampling*
Sampling methods were approached from the perspective that homogeneity and representativeness, while important, were less critical in this instance than heterogeneity as a critical affirmation of the live-experience and political announcements of minority scholars like Ladner whose methodological anthology, The Death of White Sociology, signified the collapsing of the bold line between theory and method.

The theory/concept-driven sampling criteria I used thus included: Afro-American, female, willing participant, diverse racial identifications based on life choices regarding traditional categories such as marriage, motherhood, schooling, employment, intimate interracial relationships, and so forth. I wanted to tell the stories of Black female racial identity that went beyond the surface; by allowing them to flesh out their own stories and restory themselves as racially committed women, I was both affirming and, in a way, impelling them.

In 1980 when I began this study, sampling for *heterogeneity* was an "iffy" affair: some did it ritualistically; others begged off after acknowledging the limitations of generalizing from a homogeneous—privileged, White, college student—sample. The idea of heterogeneity was then radical. I chose as diverse a sample as possible because I wanted to respond to specific theoretical and methodological assumptions or premises. First, "sampling for maximum variation" (List, 2004), meant I wanted to reach a broad range of women. So, even though I interviewed several females in interracial relationships, for instance, they varied across class, education, and religion. The goal was not to isolate one of this category or one of that; while I did not seek to exhaust or saturate my pool with "maximum variation," I did want to tap possible nuances in the stories and constructions of women around a delimited number of stimulus themes.

Collaborators were selected after initiating contact with female psychologists, community and organizational leaders, and friends. Using this reputational approach, I informed potential participants of the purpose of the study and invited them to participate. Several persons were recruited by collaborators who, after being interviewed, felt that a particular person would provide an "interesting" interview. This recruitment process illustrates the collaborative aspect; it also indicates how many of the women provided behavioral clues to their own issues around and perceptions of commitment. For example, a fifty-five-year-old mother suggested I interview her youngest daughter, a twenty-six-year-old, indicating that she did not understand why her daughter dated so many non-Black males. The mother reported that she had once dated a White man but found that she did not like White men as intimates. The daughter, in turn, suggested that I interview her cousin, whom she considered particularly interesting: the cousin did not date Black men at all; she was engaged to a White male (she later married him).

Interestingly, each of these collaborators revealed her sense of propriety and the boundaries of enlargement: the mother could deal intimately only with Black men; the daughter could date White men (she later had her first child by a White man and then married a Black man) but would not abandon intimacy with Black men; the cousin would not deal at all with Black men and chose a White mate. In short, I used the sampling procedures discussed here to expedite the theoretical work and to join the growing number of researchers who challenge the adequacy of classical research techniques for answering certain types of questions, particularly with minority populations or individuals (Engram 1982).

*Interviews*

I interviewed more than fifty women, but retained only fifty as formal cases. Most were interviewed between June 1982 and July 1984. Some were referred to me by friends and families, and others were self-selected because of an interest in the study or because they wanted an opportunity to share their thoughts. All were living in the New England region. Conversations with fifteen additional women about various parts of the study enriched and broadened my understanding of the initial interviews.

The women were interviewed in various settings: homes, offices, parks, shelters for battered women, and mental health settings. The interview schedule was an open-ended instrument. The interview questions were broad, focusing on background, their challenges, thoughts about Black male/female relations and the notion of racial commitment—define it and how it relates or does not relate to their lives. Semi-structured, the interviews were conversational, even supportive. Some of the women were interviewed only once; others were interviewed on repeated occasions as issues arose that bore on their perspectives and stories. Because the research was collaborative, they often initiated a conversation or sent a person to be interviewed. The crucial criterion for sending them was the collaborator's perception of racial commitment as a pertinent issue occurring in the life of the new recruit. For example, one woman whose dating patterns had enlarged to include Latino and White males, wanted me to interview her cousin who had stopped dealing with Black men and was about to marry a White male. Interestingly, the rationale for sending her cousin to me was a belief that the cousin was confused about herself as a Black woman. The next interview with the initial collaborator focused on her thinking about confusion in Black women. This process is discussed further below as part of "theoretical sampling" used in the interpretation and enlargement of the data.

*Ethnography and participant observation*
I saw many of the women in social and professional situations outside of the interview per se. Because of the collaborative and relational issues we covered during the interview, we often continued aspects of their narratives in other places. For instance, I was called to Eartha's mother's home late one evening as a friend and therapist because another sister was in marital crisis. After the crisis had quieted down, Eartha and I were talking in another room about Black male-female relationships generally when she reinitiated part of her narrative, explaining some of the choices she was making in terms of the present incident.

This incident also points to the issue of phenomenology in ethnographic work. Phenomenology, particularly the work of Alfred Schutz (Gresson, 1978) on "contemporaries" and "consociates" influenced my approach to the subjective experiences and interpretations of these women and the people in their lives, including myself. Schutz viewed "contemporaries" as people bound by the same sociohistorical context; and "consociates" were people who actively co-constructed the realities to which they ascribed value. Thus, as a 21$^{st}$ African American male, I am a contemporary of, say, Michael Jackson. However, I am a consociate of the editor of this volume, Joe Kincheloe. Whatever the experiences I have similar to Jackson's as an African-American male, they are only imagined or imputed. However, Kincheloe and I have actually struggled against various forms of oppression in direct ways. We are consociates.

198

This distinction between consociate and contemporary is important to note because more and more critical and postcritical ethnography (Noblit, Flores, & Murillo, 2004) has taken on this complex dimension as researchers seek to identify their audiences as well as their subjects. This is to say, what *knowledge* are you as researcher not only identifying/gaining an understanding of, but what *knowledge* are you also helping to create and how will you talk and write about it?

For example, one participant in my study, Akia, felt I was misunderstanding and violating the tricky relationship I had assumed with these women, and Black women, generally. As she said, "Damn it, Aaron, if you who read feminist literature, do this, what hope is there?" Her comments exposed the fact that so much sociological and anthropological fieldwork in the past failed because of a built-in betrayal potential. It wasn't so much an issue of bias in this case, as a divided loyalty—the continued commitment to the disciplines in which we were working and seeking to gain power, prestige and wealth (Menzies, 2001).

Akia's comments spoke to the vulnerability created for those we research when they choose to trust us. I made one critical assumption about the shared or modal experiences of these women—that is, those who agreed to talk with me: they had some experiences that they wanted to work with and felt drawn to share themselves and their concerns with me. Since these women all had both the personality and position to refuse me access, as a few did, they were not controlled by me; they were comfortable relating to me. They accepted the vulnerability of openness and relatedness.

Another collaborator, Regina, felt fear that the things I might discover might poison my affection for and faith in some Black women. She was raising, in a different way, Schutz's ideas of the difference in perspective that marks a consociate versus a contemporary. This Black woman recognized that I am potentially able to "act like a Black man" and to disidentify with the collaborators when their beliefs and behaviors cross my own identity matrix. This actually happened when I began analyzing and writing up the field notes.

*Interpreting the narratives* Grounded theory (Glaser & Strauss, 1967) is a method of analysis that builds on the assumptions of collaborative research, especially the interpersonal relationship between myself and the collaborators. Because I was caught up in the cultural context under study, my own values, views, and beliefs had to be noted and often set aside, although I strategically introduced these when appropriate. The monitoring of my own "stuff" is referred to as "bracketing" in grounded theory (Hutchinson, 1988).

Grounded theory is a method for generating an over-arching theory about a phenomenon. In this instance, "Black female racial commitment" was the phenomenon in question. The paucity of existing data in the 1980s and the ideologically charged nature of most social science research on African Americans at the time (i.e., the "Black matriarchy") and even now (i.e., "crack mothers") influenced my decision to use this methodology. Briefly, the stages in grounded theory included:

*The Research Question*—this was initially "How do Black women understand their own and others' racial commitment and the influences on it?"

*Data Acquisition*—using interviews and participant observation.

*Data Coding*—analysis of the interviews and recorded observations and reflections—coding—followed the three-stage process characteristic of grounded inquiry: open, axial, and selective coding. In the open coding phase, I essentially identified the variables—factors influencing and relevant to—racial commitment. These included such things as family history, group expectations, friendships, reference groups, political perspectives, definitions of race, racism, and self-other dependence. These ideas were labelled, categorized, and related to each other in a heuristic, preliminary fashion.

Axial coding involved the use of a "coding paradigm." This is a system of coding, guided by playing with the data in new ways, aimed at identifying possible causal relationships among the categories. Here, I was trying to understand the sense these women made of inherited and received notions of "racial commitment" and their own growth, changes, and positions. For example, the middle-aged, divorced mother who told a story of a single date with a White male in the context of raising her own concerns and questions about her daughter's almost exclusive dating of non-Black suggested several categories: exploration as commitment; rejection of choices as commitment; renegotiation of choices as commitment. Her story also indicated that choices—whether approaching or withdrawing from traditional values of "racial uplift"—were ultimately viewed as commitment and the ground for assessment. Thus, commitment to self was itself an expression of racial commitment; one marked by a shift from others' expectations and definitions to a personal definition constructed on subjective needs, experiences, and values.

The exciting moment came as these various stories rehearsed each other in terms of some of these recurrent themes/categories/relationships. Additional excitement for me occurred as I saw overlaps and reinforcement for the categories and flow of the emerging picture with earlier cited work by Gilkes, Kanter, and Jackson; and literary scholarship by Audre Lorde, Alice Walker, Mary Helen Washington and others. This was all happening during a period when there was very little overlap between racially radical and critical theories, especially around the ideas of dialectics, difference, and indeterminacy. So few established concepts adequately captured the subjective energy in these women's stories.

Selective coding, the final stage, involved the identification and selection of the core category and relating it to other categories. Trevor Barker and his colleagues (undated) have observed regarding this process: "The core category is the central phenomenon around which all other categories are based. Once this has been identified, the storyline is generated as a restatement of the project in a form that relates to the core category. Validation is done by generating hypothetical relationships between categories and using data from the field to test these hypotheses. Categories may be further refined and reclassified and the storyline may be further refined. This completes the grounding of the theory."

For example, during a particularly heated moment in her narrative, Eartha declared that she wanted to leave the planet; I refer to this as the "alien" or alienation theme or code. I later coded her material at higher levels of abstraction, describing the level one codes. So the "alienation" code shifted to "earthling" after relating it to another incident in which she referred to herself as an "earthling," while explaining her approach to people across cultures, races, classes, and sexualities. I coded these incidents as "earthling," and later, after further analysis of other incidents and her analysis of them, saw the major category of "earthling" as an expression of her separation-individuation journey or narrative: through various incidents—identified by me as incidents involving losses with specific Black men—she reached an understanding of her essential difference from stereotyped "traditional Black women." She embarked on a journey, traveling with a Jazz festival and reading fortunes, during which she met and engaged all sorts of unique, highly independent people. Throughout this journey, she continued to encounter and resist racial oppression both from within and outside of the African American context. Refusing to be defined into notions of racial commitment characteristic of this cultural context with respect to certain relational choices, she identifies herself as an "alien" ("earthling") and views her racial commitment as self-care and modeling options to others like her.

This construct developed in this sequence:

Level 1: alien

Level 2: relational self-concept

Level 3: commitment identity (relationship with self-other)

Description of self as alien is coded as feeling toward the world she experiences as oppressive and contradictory. "Alien" is a construct for the concept of alienation which includes ideas of normlessness, helplessness, powerlessness, isolation, and self-estrangement (Seeman, 1959). This relational self-concept was important. As one of the most detailed narratives, Eartha's material was a springboard for much of the initial theoretical sampling. Searching the narrative material for other representations or instances of relational self-concepts, I found a master category: earthling. This explained her identity, and her relationship as a committed Black woman to herself, the racial grouping, and the world at large.

Level three codes, illustrated in this case by "earthling," were theoretical constructs that drew on more than the data: they also included knowledge I brought to the project, emic (insider) and academic knowledge, etic (outsider). Working with codes in this way enabled me to both organize the data itself and to begin to relate the data in ways that promoted theory building. Theoretical sampling, a principal feature of grounded theory, was implicated in this coding. As the continual collecting, coding and analyzing of data in strategic ways, it enabled my accounting for all of the data gathered. By working with what data are collected in this way, one is able to identify new questions, pursue new data, and make additional refinements in the theorizing.

For example, I did not fully recognize initially the theoretical significance of the fact that most of the women who actually chose to participate in the study were engaged in racial commitment work with me. This is an important point: late in the study I realized that most of these women were not only clarifying, refining, and renegotiating their understandings and positions on "racial commitment, they were also trying to help me as a Black male to understand and communicate to my ultimate audience—the "Black Community"—the interactive, dialectical and shifting character of racial commitment in American society.

As my understanding of this larger dimension of racial commitment among these women expanded, I asked other questions and looked for other evidence in their narratives or lives that helped me understand this collusive feature of commitment processes. Interestingly, Audre Lorde had seen precisely this feature when, in an interview with Adrienne Rich, she spoke about the collusive bond forged by minority men and women (cited in Gresson, 1995). Her point was that racial oppression set up certain structural and relational conditions that encourage particular forms of shared narrative creation. These become racial narratives such as described by Blacks, Jews, Irish and other related groups. Something akin to racial narratives regarding racial commitment was co-constructed during the interviews and participant observations.

The theory of Black female racial commitment/individuation consisted of a core category, "self-other advocacy," that incorporated reflection, existential events, crisis, and investment of the self on behalf of self and others. Among the categories this core was related to were: social oppression (within and without group); self care/survival challenges; and enlargement of the community of concern. Variations among the collaborators' "self-other advocacy" were related to the nature of the experienced within group care, the pressures to remain constrained by traditional beliefs about racial uplift, opportunities for sharing and exploring alternative scripts and stories of self-other care as racial commitment.

Classical formulations of commitment theory have lacked a dialectical understanding of the integrative role played by women and its consequences for the psychological state of commitment. Black female individuation behavior is significantly integrative: it seeks to be inclusive of both personal and collective (in and out-group) conflicts and contradictions. Because of this tendency, Black female integration efforts, especially during periods of increased cultural upheaval, may tend to reflect the contradictions embedded in the culture as a whole.

The contradictions implicit in oppression seem to modify the popular description of commitment as a process of moving toward the in-group and away from the out-group. Among the oppressed there is a dual approach-avoidance process—one toward the in-group and one toward the out-group.

## DISCUSSION: THE RESEARCH AND THEORY

The issues generated by the construction of a theory were twofold. First, did the "theoretical sampling"—the constant comparing of categories and themes—sufficiently play through with the sample and data collection methods chosen? The "core category" or variable has to be a social psychological process which explains most of the variation in the data. The idea I found that met this requirement was "self-other advocacy." It occurred often in the stories; it linked much of the other material together; and it also explained much of the variation in the data.

I was able to relate this process—advocacy as rationale and agency on behalf of self and other—to categories created by the various coding stages. But how could I ensure rigor and ground the study empirically? My task was not to meet the experimental design (positivist) criteria for rigor or tightness; it was to show that the women's beliefs and behavior could be understood in non-pathological, non-recriminating terms. Moreover, I wanted to show that the continued experience of Black female racial commitment claimed by some of the more prominent Black feminist and progressive leaders was empirically grounded, at least in subjective terms. The degree of fit among the coded data or categories gave some credibility to this possibility and perspective.

The theory also seemed to work; it had relevance to some identifiable relational or social psychological process. In this instance, the self-other advocacy embedded in the choice to differentiate from the societally-forced notions of racial commitment was an act of commitment on the behalf of self and others who also had experiences and circumstances that might lead them to prefer to make similar choices.

Among the oppressed there is a dual approach-avoidance process—one toward the in-group and one toward the out-group. Beyond a scholarly interest in commitment issues, there was a personal concern: I wanted to learn more about the scope and content of Black female thought about racial matters. In my book, *The Dialectics of Betrayal: Sacrifice, Violation and the Oppressed,* I had focused on the scholarly discussions then occurring among Black academics and activists about in-group relations. This served as a theoretical context for the new inquiry. Before getting to this, however, let me explain the strategy of the study in terms of (1) theoretical and conceptual issues and (2) methods and methodology.

I began this study before critical discourse on "racialized" identities; that is, the obvious differences within socially defined groups was given less attention—we assumed despite evidence to the contrary that "Black" and "White" referred to some *essential* core. The ideology of essentialism dominated much scholarship and activism. In the late 1970s and early 1980s, only a few social and behavioral scientists concerned with racial identity issues were addressing in a sustained way the socially constructed nature of race (e.g., Gresson, 1995). While it was well understood that heterogeneity or difference was characteristic of Black communities, most still resonated to the idea of a "Black core."

"Difference" was seen as a choice to not relate to the core assumed to be there. At this point, the long tradition of intra-racial discord, called racial self-hatred by early social psychologists, had not been studied by scholars like psychologist William Cross (1991) or rhetoricians Mark McPhail (2002) or Dexter Gordon (2003). Influenced by some radical Black feminists (Ladner, 1973; Rogers-Rose, 1980; and Myers, 1980) and White Marxist feminist like Zillah Eisenstein (1979), I proceeded to formulate a research strategy that emphasized the twin notions of heterogeneity and agency-as-work.

These formulations contained decisions that were conceptual, theoretical, and ethical. Among design concerns I faced were sampling, data collection, analysis, and presentation. Within this study, I wanted to tell a holistic story—to find the unity within the diversity. This was my bias; this was my pain: fear of the loss of Black women to Black men in the face of tremendous critical—structural, material, cultural, and psychological—obstacles to the maintenance of the myth of racial oneness both imposed from without and embraced from within—during the early centuries of Euro-American oppression. My social responsibilities were to both these women and the fragile "Black community"—including me—that they had traditionally sacrificed on behalf. This social responsibility, as one researching from within, however, introduced issues of an intensified, if not altogether different, order than that associated with White researchers. Moreover, emancipatory action as an objective was equally as challenging for me to address in terms of researcher bias, contamination, and trust (Lather, 1986; Merchant & Willis, 2001).

I approached this study as an interpretive effort; I wanted to understand. This is important because I later evaluated what I understood. This happened because I became a participant and found myself being forced to split. I did not yet see my perspective as emancipation. By approaching the problem of Black women's racial commitments from these perspectives, I sought a research design that allowed me to collaborate with these women, as supportive to Black males and the community. I had a good deal of success: I gained the support of professional women who put me in touch with prospective interviewees; talked with me about my findings and experiences; and a number of interviewees returned to talk further with me or gain support me for other initiatives. For example, one woman who had been in therapy with me, asked to participate in the study in order to tell stories of women who had been battered, forced to give their children to their fathers, and seek shelter in mental health facilities while they regained their strength and made plans for the future. This woman called me a year after we had interviewed to come to an inner-city shelter for women and their children to provide counselling—not as a part of the study, but as a friend and ally—to a particular family. This former informant also wanted support in gaining better and more services for women like those in the shelter.

*Writing to Communicate and Validate*
This research was featured in my 1995, *The Recovery of Race in America*. Interestingly, this research proved more amenable for interpretation and presentation within communications rather than psychological or social science paradigms. In communications, I was able to talk about their communications as persuasive or non-persuasive to others and themselves. However, efforts to discuss the women's narratives as psychological phenomena drew me and the analysis into somewhat more essentialist, psychological evaluations. This was not my goal, but the effort to force my work and purpose into even a narrative paradigm was problematic because I was drawing on etic as well as emic resources.

These women's narratives were strategic for yet another reason. Historically, according to Kenneth Mostern (1999), autobiography was especially pertinent to the construction of racial identity. Since the categories ascribed to people defined as "Black" were constructions or abstractions, it was up to specific African American people to negotiate their identities in the contexts of their evolving, concrete— lived—experiences. The women, relating to me among others, were doing precisely this. Like more famous figures such as W.E.B. DuBois, Zora Neale Hurston, Malcolm X, and Angela Davis, these narratives attempted to construct and transform the shared meanings of racial commitment. What emerged from the interviews and encounters with these women were themes and issues and reasons that ultimately assumed the shape of a redemptive narrative.

The collaborative dimension cannot be overstated, nor the feeling that the fact that I was a Black male talking about these issues took us into very special places. Collusion as a researcher-researched notion assumed an unanticipated but crucial place in the forging of a story. I realized that racial commitment was expressed in the very decision to participate or not participate: those who participated reacted to me as a *Black* male, assuming a connection and commitment; those who ultimately refused, five in all, did so because of the visible pain and, sometimes, anger inter-action with me had stimulated. I had some nerve: trying to understand/study Black women. Only years later did I see/feel fully my own enmeshment with these Black women. I did, however, have glimpses of the peculiar bond I had forged with them. One night during a gathering with a group of Black male friends at the home of one of my closest friends, I spoke on the topic of Black male sexism and the hurt-ful ways we sometimes treated our women: two of the males there actually wanted to fight with me for saying these things.

On another occasion, when I was temporarily unemployed while writing up my dissertation study in Atlanta, my late mentor, a famous Black male gerontologist and University administrator, chided me gently: 'Aaron, you worry about these Black women, but if you were a Black female instead of male, you would have a job right now.'

The stories I shared with women, such as the above, helped enlarge the scope of their shared storytelling and often revealed some of the processes/events pertinent to commitment issues. For example, my candor about my own painful experiences with domestic violence as a child, led one collaborator, whose mother had asked me to interview her because she stopped dating Black males, to tell me a powerful story: her last Black boyfriend had threatened to beat her with his belt once just around the time that her sister had been killed by her husband with their toddlers present. She described in vivid detail how she had told him that if he did not kill her, she would kill him if he did beat her. Narrative episodes such as this were per-tinent to gaining a greater understanding of individuating behaviors, especially when these experiences were presented by the collaborators as clarifications of their ongoing renegotiation of commitment dynamics such as family disapproval of interracial dating.

This particular collaborator's narrative and my frequent involvement with the family yielded a massive amount of material. Her case was one of the richest sources of the data used to develop the categories and directions giving shape to the theory. Over involvement with the collaborators, enmeshment in the cultural context, and overwhelming by the massive amounts of collected data are all issues in this kind of semi-ethnographic, open-ended, and phenomenological investigat-ing. I struggled with all of these; and the results were not always satisfactory. But it helped immensely to have chosen grounded theory as the principal methodological strategy.

## CONCLUSION

Grounded theory (Glaser & Strauss, 1967) was the primary method informing my data analysis. The idea of "theoretical sampling" allowed me to play around with ideas drawn from the Black feminist and broader feminist scholarship on identity and personal agency. Black women literary scholars, in particular, were writing about the need for Black women to find and/or raise their individual and gendered voices (Gresson, 1995). This was the theoretical and conceptual context informing my formulation of a strategy that might uncover the lived-experiences—as self-understandings, rationales, and desires—of the women as their reflected upon their differentiating and reintegrating activities.

I began with some core theoretical concepts—notably self stories of fidelity and betrayal to traditional female loyalty—that were emergent at the time. These ideas were taken from my research on Black scholars' debates marking the 1970s and early 1980s (Gresson, 1982). I did not know where these issues fit precisely in the lives of the women I identified, but the issues themselves were clues to sampling. In grounded theory, which can be a complex process, the gathered data are constructed into concepts and tentative linkages are made between these and new, gathered data. In my study, I was not so much concerned with evolving a holistic picture as I was obtaining an enlarged vision of the "enlarged space" Black feminists like Mary Helen Washington, Audre Lorde, Alice Walker, and Joyce Ladner were seeking for representing the lives of Black women as self-referential and normative.

I did gradually move toward a core category, *the self-other recovery metaphor*, that allowed me to talk about these women as individuated—separated yet engaged and related—in their racial identities around matters seemingly divisive to the notion of a solitary Black community and racial core. The essence of this core concept was the collaborators' efforts to bring their own emergent race identity-experiences into some conscious harmony with the idealized or imagined Black male/community as materialized by me.

I did not fully see this process at the time, lacking the "native" researcher perspective that was just beginning to be articulated in some anthropology scholarship (Kuhuna, 2000). More precisely, the relationships I had established with these women did not lend themselves to the more detached, interpretive work I was required to take up in the formulation of a grounded theory. By becoming an integral part of the process, I was not able to detach myself in ways that allowed me to probe or dig deeper into their worlds in an "objective" rather than "subjective" way. This resulted in a truncated discourse and opened the way for biased and other evaluations on my part. These were evident during the interpretation and presentation phases.

This study was an important one to me personally and professionally. Personally, I was very much interested in better understanding the Black female-male relationship that I was living in 1980s New England. Professionally, I wanted to better prepare myself for clinical work with both Black males and females; and to strengthen my qualitative research skills. This study helped me achieve both goals.

When the study was finished, I was able to successfully defend the thesis before my committee. I had produced an acceptable, if more than a little disquieting, product.

This was 1985. Grounded theory and consensual interviewing and related techniques were not common approaches in studies focused on minority subjects. Publication of my work was another matter. For mainstream journals, my work was too loosely rigorous for a field trying to affirm its place along side clinical psychology and the more experimental sociobehavioral sciences. The other possible outlets, the newly emergent feminist book series, were interested but very fearful of appearing insensitive to attributed Black female proprietary rights to talk about Black women. A Black male was especially anathema in this context since this group was then the major conflict point for many feminists (Gresson, 1982). It was not until 1992 that I first published any of my results. This was a painful experience because I chopped up so much of my narrative material and critical perspective in order to fit the material into the format of the anthology in question. Suffice it to say that the over-arching point to be made here is that one be very careful in the writing phase.

In sum, qualitative research methods can be very helpful when studying complex, racialized, sexualized phenomenon within mainstream disciplines where little empirical and theoretical work exists to guide one in formulating hypotheses for testing. It is even to be preferred over quantitative methods in some instances where the enhancement of voice and agency are primary interests. There are cautions to using these methods, however; a major one, the one I encountered in my own work, is "going native" or getting too enmeshed in the phenomena under study. An emergent literature on "the native in qualitative research" (Merchant & Willis, 2001) can be helpful in this regard.

## REFERENCES

Alridge, D. (2003). The dilemmas, challenges, and duality of an African American educational historian. *Educational Researcher, 32*, 25-34.

Akhtar, S., & Kramer, S. (Eds.). (1998). *The colors of childhood: Separation – individuation - Across cultural, racial and ethnic diversity.* New York: Jason Aronson.

Baehr, A. (2004). *Wounded healers and relational experts: A grounded theory of experienced psychotherapists' management and use of countertransference* (Unpubl. Ph.D. thesis, Penn State University).

Berger, P. and Luckmann, T. (1966). *The social construction of reality: A treatise in the sociology of knowledge.* Garden City, New York: Anchor Books.

Chaudhry, L. (2001). "You should know what's right for me!": A hybrid's struggle to define empowerment for critical feminist research in education. In B. Merchant and Willis, A. (Eds.) *Multiple and intersecting identities in qualitative research.* (pp. 33-42). Mahwah, NJ: Lawrence Erlbaum.

Cross, W. (1991). *Shades of black: Diversity in African-American identity.* Philadelphia: Temple University Press.

Eisenstein, Z. (1979). (Ed.). *Capitalist patriarchy and socialist feminism.* New York: Monthly Review Press.

Fine, M. (1998). Working the hyphens: Reinventing self and other in qualitative research. In N. Denzin & Lincoln, Y. (Eds.), *The landscape of qualitative research.* (pp. 129-154). Thousand Oaks, CA: Sage.

Fishbane, M.D. (2001). Relational narratives of the self. *Family Processes. 40,* 273-91.

Gilkes, C. (1982). Successful rebellious professionals: The black woman's professional identity and community commitment. *Psychology of Women's Quarterly. 6,* 289-311.

Glaser, B. & Strauss, A. (1967). *The discovery of grounded theory.* Chicago: Aldine.

Goffman, E. (1986/1963). *Stigma: Notes on the management of spoiled identity.* New York: Simon & Schuster.

Goffman, E. (1973/1959). *The presentation of self in everyday life.* Woodstock, New York: Overlook Press.

Gresson, A. (1977). Minority epistemology and the rhetoric of creation. *Philosophy and Rhetoric, 10,* 244-262.

Gresson, A. (1978). The sociology of social pathology: Focus on black education. *The Black Sociologist. 6,* 25-39.

Gresson, A. (1982). *The dialectics of betrayal: Sacrifice, violation and the oppressed.* Norwood, NJ: Ablex.

Gresson, A. (1992). African-Americans and the pursuit of wider identities: Self-other understanding in black female narratives. In Rosenewald, G. & Ochberg, R. (Eds.), *Lived stories: The cultural politics of self-understanding.* (pp. 165-174). New Haven, CT: Yale University Press.

Gresson, A. (1995). *The recovery of race in America.* Minneapolis: University of Minnesota Press.

Gresson, A. (2004). *America's atonement: Racial pain, recovery pedagogy and the psychology of healing.* New York: Peter Lang.

Guthrie, R. (1998). *Even the rat was white: A historical view of psychology.* New York: Allyn and Bacon.

Hull, G., Scott, B. & Smith, B. (1982). (Eds.) *All the women are white, All the blacks are men, but some of us are brave: Black women's studies.* Old Westbury, New York: Feminist Press.

Hutchinson, S. (1988). Education and grounded theory. In *Qualitative research in education: Focus and methods.* (pp. 123-40). Sherman, R. & Webb, R. (Eds.). New York: The Falmer Press.

Jackson, J., McCullough, W, & Gurin, G. (1988). Family, socialization environment, and identity development in black Americans. In McAdoo, H. (Ed.), *Black Families.* 2nd ed. (pp. 242-56). Newbury Park, CA: Sage Publications.

Johnson, P. & Duberley, J. (2003). Reflexivity in management research. *Journal of Management Studies, 40,* 1279-1303.

Kanter, R. (1972), *Commitment and community: Communes and utopias in sociological perspective.* Cambridge: Harvard University Press.

Kincheloe, J., & McLaren, P. (1998). Rethinking critical theory and qualitative research. In Denzin, N. & Lincoln, Y. (Eds.), *The landscape of qualitative research: Theories and issues.* (pp. 260-299). Thousand Oaks, CA: Sage.

Ladner, J. (1971). *Tomorrow's tomorrow: The black woman.* Garden City, NY: Doubleday.

Lather, P. (1986). Research as praxis. *Harvard Educational Review, 56,* 257-277.

Mehra, B. (2001). Research or personal quest: Dilemmas in studying my own kind. In Merchant, B. & Willis, A. (Eds.), *Multiple and intersecting identities in qualitative research.* (pp. 69-82). Mahwah, NJ: Lawrence Erlbaum),

Mehra, B. (2002, March). Bias in qualitative research: Voices from an online classroom. *The Qualitative Report, 7*(1). Retrieved [February 22, 2006], from http://www.nova.edu/ssss/QR/QR7-1/mehra.html

Menzies, C. (2001). Reflections on research with, for, and among indigenous peoples. *Canadian Journal of Native Education. 25,* 19-36.

Merchant, B. & Willis, A. (Eds.) (2001). *Multiple and intersecting identities in qualitative research.* Mahwah, NJ : Lawrence Erlbaum.

Merriam, S. (1998). *Qualitative research and case study applications in education: Revised and expanded from case study research in education.* San Francisco, CA: Jossey-Bass.

Mostern, K. (1999). *Autobiography and black identity politics: Racialization in twentieth-century America.* New York: Cambridge University.

Myers, L. (1980). *Black women: Do they cope better?* Englewood Cliffs, NJ: Prentice Hall.

Seeman, M. (1959). On the Meaning of Alienation. *American Sociological Review, 24,* 783-91.

Stewart, J. (2004). Perspectives on reformist, radical, and recovery models of black identity dynamics from the novels of W.E.B. DuBois. In Stewart, J. (Ed.), *Flight in search of vision.* (pp. 107-127). Trenton, NJ: Africa World Press.

CHRISTINE A. LEMESIANOU AND JAIME GRINBERG

# 9. CRITICALITY IN EDUCATION RESEARCH

## INTRODUCTION

In this chapter we develop a critical framework to ground research work under-taken by researchers, practitioners, and policy makers. We address four fundamen-tal issues that should guide every research project: ways of knowing, what counts as real, marginalized methods of inquiry and power relations. As we will elaborate, consideration of these four issues should precede the specific decision-making re-garding the procedures of inquiry endemic to all research projects—the focus here is on the contributions of critical theory and critical epistemologies to a burgeoning conversation on the politics of research and the challenges and opportunities such endeavors raise. First, we present some data from a graduate student's research project to guide our discussion of the four issues. Subsequently, we provide the theoretical backdrop from which the critical paradigm emerges, and finally, we conclude this chapter by revisiting a 2000 special edition of the journal *Educa-tional Researcher*.

We begin here with some selected excerpts from semi-structured interviews conducted by a graduate student with a female participant in an Anger Manage-ment program mandated by the court. These interviews were part of an extended research project that also involved a 10-week ethnographic observation schedule of the program's sessions. The research project focused on emotions, identity con-struction and stigma. This project (Young, 2005) was completed in partial fulfill-ment of the requirements of a graduate course in Qualitative Research Methods in the Department of Communication Studies at Montclair State University.

Q: Tell me about your life . . . For starters, what was your childhood like?
Bonnie: *You probably wouldn't guess it but I was the happiest child. I was in Girl Scouts and 4H, and I always had good times with friends . . . I never thought my world would fall apart . . .*
Q: But it did?
Bonnie: *Yeah . . when I was thirteen my mom left and everything just fell apart . . .*
Q: It seems that you don't express anger in these sessions. Why is this?
Bonnie: *Well, I really don't know these guys. I mean, I've been with the group for a few weeks but they don't really know who I really am. So . . . I don't really feel like pouring my heart out here. Ya know?*
Q: Have things changed for you since you started with this class?

Bonnie: . . . *Once I got away from him . . . I started over, and it's been getting'*
*better ever since. . . My whole life is changed . . . But I admit, I'm getting' some-*
*thin' outta' this class . . . I mean, now I'm always stoppin' myself before I get*
*mad . . . Before I would just kinda' keep it down, but now I'm really thinkin'*
*about it, and it's not worth getting' all worked up over . . . Nothing is.*
Q: So, was there a time when you did let things get to you?
Bonnie: *Oh god, yeah, before this whole thing happened . . . Before the thing*
*with my ex and the cops . . . I was like a ticking bomb . . . I wasn't just angry, I*
*was depressed and anxious all at the same time . . . I was a mess.*
Q: Do you think men and women differ in how they express anger?
Bonnie: *Yeah . . . I mean . . . for guys it's OK to get all bent outta' shape . . .*
*Well, maybe not these guys, but you know . . . Like . . . it's no big deal—if a guy*
*punches a wall but if a girl does it, she's f.... crazy . . . I guess that was my*
*problem . . . I got as angry as anyone else but it wasn't okay . . . Like, everyone*
*always expected me to just shut up about it and not be me . . . So, I guess I'm not*
*your average girl.*
Q: If you could say anything to this group, what would it be?
Bonnie: *That they're only going to get better if they admit to their problems. I*
*think some of the guys that graduated learned from the class but this new group*
*. . . they're hang up on blaming the cops and the judges . . .*
Q: Anything else?
Bonnie: *I'm kind of sick of them bashing women . . . Maybe that's why I don't*
*say much . . . It's like a boys club . . . All the joking about women and sex . . .*
*It's really patronizing . . . it's like they have no clue. . . I mean, what am I? In-*
*visible?*

The interview excerpts above, although presented here in isolation from the rich
fieldnotes that accompanied all the interviews, raise some fundamental issues.

First, there are epistemological issues that inquire into the nature of knowing
and the manner in which a researcher can come to understand another person's
experiences. Can the experiences of women, or other marginalized groups, form
the basis of knowledge? Definitions of knowledge building arise from particular
paradigms that guide research and impose limitations on the methods of inquiry
employed and the interpretation of research data. Logical positivism, for instance,
has privileged patriarchal bodies of knowledge and requires a separation between
the subject and object of research and extols scientific objectivity. In this case, the
knower (student researcher) and the known (Bonnie) should be understood as distinct entities without a reciprocal relationship. The student here simply becomes a
reporter of Bonnie's reality and the researcher's identity positions, or the relationship of those identity positions relative to Bonnie, do not impact on that reality or
its interpretation. But as Haraway (1991) succinctly summarizes "accounts of a
'real' world do not, then depend on a logic of 'discovery,' but on a power-charged
social relation of 'conversation.' The world neither speaks itself nor disappears in
favor of a master decoder" (pp. 189-190). Alternative paradigms, such as the interpretive paradigm or the critical paradigm, which is the focus of this chapter, (see
Lincoln & Guba, 2000) propose more critical epistemologies that validate situated

knowledge, undermine the "view-from-nowhere" objectivism, and intricately connect the knower with the known.

Second, what is the reality of Bonnie's life experiences and can this reality be captured in an objective manner? Ontological assumptions about what is real similarly guide a research project (see Burrell & Morgan, 1979). Positivism assumes there is a single, objective world of facts and universal laws that can be captured without bias if the researcher uses the proper scientific methods and techniques (control groups, randomization, etc.). Such an examination of an Anger Management group and its interactions might focus on the pedagogical strategies administered during the sessions, attempt to assess their pedagogical value through a survey instrument in a pre- and post-test semi-experimental research design, and report aggregate data that either validate or disconfirm the overall usefulness of anger management programs. Is it possible that the production of a unitary and coherent narrative about lived experience can be challenged? In this specific context we have Bonnie, who is the only female participant and whose "reality" is marked by significant feelings of exclusion and marginalization. Would not such a research project, the questions it asks and the manner in which it frames questions potentially make Bonnie, to use her own words, even more "invisible?" As Marcuse (1969) argued: "The real field of knowledge is not the given fact about things as they are, but the critical evaluation of them as a prelude to passing beyond their given form" (p. 145). A critical approach insists that research is ultimately a political project that requires reflection and the interrogation of forms of domination and subordination.

Third, what are appropriate methods of inquiry that can provide insights into Bonnie's experiences and struggles? Methods of inquiry that take for granted an a priori reality ready to be uncovered have traditionally employed specifically stated hypotheses and mainly quantitative methods, in the form of experiments or survey research, that would provide verification of the hypotheses (see Lincoln & Guba, 2000). While these methods have been productive in the realm of education research, they have been historically privileged in the production of scientific knowledge and have been questioned by feminist and postmodern theorists extensively (e.g., Giroux, 1997; Harding, 1991; Hartsock, 1983). Conversely, other methods of inquiry such as narratives, autobiography, discourse analysis, case studies, and interaction analysis have been marginalized as legitimate research designs. We certainly do not mean to revisit here the dichotomy of quantitative and qualitative research methods, a heuristic that has outlived any usefulness. In problematizing methods of inquiry, we need to go far beyond typical issues that concern the codification and presentation of data. As Deleuze and Guattari (1987) point out, numbers can have "countersignifying" possibilities when the focus is on "arrangements rather than totals, distributions rather than collections" (p. 118), that is when such numbers aim to understand and expose the relations of production, distribution, and consumption rather than reaffirm the existing order of things. Harding (1987) addresses these issues explicitly within a framework that distinguishes methodology from methods of inquiry. Methodology, she argues, presupposes that the research is grounded theoretically and is consistent with fundamental ontological and

213

epistemological assumptions. By contrast, methods of inquiry involve the techniques of data collection and analysis that lend themselves to the particular questions and phenomena and the most appropriate ways of addressing them. These clearly involve the demarcation of boundaries, grids of organization and classification, and the reproduction of a social order from a specific vantage point that is embedded within social, political, economic, and cultural frameworks. Thus, a critical stance to research problematizes not only the questions we ask but also the very modes of inquiry, their presuppositions, and byproducts, which may at times normalize and neutralize.

Which brings us to the fourth issue, how are Bonnie's experiences embedded within broader social structures and power relations that shape her life and other group members' lives? An examination of Bonnie's reality from a disinterested, impartial, and value-free positivist perspective fails to take into account that societies are historical products of human activity and, thus, structured in a hierarchical order that oftentimes reproduces existing relationships of power and the status quo (see Burrell & Morgan, 1979). Bonnie's articulate expressions of "anger" should not be treated in an acontextual manner—rather, they form the springboard from which the gendered manner in which emotions have been historically constructed and valued in society can be unpacked. Understanding Bonnie's experiences requires, among other things, a critical examination of a social order that legitimizes, and indeed demands, certain emotional expressions for men and others for women (see Hochschild, 2003 for an in-depth study of gendered emotional labor) and critical interrogation of techniques utilized for emotional diagnosis and control (such as an anger management program which in this specific case seems to be reifying the cultural order and inadvertently subjecting Bonnie to further violence). Such a research project also requires that the researcher critically examine the purpose of research and who benefits from the research. Research can become a dialogic process that exposes the hegemonic manner in which states, institutions, and practices function. According to Gramsci (1971), "the state is the entire complex of practical and theoretical activities with which the ruling class not only justifies and maintains its dominance, but manages to win the active consent of those over whom it rules" (p. 178). Research is a process that unveils forms of subjugation and oppression, whether motivated by class, gender, race or sexuality difference, and can ultimately become an emancipatory project that is closely linked to political action.

Although many might consider the above four issues to be a matter of commonsense, it should not be surprising to find both education practitioners and scholars who disregard these issues when engaged in the ongoing struggle to produce relevant research that also makes a strong commitment to rigor. The remainder of this chapter revisits these fundamental research issues of epistemology, ontology, methods of inquiry, and axiology in more depth and proposes that research that obscures such considerations is constrained as an agent for positive social change.

## A CRITICAL APPROACH TO EDUCATION RESEARCH

Our view of the research process can be summarized with a simple metaphor: that of mapping. Producing research or maps are both highly volatile processes and engender the politics of representation. Consider that cartographic practices have historically allowed us to tell certain stories that highlight certain aspects of the territory and minimize the importance of others (Woodward, 1985). Maps, very much like research, incorporate the unraveling of historical events as much as the geographic locations of objects. Yet to treat a map as an accurate representation of reality, of a territory, is very problematic (Wood & Fels, 1992, p. 108):

> It is of course an illusion: there is nothing natural about a map. It is a cultural artifact, an accumulation of choices made among many choices every one of which reveals a value: not the world, but a slice of a piece of the world; not nature but a slant on it; not innocent, but loaded with intentions and purposes; not directly, but through a glass; not straight, but mediated by words and other signs; not, in a word, as it is but in . . . code.

Similarly, to treat research and its knowledge products as "real" fails to recognize that there is a situated researcher (epistemology), who asks specific questions that define the bounds of reality and inclusion/exclusion (ontology), utilizing selected research methods, for specific purposes and in specific contexts (axiology). While critical theory is by no means a unified set of propositions, a critical stance to research shares some basic tenets on these four issues (see Kincheloe & McLaren, 2000 for an extended discussion of theoretical divergences in critical theory). The following section elaborates on these tenets in the specific context of education research.

*Mapping Knowledge*

The ongoing struggle to reframe the academic "canon" across educational levels is but a starting point where we can investigate the working of contested methodologies and epistemologies. Involved in this struggle we often find education researchers and teachers, schools and their administrators, libraries, and broader communities of parents, students, political leaders, religious and legal organizations and other interest groups. The numerous attempts to ban books from schools and libraries, whether these challenges are brought forth on the basis of sexual content, gay-positive themes, racism, offensive language, violence, promotion of evolution, or misrepresentation of traditional values reveal that there is no universal understanding of knowledge and that various contenders apply situated and contingent interpretations regarding knowledge and truth. Books such as Darwin's *The Origins of Species*, Steinbeck's *Of Mice and Men*, Angelou's *I Know Why the Caged Bird Sings*, Twain's *The Adventures of Huckleberry Finn*, Lee's *To Kill a Mockingbird*, or Corville's *Am I Blue?* continue to be challenged in public schools and libraries today in efforts to define the canon.

Education too, as a discipline, is constantly striving to define its bounds. In this direction, feminist standpoint theorists have generated tremendous insights into the dynamics and politics of truth and method in the growth of scientific knowledge. Drawing from Marxist tenets, Hartsock's (1983) standpoint theory offered an initial critique of masculine epistemologies, such as positivism, and proposed that identity positions both structure and constrain our understandings of the social world. These paradigms result in normative narratives that shape how members of both dominant and marginalized groups navigate and interpret social reality and their experiences. What has traditionally been defined as the "canon" has functioned predominantly from a patriarchal, eurocentric, colonial, rational viewpoint and has represented the dominant class's interests and worldviews. She further proposed that privileged class, gender, and race groups produce only partial theories of reality since their very survival is not dependent upon a broader understanding that incorporates the subjugated subject's view of the world. The extension of this argument also posits that oppressed groups produce theories that include a broader array of interests and values since they have to contend with the dominant worldview. Oppressed groups have to "struggle for their own understandings which will represent achievements requiring both theorizing and the education which grows from political struggle" (p. 553). Knowledge is inevitably situated and positioned and there are multiple standpoints from which legitimate knowledge and meaning are produced. More importantly though, knowledge also functions as a means of legitimating existing power relations which a critical project aims to expose. Thus, in order to expose privileged ways of knowing in education research we must ask:

- What counts as knowledge?
- What are the historical, political, economic, cultural and social conditions under which it was produced and regulated?
- How, and by whom, was it legitimized?
- For whom does it speak?

Of course there are significant divergences in feminist standpoint epistemologies that are beyond the scope of this discussion. Two interrelated issues, however, promulgated by poststructuralist and postmodern critics complicate the above propositions. The first critique questions whether all women share the same standpoint (for extensive discussions see Collins, 2000a; Harding, 1991; hooks, 1984). Many feminists would question whether the privilege afforded a white, affluent, heterosexual woman in academe produces a standpoint that is representative of all women's experiences. How can a feminist epistemology support knowledge that embraces both diversity and truth claims? Collins gets around the problem of relativism by proposing that truth and meaning is what is validated by different interpretive communities (2000b, p.56). Thus, our production of knowledge needs to acknowledge difference in a broader sense, going beyond monolithic definitions of "woman" or other traditional dualisms of gender, class or race, and seek to engage critically with the issues and questions of different oppressed groups in the realm of education and schooling.

The second critique tackles directly standpoint epistemology's assertion that women's standpoint can reveal the truth about social reality, what has alternatively been labeled as "epistemic privilege." Indeed, if women's or other oppressed groups' experiences are just as embedded in social structures and socially constructed as are the dominant group's experiences, then a defense of epistemic privilege is not possible. This argument follows to a great extent Foucault's tenets in his genealogical work that investigates discursive formations. How can a feminist epistemology see humans as embedded within social structures and discursive formations that re-construct them as agents of knowledge, and yet also assert that marginalized groups can escape these discursive formations but dominant groups cannot? Harding gets around the postmodern challenge to epistemic privilege by arguing that the experiences of marginalized groups should "provide the scientific problems and the research agendas—not the solutions—for standpoint theories. Starting off thought from these lives provides fresh and more critical questions about how the social order works than does starting off thought from the unexamined lives of dominant groups" (1993, p. 62).

While the contradictions of standpoint theory have not been fully resolved, three key points can summarize what standpoint epistemologies have contributed to questions of knowledge. First, that perhaps a definitive, absolutist definition of knowledge should continue to escape us in an otherwise unstable and transformative world; second, that definitions of knowledge should remain local, contingent upon not just individual knowledge but also on a body of knowledge as the by-product of scientific communities and their practices which should be constantly scrutinized even if they appear to be favoring plurality; and third, that the knower is inescapably connected to the known. A more ethically grounded epistemology should demand that the knower subject herself to the same scrutiny to which the known is subjected.

In the educational research context, these key points become crucial. What feminist epistemologies have achieved so far, is clearly not a coherent metanarrative on the production of knowledge, but rather the inevitable conclusion that all knowledge is situated. As a result, several spaces have opened up whereby aspects of a predominantly female material and social world that were previously invisible have become legitimate spaces from where questions can emerge, knowledge can be generated, and reality can be transformed. It is only recently that women's experiences with sexual harassment and date rape have found a "name" and become part of a shared reality; and, it is only recently that these "named" practices have been deemed as criminal in the realm of policy. Education research that has made the crossroads of gender and schooling its focus has emerged and has expanded into more complex examinations of gender, social class, and race (e.g., Aggleton, 1987; McRobbie & Garber, 1976). And, as exemplars of the self-reflexive nature of standpoint epistemology, education research has also turned inwards—whereby education researchers argue that teachers have historically been constrained by education policies and completely marginalized from such policy formulation because experiential ways of knowing have been deemed unscientific (see Gitlin, Burbank & Kauchak, 2005; Smyth, 2005).

Standpoint epistemologies can make an ongoing contribution to education practice, research, and policy where previously disenfranchised groups can become agents of legitimate knowledge and their questions legitimate spaces for investigation. As West (1993) points out: "Even the critiques of dominant paradigms in the Academy are *academic* ones; that is, they reposition viewpoints and figures within the context of professional politics inside the Academy rather than create linkages between struggles inside and outside of the Academy" (p. 41, emphasis in original). Interrogating the standpoints from where knowledge production takes place is as crucial to a critical project as is the interrogation of the "commodification of difference." In the process of embracing the politics of difference, education researchers and practitioners must be vigilant not to co-opt difference in a manner that "strips it of political meaning but reformulates it as merely a matter of style" (Collins, 2000b, p. 61).

## Mapping Reality

How human beings and reality are apprehended and represented are clearly central considerations of a critical stance. If knowledge is situated in specific circumstances and contingent, then by definition the education researcher and practitioner must worry about whether her work excludes or erases. The education researcher and practitioner must also worry about an omnipotent authorial gaze and voice assumed during and after the research engagement (what questions are asked, how interaction flow is directed, what interpretations are attached to data, where and in what format products of research appear). A critical stance that aims to avoid essentialization or the production of oppressive knowledge must inquire into the manner in which power is both deployed and confronted in the research project:

- What is the position of the researcher vis-à-vis that of the researched and are they
- Involved in a dialogic process?
- Does the interrogation engage in thick description?
- How are reflective practices evidenced in the research project?
- How "layered" is the interrogation of the real?
- How are the products of the research ultimately presented?

Resisting the privileged position of the observer is paramount in what Geertz (1973) identified as thick descriptions that focus on the embodied knowledge of the researched and not the superior analytic power of the researcher. In this respect, the researcher, researched, and research are mutually implicated in constituting what is "real" in a process that Haraway (1991) characterizes as "interpretation, translation, stuttering, and the partly understood" (p. 195). A critical stance to education research proposes the co-construction of accounts that are sensitive to local knowledge and the actors' negotiated meanings (Geertz, 1983).

The translation process whereby local knowledge becomes scholarly knowledge is particularly fraught with danger for education researchers and teachers as it is deeply rooted in power relations. One way to mediate the power of ultimate authorship and potential erasure of local language and meaning is for researchers to check understandings and interpretations against those of others, and thus become "reflective practitioners" (Schön, 1983):

A practitioner's reflection can serve as a corrective to overlearning. Through reflection, he [sic] can surface and criticize the tacit understandings that have grown up around the repetitive experiences of a specialized practice, and can make new sense of the situations of uncertainty or uniqueness which he may allow himself to experience (p. 61).

Reflexivity has presented a powerful heuristic for a critical approach to research and has been variably attended to by theorists (e.g., Bourdieu, 1990; Schön & Rein, 1994). In Bourdieu's work, the "habitus," the enduring dispositions that position the self, can only be challenged reflexively once we acknowledge the "complicity of the unconscious" (p. 136). In education research, critical reflexivity raises serious issues regarding the role that schools play in the reproduction of social class, gender roles, and ethnic and racial prejudice.

The practice of reflexivity in schooling practices and teacher-student engagements can offer deep insight. We do not mean to advocate here a version of reflexivity that is based on modes of self-surveillance and control which ultimately lead to normalized practices in education; rather, we embrace reflexivity that recognizes that any examination of the social world requires challenging even seemingly taken-for-granted constructs such as "effective" educational practices, "special education" or "gifted" programs, and even "education." Further, critical reflexivity also recognizes the construction of artificial "boundaries" for research purposes. The questions we ask, and the manner in which we ask them, inevitably draw boundaries to our investigations of a complex and layered reality. Subsequently, the questions we deem irrelevant obscure aspects of that reality and produce accounts of the real that are ideologically and politically charged. The research accounts we produce have implications for those they speak of, and for. Recognizing that any research endeavor cannot map the real entirely since the human condition is far too multifaceted to be captured, many theorists advocate that researchers should apply some measure of "layering" to empirical investigations. Scheff (1997) refers to this as part/whole analysis whereby parts are considered in relation to their "nested contexts" and vice versa and Smith (1992) refers to such layering as the "production of scale," a mechanism through which varied structural and historical forces can be examined and their reproductive power problematized. As Freire (1985) argued, "Without critical reflection there is no finality, nor does finality have meaning outside an uninterrupted temporal series of events. For men [sic] there is no "here" relative to a "there" that is not connected to a "now," a "before," and an "after" (p. 70). Thus, the histories and geographies of the world researchers attempt to map cannot be ignored nor taken-for-granted—to do so, would be the equivalent of empirical ethnocentrism.

The critical approach to education research has produced some compelling accounts. An example is the collection of ethnographic works edited by Levinson, Holland and Foley (1996), which is particularly noteworthy for the theoretical and methodological rigor these studies bring to the critical ethnographic project and the varied spaces of interrogation of schools and schooling practices the studies open up and legitimize. Also noteworthy are the varied forms of voice and authorship these research projects embrace, which indicate what Foley (2002) sees as different reflexive practices and narratives in education ethnographies: theoretical, confessional, textual, and deconstructive narratives. From a critical stance, the representation of research accounts and the power afforded the researched to participate in this reflexive process are central issues that expand into a broader examination of methods of inquiry.

*Mapping Methods of Inquiry*

For over a century mainstream educational research in the US has been dominated and grounded in the paradigm of positivism. This tradition of research was frequently conducted through experimental and descriptive methods. It is important to note that these studies have generated knowledge that advanced our understanding of an array of important issues and has contributed to educational psychology, educational sociology, educational administration, special education, comparative education, and educational policy, among many areas of study. For instance, coherently with Deleuze and Guattari's argument discussed above about how numbers could be use (1987), it has helped to understand and document educational inequities (Bowles & Gintis, 1976). The systematic documentation of educational inequities is paramount for a critical analysis of educational opportunities that help interrogate how the system and organization of schooling and curricula function and in favor of whom, thus also informing the analysis of how power operates in education. This also has been done utilizing post-positivist approaches as in the use of portraits and cases informed by a critical perspective, including how emancipatory practices could alter these arrangements (e.g., Goldfarb, 1998; Goldfarb & Grinberg, 2002).

Throughout the 20th century positivist methods, mostly quantitative, grew in sophistication and complexity. However, following the discussion of feminist standpoint, at least two shortcomings were important to consider: (1) the construction of human beings, in particular children, youth, and teachers, as objects of study categorized a priori, and (2) the question of "construct" validity. It is to the second that we turn to question (Cherryholmes, 1993):

- Do the methods and instruments used really "measure" the concept or construct or are these constructs being created through the instruments and research methods, as it has been the case with "intelligence?"
- Does the research and its instruments answer the questions and problems that are asked or are these instruments defining the scope of the question or questions?
- And, more importantly, can always this line of research answer all of the important educational questions with which we are concerned from a critical standpoint?

These are not only questions of methodological rigor and approach, but also questions of meaning, relevance, and value (e.g., Cherryholmes, 1988). As already discussed in this chapter, knowledge produced in this tradition has felt short in terms of addressing issues of teaching practices, curricular organization, and intellectual engagement because it cannot adequately explain meaning and because by generalizing it ignores localized contextualities and situated knowledge. Furthermore, it has obscured the power of the actors or agents in terms of their own negotiation of educational experiences vis-à-vis not only the cultural or political context, but also in terms of classroom experiences, pedagogical and curricular, as well as institutional conditions, rules, and regulations of these experiences (e.g., Goldfarb & Grinberg, 2002; Kincheloe & McLaren, 2000). Thus, a positivist tradition of educational research has not and cannot answer an array of relevant questions pertaining to education, particularly in contextualized, contingent, localized environments. At the same time, it has created a hierarchical division between producers and consumers of knowledge, and contributed to create a false dichotomy between theory and practice in a field that needs to accept the intrinsic relationship between them (Grinberg, Goldfarb & Saavedra, 2005).

In that sense, other research paradigms and methodological traditions have been very relevant. For example, ethnographic approaches have not only contributed greatly to the understanding of school cultures and social contexts, but have also provided useful frameworks to analyze pedagogies and students' learning, while critical ethnographies of education help unpack power arrangements (Cherryholmes, 1993; Foley, 2002). Furthermore, an array of qualitative techniques, albeit resisted by traditionalists of positivism, have been developed and are used because they help answer different questions that many times deal more with value and meaning, and, furthermore, at times they emerge from practice and practitioners (Grinberg, 1994; Kincheloe, 2002). Phenomenology (Goldfarb, 1998; Polakow, 1993) portraits (Kozol, 1991; Lightfoot, 1983), case studies (Goldfarb & Grinberg, 2002), discourse analysis (Fairclough, 1992), historiography (Grinberg, 2005), autobiography/oral histories/narrative (Gallegos, 1998; Meier, 1995) genealogy (Labaree, 1992), semiotic analysis (Fischman, 2000), bricolage (Steinberg & Kincheloe, 1998), critical incidents (Herr, 2005), to name only a few, are valuable approaches that provide a deeper understanding of experience and meaning, and, when grounded in critical frameworks, problematize relations of power within the multiplicity of voices, contexts, and discourses. This could be so because categories and themes have not been created and imposed a priori, but they can emerge from participants' experiences, observations, fieldwork, documents, and so forth, while problematizing the relationships of researcher-researched and their positionalities, thus it incorporates and includes a relevant space for participants' voices and interpretations, which are also problematized without sacrificing rigor. In addition, these approaches are popular among practitioners who engage in systematic inquiries about their classrooms, schools, and communities because it has the potential to acknowledge multiple ways of knowing in situated spaces, which can be represented in multiple textualities (Kincheloe, 2002; Steinberg & Kincheloe, 1998).

Since research is a form of representation, educational research is mediated and represented in a textual form, whether it is with language or with symbols, such as numbers or tables. The point is that the representations always convey meaning and that meaning is contextual and contingent to its milieu. For instance, action research and practitioner research also alter the traditional asymmetrical power relation between researcher and subject because research questions are asked by those involved in the daily routines and data collection is conducted by them in the environments researched (Kincheloe, 2002; Price, 2000). Furthermore, researchers are participating in the events, and often the researchers are the practitioners themselves, while occasionally, this also involves students, parents, and community members (Goldfarb, 1998; Steinberg & Kincheloe, 1998). In turn, this could further democratize the production of knowledge and questions take a different dimension of practicality, relevance, and value. Then, solutions are localized and meaningful to those involved in the experience and in the particular context. Eventually, without criticality this research can be naïve and can help reproduce oppressive and repressive educational practices, and, furthermore, it risks the temptation to trivialize its potential by attempting to generalize from one specific context to another without properly addressing how power operates.

*Mapping Power Relations*

In order to unpack how power operates and to critically judge the merits, relevance, validity, value, and meaning of a research, a number of issues have to be addressed in relation to:

- Who asks the research questions?
- What are the types of questions asked?
- For what purposes?
- For whom are the questions asked?
- Under which conditions these questions are asked?
- How are these questions asked?
- Where are these questions asked?

Therefore, we use *critical* in this context as a descriptor for a systematic approach grounded in inquiry, multiple perspectives of knowledge and knowledge creation and constitution, questioning of validation of knowledge, and for what purposes (Anderson, Herr & Mihlen, 1994). Critical also is used as a construct that analyses the assumptions upon which we determine not only how knowledge is constructed or how research is conducted, but also in terms of who has access to what knowledge (Goldfarb & Grinberg, 2002; Kincheloe, 2002). Thus, critical is also utilized as a tool to analyze power arrangements in teaching and learning, as well as connections with larger contextual issues such as gender, social class, and race, among others (Cherryholmes, 1993). The person, the researcher is not divorced from the context, from the milieu, but because he, she, or them, are immersed in it, their positionalities have to be uncloseted. Problematization is a central task for a critical approach.

In a sense, the problematization of our research work, as researchers, practitioners, and policy makers, consists of an analysis of power arrangements. Power, in a traditional sense, is the ability to make others do something that benefits us—for example, to make or convince policy makers to support educational change. Historically, convincing was usually done by force or intimidation, but presently it is also done as complex advertising or as sophisticated rhetoric where research and knowledge have been played as neutral, objective, scientific and common-sense (Anderson & Grinberg, 1998). In this context, research has become an important rhetorical tool to convince responsible agents and/or the public in support of certain agendas such as privatizing public education. These agents include policy makers, practitioners, boards of education, union leaders, scholars, families, and students. Thus, we ought to ask:

- How do we do this research and for what purposes?
- How do we represent "results"?
- What counts as meaningful, valuable, and valid research?

These questions are relevant because power operates beyond cognition through what Gramsci (1971) explained as "hegemony," which is how ideology dominates public perceptions of reality because they are a form of "common sense." Foucault (1979) further proposes that power functions by disciplining not only the mind, but also the body and soul. As Anderson and Grinberg (1998) point out, "Foucault's view of power is illustrated by Jeremy Bentham's 19th-century drawings of the panopticon, which consists of a tower surrounded by a circular structure containing cells that are visible from the tower. The occupants of these cells never know if someone in the tower is observing them, but because they cannot see into the tower, they must assume that they are being watched" (pp. 333-334). Or, in Foucault's own words (1979):

So to arrange things that the surveillance is permanent in its effects, even if it is discontinuous in its action; that the perfection of power should tend to render its actual exercise unnecessary; that this architectural apparatus should be a machine for creating and sustaining a power relation independent of the person who exercises it; in short, that the inmates should be caught up in a power situation of which they are themselves the bearers (pp. 200-201).

We argue that if in this text we interchange the surveilled person by the researcher, we can better understand how power has operated in educational research to perpetuate a positivistic approach to knowledge construction and its methodologies, tactics and strategies, as taken-for-granted, common sense scientificism where the researchers have not only internalized this technology of power, but they are also the bearers of such technologies, thus perpetuating their own epistemological, and political, limitations. Again Foucault (1979) helps us here in analyzing how power "wished to regulate, to legislate, to tell the right from the wrong, the norm from deviance, the ought from the is. It wanted to impose one ubiquitous pattern of normality and eliminate everything and everybody which the pattern could not fit" (p. 167).

Why problematize? In a critical sense, the co-optation, trivialization, and subjugation of potentially liberating research practices that emerged to challenge, and drastically alter, the ways by which institutional power arrangements have historically benefited few at the expense of the rest, must be unpacked, problematized, questioned, and challenged in order to better understand how these processes of co-optation occur; therefore, the need for questioning, interrogating, and disturbing what is considered taken-for-granted, best practices, wisdom, common-sense, and desire in the dominant discourses. A research practice by itself is neither oppressive, nor liberating, and there is nothing inherently true about it. It is the particularities, the specificities, and the context, which explain how relationships are constituted. Liberatory research practices are surrendered within institutional contexts that constrain the critique and favor their demarcation and compartmentalization, thus forcing a closer analysis of the particularities of the enactment, the operation, and conditions of these practices. As Foucault suggested:

> The longer I continue, the more it seems to me that the formation of discourses and the genealogy of knowledge need to be analyzed, not in terms of types of consciousness, modes of perception and forms of ideology, but in terms of tactics and strategies of power. Tactics and strategies deployed through implantations, distributions, demarcations, control of territories and organizations of domains. (1980, p. 77)

Thus, educational research discourses and practices, even when they foster a liberal or a liberatory rhetoric, invite us to analyze their fragmentation, compartmentalization, segregation, demarcation, and colonization. This is particularly helpful to do considering Marcuse's suggestion that capitalism as a system of power arrangements has the extraordinary capacity of commodifying its own critique (1969). In educational terms this means the extraordinary tendency that the field has for appropriating critical discourses—packaging, incorporating, absorbing, and decontextualizing the critique, selling it as another technique—thus neutralizing them. Furthermore, we need to contextualize "problematization" within the violence of institutional discourses and practices. Building upon what Hannah Arendt (1964) called the banality of evil when explaining complacency within the Nazi bureaucratic apparatus, we need to focus on how evil power is exercised *against* the struggle to resist disciplining technologies in educational research. We have to unmask and denounce the malevolent enactment of everyday routinizations that domesticate, pathologize, and docilize individuals and groups.

A major purpose of problematizing is to understand how institutionalization, bureaucratization, compartmentalization, fragmentation, and specialization, serve to control, to domesticate, and to co-opt transformative approaches to research, their possibilities or spaces. These processes not only impair teachers, administrators, students, and professors, but also lead to the formation of discourses that rationalize and privilege ideas and practices over human relationships, over equity and justice, and over participatory and democratic approaches to research. We cannot afford to remain "neutral." Neutrality works in favor of the status quo, in favor of oppression because we choose not to denounce it, in favor of racism because we stay silent, in favor of an obsolete curriculum and in favor of a falling apart of school districts and public education because we let others make the decisions for us. Thus, educational research is always political because questions are not neutral since someone is asking the question within a particular milieu and within a system of ideas and interpretations. Analyses are not neutral, the researcher always has a positionality, and the instruments utilized for data collections are never neutral since they are also designed within a fabric of interests. This is not to shelve objectivity, but it is to accept the pragmatist notion of "solidarity" (Rorty, 1989).

A problematizing critical reading of research would also interrogate the value of the sacredness of educational research, which as with religion refers to an attribute denoting sanctity, deference, respect, and subordination. It also means that by being sacred, educational research is presented as deserving of veneration, admiration, and idolatry, thus it is untouchable, and cannot be questioned or challenged. In short what we are proposing, to problematize the sacred, is sacrilegious. The consequences could be terrifying. There will be penalties: If the sacred is violated, we can go to hell. Except that we will be sent to Hell not by a deity, but by those with the power to do so in the educational research establishment, and also with the exception that, ultimately, "hell" has been constructed in order to normalize, subjugate, domesticate, scare, and control any disruption, resistance, transgression, and public disrespect, which in educational terms often is constructed as unprofessional, immature, subjective, non-rigorous, poorly designed, narrow, non-collaborative, unbalanced, and so forth (Bourdieu, 1988). Having sacred discourses and practices in educational research facilitates the control of any outburst of contestation that may challenge the carefully crafted privilege of researchers who oversee the benevolent colonization of knowledge and common sense, as a form of hegemonizing and surveilling (Barker, 1993; Bourdieu, 1994; Foucault, 2000; Grinberg & Saavedra, 2000).

The connection between the construction of knowledge, power, privilege, science and religion has been explored among others by Toulmin (1990) in his book *Cosmopolis: The hidden agenda of modernity*. By reconstructing and contextualizing scientific progress during seventeenth century in Europe, he argued that science filled the vacuum that religious hegemony left as result of the misery of war, poverty, and disease. The breakdown of the power of the Church demanded a new Master Narrative, a new religion with its own institution, organization, procedures, hierarchies, and priests. Science and the scientific method, the modern university, and the expert scholar/researcher took on these roles. In a sense, the role is often similar to that of the librarian in Eco's *Name of the Rose* (1983), who kept control of what work or books were accessible and what books or work were not (as Aristotle's work on irony), thus of what counted as knowledge and what knowledge did not exist. We contend that in spite of the seemingly oppositional discourses between religion and science, the institutionalization of their Truths and hierarchies, as well as the ways by which power is exercised through research and its knowledge production have striking similarities. Of course, not a minor connection is that the modern university has its strong genes in the Medieval European university, which was dominated by the Church, and in which the highest degree obtainable was in Theology, comparable to a modern Ph.D., and interestingly, many of the great scientists of the seventeenth century who started to shape the modus operandi of scientific knowledge production, were educated in Jesuit universities (Toulmin, 1990).

In comparing the Church and the modern university we find that there are some common elements in place. The hierarchical organization is in place, having Deans, Chairs, and then senior faculty "mentoring" and socializing "novices" (Bourdieu, 1994). The scientific method is sacred and several scientists are sacred too. Even nowadays, the university's blessing of scientificism and scientocracy is so dominant, so prevalent, so penetrating, that even qualitative studies tend to be framed within the scientific method and justified within the scientific language and constructs such as with issues of validity and reliability.

Therefore, problematizing the sacred is not just about questioning practices, but it is also about displacing privilege and, in spite that there isn't any intention to offend anyone, by practicing problematization there is an element of "insulting" or "disrespecting" authority. But, can it be done otherwise when insult and disrespect are constructed and defined by the privileged, aiming at controlling and containing resistance? In the modern university and in the research community often questioning authority, doubting what is being said or done under the protection of these authorities, and deconstructing their discourses and practices, is not an option often exercised. Problematizing could be heretical, although the dominant discourses and practices grounded in a positivist common sense do need the heretic criticality in order to keep defining themselves as the sacred (Barker, 1993; Foucault, 2000).

Potential critical changes are commodified and absorbed within the Church, or the University and its disciplines, it is contained, arranged, localized, and categorized, in order to effectively oversee subversion and heresy, therefore perpetuating their own advantaged position in the hierarchy and it secures an advantage in favor of those on top of the hierarchy, the high priests or the modern researchers. Problematizing, as suggested above, is sacrilegious because it may disturb these power arrangements. The church, as well as the modern American university, responds yet to a greater power, to which they gratefully submit and serve, but that is not the power of a deity, it is the power of the agencies and foundations (often responding to corporations that created them in the first place).

For too long educators have been too complacent in responding to the audiences of legislators, business organizations, and CEOs who often are the central part of the problem, not of the solution, because in a circular way they are immersed in the discourse-practices that generate Truth and support such system of Truth generation because it benefits their own interest. These audiences should feel uncomfortable and threatened by an analysis that refocuses the responsibilities of failure on them, and by a critique that deconstructs the taken for granted discourses about the purposes of education. If these audiences feel insulted, it is because they recognize that they have been central to maintaining their own privilege and that of their social group. Our role as public intellectuals is to challenge these power arrangements by asking questions and researching how they operate, not by accommodating them in a dialogue or conversation ruled by their terms. For too long our role as educational researchers served to collude with the establishment and neglected our social, moral, and political responsibility as public intellectuals (Bourdieu, 1994). Problematizing the sacred methods, practices, and discourses of research and knowledge (and truth) construction in specific and contextualized spaces is one way to interrupt unjust, unequal, oppressive, silencing, and subjugating practices and it also serves to interrogate and interrupt the privilege and control of hierarchies of research (including its validities and reliabilities) in and out of the university. And then, we have also to question our own positionality as public intellectuals and researchers because, as Baynes, Bohman, and McCarthy (1987), argued that we researchers and intellectuals do not necessarily represent "the voice of Reason or Truth... [And do] not stand outside of every system of power... Criticism is then an instrument of struggle, with which the critic seeks to change, if only for the moment, the balance of power in the present regime of truth" (p. 98).

To conclude, we will discuss below the case of research in educational history as an example of how power operates within a community of researchers where its approaches are often non-positivistic, yet could also contribute to the construction of common sense and taken-for-granted ways of knowing.

## THE CASE OF RESEARCH AND RESEARCHERS IN THE HISTORY OF EDUCATION

A special issue of *Educational Researcher* (ER) in the year 2000 was dedicated to the discussion of the state and future of research in the history of education. This journal is one of the most circulated and read journals of educational research in America, and the American Educational Research Association (AERA) publishes it, which is the one of the largest organizations of educational researchers in the world. What is published in ER represents the mainstream of the discursive struggles over knowledge and method, epistemology and politics in educational research, thus constituting its common sense. Several researchers (Donato & Lazerson, 2000; Dougherty, 2000; Mahoney, 2000; Tyack, 2000) discussed what have been the dominant perspectives and relevant work done in the past four decades while providing interesting suggestions for research and programmatic agendas for this decade. For reasons of space we will not repeat or summarize their arguments here. However, we are interested in problematizing their arguments as examples of how criticality helps unpack how power operates in the constitution of educational knowledge.

In this issue of ER, Donato and Lazerson (2000) eloquently advocated the need for collaborative work with scholars grounded in other disciplines. Although research on educational history could be informed or could inform educational sociology, anthropology, philosophy, and so forth, it does not abandon the notion of historical work as a discipline carefully crafted and epistemologically and methodologically distinct from other disciplines, something that other disciplines also cultivate in order to maintain their own power arrangements in academic and institutional terrains. This construction has historical roots in the constitution of history as an academic discipline housed in the modern university. Such constitution, according to Novick (1988), is not only a result of methodological and epistemological developments, but it is also and foremost the result of political struggles over control and legitimacy, over who determines the rules of objective and scientific production of historical knowledge. These rules distinguish the professional historian (university professor) from the amateur historian (outside the sanctuary and sanctity that the university offers). History of education as a discipline is part of this constitution, not divorced of it. Maybe, new boundaries could be defined as educational cultural studies where other scholarly approaches could inform historical work and vice-versa, such as discourse analysis, semiotics, autobiographies, and/or genealogies.

This disciplinary exclusionism in Donato and Lazerson and the respondents is necessary since the attempts of the essays have been to reposition educational history as a potentially relevant area of scholarship attempting to better inform and shape educational policy, and thus regain status and privilege. Abandoning such boundaries may imply that educational history has no relevant place, or that it is destined to whither away. However, if there is commitment to continue with the research agendas suggested by Donato and Lazerson, then different forms of scholarship such as genealogy, biography, oral history, and autobiography, often neglected as historical scholarship, and areas of study such as cultural studies or folklore and religion are necessary (See Morcillo, 2000, for an excellent connection of these approaches). Furthermore, an important contribution of women studies and herstories to educational history, or the work done on the experiences of underrepresented populations, different ethnic groups, histories of disabilities, and/or histories of populations constructed as "other," (Grinberg & Saavedra, 2000) is that of looking into everyday experiences, the routines, meanings, and formation of identities vis-à-vis education (Finkelstein, 1992). Such work demands not only a different type of conceptualization and a different type of theoretical analysis, but also a more comprehensive and less traditional methodological approach.

Another theme that emerged in Donato and Lazerson (2000) is the essentialization of categories such as women, Latinos, and so forth. Essentialization is a typical phenomenon in educational research. By essentializing these categories the result is a limited analysis of power relations within these categories. For instance, the educational experience of an educated affluent African-American woman is probably different from the educational experience of the African-American woman who cleans the bathroom of the educated affluent woman. Furthermore, post-colonial critiques (e.g., Carlson, 1998; Dhillon, 1999; Fanon, 1952; Gallegos, 1998) unpacked the dynamics of internal colonization and the role of the colonized minorities that operate as educational brokers in perpetuating oppression, marginality, and asymmetric access to knowledge in order to advantage themselves at the expense of their own ethnic, gender, and/or racial entourage (Carlson, 1998; Cordova, 1997; Darder, 1997; Gallegos, 1998; Grinberg & Saavedra, 2000; Grinberg, Goldfarb & Saavedra, 2005). At this intersection of dessentialized categories, of different standpoints, and of different experiences is where the advocacy for crossing categories could have been made more explicit.

As an example of how power operates to define knowledge through essentialising categories, in the subsection on the educational history of Latinos in the same journal issue (p. 8), there was only one work cited on the history of Mexican-Americans. Yet, as Donato (1997) has remarked, the Southwest has been a problematic area to study since many Hispanics are not Mexican-Americans, but are Chicanos (Mestizos, the mix of Spanish colonizers and American Indians). For instance, in Northern New Mexico and Southern Colorado, many Hispanic groups consider themselves Spanish-Americans, who never recognized Mexican sovereignty and who were well settled for almost 300 years before becoming part of the American territory (North-American) (Grinberg & Saavedra, 2000). Thus, for these groups it is not a history of education of immigrants as it is for many Latinos/as, but a history of education, colonization, dispossession and accommodation, where there were winners and losers not only in terms of Anglo-Hispanic categories, but also within Hispanic populations. Moreover, the problem was also one of a struggle of a colonizing, privileged population of aristocratic descendants of Spanish conquerors, and their losing ground to the new colonizer after the Treaty of Guadalupe Hidalgo (Grinberg & Saavedra, 2000). In this equation some of the old privileged classes maneuvered to maintain their privilege at the expense of their own, becoming agents for the new colonizing power. Therefore, although Hispanics had agency, it is important to study in favor of what this agency operated and under what circumstances. At times, this agency perpetuated colonization in a symbolic way by benefiting a class of educational brokers who acted as colonized minorities (Carlson, 1998; Cordova, 1997; Gallegos, 1998; Grinberg & Saavedra, 2000). In addition, certainly Hispanics and Mexican-American educational histories are different from Cuban, Dominican, Puerto Rican, or other Latino/a histories and those of many other immigrants of the late 1890s and of the late 1990s. Thus, advocating for a critical lens in a more regional and localized work could be extremely relevant.

Another issue we want to address from a critical perspective is the coinciding argument of all the authors in this issue of ER about making educational history more relevant to policy makers. There are two aspects to consider. First, as Jay Featherstone (1991) has argued, we live in the "United States of Amnesia" (p. xi). This means that the cultural context is not one in which history seems to be relevant to the conceptualization or to the unpacking of the present in terms of its constitution, its master narratives, regimes of truth, and contradictory discourses. It also means, that often when historical research on education is used, it has been mostly utilized to support and legitimize already defined agendas by interest groups. Institutions of higher education, which are the places where most educational historians reside, have an intentionally constructed entanglement with the practice of shaping social policy and providing the know-how knowledge for social engineering, thus always working to improve the system, making it effective and efficient, but not transforming it (see Popkewitz, 1991, for an excellent discussion of this topic). Perhaps, an alternative line of scholarship grounded on a critical perspective will be one that represents total independence from the agendas of the American universities and abandons the temptation of corrupting educational history and selling out to the corporatization of higher education and the role of external foundations and agencies that shape what can be asked and for what purposes.

By doing a comprehensive review of the state of educational history as a discipline, Donato and Lazerson (2000) had to make choices, organize thematic issues and highlight relevant pieces of work. By doing so, they also established the notion of authority in the field. This means that the works cited comprise the relevant and influential work in educational history. By virtue of participation and by virtue of being cited, the work and the scholars are positioned as the ones who determine what counts as relevant work, what counts as good scholarship, and what the agendas should be about if ones' work is to be considered good scholarship.

This is not a critique of the work cited and the scholars who participated in that particular issue of ER since indeed their work is generally of superb quality, but it highlights how a field of study constitutes its power arrangements (e.g., Anderson & Grinberg, 1998; Foucault, 2000) and how behavior in terms of procedures and methods, and minds in terms of questions, topics, and conceptualizations, are controlled. In short, Donato and Lazerson and their respondents have done an outstanding job, but by doing so they also contributed to privileging individuals, research methods, epistemological grounding, and neglected to raise critical issues about disciplinary and institutional relationships. If some form of research in the history of education is to be relevant in critical terms, the alternatives are: (1) to expand the ways by which data are gathered and represented by using more models and connections; and (2) to abandon its own imposed disciplinary boundaries, challenge the disciplinary boundaries of other fields, and engage in a type of scholarship relevant to the advancement of a just social and educational theory and practice by problematizing and disturbing what has been taken for granted, including the routines of knowledge constitution (Foucault, 1990).

Therefore, the example of problematizing the constitution of knowledge in the history of education brought us back to the argument that there is not one categorical truth regarding what is meaningful, valuable, and valid. Issues of method, paradigm, and representation are part of tactics and strategies of power, which in a critical stance obligate us to ask:

- In favor of whom are we doing it?
- Who benefits?
- Who are the winners and losers?

We as scholars and practitioners of educational research have to be alert and problematize even research approaches that seemingly are humane and progressive, and incorporate voice and meaning, including the researchers' standpoint and positionality, as Anderson and Grinberg (1998) have argued:

> More recent discourses calling for collaborative action research and teacher and administrator study groups can either open up authentic spaces or discipline school professionals through what Foucault calls pastoral power... based on the religious practice of the confessional, reaches inside people's minds, explores their souls, and makes them reveal their innermost secrets... The point here is not that one or the other disciplinary practice is better or worse but that neither is inherently good or bad (p. 343).

## REFERENCES

Aggleton, P. (1987). *Rebels without a cause*. London: Falmer.

Anderson, G. & Grinberg, J. (1998). Educational administration as disciplinary practice: Appropriating Foucault's view of power, discourse, and method. *Educational Administration Quarterly, 34*, 329-353.

Anderson, G, Herr, K., & Mihlen, A. (1994). *Studying your own school.* CA: Corwin Press

Arendt, H. (1964). *Eichman in Jerusalem: A report in the banality of evil.* New York: Viking.

Barker, J. (1993). Tightening the iron cage: Concertive control in self-managing teams. *Administrative Science Quarterly, 38*, 408-437.

Baynes, K., Bohman, J, & McCarthy, T. (Eds.) (1987). *After philosophy: End or transformation?* Cambridge, MA: MIT.

Bourdieu, P. (1988). *Homo academicus.* Stanford, CA: Stanford University Press.

Bourdieu, P. (1994). *Academic discourse.* Stanford, CA: Stanford University Press.

Bourdieu, P. (1990). *In other words: Essays towards a reflexive sociology.* Chicago: University of Chicago Press.

Bowles, S. & Gintis, H. (1976). *Schooling in capitalist America: Educational reform and the contradictions of economic life.* New York : Basic Books.

Burrell, G., & Morgan, G. (1979). *Sociological paradigms and organizational analysis.* London: Heinemann.

Carlson, D. (1998). Self education: Identity, self, and the new politics of education. In D. Carlson & M. Apple (Eds.), *Power/knowledge/pedagogy: The meaning of democratic education in unsettling times* (pp. 191-200). Boulder, CO: Westview Press.

Cherryholmes, C. (1993). Reading research. *Journal of Curriculum Studies, 25*, 1-32.

Collins, P. H. (2000a). *Black feminist thought.* New York: Routledge.

Collins, P. H. (2000b). What's going on? Black feminist thought and the politics of postmodernism. In E. A. St. Pierre & W. S. Pillow (Eds.), *Working the ruins: Feminist poststructural theory and methods in education* (pp. 41-73). New York: Routledge.

Cordova, T. (1997). Power and knowledge: Colonialism in the academy. *Taboo, The Journal of Culture and Education, II*, Fall. 209-234.

Darder, A. (1997). Creating the conditions for cultural democracy in the classroom. In Darder, A., Torres, R., & Gutierrez, H. (Eds.) *Latinos and education: A critical reader.* NY: Routledge.

Deleuze, G., & Guattari, F. (1987). *A thousand plateaus: Capitalism and schizophrenia* (B.

Massumi, Trans.). Minneapolis: University of Minneapolis Press.

Dhillon, P. (1999). (Dis)locating thoughts: Where do the birds go after the last sky? In T. Popkewitz & L. Fendler (Eds.), *Critical theories in education* (pp. 191-207). New York: Routledge.

Donato, R. (1997). *The other struggle for equal schools: Mexican Americans during the civil rights movement.* New York: SUNY.

Donato, R. & Lazerson, M. (2000). New directions in American educational history: Problems and prospects. *Educational Researcher, 29*, 4-15.

Dougherty, J. (2000). Are historians of education "bowling alone'? Response to Donato and Lazerson. *Educational Researcher, 29*, 16-17.

Eco, U. (1983). *The name of the rose.* San Diego, CA: Harcourt Brace Jovanovich

Fairclough, N. (1992). *Discourse and social change.* Cambridge, UK: Polity.

Fanon, F. (1952). *Black skin, white masks.* New York: Grove Press.

Featherstone, J. (1991). Foreword. In K. Jervis & C. Montag (Eds.), *Progressive education for the 1990s* (ix-xiii). New York: Teachers College Press.

Finkelstein, B. (1992). Education historians as mythmakers. In C. Grant (Ed.), *Review of research in education, 18,* (pp. 255-297). DC: AERA.

Fischman, G. (2000). *Imagining teachers.* NY: Rowman & Littlefield.

Foley, D. E. (2002). Critical ethnography: The reflexive turn. *International Journal of Qualitative Studies in Education, 15*, 469-490.

Foucault, M. (1979). *Discipline and punish: The birth of the prison.* New York: Vintage.

Foucault, M. (1980). *Power/knowledge: Selected interviews and other writings by Michel Foucault, 1972-1977* (C. Gordon, Ed.). New York: Pantheon.

Foucault, M. (1990). *Politics, philosophy, culture: Interviews and other writings, 1977-1984* (Edited by Lawrence Kritzman). Great Britain: Routledge.

Foucault, M. (2000). *Power: Essential works of Foucault, 1954-1984, Volume III* (P. Rabinow, Ed.). New York: New Press.

Freire, P. (1985). *The politics of education: Culture, power and liberation* (Trns. D. Macedo). Boston, MA: Bergin & Garvey Publishers.

Gallegos, B. (1998). Remember the Alamo: Imperialism, memory, and postcolonial educational studies. *Educational Studies, 29*, 232-247.

Geertz, C. (1973). *The interpretation of cultures.* New York: Basic Books.

Geertz, C. (1983). *Local knowledge.* New York: Basic Books.

Giroux, H. (1997). *Pedagogy and the politics of hope: Theory, culture, and schooling.* Boulder, CO: Westview.

Gitlin, A., Burbank, M. D., & Kauchak, D. (2005). The struggle for legitimate knowledge: Teachers' thinking on research. In F. Bodone (Ed.), *What difference does research make and for whom?* (pp. 111-128). New York: Peter Lang.

Goldfarb, K. (1998). Creating sanctuaries for Latino immigrant families: A case for the schools. *The Journal for a Just and Caring Education, 4*, 454-466.

Goldfarb, K. & Grinberg, J. (2002). Leadership for social justice: Authentic participation in the case of a community center in Caracas, Venezuela. *Journal of School Leadership, 12*, 157-173.

Gramsci, A. (1971). *Selections from the prison notebooks* (Eds. And Trans. Q. Hoare & G. Nowell-Smith). London: Lawrence & Wishart.

Grinberg, J. (1994). From the margins to the center: Teachers' emerging voices through inquiry. In R. Martusewicz & W. Reynolds (Eds.), *Inside/out: Contemporary critical perspectives in education* (pp. 121-137). NY: St. Martin's Press.

Grinberg, J. (2005). *Teaching like that: The beginnings of teacher education at Bank Street.* New York: Peter Lang.

Grinberg, J. & Saavedra, E. (2000). The constitution of bilingual/ESL education as a disciplinary practice: Genealogical explorations. *Review of Educational Research, 70*, 419-441.

Grinberg, J., Goldfarb, K., & Saavedra, E. (2005). Con coraje y con pasion: The schooling of Latinas/os and their teachers' education. In P. Pedraza & M. Rivera (Eds.), *Latino education: An agenda for community action research* (pp. 227-254). Mahwah, N.J.: Lawrence Erlbaum Associates.

Haraway, D. J. (1991). *Simians, cyborgs and women: the reinvention of nature.* London: Free Association Books.

Harding, S. (Ed.). (1987). *Feminism and methodology: Social science issues.* Bloomington, IN: Indiana University Press.

Harding, S. (1991). *Whose science? Whose knowledge? Thinking from women's lives.* Ithaca, NY: Cornell University Press.

Harding, S. (1993). Rethinking standpoint epistemology: What is 'strong objectivity'? In L. Alcoff & E. Potter, (Eds.), *Feminist epistemologies*, (pp. 49-82). London: Routledge.

Hartsock, N. C. M. (1983). *Money, sex, and power.* New York: Longman.

Hochschild, A. R. (2003). *The managed heart: Commercialization of human feeling.* Berkeley, CA: University of California Press.

Herr, K. (2005). Administrators mandating mediation: tools of institutional violence cloaked in the discourse of reconciliation. *Journal of leadership in education, 8*, 21-33.

hooks, b. (1984). *Feminist theory: From margin to center.* Boston: South End Press.

Kincheloe, J. (2002). *Teachers as researchers: Qualitative inquiry as a path to empowerment (2nd. Edition).* New York: Routledge.

Kincheloe, J. L., & McLaren, P. (2000). Rethinking critical theory and qualitative research. In N. K. Denzin & Y. S. Lincoln (Eds.), *Handbook of qualitative research*, (pp. 279-313). Thousand Oaks, CA: Sage.

Kozol, J. (1991). *Savage inequalities: Children in America's schools.* New York: Harper.

Labaree, D. F. (1992). Power, knowledge, and the rationalization of teaching: A genealogy of the movement to professionalize teaching. *Harvard Educational Review, 62*, 123-154.

Lightfoot, S. L. (1983). *The good high school: Portraits of character and culture.* New York : Basic Books.

Levinson, B. A., Holland, D. C., & Foley, D. E. (Eds.) (1996). *The cultural production of the educated person: Critical ethnographies of schooling and local practice.* New York: SUNY.

Lincoln, Y. S., & Guba, E. G. (2000). Paradigmatic controversies, contradictions, and emerging confluences. In N. K. Denzin & Y. S. Lincoln (Eds.), *Handbook of qualitative research,* (pp. 163-188). Thousand Oaks, CA: Sage.

Mahoney, K. (2000). New times, new questions. *Educational Researcher, 29*(8), 18-19.

Marcuse, H. (1969). *Negations.* Boston, MA: Beacon.

McRobbie, A., & Garber, J. (1976). Girls and subcultures. In S. Hall & T. Jefferson (Eds.), *Resistance through rituals* (pp. 209-222). London: Routledge.

Meier, D. (1995). *The power of their ideas: Lessons for America from a small school in Harlem.* Boston, MA: Beacon Press.

Morcillo, A. (2000). *True Catholic womanhood.* DeKalb, IL: Northern Illinois University Press.

Novick, P. (1988). *That noble dream: The "objectivity question" and the American historical profession.* Cambridge: Cambridge University Press.

Polakow, V. (1993). *Living on the edges: Single mothers and their children in the other America.* Chicago : University of Chicago Press.

Popkewitz, T. (1991). *A political sociology of educational reform: Power/knowledge in teaching, teacher education, and research.* NY: Teachers College Press.

Price, J. (2000). *Against the odds: The meaning of school and relationships in the lives of six young African-American men.* Stamford: Ablex.

Rorty, R. (1989). *Contingency, irony, and solidarity.* New York: Cambridge University Press.

Scheff, T. J. (1997). *Emotions, the social bond, and human reality: Part/whole analysis.* New York: Cambridge University Press.

Schön, D. A. (1983). *The reflective practitioner.* New York: Basic.

Schön, D. A., & Rein, M. (1994). *Frame reflection: Toward the resolution of intractable policy controversies.* New York: Basic.

Smith, N. (1992). Contours of a spatialized politics: Homeless vehicles and the production of geographic scale. *Social Text, 33*, 54-81.

Smyth, J. (2005). Policy research and "damaged teachers": Towards an epistemologically respectful paradigm. In F. Bodone (Ed.), *What difference does research make and for whom?* (pp. 141-160). New York: Peter Lang.

Steinberg, S. & Kincheloe, J. (Eds.)(1998). *Students as researchers: Creating classrooms that matter.* PA: Palmer Press.

Toulmin, S. (1990). *Cosmopolis: The hidden agenda of modernity.* New York: Free Press.

Tyack, D. (2000). Reflections on histories of U.S. education. *Educational Researcher, 29*, 19-20.

West, C. (1993). *Race matters.* Boston: Beacon Press.

Wood, D. & Fels, J. (1992). *The power of maps.* New York: Guilford Press.

Woodward, D. (1985). Reality, symbolism, time, and space in medieval world maps. *Annals of the Association of American Geographers, 75*, 510-521.

Young, A. M. (2005). *Expressions of a "mad" woman: The observations of a lone woman in anger management.* Unpublished manuscript, Montclair State University, New Jersey.

WOLFF-MICHAEL ROTH

# 10. CONVERSATION ANALYSIS

*Deconstructing Social Relations in the Making*

"The university makes us go through all this," the secretary tells me after I complained about the paperwork associated with getting a student to graduate. I respond, "We all are the university, you, I and everybody else. The university only exists in and through our actions. Thus, we can change the university by changing our actions."

This or similar little episodes may be familiar to readers. It exhibits two very different attitudes about social life, social organization, and social relations. One the one hand, there is the belief that organizations and relations exist out there, independent of our actions and interactions. We are but dopes filling the slots provided in the collectivity (group, organization, or society) in and of which we are a part, made to operate by internal (psychological) laws and genes. We simply play the roles that someone else created—teacher, administrator, or student—animated by some internal mechanism. What I told the secretary, on the other hand, is a very different orientation. Social organizations such as the university only exist in and through our actions and, relevant to the present chapter, to our interactions with the surrounding social and material world (Boden, 1994). We best think of them as fields that provide resources and constraints to our actions. Without the structures constituted by resources and constraints, it makes little sense to talk about action; but without actions, it does not make sense to talk about structures that are both prerequisite conditions and outcomes of our actions. We continuously produce|reproduce social life by interacting with others, not only as it pertains to the particular relationship with another person but also as it pertains to society at large.[1] But how do we do this? To provide a gloss of this chapter's topic, we produce|reproduce social structure in and through conversation. This chapter is about conversation analysis, an analytic process that can be used to reveal how we continuously produce|reproduce society and social relations in and through everyday face-to-face interactions.

## A DEMONSTRATION

*Event: Reading/Interpreting a Graph*

To provide some concrete situation, which we can take as a form of ground against which theoretical and methodological considerations can be checked, let us take a look at the following episode involving Anne and Dan. Dan has asked Anne to

*K. Tobin & J. Kincheloe, (eds.), Doing Educational Research—A Handbook, 235–267.*

interpret a graph displaying birthrate and death rate of some population (the graph can be found in the offprints in Figure 10..1). As part of the arrangement that brought them together, she is supposed to tell Dan how the birthrates and death rates affect the population. (The transcription conventions are discussed in the text and are also available in Note 2.[2])

**Episode 1**

```
01 A:    ((Fig. 1a)) SO Υ(0.43)           /
02              ≤((puts paper down))ʃ
03       (0.43) ((hits table hard with hand)) (0.54) HERe
04       (0.21) we have the ((Fig. 1b)) (2.11) ((Fig. 1c))
05       dEATh rate ((Fig. 1d)) increasing (0.68) an the
06       BIRTHrate ((Fig. 1e)) increasing ((traces
07       birthrate)) and the birthrate is increasing
08       (0.76) fA:Ster (0.87) than the death rate. (1.80)
09       So they are bOTh increasing but the birthrate
10       envi- increasing faster than the death rate so
11       preSUMmably that means that the population is
12       increasing. ((Fig. 1f))
13       (0.93)
14       is that right then?
15       (0.96)
16 D:    u:m::
17       (0.44)
18 A:    Υ((Fig. 1f, circles))/
         ≤round Υthis⁄region?.ʃ
19 D:              ≤hhh ʃ
20       (0.78)
21 D:    um ((Fig. 1g)) YEAh if you take- (0.20) well
22       shall I think I should (stay out?)- if you took
23       □birth minus the death⁄
24 A:    ≤((Fig. 1h, circles ))ʃ
25       (0.56)
26 D:    OR the birth plus the death (0.11) rate which is
27       negative, you are gonna get s:omething positive
28       (0.78) u growth rate right?
29 A:    yea ΥI'M□ looking at the slopes of the curves=
30 D:    ≤so ʃ                   =oh, okay.
31
```

In this episode, we notice how Anne signals in three ways that she is ready to start: first she says louder than normal "SO"; then, she lays the sheet with the graph and instruction flat on the table, which gets her ready to use the hand for pointing (Figure 10..1a–b); after a very brief pause, she hits the desktop with her

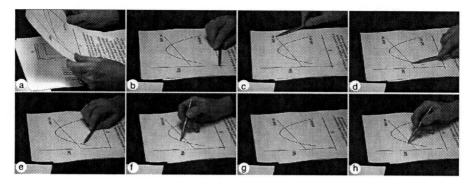

*Figure 10.1. The video offprints feature Anne's hand(s) at different instances during a session in which she interprets a graph from biology.*

palm. She then describes the two lines labeled death rate (line 05) and birthrate as "increasing" (line 06), stressing (see underline in transcript) or pronouncing certain syllables much louder than normal (see capital letters with or without underline). She then compares the two increases (line 07–line 08), notes that birthrate is increasing faster than the death rate (line 10), and draws the tentative ("preSUMably") conclusion that the population will increase (line 11–12). There is a pause of nearly a second (line 13), after which Anne asks whether she is right (line 14). There is another pause of nearly one second, after which Dan gives off a drawn out (indicated by colons) ":m::", followed by another pause (lines 15–17). Does Dan not want to answer? Or has he not understood Anne's question? Anne specifies, "Round this region?" with a rising pitch at the end (indicated by question mark), which we hear as a question. There is another pause before Dan begins to speak, hesitatingly at first as indicated by the "um," "YEAh," sudden stops (indicated by n-dash in "if you take–"), and hearable pauses (indicated by "(0.20)").

These emphases and louder than normal utterances give the talk a measured, rhythmic structure, which, as Anne has not and could not have prepared what she said, is an emergent and contingent phenomenon. The circling gesture can be seen as a signal that Anne wants to get in and say something (line 24), but Dan does not stop talking (line 23). Then, when he does stop, Anne does not begin, which leaves a pause, after which Dan eventually picks up again and continues his explanation (lines 26–28).

When Dan seemingly finished his explanation, as indicated by the query "right?" (line 28), Anne weakly acknowledges uttering a "Yeah," which she immediately follows suggesting that she is looking at the slopes. She stresses her own focus ("I'M"), the slopes of the curves, which therefore can be heard as a contrast to something he just has explained. That there is a difference between Anne's looking at slopes and what he has explained can be seen from Dan's acknowledgment of the contrast evoked, "Oh, okay."

*A First Analysis*

Now that we have moved step by step through the transcript, we can now gloss the event it represents in the following terms. In response to Dan's request, Anne provides a tentative inference for a small section of the graph and then asks Dan whether she is correct. Dan initially hedges but eventually accedes, providing at least a partial answer about the relationship between birthrate and death rate. If we are told that one of the two is a university science professor and the other a student in the same department, we tend to bring our background knowledge to the situation to attribute these roles to the individuals. Who is who? Often in social life we use roles to explain what people do and say. In this situation, readers do not have this information beforehand and have to infer structure from the (verbal, gestural) actions. Let us take a look at the situation.

Dan has asked Anne to provide an interpretation of the graph from a second-year university ecology textbook. Anne begins the interpretation, then stops and asks whether she is right. Together, these pieces of information provide indications that Anne is not sure about the graphs; she is not knowledgeable about them. Dan does not want to answer, he hedges, like teachers hedge when students want to know how they are doing before having completed the task. But Anne insists, both asking and leaving pauses rather than continuing with the task. Eventually, Dan responds. All of this seems to suggest that Dan knows how to read and interpret the graph; Anne, on the other hand, does not know it. Everything we know from the literature on graphing is that graphing is a general, generic skill scientists have. Knowing this leads us to infer that Dan is the professor and Anne the student. But let us look again.

The fact is that Dan is a student—and not even one of the top students—and Anne a professor, both from in the same physics department. They know one another. Dan currently completes a co-op internship during which he recruits physics professors for a project concerning experts doing interpretations of graphs from their own and another field. In this situation, using the sociocultural roles two individuals take in society would have led us to an inappropriate prediction about who knows about graphing and who does not. The psychology and cognitive science literature on science and graphing would have suggested, too, that Anne, qua scientist, will be the expert and Dan, qua student of science, the novice.

However, in this situation, the matter of who knows or is presumed to know is played out in a situated way. Anne displays uncertainty ("presumably," "Is that right?"), whereas Dan displays certainty. After hedging, to which social actors may attribute after the fact the waiting of the person in the know in the face of a question by a student, he does provide an answer. That is, the social actors in this situation constructed the unequal relationship as the event is unfolding. Anne displayed uncertainty about the graphs; Dan displayed certainty. They displayed these different degrees of certainty to one another, but they also displayed intelligibly for all those who overheard the situation or who, as we analysts, have the privilege to see the videotape or transcript. Here, they do not draw on their roles as a resource. As it happens, they draw on the particular situation as a resource to construct knowledge inequality in the reverse of what one might have expected on the basis of their social position and science experience. Here, Dan has invited Anne to the think-aloud session; he is the researcher and she is the one from which information is to be elicited. Anne shows that she expects him to know the answer to the question he asked.

This in itself is a reversal of many other interview situations where the interviewer does not know the answer—interviews journalists conduct with scientists, for example. Anne knows that the present situation is part of a scientific study, which involves tasks that cognitive scientists pose but to which they already have some standardized answer. Her query as to the correctness of her first inference makes sense against the background of the interview situation. But this alone would not *explain* the situation either. Dan is still the undergraduate, and the scientist had been invited qua expert, and as such, may know more about the topic than even the best cognitive scientist. One way out of the quagmire of wrong causal predictions is based on social position, expertise, and so on is to assume the actors being involved in making assessments as a matter of course.

In this short episode we also see that the content of interview responses cannot be taken as if it represented knowledge as such; rather, what is being said during an interview (think-aloud protocol) is the outcome of an activity, the nature of which constitutes the background of which the social actors are aware. What they say is said given their awareness of the situation and cannot be separated (abstracted) from it. This constructive nature of talk characterizes all interview situations, even if they are conducted under the most strictly controlled conditions and protocols (Maynard & Schaeffer, 2000; Suchman & Jordan, 1990) and school examinations (Maynard & Marlaire, 1992).

We have seen that in this situation Anne displayed uncertainty with respect to knowledge and Dan displayed certainty. This, however, was not always the case in the interaction over and about this particular graph. There were moments when both emerged as knowing something—including the moment when Anne responds positively after Dan had sought confirmation that she understood his elaboration (line 29). It is worthwhile here to take a closer look. Dan actually makes some contradictory statements. First he suggests that death rate should be subtracted from birthrate (line 23) and then he suggests they had to be added (line 26), but that death rate was to be taken as negative (lines 26–28). This may at first be quite confusing. However, we need to remember that both are members of a physics department. In physics, quantities such as rates or forces are signed, that is, they are considered not only in their values (like 2 deaths/month) but also together with their direction. Here, death rate is a rate that decreases the population. Thus, a physicist would write death rate = - 2 deaths/month. This is just what Dan says, and which Anne acknowledges. This example also shows us that we cannot get everything about the social relation between the two from the transcript or videotape. We also need to do the ethnographic work that provides us with the understanding of *this* situation as well as what the interaction participants assume about the levels of intersubjectivity they bring, the sense that is common to them, what is truly their common sense.

We can see therefore that actors do bring background information and sensitivity to context to the social situation, but this background information cannot be used to construct causal explanations about how events will unfold. Rather, both the professor-student and interviewer-interviewee relations are resources for the two participants in constructing their interaction. Whether and how this background knowledge is brought to bear on and therefore structures the unfolding event is a matter of contingency, depending on the situation itself, which, because of the contingent nature, neither the participants nor the analyst/theoretician can predict. If the outcome of interactions were known beforehand, there would not be any need to interact; there would be no need to conduct think-aloud protocols or interviews.

This then is a very productive way of approaching interactions that also allows us to understand other situations. For example, educators have long been familiar with the phenomenon of a gap between the lessons a teacher plans and the way a lesson actually unfolds—this gap is captured in the distinction between planned and enacted curriculum (Tobin & McRobbie, 1996). Although a teacher might know her students, she can never foresee exactly how the curriculum will actually unfold. The enacted curriculum is always a *collective* achievement of teacher *and* students, emerging from their transactions in praxis, whereas the plans only involve the teacher, her understandings (students, subject matter) and expectations. Conversation analysis constitutes an important tool (method) that allows us to analyze and understand how such events as the enacted curriculum emerges as the result of situated actions, themselves contingently drawing on the social and material resources available in the setting. Rather than being dopes, teachers, students, and all other social actors who participate in our research are understood to be highly competent social actors who coparticipate in making social structure emerge in and through their situated activity. Because participants act, social structure is always constructed. But participants always draw on existing resources; therefore what emerges from their actions already exists as possibility in the situation. It is not completely new. Situated action therefore also reproduces social structure. That is, conversation analysis allows us to get at the simultaneously occurring and in fact mutually presupposing production and reproduction of social relations, social structure, social organizations, and society at large.

*Itinerary*

In this first part of this chapter, I already presented some basic ideas about how conversation analysis is conducted. Prior to the transcript and offprints, there already had to have been (a) the real-life event and (b) the recording activity. The association between the original event and the tape is an innocent, one-to-one relation—this is evident from the fact that the event only happened once, in real-time through, whereas the tape is iterable, it can be played over and over again (Ashmore & Reed, 2000). The tape is then transcribed, which constitutes a translation into a different medium, and therefore cannot be taken innocently as a process of one-to-one matching (e.g., Latour, 1999). The transcription makes use of a notation system designed to symbolize as many interesting elements as possible in the written medium that are present on the tape (see Note 2). As analyst, I then "work up" the transcript in elaborating and explicating what is and can be seen. My text is therefore both descriptive (what I have seen) and pedagogic—it teaches my readers how to see events they are familiar with in the transcript.

In the following sections, I first introduce conversation analysis (CA) and some of its key ideas and continue my analysis of the episode with the intent to show how various aspects of conversation analysis are done. In attending to what I am doing and in verifying what I am saying, readers already engage in conversation analysis as praxis. I could have taken many other episodes from the same or other tapes involving the two participants to show the same phenomena, or other tapes featuring Dan with other certain other professors, or another student interviewing professors and scientists. I stay with this transcript because readers are already familiar with it and because it allows me to limit the amount of background information that has to be provided.

## CONVERSATION ANALYSIS: DISCIPLINE AND PHENOMENA

### A Brief History

Conversation analysis emerged during the 1960s from the seminal efforts of Harvey Sacks and Emmanuel Schegloff who, influenced by Ervin Goffman and Harold Garfinkel, strived to study social structure through the analysis of commonsense activities. The then recent emergence of cheap audio recording technology provided a tool with which to capture natural phenomena produced in and through talk-in-interaction. These early researcher noted that the details of recorded talk have to be recovered during transcription; Gail Jefferson did, during the early days, a lot of the transcriptions for Sacks before becoming an important CA scholar in her own right. The seminal texts that founded the discipline include "A simplest systematics for the organization of turn taking for conversation" (Sacks, Schegloff, & Jefferson, 1974) and *Lectures on Conversation* (Sacks' (1992a, b), which began their life as widely circulated lecture notes.[3] Another text, "On formal structures of social action" (Garfinkel & Sacks, 1986) articulated the theoretical commitments common to ethnomethodology and conversation analysis.

Over the years, conversation analysts have investigated numerous issues including four overlapping but analytically distinguished types of interactional organization: *turn-taking*, *sequence*, *repair*, and *preference* organization. In the following two sections, I discuss these four types of organization and then turn to describe *formulating*, a pervasive feature of everyday talk.

### Turn-Taking and Sequencing

Turn-taking as an organizational feature of interactions is one of the fundamental ideas underlying conversation analysis. Normally, one person speaks at a time and change to the next speaker occurs with minimal overlap or gap. Change over generally occurs at the completion of a grammatical unit, which may be a sentence, clause, phrase, or lexical construction (Sacks et al., 1974). Thus, although there are lengthy pauses during Anne's articulation of an interpretation—here 2.11 (line 04) and 1.80 seconds (line 08), but lasting up to 10 seconds in other parts of the transcript—Dan does not begin to speak (see the 8.18 seconds in Episode 2 below). The pauses are prior to the end of a unit. However, the events following the completion of the inference (line 12) show that Anne expected Dan to comment. When the comment did not come forth, Anne explicitly requested it (lines 14, 18). Fundamental to the enterprise of conversation analysis and the understanding of the intersubjective nature of conversation is the phenomenon of *recipient design*. That is, utterances are designed for others; they therefore imply their own intelligibility and therefore intersubjectivity. Anything a person says in conversation to another is inherently assumed to be understandable, and therefore cannot be entirely new in its form or content. A particular form of recipient design leads us to sequencing and its realization in adjacency pairs.

The idea sequencing of sequencing is related to that of turn-taking and recipient design. Analytically, conversation analysts get at sequencing, among others, through the study of *adjacency pairs*—greeting-return greeting, summons-answer, question-answer, and invitation-acceptance/rejection. In Episode 1, Anne twice formulated a question and, according to the adjacency pair organization, should expect a response. Similarly, in the following, Dan invited Anne to begin by talking about a particular aspect of the graph, "region one," that is, the area to the left of the left intersection (from Anne's perspective). According to the adjacency pair organization, he should expect an acceptance or rejection. In Episode 2, Anne accepted the invitation and began to describe the birthrate curve as lying below the death rate curve.

**Episode 2**

```
01 D:    so start in region one and (0.71) talk about (0.68)
02       conservation of the species in that area.
03       (2.95)
04 A:    WELL HERE the BIRthrate (2.32) the BIRth of RAte
05       (0.31) in numbers per year presumably (1.38) is
06       still below the death rate (8.18) but it (0.43) s:o
07       (1.10) but it is rising- what I see is- there wa-
08       this is increasing.
```

The two parts of a pair are connected by means of *conditional relevance*, not as a mere latching of the two parts, but as the "participants' prospective and retrospective production and calibration of joint understanding" (Lynch & Bogen, 1996, p. 275). After the first part initiates the adjacency pair, the next utterance is heard as a second pair part. If it is absent or does not fit, the second speaker is accountable for it. Thus, when Dan does not answer Anne's question or Anne does not follow Dan's invitation, they have to account for the deviation from the expected organization. On the other hand, the speaker may take the non-occurrence of the second part of the sequence as an indication of trouble. Here, Anne may take the non-response as an indication that the question was unclear; this then calls for *repair*. From Dan's perspective, because he is supposed to generate a think-aloud/interview protocol, providing Anne with answers is the response is not the *preferred* course of action. We now turn to repair and preference.

*Repair and Preference*

Repair in conversation is a both a well-studied phenomenon and an analytic concept in conversation analysis (Schegloff, Jefferson, & Sacks, 1977). Episode 1 exhibits several instances of conversational repair. After Anne has made her inference about the consequences of the relation between the slopes of birthrate and death rate, there is a pause. Such pauses are opportunities (resources) for anyone to take the conversational floor. The pause is the outcome of a collaborative effect: Anne does not continue to speak, perhaps because she expects or anticipates a response; Dan does not begin, perhaps anticipating or expecting that Anne will continue. Anne then asks the question, "Is that right then?"

**Episode 1 (excerpt)**
```
12       increasing. ((Fig. 1f))
13       (0.93)
14       is that right then?
```

This question allows us to retroactively hear the pause from her perspective as waiting for a comment that would deal with the uncertainty she had articulated ("presumably" [line 12]. Her query would be understood as functioning as a repair: Anne anticipated or expected a comment and, as it was not forthcoming, articulated what she expected to happen. Dan did not comment, perhaps did not understand the cue that a comment was expected; the explicit articulation of a request for comment then constitutes a repair.

**Episode 3**
```
01 D:    now if you are in region two (0.86) your
02       ↑bIRthrate's lARger/
03 A:    ≤OH this is (mean?)[
04       (0.46)
05 D:    so your population's gonna go up s:o you're gonna
06       increase until what time?
07       (1.83)
08 A:    if you=are in region two?=
09 D:            =Yea
10       (1.19)
```

A repair move can also be discerned in Episode 3. Dan has completed one of his tutoring moves (lines 01–02, 05–06), which ended with a question. Anne, however, did not respond but asked a question in turn, "if you=are in region two?" (line 08). Dan responded by saying, "Yea" (line 09).

Let us work our way backward. Dan responded with an affirmative to a question, which had taken up a particular region of the graph as the topic of the talk (line 02). Her query therefore seeks confirmation as to the nature of the region talked about, which Dan confirmed. That is, Anne's question (line 08) sought to repair an uncertainty about the current focus by proposing one of the three areas as candidate. Dan confirmed the proposed candidate area as the one he was talking about (line 09).

Anne did more than clarifying the region her question pertains to. At the end of her utterance, the pitch moved upward. Raised pitches at the end of an utterance are resources for hearing what has been said as a question. That is, Anne both repaired a possible misunderstanding or lack of understanding of the original question, and reiterated the question at the same time. The fact that Dan began to respond indicates that he heard Anne's utterance as a request to respond.

The fundamental ideas underlying preference organization are that (a) when alternative (discursive) actions are possible, the *preferred* one is generally expected and chosen and that (b) the difference between preferred and *dispreferred* is demonstrated in the way the turn is shaped (Pomerantz, 1984). The preferred action is frequently made available by the first speaker in a turn and, if a rejection occurs, has to be (and generally is) accounted for by the respondent. For example, in Episode 1, there is a moment in which repair was interactively made necessary and then achieved; it immediately followed the request to comment on the inference (line 14).

**Episode 1 (excerpt)**

```
14        is that right then?
15        (0.96)
16 D:     u:m::
```

Anne now had asked explicitly for the comment, but a conversationally lengthy pause developed. Dan does not respond, although he was asked an explicit question. When he eventually does respond, it does not actually constitute the word but a drawn-out "u:m::." Preferred responses usually are given immediately. Pausing and delaying responses by producing verbal tokens such as "uh" or "um" indicate a *dispreferred* answer was called for. Teachers who do not want to reveal correct responses right away may act in this way. The same pauses and verbal tokens may be taken as an indication that the person queried does not have a pat answer or that the question was clear. Rather than selecting one or the other possible interpretation, analysts interested in the online production of social structure look for the actions of other members in the situation. Here, after another pause, Anne utters "Round this region?" and produces a circular movement near to and a little to the right of the left intersection point.

She has asked whether her inference is right, and now indexes verbally and gesturally to a particular area on the graph. If Dan had not understood which area the question "Is this right then?" referred to, the actions in line 18 in Episode 1 would have repaired his lack of understanding.

**Episode 1 (excerpt)**

```
14       is that right then?
15       (0.96)
16 D:    u:m::
17       (0.44)
18 A:    ϒ((Fig. 1f, circles))/
         ≤round ϒthis□ region? {
```

*Formulating*

A pervasive feature of talk in interaction is participants' attention to formulate what is going on (Garfinkel & Sacks, 1986). Thus, the verbal contributions to interactions are not just about informational content regarding the current topic but also co-articulate what is being done or what has been done. *Whatever* a person says provides materials that others can use for *making out* what he or she means to say. This is particularly the case when trouble is apparent.

There is always more to a situation than participants can say in so many words. Thus, in the episode, Anne provided her reading of the two lines, compared the two, and then drew an inference about the effect on the population for a case where "birthrate is increasing (0.76) fA:Ster (0.87) than the death rate" (Episode 1, lines 07–08).

**Episode 1 (excerpt)**

```
07       birthrate)) and the birthrate is increasing (0.76)
08       fA:Ster (0.87) than the death rate. (1.80) So they
```

When she requested an assessment, Dan articulated the result of the comparison between the two rates when birthrate is larger than death rate. In response, Anne said that she was looking at the slopes of the curves. Here, we can understand her contribution as *formulating* what she has done and still is doing—looking and talking about the slopes of the curves. That is, when Dan apparently did not understand what she had done—draw an inference from the fact that the slope of birthrate is larger than that of the death rate in the particular region—she formulated what she was doing, that is, looking at (and talking about) the slopes rather than the values of the two curves.

Formulating is a pervasive feature. In other parts of their session, for example, Anne formulated long pauses and Dan's hedges as her having missed something. Just prior to the following episode, Anne again requested a comment about whether she had been right with her inferences. After hedging in a manner almost identical to Episode 1, Dan provided in Episode 4 a hesitating assessment, "I think tha:t's correct?" and continues, "Is that what it says on the graph?" There is an ever lengthening pause without a response from Anne, which Dan interrupted with a token that invites Anne to respond "Or?" (line 05). After a brief pause, Anne initiated a repair move, "you mean here?" and, while moving her right hand until it points to the text, uttered "that's what you say?" Dan overlapped this utterance, acknowledging her repair regarding the nature of the thing being talked about and pointed to (line 07) and reiterating his earlier question, "yea, does it say?" (line 08). While still pointing to the lower part of the caption, Anne queried, "You want me to look there?" (line 09).

**Episode 4**

```
01 D:     yeah that- yeah (.) I think tha:t's
02        correct. (0.32) Is that what it says
03        on the graph?
04        (2.75)
05        °Or?°
```

```
06        (0.39)
07 A:     you mean here?
08 D:     ⌜that's what you say?/
09 A:     ⎵((rH moves to text))∞
          ≤yea, does it     ⌜⌜say?/
                            ≤You ⌜want me
          to look there? ((still pointing to
          text))
```

In this episode, Anne twice formulated what she heard Dan to mean without that he had said this in so many words. Framed in question form, she articulated Dan to "mean" attending to a particular part of the instructions (line 07), which she immediately thereafter pointed to. She formulated a second time what he was doing, "that's what you say?" In line 09, again, she formulated hearing Dan as instructing her to look somewhere at the lower part of the instruction. Dan had not done so, but Anne made available to Dan that she heard him saying so, and in this, she also told everybody else viewing the tape and reading the transcript.

A second aspect of formulating can also be found in this episode. In saying, "is that what it says on the graph?," Dan was doing something. In line 09, Anne explicitly articulated what he was doing. Without saying it in so many words, Dan exhibited what he was doing to Anne (and the analysts). We do not need to infer what he was doing. Anne articulated it for us: Dan is "doing [wanting me to look there]," where I have drawn on a recommended denotation practice to bracket the gloss of what is being done (cf. Garfinkel & Sacks, 1986). That is, in the present situation we do not imbue actors with intents or interpret what they have done; one of the participants, here Anne, has *formulated* what was being done. This is important, for her subsequent actions take into account what she has seen and heard Dan to have done rather than what we, the analysts, might have seen him do and say.

PROSODY AS RESOURCE IN AND FOR INTERACTION

Educators and educational researchers are singularly focused on words and the language (discourse) they constitute. But at the origin, there are not words. Anyone who has tried to transcribe a video- or audiotape recorded under everyday, noisy classroom conditions knows that there are moments when intent and prolonged listening does not allow hearing *what* is being said; all one can hear are indistinct sounds. At the origin of utterances, words, and language are therefore sounds. As part of our cultural upbringing, we learn to hear sounds in particular ways, as motorcycles, musical instruments, or voices. More so, we learn to hear them as approaching motorcycles, musical instruments playing a tune rather than being tuned, and as voices articulating words. But words do not suffice in the constitution of interaction—the increased number of misunderstanding in email conversation, and the use of specific signs to put expressions in relief (e.g., smiley faces, typographic reproduction of faces) should alert readers that face-to-face communication has a variety of other symbolic means for producing conversational resources. A related familiar, folk psychological notion is that of "body language"; that is, bodies as a whole or in part move, and these movements are seen as part of communication. One known but in education little studied communicational resource is prosody (intonation), which speakers use to indicate syntax, turn-taking, utterance type (question, statement), attitudes, and feelings.

Prosodic features include speech intensity (a measure how loud someone speaks), pitch or frequency of the voice, and duration (words can be spoken fast or drawn out, between words there may be pauses). Changes in these features, individually or in combinations, produce stressed or emphasized syllables. Thus, a word spoken much louder or at a much higher pitch than the surrounding talk will be heard as having been emphasized or received stress. In a conversation analytic approach, these features are understood as resources that both speaker and listener use for making sense.

*Prosody and Temporal Structuring*

Time is often treated as a factor that conditions events and their unfolding in time; it is taken in the physicists' manner, an external and objective frame external to interactions. Yet numerous scholars in disciplines such as sociology (e.g., Bourdieu, 1990) or organization science (Orlikowski & Yates, 2002) view time as a resource for action, giving recognition to the fact that temporal structures are shaping and being shaped by ongoing human action. Time is therefore neither external and determining nor entirely shaped and determined by human action. As other resources, temporal structures restrain and enable the production|reproduction of culture and are both the medium and an outcome of cultural practices. Conversation analysis is a method that allows us to get at such phenomena as a brief look at an excerpt from Episode 1 shows (lines 05–07).

Anne achieves the emphasis of "bIRTH" both by the greater speech intensity and a significant rise in pitch; the lengthening of the phoneme and a corresponding sudden rise in pitch are responsible for the emphasis on "ing" (Figure 10..2).[4] In the second occurrence of "birth," however, emphasis is due only to the rise in pitch. None of the phonemes making up "increasing" stand out in loudness, pitch, or length when compared to the pronunciation of the immediately preceding "rate is." This leads us to the transcript as provided, "an the bIRTHrate increasing and the birthrate is increasing" (lines 05–07).

**Episode 1 (excerpt)**

```
05 A:    dEATh rate ((Fig. 1d)) increasing (0.68) an the BIRTHrate
06       ((Fig. 1e)) increasing ((traces birthrate)) and the
07       birthrate is increasing (0.76)
```

One of the functions this stressing of syllables has is similar to pointing; it is making salient current features in the setting or in the semantics of the utterance itself. Thus, Anne marks the words birth and death, which are thereby marked as the semantically important items. Throughout the transcript, Anne employs this device and thereby makes salient to herself and her audience what is the momentarily salient element.

A first look at the transcript reveals regular emphases that appear to structure the performance; these emphases are also related to the particular verbal tokens. For example, in lines 05–06 of Episode 1, corresponding items are stressed "dEATh

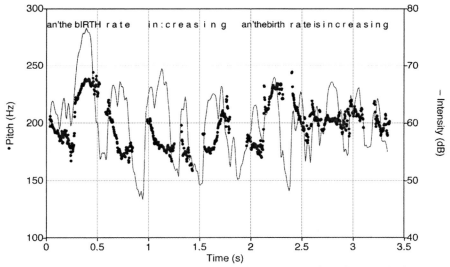

*Figure 10.2. Speech intensity (dB) and pitch (Hz) for an excerpt from the episode (lines 05–07). That a part of the utterance "bIRTH" is much louder than normal is evident from the peak of intensity. The emphases usually fall where two or three of the variables intensity, pitch, and phoneme length are larger than in the surrounding talk.*

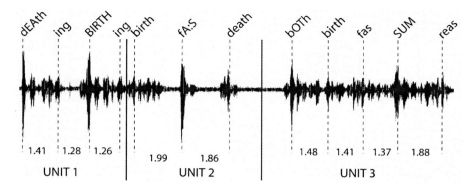

*Figure 10.3. The emphasized syllables have been added to the waveform of the opening section of the episode; dotted lines mark the center of the emphasized syllables and numbers denote the time in tenth of a second between adjacent emphases within a speech unit.*

rate increasing (0.68) and the BIRTHrate increasing." A plot of the waveform of her voice allows us to mark the stresses in time (Figure 10.3). We immediately see the rather regular temporal appearance of the stresses during the different sections of Anne's initial reading and interpretation of the graph. During the first descriptions, the temporal distances between stressed syllables are from 1.3 to 1.4 seconds, in the next part where Anne compared birthrate and death rate, the stressed syllables are separated between 1.9 and 2.0 seconds, and in the final section, all but one distance lie between 1.4 and 1.5 seconds.

Here, the emphases are on semantically similar items and occur in regular intervals. Both are resources for structuring the delivery. This delivery appears to served Anne in pacing herself through this unknown thicket of the graph; her thinking aloud took on structure, her thinking became structured in and through the delivery. It was also a resource to the person who is the intended audience; it is a resource for attending to those things that currently are to stand out.

Time and temporality are also of particular issue in and during interactions, that is, in the interval between the actions of the participants. It is in the mastery of the intervals that cultural competence plays itself out (Bourdieu, 1990). For example, in the transcript there are two instances (lines 13, 15) where the pause after a completed sentence unit reaches what has come to be known as the *standard maximum silence* of about one second (Jefferson, 1989).

**Episode 1 (excerpt)**

```
12      increasing. ((Fig. 1f))
13      (0.93)
14      is that right then?
15      (0.96)
16      u:m::
```

249

A brief reflection shows that silences in interaction are always produced collaboratively. The fact that Anne asks whether she has been right in the as tentative marked inference suggests she was expecting a comment. Dan had not shown any indication that he understood this intent in the growing pause. There is another pause developing, followed by Dan's production of "u:m::" (Episode 1, line 16), a signal that answering is the dispreferred action or that there is uncertainty about what the question is. Anne's uncertainty about whether Dan was aware of her expectation was heightened by the fact that another pause begins to develop again interrupted by Anne who now circles the region immediately to the right of the left intersection point and queries, "Round this region?" Another silence ensues, followed by semantically empty tokens before Dan begins to respond. From his perspective, responding when the task has been set up for Anne to provide a think-aloud protocol is the dispreferred action. He allowed the pauses to develop. For Anne, these developing pauses were resources for inferring that the content of her question had not been clear.

There are other moments when the pauses in Anne's production exceed the one-second standard maximum silence (Episode 1, lines 01–04, 04, 08; Episode 2, lines 03, 04, 05, 06, 07; Episode 3, lines 07, 10; Episode 4, line 04). But in these moments, she has not yet reached a completion point from her own and Dan's perspectives. At other moments in this and other interviews, Dan encourages the participant to think/talk aloud. That is, in these situations, he takes Anne and other participants as not fulfilling their commitment to the research protocol and therefore reminds them of the task specification that requires thinking aloud.

*Prosody, Interaction, and Emotion*

In thinking aloud, Anne explicitly addressed the activity system; she was following the instruction, which had been to think aloud so that the Dan and the social scientists he was working for could learn about graphs and graphing, particularly about expertise.

Speakers have characteristic pitch ranges. These ranges may change as a function of the overall emotional state of the person (Roth, in press). In the present situation, across the interview/think-aloud session, Anne's range lies between 175 and 200 Hertz (Hz), with occasional moments where her voices ranges between 200 and 235 Hz, particularly during the moments when a task was still unfamiliar (Figure 10.4). The pitch range for Dan's voice lies between 115 and 135 Hz, with occasional peaks reaching to 145 Hz. Variations from the normal range are resources for speakers and listeners for making sense of what is being said and for the speaker's emotional coloring at the moment.

For Anne, too, asking whether she is right or querying comes from and is associated with a particular emotional state, which expressed itself in a high pitch (Figure 10.5). Every time she asked to receive a hint or an assessment, the pitch moved into the 300–350 Hz range. On the other hand, when the same utterance "right" was used in different contexts, for example, as a form of acknowledgment, the associated pitch was in or near her normal (or peak) range.

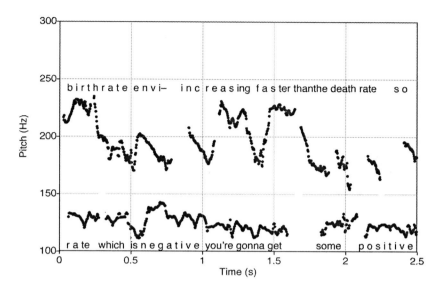

*Figure 10.4. This representation of pitch levels characterizes Anne (top) and Dan (bottom) when they speak longer stretches. For Anne, the pitch varies between 175 and 200 Hz, with peaks reaching 235 Hz; Dan's voice is characterized by pitch levels between 115 and 135 Hz, with occasional peaks reaching to 145 Hz.*

Figure 10.5 exemplifies the pitch ranges when Dan hedges ("umm," "hhh"), and when he accedes to Anne's query ("if you take– well"). In the former case, his voice stays within the pitch range (including the peaks), but in the latter case, he invariably moves into or above the pitch range normally occupied by Anne. Subsequently, his pitch descended until reaching its normal range between 115 and 135 Hz. This is a consistent pattern throughout the session and other female interviewees; it is more difficult to discern with the male participants, for their pitch ranges were similar to that of Dan.

Here, the pitch appears to articulate the express wish to meet up with the person making a request or asking a question. His voice not only matched the pitch range, but also quoted the pitch contour, both of which are expressions of alignment (or intent thereof) between speakers of quite diverse cultural background (Müller, 1996; Roth, 2005). At another level, matching pitch and pitch contour are ways of expressing empathy and solidarity, which are therefore ways of making emotions available to others and to reproduce these emotions.

## Prosody and Emotion

Stressed syllables can be heard. But, in many situations, the hearings can be cross-checked against the electronically produced measures of speech intensity and pitch.

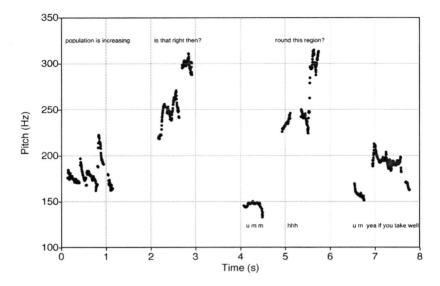

*Figure 10.5. When Dan does not accede to Anne's requests, his pitch remains in his normal range. However, when he does respond, his pitch rises into Anne's range as if trying to meet her, not only metaphorically, but literally, at least with respect to the absolute pitch.*

Stresses in speech produce a rhythm, and this rhythm together with pitch and loudness are expressions of emotions. Because these expressions are materially in the room, others notice them, who, in fact, are entrained not only into the same rhythm but also into the same emotion (Collins, 2004). At the time of this writing, I am analyzing data that show that the rhythm in the speech of an agitated African American student engaged in an argument with her teacher, is the same that other students in the class display through tapping the desk, wiggling with the leg, and nodding with their heads. The more agitated the young woman becomes the more her pitch rises and the more her rhythm accelerates. But, interestingly, the rhythm of other students' movements accelerates as well. This acceleration is subsequently reversed through the "calming" talk of a fellow student, leading to decreases in rhythm, speech intensity, and pitch. Not only the student reduced the pitch levels, but also her teacher; and the rhythm displayed in the taping and wiggling of the legs also slowed down. That is, the reduction of tension at the verbal level was also signaled through the return to normal levels at the prosodic level. Here, prosody and movements were a means to track not only the individual emotions and mood, but also the collectively enacted emotion and mood in the classroom.

The changes in pitch can be associated with changes in the emotive aspects of the situation—for example, girls in disputes over a game of hopscotch displayed disagreements both semantically and emotionally through large changes in pitch (Goodwin, Goodwin, & Yaeger-Dror, 2002). In the present episodes, Dan's hedging and resistance to responding, which can be seen at the temporal unfolding of the transcript, are also indicated at the prosodic level. As such, these forms of resistance are also available to Anne. Staying in his normal range when explicitly asked to answer a question may be heard as an indication that he resisted making a step toward her (Figure 10.5). On the other hand, every time Dan followed a request, his pitch moves way beyond his normal range into and above Anne's normal range. He was acceding, taking a step toward and empathizing with her, which was also expressed at the pitch level (Figure 10.5, right hand side).

## Hand Gestures, Body Movements

Gestures with the hands and other body parts constitute resources to interaction participants for making sense of and communicating what is going on. By their very definition, gestures are understood to be symbolic movements designed to contribute to symbolic activities, thinking and sense making. (For a good introduction and overview of gesture research, particularly from a perspective consistent with a sociocultural approach see McNeill [1992].) There are many instances of gesture use apparent just in the brief episodes featured in this chapter. However, conversation analysis does not have to limit itself to gestures, that is, the explicitly symbolic aspects of interactions, but also can turn up interesting phenomena of other body movements, which, as all actions, come to be resources in the ongoing, real-time sense-making of conversationalists. The movement or non-movement of entities in the setting can be resources in and for the constitution of participants' ongoing and developing sense, even when they do not speak a single word for long periods of time (Roth, 2004). In this vein, I already described how Anne shifted her body position and orientation and how these shifts were associated with the division of labor in the responsibility for the task of completing the interview. But let us take a closer look at the deployment and function of gestures in the present corpus.

Anne's pointing to the graph as she thought aloud oriented Dan to particular locations of the graph that corresponded in some way to her speech. As Anne progressed, in talking about the birthrate curve, for example, her hand was turning so that the pencil almost always stays perpendicular to the slope of the line where she was pointing (Figure 10.1e, f, h); similarly, when she talked about the death rate, the pencil was perpendicular to the slope of the line (Figure 10.1c, d). The pencil point marked the point of attention; the deictic gesture was a resource for attending to the point. Thus, from the speaker's perspective, pointing is both a resource for getting the work of attending done and an outcome, the result of attending. The pointing (deictic) gesture is a resource that allowed Anne to orient and focus as well as tracking her own progres-

Figure 10.1 e, f, g. are illustrations of Anne's pointing, which orients both Dan and her own attention to particular

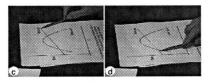

The movement from Figure 10.1 c to d constitutes an iconic gesture, that is, in its shape it reproduces the shape of the line.

sion. Thus, at the time Anne talked about the death rate for the first time, describing it as increasing, her hand had already moved along the line on the paper. The perceptual image, the hand movement, and the utterance "death rate is increasing" are three different forms in which the same idea unit expressed itself. They were not just three forms that are additive. From a sociocultural perspective, the different forms of expression are mutually constitutive and presuppose one another; in other words, they stand in a dialectical relationship (McNeill & Duncan, 2000).

It is clear, then, that when Anne was leaning forward and bringing her hand and pencil to the paper in front of her, this was an expression of the intention to attend to and talk about the graph, the part of the activity that she was responsible for. When she leaned backward and took her hands off the graph, this expressed, among other things, that she was not currently orienting to a specific aspect of the graph and to getting her part of getting the think-aloud session done. Thus, the body orientation and hand position have interactive function. They exhibit attention and focus, readiness to continue, and therefore also constitute resources for Dan concerning the interaction.

The hand gestures also have interactive function, which is made even more explicit in moments of trouble. Thus, when Dan did not respond to Anne's question about the correctness of her inference, Anne circled a particular region on the graph querying, "round this region?" (Episode 1, line 18). At this moment, her hand gesture was the dialectical complement of the utterance, providing a perceptually (but not verbally) available specificity to "this region." Here, the gesture more than the utterance was a resource for directing the interlocutor's attention to a specific physical region.

Hand gestures (movements) have other interactive functions as well. Thus, hitting the desktop hard with the palm of her hand (Episode 1, line 03) is a culturally recognizable sign for getting ready and starting an activity that has been set up in previous actions; it means something like "okay, let's get going." Here, Anne has completed reading the captions and instructions and now sets out to engage in that part of the task described in the text. In line 24 (Episode 1), while Dan continued talking, Anne moved forward, then brought her hand to the graph and circled the same region as previously.

**Episode 1 (excerpt)**

```
23 D:    ↑birth minus the death/
24 A:
```

```
         ≤h            ((circles ))∫
```

In this movement, she indicated readiness to talk, but she refrained, as Dan did not stop until uttering "death." At the same time, this gesture again meant she reiterated the region that her question had been about; there was no need to reiterate the question verbally. Consequently, a pause began to develop. From Dan's perspective, Anne appears to have indicated intent to speak; from Anne's perspective, she has expressed what she wanted to express and therefore she does not need to talk leaving the turn to Dan. He then took the opportunity provided. The pause here is a resource that allowed him to take the next turn, which in fact constituted a continuation of the immediately preceding one.

This hand movement toward the graph as an instance of the intent to speak is further put in relief, for throughout the session, there was clear division of labor with respect to the responsibilities for the textual and graphical part of the sheet. Anne was responsible for the graph, and Dan for the contents of the text. In their bodily, gestural, and verbal interactions, these different responsibilities were expressed in different modalities. Thus, Anne's forward movement and hand gesture to the graph meant she not only pointed out something but also was ready to act toward (talk about) something that fell within her realm of responsibility. When she leaned back, taking her hands away from the graph (or pointing to the text), the salient issue pertained to Dan's part in the division of labor of researcher and researched.

## A MICRO COSMOS OF SOCIETY AND SOCIAL RELATIONS IN THE MAKING

### Members and Researchers

In much of the education literature on classroom interactions, intersubjectivity is treated as something that independent individuals have to achieve. From a traditional psychological and radical constructivist perspective, this is a difficult task given that these approaches treat human beings more or less as monads. However, it should be evident that human interaction generally and conversation in particular presuppose intersubjectivity to the same extent that it produces intersubjectivity. Conversation analysis is both based on and allows articulation of the fundamentally intersubjective nature of human interaction. For example, it did not make sense for Anne to ask Dan in Episode 1, "is that right then?," unless she could presuppose that Dan already understood the words she was and would be using. More so, she had to presuppose that Dan understood her to ask a question rather than to make a statement, to beg for something, etc. Similarly, in responding at all, Dan not only had to assume that Anne heard the sounds he produced as words, but also that she already understood what he was saying. In this sense, he could not say anything that was radically new; whatever he could usefully contribute to the interaction already was presupposed as intelligible. Not only words, but also hand and arm movements used in pointing and iconic gesturing were presupposed as material forms that signify and denote. At the same time, these actions introduced new elements in the sense that they oriented participants to particular locations in the setting. In summary, then, intersubjectivity is both condition for and outcome of

255

the communicative interaction; intersubjectivity is continuously produced|repro-duced.

Intersubjectivity as a presupposed condition of the interaction is particularly important if we consider the emergent nature of the interaction. Frequently re-searchers formulate what their participants do in terms of intents. This in itself is not inappropriate, for, as I show here, interaction participants make available to each other not only actions but also intents in and through their actions. It would be inappropriate, therefore, to suggest that the intents *predate* the actions observed. Anyone taking a little time out during a meeting and observing what is going on will note that events continuously unfold. There is generally too little time to ar-ticulate a response prior to speaking. What *exactly* a speaker wants to say is said *in* the moment of speaking. Just like Anne, human beings generally think as they go, their thoughts (and cognition) being *in* their actions, simultaneously made available to others and themselves. Human conduct is such that the actions themselves are such that they can be explained in terms of intents. Thus, Anne was able to provide a gloss of Dan's action: he was "doing [wanting (her) to look there]." Dan may still suggest otherwise, but the fact is that in his actions and talk, Anne found sufficient evidence supporting her formulation (gloss) of what he had done.

The rapidity and efficiency of human actions in real time cannot be understood unless we take them as providing sufficient elements that can be used in accounts of what has happened. Extending this idea, I suggest that thinking does not have to precede the actions but is expressed in the (discursive) action as it unfolds.

With ethnomethodologists, conversation analysts explicitly recognize the role the researcher's cultural competence plays during the analysis. To be able to un-derstand what is being said without saying so, the researcher, too, has to be a member in the cultural community under investigation (ten Have, 2002). Here, *member* is not used to refer to a person but rather to the mastery of natural lan-guage used in the production and display of commonsense knowledge in and of everyday activities as observable, reportable, and accountable phenomena (Garfinkel & Sacks, 1986). Thus, to articulate what is going on in talk, to under-stand what is being said and done in and through talk, the analysts need to be members (of the community, culture, tribe)—lest they misinterpret the data and articulate structures that are irrelevant to the populations and situations studied. This became very clear during an extensive three-week eight-hour-per day effort during which David Middleton, a social psychologist experienced in the analysis of discourse (e.g., Middleton & Edwards, 1990), collaboratively analyzed the present data corpus. It turned out that he misinterpreted the interactions whenever the con-tent concerned specialized knowledge of physics or advanced mathematics. For example, he was not attuned to the difference between Anne and Dan with respect to their foci of attention to slopes and values of birthrate and death rate, respec-tively; he also missed the point of Dan's adding rather than subtracting the two rates. In other parts of the transcript, Anne and Dan talked about first, second, and partial derivatives. Here again, David found himself at a disadvantage because he lacked the cultural understanding characteristic of the community of physicists. Whenever Dan and Anne presupposed specialized knowledge that remained unarticulated because it "went without saying," David missed the point of their interaction during his analysis.

## Power/knowledge

Conversation analysis is an ideal tool for analyzing how social positions and relations are produced|reproduced in and through interaction. One way of getting at power in educational contexts is through the way in which questions of knowledge play themselves out, are negotiated or contested, and come to be settled for the purposes at hand. Who knows what and when and how this knowledge pertains to the issues at hand is an important aspect of positioning, maintaining existing knowledge/power gradients, and overturning these gradients, even if only for the moment.

In line 14 of Episode 1, Anne asked Dan whether her inference was right; he eventually responded providing some elaboration. Interactionally, the authoritative knowledge was thereby attributed to Dan; in his response, he accepted. In Episode 2, Dan operated as a tutor, inviting Anne to go about the task in a particular way (lines 01–02); Anne followed this invitation, thereby coproducing the tutor-tutee relationship. This difference in knowing constitutes a difference in power. This power is not some substance that people bring to their interactions with others. Rather, it is an effect, a product of the interaction. Thus, Anne may be thought as having power that she could have played out in her interactions with Dan given that she is the professor. Furthermore, the latter is not in a more powerful situation inherently, for he depends on his participant to get his recording, and, established as part of the consent agreement, Anne can stop her participation at any point. Yet it turns out that Anne makes a request for assessment and Dan eventually accedes to it. He is in the situation that he may or may not grant the request. The asymmetric positioning of the two is a result of their interaction, initiated by Anne, but co-produced by Dan.

In other parts of the session over and about the same graph, Anne asks Dan for hints, that is, she requests help. This articulated—at least in this situation—a difference with respect to who is presumed to be knowledgeable about the topic. Although the preferred action to questions and queries is responding, not responding is also a possible action. In fact, withholding a response can be a way of controlling the situation. For example, teachers withhold answers to encourage students to think their way through some issue. Withholding something one has and could give away without material loss—here knowledge/information—is a way of producing|reproducing control and therefore power. Thus, when Anne requested a hint, Dan, after some more back and forth, eventually said, "so start in region one and (0.71) talk about (0.68) conservation of the species in that area." Dan yielded the request for help, but he controlled how this help unfolded. Both Anne and Dan acted as if he knew the answer and he was therefore in a position to grant or withhold the request. In the following brief exchange, for example, he did not provide the requested answer but responded with questions in turn.

**Episode 5**
```
01 A:    so this is a stable point, is it?
02       (0.18)
03 D:    y:- (0.20) well you tell me:hh (0.74) what do you:
04       think?
```

Here, Anne first made an assessment of the second point where birthrate and
death rate intersected, and then sought confirmation whether the situation is as she
described it (line 01). Dan appeared to respond quickly, that is, in the preferred
mode, but then suddenly stopped the somewhat extended "y:" sound. There was a
brief pause, followed by a request for her to tell him, which was, after a lengthening pause without response, followed by a question, "what do you: think?" (lines
03–04). Here, he did not respond directly, which would have been the preferred
action, but twice attributed the responsibility for providing a full assessment to the
person making the original assessment request—this is a typical prerogative of
teachers. To reiterate, he is in the know and, here, does not reveal this knowledge
to the person asking, who nevertheless participates in attributing knowledge to
him. But both contribute to conferring this special power to him.

We notice other features related to differences in position and positioning. For
example, at one point in the episode, Anne ended up "complaining" to or "chiding"
Dan. This complaint is enacted in, arises from, and is acknowledged interactively.
Anne had provided a description of the slopes of the two curves, and draws an inference. She then asked Dan whether what she has said is right. He gave a description of what to do—subtracting or adding the rates—then uttered, "so" (line 30), as
if expecting Anne to continue or draw her own conclusion from what has been
said. Anne, however, suggested that *she* is looking at the "slopes of the curves"
(line 29).

**Episode 1 (Excerpt)**
```
29 A:    yea ⌈I'M⌉looking at the slopes of the curves=
30 D:       ⌊so ⌊            =oh, okay.
31
```

Here Anne stressed the personal pronoun "I" together with the truncated auxiliary verb "am." In this, Anne emphasized what she has done, which Dan heard as a
contrast with what he had said. Here, the "oh" signaled the surprise, the novelty of
the information that Anne just has provided. So in effect, Dan did not provided an
answer to her question, but in his response talked about something else. Anne said,
"I'M looking at the slopes of the curves," which contrasted the curves that Dan had
talked about. Anne not only provided information about the difference between
their respective contributions, but she also did relational work—she chided him for
not having responded to her question.

## TECHNICAL ISSUES

*Transcription*

Many researchers collect their videotapes and then select some for transcription and analysis. In my research team, we proceed differently. We transcribe the tapes in their entirety as soon as possible after they have been recorded. This has the advantage that we can direct our cameras in subsequent recording sessions in order to extent our database concerning interesting issues. The first transcripts are done quickly and therefore rough, because we do not spend a lot of time trying to get every single word; we do not transcribe pauses and overlaps (e.g., Figure 10.6). The Figure 10.shows that there is little detail and even many missing element when the transcript is compared to Episode 1 and Figure 10.1. Video offprints are added into the transcript, especially where participants make extensive use of gestures or where other aspects of the talk can be understood better (or only) with the image present. At this stage, a screen print of the video image is created, which is then directly inserted into the transcript.

In subsequent analyses, the transcripts are enhanced. Pauses are inserted, and transcription conventions are used. I also use a font that spaces letters equally. At this stage, programs that create a visual representation of the soundtrack—intensity or waveform—are useful because the pauses can be measured more quickly and accurately. Also, overlapping talk can be isolated and the exact points of overlap determined. Video offprints are imported into a painting program such as Adobe Photoshop, changed to gray-scale, and, if necessary, elaborated and touched up. At this stage, I also produce the high quality video offprints; publishers generally require a pixel density of 300 pixels per inch. Depending on the ultimate use of the image, I choose the specific size: about 1 inch (2.54 centimeters) wide when the

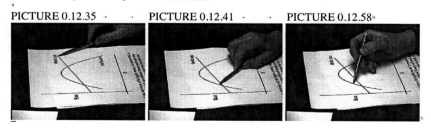

A: ? here we have the death rate increasing (PICTURE 0.12.35) and the birth rate increasing (PICTURE 0.12.41) and the birthrate is increasing faster than the death rate ? presumably that means that the population is increasing (PICTURE 0.12.58) is that right then
D: Well ? birth + death your ?
A: I'm looking at the slopes of the curves ?

PICTURE 0.12.35     PICTURE 0.12.41     PICTURE 0.12.58

*Figure 10.6. As soon as possible after recording, a rough transcript often including many passages marked as undecipherable. The video offprints is labeled using time into the tape (h:mm:ss) so that the exact moment can easily be found again in the Quicktime™ movie file.*

259

image is inserted in the transcript (see Episode 2), larger or smaller producing figures containing single or multiple off prints. The ultimate result is saved in the program specific file type as well as in JPG-compressed form. (This format can easily be shared across platforms and, most importantly, is acceptable to publishers.)

Generally, I do my own transcripts from the initial stages through all transformation to the most refined ones such as those featured in this chapter. Transcribing allows me to really get to know the tapes. Furthermore, while transcribing, I already annotate and comment on the transcript and salient episodes. The amount of time spent doing the rough and subsequent fine transcripts is more than returned in the detailed knowledge I develop in and about the database. This intimate familiarity with all aspects of the tapes and transcripts leads to the fact that I learn many different things, which can be reported to different audiences, leading to a number of publications rather than only one.

*Listening and Hearing*

While constructing the transcription, the conceptual differences between listening and hearing are quite evident. These differences actually allowed me to develop a better appreciation of words in communication. In western cultures, words and language receive preferential treatment—the term (phal-) logocentrism highlights this (Derrida, 1982).[5] Those who attempt to transcribe video- or audiotapes can easily experience the questionable nature of the central status words take. There are frequent moments during transcription, where listening does not allow us to make out what has been said (we then put question marks in parenthesis to mark those places). Even repeated listening may not help. We experience time and again that when someone else tells us what has been said or what he or she has heard, we too can hear it. All of a sudden, what has been but an undecipherable noise becomes a more or clear articulation. That is, sounds hit our ears; it is our long-time experience in a particular linguistic context that allows us to hear certain sounds *as* words rather than as noise. It is similar to other moments in everyday life: We hear a motorcycle approaching or receding rather than just noise.

We can draw from this the lesson that prosodic features are just as legitimate resources in collective sense-making activity as are the sounds we hear as utterances. Similarly, we use bodily configurations and gestures all of the time as resources for attributing intention and attitude (boredom, interest) to others who may "pick up" the same body movements and gestures so that we collectively express the same attitudes and intentions to one another. A classroom full of students express, in the way they lean back, yawn, orient their bodies, and so forth their interests, emotions, and intentions. We may adapt to or do something about it, that is, use these displays as resources, and thereby produce and reproduce forms of culture.

From this we can learn that all communication involves material signs, which always appear in material contexts. Culture, social relations, and social structure, which, as I suggested, are the outcomes of human interactions, are therefore instantiated in material communicative forms. It is by interacting with such material forms that we come to know about and learn cultural forms, even emotions, both how they express themselves materially and the corresponding sounds that we hear as their names. There is no mysterious transmission of cultural practices and signification. Communication, in whichever form it occurs, is always materially available in the setting so that all participants, all those present, can access it and, qua resource, draw on it in subsequent action.

*Analytic Process*

Colleagues and graduate students frequently ask me how I do my analyses. Normally, my analytic process begins with some noticing, often while I transcribe. For example, when I started looking at the videotapes and rough transcripts of this database, in particular the session involving Anne and Dan, I went, "Wow, something is going on here." Contrary to what one might expect from a scientist invited to provide an expert reading of a series of graphs, Anne and some of her colleagues began to ask the interviewer about the "correct" interpretation. In some instances, the interviewer began to articulate such a reading or guide the interviewee to a standard reading. To better understand the interactions, I first transcribed an entire session in detail, that is, yielding about 30 pages of transcript as exemplified in the episodes presented here. In the process, I came to hear the tape over and over again, becoming attuned to the slightest change in the voice and became familiar with the recorded events. As I listened to the tapes, an increasing amount of detail became apparent to me. I took notes and wrote small analyses as I went along working my way second by second through the tapes. It turns out that in such work, I come to hear certain what is being said in parts of the tape that previously I could not understand despite intent listening.

As I go along, I also use the PRAAT software, which allows me to check the accuracy of the transcript, and also to get an impression of the various prosodic features. I produce graphs of intensity and pitch, add the words matching them to the other physical features, and print them to be able to take rapid notes on the printed version. In working my way through the tape(s), I also check for the occurrence of the same or contradictory patterns to those I previously noted.

Conducting sessions involving others is helpful for noticing new types of events. In my research group, we often meet to collaborative analyze a tape that someone brings to the session. These sessions are organized according to the principles of *Interaction Analysis* (Jordan & Henderson, 1995). We play the tape, and whenever someone sees something of interest, we stop and begin to talk about what we have seen. We replay the episode of interest as often as we deem necessary until we all feel to have said as much as we could. We then move on until someone calls for another stop. We usually do not get very far into the tape, and many times we did not get farther than 90 seconds or a few minutes; this is how rich even the shortest moments of human interaction can be.

Eventually I come to the point where do not seem to have any more new insights. I then begin to go back through the notes, looking for patterns and organizing themes. I begin to write notes about my notes, leading to more comprehensive and encompassing statements about the events and the ways of participants to make sense of the situation they find themselves in. I also read related articles and books; new theoretical understanding and acquaintance with empirical research often leads me to new insights about what is going on in my own data. I usually work for many days, generating hundreds of typewritten pages of analysis, descriptions, theoretical commentaries, worked up transcripts.

*Technologies and Tools*

Conversation analysis began with audio recordings. As VCR and digital video technology became readily accessible and affordable, an increasing number of researchers not only used these means for doing research but also extended the analysis of interactions to include body movements and positions (e.g., Heath, 1986). These recording means can be understood as part of the "estranging" task all anthropologists have to complete when they attempt making the familiar look strange (ten Have, 2002). For many researchers, a digital camera will be a technology of choice. It allows recording in stereo, it is small enough to be taken into most places, and it is relatively unobtrusive. The stereo feature comes in handy during transcription, especially of multi-person talk. Using headphones one can hear the different directions of the voices, which aids in recovering who spoke and what was said. When using external microphones, depending on the make, the digital stereo feature may be lost.

For those using Macintosh computers, iMovie provides an ideal tool for digitizing video and for creating a variety of formats for self-contained movie files, which, because of their smaller size, are more easily stored on CD and shared. Self-contained movie files can be scanned rapidly, which is of great advantage for quickly finding episodes. For those who use archiving and analysis software to label episodes, they will need self-contained movie files. Finally, transcription programs require self-contained movies. A commercial version of Quicktime™ has been useful in our research. It permits the creation of shorter clips even after the production of self-contained movie files and the creation of self-contained sound tracks that are required for the analysis of prosody.

*CLAN* is a free, multi-platform piece of software developed at the University of Pittsburgh, which I have found quite useful for some purposes (http://childes.psy.cmu.edu/clan/). It can be operated both for transcribing and for conduction conversation analysis. Another transcription program designed to facilitate the transcription and analysis of video data is called *Transana*, and it is freely available (www.transana.org). At the moment of this writing, it is only available for PC users, but a Macintosh OS-X version is announced. Transana is available as both a single-user application and a multi-user version, which allows a local workgroup to share access to a single dataset. It provides a way to view video, create a transcript, and link places in the transcript to frames in the video. It provides tools for identifying and organizing analytically interesting portions of videos, as well as for attaching keywords to those video clips.

262

After having used a number of different software packages, I have found *PRAAT* (http://www.praat.org) the most useful and reliable across the voice ranges for which I conduct prosodic analysis—from seventh-grade students to practicing adult engineers, technicians, and scientists. Its multi-platform availability is of advantage to all those who collaborate a lot, which frequently has to occur across platforms. Furthermore, PRAAT allows creation of graphs in postscript and PICT formats (on the Macintosh platform), which can be shared between programs on the same machine and with collaborators.

## POSSIBILITIES AND CONSTRAINTS

Conversation analysis has developed as, and continuous to be, among others, a rather specific analytic endeavor concerned with the emergence of social relations and societal structure in and through *talk-in-interaction*. Over the decades, numerous researchers have found among its methods useful analytic tools to investigate a variety of phenomena not for the purpose of contributing to CA independent of the setting—the interests of "pure" CA (ten Have, 1999)—but to contribute to understanding phenomena in their own disciplines, that is, applying CA to the problems and in the settings of interest. The concerns of these researchers have a decidedly applied character and perspective, concerned with various forms of institutional interactions. In this chapter, I exemplified a variety of concepts and procedures that readers might find useful as resources in their own analysis of interesting social and institutional phenomena.

Most generally, educators—even those who are not committed to social and cultural criticism—are in the business of contributing to change, for example, their students' knowledge and identity, and their and their students' world. Conversation analysis is a very powerful tool as it allows us to explicate the ways in which conversationalists produce|reproduce social order in ongoing, contingent, and highly efficient ways. That is, it is a powerful tool especially for the critical educator interested in how power/knowledge and social inequalities are brought about maintained in an ongoing manner. Its power arises from the fact that even if deconstruction is not part of a researcher's methodological agenda, it is a perspicuous factor of the ultimate descriptions a researcher arrives at (Lynch & Bogen, 1996). Employed in concert with my video-based ethnographic efforts, CA has developed into my tool of choice.

Conversation analysis is, however, not a methodological panacea. CA does not provide us with the whole picture. Similar to the limitations that have been attributed to ethnomethodology (Chua, 1977), CA allows us to get at how social actors produce|reproduce social relations, social orders, and ideology; that is, it is concerned with the local organization of social order. In this orientation, it does not allow us to understand the determinations of structures from outside of the actors' situation. That is, for example, CA can help us in explicating and understanding how Anne and Dan produce|reproduce social relations in an interview/think-aloud-protocol situation, using a variety of cultural resources at hand, but it cannot get at the social phenomenon of social scientists conducting interviews and think-aloud

263

protocols; only a cultural-historical (Marxist) analysis of the division of labor leads us to the emergence of the phenomenon and its interpenetration with society as a whole. CA is, in a sense, loyal to the local and particularities of everyday life and therefore fails to move beyond the everyday and make connections with the mac-rolevel of society and imposes an ideological description on situations and people it studies (Smith, 1999). That is, CA can get at the use and deployment of re-sources in the setting, but it cannot normally get us at the (external, structural) de-termination of some of these resources. Together with a critical (e.g., Marxist) the-ory, conversation analysis—as ethnomethodology (Freund & Abrams, 1976), can be used to provide a critique of ideology and the production and dissemination of social information. Both forms of research see social knowledge inextricably linked to the situations in which and how it is produced. Critical educators, there-fore, will want to appropriate CA into a critical theory that allows for and legiti-mates more activist stance to social life than is taken by CA and ethnomethodol-ogy.

## NOTES

[1] In the work of my research group, we have found it helpful to unite pairs of mutually constitutive and presupposing mutually exclusive terms but to separate them with the Sheffer stroke "|." This creates a unit that embodies a contradiction, which in turn constitutes the motor of change (Goulart & Roth, in press).

[2] Conversation analysts make use of a transcription notation system that Gail Jefferson (e.g., 1989) developed over a period of years. Those listed below are the most commonly used. More complete discussion can be found in Heritage and Atkinson (1984), ten Have (1999), or Psathas and Anderson (1990).

| | |
|---|---|
| A: ⌈I'm⌉ looking | Brackets indicate the extent to which speech or |
| D: ⌊Oh ⌈ | actions overlap. |
| A: curves= | Equal signs are used when there is no audible gap |
| D:      =Oh | between two utterances next. |
| (0.56) | Pause measured in hundreds of a second are enclosed in single parentheses. |
| (.) | A dot in parentheses indicates a slight pause, less than 0.10 seconds long. |
| Faster | Underline indicates emphasis or stress in delivery. |
| YEA | Capital letters are used when a syllable, word, or phrase is louder than the surrounding talk. |
| A: S:o:: | When a sound is longer than normal, each colon indicates approximately 0.1 of a second of lengthening. |
| A: Envi- | The n-dash marks a sudden stop in the utterance. |
| .,? | Punctuation marks are used to capture characteristics of speech rather than grammatical features. |

| `.hh::` | A dot prefixed "h" denotes inbreath; without dot, exhalation. |
|---|---|
| `(stay out?)` | The question mark following items enclosed in single parentheses denotes an uncertain hearing. |
| `((circles))` | Double parentheses enclose transcriber comments. |
| `°Or?°` | Degree signs enclose utterances produced with low speech intensity. |

[3] At the time of this writing, the ISI Web of Knowledge lists at least 1264 citations for the "A simplest systematics. . ." and over 870 citations to the *Lectures*.

[4] For the technical aspects of working with image and sound tracks, see the section below. Having tried out a number of different packages for working with the sound track, I have found PRAAT the most useful, versatile, and platform independent. The curves for the pitch and intensity graphs were produced within PRAAT and then saved in image format to receive further treatment in a graphics package (e.g., addition of text).

[5] "Tympan" (Derrida, 1982) explicitly links the penetration of the ear by words, on the one hand, and the penetration of thought by a binary logic, on the other.

## REFERENCES

Ashmore, M., & Reed, D. (2000). Innocence and nostalgia in conversation analysis: The dynamic relations of tape and transcript. *FQS: Forum Qualitative Sozialforschung/ Forum Qualitative Social Research* [Online journal], *1* (3). Available at URL: http://www.qualitative-research.net/fqs-texte/3-00/3-00ashmorereed-e.htm. (Accessed December 17, 2004)

Boden, D. (1994). *The business of talk: Organization in action*. Cambridge: Polity Press.

Chua, B. (1977). Delineating a Marxist interest in ethnomethodology. *The American Sociologist, 12*, 24–32.

Derrida, J. (1982). *Margins of philosophy*. Chicago: Chicago University Press.

Freund, P., & Abrams, M. (1976). Ethnomethodology and Marxism: Their use for critical theorizing. *Theory and Society, 3*, 377–393.

Garfinkel, H., & Sacks, H. (1986). On formal structures of practical action. In H. Garfinkel (Ed.), *Ethnomethodological studies of work* (pp. 160–193). London: Routledge & Kegan Paul.

Goodwin, C., Goodwin, M. H., & Yaeger-Dror M. (2002). Multi-modality in girls' game disputes. *Journal of Pragmatics 34*, 1621–1649.

Goulart, M.I.M., & Roth, W.-M. (in press). Margin|centre: Toward a dialectic view of participation. *Journal of Curriculum Studies*.

Have, P. ten (1999). *Doing conversation analysis: A practical guide*. London: Sage.

Have, P. ten (2002). The notion of member is the heart of the matter: On the role of membership knowledge in ethnomethodological inquiry. *FQS: Forum Qualitative Sozialforschung / Forum Qualitative Social Research* [Online journal], *3* (3). Available at URL: http://www.qualitative-research.net/fqs-texte/3-02/3-02tenhave-e.htm (Accessed December 21, 2004)

Heath, C. (1986). *Body movement and speech in medical interaction*. Cambridge: Cambridge University Press.

Heritage, J., & Atkinson, J. M. (1984). Introduction. In J. M. Atkinson & J. Heritage (Eds.), *Structures of social action: Studies in conversation analysis* (pp. 1–15). Cambridge: Cambridge University Press.

Jefferson, G. (1989). Preliminary notes on a possible metric which provides for a "standard maximum" silence of approximately one second in conversation. In D. Roger & P. Bull (Eds.), *Conversation: An interdisciplinary perspective* (pp. 166–196). Clevedon: Multilingual Matters.

Latour, B. (1999). *Pandora's hope: Essays on the reality of science studies*. Cambridge, MA: Harvard University Press.

Lynch, M., & Bogen, D. (1996). *The spectacle of history: Speech, text, and memory at the Iran-contra hearings*. Durham: Duke University Press.

Maynard, D. W., & Marlaire, C. L. (1992). Good reasons for bad testing performance: The interactional substrate of educational exams. *Qualitative Sociology, 15*, 177–202.

Maynard, D. W., & Schaeffer, N. C. (2000). Towards a sociology of social scientific knowledge: survey research and ethnomethodology's asymmetric alternates. *Social Studies of Science, 30*, 323–370.

McNeill, D. (1992). *Hand and mind: What gestures reveal about thought*. Chicago: University of Chicago.

McNeill, D., & Duncan, S. D. (2000). Growth points in thinking for speaking. In D. McNeill (ed.), *Language and gesture* (pp. 141–161). Cambridge: Cambridge University Press.

Middleton, D., & Edwards, D. (1990). *Collective remembering*. London: Sage.

Müller, F. E. (1996). Affiliating and disaffiliating with continuers: Prosodic aspects of recipiency. In E. Couper-Kuhlen & M. Selting (Eds.), *Prosody in conversation: Interactional studies* (pp. 131–176). Cambridge: Cambridge University Press.

Orlikowski, W. J., & Yates, J. (2002). It's about time: Temporal structuring in organizations. *Organization Science, 13*, 684–700.

Pomerantz, A. (1984). Agreeing and disagreeing with assessments: Some features of preferred/dispreferred turn shapes. In J. M. Atkinson & J. Heritage (Eds.), *Structures of social action: Studies in conversation analysis* (pp. 57–101). Cambridge: Cambridge University Press.

Psathas, G., & Anderson, T. (1990). The "practices" of transcription in conversation analysis. *Semiotica, 78*, 75–99.

Pozzer-Ardenghi, L., & Roth, W.-M. (in press). Photographs in lectures: Gestures as meaning-making resources. *Linguistics & Education, 15*, 275-293.

Roth, W.-M. (2004). Perceptual gestalts in workplace communication. *Journal of Pragmatics, 36*, 1037–1069.

Roth, W.-M. (2005). Becoming like the other. In W.-M. Roth & K. Tobin (Eds.), *Teaching together, learning together* (pp. 27–51). New York: Peter Lang.

Roth, W.-M. (in press). Mathematical modeling 'in the wild': A case of hot cognition. In R. Lesh, J. J. Kaput, E. Hamilton, & J. Zawojewski (Eds.), *Users of mathematics: Foundations for the future* (pp. •••–•••). Mahwah, NJ: Lawrence Erlbaum Associates.

Sacks, H. (1992a). *Lectures on conversation* vol. 1. Oxford: Basil Blackwell.

Sacks, H. (1992b). *Lectures on conversation* vol. 2. Oxford: Basil Blackwell.

Sacks, H., Schegloff, E., & Jefferson, G. (1974). A simplest systematics for the organization of turn taking for conversation. *Language, 50*, 696–735.

Schegloff, E., Jefferson, G., & Sacks, H. (1977). The preference for self-correction in the organization of repair in conversation. *Language, 53*, 361–382.

Smith, D. (1999). *Writing the social: Critique, theory, and investigations*. Toronto: University of Toronto Press.

Suchman, L. A., & Jordan, B. (1990). Interactional troubles in face-to-face survey interviews. *Journal of the American Statistical Association, 85*, 232–244.

Tobin, K., & McRobbie, C. J. (1996). Cultural myths as constraints to the enacted curriculum. *Science Education, 80*, 223–241.

## WEB-BASED RESOURCES

Charles Antaki's website (Loughborough)—with practical guides to doing CA. URL: http://www-staff.lboro.ac.uk/~sscal/sitemenu.htm.

Many conversation analytic and ethnomethodological websites (individuals, resources) are indexed at a site for ethnomethodology and conversation analysis (ETHNO/CA NEWS) maintained by Paul ten Have URL: http://www2.fmg.uva.nl/emca/.

Some readers may find Transana helpful for transcribing and linking video and transcript. It is available at URL: http://www.transana.org. Only the PC version is currently available (December 2004).

The downloadable files and manuals for the CLAN software can be found at URL: http://childes.psy.cmu.edu/clan/.

PRAAT is a freely available program designed for linguists and has many features
(http://www.praat.org/). I found it to give the best analyses of pitch, which depend both on the algorithm a program uses and the parameters chosen by the analyst.

Emmanuel Schegloff, a leading scholar and practitioner of conversation analysis, has made numerous papers available in PDF format on his website at URL:
http://www.sscnet.ucla.edu/soc/faculty/schegloff/.

Chuck Goodwin is an applied linguist who uses classical conversation analytic procedures, but also analyses body movements, body positions, and gestures as well as prosody. A number of his papers and chapters are available online at URL: http://www.sscnet.ucla.edu/clic/cgoodwin/.

267

DAVID W. JARDINE

# 11. ON HERMENEUTICS: "OVER AND ABOVE OUR WANTING AND DOING"

My real concern was and is ... not what we do or what we ought to do, but
what happens to us over and above our wanting and doing.

Hans-Georg Gadamer, from Truth and Method (1989, p. xxviii)

I

The hermeneutic phenomenon is basically not a problem of method at all. It
is not concerned primarily with amassing verified knowledge, such as would
satisfy the methodological ideal of science–yet it, too is concerned with
knowledge and with truth. But what kind of knowledge and what kind of
truth? (Gadamer, 1989, p. xxii)

I have retained the term "hermeneutics". . .not in the sense of a methodology
but as a theory of the real experience that thinking is. (p. xxxvi)

If hermeneutics is, as Hans-Georg Gadamer suggests, "basically not a problem of
method at all," it would seem rather difficult to make a case for hermeneutics as a
research method in education.

Hermeneutics may not provide us with a method, but it does give researchers
and teachers and students an image of how human understanding operates in the
world. It articulates how the world is a *living* world of *living* ancestry that perennially has to take up the task presented by the arrival of the new and the young into
that living world. As such, it provides a way to re-think what we experience in our
day to day lives as teachers, what we understand teaching to be, what we imagine
about the relations between the young and the old, what we understand knowledge
and tradition and language and conversation and art and play and imagination and
words and images and the methods of the sciences to be. This by-no-means- exhaustive array of topics are all dealt with in *Truth and Method*, Gadamer's profound, beautiful and terribly difficult work, originally published in German in 1960
and first translated into English in 1975.

In this chapter, I want to show how hermeneutics has a special affinity to education. It is not simply that hermeneutics is particularly well suited to education as an
object of scholarly investigation. More than this, hermeneutics, as a way of conducting research, is educative in its intent. It wants to listen, to affect and to invite,
not merely inform. But there is an even strong affinity between hermeneutics and
education. Hermeneutics is also, I suggest, a way of conducting classroom life. My

*K. Tobin & J. Kincheloe, (eds.), Doing Educational Research—A Handbook, 269–288.*

work has been focussed for several years now on classroom events–not only inter-preting them using hermeneutics as a way of understanding, but showing how, in effective, intellectually stimulating classrooms, *teaching and learning themselves can be hermeneutic in character* (e.g., Jardine, Clifford & Friesen, 2006). This itself is a hermeneutic point. Our choice of research methodologies is, of necessity, a choice regarding how understanding happens and what sort of voice is given to the "object" of such research. Therefore, our choice of research methodologies is a deeply pedagogical choice *at the outset*, before any research project has begun.

This case regarding the pedagogical character of hermeneutics can be made be-cause hermeneutics has, at its heart, the belief that understanding occurs and can be properly cultivated and cared for only in the often contentious, often transforma-tive, *relationship between* the young and the old, the new and the established, be-tween ancestral bloodlines and what Hannah Arendt (1969, p. 177) called "the fact of natality." "*The true locus of hermeneutics is this in-between*" (Gadamer, 1989, p. 295), as one might expect from a theory of experience named after a god of bor-ders and boundaries who, sometimes trickster in intent (Jardine, Clifford & Friesen, 2003), sometimes monstrous (e.g., Jardine, 1998; Jardine & Field 2006; Jardine & Novodvorski, 2006), shuttles messages between heaven and earth, be-tween the gods and humanity.

II

For those who have struggled to find their way through the first part of Gadamer's *Truth and Method*, it is often very difficult to understand exactly why, in introduc-ing hermeneutics, he begins by talking about "aesthetic experience." This seems very far away from anything that might help us understand the classroom, or the curriculum or how to do educational research.

Gadamer's talk of "aesthetic experience" is not about developing a theory of "art appreciation" (although it certainly has a profound relevance for such devel-opment). He is discussing aesthetic experience as an introduction to the nature of hermeneutics. He is pointing to a commonplace experience that any teacher knows about full well. Before we adopt any methodological stance, before we "do" any research, before we know it, we enter a classroom and something that a student says, some work that they have produced, something they have written, some ques-tion they ask, the look in one child's eyes, some sketch posted on a bulletin board– these simple things sometimes *strike* us, *catch* our fancy, *address* us, *speak* to us, *call* for a response, *elicit* or *provoke* something in us, *ask* something of us, *hit* us, *bowl* us over, *stop* us in our tracks, makes us *catch our breath*.

This initiatory phenomenon of hermeneutics must be thought about phenome-nologically and experientially:

> Things announce themselves, bear witness to their presence: "Look, here we are." They regard us beyond how we may regard them, our perspectives, what we intend with them, and how we dispose of them. (Hillman, 1982, p. 77)

Rich and memorable experiences catch our attention and ask things of us. As such, the venture of coming to understand such things is characterizable as "more a passion than an action. A question *presses itself upon us*" (Gadamer, 1989, p. 366, my emphasis) and places us and our being-in-the-world into question.

This is what Gadamer means by suggesting that, at the core of hermeneutics, at the core of "what happens to us over and above our wanting and doing," is something akin to an "aesthetic experience." Aesthetic experience, Gadamer suggests, is the experience of being drawn out of our subjectivity and into a teeming world of relations that lives "beyond our wanting and doing." The task posed to understanding at such a juncture cannot be simply one of corralling that teeming world back into the confines of our constructs.

In these aesthetic moments we are drawn out of ourselves and our constructions and our methods and our "our"-centeredness and get caught up by something, charmed by it, drawn into *its* sway, into *its* play, into *its Spiel*. (This is why, after exploring aesthetic experience, Gadamer then turns, in *Truth and Method* [1989, pp. 101-9] to the ways in which play is a clue to understanding what happens to us in understanding the world). Such events–such moments of "opening" and of "venture"-- "would not deserve the interest we take in [them] if [they] did not have something to teach us that we could not know by ourselves" (Gadamer, 1989, p. xxxv). Like monsters in fairy tales, they wouldn't whisper to us or stop us in our tracks if they didn't have something to tell us.

Hermeneutics is, therefore, implicitly a critique of a particular way in which constructivism has been conceived. We can only suggest what is entailed here (e.g., Jardine 2005, Jardine, Fawcett & Johnson, 2006, Jardine, 2006).

There are some lines from a poem by Rainer Marie Rilke that Gadamer cites as the frontispiece of *Truth and Method*: "Catch only what you've thrown yourself, all is mere skill and little gain. But when you're suddenly the catcher of a ball thrown.—towards you, to your center—why catching then becomes a power–not yours, a world's." What addresses us does so from beyond our wanting and doing, beyond our constructs. We experience the limits of our experience by experiencing something that calls us to go beyond the limits of our experience. Less philosophically put, we live in the world and that world houses us and our thinking and experiencing. We do not house it in our constructs. This, of course, is an *ecological* and a *pedagogical* point as much as it is a commentary on research methodologies in education.

Gadamer put it so simply: "something awakens our interest–that is really what comes first!" (Gadamer 2001, p. 50). "Understanding," Gadamer insists, "begins. ..when something addresses us." (Gadamer, 1989, p. 299). Hermeneutics goes further even than this. It wants to show that, within this beginning, originary experience of being addressed is some sort of "truth claim," (Gadamer, 1989, p. xxii) although, of course, what is meant here will need the rest of the chapter and more to fill out.

III

In a chapter on hermeneutics as a "research method" in education, you might expect someone to tell you *how to do it*. But this way of proceeding towards understanding–starting with explicitly laying procedures on the "how to" of understanding--is a contentious matter in hermeneutics itself and understanding why this is so helps in our understanding of hermeneutics and its ways.

There is a brief, lovely, difficult passage from *Truth and Method* (1989, p. 21) that will help us here: "Youth demands images for its imagination and for forming its memory. Thus [Giambattista] Vico [b. 1668] supplements the *critica* of Cartesianism with the old *topica.*" Gadamer is suggesting that anyone new to something ("youth," so to speak–Vico's *pedagogical* point is not necessarily or solely a *chronological* one) cannot begin the task of coming to understand through being told what *method* to use (*critica*, from Rene Descartes [b. 1596] *Discourse on Method [1955]*). A method has no face, no body, no memories, no stories, no blood, no images, no ancestors, no ghosts and spirits, no monsters, no familiars. It doesn't help us get our bearings and learn our way around, because there is no "place" to it. The young, as Jean Piaget so well attests, are imaginal, playful, bodily beings in their coming to understand (see Jardine, 2005).

Hermeneutics does not begin its work by beginning with method. It does not begin by characterizing understanding as an action or set of actions we can marshal. It begins, rather, with *topica*–great image-filled, sensory, alluring *topics* that address us and draw us into their sway and ask things of us. To re-cite Gadamer's claims, "*something* awakens our interest"(2001, p. 50, emphasis added), "*something* addresses us" (1989, p. 299, emphasis added).

The first question in hermeneutics is "What is your topic?" because in pursuit of an answer to this question, memory is formed, images are entertained, thinking is enriched by traversing the terrain, the place, the topography, with all is shapes and ancestors and old stories and vital new arrivals. Hermeneutics begins substantively, with a topic that addresses us and draws us in. "*What* is being investigated itself holds part of the answer concerning *how* it should be investigated" (Smith, 1999, p. 39). Part of the task of hermeneutics is learning how to "entrust ourselves to what we are investigating to guide us safely in the quest" (Gadamer, 1989, p. 378).

This probably seems really odd on the face of it because this description of hermeneutics still has no face. Hermeneutics can only start to substantively and imaginatively appear in the face of "a case" (even though hermeneutics does not produce "case studies"). It is always *something* that happens that awakens our interest in pursuing interpretation.

There is always a story that happened once upon a time.

IV

A former student teacher phoned me in a panic late one August, excited that she had been offered a job in an Early Childhood Education classroom starting the next week and, of course, apprehensive about all that might entail. She phoned, I suspect, as much for reassurance as for advice. Eight weeks later, well into the school year, she phoned again and recounted the experience of going to her new school just days before the children were to arrive.

The principal was not available when she arrived, and she was instructed by the school secretary that her room was "down there, Room 10." She had walked down the hallway to what was to be "her room" and paused. The door was shut and she spoke of this shut door being "imposing," "as if something was going on in there already" that of which she was not yet part of, something to which she did not yet "belong." As she told it, she knew that when she opened that door, somehow, "everything would be different," things would be, in her words "turned around." She sensed that, once she "stepped in," she would be finally "crossing over" from student to teacher: "once I entered the room, I knew that would be *it.* "

Here is where hermeneutics can start to work. This incident, in its very commonplaceness and simplicity, was full of address for me when it occurred. These new teacher's words sound familiar. "Something is going on," (*im Spiele ist*)," "something is happening" (*sich abspielt*) (Gadamer, 1989, p. 104) (note how both these etymological twists in the German terms dovetail with *Truth and Method*'s interest in play, *Spiel*–a love of etymology gets cultivated as you become practiced in hermeneutics [Smith, 1999, p. 39]).

I expect, at first blush, that we have all had similar experiences to the sorts of things this new teacher seems to be articulating or alluding to. In some sense, and to some degree, we all understand what this new teacher is talking about. On the face of it, we sort of "get" it. Her tale is familiar, familial, something with which we already have deep, unvoiced "kinship" (Wittgenstein, 1968, p. 36), something to which our own lives and what we've experienced of the life of teaching somehow bear a "family resemblance" (p. 32). We live together in a world in which such things are not especially extraordinary to say.

In the face of this *prima facie* sense of kinship, the hermeneutic question is this: How are we to do justice to this particular episode that happened to a particular teacher at a particular time and place, while at once respecting the undeniable sense of kinship we experience in hearing this teacher's tale? Again, the moment of address occurs somehow "between" this new eruption of life and some older that is awoken.

Hermeneutics requires that we attempt to experience this happenstance incident as, so to speak, "speaking to us," having something to say to us beyond what we might be able, as yet, to say of it. Imagine this. I stood at the closed door and knew that when I walked through, everything would be different. This incident, taken up hermeneutically:

> draws us [*both* parties to that telephone call]—outside of ourselves [this is not "teacher narrative" owned by any one of us] and imposes its own presence on us. [It] no longer has the character of an object that stands over against us; we are no longer able to approach this like an object of knowledge, grasping, measuring and controlling. Rather than meeting us in our world, it is much more a world into which we ourselves are drawn (Gadamer, 1994, pp. 191-192)

Those new teacher's comments seem "surrounded" by living *worlds* of relations, worlds full of images, faces, concepts, rituals, bloodlines, invocations, spooks and sprits. They are "familiar." And those surroundings seem to already surround me, since it seems that I am already living in a familiarity with that world.

Hermeneutics is therefore pointing to something very commonplace, but also something very odd to articulate in the context of research methodologies: "a hitherto concealed experience that transcends thinking from the position of subjectivity" (Gadamer, 1989, p. 100).

To cite again from Rilke's frontispiece "Not yours, a world's."

V

At this juncture, part of the work of understanding hermeneutics is to understand aspects of its reflections on the treatment usually given to such incidents in most research methodologies that we have inherited. Hermeneutics is, in part, a critique of the ways that the human sciences have methodologically, epistemologically and ontologically "aped" the natural sciences to terrible, damaging, effect. More bluntly put, hermeneutics provides a critique of how *education* has become spellbound by a weak and intellectually dull-minded version of the methodologies of the natural sciences. Differently put, the following ancestral exploration can be read as a description of the situation that teachers and students often experience at school. We can only untangle a few small threads of this inheritance in this context.

"A substance is that which requires nothing except itself in order to exist" (Descartes, 1955, p. 275). This is a longstanding definition, cited here from Descartes (seventeenth century) but winding its way back into the work of Thomas Aquinas (thirteenth century) and from there, back into Aristotelian metaphysics (third century B.C.E.). I cite it here because for much work in educational research (quantitative and qualitative alike), the fundamental given (the root of the notion of "data" as "that which is given or granted") in research is *not* that original, ambiguously alluring familiarity that first strikes us when we hear this new teacher's words about going to her school for the first time. What is given in those methodologies for which this Cartesian idea of substance holds sway is *not* a world into which we are drawn. Rather, what is strictly given is this new teacher's words is an "isolated incident."

The literal text produced by this particular teacher at this particular time in this particular situation-this, severed from all its abundant familiarity, severed from our interest in it, severed from what we think it means or what worlds it reminds us of– this "that which requires nothing except itself in order to exist." This is the substance of (most forms of) research. In light of this pronouncement about the substance of this incident, all that compelling familiarity is henceforth understood to be *subjective*, an added, distortive, contaminating "extra" that we "bring" to the in-fact isolated, "in itself" thing and somehow lay over top of it as a layer of subjective response or the like. What was initially experienced as the address of something from beyond the confines of subjectivity is, in this way, rendered subjective (see Gadamer's discussion of the "subjectivization of aesthetics" [1989, pp. 42-80]; see also Jardine & Batycky, 2006). Both quantitative and qualitative methodologies fall for this move.

Against this premise of isolated substances, we make this incident into something portioned off from anything else except itself. We have to rescue it from its familiarity, because the familiarity it evokes in us is, we presume, a *contamination* of its being what it in fact is. Therefore we must begin by systematic acts of severance aimed at retrieving the given ("the isolated incident") out of the amorphous web of interweaving meanings in which it was originally embedded and in whose abundant embrace it first appeared. We must sever any interconnections that are already at work before the methods of our inquiry are enacted. We must (ideally, at least) put out of play any understanding of or connection to this instance that we may have as researchers. We must suspend any spontaneous familiarity or sense of kinship that it evokes in us, any sort of aesthetic appeal or experiential reminders or reminiscences. We must also put out of play any interconnections we see or suspect between this instance and any other meanings or tales or stories or narratives. We must stop dreaming that the world has something to say to us.

These two acts of severance-this instance from us and our lived familiarity with and attraction to it, and this instance from any and all other instances-will allow it to become a self-identical substance, something that stands "without us" and without reference to any other incident. Thus severed, it no longer signifies or signals anything beyond itself. It becomes, as far as we know thus far, "an isolated incident," just itself and nothing more.

This is a fascinating process to which we subject both the instance and ourselves. It is, as we have alluded, akin to a sort of purification ritual (Bordo, 1988, p. 108) that both we and the instance must undergo. Regarding the instance itself, ambiguous linkages and telltale signs and marks of potentially violating interconnectedness are systematically eliminated, producing of a sort of virginal, untouched instance. And regarding ourselves, we can no longer approach this instance with the moist and fleshy and playful and imaginative familiarity with which we began. We must now simply "behold" it with what Alfred North Whitehead named the "celibacy of the intellect" (cited in Fox, 1983, p. 23). We must remain strictly within the parameters of the methods of severance we have enacted, for any other interconnection would despoil or defile the instance we have so carefully and methodically isolated and purified. Our connection to this instance thus becomes gutted. We understand it "from the neck up" and only within the bounds that our severing and isolating methodology allows. We deny that it is our kin. We begin our work with "abandonment" (Arendt, 1969, p. 188) and "betrayal" (1969, p. 196).

"I don't know anything. I've never seen it before. It's not mine. It doesn't point to me. I'm not implicated." Severance has freed us from our kinships and dependencies. I'm just an anonymous, replaceable, controllable, predictable, methodwielder now. My only connection to this incident will be forged *after* and *as a consequence of* and *solely within the parameters of* my "methodology."

There is an aside here that is simply astounding. The researcher has been purged of dark and lingering familiarities and the incident, too, has been isolated from its world of relations.

This spins us back to Descartes and his Aristotelian notion of substance. Isolated, purified, self-identical substances–*objects*, one might say—*contain no contradictions*:

> Descartes' emphasis on clear and distinct ideas . . .served to canonize the Aristotelian principle of non-contradiction. Since the Cartesian paradigm recognizes no self-contradictions in logic, and since logic (or geometry), according to Descartes, is the way nature behaves, the paradigm allows for no self-contradiction in nature (Berman, 1983, p. 23).

The clean and clearly isolated instance is what it is without reference to anything else (the principle of identity [A=A] that underwrites the principle of non-contradiction [it either is A or it isn't A]). The isolated incident is what it is only *without* all its relations. Individual, self-contained, autonomous, self-existing things come first.

A more direct and familiar way of putting this process is that, through these severances of the original familiarity in which we were immersed and which addressed and charmed us in the first place, we render this instance into *an object* and, correlatively, render ourselves into a *knowing subject* which has this object, not as something to which we belong and have a kinship or relation, but as something standing over against us and is allowed, now, to appear only within the confines of the methods that knowing subject wields. The instance as object now no longer draws us into a world. It no longer is experienced as fitting into a complex fabric of interrelations in which I ambiguously belong with it, but rather "stands out," isolated from what surrounds it.

From this original severance thus begins a long series of correlative purification movements between this instance and myself as inquirer. "Subject and object precipitate out simultaneously. Yet even while separate, they remain interdependent, because the breakdown in the world [i.e., the tearing of the instance out of the fabric of familiarity in which it originally lived] corresponds to a breakdown in understanding" (Weinsheimer, 1987, p. 5). Once divested of the original, intimate knowing, I can no longer claim to understand this now severed object. That original allure never was *knowing the object*. It was just subjective. Although I might have experienced this original allure as a matter of the object drawing me into *its* orbit, in fact (according to the ontological assumptions of this way of proceeding) it was a matter of *me* drawing the object into *my* orbit.

In this way, "both subject and object are derivative and secondary, in that both precipitate out of the more primordial unity of being at home in the world" (Weinsheimer, 1987, p. 5), a "being at home" bespoken by the fact that I somehow "already understood" what this teacher said before the specific work of rendering it an object of research even began. This precipitated subject and precipitated object "are [both] determined negatively: the knowing subject [now severed from our original senses of familiarity] no longer understands and the object [now severed from its living context of familiarity and kin] no longer fits" (p. 5).

Now "real research" can finally begin because we finally have an "object" to research. Before these severances, we had a *topica*. Now, as a consequence of *critica*, we no longer have a topic. We have an object-domain to which we do not belong and in relation to which "belonging" doesn't even make sense.

These fundamental acts of severance and the convoluted sequence of correlative purification transformations in both the object of inquiry and the inquirer, give subsequent research peculiar and deliberate anonymity and rootlessness. When we hear this new teacher's talk about the anxieties of opening the classroom door for the first time and entering in, all we can do is set up a research project in which we can collect a lot of new teacher's talk and then check whether or not a significant number of "respondents" will cite the same experiences, use the same words and concepts, speak in the same terms in their reports of their own experiences as beginning teachers. Because we have actively and intentionally reduced this instance to an isolated incident, it becomes essential to collect more and more incidents in order to raise this first incident out of its isolation. An interesting turn of events: we raise these incidents out of their isolation through first isolating them and then rescuing them (us?) from their (our?) isolation by finding frequently occurring themes.

Because we have actively and intentionally restricted ourselves to that knowledge produced methodologically, it becomes illegitimate to engage these instances in ways other than simply collecting them and looking for surfaces features. This first instance becomes significant (that is to say, it points to something beyond itself) only insofar as it can now be shown to reoccur in a (mathematically) significant number of other equally actively isolated incidents. Significance thus becomes intimately linked with *frequency*. This happens to the extent that, even in qualitative studies, some still ask how many people they should talk to in their research interviews and how many transcripts must mention some term before my qualitative understanding is adequately and warrantably "saturated."

The interest of such a mathematization of significance is not to better understand the world(s) into which this incident has drawn our attention. The purpose is not to cultivate a place of commiseration and conversation and reflection and thinking and scholarly investigation into this *topica* that has addressed us. Rather, the purpose is to be better able to control, predict, and manipulate the future reoccurrences of such talk (Habermas, 1972). Obviously, however, we might be able to say with great assurance what the future statistical likelihood is of a beginning teacher using the terms we have coded and counted, without having considered for a moment *what is being said,* what worlds are being invoked by such terms.

Above, we mentioned that, following upon the methodical severances of our familiarity with the world, there is a correlative negative determination of both object (which now no longer fits) and subject (who now no longer understands):

> The cognitive remedies for these twin defects are likewise correlative. The object is disassembled, the rules of its functioning are ascertained, and then it

is reconstructed according to those rules; so, also, knowledge is analysed, its rules are determined, and finally it is redeployed as method. The purpose of both remedies is to prevent unanticipated future breakdowns by means of breaking down even further the flawed entity and then synthesizing it artificially. Thus Gadamer speaks of "the ideal of knowledge familiar from natural science, whereby we understand a process only when we can bring it about artificially" [Gadamer, 1989, p. 336]. (Weinsheimer, 1987, p. 6).

Once these "cognitive remedies" are enacted, we can (within mathematically prescribed limits) predict the reoccurrence of such incidents and therefore we no longer are "taken aback" by such reoccurrence. Such incidents will not allure us again and catch us off guard, with all the disorienting and disturbing consequences that such allure can have. These remedies prevent the possibility of understanding being provoked by something unwittingly and without methodical anticipation. Thus, "objectification" protects us from dangerous unanticipated turns that the world might take. This is precisely the strength of this sort of research. It rules out of consideration unanticipated ("uncontrolled for") interchanges with the world.

Of course, the methodical attainment of such objectivity does not altogether prevent playful, risk laden, unanticipated interchanges. Things still happen. However, their happenstance occurrence is divested of any claim of or access to truth.

Truth and method become identified.

## VI

Hermeneutics doesn't drag us through difficult terrain like this in order to "philosophize." It does so because this terrain is *one of the things that has happened to us.* Reflecting on such matters helps us think through what has happened to our ability to understand what comes to meet us in our experience. Doing a hermeneutic study requires this sort of work because hermeneutics contends that we have inherited a world full of images and assumptions and desires that affect how we might imagine the very existence and status and worth and place of those new teacher's comments.

Hermeneutics steadfastly holds that these incidents happen and have their meaning and significance *in the world.* Part of the real work of hermeneutic research is to let us deeply experience how deliciously and terribly difficult is the task of wanting to *understand* the great inheritances of human life in the midst of which this new teacher's words appeared. Hermeneutics isn't a psychology. The inner thoughts and feelings of this student's private interiority are not its topic. Her comments' arrival makes *the world* of teaching "waver and tremble" (Caputo, 1987, p. 7). Her comments call ancient tales to account. And her comments do so "beyond [her] wanting and doing."

It is precisely the identification of truth and method that hermeneutics works against. The title of Gadamer's major work is not as simple as it seems. Hermeneutics suggests that there is a "truth" to be had, an understanding to be reached, an experience to be savoured in the provocative, unmethodical incidents of our lives that address us, a truth which is despoiled and thus left out of consideration by the methodical severances and isolation requisite of much qualitative and quantitative research work.

So, to begin again elsewhere. This new teacher's comments arrive. I've heard this before, somewhere. Something is going. "In this short passage, we have an embarrassment of symbolic riches" (Turner, 1987, p. 18)—multiple meanings, "interweaving and criss-crossing" (Wittgenstein, 1968, p. 32) (*textus* originally means "to weave," like textiles):

> The term "initiation" in the most general sense denotes a body of rites and oral teachings whose purpose is to produce a radical modification of the person to be initiated. Initiation is equivalent to an ontological mutation of the existential condition. The novice emerges from his ordeal a totally different being: he has become *another* (Eliade, 1975, p. 112).

Are this new teacher's words signs of initiation and transformation? Are they heralds of "becoming *another*"? The hermeneutic question at this juncture is not "Is this what is somehow 'really' going on in this teacher's words?" as if there was some objective template in the world against which such a claim could be measured. The hermeneutic question clusters like this: "What *difference* does it make if we read these words this way? What possibilities open up? What images and tales and ways of acting in the classroom become warranted? What dangers arrive? What dragons be here?"

We are not "amassing verified knowledge" (Gadamer, 1989, p. xxii) here. We are playfully teasing out a territory and learning its ways and asking what relief might be found in allowing this new teacher's words to "world" (Heidegger, 1962) in this way. This teacher's words can be heard to re-tell ancient and power-laden narratives of initiation and transformation, "insiders" and "outsiders," thresholds and boundaries, liminal spaces and monsters. They are full of images of rites of passage and moving from child to adult and back again (because, of course, once she "enters the room" and turns around, the child will be at the door wanting in). And let's add to the mix the offhand comments of an elementary school principal: "I enjoy having student-teachers in the school. It keeps things lively, keeps us on our toes. And anyway, it's our responsibility. The profession needs new blood." If these moments are allowed to "expand to their full breadth of illuminative meaning" (Norris-Clarke, 1976, p. 188), this principal's words, along with that new teacher's words, echo down into a rich "implicate order" (Bohm, 1983) of metaphors, mythologies and traditions. They contain images of education's relation to and responsibility for the young, as well as images of the mysterious "liminal period" (Turner, 1969) indicated by the hyphenation "student-teacher." The movement through such "threshold times" (Mahdi, et al., 1987, p. ix) is full of "ambiguity and paradox, a confusion of all customary categories" (Turner, 1987, p. 7) and as such, the tales told of such times lend themselves to a discourse that is itself "incurably figurative and polysemous" (Clifford, 1986, p. 5)–just the sort of thing that Vico suggests the young need for the cultivation of their memory and character. Just the sort of literature that might help a student-teacher understand the terrible ambiguity of her task.

Ok, here's a warning It is easy to have a hermeneutic meditation get out of hand. Hermeneutics is necessarily, not accidentally, prone to exaggeration (Gadamer, 1989, p. 115) and hyperbole (Hargreaves, 2005)--flights of over-abundant fantasy. We don't know yet if we are going too far, whether there is any truth to be had. But this much is true about doing hermeneutic work: it has *already begun.* The unfolding and exploring and articulating of and writing about the venture into these worldly possibilities *is* the work of "doing" hermeneutics. We have already started to lay out the shapes of a possible way to understand the experience of teaching and its manifestation in the ordinary talk of a new teacher and an old principal.

This much is true as well. Interpretive research begins with a different sense of the given. Rather than beginning with an ideal of clarity, distinctness, and meth-odological controllability–all consequences of the presumption of isolated sub-stances--and then rendering the given in light of this ideal, hermeneutics begins in the place where we actually start in being granted or given (*datum*) this incident in the first place. Hermeneutics begins (and remains) with the evocative, living fa-miliarity that this tale started to evoke in the first place–that address, that strange familiarity or weird seemliness, that old memory of having read words like this before, felt moments like this in the hallways of schools. The task of interpretation is not to clarify and straighten out this mess. It is, rather, to bring out this evocative given in all its tangled ambiguity, to follow its evocations and the entrails of sense and significance that are wound up with it and not "betray" it (see Caputo, 1987) with promises of isolation and clarity and cleanliness.

Hermeneutics suggests that these striking incidents make a claim on us and open up and reveal something to us about our lives together and what it is that is going on, often unvoiced, in the ever-so commonplace and day-to-day act of being and becoming a teacher. In this sense, our unanticipated, unmethodical being in the world–this happenstance phone call from a former student and her tale of walking down a hallway and standing by a closed door--can, quite literally in certain in-stances, make a claim to some sort of truth.

Teachers are drawn to this story of this student-teacher because it "rings true" to the lives they have led, to moments they have faced, to monsters in education's closet.

Something is waking up here at the edge of familiarity.


VII


We need to ask here the inevitable question: How do I know that this reading I have given this instance is reliable? "What kind of truth" (Gadamer, 1989, p. xxii) are we dealing here? How do I know I'm not just delusional, spooked by Descartes' demons or black biles?

Well, I don't know all by myself or in advance or through the assurance of hav-ing properly applied a particular method. I cannot separate out in advance which features of my reading of this incident reveal nothing more than idiosyncrasies of my individual experiences. "This separation must take place in the process of un-derstanding itself" (Gadamer, 1989, p. 296) and a hermeneutic study, in part, is the articulating of this process, not simply the articulating of the *end-product* of this process. I can only find out about the revelations and distortions that my life brings to the images haunting that phone call from a new teacher by *working such matters out*. And I have to work these matters out *in public*–in writing, in talking to colleagues, in reciting this incident to new student teachers and listening to the buzz that is created, in reading more and thinking more, and therefore in letting the potential distortions of my subjectivity work themselves out into a worldly territory that can comfort and contain and cultivate and limit and, sometimes, humiliate them.

This incident happened 15 years ago, and it still has me in its grip. I'm still "working on it."

Interpretation thus becomes a movement of shaping and making something of this instance and its human topographies, while, at the same time, shaping and making something of myself in the midst of this world in which I work as a teacher, a writer, a scholar, a parent, and so on. Differently put, I become someone in the process of coming to know about the world in which I live. This is why Gadamer (1989) links up hermeneutics, understanding, and the cultivation of character (*Bildung*). I have to let my pre-understandings and prejudices and presumptions fully engage this new teacher's words. I have to bring what I thought I knew about this world of teaching under the witness of these words and see what happens. Hermeneutics is thus not a form of methodological imperviousness but is, rather, precisely the opposite. I must let what I have come to know about this world be susceptible to being supplemented, enhanced, transformed, further-changed, embarrassed, perhaps even humiliated, in confronting what this teacher's text has to say (Gadamer, 1989, p. 299) about this world of teaching. I don't get to say all by myself what will happen, how things will work out, how comments will be understood or whether the work will continue. Teachers know all about this.

Hermeneutics is therefore already operating in a pedagogical space. The fact that I happened to have read and vaguely remembered Mircea Eliade's work on initiation, the fact that I happened to have been called by this teacher and to have been struck by what she said-all of these "happenstances" make possible the interpretation that will then ensue (Weinsheimer, 1987, p. 78). The interpretation that results is thus unavoidably linked to me. It is not something produced by an anonymously wielded method that anyone could wield and get the same results. However-and here is the paradox-*what* the interpretation is henceforth *about*, is not "me" but that topography *of which* I have had certain experiences: initiation. Initiation and its kin form a world in which I am "housed." They are not housed inside of me.

This hermeneutic insistence is rooted in Edmund Husserl's (1970, pp. 12-13) phenomenological admonishment that "consciousness is always consciousness *of* something." Human experience is *intentional*, not psychopathological. Therefore, when students say that they are interested in children's experiences, the hermeneutically proper question is "Children's experiences *of what*? What is the topic, what is the terrain, in which you wish to meet children and understand their ways?" Hermeneutically conceived, people don't "have" experiences. They have experiences of something and therefore, "experience" does not delineate an interiority that has to be deciphered through matching up this new teacher's comments to her real, inner, private, individual, "moist gastric intimacy" (Sartre, 1970, p. 4). Hermeneutically, we are *had* by experience. We suffer it or undergo experiences. We do not possess them. Experience, hermeneutically conceived, is something that happens to us over and above our wanting and doing. To re-iterate something that might now be a bit clearer, hermeneutics is concerned with "a hitherto concealed experience that transcends thinking from the position of subjectivity" (Gadamer, 1989, p. 100).

Even though interpretive work is not possible without a living connection to its topic, it is *the topic* that is the centre of interpretive work. My experiences with such topics are not "interior states" that subjectivize the living phenomenon of initiation and rites of passage into something of *mine* (any more than I would subjectivize that new teacher's words into her property). On the contrary, for hermeneutic work, my experiences are best understood as ventures or journeys through something. In *Truth and Method*, this is why so much discussion occurs regarding the difference between the two German terms for "experience": *Erlebnisse* (1989, pp. 60-80) and *Erfahrung* (pp. 346-361). *Erlebenisse* is etymologically linked to the intimacies of one's inner life (*Leben*, to live). *Erfahrung* contains the roots both of a journey (*Fahren*) and of ancestry (*Vorfahren*).

This latter usage says that our experience is worldly and haunted by those who have journeyed before us. It suggests that, in the classroom, we do not meet students as isolated individual subjectivities. We meet them as worldly beings in the world, say, of poetry or mathematics or the like.

## VIII

The question remains: What kind of truth is being proffered by a hermeneutic study? Clearly, the truth of a hermeneutic study cannot be that its claims match up to some objective state of affairs. The reliability of a hermeneutic study is not that it matches up to a world that existed "in and of itself" before that interpretation ensued. If this were the case, interpretation would be an overlay. Hermeneutics is not "objective research" in this dated sense. Its "truth" is not found in its correspondence to objective states of affairs.

Hermeneutics draws the pre-Socratic image of *alethia* for its understanding of the "truth" of hermeneutics. First, *alethia* means to open up what was previously shut, to show what was previously concealed, to uncover that which was covered over, to make present that which was absent, to say that which was silent. It was precisely this sense of "something opening up" that that new teacher's comments provoked. Something seemed to be an open question again, not a closed concept. To understand those ordinary comments as true is to cultivate in ourselves the ability to experience them as an opening into a heretofore closed or occluded field of relations and memories and ancestries and conversations and contestations. Initiation, it seems, is not a closed case. It is still "open for the future" (Gadamer, 1989, p. 340) and these incidental comments of a new teacher have effected such opening into a world. These comments are, in this sense, "true." They are true because, insofar as it is part of the living human inheritance, "initiation" it is not isolated or fixed or finished but is, rather, open to being taken up anew in ways that are beyond our wanting and doing. When we are able to experience it this way, as "standing in a horizon of . . . still undecided future possibilities" (Gadamer, 1989, p. 112), we are able to experience its truth. When it is just a dead theme under which teacher's comments silently "fall," it is no longer true in this "hermeneutic" sense. There is nothing "true" about a "theme" under which instances fall except in those moments where some incident opens up to questions and susceptibility and risk what the theme might mean in ways that render it "in play" again, open, again, to the arrival of the new case and the difference that new case might bring.

But there is a fundamental caution here in hermeneutic work. Opening up, of necessity, closes off as well. These glimpses of the living human inheritance are susceptible to calcification, sedimentation. Opening up does not "amass" like verified knowledge. *Alethia*, as a privative term, always reminds us that truth, in this hermeneutic sense, is a dance between revealing and concealing, between opening up and closing off:

> One has to ask oneself whether the dynamic law of human life can be conceived adequately in terms of progress, of a continual advance from the unknown into the known, and whether the course of human culture is actually a linear progression from mythology to enlightenment. One should entertain a completely different notion: whether the movement of human existence does not issue in a relentless inner tension between illumination and concealment. Might it not just be a prejudice of modern times that the notion of progress that is in fact constitutive for the spirit of scientific research should be transferable to the whole of human living and human culture? One has to ask whether progress, as it is at home in the special field of scientific research, is at all consonant with the conditions of human existence in general. Is the notion of an ever-mounting and self-perfecting enlightenment finally ambiguous? (Gadamer, 1983, pp. 104-105)

In making something of the vivid intersections between this new teacher's comments and the bloodlines of blood sacrifice and the like, we necessarily close off other possibilities, turn our backs on other options (options which a future voice may later open anew). Truth in this human inheritance is not to be had through full, final presence, but through the living inner tension between illumination and concealment. This makes hermeneutic truth very fragile, very mortal, very close to what happens to us. This initiation-venture regarding this new teacher's comments will not last forever; it will not be always and everywhere proper and appropriate. It's telling character is out of our hands because, after all, we do not and cannot know what will come of this moment of opening. Thus "truth has in itself an inner tension and ambiguity"(Gadamer, 1977, p. 227). A hermeneutic study, therefore, doesn't get everything out in the open by the force of its methodical will. Rather, a hermeneutic study always alludes to concealment, unfinishedness, darkness, frailty and invalidity (e.g., Jardine, 2000).

Second, *alethia* means to liven up, to enliven, to see the life in or breath life into what previously was dead (lethal), lifeless, boring, obvious, flat, deadly, deadening (great terms for teachers to consider when reflecting on classroom life). This is the most phenomenological characteristic of *alethia*. It is linked to the adrenaline rush of insight, the giddy breath of generativity and newness ("the new, the different, the true" [Gadamer, 1977, p. 44]) and liveliness, the weird feel that something has *happened*. Opening (sense one of *alethia*) is a *movement*, an animation, a happening upon in which something seems to turn around and face me and demand, claim, address in a voice that is not my own. This means something very simple. The topic I've ventured into has *its own life* "beyond my wanting and doing."

There is a wonderful mythopoetic expression of this phenomenon in Clarissa Pinkola-Estes' re-citing of the tale of *La Loba*:

> The sole work of *La Loba* is the collecting of bones. She is known to collect and preserve especially that which is in danger of being lost to the world. . .. [H]er speciality is said to be wolves.

> She creeps and crawls and sifts through the *montanas*. . . and *arroyos*. . . looking for wolf bones, and when she has assembled an entire skeleton, when the last bone is in place and the beautiful white sculpture of the creature is laid out before her, she sits by the fire and thinks about what song she will sing.

> And when she is sure, she stands over the *critura*, raises her arms and sings out. That is when the rib bones and leg bones of the wolf begin to flesh out and the creature becomes furred. *La Loba* sings some more, and more of the creature comes into being; its tail curls upward, shaggy and strong.

> And *La Loba* sings more and the wolf creature begins to breathe.

> And *La Loba* sings so deeply that the floor of the desert shakes, and as she sings, the wolf opens its eyes, leaps up, and runs away down the canyon (Estes, 1992, pp. 27-8).

This can be read as an expression of the deep experience that hermeneutic writing and research entails. Sometimes those moments that address us–a child's comment, a passage read in a book–just lie there like dry bones. Sometimes we have to just collect them and protect them and wait. Sometimes we sing over them a bit and something stirs and then fails right in front of our eyes. Like I've already mentioned, that new teacher's phone call was 15 years ago, and I'm still carefully and patiently musing over it, hoping that it will come to life again, hoping that the song sung, this enchantment, this book chapter, will result in a re-enchantment (Berman, 1983) and a reanimation of the world. *Part* of this is out of my hands because my work is on behalf of a life that is not my work, on behalf of a "topic" that lives "beyond my wanting and doing."

This sense of *alethia* as "enlivening" is therefore also privative, and it necessarily hides its inverse. By courting natality and life and liveliness, we necessarily concede mortality to understanding. Our explorations of initiation, our conversations with teachers and their mythic dreaming, our work, our insights, our writing, our lives–none of this will last forever and this not-lasting is not a failure. It is, rather, an insight. A hermeneutic study must not aspire to an ever-mounting enlightenment because, philosophically, hermeneutic experience and understanding are most fundamentally "an experience of human finitude" (Gadamer, 1989, p. 357).

This links to Hannah Arendt's great and terrifying insight into the life and breath of education itself:

> We are always educating for a world that is or is becoming out of joint, for this is the basic human situation, in which the world is created by mortal hands to serve mortals for a limited time as home. Because the world is made by mortals it wears out; and because it continuously changes its inhabitants it runs the risk of becoming as mortal as they. To preserve the world against the mortality of its creators and inhabitants it must be constantly set right anew. The problem is simply to educate in such a way that a setting-right remains actually possible, even though it can, of course, never be assured. Our hope always hangs on the new which every generation brings; but precisely because we can base our hope only on this, we destroy everything if we so try to control the new that we, the old, can dictate how it will look. Exactly for the sake of what is new and revolutionary in every child, education must be conservative; it must preserve this newness and introduce it as a new thing into an old world. (Arendt, 1969, pp. 192-3).

Hermeneutic truth, therefore, does not progressively amass. In terms of humanity's efforts to understand itself–say, for example, this great movement from student to teacher–we are not getting anywhere. Even though many research methods have amassed great archives of verified knowledge, we still face, in our lives as students and teachers, the great, unfinished tales of such movement. To know of these matters "in truth" is to know that what such matters will turn out to be is necessarily "yet to be decided." There is an empty chair at the table (see Jardine & Batycky, 2006). *This* is the truth of things.

Finally, a third sense of hermeneutic truth. After dying, *Lethe* was the river one's "soul" crossed when ferried into the underworld (parallel to the Roman River Styx) and such crossing involved forgetting what one had undergone or experienced. *Alethia*, as the privative of "forgetting," thus means remembering what was forgotten, recovering what has been lost. When I talked to this new teacher on the phone, when I recite this happenstance event to others and draw out the threads of thresholds and passages and the like, the first response tends to be "oh, yeah, right," as if something is quite literally *recognized*. This difficult sense of breath-intake is key to hermeneutics. A new piece of knowledge is not amassed. Rather, it is as if something lost has been found again, something old is remembered. And "re-membered"is triple here: "1. 'bringing back to memory' 2. 'gaining new members.' 3. 'putting back together'" (Jardine, 1992, p. 14).

And, like senses one and two, this third sense, too, hides the seeds of its own demise. Things get forgotten or repressed or sublimated or lost, members arrive and die off, things put together fall apart. The centre does not hold forever. The living truth of things must "always must be renewed in the effort of our living" (Gadamer, 1989, p. 100-111).

## IN CONCLUSION

The truth of [hermeneutic] experience always implies an orientation to new experience. "Being experienced" does not consist in the fact that someone already knows everything and knows better than anyone else. Rather, the experienced person proves to be, on the contrary, someone who...because of the many experiences he has had and the knowledge he has drawn from them, is particularly well-equipped to have new experiences and to learn from them. Experience has its proper fulfilment not in definitive [amassed] knowledge but in the openness to experience that is made possible by experience itself (Gadamer, 1989, p. 355).

Amassed verified knowledge makes us less and less interested in what the new case might have to say. We become, not "experienced" but "experts" whose cynicism and condescension increases as that mass increases. Our understanding becomes "saturated" because we have seen enough that we feel able to close down the venture and end it. "Been there, done that," as the saying goes. As experts, we become less and less susceptible to the difference that the new case might bring. For example, living in a classroom where young children are learning to write or where young adults are learning to be teachers brings no exhilaration and pleasure because, as a consequence of our amassment, nothing can possibly happen that will speak to us from beyond the amassed consequences of our wanting and doing. Worlds become more and more of a closed case. We become more and more impervious to being interrupted. This is not a version of understanding that bodes well for pedagogy.

To become good at hermeneutics, you have to enter into the process, not of amassing verified knowledge and attaining "expertise," but the process of *becoming experienced*. Hermeneutically understood, the more experienced I become, the *more* susceptible I become to the difference that the next case might bring, the *more* susceptible I become to being addressed. Understanding, understood hermeneutically, means the cultivation of susceptibility in ourselves and others.

A good hermeneutic study opens up our ability to experience "the fecundity of the individual case" (Gadamer, 1989, p. 38) that comes to meet us in the world. This, I suggest, bodes well for treating education as a hermeneutic endeavor.

## REFERENCES

Arendt, H. (1969). *Between past and future*. New York: Penguin Books.
Berman, M. (1984). *The reenchantment of the world*. New York: Bantam Books.
Bohm, D. (1983). *Wholeness and implicate order*. New York: Ark Books.
Caputo, J. (1987). *Radical hermeneutics*. Bloomington, IN: Indiana State University Press.

Clifford, J. (1986). Introduction. In Clifford, J. & Marcus, G. (eds). *Writing culture: The poetics and politics of ethnography.* (pp. 2-11). Berkeley, CA: University of California Press.

Descartes, R. (1955). *Descartes selections.* New York: Scribners.

Eliade, M. (1968). *Myth and reality.* New York: Harper & Row.

Eliade, M. (1975). *The quest.* New York: Harper and Row.

Estes, C. P. (1992). *Women who run with the wolves: Myths and stories of the wild woman archetype.* New York: Ballantine Books.

Fox, M. (1983). *Original blessing.* Santa Fe: Bear and Co.

Gadamer, H.G. (1977). *Philosophical hermeneutics.* Berkeley, CA: University of California Press.

Gadamer, H.G. (1983). *Reason in the age of science.* Boston: MIT Press.

Gadamer, H.G. (1989). *Truth and method.* New York: Continuum Press.

Gadamer, H.G. (1994). *Heidegger's ways.* Boston: MIT Press.

Gadamer, H.G. (2001). *Gadamer in conversation: Reflections and commentary.* Edited and translated by R. Palmer. New Haven, CT: Yale University Press.

Hargreaves, A. (2005, October). Review of back to the basics of teaching and learning. *Education Canada.*

Hillman, J. (1982) Anima mundi: Returning the soul to the world. *Spring, 40,* 174-188.

Hillman, J. (1989). *Healing fiction.* Barrytown: Station Hill Press.

Hillman, J. (1991). *Inter/Views.* Dallas: Spring Publications.

Husserl, E. (1970). *The Paris lectures.* The Hague: Martinus Nijhoff.

Jardine, D. W. (1992). *Speaking with a boneless tongue.* Bragg Creek: Makyo Press.

Jardine, D. W. (1998). Student teaching, interpretation and the monstrous child. In Jardine, D. W. (Ed.). *To dwell with a boundless heart: On curriculum theory, hermeneutics and the ecological imagination.* (pp. 123-134). New York: Peter Lang Publishers.

Jardine, D. W. (2000). Learning to love the invalid. In Jardine, D. W. (Ed.). *Under the tough old stars: Ecopedagogical essays.* (pp. 193-200). Brandon, VT: Holistic Education Press.

Jardine, D. W. (2003). The profession needs new blood. In Jardine, D., Clifford, P., & Friesen, S. (Eds). *Back to the basics of teaching and learning: Thinking the world together.* (pp. 55-70). Mahwah, NJ: Lawrence Erlbaum and Associates.

Jardine, D. W. (2005). *Piaget and Education.* New York: Peter Lang Publishing.

Jardine, D. W. (2006). Cutting nature's leading strings: A cautionary tale about constructivism. In Jardine, D., Friesen, S. & Clifford, P. (Eds). *Curriculum in abundance.* (pp. 123-135). Mahwah, NJ: Lawrence Erlbaum and Associates.

Jardine, D. W. & Batycky, J. (2006). Filling this empty chair: On genius and repose. In Jardine, D., Clifford, P. & Friesen, S. (Eds). *Curriculum in abundance.* (pp. 213-225). Mahwah, NJ: Lawrence Erlbaum and Associates.

Jardine, D., Clifford, P. & Friesen, S. (2003). Whatever happens to him happens to us: Reading coyote reading the world. In Jardine, D., Clifford, P., & Friesen, S. (Eds). *Back to the basics of teaching and learning: Thinking the world together.* (pp. 41-52). Mahwah, NJ: Lawrence Erlbaum and Associates.

Jardine, D. & Field, J.C. (2006). Disproportion, monstrousness and mystery: Ecological and ethical reflections on the initiation of student-teachers into the community of education. In Jardine, D., Friesen, S. & Clifford, P. (Eds). *Curriculum in abundance.* (pp. 107-119). Mahwah, NJ: Lawrence Erlbaum and Associates.

Jardine, D., Friesen, S. & Clifford, P. (2006). (Eds). *Curriculum in abundance.* Mahwah, NJ: Lawrence Erlbaum and Associates.

Jardine, D., Johnson, B., & Fawcett, L. (2006). Further thoughts on cutting nature's leading strings: A Conversation. In Jardine, D., Friesen, S. & Clifford, P. (Eds). *Curriculum in abundance.* (pp. 139-148). Mahwah, NJ: Lawrence Erlbaum and Associates.

Jardine, D. & Novodvorski, B. (2006). Monsters in abundance. In Jardine, D., Friesen, S. & Clifford, P. (Eds). *Curriculum in abundance.* (pp. 103-5). Mahwah, NJ: Lawrence Erlbaum and Associates.

287

Mahdi, L., Foster, S., & Little, M. (1987). *Betwixt and between: Patterns of masculine and feminine initiation*. LaSalle, IL: Open Court.

Norris-Clarke, W. (1976). Analogy and the meaningfulness of langauge about God: A reply to Kai Nielsen, *The Thomist, 40,* 176-198.

Sartre, J.P. (1970). Intentionality: A fundamental idea in Husserl's phenomenology. *Journal for the British Society for Phenomenology, 1,* 3-5.

Smith, D. G. (1999). *Pedagon: Interdisciplinary essays on pedagogy and culture*. New York: Peter Lang Publishers.

Turner, V. (1969). *The ritual process*. Chicago: Aldine.

Turner, V. (1987). Betwixt and between: The liminal period in rites of passage. In Mahdi, L., Foster, S., & Little, M., (Eds). *Betwixt and between: Patterns of masculine and feminine initiation*. pp. 3-41, La Salle: Open Court.

Weinsheimer, J. (1987). *Gadamer's hermeneutics*. New Haven, CT: Yale University Press.

Wittgenstein, L. (1968). *Philosophical investigations*. Cambridge: University of Cambridge Press.

REBECCA J. LLOYD AND STEPHEN J. SMITH

# 12. MOTION-SENSITIVE PHENOMENOLOGY

Sometimes I just have to see the ocean to gain inspiration. I want to get close and hear the water caressing the beach, the sound rippling through me. Today I stand for about 5 minutes of real time in what feels like an eternal moment. My heart rate is elevated from the run that brings me to the beach, pulsing into the freshness of the waves moving in my direction. My gaze stretches to the horizon, to the place where gravity plays with the wind, and back to the ripples inches from my feet. The sensory experience of being close to water affects the way I feel on many levels. The more I see and hear the natural flow of water, the more I feel at ease with the natural movement of thought. (Rebecca Lloyd's journal, 2001)

This opening journal entry was written when Rebecca, the first author of this chapter, was first introduced to phenomenology. It was written on a particular day when she needed to take a break from academic readings and shift her attention to the topic of her first phenomenological inquiry (Lloyd, 2004).

As Rebecca and others have found, becoming a phenomenologist is no easy task. It is premised on immersion in a scholarly tradition that values lived experience, and it signals a commitment to taking up the ways, both traditional and creative, of describing the meanings that these lived experiences hold. Phenomenology is a scholarly and methodological undertaking, as might be said of any other research endeavour. Becoming a phenomenologist, however, is something yet again. It is about more than pursuing a research method, more than facility with the procedures and techniques that the phenomenological tradition makes available. Becoming a phenomenologist is a way of remaining in touch with lived experience just as one tries to apprehend its meanings. The phenomenologist considers how events and actions constitute lived experience, how researcher activity accesses the inherent meanings of lived experience, and how a research practice that is methodologically explicit can render these meanings accessible to others, all the while living in the midst of the experience.

"Phenomenology is a method; it could also be called an attitude" wrote Jan Hendrik Van den Berg (1972, p. 77). He went on to say how the phenomenologist adopts a way of observing life that differs from scientific protocols putting observers at objective distance from the things of interest. The phenomenologist mistrusts observational categories and any "opinions" that get in the way of an open, receptive sense-taking of the incidents, events or "phenomena" in question. The phenomenologist would have any interpretation "spring from this life."

*K. Tobin & J. Kincheloe, (eds.), Doing Educational Research—A Handbook, 289–309.*

> If he [sic] intends to write a discourse on swimming, he will want, first of all, to swim–and repeat his swimming until he knows and can express what swimming is. Only he who knows the sea, the river, the stream, the lake, physically can know what it is really like. (Van den Berg, 1972, p. 77)

The requisite attitude is best expressed as a *disposition* in order to emphasize the level of physical attentiveness necessary. It is comprised dispositionally of postures, positions, gestures and indeed expressions, depending upon the degree of physical engagement and attentiveness that the subject matter requires. Martin Heidegger (1968) wrote:

> We shall never learn what 'is called' swimming, for example, or what it 'calls for,' by reading a treatise on swimming. Only the leap into the river tells us what is called swimming. (p. 21)

Rebecca was interested in the flow experience and disposed to experiencing flow in her own movement. Her interest lay with those moments of life when actions appear effortless, when there is synchrony between them, and when a joy in movement is experienced. Contextually she was interested in the flow experience of exercise pedagogy, particularly in fitness classes and one-on-one training sessions when there are moments of joyful movement with others. Rebecca knew such moments of flow in these contexts as a fitness leader and trainer, and as an athlete and dancer she knew 'in her bones' the possibilities of experiencing flow with others. Still, Rebecca wanted to know more about the possibilities of flow, not just as a performer, and not simply as one who teaches fitness and is employed as personal trainer, but as a doctoral candidate in education with an interest in the pedagogical relation that is defined in moments of intense flow. Instead of putting her lived experiences of flow behind her, however, Rebecca needed inspiration for this study and a dispositional consciousness of how to approach it. She needed a sensory reminder of flow and its interactive possibilities. She recalls wanting to loosen her stiffening 'academic' ideas of flow by literally running to a place where the reminder of flow is evident and where the prevailing flow motions kindle a phenomenological imagination of its interactive possibilities. Beginning a phenomenological inquiry of flow interactions required adopting the movements that activate a sense of flow. It required connecting actively with a waterscape where one can sense the moods, motions, and gestural formations of flow phenomena.

No research text suggested running to the beach and entertaining the elemental motions of ocean. No research text suggests making soup, folding laundry, gardening, walking the streets, or any of the many 'diversions' that occupy researchers of all stripes. But those are precisely the activities that inspire writers of a phenomenological bent when there is a sensed connection between the postures, positions, gestures, and expressions that such activities require and the physiognomic aspects of the topic at hand. Flow, as a phenomenological topic, indicates a topology of being in flow motion. It recalls lived experiences of flow through the mediation of places where flow can be activated and where a sense of writing about flow can be enlivened.

Stephen, the second author of this chapter, had a related sense of his research topic. He focused initially on a physical education curriculum geared to flow experience (Smith, 1982) and subsequently on how children's decision-making in physical activity enhances the possibilities of flow (Smith, 1988; Smith 1997a). Running was one of his lived flow experiences.

Running is a good time for writing. Writing on the run. My thesis question of the educational significance of physical play preoccupies me, even as I think about running. But once up and running, unlike sitting at my writing desk where ideas of physical play shoot in all directions, there is a different, more agreeable questioning of the physicality of play. The agitated mood of the office, with its jabbing, niggling, galling incomprehensions, is massaged by the flow motions of the run. Running imposes its own feeling for the question that is ever on my mind. The question bounces around while running, up and down, in cadenced stride. It runs ahead, turns around, and waits until I catch its pulsations. It becomes heavy, weighing me down momentary, before a burst of speed pitches the question back into its rightful, energetic place.

Writing is a little like running. I write with a running hand words that run together, around in circles, or off the page. I run into difficulties as I write, running around them, and often away from them. Running up against writer's block. I take a breather from my writing, time out to collect my thoughts. I run over what I've written and, in these pulsing motions, my writing is directed, enlivened, projected. I write over that which ran by me and in this writing the flow of running returns. Writing contains the flow motion I have experienced while running. Its prose fleshes out this lived experience of physical play. Writing engulfs my running, clearing a space where running finds its phenomenological place. (Stephen Smith's personal writing, 1979)

Writers have long sought solace and recuperation in physical activity. Certain phenomenologists, with their interests in catching the salient aspects of lived experience, have taken to heart the physical affinities of writing and those somatic practices that bear the postural, positional, gestural and expressive features of their topics. David Levin (1985) and Kenneth Shapiro (1985), for instance, follow the phenomenological admonition of returning to the things themselves, corporeally, physically, tangibly, palpably, kinaesthetically in texts "destined to bring back all the living relations of experience" (Merleau-Ponty, 1962, p. xv). They follow a tradition of describing conceptually that which has been lived perceptually in the "flesh" and which carries the "flesh of the world" to phenomenological apprehension (Merleau-Ponty, 1968). In fact, they follow a long tradition of thinking that remains in touch with bodily motions. Berel Lang (1995) writes of Aristotle:

Long after the immobility of death caught him, holding him to one place in the earth, we think of him still, first, as the Peripatetic, the teacher who walked as he taught, whose mind was so active that it seemed to grow feet.

But here, too, most of us recall this feature as a quirk, an accident of posture or patience; thus we persist in keeping the body the captive of the mind, its servant, even–at some points–its symptom. Only a few obscure students, rarely heard, are willing to acknowledge their loss. These understand how much more they would have been able to learn from the master–if only they had the opportunity to watch, under the cloak of his words, that extraordinary walk (Lang, 1995, p. 14).

Recall also the European wanderings of Jean-Jacques Rousseau, the evening walks of Immanuel Kant in Königsburg, Søren Kierkegaard's on-foot explorations of Copenhagen, or Martin Heidegger's walks though his beloved Black Forest (Solnit, 2000, pp. 15-29). How much more might we understand their ideas if we literally followed in their footsteps?

Our own topics of phenomenological inquiry take us a step farther. We regard this scholarly work as a necessary, ongoing blend of lived, living and still-to-be-lived experiences. Phenomenology that moves, emotes, and motions to the significance of its topic begins and ends in the register of movement appropriate to that topic. On the topic of flow, phenomenology is inherently moving, flowing, defining itself around the motions constitutive of flow. Elsewhere flow is variously turned into a cognitive construct, a behaviour, a quality of motion, an extra-human force, or a property of physical environments. Fragmentary views, these reductions fall short of the phenomenological reduction which would, in the silences of primary, movement consciousness, show "not only what words mean, but also what things mean: the core of primary meaning around which the acts of naming and expression take shape" (Merleau-Ponty, 1962, p. xv).

Consider now the disposition of another phenomenological expert. Max van Manen (2002) describes the setting, position and sentience constitutive of his inquiry into the seemingly inactive phenomenon of writing phenomenologically. He begins:

I am sitting at my keyboard, mulling over some last words. As I stare out of the window into the dark winter evening, I barely notice the lights of the cars that are crossing the bridge spanning the banks of the river. In fact, I am scarcely aware that I am looking out of the window, until casually my son walks into the room. "Hi, what are you doing?" he queries. Awoken, as if from a daydream, I say, "I am writing." "Oh no, you aren't. You are just looking out of the window." He laughs, teasingly, and leaves.

It is true. I was staring out of the window. And yet, while I may have been observing the traffic, following some cars or trucks with my eyes, I did not really see them. My thoughts were elsewhere. More accurately: I was elsewhere. Where? One way to say it is that I was caught up in the words that I was writing, silently chewing them and then spitting them onto the keyboard, onto the computer screen. But is this writing? Am I writing? Well, yes and no. I am producing words, a text even. Yet, these are just words. This is not really writing. So my son was right. But when could I say that I am actually writing? I wonder if there is an actual moment that I can say: "Now. Now I am writing!" (van Manen, 2002, p. 1)

Max van Manen's words on writing beg the question of how far removed the writer can be from the subject of writing and still be writing of its livedness. Alternatively, they ask: what experiential attunements, sensory awarenesses, kinaesthetic connections, in the writing process itself, make possible a moment of textual connection to the subject of writing? What, indeed, are the movements of dispositional attunement to the topic at hand when one can say "Now. Now, I am writing?" Max van Manen goes on to address the "writerly space" of phenomenological reflection where we step out of "the ordinary world of daylight [to] enter another, the textorium, the world of the text" (van Manen, 2002, p. 3). The "textorium" we enter is a space of solitude, detachment from the practical tasks and responsibilities of the day, withdrawal to the office space or computer desk. A writer's retreat. We take leave of the immediacy of lived experience, its sociality and mimetic resonances, for the sake of discerning its portended meanings. But this leave-taking is no escape from reality. It is for the sake of lending greater reality to that which is lived, defining, through the licence of a textual methodology, the most salient, reverberating, touching aspects of the phenomena of daily living, and re-engaging life with a heightened awareness of its sensibilities. On the one hand:

> The phenomenologist as writer is an author who starts from the midst of life, and yet is transported to that space where, as Robert Frost once said, writing is "like falling forward into the dark." Here meanings resonate and reverberate with reflective being. (van Manen, 2002, p. 7).

On the other hand, the phenomenologist as researcher is a "reflective being" thrown back into "the midst of life" to the lived spaces and times of the topic at hand. "One writes to make contact, to achieve phenomenological intimacy with an object of interest" (van Manen, 2002, p. 245).

Motion-sensitive phenomenology emphasizes the *transposition* of the actions of living into the activity of writing and the latter's capacity to not simply re-enact or represent times and events past but to rejuvenate the ongoing practice of living well. Phenomenology, as the study of lived experience, recalls the details of life; but, as the study of living and still-to-be-lived experience, it inspires and invigorates us in the lives we lead. It is not "passive" in the sense of simply being inactive; on the contrary, there is a "receptive passivity," a "pathic" register of activity, a dispositional attunement, in other words, a motion sensitivity, that phenomenology cultivates (van Manen, 2002, pp. 250-251). A study of flow must then connect us with the motions constitutive of that experience in a practice that flows back and forth between swimming and writing, running and writing, walking and writing, in fact, between any number of activities and the activity of writing phenomenologically that transposes the flux of life into a heightened understanding of flow motion.

## DOING MOTION-SENSITIVE PHENOMENOLOGY

We pursue a method of motion-sensitive phenomenology though continuing reference to Max van Manen's work for a number of reasons. First, Max van Manen is widely recognized as one of the foremost phenomenological scholars in North America (Pinar, Reynolds, Slattery, & Taubman, 2000). Second, he has published a number of treatises on phenomenological method, in addition to the aforementioned text, which are widely used in education, health care and the human sciences (van Manen, 1984; 1990; 1997). Third, Max van Manen has long concerned himself with the action reference of phenomenology, whether that be, say, the expressive "tone of teaching" (van Manen, 1986) or its bodily expressed "tact" (van Manen, 1991). Max van Manen's procedures for undertaking "lifeworld phenomenology" enable us to be sensitive to motion and to the active register of a flow consciousness.[1]

The practical steps of the inquiry process include: orienting to a phenomenon of interest; asking specific "what" questions that will bring one closer to the heart of the phenomenon; defining reflective modes that facilitate the answering of such questions; deepening understanding by consulting philosophical and phenomenological texts; re-grouping and organizing the inquiry through inherent theme structures; and lastly, re-writing the transition segments so the text appears to be seamless (van Manen, 1990). To these steps we bring a motion-sensitivity needed in the phenomenological description of flow motion and, by this example, a sensitivity indicative of phenomenology writ large. Accordingly, we reframe Max van Manen's steps of inquiry as a practice, both actual and textual, of making sense of flow phenomena (i.e. sensing), discerning the essences of flow (i.e. essencing) and, in the process, cultivating a heightened flow sensitivity to the motions of others (i.e. sensitizing).

### Sensing

The latitude of phenomenological inquiry enables us to "question something from the heart of our existence, from the center of our being" (van Manen, 1990 p. 43). Even small phenomenological inquiries require "that we not simply raise a question and possibly soon drop it again, but rather that we 'live' this question, or better, that we 'become' this question" (p. 43). We must have a sense, from the outset, that the inquiry is significant and that the question is one that carries us to the heart of what moves us most deeply.

The question we asked in a study of interactive flow in exercise pedagogy (Lloyd, 2004; Lloyd & Smith, 2006) was: "What is the nature of flow in exercise instruction and what makes such an experience pedagogically justified?" We were mindful, in asking this question, of flow as a motivational psychological theory of engaging activity that has been extensively researched by Mihaly Csikszentmihalyi (2000) for over 30 years. He characterised flow in terms of the intrinsic motivation of the participant, as a match between the level of inherent challenge in the experienced activity and the participant's skill level, as full immersion in activity such that self consciousness disappears, and as a lack of worry and anxiety on the one hand and boredom on the other so that all that exists is the merge of action and awareness. We can thus make psychological sense of flow, in Mihaly Csikszentmihalyi's terms, as an experience subject to certain defining characteristics. But what sentient properties does this experience hold? What is the sense of immersion and what are the feelings of fluidity? What sense of ourselves and of our relations to others do we have in flow motion? These questions prompt a participatory exploration of flow rather than the empirical detachment that Mihaly Csikszentmihalyi and his associates have adopted (Csikszentmihalyi, 2000; Jackson & Csikszentmihalyi, 1999). They require stepping into flow, immersing ourselves in flow motions, in order to sense and make sense of the bodily experience of fluid movement.

The data of flow need to take on a sensory quality indicative of flow consciousness. This is no easy task and requires not just a bracketing of assumptions, theories and conceptions of flow, or what the phenomenologists have called the *époche*, but also the textual practice of participatory consciousness. It requires learning to write in flow. The primary author's struggle with her former objective, behavioral mode of analysis, for example her masters thesis research (Lloyd & Trudel, 1999), required dedicated time to a writing process that begins to express the incarnate intentionality, which is to say, the corporeal and intercorporeal feelings and sensations of flow consciousness, Here is one such textual reflection that oriented Rebecca toward the phenomenon of interactive flow.

A drumbeat traveling into my watery glide to the shore from the red tide is pulling me away from the shower I so desperately need to rinse the slimy salt from my body. It draws me toward a small gathering of people. At the heart of the enclosed circle I see a demonstration of Capoeira–a Brazilian martial art based on interactive movements where each action or gesture has a specific reaction.

The space between the martial artists is close although they always have enough room to finish a fully extended fan kick or an inverted one-arm supported kick. Every now and then they tap each other gently on the shoulder or back as if to say, "you're it." The tap lasts a moment with an immediate, almost seamless, exchange of positions. It is a game of two continuously moving bodies merging into one awareness with a specific set of rules. The pace is quick with little time to think of strategic moves. A rhythm of thrusts and parries, kicks and counters, is generated by these sweating bodies, sparkling in the sun.

Later I do a trial class of Capoeira. I think that, as a dancer, I have the flexibility and body awareness to jump right into the moves, but as I begin to sense the interactive nature of the art and the rhythm of two people connecting I realize I need to be more aware of how my body moves in relation to my partner. I can't do the fancy kicks whenever I feel like it. I have to learn how to lunge and move from side to side to pick up the first phase of interactive rhythm. Still, I enjoy my introduction to Capoeira as it helps me recall the beauty, interactive awareness and holistic connection of the performers I observed at the beach last Sunday. (Rebecca Lloyd's Personal Journal, 2000)

This writing sample indicates the movements of interactive flow in differing types of physical activity, whether they be spectacular transitions between one-arm supported postures, reaches or kicks in Capoeira, or the final glide to the shore in surfacing from the fluid, repetitive movements of swimming. It records Rebecca's inclination to adopt the postures, positions, gestures and expressions of flow motion that can be observed and made kinaesthetically meaningful. She is moved to experience interactive flow as moving responses to something, some action, some medium, and some body.

While orienting to interactive flow through observation, participatory consciousness and journal reflection, note is taken of Max van Manen's suggestion to make sure that the descriptions of lived experience articulate fully the meaning of the phenomenon, especially where "[o]rdinary language is in some sense a huge reservoir in which the incredible variety of richness of human experience is deposited" (van Manen, 1997, p. 61). Becoming mindful of the words we use challenges us to think creatively and imaginatively of significant flow data. We immerse ourselves, through daily action, interactions and journal reflection, in waterscape words of flow,

"Waves" beckon to us, speak to us, and suggest to us some elemental sense that suffuses flow motion. They remind us of rhythms of life, oscillations of energy, pulses, circulations, ebbs and flows.

Each time at the ocean I am mesmerized by the changing shapes, solicitous colors, and evolving atmosphere that ebb and flow with the tide. This is not simply human imagination or projection, but receptivity to an inherent expressivity of the waves.

It strikes me, particularly through the memory hints of previous connections, that the ocean speaks with some kind of primordial, amniotic power. Many of our gestures must surely originate in this briny wash, both as evolutionary fact and continuing natural affiliation. The wave of a hand draws its gestural power from the cresting of the sea; a caress traces the sensuous swell of a forming roller; while a kiss is a lapping of wetness that draws one into a fluid embrace.

Between the sitting on the beach and motions of the water, there is the beckoning of the sea toward a more intense connection with the world. I begin to wonder how separate the reality of the seascape is from our consciousness, from our perception of it. It beckons us and we participate, but this gesture of solicitation has an independence and a reality separate from us into which we enter, as into a relationship. Gesturing lies, as Rembrandt once said, "in the curtains," which is in the folds and creases of human habitation. It's in the pattern and form of the waves.

In the gesturing of the waves there is an absence of self-consciousness or, better still, a filling of the void that often marks our passage through everyday events. This elemental gesturing is not defined as an act of consciousness, but as an opening to the world which fills us with the world's flesh, as Merleau-Ponty might say, or with its fluid, which is more apt. It is a transcendence of self and an openness to the world beyond the narrow definition of the sensual or sexual. It is the critical moment of recognition of our being in the universe which is ironically reflected back in the form of touch by what we are actually able to truly see and feel.

The idea of 'flow motion' opens up a space for contemplating not only the gestures of human form—which include the constitutional gestures arising from birth and heredity, the habitual gestures arising from environment, custom, and simply growing up, and the fugitive gestures that spring from temporary emotion—but also gestures of rhythm and unity which are much more about world attunement and receptivity to the things of a supposedly more 'natural order' of living. Within this space one might think differently about those attunements and receptivities that have a physical basis to them and, instead of being confined to a de-natured sense of language acquisition, it might be possible to trace them out as full-blown gestures of form, rhythm and unity. Seascape gestures, waves, might provide, in other words, paradigmatic examples of a range of natural expressions (Smith, 2001, email communication).

We attend to waves and to other words of flow motion, such as rushes, ebbs, immersions, floats, pulses, runs and swims and dives, in order to sense something elementally constitutive of the phenomenon.

The senses of flow motion are further stimulated through literary and poetic texts. Max van Manen (1997) writes that poetry "allows the expression of the most intense feelings in the most intense form" and a poet "can sometimes give linguistic expression to some aspect of [non]human experience that cannot be paraphrased without losing a sense of the vivid truthfulness that the lines of the poem are somehow able to communicate" (p. 70). Poetic descriptions of fluid, seascape-formed gestures of flow draw us to "oceanic memories that continue among all humans who have landed. The pulsing waves of ancestral amphibians are recorded in every undulation of an organ, in every sweep of tissue, in every course of blood" (Conrad-Da'Oud, 1995, p. 311). Poetry can evoke the sense of flow motion where there is "no inside, no outside, no up or down, no 'body,' only wave motions, many kinds—short waves—long waves—dancing waves" (Conrad-Da'Oud, 1995, p. 309). Narrative, story, fiction, the novel, can likewise evoke flow motion and reveal gestural meanings otherwise hidden from phenomenal view. Milan Kundera's (1990) description of a wave between an elderly lady and a lifeguard captures well the duration of an interactive, fluid gesture.

She walked around the pool toward the exit. She passed the lifeguard, and after she had gone some three of four steps beyond him, she turned her head, smiled, and waved to him. In that instant I felt a pang in my heart! That smile and that gesture belonged to a twenty-year-old girl! Her arm rose with bewitching ease. It was as if she were playfully tossing a brightly coloured ball to her lover. That smile and that gesture had charm and elegance, while

297

the face and the body no longer had any charm. It was the charm of a gesture drowning in the charmlessness of the body. But the woman, though she must of course have realized that she was no longer beautiful, forgot that for a moment. There is a certain part of all of us that lives outside of time. (Kundera, 1990, p. 3)

The poetics and prose of flow motion orient us to bodily senses, metaphors and meanings that are too often dulled in the arduous, painstaking work of objectifying experience (Markula & Denison, 2000). These insights, having to do with waves and floats and flows, suggest motions of a lived body responding to the motions of another living being. They bring attention to a "structure of comportment" (Merleau-Ponty, 1963) and a "bearing of thought" (Heidegger, 1965) that resonate with the phenomenon of flow motion; in fact, they intimate how "each body's movements all day long form part of the skeleton of meaning that also gives any aberrant or spectacular bodily action its luster" (Foster, 1995, p. 5).

It is with such phenomenological attentiveness that Rebecca began to write about teaching fitness. The following journal entry illustrates the emerging focus on an interactive sense of flow motion.

I have the pleasure of training Ben, an 80-year-old client, every Tuesday. Ben started personal training six years ago when he experienced a mild stroke which now limits his cardiovascular capacity and the use of his right arm. Physical activity, whether it be running, skiing or biking has always been a part of his life, so Ben has hired me as his personal trainer to help monitor and guide his recuperation.

One of Ben's goals is to increase his aerobic endurance and capacity. We go for a 30 min light power walk/ jog/ run and look for small windows of opportunity where he can do intervals of increased intensity. We include natural inclines such as hills in the neighbourhood or landmark distances such as sprinting between benches in the park loop.

Today turns out to be one our special days....

Ben greets me warmly as I meet him in front of the garage door of our gym. It is his favourite spot and he is always 2 to 3 minutes early so I do my best to make sure our sessions start right on time if not before. Today Ben is wearing his red polar fleece jacket and looks quite cozy. We trek outside past the smiling front desk staff and Ben salutes them with his good arm. I don't know what it is about our outside walk/runs but everyone who walks or drives by immediately smiles when they see us together. I think our shared activity gives them a sense of connection to taking the time to appreciate the good things in life such as exercising and enjoying the fresh air. We wait for the first crosswalk patiently and enjoy the weekly update of what we've been up to. Ben tells me he went swimming twice, played tennis once, and saw Jane, his other personal trainer, last Friday. He is feeling good and we start our steady light jog.

As I turn my shoulders towards him and reach in the direction of his hips I ask, "Ben, can you hear the sound of your right foot? Listen to it as it rolls through and connects with the ground." Ben changes his heavy-footed impact and lightens up the motion. His upper body starts to soften but his hip flexors appear to be tight since his hip elevates slightly as his foot passes from a back extended position to a forward heel reach.

We approach another crosswalk. Ben just looks for a moment and then darts out before me. He likes to run out on the road. There are times when I have reached out and grabbed the back of his shirt in his moments of glee, watching the approaching traffic for fear we might not reach the other side in time. Ben even plays games with pedestrians. He likes to be the fastest person on the sidewalk. If there is another walker or jogger nearby, his focus is fixated ahead, pushing forward until we pass.

The sound of Ben's jog is a syncopated thud. The right foot often lands flat-footed and the left quickly passes through to complete the cycle. It changes a little when I point out the sound or cue ease in the hips, but it is something that requires specific thought to refine—until we get to the light on Broadway. There is something different between that traffic light and the quieter street crossings. It gives so little time to cross safely to the other side.

Ben asks me to run ahead and get the light ready so we don't have to stop. I run up, press the button, and it changes immediately. Ben, who is 10 steps behind, seizes the moment and overtakes me in a joyous stride. I feel the presence of a young, eager boy, speeding by my side. He floats across. The only sound is the swoosh in the air as he zooms by. I look up and see both of his arms swinging and he continues to run until the loud breaths catch him. The strident exhales return us to our walk and his heart rate starts to slow down.

Ben's sprint transcends time, his physical presence, the grounding reality of a heavy right foot, and the dysfunction of a right arm. His youthful energy catches him in a glide across the street to the other side and beyond. I push to catch up with him, laughing in the moment. It is not unlike Agatha's wave, in Kundera's (1990) Immortality, flowing though her body cultivating a sense of childhood youth in a motion that transcends old age. (Rebecca Lloyd's journal, 2003)

Moments such as these happen from time-to-time, yet they need not be sheer happenstance. A kinaesthetic attentiveness, wherein our bodily motility brings about a physical communion with others, creates moments of vitality, energy and seemingly transcendent motions of flow beyond the repetitive drudgery of daily tasks or, in this case, beyond the heavy-footedness of running. When Rebecca shared her written description of the walk/run outings with Ben he explained that:

Everything feels different when I run across the street. I feel energized in a way that just plain running doesn't. It's a liberating moment from what running usually is for me. Running up the street can be pretty boring...When I ask you to run up and get the light it is no longer routine. I get incentive in taking a risk, like going down a steep ski slope, and that I can do it. Running becomes more natural because I suddenly get the feeling of freedom. The fact that I can't continue is age-related. The feeling of running at that point is tremendous. It's not an out-of-body experience, but something that approaches it....Twenty years ago I could do a six-minute mile, now that's no longer possible. Any moment I can go back to that feeling and throw myself over the road, figuratively speaking, it feels good. It feels very good. (Client Response, 2003)

Before writing about Ben's youthful run across the street and asking him to read it, he told Rebecca that he was unaware of any physical transformation. But after reading the passage, Ben became increasingly excited about moving as if he were a youth again and shortly after decided he would focus on increasing the motion and strength in his right arm in the gym. He and Rebecca started incorporating two-arm cable triceps extensions and biceps curls, along with range of motion active stretches. Ben's swinging arm motion in that fleeting moment of running across the street filled him with a sense of possibility in a part of him that he once thought was disabled.

Noticing and noting a flow motion allow one to experience it again with increased frequency and sensory awareness. We sense the motion aesthetically through writing up its duration in phenomenological notation, and we sense the motion kinaesthetically through running down, running over, running with the notation of that moment in an active register of flow motion. Phenomenological data draw attention to the rhythmical swing of arms and legs, to running together, to the full-bodied grace of youth, to fluid motion and wave-like surges of emotion that cultivate a deeper relation with the world at large. Phenomenology, in the givens of experience and the give and take of experiential description, begins to disclose a "primordial choreography" and "poetizing motility" (Levin, 1985, p.15).

*Essencing*

Ben's transition from doing a lop-sided run to a floating glide across the street provides but one example of flow motion. The point of motion-sensitive phenomenology is not merely to generate further examples; it is to deepen the sense of motion that the example above contains. It is to catch the essential, sentient, sensible meaning of this evocative moment of flow motion. We thus pursue a phenomenological reduction that attends to its essential characteristics.

This is a method of "existential reflection" (van Manen, 1997) in which attention is paid to the following aspects of lifeworld experience: to the sensing and essencing of body awareness or corporeality, spatiality, temporality and relationality. These experiential foci are the "fundamental existentials" of all conceivable experience (van Manen, 1990, pp. 101-106) and, indeed, come close to the elements of movement first articulated by Rudolf Laban and since incorporated in a range of movement disciplines (Hodgson, 2001). They refer to the conjunction of behaviour and attitude, motion and emotion, position and disposition, gesture and gists of meaning, expression and impression. Corporeality, spatiality, temporality and relationality are the general structures of lived experience indicative of what is essential to this and any other experience of flow motion. What characterizes a particular experience are the distinctive corporealizing, spatializing, temporalizing and relating motions involved.

We ask, in our focused exploration of interactive flow in exercise pedagogy, what is the particular and distinctive sense of the teaching body? Where and how does my body move, not just on the external surfaces of objective space and time, but in terms of the kinaesthetic registers of expansive and contractive spaces and the bodily feeling and muscular-skeletal sensing of physical effort (Cohen 1993; Laban & Lawrence, 1974)? What is it to become aware of the movements of another body while teaching movement? How does somatic connectivity change, strengthening or weakening the teaching connection, not just in relation to spatial proximity and distance, but also in creating and giving space, standing back or making contact, reaching out, touching, and at times making deep contact with others? And in being not just on time but in time with another: What is the effect of teaching quick, effervescent movement over slow, penetrating movement? How do instructor movements of varying effort, whether forceful or light, staccato or sustained, jerky or flowing, influence client postures, positions, gestures and expressions?

In questioning the lived body, lived time, lived space, and the lived other as the existential heuristics of experiencing flow, we show flow motion to be essentially about pedagogical interaction. For example, within a walk-run routine, Rebecca was able to see, feel and move with Ben's moment of flow motion as she ran by his side. She was able to do this because she was moving and predisposed to feel movement. She did not assume an objective distance, analyzing his gait through passive observation, in what Max van Manen describes as the phenomenological "gaze of wonder [that] sweeps us up in a state of passivity" (van Manen, 2002, p. 251). She felt kinaesthetically the glide wash over her as she reciprocated his joyous stride. She wasn't vicariously feeling Ben's flow by imagining herself enjoying a youthful run across the street. She was able to step interactively into the time and space of her client's experience. She departed from the predominantly visual mode of observation in which "the seer is caught up in what he sees, it is still himself he sees: there is a fundamental narcissism of all vision," (Merleau-Ponty, 1968, p. 139). She observed synaesthetically and kinaesthetically, to which we can add the neologism "kinethically" as an indication of participatory observation that is now especially mindful of the quality of another person's movement experience..

Motion-sensitivity affords a multi-sensory, inter-subjective, inter-corporeal, intertwining of what moves and moves us. Phenomenological reflection seeks to catch this motion sensitivity, virtually, vicariously, reciprocally, in an essencing of the senses of flow motion. It is an agogic stress that phenomenology provides initially–a stress on momentary duration, a notation of sustainment, which is not so much a pause for thought as it is an extension of the lived experience by sensitive touch, contact and direction. Before there is a logic of the phenomenon of flow motion there is the phenomenagogic accent on the flow moment. Note is taken of what might so easily pass unnoticed. Phenomenology, as a reflective, textual practice, then brings the moment agogically and even pedagogically to mind. [2]

We pursue the agogic, phenomenogogic and phenomenologic essencing of flow motion in order to provide an alternative approach for athletic trainers and physical educators who are generally entrenched in technical, managerial and narrowly biomechanical representations of the human body. Richard Shusterman (1999) points out that enthusiasts of bodily training tend to "see the body as a moving mechanism, with joints as its components and flesh to cushion the skeleton" and objectify the body "as though they were already separated from it" (p. 7). To observe a client in this way affects how movement is understood and analysed. Personal trainers typically assume "the gaze of a coffin maker" in sizing up what is "tall, short, fat or heavy" and unfortunately "[l]anguage keeps pace with them. It has transformed a walk into motion and a meal into calories" (p. 7). But can we really learn what is essential "about the living body from a dead body" (Pronger, 1996, p. 428)? Can knowledge of movement be based on bodies whose owners have "vacated the premises" (p. 438)? Even the movement terminology of physical education curricula has a tone of bodily detachment such that body awareness–what the body can perform, space awareness–where the body can move, movement quality–how the body moves, and relationships–with whom or what the body relates (Pangrazi & Gibbons, 2003), externalize the movements and motions of the lived body, severing them from the senses of moving bodily in concert with another.

Phenomenological inquiry, with its bracketing of the objective form and function of movement for the sake of attending to the corporeal, spatial, temporal and relational stresses of flow motion, deals essentially with the "vitality of the pedagogical relation" (van Manen, 1992). It highlights an energy, aliveness, and "animate consciousness" (Sheets-Johnstone, 1999) evident in motions that flow back and forth, to and fro, reciprocally, interactively, responsively. It divines an essence to flow motion that enlivens that motion, actively and interactively in the moment of flow and, let us say, hyperactively in that moment's textual duration. It is not necessarily the case that "every word kills and becomes the death of the object it tries to represent" (van Manen, 2002, p. 244), nor is the opposite case necessarily so, that "we write to taste life twice, in the moment and in retrospection" (Nin, 1976, p. 149). Writing with motion-sensitivity may breathe life into bodies that have been deadened to touch, contact and tactful engagement with other bodies. Textualizing flow motion may reclaim a sense of fluidity just when "as we walk upon the earth, drawn into clasping and grasping, and finding a purchase for ourselves through firm hands and erect, hardened bodies, we become deadened to 'our home'. We are no longer wet" (Conrad Da'Oud, 1995, p. 311).

Essencing has us look with motion-sensitivity to further instances of interactive flow. We are mindful now of representations of motion that abstract the body, its space and time, and that distance it from other bodies. We are conscious particularly of the dispositions of movement that such texts represent–the transposed poses, postures, positions, gestures and expressions–which incline us not to sense flow motion. We look askance at the customary crossed-armed postures or arms akimbo positions of authority so evident in personal training and seek instances of more fluid, interweaving, interpenetrating, folding, enfolding, unfolding motions of responsiveness. The following excerpt from Rebecca's thesis (Lloyd, 2004) illustrates movement toward an essential connectivity.

> May is a client who responds well to managing gestures. As she is lying back on the leg press, she begins her descent and stays there a little too long. The weight stack clangs together and she starts to talk about her legs and the last time she did something like this. I ask May to keep going. Not with my words but with my hand. My arm sweeps down to the depth of her knee flexion and my wrist rolls up following the upward lift of my elbow into a complete arm and finger extension. My signal sends a message: Travel up and keep the pace. May pushes up and continues to bend her knees in a 30 to 40 degree angle. May is almost going low enough but is shying away from a depth that will challenge her gluteus maximus. Her knees show hesitancy and she is quick to get out of the compressed position. I gesture to May to come down lower by beckoning her with an in-coming wave, a gathering motion of my hand. I call her knees to bend and they comply with an approximate 60-degree flexion. May's knees are responsive to my wave. My hands guide the depth and extension of the movement. As long as my hands continue to move, May repeats the motion. I see her legs start to quiver and I suggest that she take a break. We made it up to twenty. A set well done!!! (Personal Journal, 2003).

Rebecca's hands guide the path of May's motion with fluid motility. She attends to the tempo, pattern, and bodily signs of fatigue, her fingers showing the desired grace and pace of the exercise. Her hands are not rigid or stiff as a pointing motion might be. They are alive, tracing a "primal sensibility" (Sheets-Johnstone, 1999, p. 136) which is conveyed to May's movement. These hands that wave with the intentionality of flow motion are different than fingers that reach with managing intent. They have the capacity to touch and be re-touched. Like the extension of a dancer's hand in an arabesque, they are not stiff. There is animation in the way the fingers sweep away from the body as if gliding over the top of water. These hands make contact beyond the span of the limbs.

Michelangelo's painting of the Sistine Chapel shows fingers with such tactile dexterity. God's and Adam's fingers aren't stiff or connected across space in a straight line. The inter-connection is apparent in the flowing movement of flesh across sensitive space. David Levin (1985) picks up on the "awesome dimensions" of this gesture:

> In his depiction of "The Creation of Man," we see the hand of God reaching down from the heavens and the hand of Adam as it reaches up from the earth. Their arms are *stretched to the limit*, their fingers touch. The meeting of hands, that 'point' where they meet, initiating a binding contact, is even of

awesome dimensions. It can move us with the might of a thunderbolt. It can shake us with the strength of an earthquake. The gesture extends the mystery of their communication across all generations of mortals and across the infinity of space which separates us from the Creator. The painting re-presents an experience of primordial presence as it is bodied forth in its archetypal gesture. (p. 135)

God's and Adam's fingers reach toward each other with touching sensitivity. They are not stretched to the limit like managing hands. They are mutually interconnected with curvatures of fluid somatic sensibility and other-directed sensitivity. Accordingly, when we revisit Rebecca's fluid hand reaching out to guide the pace and outer shape of May's leg press motion, we realize that even fluid, folding hands have the propensity to be 'one-sided.' The beckoning incoming wave followed by the rippling extension of Rebecca's fingers and hand conducted May's motion. The pace did not come from May's desire to do just one more press; May moved in response to an external gesture. Helping clients respond to their own desires, sensations, and bodily awarenesses requires a shift from one-sided movement instigation to motion sensitivity to energy that flows in and out, and back and forth.

*Sensitizing*

The sensing and essencing of flow motion that we have described sensitizes us to further instances and pedagogical possibilities. Phenomenologically we write and re-write our reflections on movement experience in relation to inherent theme structures, meanings lifted from one example and related to another. We write, keeping in mind the test of high quality phenomenological writing as the "eureka factor" (Dukes 1984, as cited in Creswell, 1988) or the degree to which the text resonates with a reader experience. We organize this writing around themes that clear a path of understanding the phenomenon (van Manen, 1997, p. 29). We indicate, thematically, the layers of emotive, kinaesthetic, synaesthetic, somaesthetic depth to the experience of interactive flow in exercise pedagogy, through continuing referral to water and its flow motions.

Let us begin with floating. It means to "go with the flow" of the currents and natural movements of water. Yet already we sense floating to be far removed from the phenomenon of interactive flow described so far. Mihaly Csikszentmihalyi (2000) reminds us that going with the flow is "an expression used by the counter-culture of the 1960s" which is in "some ways antithetical to what flow means" (p. xviii). Susan Jackson and Mihaly Csikszentmihalyi (1999) explain that "going with the flow" implies "a laissez-faire attitude, where one is taken along as if on a ride that requires no effort of one's own" (p. 115). The sensing of flow motion happens when we move with and through the environment in which we are immersed. There can be effortless sensations, but these are a result of combinations of effort and relaxation, or what Moshe Feldenkrais (1980) called "pleasurable exertion" where "one is able to make contact with one's own skeleton [...] muscles and [...] environment practically simultaneously" (Feldenkrais, 1980, p. 77). A sensitivity to flow motion does not mean to "stand outside oneself" (Ackerman, 1999). It may be that teaching group fitness on a stage can be likened to floating on waves of energy from a sea of bodies moving to the pre-crafted and pre-choreographed sequences cued and managed by the presenter. But the flow motion we have explored indicates a greater *depth* of interaction.

Sensitizing to flow suggests swimming rather than floating. Here fluidity surrounds and supports the flesh as the body is propelled forward in bubbling, wake-producing strokes. Bodily experience dissolves in the inter-connection of one's flesh with the buoyant world, creating a "solidity, so to speak; which even water presents" (Bergson, 1975, pp. 211-212). By immersing ourselves in the movements of others, either particular individuals within a group or personal training clients, we can adopt a similar solidity.

> I only started to feel specific responses, comparable to the way synchronized swimmers adjust their strokes, when I immersed myself in my personal training client's body. Motions that I taught with Platonic understanding, i.e. the 'ideal' way to demonstrate them, describe them, and perform them, were not uniformly or 'ideally' represented in the motions of my clients. Martha's squat differed from Leo's, Suzie's, Ben's, and Frank's squats. After I demonstrated 'set up' where I would ask my clients to assume the position I just performed and continue the motion with a steady tempo, I learned that each person has a unique understanding of the motion, history associated with the motion, internal desire to repeat the motion, and level of somatic awareness and interest to refine the motion. (Rebecca's Personal Journal, 2002)

Delving beneath superficial sensations creates bodily encounters that are lasting, life changing and life affirming. Jumping into a pool, off a dock, or into the ocean can be a quick, tingling burst if the intention is to re-surface and jump joyfully in again. It can also be the entry point to another place–a deeper dimension of the carnal world that lies below the surface and surrounds, immerses and embraces movement consciousness. The longer one sustains a plunge, the more time one has to become absorbed in everything the water-human merge has to offer. Time below the surface permits the aesthetic and emotional qualities of the moment to 'sink in'.

The deeper one goes into the ocean depths, the more one approaches the human limits of being alive. In fact, as dives go increasingly deeper[3] the parasympathetic and sympathetic nervous systems start to work in conjunction instead of opposition, a biological response similar to that of reptiles. There is an incredible amount of bodily effort to sustain the pressures of the ocean depths and return to the surface. One must prepare diligently to survive such descents. One might wonder, if diving requires so much effort, then why take the plunge? Wouldn't it be more enjoyable to move within the shallows and observe radiant, tropical fish while breathing with the help of a snorkel? Divers think otherwise. A depth meter is an essential part of every deep-sea dive to counter the pull of wanting to go just a little deeper. Once one leaves the surface and glides downward, there is no natural feeling of how deep one should go. If a critical depth is passed, there may not be enough oxygen left to make the journey upward. Funnily enough, the journey to the surface is not the primary thought of a diver who feels "at home" with the fish. Perhaps Freud was right in expressing the "oceanic feeling" we crave as an infant (Ackerman, 1999) or in this case, what we crave as a child-like adult experiencing flow in depth. This bliss in merging with the ocean depths can either be attributed to connecting to a primordial state of being or to the early stages of nitrogen narcosis[4] and oxygen poisoning. If one has never plunged into the ocean depths can one have the sense of belonging that the water brings, "the embrace of the depths...a deep immersion the ultimate gentle release, a homecoming in an element" that can bring "only joy" (Ecott, 2001, p. 135)?

"The embrace of the depths" is a very fitting phrase for the joyful sensation of deep immersion. Any workaholic, artist, writer, or musician can relate to the feeling of complete intoxication with a project. Once the activity is begun, it is possible to be drawn so deeply into the experience that there is no longer a natural moment to surface, re-group, and reflect. The worry is that an individual may willingly delve into the bliss of prolonged deep activity knowing full well that there are potential physical or stressful hazards for overall wellness. What, then are the ethical implications of engaging in deep pedagogical flow. Is the client ready for such deep penetration? What sensitivities are needed to the moods and feelings of the client?

Diving sensitizes us to the interactive motions of deep flow in exercise pedagogy. Reflections on gestural moments of flow motion, beyond moments of physical resonance, require a critical sensitivity. We ask: Are the hands of helpfulness guiding and affirming the other's motions? Do they nurture the others postures, positions, gestures and expressions? Do these hands respond to another living, breathing, moving body in holding, supporting, molding, shifting, shaping and so setting in place new patterns of exercise motion? Do they bring vitality to these movement patterns? Do they draw one into an "embrace of the depths" of human interaction where one can feel and guide the client's motions as if they were one's own? Do they express a "chiasm of the Flesh" (Merleau-Ponty, 1968), crisscrossing motions, gestural reciprocity, where who moves and who is moved overlap and approximate one being?

Describing flow motion from the "surface" to the "depths" helps us discover how exercise pedagogy can move from an elevated stage of one-sided instruction to motions of deep, other-directed absorption (Lloyd, 2004; Lloyd & Smith, 2006). Within this thematic structure we become sensitive to the "pedagogical tact and thoughtfulness" (van Manen, 1991) pertaining to a particular region of lived experience and, in so doing, shed some light on what it means to move, be moved and sustain, textually and phenomenologically, the flow motions of pedagogical relationship.

CONCLUSION

Motion-sensitive phenomenology, involving sensing of, essencing of, and sensitizing to, the potential depth of flow experience in exercise settings provides a guide for human science research into the larger realm of movement education. At a time when movement is more often that not observed mechanically as "motor skill" acquisition, when "[m]ovement research and movement education have been neglected in our time" (Rudolf Laban as cited in Moore & Yamamoto, 1988), it is necessary to consider meaningful and thoughtful motion in meaningful and thoughtful ways. The Husserlian "I move" is central to human and other-than-human consciousness. Movement in all species of living things precedes its consciousness awareness such that, even the Merleau-Pontyean "I can do" is, in the first moment of awareness, a primal, animate consciousness (Sheets-Johnstone, 1999,pp. 134-135). What I think "I can do" is a conscious apprehension, a comprehension, of preconsciously thinking in movement. I move, therefore I am. To become motion-sensitive is thus to become attuned to "our wordless kinetic beginnings and our wordless celebrations of movement" (p. 225). It is to rediscover in movement a grounding of the phenomena of life, a preconsciousness of the pulses of living, a positioning and gesturing of ourselves within flow. certain motions, and agogic accent on moments of deep, interactive movement experience.

Motion sensitivity naturally lends itself to a phenomenology which is, as Maxine Sheets-Johnstone points out, "virtually nowhere to be found in phenomenological studies" (p. 269). The search for essences must take on a new dynamic, spatial, temporal and relational tone. We can no longer seek to elucidate an "end-state" (p. 269) as in determining the fixed nature, meaning or essence of "lived experience," but open the door to exploring the pulse of "living experience," its senses, incarnate essences and sensitive registers of meaning. The present chapter is but a step or stroke in this direction–a running step, a swimming stroke, a waving hand–amidst strokes of the computer keyboard that sustain certain moments of flow motion.

We have focused on particular instances of flow motion in this chapter with two sets of examples: those drawn from the flows of running, swimming and diving and those drawn from teaching the motions of flow to others. Our interest is sensuously, essentially and sensitively phenomenological *and* pedagogical. We began the chapter by blurring the boundaries between the flow motions of physical activity and the flow of writing phenomenologically. We conclude the chapter having blurred the divisions between lived experience, a textual practice, and a teaching relationship. Phenomenology and pedagogy are interwoven. The postures, positions, gestures and expressions of flow motion transpose to phenomenology and pedagogy though the durational accents that writing a text for others and being physically with others provide. Doing motion sensitive phenomenology is more than a research undertaking. It is a textual practice of moving kinaesthetically, aesthetically and ethically with others.

# NOTES

[1] The following discussion extends earlier methodological outlines of the applicability of "lifeworld phenomenology" to the phenomena of the play, game and sport regions of the world. (Smith, 1992; Smith, 1997b.)

[2] The term "agogic stress" is the special accent given a note in music by slightly increasing its duration. It's about subtle, nuanced tempo and rhythm changes as a result of phrasing. It differs from the dynamic accent of loudness and the tonic accent of pitch. "Agogy" is the suffix for leading forth, guiding, or bringing, taking, promoting or stimulating that which any prefix names. Thus, we use the neologism "phenomenagogy" as sensitivity to movement duration, and "pedagogy" as sensitivity to the durations of moving with others.

[3] In 1976, Jacques Mayol, the real-life hero who inspired the popular theatrical film production Big Blue, was the first to descend to 312 feet (100 meters), a depth once considered to be a physiological impossibility for humans. It was thought that pressure at that depth would cause the thorax surrounding the lungs permanently to collapse, but Mayol – sometimes admiringly referred to as *Homo aquaticus* – not only survived with his lungs and chest intact, but has continued to press the limits in competition with several others who aspire to be "the deepest man alive" (Earle, 1995, pp. 16-17).

[4] Nitrogen under pressure causes a peculiar euphoric effect much like the dreamy state induced by laughing gas, nitrous oxide. At about 100 feet and deeper, divers get "high," often experiencing a tranquil, giddy "buzz." Some divers happily hallucinate, become forgetful or confused which way is up, or decide that the regulator is a nuisance and offer it to passing fish (Earle, 1995, p. 53).

# REFERENCES

Ackerman, D. (1999). *Deep play*. New York: Vintage Books.

Berg, J. H. van den (1972). *A different existence*. Pittsburgh: Duquesne University Press.

Bergson, H. (1975). *Creative evolution*. Westport, CT: Glenwood Press.

Cohen, B. B. (1993). *Sensing, feeling, and action: The experiential anatomy of body-mind centering*. Northampton, MA: Contact Editions.

Conrad-Da'Oud, E. (1995). Life on land. In D. H. Johnson (Ed.), *Bone, breath, & gesture: Practices of embodiment* (pp. 297-312). Berkeley, CA: North Atlantic Books,.

Creswell, J. W. (1998) *Qualitative inquiry and research design, choosing among five traditions*. Thousand Oaks, CA: SAGE Publications.

Csikszentmihalyi, M. (2000) *Beyond boredom and anxiety. Experiencing flow in work and play*. San Francisco: Jossey-Bass.

Ecott, T. (2001) *Neutral buoyancy: Adventures in a liquid world*. New York: Grove Press.

Feldenkrais, M. (1980) *Mind and body. Your body works*. Copyrighted newsletter by Moshe Feldenkrais.

Foster, S. L. (1995) *Choreographing history*. Bloomington and Indianapolis: Indiana University Press.

Heidegger, M. (1965). *On the way to language*. New York: Harper and Row.

Heidegger, M. (1968). *What is called thinking?* (J. G. Gray, Trans.). New York: Harper and Row.

Hodgson, J. (2001). *Mastering movement: The life and work of Rudolf Laban*. London: Methuen.

Jackson, S. A., & Csikszentmihalyi, M. (1999). *Flow in sports: The keys to optimal experiences and performances*. Champaign, Il: Human Kinetics.

Kundera, M. (1990). *Immortality*. New York: Perennial Classics.

Laban, R. & Lawrence, F. C. (1974). *Effort*. London: Macdonald & Evans.

Lang, B. (1995) *Mind's bodies: Thought in the act*. Albany: State University of New York Press.

Levin, D.M. (1985) *The body's recollection of being*. London: Routledge.

Lloyd, R.J. (2004). *Interactive flow in exercise pedagogy*. Unpublished doctoral dissertation, Simon Fraser University.

Lloyd, R. J. & Smith, S. J. (2006). Interactive flow and exercise pedagogy. *Quest, 58*, 222-241.

Lloyd, R. J. & Trudel, P. (1999) Verbal interactions between an eminent mental training consultant and elite level athletes: A case study. *The Sport Psychologist. 13*, 418-443.

Manen, M. van (1984). Practicing phenomenological writing, *Phenomenology + Pedagogy, 2*, 36-69.

Manen, M. van (1986). *The tone of teaching.* Richmond Hill, Ontario: Scholastic.

Manen, M. van (1990). *Researching lived experience: Human science for an action sensitive pedagogy.* London, Ontario, Canada: The Althouse Press.

Manen, M. van (1991). *The tact of teaching.* Albany: State University of New York Press.

Manen, M. van (1992). The vitality of the pedagogical relation. In B. Levering, S. Miedema, S. Smith & M. van Manen (Eds.) *Reflections on pedagogy and method,* vol. 2 (pp. 173-192). Montfoort: Uriah Heep.

Manen, M. van (1997). From meaning to method, *Qualitative Health Research: An International, Interdisciplinary Journal, 7*, 345-369.

Manen, M. van (2002). *Writing in the dark: Phenomenological studies in interpretative inquiry.* London, Ontario, Canada: The Althouse Press.

Markula, P. & Denison, J. (2000) See spot run: Movement as an object of textual analysis *Qualitative Inquiry, 6*, 406-432.

Merleau-Ponty, M. (1962) translated by Colin Smith, *Phenomenology of perception* (C. Smith, Trans.). London: Routledge & Kegan Paul.

Merleau-Ponty, M. (1963). *Structure of behavior.* Boston: Beacon.

Merleau-Ponty, M. (1968). *The Visible and the invisible* (A, Lingis, Trans.). Evanston, Illinois: Northwestern University Press.

Moore, C-L. & Yamamoto, K. (1988). *Beyond words: Movement observation and analysis.* New York: Gordon and Breach.

Nin, A. (1976). Letter to a young writer. *The journals of Anais Nin.* (G. Stuhlmann, Ed.), Vol. 5, 1947-1955. London: Quartet Books.

Pangrazi, R.B. & Gibbons, S. (2003). *Dynamic physical education for elementary school children,* Canadian Edition. Toronto, Ontario: Pearson Education Canada.

Pinar, W.F., Reynolds, W.M., Slattery, P. & Taubman, P.M. (2000) *Understanding curriculum.* New York: Peter Lang.

Pronger, B. (1995) Rendering the Body: The implicit lessons of gross anatomy. *Quest, 47*, 427-446.

Shapiro, K.J. (1985). *Bodily reflective modes: A phenomenological method for psychology.* Durham: Duke University Press.

Sheets-Johnstone, M. (1999). *The primacy of movement.* Philadelphia: John Benjamins.

Shusterman, R. (1999) Somaesthetics: A Disciplinary Proposal. Published in: *Journal of Aesthetics and Art Criticism.* Retrieved December 2003 from http://www.temple.edu/aesthetics/somaesthetics.html.

Smith, S. J. (1982). The phenomenology of play behaviour and its educational significance. Unpublished M.Ed. dissertation, University of Queensland.

Smith, S. J. (1988). Risk and the playground. Unpublished doctoral dissertation, University of Alberta.

Smith, S. J. (1992). Studying the lifeworld of physical education: A Phenomenological orientation. In A, Sparkes (Ed.), *Research In physical education and sport: Exploring alternative visions* (pp. 61-89). London: Falmer.

Smith, S. J. (1997a). *Risk and our pedagogical relation to children: On the playground and beyond.* Albany, NY: State University of New York Press.

Smith, S. J. (1997b). The phenomenology of educating physically. In D. Vandenberg (Ed.). *Phenomenology in Education Discourse* (pp. 119-144). Durban: Heinemann.

Solnit, R. (2000). *Wanderlust: A history of walking.* New York: Penguin.

LEILA VILLAVERDE, JOE L. KINCHELOE AND FRANCES HELYAR

# 13. HISTORICAL RESEARCH IN EDUCATION

INTRODUCTION: HISTORIOGRAPHY, PHILOSOPHY, AND THEORY (LEILA
VILLAVERDE)

The study of history is often regarded and studied as a detached endeavor, a quest
for facts through an objective disposition. Historical writing tends to encapsulate a
grand narrative, one that explains the events of the past without agents or producers of knowledge; both technicist and positivistic language usually frame such historical writing. Historiography exposes the frames and parameters of historical
writing in order to further one's understanding of the circumstances of the past.
Historiography offers a method of intervention in the comprehension of and living
in socio-cultural political events. It is the careful study of historical writing and the
ways in which historians interpret the past through various theoretical lenses and
methodologies.

The key element in historiography is the ability to discern how history is mediated by philosophy, ideology, and politics. Such clarity makes history intelligible
and accessible, denoting its contemporary presence and significance. Having own-
ership over the past links the self to others and vice versa, grounding the present
with critical consciousness and the future with proleptic responsibility. Historiography is a consuming project, demanding astute attention to detail in how and what
is present and excluded. Yet as students of history emerge from the heuristic process, they have a better chance of sustaining the will to change/ transform the pub-
lic/ private space in the 20th century. In this chapter we will discuss the theory of
historiography, its philosophy and methodologies, and outcomes.

*Theory of Historiography*

Methods within historiography are informed by a theory or theories that construct a
set of parameters helpful in asking questions about history, particularly about the
relationship between people, events, and the times that create history. In other
words the process of doing historiography does not happen in a theoretical vacuum; it is not just methods, but praxis (informed action). Wehler, a social historian
from the University of Bielefeld, coins the term historical social science and believes such a historian "approaches society with clearly formulated questions related to social change," and aims to progressively transform social structures (Iggers, 2005, p. 70).

Wehler stresses the goal and purpose of doing historical social science and situates this method in the Frankfurt School's Critical Theory where political respon-

*K. Tobin & J. Kincheloe, (eds.), Doing Educational Research—A Handbook, 311–346.*
© *2006 Sense Publishers. All rights reserved.*

sibility, human agency, and intellectual efforts are privileged, as well as prioritized. Often an explicit and articulated position on historical events is read as biased, as partial accuracy, yet this assumption presupposes there is a neutral way of reading, understanding, or knowing history. Such practices only further curtail an individual's ability to critically interpret or narrate a situated history. Theory and/ or ideology can be regarded as a process through which particular knowledge is produced, public consciousness affected, and reading practices renegotiated. It can facilitate or close off a fluid representation of historical events or figures.

Many perceive theory and history to be mutually exclusive entities, at least those situated in more traditional discourses of history. Others discuss the necessity to highlight or integrate theory into history particularly as an attempt to sustain history in the university, as an academic discipline. However history is understood, past or present, there are compelling articulations for how theory works through and informs the discourse, appreciation, and writing of history. Koselleck (2002) cites seven essential elements (*conceptual history, structural history, chronology, historical conflicts, temporal series, teleology, and monocausality*) in the formulation of theory in history. These elements are also fundamental in doing and studying historiography. Each concept is discussed for its importance to the theorizing of historiography.

Koselleck (2002) illustrates *conceptual history* as "...rather, a question of theoretically formulating in advance the temporal specifics of our political and social concepts so as to order the source materials" (p. 5). The main focus of conceptual history is to organize the overarching themes in a historical period in order to stress recurring patterns in social movements or developments. Conceptual history is structured by topics or issues casting a wider net over space/ time boundaries. Once these patterns are articulated new ways of investigating the past can be uncovered and new lenses of interpretation can be applied. *Structural history* is situated within a theory of periodization, which asks questions about the historical determination of time (p. 6).

Structural history as a lens underscores the technical expressions of space and time. How we use language to denote time, era, epoch, and so on, as well as the way in which we employ language to shape time in action (friction, ruptures, resistance, combat, etc.) facilitates a critical awareness of temporality, of time lived and revisited. Time is carefully studied to comprehend the conditions of the events of history. We often run the risk of supplanting present values and beliefs on past events without careful recognition of the trappings in simulated time travel. Koselleck cautions his students to be mindful of this phenomenon, thus emphasizes the usefulness in applying structural history. *Chronology*, his third element in the theorizing of history, questions the recurrent narration of history as neatly organized sequences. Koselleck argues:

We must, rather, learn to discover the simultaneity of the nonsimultaneous in our history...And since the large scale problems of developing countries are coming back to haunt us today, it becomes imperative to gain theoretical clarity about the nonsimultaneity of the simultaneous and to pursue related questions. (p. 8)

Interrogating historical chronology invites an intertextual understanding in the construction of history, emphasizing various interpretations and perspectives of any historical event or movement. History shifts dramatically from a positivist epistemology to a constructivist one. *Historical conflicts* is the next element in Koselleck's list. Controversies, disputes, and tensions in history are at the core of historical writing, unresolved conflicts in particular, those that tend to mutate and change form with the times, sustain students in their continuous pursuit of history. "A historical theory of conflicts can be...developed only by bringing out the temporal qualities inherent in the conflict...In historiography, conflicts are usually dealt with by introducing opponents as stable subjects, ...fixed entities whose fictive character can be recognized..." (Koselleck, 2002, p. 9). In other words, events of the past are told through a story of numerous characters where relational interactions are as central to the story as the characters themselves. This kind of storytelling, mainly focusing on conflicts between places, people or ideas renders a partial story that can rely heavily on the reconstructed history based on the available documents.

Understanding the limitations of historical conflicts deters the student and researcher of history from replicating fixed or fictive entities. Koselleck then turns to his concept of *temporal series* to demonstrate the study of a subject through time as a continuous entity. The boundaries of time and space provide a heightened magnifying lens on the selected topic of history bracketing certain information and allowing for closer measuring of the quality of experience. He states, "Moreover, excluding certain questions under certain theoretical premises makes it possible to find answers that would otherwise not have come up; a clear proof of the need for theory in our discipline" (p. 10). *Teleology*, the study of final causes, results, or predetermined outcomes, is the next element in the construction of a theory of history. According to Koselleck the field of history presupposes a teleology, yet whether the historian supports or disputes the finality of history, the way in which history is told/ written is the operative strategy in teaching through history. He contends the following:

If every historian remains rooted in his situation, he will be able to make only observations that are framed by his perspective. These, however, evoke final causes. A historian can hardly escape them, and if he disregards them he relinquishes the reflection that teaches him about what he is doing. The difficulty does not so much lie in the *final causality* deployed but in naively accepting it. It is possible to come up with as many causes as one wishes for any event that ever took place in the course of history. There is no single event that could not be explained causally.... Stated more concisely: everything can be justified, but not everything can be justified by anything. (pp. 11-12)

Both issues of finality and the author's perspective or position are pivotal factors in the interpretation and analysis of history. Unless the student of history is aware of these conditions she/he will be unable to critically grasp history as a holistic inquiry instrumental to both present and future identity formation and social change. Koselleck's final concept of monocausality, where history is explained through one major causal agent, requires reflexivity and critique. Once again Koselleck cautions his reader in being overly singular in their historical approach. He is not negating that one cause may be predominantly useful in comprehending history; instead that one should not use one cause as default nor exercise ideological tunnel vision. He advocates the investigation of multiple causes and conditions. The seven elements in the theory of history provide cautions and directions on what are necessary contentions in the study of history. The theoretical construction here allows for the student of history to delineate the larger constructs which inform the ways she/he makes sense of past, present, and future.

Another useful theoretical structure through which to examine history is ontology. Ontology is a branch of metaphysics that focuses on how things are the way they are, subjective existence, and the relationships that exist between the self and society. By prioritizing being and existence and using it to conduct historical studies, events and people of the past take on a larger human quality. The quality and nuances of experience are centralized not objectified. Ontology affords another theoretical impetus for the purpose of doing historiography.

*Philosophy and Methodology*

Philosophy can be used as a conduit, a solution to the theoretical and practical problems raised in the study of history. To fully grasp how philosophy can serve as a method, one must understand what philosophy produces. It helps to focus on what happens to how the world is perceived when one believes in the tenets of any philosophy. How do the tenets explain reality or human nature? How do these tenets help to clarify the moments in lived experience that may be either accepted or not, yet not fully understood? How can one investigate phenomena that have never been questioned or regarded as questionable? Philosophy provides language and structures through which to understand reality, a platform from which to decode perception, intentions, texts, and experiences. Philosophy offers specific guidelines for what to ask, how to ask it, how to detect a problem and how to theorize solutions or possibilities. The sole adherence to any one philosophy can also provide limitations and blindspots in understanding historical phenomena. On the other hand, the integration of several philosophies may address the conceptual restrictions of any one set of tenets.

Methodology provides guidelines for action in the study of a variety of events, people, conditions, ideas, documents, and so on. What follows are three methodologies, critical interpretation, meta-analysis, and asking unique questions, all of which are integral to engaging in historiography. Critical interpretation is encouraged while grounded within a serious research of primary and secondary sources. The author uses this process of research to inform his/her questioning and critical analysis of events, people, policy, norms, beliefs, and values; one "can't overlook how ideology frames, constructs, and defines what is seen and/ or obscured" (, Tierney, 2003, p. 305). Similar to hermeneutics, the pursuit is of meaning, whether it is through textual analysis, conceptual analysis, post-structuralist criticism, discourse analysis, literary criticism, or phenomenology. There is an active engagement with history and self, a deep reflection and critique of one's place in history and the social consequences of such, and the search for knowledge otherwise excluded, yet central to more equitable social change.

Meta-analysis is another cornerstone of historiography; it illustrates the investigation of how existing analysis is produced. It is a crucial process in discovering what has been excluded and included, as well as the reasons for such decisions. This process may involve thick description of an event or viewpoint in order to tease out/ discern ideological clues and notations in language and judgment. Through this process the interpretative work of history is made evident and accessible to the reader. The interpretation of historical writing and primary or secondary resources allows for the author to contextualize his/ her viewpoint of what occurred, of how history is told and retold. The author can expose the rich layering and complex structuring of social phenomena.

Since historiography often includes the writing of other historians, the historians themselves may become part of the researched subject. In essence one is a participant in thinking about his/her own thinking. The context from which the historian wrote is as important as what the historian made of it. White (1990) contends, "[Historians] too must be 'deconstructed,' their 'blindness' specified, and their places in the *epistemes* of their epochs determined before they can enter the lists as possible models of historical reconstruction and analysis" (p. 186). Meta-analysis instills a critical distance through which to create a bird's eye view of the entire slice of history while simultaneously producing an insider's perspective. The spatial and temporal shifts in the historiographer's position lend themselves to insights not previously attainable.

Asking unique questions is also an important part of the process in historiography. Borrowing from Kincheloe and Steinberg's (1993) features of postformal thinking, the first is etymology that focuses on the origin and historical development of what we know. They state, "Problem detecting and the questioning that accompanies it become a form of world making in that the way these operations are conducted is contingent on the system of meaning employed" (p. 305). This process also leads to seeing connections between otherwise disparate things or events. The inquiry based method is at the core of a meaningful research endeavor; it fuels curiosity, and recognizes problematic practices and beliefs before considered 'natural" or part of the "norm".

For example to see slavery as a functional necessity in a capitalist society only presents part of a story from a particular position of power and a distinct orientation in defining the value of human life. A historiographer would expose this as well as focus on the human suffering which was the high cost and expense of such racist and sexist practices. The method and philosophy of historiography can raise critical consciousness and awareness in increasing the stakes of personal and collective involvement in history.

One place where philosophy and methodology can be theoretically worked out is in our imagination. Villaverde (1999) has previously argued the imagination as a pedagogical space, an often unused dimension of our thinking/ theorizing space. White (1987) connects the narration/ interpretation/ analysis of history to the use of one's imagination in the following way:

> Because history, unlike fiction, is supposed to represent real events and therefore contribute to knowledge of the real world, imagination…is a faculty particularly in need of disciplinization in historical studies. Political partisanship and moral prejudice may lead the historian to misread or misrepresent documents and thus to construct events that never took place. On the conscious level, the historian can, in his investigative operations, guard against such errors by the judicious employment of "the rules of evidence." The imagination, however, operates on a different level of the historian's consciousness. It is present above all in the effort, peculiar to the modern conceptualization of the historian's task, to enter sympathetically into the minds or consciousness of human agents long dead, to empathize with the intentions and motivations of actors impelled by beliefs and values that may differ totally from anything the historian might himself honor in his own life, and to understand, even when he cannot condone, the most bizarre social and cultural practices. This is often described as putting oneself in the place of past agents, seeing things from their point of view, and so forth, all of which leads to a notion of objectivity that is quite different from anything that might be meant by that term in the physical sciences. (p. 67)

White warns the reader that imagination can also be dangerous if one takes great artistic license in the construction of historical narrative. Yet he strongly believes the actual objects or events of historical study place parameters on what can be imagined without additional corroboration from research. Contextual understanding is crucial in historical interpretation and study. In the journey back through time a combination of artifacts and discourse represent the conditions of a particular time and are essential to the historian's particular explication of any era or event. Utilizing the imagination is not an excuse to be romantic or essentialist, but rather an opportunity to use language, to stretch what language can do in capturing the nuances of time, lived experience and the sociopolitical context of history, always being authentic to the primary sources discovered. According to White (1990) historical interpretation should at least not deny the reality of the events it treats. Too often "objectivity' is confused with objective distance and critical separation out of which a telling of history comes forth that uncovers otherwise hidden nuggets of knowledge. If history is to teach us something as White and Kant propose, then we cannot assume it is a monolithic grandiose teacher, but rather a variety of teachers with distinct ideologies, interpretations, and methodologies.

White further discusses the progression of aesthetics, imagination, beauty and the sublime using Kant, Burke, and Hegel to explain the prioritization of the beautiful and the disengagement with the sublime. The sublime (a precondition to histo-riography, according to White 1990) is usually described as the awe producing events or experiences that weigh on the horrific or produce terror. Many accounts of history gloss over the sublime, the gruesome and appalling details of war, colo-nialism, power, disregard for human life, struggles over civil rights and equity. Preference for the 'beautiful" particularly in renditions of history can be danger-ous; dangerous in that it covers/ camouflages lived pain, suffering, struggle, loss, and the abuse of power. These troublesome pockets of time are what Giroux and Macedo call dangerous memories, those events once remembered that can cause great anger or frustration precisely because of the simultaneous discovery of the intentional suppression and at times destruction of primary resources. These memories may also attempt to politically domesticate public attitudes towards his-tories already difficult to deal with, "but a memory, whether real or only felt to be so, cannot be deprived of the emotional charge and the action it seems to justify by presenting a historical-real that has remembrance as its only purpose (White 1990, p. 80). Historiography can offer a more in depth and comprehensive account of social movements or experiences.

Regardless of which methodology is chosen or what philosophy informs this methodology, we must also accept the past will always be in part unknowable. If we fall prey to thinking it is completely knowable by investigating the most minute section or detail after detail we enact a positivist approach to historiography and any other kind of study/ research. To know in detail and only in detail fragments understanding, detail and whole must always relate to one another in heuristic bal-ance; it's how one studies the past that makes the considerable difference.

## Outcomes of Historical Research

What is the outcome of historiography? Stated simply, the purpose of historical research is knowledge production, learning that is politically situated and made useful for the transformation of culture and society. More explicitly, the purpose is to make the construction and content of history known and exposed. History is narrated through the author's poignant analysis and commentary. But by carefully piecing history back together, paying close attention to the implicit and null ele-ments of history, a new perspective surfaces. The insight and interpretation of his-tory is founded and crafted through the author's ethical referent, theoretical framework, and philosophical method. Historiography affords the ability to ask fundamental questions about the responsibilities of governments, societies, com-munities, and individuals in times of crisis. By assuming history is a collection of facts unfiltered by specific agendas truncates the comprehension of history often producing historical amnesia and political apathy which usually also renders his-tory static, as well as one-dimensional. The need is to remember in a pedagogically productive manner. "To the historian equipped with the proper tools, it is sug-gested, any text or artifact can figure forth the thought-world and possibly even the world of emotional investment and praxis of its time and place of production" (White 1990, p. 187).

Another important outcome of historiography is the appraisal of history's meaning, its description and assessment, the exposition of its situatedness, as well as a renewal of dialogue with events and significant figures of the past. How the past is articulated and hypothesis established would complement and reconstruct what is read and studied as history. As the student of history unfurls the rich content learned through historiography, she/he must be cautious of relativism and absolutism. As the student decides on the topic of inquiry and proceeds in the research process, often there is a propensity to either perceive everything as important or to generalize/ universalize from a singular social/ cultural pattern.

Historiography focuses on human agency, the ability to extract the power of individual stories and collective endeavors in changing culture and society. This historical method allows for active participation in the past through ways that can thoughtfully inform the process in which we approach and transform present and future. It provides more viable connections between thoughts and being, ideas, events and self. It invites individuals to be intricately involved in the course of history. Historiography extracts the social and political spirit through textual analysis and questions of past practices. Through these particular triangulations history is unified, it is seen through holistic kaleidoscopes. Too often history is presented as a set of dates on a chronological timeline, fragmented, and objectified. By connecting the dots, so to speak, the reader is forced to think and make lasting meaning about the impact of people's contributions to the past and the potential impact on both present and future. Education and learning are made accessible when students are able to pose and examine questions about the problems facing their own communities present and past. Distancing the student from the events of the past produces a type of alienation and immobilization in developing one's empowerment and imagination. The more we create disconnected individuals, the further we support an incomplete construction of the past.

## FOUR DIMENSIONS OF A CRITICAL HISTORIOGRAPHY: CRITICALITY, AN AFFIRMATIVE PRESENTISM, THE BRICOLAGE, AND MULTILOGICALITY (JOE L. KINCHELOE)

### Laying a Foundation for a Critical Historiography

Picking up on the historiographical foundation constructed in Part I of this chapter, we will now turn to the critical dimensions of historical research. "Critical" in this context is used in the critical theoretical sense of the term. Emerging in the work of the Frankfurt School in post World War I Germany, critical theory along with approaches to scholarship emerging from the work of W.E.B. DuBois addressed the frustration produced by positivist methods of studying social, cultural, political, economic, psychological, and educational phenomena and the oppression of unbridled capitalism. Critical scholars from diverse disciplines were impressed by critical theory's approach to the social construction of human experience (see Kincheloe, 2004 for more insight into these issues of criticality).

Buoyed by critical insights, such scholars came to view their disciplines as manifestations of the discourses and power relations of the socio-historical contexts that produced them. The discourse of possibility implicit within the constructed nature of social experience suggested to these scholars that a reconstruction of the humanities and social sciences could lead to a more egalitarian and democratic social order. In such a context historical research took on a new usefulness, a new sense of what could be. In a critical modality history could escape a necrophilic concern with the past for its own sake and become a part of a contemporary conversation about social change and democracy.

Thus, critical theory revolutionized the notion of theory itself. In a critical context theory would not longer be viewed as a universal body of intractable truth but as a guide to the socio-cultural, political, psychological, and educational domains. In historiography critical theory does not determine how we see the world but helps historians gain new lenses for viewing educational phenomena and new strategies for exploring them. Critical theory is particularly concerned with issues of power and justice and the ways that the economy, matters of race, class, gender, sexuality, religion, and other forces shape both educational institutions and individual consciousness.

A critical historiography in education helps educators locate who they are, the goals of their pedagogy, and their political orientation to the educational act. In a critical historical context educators begin to learn the reasons for the multifaceted origins of public education. They find that schools were formed for competing purposes: the regulation of the poor, immigrants, and other "social threats" as well as for the democratic desire to educate an enlightened citizenry. Throughout history, education has served both causes concurrently. In this context educators can begin to make the choice as to which educational god they want to serve and build their pedagogies around their preferences.

In an essay (Kincheloe, 1991) I published fifteen years ago on educational historiographical methods, I addressed this issue of historian subjectivity and ways of seeing. The means by which power and culture shaped the perspectives of historians and thus the histories they produced were not deemed to be an important dimension of historiographical—especially educational historiographical—literature in the early 1990s. While strides have been made such concerns still are relegated to the periphery of historical scholarship. Even those deemed revisionists in the radical scholarship of the 1960s and 1970s were not especially concerned with issues of the subjectivity of the historian.

As Thomas Kuhn (1962) wrote over four decades ago, members of scholarly disciplines come to see themselves as responsible for the pursuit of common goals—objectives that form the core of so-called disciplinary matrixes. These disciplinary matrixes reflect their assumptions in the questions and methodologies employed in analyzing the concerns of a particular discipline of knowledge. What I then called a critical meta-analysis involves the myriad of ways that ideology, discourse, culture, and positionality shape this disciplinary matrix. In this context, I believe, that there are many engagements that are necessary to move educational historians and educational historiography to new insights into the limitations of the discipline and our ways of "doing historical research."

In this conceptual domain critical historians of education take an important cue from African American historians of education of the first half of the twentieth century: W.E.B. DuBois, V. P. Franklin, Carter Woodson, Horace Mann Bond, and many others. These historians saw no conflict between their scholarly goals of race uplift—the effort to improve the living conditions of people of African descent—and rigorous scholarship. They viewed themselves as scholars with profound connections to the black community. Critical historians, like these African American scholars, maintain close connections to marginalized individuals and communities and view their work as part of larger efforts to improve the lot of the oppressed (Blant, 2000; Alridge, 2003). As the famous liberation theologian, Enrique Dussell has maintained, what meaning does scholarship have:

> For a Hindu beggar covered with mud from the floods of the Ganges; or for a member of a Bantu community from Sub-Saharan Africa dying of hunger; or for hundreds of thousands of poor marginalized in the suburban neighborhood like Nezahualcoyotl or Tlanepantla in Mexico.... (Dussell quoted in Mignolo, 2001, p. 34).

Critical historians of education embrace a history that provides insight into problems that matter, that can help change the lives of those in need. Drawing upon the spirit of Paulo Freire, we proclaim a historiography for a pedagogy of the oppressed. Such an approach to history is grounded on an emancipatory reason that we referenced earlier as postformalism. As a form of emanicipatory reason, postformalism is a multilogical alternative rationality (Aronowitz, 1988) that employs forms of analysis sensitive to signs and symbols, the power of context in relation to thinking, the role of emotion and feeling in cognitive activity, and the value of the psychoanalytical process as it taps into the recesses of (un)consciousness. In the character of critical theory, postformalism attempts to democratize these ways of making meaning. In this effort postformal historians study issues of purpose, meaning, and value. Critical historians, thus, believe that the compelling interpretations that emerge from these purposes and scholarly processes can produce knowledges that provide a basis for just action in the present.

The knowledges that critical historians produce lead to action by working to decolonize the mind. Hegemonic, ideological, and discursive forms of power emanating from power centers in the Western world have worked to shape the consciousness of a wide range of individuals. The history of education that comes out of this mindset is many times blinded by the intense white light of dominant power. The result of such history is to exclude the experiences and insights of those who have not been well served by educational establishments. Historical knowledges produced by critical historians cannot predict the future or provide educators with a blueprint for the "correct" way of educating. Nevertheless, critical history of education can help us understand how situations came to exist in a way that informs our actions (Murphy, 1997; Parker, 1999). Thus, a critical history is a pragmatic history—a story of the past with consequences for the present and future.

Such a pragmatic history by nature connects the past, present, and future. History is changed by the events of the present. When we study histories written about gender and education in the late nineteenth century, we are amazed by the assumptions about gender that shaped such chronicles. The changing role of women in the last half of the twentieth century forced historians to rewrite earlier histories of the schooling and education of women. Thus, critical historians aware of the co-constructed relationship of past, present, and future and the role of power in shaping everyday events continuously gain new perspectives into old concerns. Such critical histories expose oppressive assumptions, the fingerprints of power on archival manuscripts, and the cultural logics of established historical interpretations. This critical expose opens a stargate to an alternative future, as it sheds a revealing light on the foibles of the old regime. Even in light of the critical historian's understandings of the complexities and ambiguities of reconstructing the past, she still insists that compelling historical interpretations can lead to social and educational change (Parker, 1999; Barros, 2004; Bentley, 2005). A critical historical consciousness leads to enhanced human agency that helps individuals and groups navigate their way through a maze of socio-cultural, political, economic, and educational structures that too often serve to regulate and discipline.

To get to this point critical historians often start their research with a basic question: what groups and individuals are advantaged and what groups and individuals are disadvantaged by particular historical educational plans and organizations? Here critical historians begin to identify the power relations that shape educational issues. In this context a literacy of power becomes especially important. Such a literacy involves a complex understanding of a variety of the ways power operates to marginalize and oppress. Critical historians are thus obligated to understand hegemonic, ideological, discursive, disciplinary, and regulatory modes of power and the ways they affect human efforts to shape their own lives. Understanding such power dynamics does not make the critical historian's task any easier. Power in a critical complex sense does not play out in some paint-by-numbers formula. Every circumstance is different and while hegemony may exist, it may manifest itself in unique and perplexing ways.

Historians operating in the critical sense outlined here struggle for accuracy even when events elude their initial expectations. Many of us operating in this critical historical domain have often heard conservative critics argue that social theory informed history allows particular worldviews to dictate their interpretation and their narrative. This is the case only if one is an inept historian. Social theory in the critical sense of the term helps historians formulate questions, rethink what counts as a source, develop interpretive strategies, expand one's toolbox of methods, and develop unique narrative styles (Parker, 1997; Gale, 1999). Critical theory does not dictate what it is one finds in the process of historical research. In fact, if it works properly it expands the possibility of finding new sources and developing innovative ways of making sense of the past and its relation to the present. Any historian—no matter what his or her ideological/theoretical orientation who looks only for and uses evidence that supports some larger political point has committed an unnatural act against Clio (the Greek muse of history).

I have been confronted with these accusations of "cooking the research" so often in my career as a critical educational researcher that I feel it important to address these matters in more detail. Let there be no ambiguity about this tenet of critical historiography: dishonestly picking and choosing historical data to marshal support for a specific political, social, or educational agenda is bad history. Critical historiography is concerned with asking questions of the past—not dictating answers about it. These questions take us where they will, and we must have the courage to venture into these uncharted hermeneutic domains. In this interpretive netherland critical historians must avoid the deterministic sirens imploring us to view only macro-structures while ignoring the lived complexity of everyday life as well as the criticalists who would move us to see only the oppressive dimensions of schooling in lieu of expressions of education's democratic impulse.

Concurrently, critical educational historiography as it focuses on race, class, gender, sexual, religious concerns must not lose sight of the reformulation and intensification of the power of new twenty-first century forms of capital-driven global colonialism. Such structures exert new forms of regulation on peoples around the planet as they co-opt education for their own insidious designs. An exploration of these new phenomena must be carried out in diverse locales with concentrated attention paid to the ways particular individuals and groups have resisted their intrusions. The critical historiography here searches for new formulations and articulations of power and oppression, but always within a dialectic shaped by the interaction of individual and structure. Individual and structure simply cannot be considered as separate dynamics because of their co-constructive relationship. Structure shapes the individual, as the individual shapes the structure (Castro-Gomez, 1998; Bentley, 2005). One cannot study the history of schooling nor walk into a contemporary school without noting the omnipresence of this process. The dance of the subject and the macro-structure is a key dimension of the critical complexity referenced earlier.

A key dimension of doing historical research in education involves anticipating and addressing the complexity of history and historical research. Contrary to naïve objectivist assertions, history is much to complex to be known in some final, comprehensive, and intractable manner. Historians—no matter how brilliant they may be—cannot escape the blinders of her particular historical era. Our Zeitgeists shape us in ways we can never completely understand in our lifetime. Even the documents historians validate as "authentic" are soaked with dominant power and shaped by the subjective perspectives of their producers. Often when critical historians address such complicating factors, they are accused of relativism and the attempt to kill history. Understanding the ways that the construction of a historical narrative is in part a creative act, a feat of the imagination does not take away from the usefulness of historical scholarship. Indeed, it provides us with a more accurate picture of the historiographical process and how history may be either distorted or used in a socially beneficent manner.

All historical research is ensnared in this web of complexity, whether we like it or not. Historical narratives assume particular epistemological, ontological, political, ad infinitum positions—whether the historian is conscious of them or not. Based on these commitments historians choose to include particular data in their narratives while excluding other information. So much happened in the time and place about which one is writing that the historian is forced to use a set of subjective criteria to select what is and is not important. Critical historians attempt to make these criteria open for inspection by their readers. Objectivist historians often act as if they don't exist, arguing that they made no subjective choices—we're just telling the story as it really happened (Murphy, 1997; Norkus, 1999). Of course, no one can do that in some objective, disinterested manner, even when we're attempting to describe something that happened in the present. Human beings always see the world from a particular vantage point—the authors of this chapter included.

In light of the previously mentioned critical theoretical goals and issues of complexity, the history of education we are promoting here moves historical scholarship to a new level of scholarly rigor. We are not defining rigor here in some positivistic follow-the-standardized-procedure modality. Our definition of rigor involves an awareness of the influence of one's own subjectivity on historical research, the complexity of the past, the power dynamics at work in all phases of historical research, the dynamics of a useful history that promotes the social good, and the multiple dimensions of historical narratives. I have argued in many places that such rigor demands a multilogical approach to scholarship and social action.

As discussed earlier in this chapter, postformalism calls on historiography to bring multiple perspectives to its work. This concept of multilogicality rests at the heart of a critical multiculturalism and an evolving notion of criticality. I have expanded these notions in my description of the research bricolage (Kincheloe, 2001, 2005; Kincheloe and Berry, 2004). A complex mode of research is grounded on this multilogicality. This assertion is not some esoteric, academic point—it shapes social analysis, political perspectives, curriculum development, teaching and learning, and the field of educational history. Acting upon this understanding, critical historians understand that historical observations hold more within them to be analyzed than first impressions sometime reveal. In this sense different frames of reference produce multiple interpretations and multiple realities. The mundane, the everyday and the historical dimensions are multiplex and continuously unfolding—while this is taking place, human interpretation is simultaneously constructing and reconstructing the meaning of what we observe. A multilogical educational history promotes a spatial distancing from reality that allows an observer diverse frames of reference.

Drawing upon this postformal multilogicality in this historiographical pursuit, critical historians, like liberation theologians in Latin America, make no apology for seeking the viewpoints, insights and sensitivities of the marginalized. The way to see from a perspective differing from that of the positivist guardians involves exploring an institution such as education from the vantage point of those who have been marginalized by it. In such a process subjugated knowledges once again emerge allowing historians to gain the cognitive power of empathy—a power that enables them to take pictures of reality from different vantage points. The intersection of these diverse vantage points allows for a form of analysis that moves beyond the isolated, decontextualized and fragmented analysis of historical reductionism.

Cognitively empowered by these multiplex perspectives, complexity-sensitive, multilogical historians seek a multicultural dialogue between Eastern cultures and Western cultures, a conversation between the relatively wealthy Northern cultures and the impoverished Southern cultures and an intracultural interchange among a variety of subcultures. In this way forms of knowing, representing, and making meaning that have been excluded by reductionist and often white patriarchal elitist history move us to new vantage points and unexplored perspectives. Understandings derived from the perspective of the excluded or the "culturally different" allow for an appreciation of the nature of justice, the invisibility of the process of oppression, the power of difference and the insight to be gained from a recognition of divergent cultural uses of long hidden knowledges that highlight both our social construction as individuals and the limitations of monocultural ways of meaning making.

In our critical historiographical use of multilogicality we begin to uncover the ways that race, for example, is embedded not only into the topics that historians of education traditionally chose to study but also in the construction of history as a discipline. By the seventeenth and eighteenth centuries race had emerged as a colonial construct characterized by white conquerors and the "colored" colonized. This hierarchy was built into a meta-philosophy of history that assumed hierarchical distinctions between diverse groups of people. Such inscriptions can be easily seen in the historical productions of the centuries following the advent of colonialism, yet they were often oblivious to the historians and their readers. A critical multilogical historiography of education seeks to identify and expose tacit assumptions such as these.

A multilogical historiography promotes a displacement of a monological perspective from the centers of various power blocs—racial, class, gender, sexual, religious, national, etc. In this way diverse ways of seeing and being are valued and employed in the historical topics chosen, interpretive strategies devised, and the historical research methods engaged. By recognizing the power of difference we begin to understand the limitations of the epistemological assumptions behind much Western historiography. In this context we discern that objectivist forms of history are built on an epistemological house of cards that collapses quickly when reductionistic truth claims are seriously questioned. Thus, critical historiography's view from the bottom, its respect for subjugated knowledges moves educational historians to listen to colonized peoples, racially marginalized individuals, men and women who did not benefit from the promises of schooling, and other peoples occupying the lowest rung of the socio-economic ladder. In such a context such individuals' ways of seeing and making meaning can inform our understanding of the world, society, education, the construction of selfhood, and, thus, the study of history in dramatic new ways.

In this critical multilogical context educational historians enter a new domain of practice. In this zone of critical multilogicality such historians if they are operating in North America work in solidarity with Asians, Africans, Latin Americans, indigenous peoples, and subcultures within their own societies. In their "interracialism" and "interculturalism" they understand that there is far more to history than the socially constructed notion that civilization began in ancient Greece, migrated to Europe, and reached its zenith in the contemporary U.S. In histories that emerge in various fields, education included, this assumption exists in an influential and unchallenged state. Critical multilogical historians challenge this monological Eurocentrism and search for the ways it insidiously inscribes the "doing of educational history." At this point educational historians look for various forms of indigenous knowledge both as a focus for historical research and for their epistemological and ontological insights. Not only do we learn about such knowledges and the cultures that produced them, but we also use their ways of seeing and being to challenge Western monological perspectives. Here critical multilogical historians question reductionist notions of historical objectivity and superficially validated historical facts.

Historiographical multilogicality is a break from the class elitist, white-centered, patriarchal histories that have dominated Western historiography for too long. While many successful efforts have been made to get beyond elite, white, male histories, critical historians want to go farther—they want to understand the colonial impulses that work to exclude important histories of education from non-Western and subjugated domains and how these domains shape normalized history. Learning from indigenous knowledges, African, Islamic, Asian, and Latin American philosophies of history, critical historians learn new ways of practicing their craft. Those who have suffered under existing political economic and social arrangements are central to the project of critical historiography. Because those who have suffered the most may not have left written records—the bread and butter of traditional historiographical source material—critical historians employ oral history that grants voice to those peoples and perspectives lost to traditional educational history.

Critical oral history exerts a democratizing effect on educational history, as it welcomes the perspectives of those who have not been the beneficiaries of schooling (Parker, 1997, 1999; Mignolo, 2001). In this context it opens new domains of inquiry to educational historians, moving the educational historian to look to sources of evidence previously dismissed. In my own interviews with students who were deemed to be failures in the schools they attended, I uncovered idiosyncratic ways of expressing their frustrations that would be overlooked by more traditional educational historians. For example, in studying the educational life histories of several school dropouts in Pennsylvania, I was allowed access to former students' personal writings that provided new insights into the ways they had been misevaluated in school. Their writings gave me profound insights into who these students were, what they suffered in school, and the compelling talents they possessed that were never uncovered by standard educational practice.

325

## Critical Historiography: An Affirmative Presentism

A key dimension of a critical educational historiography involves what might be referred to as an affirmative presentism. In more traditional forms of historiography presentism is viewed as a venal sin. The fallacy of presentism, as it is labeled, occurs when a historian infuses the past into present—e.g., the U.S. is in the same shape of the Roman Empire and will fall just like it did if we continue our sinful ways. At the same time the charge of presentism can also be made when historians interpret the past using frameworks developed in the present—e.g., in the eleventh century the Iraqis knew that someday they would face threats from Russia. Obviously, in both of these cases a historiographical mistake is being made. A presentism that simply imports contemporary modes of understanding and frames of reference to the past produces anachronistic interpretations of history.

What historiographers have traditionally labeled historicism provides the grounding for the historical craft's disdain for mixing past and present. The key argument of historicism is that each epoch possesses its own unique *Zeitgeist* and, thus, must be viewed on its own terms, values and belief structures. In viewing the past historicism posits that all present-day values must be set aside. If such values are employed either consciously or unconsciously, then the historian has fallen into the briar patch of presentism. To stay out of such a briar patch, historicism maintains that the purpose of all history is to understand the mindset of people living in the past and to see the cosmos through their eyes.

Critical historians advocating an affirmative presentism discern many flaws in these anti-presentist and historicist arguments. While understanding that anachronistic judgments can be made by applying the ways of seeing of one era to another, an affirmative presentism understands the complexity of the historicist notion of seeing the past through the eyes of those historical figures who lived in it. No historical era is made up of one perspective—indeed, there are always multiple and conflicting viewpoints coming from a wide diversity of groups. If the objective historian is to examine a historical era from the perspective of those who lived during it, which group's perspective is chosen? Students? Teachers? Administrators? Defenders of the educational status quo? Critics? Given the nature of historical sources, historians will often unconsciously embrace the perspective of those who left written records. Of course, the authors of these sources tend to be the most privileged members of the social order under study.

This question of sources raises a whole new set of problems for historicists who seek to represent "the past as it really was." The historical sources to which historians have access are always subjective, idiosyncratic perspectives of particular groups of people viewed through the researcher's presently constructed interpretive lenses. What sources does a historian choose to include as part of her narrative? What sources does she choose to exclude? All of these questions make the historical research process much more complex than historicists and other groups of historians originally thought it was. In addition, we can never completely grasp a moment of the past in the way it was experienced by even one group of people because we know many things that happened in the following months, years, decades, and centuries. The consequence we assign such historical moments is always shaped by the historical hindsight not possessed by the historical participants (Parker, 1997; Castro-Gomez, 1998; Alridge, 2003).

Thus, educational research—even some educational historical research— isolates past from present. The temporality of education, the time related processes of which educational processes are a part is often overlooked in educational research. One role of historical research in education—its place in the multiperspectival bricolage that Kathleen Berry writes about in this volume—is to help researchers understand the inescapable relationship between past and present in all knowledge production. One's socio-cultural, political economic location in the present will always influence one's research no matter if she is a historian, ethnographer, semiotician, or statistician in education. An affirmative historiographical presentism in this context understands that the present always affords the past with meaning. This should not make us give up the effort to produce great educational history but should make us better historians as we study this hermeneutic process. For example, the textbook battles in the mid-1970s led by right-wing religious conservatives take on a new type of historical importance after the political and educational victories of right-wing operatives in the subsequent thirty years.

Present events, thus, construct the importance of past events. An educational historian needs to know how this process takes place. Humans grant meaning to both present and past events by our decisions about which ones are important and by how we narratively position them. Processes such as the emergence of hyperreality and globalization demand a rethinking and rewriting of history. History, thus, changes history (Valdes & Hutcheon, 1994; Barros, 2004). After 9/11 the history of relationships between the Muslim world and Europe took on new importance. The point is made over and over again—many historians may want to pristinely separate present and past but such segregation is simply not possible. Critical historians in this context dismiss the segregationist effort and work to understand the complexity of the relationship.

Appreciating that our knowledge of the educational past is always partial— dependent upon what happens next—critical historians promoting an affirmative presentism understand the hermeneutic limits on any historical research. We all live and operate in a particular social, cultural, political economic [fh: Joe intends this to be a phrase, political economic, not political & economic], discursive present and it is that spatial and temporal locale that creates the horizon on which we view the past. The better we understand our present situation, the more rigorous our historical scholarship will be. The more rigorous our scholarship, the more compelling our interpretations of historical moments will become. And the more rigorous our interpretations become, the greater use value they provide critical historians for informing critical action in the present. How did the present situation come to be? critical historians ask. What social, cultural, political economic situations induced individuals to make particular decisions about educational purpose, curriculum content, school policy, teacher prerogative, etc?

Embedded in these presentist oriented questions—and all historical questions for that matter—are projections of the future. Often without consciously understanding the teleology they embrace, Western historians have assumed a future dictated by Western epistemologies and ways of seeing the world. Critical historians with their study of the interaction of the past and present expose such Eurocentric/Amerocentric inscriptions that shape educational history and contemporary educational affairs. The process of engaging in an affirmative presentism is never easy, as critical historians must always search for what is not readily apparent to someone from a different era. If we are to produce a usable history that informs—not directs—contemporary emancipatory action, we must focus on historical disjunctions, naive attributions of cause and effect, the lost pathways of particular historical processes, forgotten options that seemed plausible to people of the historical era being studied, etc. Devoid of these complicating dynamics, the critical histories we produce may be too simplistic, too reductionistic in the ways we think that they might inform present educational practices (Valdes & Hutcheon, 1994; Murphy, 1997; Parker, 1997; Blaut, 2000; Cooper, 2005).

As critical historians we take on the challenge of engaging a historiography that is unafraid to address the relationships connecting the past, present, and future—even as we understand how complex such interconnections may be. Healing racial, class, gender, and religious divisions, for example, requires an understanding of the historical ways such conflicts oppressed and caused suffering among particular groups. Without such knowledge paths to an emancipatory future are much harder to forge. Thus, critical historians who embrace an affirmative presentism become brokers that work to connect past, present, and future. As time brokers critical historians don't predict the future, they do not gain access to some mystical crystal ball. The hermeneutic relationship connecting past, present, and future is much too complex for such a positivistic notion. As previously noted, critical educational historians gain insight via their historical work that helps guide their own actions as well as the actions of their readers in the present and future (Parker, 1999; Barros, 2004; Gresson, 2004).

In this context of affirmative presentism critical educational historians pay close attention to the African concept of *sankofa* (Alridge, 2003; Hotep, 2003). *Sankofa* refers to going back to understand the past for the purpose of moving forward. In this African framework the past is not something lost to the ages but inseparable from the present and the future. In this context *sankofa* becomes a key historiographical concept as it provides compelling multilogical perceptions of how the present came to be and the possibilities the future portends. Employing this notion an affirmative presentism interrogates the cultural significance of the histories we produce. There is a profound difference between an anachronistic presentism that applies the tacit ways of seeing of the present to an interpretation of the past and its meaning and an affirmative presentism that understands the ways that present and past are intertwined in complex and often confusing ways.

Understanding this omnipresent entanglement, critical historians continuously study the ways that present forces shape their relationship to the past. This dynamic is a crucial aspect of a critical historiography. Indeed, critical historians maintain that it is important to not only understand these forces but to also let their readers know about them. This is where an understanding of a critical epistemology—an appreciation that knowledge is always a product of a particular vantage point—becomes extremely important in historical and other forms of educational research. It is in this context that we wish that contemporary devisors of standardized, allegedly value neutral curricula in Western schools had a greater historical consciousness of how past and present are intertwined. Such a perspective could help them discern the ways that historical and social forces continuously shape the nature of what we consider objective educational research. While a presentist-oriented history is always dangerous, it is inevitable. The point of our affirmative presentism is to acknowledge and study the relationship between past, present, and future in ways that can promote a more rigorous form of educational history that can be used in ways to promote the social and educational good.

## AN EXAMPLE OF THE BRICOLAGE IN EDUCATIONAL HISTORY: "DEMOCRACY, FREEDOM AND THE SCHOOL BELL" (FRANCES HELYAR)

Once upon a time it was possible for the researcher to describe the history of education as a straight narrative. That action led to this development, which led to that innovation and those consequences. Of course, history was never that simple; different historians produced widely varying accounts of the past and its relationship to the present. Today the researcher-as-bricoleur uses new and often multiple tools and methodologies to explore the same source materials, as well as some that have never been examined, in order to come to a deeper understanding of educational history. By weaving together a historiographical approach in which the researcher self-consciously examines not just the past, but also the way the past has been interpreted by others, combined with various other disciplinary approaches, the result is a richer tapestry of images, a broader narrative canvas, and a more complex conceptualization of education as it exists in the present—indeed, an affirmative presentism.

What follows on the next few pages is an example of this type of research. The initial impulse was to look at freedom, democracy and educational history. But when this project began, the 2004 presidential election campaign was in full swing. The rhetoric swirled and the promises abounded. At the same time, I read William Reese's Power and the Promise of School Reform: Grassroots Movements During the Progressive Era (2002). The image that stayed with me was from that book's opening passage: a ship arrives in Toledo harbor carrying the new school bell. I began to think about that bell as a symbol, and to recognize that as such it was an image with rich and varied associations. Thus by using semiotics as a starting point I was able to embark on a study using multiple disciplines in a bricolage approach that combines historical research with the disciplinary knowledges of sociology, ethnography, political science, educational psychology, and more. The accompanying poems were written for oral presentation, to give a sense of the content of the text without resorting to a more traditional abstract.

Freedom is the expressed goal of democratic nations in twentieth and twenty-first century political and social discourse. The terms freedom and democracy are intricately entwined; they appear repeatedly, for example, in the promotional mate-

329

rial of the U.S. Republican Party (on average, the word democracy shows up on over thirty percent of the pages in the Republican Party Platform (Republican National Committee, 2004), while freedom appears on about seventy-five per cent). The U.S. Democratic Party mentions freedom and democracy in equal proportions (Democratic Party, 2004). Democracy as a search term generates 145 million hits on Google; freedom generates 415 million. The construct of each word in general Western discourse relies upon the notion that freedom and democracy are both homogeneous. In reality, however, the two concepts are equally complicated and multifaceted. Economic freedom is not necessarily the same as political freedom, and political freedom is not the same as social freedom. Democracy has gradations: "all the people" represented by government may exclude a significant portion of the population, whether by race, gender, class, sexuality or other factors. Government practices may be overtly democratic, but populations are often willing to cede control in order to procure economic or other gains. Since the publication of Antonio Gramsci's work on hegemony, critical scholars understand that neither freedom nor democracy exist in any pure form.

The bell is an important symbol associated with freedom and by extension, democracy in American folklore. Peter, Paul and Mary sang about the "Bell of Freedom" during the 1960s (Hays & Seeger, 1949). The Liberty Bell serves as an enduring example, as a result of its association with the American Revolution. "Let Freedom Ring" (Hirsch, 1997, p. 165) is one title by which E.D. Hirsch introduces the bell, including it in his list of vital knowledge for first graders. In educational history the bell appears regularly in accounts of schooling, both theoretical and narrative. William Reese opens his study of grassroots movements in education during the Progressive era with the story of the arrival of a new school bell by boat to the city of Toledo. The scene is a celebratory one, but as Reese makes clear, the bell is not a symbol of freedom. It will ring out the hour to tell citizens when to begin and end their work and school days, imposing virtues valued by the elite upon public institutions (Reese, 2002). This tension between the ideal of freedom as symbolized by the bell and the actual function of the bell as a means of control mirrors the tension between the homogeneous notion of freedom and democracy, and the way freedom and democracy are actually experienced in the history of education.

The bell metaphor is an apt tool to dismantle the history of education in the twentieth century, and the course of education in the twenty-first. If the bell is a metaphor for freedom, and freedom is a hallmark of democracy, then a series of questions about school bells serves to frame an interrogation of developments in education over the last hundred years: What does the location of the bell signify? What does the lack of a bell signify? What does the shape of the bell signify? What does a broken bell signify, and what does the sound of the bell signify? Finally, who rings the school bell? By examining these questions using critical educational historiography, it is possible to approach an understanding of the complexity of developments in education, and indicate that this complexity continues into the twenty-first century.

These framing questions came late in the process of preparing this piece, which began with brainstorming about bells in general, and then bells in relation to education. During the brainstorming process the various directions of the research became clear. This is a semiotic study in which the bell is a symbol on many different levels. Thinking about church bells, the Liberty Bell, plantation bells, the hand-held school bell, and the automated school bell led to thoughts of time and marking time, social control, Pavlov's dogs, wedding bells, John Donne, Hemingway and even Motley Crüe's "Smoking in the Boys' Room" (the last three of which I didn't use in the end). I investigated each to see how it related to developments in education. Cultural studies, poststructuralism, sociology, history and psychology all came into play. Much later in the process when I felt I had explored the metaphor sufficiently, I organized the results loosely by three senses: sight, touch and hearing.

*What Does the Location of the Bell Signify?*

High atop the school tower sits the ringing bell,
Where once it rang from steeples keeping us from hell.
Now it's not salvation but a better life through school
**For it's through education that we learn the Golden Rule.**
The growth of cities and the corresponding growth in the numbers of urban children was a major factor in the development of Common Schools in the U.S. How should these children be prepared for the future? How should they be controlled in the present? Parents no longer held sole responsibility for these tasks, nor did the church have as great an influence as in the past. In fact, cities placed added burdens on extant institutions, ranging from the insistence that they provide the social discipline essential to life amidst crowded conditions to the suggestion that they convey every manner of vital specialized knowledge. One result was that statements of educational purpose tended to broaden significantly. (Cremin, 1988, p. 7)

The school in an urban setting called for a bell the sound of which was capable of being broadcast over a wide area. The Toledo school bell described by Reese (2002) had a place of honor alongside a brass town clock at the top of the tower of the new high school. Where in most communities the bell once stood atop a steeple calling worshippers to church, here education was usurping the role of religion as a locus of control in the community. In addition, schools assumed more responsibility within urban communities, to the extent that they became social centers and welfare agencies (Spring, 2005; Reese, 2002). Thus the location of the urban school bell atop a tower signifies a shift in the nature of society during the 20$^{th}$ century from religious to secular, so that one theologian maintained that the secular religion of Americans was not an implicit set of common values expressed diversely through the three great religious communities but rather a fourth religion standing alongside the three, with its own theological and educational apparatus centered in the public schools. (Cremin, 1988, pp. 61-2)

The shift was not a permanent one, however. The Federal legislation No Child Left Behind includes provisions allowing faith-based organizations to become more involved in schools and schooling, presented under the aegis of local free-

331

dom. The U.S. Department of Education's website contains a section devoted to local freedom for schools, and it includes a page titled "No Child Left Behind and Faith Based Leaders." The page highlights a quote from George W. Bush saying, "The indispensable and transforming work of faith-based and other charitable service groups must be encouraged. Government cannot be replaced by charities, but it can and should welcome them as partners" (U.S. Department of Education, 2004). Thus in the twenty-first century, the effect of "compassionate conservatism" with its focus on faith-based initiatives is to place church bells alongside school bells.

This is an instance where the present-day intruded upon a study of the past. My first impulse was to stop at the shift from religious to secular, but a reading of No Child Left Behind made that impossible. The reform document highlights the ebb and flow of educational developments and their complexity. The passage that follows and its description of automated school bell systems arises from my visits to schools in which I was surprised by the sound of the bell; they were unlike any sound I'd ever heard and somewhat startling. The world of school had definitely changed since I was a student. As a result of this ethnographic observation, I wanted to know who makes these bells and how they are marketed, and wondered whether or not the changes in the sound of the school bell resulted in a change of the effect of the school bell.

Ain't no bell in this school, least not one we can see
And yet it rings and rings and rings, alarming you and me.
So classes start and classes end; it's Math and ABCs,
And this will help us when we start our work in factories.

Throughout the twentieth century, the school bell was central as a mechanism for controlling students. Cuban (1993) describes the way a 1926 handbook for a Washington, D.C. high school spells it out:

> [S]tudents were told to go to their section (home-room) for opening exercises by 8:55 a.m. 'In classrooms absolute quite must prevail at this time,' the handbook stated, because the students must have the 'proper attitude' and 'frame of mind necessary to start the day right.' At 9:10 the bell rang to start the students' seven-period day – 'six recitation periods' and lunch. Students had 4 minutes to move from one class to another. (pp. 107-108)

In contemporary schools the school bell is no longer visible. Instead it is hidden within the architecture of the school, and students experience it as a sound alone with a tone often more comparable to an alarm than to the tolling of a bell. Even this sound is changing in the twenty-first century as bell systems become increasingly computerized. One manufacturer promotes the benefits of its products saying that administrators can "Save thousands of dollars over out-of-date mechanical bell technology with low-cost standardized PC-based technologies" and "Never be stuck with ordinary school bell sounds again" (Acro Vista Software, n.d.). No matter the tone of the modern school bell, however, it always sounds with an impersonal efficiency, releasing "thousands of students into hallways six to 10 times a day for three to five minutes of chaos" (Rettig & Canaday, 1999, p. 14). Its function is automated so that only a technician can repair it. Moreover, particularly in the high school, the school bell rings not just to begin and end the school day but also to mark the beginning and end of each period, serving as an aural separation of discrete subject areas one from the other. In this way the twenty-first century school bell has a direct relation to the highly controlled organization of the nineteenth century Lancasterian system of schools (Spring, 2005), the efficient and cost-effective platoon schools of the Gary Plan (Mirel, 1999), and the curriculum reforms of various eras that discourage integration of school subjects. The question becomes, by regimenting students' every move, are these schools democratic? If they keep children away from a life of crime and give them the tools they need to meet the demands of living in an adult world, the answer is yes. If they remove children's ability to think critically or to imagine a life outside of a regimented existence, the answer is no.

The complexity of educational research engulfs in a discussion of the "doing" of pedagogical research. For example, educational scholars find it difficult to speak definitively about the purpose of education; different interests define the purpose differently. Through a hermeneutic analysis I try to peel back the layers of meaning. The result is not a positivistic arbitration; I cannot determine which of the purposes of education is the "true" one. Indeed, I can only attempt to present a variety of perspectives. Of course, I have my own biases and preferences and they are ever present in my writing. The more aware I am of these dynamics, the more compelling, more informed by historical research will be.

## What Does the Lack of a Bell Signify?

No school, no bell. Not fair? Oh well.

Among the recurring problems of education throughout the twentieth and into the twenty-first century, particularly in the urban setting, is the insufficient number of school buildings, inadequate buildings, and in some cases, overcrowding in the schools. Whether the goal of education is to challenge the status quo or strengthen the established order, such problems are major impediments. If there is no school building, there can be no school bell. The problem can take on racial and ethnic dimensions as it did in Boston in the mid nineteenth century where black schools were housed in African American church basements (Spring, 2005) or as in Detroit in 1924 with the controversy emerging from the suspicion that school budgets were being spent on elaborate buildings in areas of high immigrant population (Mirel, 1999).

Even if there was a school building, the school may not have had a bell. Throughout the history of the American republic, the existence of inadequately funded and segregated schools calls into question the country's democratic identity. No bell of freedom rang in the antebellum American South where it was illegal to educate slaves, or in California of 1872 where the school code excluded all but white children from admittance to public schools (Spring, 2005). The effect of such legal sanctions was that equal educational opportunity did not exist for every child. In a broad sense, schools became the battleground for conflicting ideas about social goals and norms, raising the question "how should the legitimate but often unclear and conflicting demands of liberty, equality and comity be resolved in and through programs of education?" (Cremin, 1988, p. 13).

Our school is progressive, and so we have no bells,

But if we did, you know that we would forge them by ourselves.

In a more literal sense, the lack of a school bell could also be a choice, turning away from traditional pedagogy to a progressive approach. Cuban describes the changes in a rural Michigan school in 1939 in which the newly progressive teacher cites the abandonment of the school bell as evidence of her conversion (Cuban, 1993). Even this transition,however, is complicated. The Michigan passage is followed by a long quote from John Dewey himself, expressing skepticism that much had changed in American schools. Helen Parkhurst took as fundamental principles of the Dalton School freedom and cooperation, and to that end, she refused to allow bells in the school (Semel, 1999). But although the Dalton School may have started as a progressive school and Parkhurst may have espoused progressive principles in education, in the actual running of the school she was autocratic and controlling—qualities that eventually led to her downfall. Thus, her choice to abolish school bells and escape the tyranny of their regulation seems merely cosmetic and not reflective of a theory put into practice in a consistent way throughout the school. Just because Parkhurst called her school democratic did not make it so.

Although many progressive schools may have lacked a bell to signal the beginning and end of the day, it did not necessarily mean that bells were banned from the schools entirely. In fact, it was more likely that the bell would become an object of study. How does it work? What are its parts? What is it made of? When the children of the City and Country School needed an electric bell to call a Special Delivery postman to carry important messages, they installed it themselves (Semel, 1999), illustrating the difference, in theory, between a progressive and a traditional system of education. While one of the goals of traditional education may have been to create citizens for a democratic society, the goal of the progressives was to create a democratic society within the school.

If the bricolage approach to research involves making connections between apparently disparate ideas, there is joy in the discovery that those connections are not tenuous at all. Once I undertook a semiotic study of the bell, I was surprised at how many interpretations of the symbol I could find, and how they helped to expand my understanding of developments in the history of education. The bell curve and the Liberty Bell are two that would seem to be obvious, but in examining them in the following short passages, I attempted to use starting points different from Herrnstein, Murray and Hirsch.

*What Does the Shape of the Bell Signify?*

The bell curve is a funny thing, you'd think it was unchangeable.

Use hammer and a little heat, the bell curve's rearrangeable.

The shape of the school bell is the bell curve, and in the 1990s Herrnstein and Murray used this shape in order to explain the relationship between intelligence and class (and racial, though they denied it) structure. Intelligence is defined as a "general way to express a person's intellectual performance relative to a given population" and intelligence quotient is "a universally understood synonym for intelligence" (Herrnstein & Murray, 1994, p. 4). By stressing that IQ is the only way to measure intelligence and by thus reducing intelligence to a "single number capable of ranking all people on a linear scale of intrinsic and unalterable worth" (Gould, 1996, p. 20), Herrnstein and Murray re-imposed a racist, elitist interpretation of intelligence that echoed Edward Thorndike's narrow assumptions favoring nature over nurture (Spring, 2005). They set up an "us" versus "them" scenario, in which "we" have plenty to fear:

> The American family may be generally under siege . . . but it is at the bottom of the cognitive ability distribution that its defenses are most visibly crumbling. (p. 190) . . . [S]omething worth worrying about is happening to the cognitive capital of the country" (p. 364) . . . . The threat comes from an underclass that has been with American society for some years (p. 518) . . . . Trying to eradicate inequality with artificially manufactured outcomes has led us to disaster. (Herrnstein & Murray, 1994, p. 551)

Cloaked in a so-called scientific rationale, this educational determinism relies on the notion that the bell is made of a non-malleable substance. Herrnstein and Murray characterize their "facts" as irrefutable and unassailable, in spite of the origins of many in the literature of white supremacists (Kincheloe & Steinberg, 1997). But just as intelligence is not one fixed entity (Gardner, 1993; Gould, 1981; Kincheloe, 2004), the bell is malleable, both in reality and metaphorically; it can be shaped in any number of different ways.

*What Does a Broken Bell Signify?*

Ding dong, the Liberty Bell, the sound of freedom's ring. The trouble is, a bell that's cracked is never going to ding. There is obvious irony in the fact that the Liberty Bell endures as a symbol of American democracy. The inscription inside, "Proclaim liberty throughout the land unto all the inhabitants thereof" (Hirsch, 2002) speaks to an ideal that has yet to be met in America. Because it is cracked, the bell has not sounded since the mid-nineteenth century. Democracy is flawed; freedom cannot ring because it has no voice. In the first edition of What Your First Grader Needs to Know, this irony is perfectly captured with the juxtaposition of a passage about the Liberty Bell, "a symbol of our country" (Hirsch, 1991, p. 131) with a passage titled "Freedom for All?" describing the denial of freedom for women and slaves by the men who signed the Declaration of Independence. The school as the provider of equal opportunity also has a cracked bell. Segregation, exclusion laws, language policies, and standardized testing are among the institutional means by which equal opportunity is denied.

When I began my original brainstorming about bells, ideas about their sound dominated, perhaps because as I wrote, I heard the hourly tolling of a church bell outside my window. Once I had imagined when and where different people heard bells in the past, and where people hear them today, I developed a list of questions that required historical research. By understanding the origins of bells and the changing nature of their use, I'm able to increase my understanding of their literal and metaphorical significance in education.

*What Does the Sound of the Bell Signify?*

The sound of the bell is many things:
Plantation, incarceration,
Emancipation, regulation
Domination,
Salvation.
The sound of a bell is replete with meanings. The ringing of a bell is a form of civic communication, and when not ringing from schools and churches, it often signals a warning. Fire and other alarms become an important part of public safety, inherently democratic because they serve to warn everyone who can hear them regardless of class, race or other consideration. In pre-industrial times, the sound of the town crier's bell heralded important events and served to draw the community together. One of the most frequent functions of a bell is to indicate time, and its use grew concurrently with the introduction of clocks signaling the shift from marking natural time (the rising and setting of the sun) to a preoccupation with the more specific marks of minutes and hours, as required in an industrial setting. Where the Puritans originally believed that clocks marked God's time, eventually "aural time was used to announce not just God's time but increasingly to regulate the time of schools, markets and factories" (Smith, 1996, p. 1449). Public clocks served a valuable purpose in situations where industrialists, hoping to increase production, manipulated the factory clocks to lengthen the workday. The solution was a public clock marking the "true" time (Hensley, 1992). A worker could ignore the sound of the factory bell in favor of the public bell, erected for the public good.

Just as church bells peal to celebrate the conclusion of a wedding, the ring of the school bell at the end of the day can be cause for celebration for the student:

Sitting here watching the clock tick away
Tick-tock-tick-tock every day
Waiting for the stupid little bell to ring
So I can go home and do my thing . . . . (Hynds, 1997, p. 29)

This function of marking time connects the school bell with the factory bell, and both serve a major function in controlling human capital (Reese 2002). Embedded in the school and the factory are rewards for heeding the ringing of the bell and getting to class and to work on time. The closing bell in each setting brings a feeling of relief.

If a common culture existed, the bell would sound the same to everyone. But just as democracy and freedom have multiple dimensions, the sound of the school bell does not hold the same meaning for all who hear it. The sound has a particular set of associations for the prisoner whose day is regulated by the jailhouse bell. For the slaves or the sharecroppers who once rose and slept at the bidding of the plantation bell, that sound brought "thoughts of another day of unremitting and unrequited toil in the cotton fields" (Kester, 1969, p. 39). The school bell may have been the transformative sound of democracy, of equal access to education where before there was none, but it also may have been the sound of exclusion if it rang from a racially segregated or under funded school. It may have been the sound of assimilation or deculturalization (Spring, 2005). The pealing of the bell echoes the celebratory sound of the original Liberty Bell, but when the bell rings in Puerto Rico or the former Mexican territories, it can also be symbolic of the imperialism of the colonizing power of America. The ringing of the bell may have become a secular call, but echoes of its earlier significance as a call to church remain, and in the twenty-first century tower of education, the double peal of the school bell alongside the church bell has a different sound for different people. To the compassionate conservative and the fundamentalist Christian, the two bells ring in harmony; school and faith are inextricably linked. To the secular humanist, however, the combined sound is dissonant, disturbing and in violation of the First Amendment of the United States Constitution.

The elite does the ringing, the worker responds,
And it's always been that way, I fear,
But the ring of the Common School bell is a sound
That everybody can hear.

Historically and in class terms, whether on the factory floor or in the dining room, the elite used the bell to summon the worker. In this sense, the bell of the Common School was indeed democratic because it was used to supposedly eliminate distinctions between the rich and the poor. The workers and the elite may have had different notions of why schools were created in the first place, whether to provide equal opportunity for all or to prepare a compliant workforce (Spring, 2005). With the introduction of vocational education and the development of separate streams that separate the elite from the working class, however, the school became a site of further social and economic alienation of one group from another, and the school bell did not call all students to the same education.

The school bell rings, I salivate. No, that's the other bell, no wait,
I'm all confused, I'm in a state, I'm either hungry or I'm late.

The sound of a ringing of the bell is the sound of a stimulus-response experiment, and it suggests another significant development in education. Behaviorism, with its effect of excluding individuals from educational opportunities based on measured intelligence or scores on standardized tests, does not meet the critical definition of democratic. But couched as it was within the language of freeing every individual to match one's own intelligence with social needs (Spring, 2005), social efficiency practitioners such as Edward Thorndike could justify the use of behaviorism in a school setting, thus ushering in a century of scientific management of schools. If the ringing of the school bell made education available to a larger number of students, the resulting increased opportunity was indeed democ-

ratic. If the sound of the bell served to control the students and curtail their freedom of movement and freedom to choose their course of study, propelling them
into predetermined careers from an early age, however, the bell is broken.

Research grounded on the bricolage often takes the researcher outside of her
comfort zone. In my experience, the Securities Exchange Commission's website
was a mysterious place which became a rich source of information, particularly in
the annual reports of publicly traded companies. It may take some effort to learn
how to locate the data, but finding the information as presented in a corporation's
own marketing materials is worth the effort. In this case it introduces a new perspective, which should be the goal of all educational research. Media reports also
offer an alternative perspective on a given phenomenon.

*Who Rings the School Bell?*

Who rings this bell, I think I know. It's not as schools intended, though,
For business makes the clapper sound, and money jingles all around.
During an era of child labor, the ringing of coins drowned out the sound of the
school bell. Sharecropper's children in the late 19th century, for example, may have
had access to education, but not necessarily the opportunity to participate because
there was money to be made through their labor: "When the child can be spared
from the labor in the field, the schoolhouse doors swing open; but when cotton
beckons, the doors close in the face of thousands of youngsters who are an integral
part of American life" (Kester, 1969, p. 46). In the twenty-first century the sound
of the school bell is not just the call to the classroom, it is also the ringing of the
cash register. Fast-food restaurants and computer software manufacturers insinuate
themselves into the lives of students, while school administrations acquiesce. Thus
in September 2005 McDonald's introduced its "Passport to Play" physical education curriculum, saying "With the guide and materials we provide, approximately
seven million children in grades 3–5 will learn about and play games from 15
countries around the world" (McDonald's Corp, n.d.). Those same seven million
children become a captive audience for McDonald's promotions. Similarly, Microsoft captures the market for computer hardware and software with its School
Agreements, . . . a subscription licensing program specifically created to address
the unique needs of primary and secondary schools and districts. With the simplicity of counting computers just once per year, School Agreement makes it easy for
you to license all of your computers, whether in a single school or throughout the
entire district (Microsoft Corp., 2005).

Notwithstanding the lawsuits charging market monopolization reported in Microsoft's 2005 Annual Report (United States Securities and Exchange Commission, 2005), by gaining exclusive access to schools the corporation ensures that a
sizeable segment of its target consumers are familiar with its products from an
early age. In an era in which school under funding is the norm rather than the exception, profit and education thus are inextricably linked, whether promoted by the
neo-conservatives who encourage business involvement in government, including

education, or by the neo-liberals who espouse education as a means to increasing wealth (Spring, 2002).

The ring of the school bell, however, is replaced by the ring of the cash register in more ways than just these. For-profit schools and school management businesses proliferate in America, bringing to the forefront the conflict between competing notions of the purpose of education, articulated by David Labaree (1997) as a conflict between democratic equality, social efficiency and social mobility goals. Christopher Whittle (the founder of Channel One, a technology that introduced commercial advertising along with packaged news shows to schools across the country) has as his main project Edison Schools, which has transformed over the years from a national network of for-profit schools to a public company (Whittle, 1997) and then to a privately-held business managing public schools (Mazzacappa, 2005). The language Whittle uses to describe his project reflects a melange of characterizations. If he sees Edison as "just the first colony in a new academic world," then he is a colonizer and American children are the colonized—replete with all the associated meanings of the term. If his schools "are simply its Model T's" then the education system is a factory, and the schools and children in them are simply widgets. Whittle may say that "parents he meets don't care if he makes a profit or not if he can help educate their children" (Baum, 2005). But make no mistake, Whittle himself certainly cares whether or not he makes money— otherwise he wouldn't be in business.

Whoever rings the school bell determines what definition of democracy prevails in education. Once that task fell to the schoolteacher. The bell would be a hand held model kept on the teacher's desk and rung by the teacher or an appointed bell ringer. As public education grew, control passed to headmasters, and then to school boards. The large, ward-based systems, while responsive to and representative of the electorate, were also prone to misuse of political power (Reese, 2002). The smaller at-large boards focused the power in the hands of the elite, and as state departments of education shared the responsibility, the task of bell ringing fell to the so-called experts, to scientists, technocrats and politicians. Today business leaders are just as likely as administrators or politicians to have their hands on the bell, but their grasp is not secured through democratic means, and the consequences lead to a fundamental change in the nature of education. Monica Pini (2001), in her examination of so-called Educational Management Organizations (such as Edison), outlines the way such EMOs focus on parental and community involvement in for-profit schools, thus undermining public and social support for education. Pini explains,

The logic of privatization says that anybody can sell educational services, as any other good. But education cannot be identified with any other industry, its nature is too rooted in the meaning of an authentic democracy to treat it as any business. That is why EMOs need and use such dramatic rhetoric . . . . One can wonder if the ultimate political goal of this ideological and structural process is to stop the slow but constant trend to democratize the American educational system . . . . Common people still have the opportunity to discuss social justice, wealth distribution, and educational policies in the public sphere, this is not the case in shareholders [sic]meetings. (pp. 39-40)

In spite of the rhetoric of the for-profit educators, the ring of a cash register can never be made to sound the same as a school bell.

## Conclusion: Bells, Complexity, and Multilogicality

Freedom may be the stated goal of democratic nations, but both freedom and democracy are terms too complex to fit such a simplistic equation. As the school bell metaphor demonstrates, democracy has many layers and what represents freedom to one sector of society may represent something entirely different to another. In education, each new policy, each new "ism," needs to be examined in order to determine what definition of democracy is implied. Who benefits and who loses as a result of that democracy needs to be examined as it applies to the definition. Only then can a socially just education system begin to develop, so that the sound of the school bell will indeed be a call with the same emancipatory message for all.

The process of doing historical research in education is complex and highly personal. The researcher brings to the task aptitudes and experiences that color his or her choices. Given the same topic, no two individuals choose to explore the same avenues, nor do they present their findings in identical ways. By using the bricolage and anticipating that the end result will not produce a definitive understanding of the topic, but a study that raises as many questions as it answers, it is possible to view research as a multilogical life long effort that continues well after each project is completed.

### MULTILOGICALITY AND EDUCATIONAL HISTORIOGRAPHY (JOE L. KINCHELOE)

The simplicity of bell metaphor combined with the highly complex ways it plays out in educational history illustrates the power of the multilogicality of the bricolage in a critical historiography. To conclude this chapter, we want to raise a few more points about a critical multilogical educational historiography. Such an approach in recognizing diversity on numerous levels, understands the multiplicity of positions from which historians research, write, and produce history. Historians writing from different times, places, positions of social power, inside or outside of the academy, epistemological, ontological, ideological assumptions, ad infinitum, view the world and the past in profoundly different ways. Indeed, even those writing from similar locales can view the past in dramatically divergent ways. Recognizing these dynamics does not weaken educational history but makes it stronger, more rigorous, more capable of helping produce transformative action in the present. Sandra Harding (1998) ups the ante of such informed approaches to research, calling such researcher awareness a form of "strong objectivity." While we don't use the term ourselves, we appreciate the point that Harding is making by invoking the empirical use of the term, objectivity.

340

In socio-cultural, political, psychological, and educational circumstances it is very difficult to "prove" the cause of a specific episode. Historians working in this realm—coming from their diverse positionalities—can strive to distinguish some of the circumstances that were involved with the appearance of new realities. Positivistic empirical assignment of cause-effect draws on an epistemological mode of analysis that eludes historiography. In this context educational historians can better understand that there are always multiple causes, contexts, and processes involved with historical conditions. Given the specific nature of what historians are studying, they may devise priorities within their interpretations—for example, macro-, enduring forces vis-à-vis micro-influences specific to a particular event. A central point here is that a critical multilogical educational historian—while always concerned with questions of power, justice, the improvement of educational practice, etc.—sees every new research project, every different historical era as a new situation with unique events and complex causations.

Thus, historiographical multilogicality consciously attempts to break away from more traditional modes of historical interpretation grounded on more of a monological understanding of historical processes and that are less concerned with researcher positionality. In the spirit of poststructuralist feminism, Derridian and Foucauldian discursive analysis, and indigenous knowledges/concepts such as *sankofa*, critical historiographical multilogicality refuses particular privileged readings of educational history. Here, we constantly search for new angles, new sources, new methodologies, and new topics for our research. In this context critical multilogical educational historians experiment with presentation, sometimes presenting historical events from multiple perspectives—sometimes even contradictorily and simultaneously. Such simultaneous multiperspectivalism (Kellner, 1995) constitutes a form of historiographical cubism. The previous illustrative section on "democracy, freedom, and the school bell" makes use of one form of such multiple perspectives, as Frances Helyar (the author of the section) integrates insights into her own positionality as a historian vis-à-vis the narrative about the school bell. The ways that the multiple perspectives of historiographical multilogicality might be brought to bear in a historical narrative are limited only by the imagination of the historian.

When historiographical multilogicality is run through the lenses of interracialism, social and economic justice, global democracy, and other critical discourses, the possibilities of an affirmative presentism are profoundly enhanced. In such a context an educational historian might view schooling in ways, for example, that transcend its contribution to the consolidation of the "nation-state." Escaping this Eurocentric concern, educational historians could be freed to explore more global issues that help raise new insights into unexamined functions of educational institutions. Such an approach might open a space for an ecumenical history of education that is by definition multilogical. In such an ecumenical, multilogical context the historian is much better situated to recognize the socio-cultural, political economic, and colonial interactions that have caused human suffering and the use of pedagogy for repressive purposes.

In this context, parochial perspectives of any dominant national, class, gender, racial, or ethnic group are transcended, as the dynamics of pedagogy and peda- gogical/epistemological systems are viewed in larger and multiple contexts. The subtle and sometimes not so subtle ways that diverse groups affect what forms education writ large or school classrooms take is a central concern to an educa- tional historian operating in the twenty-first century. With globalization, multiple diasporas, cultural exchanges via new technologies, and renewed imperial ambi- tions on the part of the U. S., this multilogical ecumenicalism takes on new impor- tance in educational research in general and educational historiography in particu- lar. Here, educational historians can trace complex webs of connections between these forces and those who are influenced by education (Parker, 1997; Murphey, 1997; Castro-Gomez, 1998; Bentley, 2005). With these dynamics in mind, educa- tional historians are better equipped to understand the ways that education is shaped by and produces dominant forms of power—as well as the means by which critical scholars/teachers/students can resist such forms of oppression.

While we appreciate the complex forces that can construct educational history as the story of pedagogy as told by those privileged by race, class, gender, ethnic- ity, language, sexuality, etc., critical multilogical historians still believe in the power of a rigorous history to provide an erudite, emancipatory understanding of the relationship between the past, present, and future. An ecumenical, multilogical history of education engages difference and its construction through time. In this multilogical context historians are better equipped to deal with both the complex forces that shape history as well as the way it is researched and written. As Paulo Freire (1985) argued, we must view ourselves as historical subjects—individuals who make history—as we come to understand the multiple ideological and struc- tural forces that operate to regulate us. Thus, in this Freirean context critical multi- logical historians strive to appreciate what it means to be a historical subject, gain an awareness of the ways that dominant power has shaped history, and understand the ideological and discursive dimensions of historiography itself.

## REFERENCES

Acro Vista Software. (n.d.) *Bell Commander*. Retrieved October 10, 2005 from
  http://www.acrovista.com/
Alridge, D. (2003). The dilemmas, challenges, and duality of an African American educational historian. *Research News and Comment.* Retrieved March 30, 2006 from
  http://www.aera.net/uploadedFiles/Journals_and_Publications/Journals/Educational_Researcher/320
  9/3209_ResNewsComment.pdf
Aronowitz, S. (1988). *Science as power: Discourse and ideology in modern society.* Minneapolis: Uni-
  versity of Minnesota Press.
Barros, C. (2004). The return of history. In C. Barros & L. McCrank (Eds.), *History under debate:
  International reflection on the discipline.* New York: Haworth Press.
Baum, J. (2005, September). Chris Whittle, CEO, Edison Schools. *Education Update Online.* Retrieved
  October 28, 2005 from http://www.educationupdate.com/index.html
Bentley, J. (2005). Myths, wagers, and some moral implications of world history. *Journal of World
  History, 16*(1). Retrieved March 21, 2006 from
  http://www.historycooperative.org/journals/jwh/16.1/bentley.html

Blaut, J. (2000). *Eight Eurocentric historians*. New York: Guilford.

Castro-Gomez, S. (1998). Traditional and critical theory of culture: Postcolonialism as a critical theory of globalized society. Retrieved December 3, 2005 from http://www.javeriana.edu.co/pensar/sc5.html

Cooper, F. (2005). *Colonialism in question: Theory, knowledge, history*. Berkeley, CA: University of California Press.

Cremin, L.A. (1988). *American education: The metropolitan experience. 1976-1980*. New York: Harper & Row.

Cuban, L. (1993). *How teachers taught: Constancy and change in American classrooms 1880-1990* (2nd ed.). New York: Teachers College Press.

Daniels, R. (2002). *Coming to America: A history of immigration and ethnicity in American life* (2nd ed.). New York: Perennial.

Democratic Party (The). (2004). *Strong at home, respected in the world: The 2004 Democratic national platform for America*. Retrieved October 10, 2005 from http://www.democrats.org/

Gale, T. (1999) *Critical policy methodology: Making connections between the stories we tell about policy and the data we use to tell them*. Paper Presented at the Joint Conference of the Australian Association for Research in Education and the New Zealand Association for Research in Education. Melbourne. Retrieved March 30, 2006 from http://www.aare.edu.au/99pap/gal99121.htm

Gardner, H. (1993). *Frames of Mind: The theory of multiple intelligences*. New York: Basic Books.

Gould, S.J. (1996). *The mismeasure of man* (Rev. ed.), New York: W.W. Norton.

Gresson, A. (2004). *America's atonement: Racial pain, recovery rhetoric, and the pedagogy of healing*. New York: Peter Lang.

Harding, S. (1998). Is science multicultural? Postcolonialisms, feminisms, and epistemologies. Bloomington, IN: Indiana University Press

Hays, L. & Seeger, P. (1949). *If I had a hammer*. Lyrics retrieved October 10, 2005 from http://www.inlyrics.com/

Hensley, P.B. (1992, December). Time, work and social context in New England. *The New England Quarterly, 65*, 531-559.

Herrnstein, R.J., & Murray, C. (1994). *The bell curve: Intelligence and class structure in American life*. New York: Free Press.

Hirsch, E.D. Jr., Kett, J.F., & Trefil, J. (Eds.). (2002). *The new dictionary of cultural literacy* (3rd ed.). Houghton Mifflin. Retrieved October 10, 2005 from http://www.bartleby.com/

Hirsch, E.D., Ed. (1991). *What your 1st grader needs to know: Fundamentals of a good first grade education*. New York: Doubleday.

Hirsch, E. D., Jr. (Ed.). (1997). *What your 1st grader needs to know: fundamentals of a good first grade education* (Revised ed.). New York: Doubleday.

Hotep, U. (2003). Decolonizing the African mind: Further analysis and strategy. Retrieved March 30, 2006 from: www.nbufront.org/html/FRONTalView/ArticlesPapers/Hotep_DecolonizingAfricanMind.html

Hynds, S. (1997). *On the brink: Negotiating literature and life with adolescents*. New York: Teachers College Press.

Iggers, G. (2005). *Historiography in the twentieth century: From scientific objectivity to the postmodern challenge*. Middletown, CT: Wesleyan University Press.

Kellner, D. (1995). *Media culture: Cultural studies, identity and politics between the modern and postmodern*. New York: Routledge.

Kester, H. (1969). *Revolt among the sharecroppers*. New York: Arno Press.

Kincheloe, J. (1991). Educational historiographical meta-analysis: Rethinking methodology in the 1990s. *Qualitative Studies in Education, 4*, 231-245.

Kincheloe, J. (2001). Describing the bricolage: Conceptualizing a new rigor in qualitative research. Qualitative Inquiry, 7, 679-92.

Kincheloe, J. (2004). *Critical pedagogy*. New York: Peter Lang.

Kincheloe, J.L. (2004). 21st century questions about multiple intelligences. In J.L. Kincheloe (Ed.), *Multiple intelligences reconsidered* (pp.3-28). New York: Peter Lang.

Kincheloe, J. (2005). On to the next level: Continuing the conceptualization of the bricolage. *Qualitative Inquiry.* 11(3), 323-350.

Kincheloe J. & Berry, K. (2004). *Rigor and complexity in educational research: Conceptualizing the bricolage.* London: Open University Press.

Kincheloe, J. & Steinberg, S. (1993). A tentative description of postformal thinking: The critical confrontation with cognitive theory. *Harvard Educational Review, 63.* 296-320.

Kincheloe, J. & Steinberg, S. (1997). *Changing Multiculturalism.* London: Open University Press.

Kincheloe, J. & Steinberg, S. (1996). Who said it can't happen here? In J. Kincheloe, S. Steinberg & A. Gresson III (Eds.), *Measured Lies* (pp. 3-47). New York: St. Martin's Press.

Koselleck, R. (2002). *The practice of conceptual history: Timing history, spacing concepts.* Palo Alto, CA: Stanford University Press.

Labaree, D.L. (1997). Public goods, private goods: The American struggle over educational goals. *American Educational Research Journal, 34,* 39-81.

McDonald's Corp. Good Works (n.d.) *Balanced, Active Lifestyles.* Retrieved October 17, 2005, from http://www.mcdonalds.com/

Mezzacappa, D. (2005, October 12). Edison schools can show gains over time, report says. *The Philadelphia Inquirer Online.* Retrieved October 29, 2005 from
http://www.philly.com/mld/inquirer/living/education/12877813.htm

Microsoft Corp. (2005, August 15). *Microsoft School Agreement.* Retrieved October 17, 2005 from http://www.microsoft.com/

Mignolo, W. (2001). The geopolitics of knowledge and colonial difference. Retrieved March 30, 2006 from http://www.incommunicado.info/node/view/18

Mirel, J. (1999). *The rise and fall of an urban school system: Detroit, 1907 – 81* (2nd ed.), Ann Arbor, Michigan: University of Michigan Press.

Moxey, K. (1999). The history of art after the death of the subject. *Invisible Culture: An Electronic Journal for Visual Studies.* Retrieved March 21, 2006 from
http://www.rochester.edu/in_visible_culture/issue1/moxey/moxey.html

Murphy, R. (1997). Hayden White on facts, fictions and metahistory. *Sources: Revue D'etudes Anglophones, 2,* 13-30. Retrieved March 30, 2006 from
http://www.paradigme.com/sources/SOURCES-PDF/Pages%20de%20Sources02-1-1.pdf

Norkus, Z. (1999). Between philosophy and rhetoric, or historicizing postmodernism in meta-historical studies. Retrieved March 30, 2006 from http://www.crvp.org/book/Series04/IVA-26/chapter_vii.htm

Parker, L. (1997). Informing historical research in accounting and management: Traditions, philosophies, and opportunities. *Accounting Historians Journal.* Retrieved March 21, 2006 from
http://www.findarticles.com/p/articles/mi_qa3657/is_199712/ai_n8781710/pg_2

Parker, L. (1999). Historiography for the new millennium: Adventures in accounting and management. *Accounting History.* Retrieved March 21, 2006 from
http://www.findarticles.com/p/articles/mi_qa3933/is_199911/ai_n8865215/pg_6

Pini, M.E. (2001, April). *Moving public schools toward for-profit management: Privatizing the public sphere.* Paper presented at the meeting of the American Educational Research Association, Seattle, WA.

Reese, W.J. (2002). *Power and the promise of school reform: Grassroots movements during the progressive era.* New York: Teachers College Press.

Republican National Committee. (2004). *2004 Republican party platform: A safer world and a more hopeful America.* Retrieved October 10, 2005 from http://www.gop.com/

Rettig, M. & Canaday, R.L. (1999). The effects of block scheduling. *The School Administrator, 56*(3), 14-16, 18-20.

Semel, S.F. (1999). The City and Country school: A progressive paradigm. In S.F. Semel & A.R. Sadovnick (Eds.), *"Schools of tomorrow," schools of today* (pp. 121-140). New York: Peter Lang.

Semel, S.F. (1999). The Dalton school: The transformation of a progressive school. In S.F. Semel & A.R. Sadovnick (Eds.), *"Schools of tomorrow," schools of today* (pp. 171-212). New York: Peter Lang.

Smith, M.M. (1996, Dec.). Old south time in comparative perspective. *The American Historical Review, 101*(5), 1432-1469.

Spring, J. (2005). *The American school: 1642-2004* (6th ed.). New York: McGraw-Hill.

Spring, J. (2002). *Political agendas for education: From the religious right to the Green party* (2nd ed.). Mahwah, New Jersey: Lawrence Erlbaum Associates.

Steinberg, S. & Kincheloe, J. (Eds.) (2006). *What you don't know about schools.* New York: Palgrave.

Tierney, W. (2003). Undaunted courage: Life history and the postmodern challenge. In Denzin, N., K. & Lincoln, Y. S. (Eds.). *Strategies of qualitative inquiry.* 2nd ed. Thousand Oaks, CA: Sage Publications.

United States Department of Education. (2004, July 1). *No child left behind and faith based leaders.* Retrieved October 10, 2005 from http://www.ed.gov/

United States Securities and Exchange Commission. (2005). *Form 10-K: Microsoft Corporation annual report for fiscal year ending June 30, 2005.* Retrieved October 17, 2005 from http://www.sec.gov/index.htm

Valdes, M. & Hutcheon, L. (1994). Rethinking literary history—comparatively. American Council of Learned Societies. Occasional Paper No. 27. Retrieved March 30, 2006 from http://www.acls.org/op27.htm

Villaverde, L. E. (1999). Creativity, art, and aesthetics unraveled through post-formalism: An exploration of perception, experience, and pedagogy. In J. Kincheloe and S. Steinberg (Eds.) *The post-formal reader: Cognition and education* (pp. 174-205). New York: Falmer.

White, H. (1978). *Tropics of discourse: Essays in cultural criticism.* Baltimore: Johns Hopkins Press.

White, H. (1990). *The content of the form: Narrative discourse and historical representation.* Baltimore: Johns Hopkins Press.

Whittle, C. (1997). Lessons learned. *The School Administrator,* 1997, 6-9.

Young, R. (1995). Conceptual research. *Changes: An International Journal of Psychology and Psychotherapy, 13,* 145-48.

345

GLOSSARY

*Critical theory*: a theory oriented towards creating social change through the critique of political, cultural, social, and historical phenomena. This theoretical approach was developed by the Frankfurt School, a group of social theorists, who based their work on Marxism, Neo- Marxism, psychoanalysis, structuralism, and post-structuralism.

*Epistemology:* the branch of philosophy that studies knowledge and its production. Epistemological questions include: what is truth? Is that a fact or an opinion? On what basis do you claim that assertion to be true? How do you know?

*Hermeneutics*: the study of interpretation. Historically it was a method used only to interpret and understand religious texts, since, it has been utilized to study any text including lived experience, its layered meaning, and the relationship between interpreter and the interpreted.

*Historiography*: the study and critical examination of history, historical methods, and historical writing. It employs a meta-analysis of the writing of the past using various literary methods (deconstruction, discourse analysis, textual analysis, hermeneutics, semiotics, and ideological contextualization) for interpretation.

*Objectivism*: the epistemological belief that disinterested knowledge can be produced about any phenomena simply by following the scientific method. If the method is followed rigorously no values, ideology, or other human perspectives will undermine the objectivity/validity of the knowledge produced.

*Ontology:* the study of the nature of being, existence, and reality, a branch of philosophy and metaphysics concerned with what it means to exist in a specific reality.

*Positivism*: an epistemological position that values objective, scientific knowledge produced in rigorous adherence to the scientific method. In this context knowledge is worthwhile to the extent that it describes objective data that reflect the world.

*Praxis*: central to liberatory education, it is the process through which critical analysis and action are simultaneously enacted. Praxis uses theoretical understandings, lived experiences, and pragmatic strategies to intervene in social, political, and cultural contexts.

*Reductionism*: a tendency in tradition Western research that assumes that complex phenomena can be best appreciated by reducing them to their constituent parts and then piecing the elements back together according to causal laws. This process typically involves forms of decontextualization and isolation of variables that work to undermine an understanding of the relation of phenomena under study to the world around them.

*Zeitgeist*: the German word for spirit of the times, commonly employed in historiography.

WILLIAM F. PINAR

# 14. LITERARY STUDY AS EDUCATIONAL RESEARCH

*"More than a Pungent and Corrosive School Story"*

Upon the publication of his *The Confusions Of Young Torless* in 1906, one of the most celebrated literary and drama critics of the period (Alfred Kerr) praised Robert Musil's first novel as "a book that will remain" (quoted in Rogowski 1994, p. 8). Kerr's review covered no fewer than eight columns on the December 21, 1906 issue of the influential Berlin periodical *Der Tag*. Such extensive and enthusiastic praise for the work of an unknown writer was unprecedented. Kerr judged the novel "brilliant" and "psychologically sophisticated." Musil was commended for the candor with which he treated the rituals of sado-masochistic homosexual rape practiced in the military school in which the novel is set. Of all of Musil's books, *Young Torless* is the only one to have sold reasonably well during the author's own lifetime. A century later, the novel is still assigned as high-school reading in Germany, presumably due to its focus on the problems of "adolescence"[1] (Rogowksi, 1994). It has also been taught in at least one private school in New York City (Taubman, 1992).

Given the right-wing destruction of democracy in America – intensified during the Administration of George W. Bush – it is unlikely the novel is widely taught in public high schools, even at public universities, in the United States. Homosexuality has been so stigmatized, teachers' and professors' academic freedom so challenged (the former by linking the curriculum to standardized examinations in the Bush Administration's *No Child Left Behind*), teaching a book that foreshadows fascism is, in the United States, after the fact.

Even students of educational research, including those who appreciate literary study as a form of educational research[2], might find the novel distasteful, despite its resonance with contemporary issues within schools, among them bullying, crime, and ethnic stereotyping - not to mention the homophobia - of too many adolescent boys. While set in a specific set of circumstances, the novel speaks to present generations struggling with the severed relation of school curriculum to lived experience, that of sexuality to the political order, and the love that, for too many school children, still dare not speak its name.

It has been suggested that the American novel closest to *Young Torless* is J. D. Salinger's *The Catcher In The Rye*. For one critic—Burton Pike (1961)—the two novels are markedly different treatments of the same theme, the sensitive adolescent trying to come to terms with him- or herself and society. Pike (1961) suggests, "this conflict in Musil's works between the general and the individual is a central

*K. Tobin & J. Kincheloe, (eds.), Doing Educational Research—A Handbook, 347–377.*

paradox" (p. 22). In Musil's works, the individual's inner world is the higher reality. Like the school in *Torless*, the external world usually remains sketchy and peripheral, more a source of sensory impressions than a definitive reality (Pike,
1961).

While some insist that the novel cannot be regarded as an indictment of the
nineteenth-century military boarding school (Pike, 1961), clearly it is (although
perhaps not primarily) a criticism of the school. As part of the public world, the
school fails to hold significance for its students, except as it creates "data" for the
individual to process. As schools do today (see Pope, 2001), this school seems far
from the everyday lives of its students and the community nearby. Like the political and social institutions of the Hapsburg Empire (Janik & Toulmin, 1973), the
school curriculum is severed from the lived experience of its inhabitants. When, at
the end of the novel, young Torless attempts to tell his story to the school officials,
not only language fails him, they do as well, unable to articulate the curricular
bridge he might have traveled in order to understand and articulate his experience.

The other major characters - Beineberg, Reiting, Basini, and the mathematics
teacher - are described physically but impersonally, either by the narrator or by the
other characters, often by Torless who remains a shadowy figure (Pike, 1961).
None of the characters is vividly drawn. Torless remains a presence reporting what
he sees and feels; he is not a singular subjectivity into whom we, on the outside,
have access. Pike (1961, p. x) regards the figures of Beineberg, Reiting, Basini,
and the mathematics teacher as "bafflingly complex." To me, however, their conduct renders them "perfectly queer" (Doty, 1993).

Musil's interest is Torless, a boy of "subtle mind" and "sensitivity," someday an
"intellectual" (Young-Bruehl, 1996, 155). Musil labors to make the others interesting, Pike suggests, if only to dissuade us from dismissing them outright. Musil
does not, for instance, develop the conflicts among them, or, for that matter, develop their individual characters in detail. We know enough about Beineberg and
Reiting, however, to know that they "cast unwittingly, from 1906, a long, dark,
anticipatory shadow forward to the rise of Nazism" (Pike, 1961, p. 51). (Reflecting
on this point years later, Musil acknowledged that Beineberg was a Nazi precursor:
see Young-Bruehl, 1996, p. 156].) Strangely, Pike regards it an "overstatement to
say that there is a political element in *The Confusions Of Young Torless*." Even so,
he acknowledges that the power-mad Beineberg and Reiting must be considered an
"embryonic political problem" (quoted passages in Pike, 1961, p. 51). While guilty
of reading the 1906 novel through the post World-War-II sensibility, I submit that
while hardly the only one, the political problem seems significant.

Each character seems capable of seeing things from his own perspective only.
Reiting views Basini as an object which whom he can experiment with power; Beineberg sees in Basini an opportunity to test his theories. Torless regards Basini as
the embodiment of the strangely doubled nature of things. None sees the perspective of the other. Torless seems uninterested in Reiting's intrigues and is annoyed
by Beineberg's speculations, although for a time Torless is drawn to Beineberg,
whom one critic terms a "mystagogue" (Hickman, 1984, p. 31). Beineberg dis-
guises his malevolent intentions behind a facade of (pseudo) philosophical ideas.

348

Hickman (1984) believes that Basini holds only an emotional fascination for Torless. If Torless imagines if he were to give up all questions and live from moment to moment like Basini, Hickman suggests, his own anxieties would disappear. I agree that the attachment is emotional and intellectual, but it also sexual.

The point of the novel, Pike (1961) argues, is a different and far more complicated one than the situation surrounding Basini suggests. While he is preoccupied with Basini, Pike suggests that Torless is to be more upset by the problem of irrational numbers in mathematics. Torless is upset by irrational numbers, I suggest, because they symbolize what he cannot understand in his lived experience. Basini represents an "irrational number" in the macho all-male society of the military school.

Alan Pryce-Jones (1955) calls *Young Torless* "a most alarming book" (p. v). While a "pungent and corrosive school story," it is, he asserts, "very much more." It is a "parable of power" (p. v). Pryce-Jones identifies two main themes in the book: one, a painful process of self-discovery, the other a brutal narration of bullying. To these I would add the split between institutional life and lived reality, and the creation of "others," including how this process of "creation" invites false solidarity and violence, in effect, a fraternal fascism.

While set in fin-de-siecle Vienna, the novel refracts the dawn light of Nazi Germany. It conveys the mysticism illumining rationalism, and honors that love possible between young men, despite its prohibition by the school. It is a novel about adolescent boys, boys who pretend to be interested in women, as long as this interest is enacted on the stage of male-male relations. There are echoes of colonialism, social science experimentation, voyeurism, and enslavement. As it portrays the crisis of early twentieth-century masculinity, the novel conveys the twentieth-century crisis in European civilization, a complex and multi-faced crisis concentrated in one school.

## A SCHOOL FOR BOYS

Reality itself is nothing but an embodiment of a certain blockage in the process of symbolization. For reality to exist, something must be left unspoken.

Slavoj Zizek (1991, p. 45)

Young Torless has been sent by his family to this school for specific reasons: it is well-known and respected. It boasts a religious foundation. What more could ambitious parents want for their child? Academically excellent, publicly respected *and* moral, it is no wonder that Frau Torless chose to deposit her son in this "remote" and "inhospitable" district (p. 2).[3] Not incidentally, this school is located far from civilization.

Common to coming-of-age rituals worldwide (see Gilmore 1990), the young man is removed from home. Young Torless' sense of isolation is indicated in his longing for his parents. He writes home nearly everyday; Musil tells us that only in such communication did he feel alive: everything else seemed "shadowy" and "unmeaning" (p. 3). This "longing" becomes redirected, from home to himself. Missing home becomes a more generalized "internal suffering" (p. 4).

There is a strong allegorical substratum. Torless represents an ascendant class, middle-class and secular (see p. 7). Early on, he meets a member of the aristocracy, one Prince H., whom the narrator characterizes as "effeminate" (p. 6), restating the widely held view that the decline of the Habsburg Empire is due to decadence, specifically an absence of virility. The two boys become close friends. On one occasion they argue over religion, an argument that ends the friendship. Musil tells us that Torless poured "torrents" of a "rationalist's scorn" on the "sensitive" young prince (p. 8). Afterward, the two boys never spoke to each other again. Some time later, the prince, left the school (see p. 8). Aristocracy was soon to leave the world political stage, remaining only as an ornament, a ceremonial echo of past authority.

Musil appreciates the distinction between schooling and education. Moreover, he distinguishes between education of the soul and that of the mind. He tells us that Torless' mind was "most subtle" (p. 53), that none of the books he was assigned to read had any "real" influence on his character (p. 10). His responses to classroom events were "cerebral reactions" (p. 10). Why? Musil tells us that Torless' soul[4] was severed from his mind at this stage. Musil emphasizes the "education of the soul" by distinguishing between the inner movement of the young man and the contingencies of socialization. Nowhere is this distinction made sharper than in the arena of sex-role socialization. While a tender boy, Torless feels compelled to pretend he is not, emulating his "rough," more "masculine" friends (p. 11). He avoids his mother's touch, despite yearning for it, afraid he would be seen by his friends (see p. 11).

In Torless' dilemma, we have a precise illustration of object relations theory: under panoptical surveillance, the boy performs masculinity by copying other boys and, earlier, his father (Chodorow 1978, Simpson 1994). This sex-role socialization occurs against the pull of the "other" who is the mother. The boy wants to "yield" and "regress" to the pre-oedipal period wherein he enjoyed a less differentiated, even somewhat symbiotic, relationship with the mother, and with the feminine within. To be a man, the feminine must be disavowed. Boys' physical and psychological separation from their mothers seems a nearly worldwide feature of their gendered socialization (see Gilmore 1990).

Who are his "rough, more masculine friends" at school? First is Beineberg, a "lanky" and "bony" boy with "big ears" that stuck out, and eyes that were "expressive" and "intelligent" (p. 12). By his title we note that Beineberg, like Prince H., comes from aristocracy; he represents the *ancien regime*, that remnant of medieval hierarchy, in his case somewhat militarized and thereby, presumably, vitalized. In this novel we discern how remnants of the German aristocracy could be drawn into fascism.

Torless dreads the "cramped narrowness" (p. 15) of the school; the sound of the bell slashes him like the "savage slash" of a "knife" (p. 15). Like fin-de-siecle Vienna, the school is a society whose conventions do not acknowledge the inner realities of its students. During the day school routine, Torless finds himself "shivering," shoulders "hunched up" against the "paralyzing weight" of the "constriction" of the school, including the social weight of his classmates' gendered expectations (p. 23).

To demonstrate their virility to each other, the young men leer at peasant girls in the nearby village (see p. 16). Using girls for the sake of show does not interest Torless. Musil tells us he took "no part" in these displays of "overweening" and "precocious manliness" (p. 16). The reason, Musil tells us, is that Torless' sensuality was "hidden," "more forceful," and—here racialized imagery enters the Austrian's prose—of a "darker hue" than that of his classmates, more "slow" and "difficult" in its expression (p. 16), a "terrifying, beast-like sensuality" (p. 17).

Racialization rationalized imperialism and colonization, of course (Stoler, 1995), rendering exotic and strange those of a "darker hue" whom Europeans exploited and enslaved. Torless' classmate Beineberg describes what his father—a General—brought back from India where, as a young officer, he had been in British overseas service. Not only had he returned with the "usual"—carvings, textiles, and idols—he had returned with "something" of a "feeling" for the "mysterious, bizarre glimmerings" of "esoteric Buddhism" (p. 18). This feeling would seem to be a version of Orientalism (Said 1979).

Beineberg appreciates India and its "wisdom"—for him books of Indian philosophy were not just books, but "revelations" (p. 19)—but his attitude is exploitative. He wants to apply its "spiritual powers" in order to "achieve domination" over others (p. 21). Is this the core fantasy of colonialism, of the "other" as possessing "resources" to be exported home, to the fatherland, there to increase its potency? Is Musil also suggesting that books might be more than information, that the mysticism of the East might have something important to contribute to European civilization?

## SEXUAL SERVITUDE

The theory of interpellation appears to stage a social scene in which a subject is hailed, the subject turns around, and the subject then accepts the terms by which he or she is hailed.

Judith Butler (1997, p. 106)

Although representing what is most emphatically our own, the language of our desire consequently remains for most of us irreducibly Other. In a certain sense, we do not even speak it; rather, it speaks us.

Kaja Silverman (2000, p. 51)

As in the work of Thomas Mann—whom Musil detested, jealous of his fame (Rogowksi, 1994)—there is in *Young Torless* a metaphysical quality to the young male body, as if the soul glistens on the surface of the body (see p. 19). The spirit-in-the-flesh idea—made famous in Europe by J. J. Winckelman (see Mosse, 1996, p. 29)—becomes explicit in the description of Beineberg's hands, described as "slim" and "dark" and "beautiful." Musil allows there is a "touch" of "breeding," even "elegance" about his fingers. That touch of "breeding"—recall we are in a moment when genetics, including its degraded form of eugenics, was thought to control destiny—in the "long-drawn lankiness" of the boy's body. For Torless, it was not the "ugly" but rather the more "attractive" features of Beineberg's body that left him "so peculiarly uneasy" (quoted passages on p. 21).

Torless seems drawn, as he was to the young prince at the beginning of the novel, to the aristocratic elite. Here his attraction seems homoerotic. The authority of aristocracy is fading in Europe by 1900, but it remains an object of fantasy and desire, and, in Russia in 1917, an occasion for murder. Recall that Torless represents the child of the new class, secular yet spiritual, meritocratic yet appreciative of (perhaps longing for) the aristocratic past. But he is determined that education be meaningful in terms of individuation not simple socialization, not as ornamental to an "imperial-royal" order.

Stripped of the soul, the body becomes pornographic, a provocation of desire, not of love and beauty. As one expects in a heterosexist regime, Torless flees what he feels, focused for the moment on Beineberg's hands. On these became concentrated Torless' "repugnance." Why? There was, he tells himself, something "prurient" about them. For that matter, he decides, there is "something prurient" about Beineberg's entire body. But it was his hands that sent a "thrill of disgust" coursing over Torless' skin. Shocked, Torless realized that something "sexual" had, "without warning," "thrust" its way "in" among his thoughts (quoted passages on p. 22). Here is a paradigmatic instance of homophobia. In the disavowal of desire, we see the severance of reason from the body, as desire, split-off, is now experienced as something that "thrusts" its way into his "thoughts." He comes to mistrust Beineberg (see pp. 22-23), but in doing so, it is desire for Beineberg he is negating.

Not just as a body but also as a personality, Beineberg can be seductive, as when he complains about the emptiness of the school. His irreverent questions echo the alienation of Musil as the Habsburg Empire denies historical time by ignoring the lived experience of its subjectively-existing citizens (Janik & Toumin, 1973). Beineberg raises the question social-efficiency curriculum theorists in America were posing, wondering how much of what students do in school is "going to get anyone anywhere?" (p. 25)

Unlike his American counterparts, however, Beineberg turns inward, reflecting that, despite keeping up with teachers' assignments, "you're empty—inwardly, I mean" (p. 25). Like church ritual for the secular, like the degraded language of U.S. politics, the school operates severed from the lived experience of those it presumably serves. In the estrangement of this educational institution from lived experience of its students is a temporal alienation, a severance of future from the present.

"Now" is sacrificed for "later," valuable not in itself but as preparation for college or for work. Beineberg is indignant: "Preparation? Exercise? What *for*?" He demands to know if Torless or Reiting has any idea why they study what they study. He concludes that school is "everlastingly waiting.... It's so boring" (p. 25). In this sense of waiting "everlastingly" is conveyed not only the estrangement of the school from students' lives, but as well the self-division of the contemporary conservative Christian, waiting for everlasting life by waiting for death.

For Musil, the emptiness of the present cannot be the pretext for waiting. Musil demands to understand. Moreover, Musil insists on linking the social surface with lived experience. His response is not theological (rationalizing waiting for some experience hereafter), nor, strictly speaking, political (rationalizing action now). Rather, Musil's response is, we might say, epistemological; he inhabits a "tension" that is also a "harkening" (p. 26), concepts that recall Ted Aoki's appreciation of the "tensionality" between curriculum as planned and curriculum as lived (Aoki, 2004, p. 232).

In Musil's language, there is an anticipation of the "auditory turn" (evident, too, in Aoki's *oeuvre*), in Musil's depiction of what is "not yet" as "some solemn mystery" that might become "audible." There is no privileging of any one sense, as Musil follows the auditory with a visual image, describing this attunement to the opaque present as imposing a "burden" of "gazing" at what is not intelligible (p. 26). The labor of understanding is not only, but always, psychological labor, and requires all the senses, especially the auditory.

Like Huebner (see 1999, chapter 1), Torless is possessed by a strong sense of "wonder" at the world, not only at objects, but at events, people, and even himself, enabling him to experience the world simultaneously an "insoluble enigma" to which he held "some inexplicable kinship" (p. 28). Both Lacan and Gadamer figure in the imagery of the following paragraph, wherein Musil names the distance between desire and its realization:

> Between events and himself, indeed between his feelings and some inmost self that craved understanding of them, there always remained a dividing-line, which receded before his desire, like a horizon, the closer he tried to come to it. (p. 28)

In the gap can we find what Wang (see 2004, p. 144) has described as the "third space," inaudible and invisible?

In the nineteenth century, a third sex – as sexologists hypothesized – appeared, the "homosexual." Neither man nor woman but somehow "in-between" the two, the nineteenth-century homosexual occupied, it would seem, a third space. Like the distance between understanding and experience, Torless dwelled between this "queer antithesis," pulled this way then that; it was, Musil continues, "something that tore at his soul, as though to rend it apart" (p. 29).

Sexual identity is, evidently, not the answer to this question. Musil implies Torless is not a homosexual (see p. 35) by emphasizing his sexual attraction to a prostitute named Bozena. For her part, Bozena expressed "contempt" (p. 35) for these privileged students of the nearby residential school. Does European self-division and social hierarchy sexualize the lower caste, rendering "alterity" a turn-on? To move among the inhabitants of the village and inside the house of the prostitute provokes, we are told, "fear," and this fear accompanies Torless' sense of self-abandonment; it is this that "seduced" every time, as it repositioned him as "lower than them!" (p. 36).

The poor and the outcast stimulate, then, not only sexual feeling, but self-contempt as well. Are the two related? The clue, perhaps, lies in the sexualization of self-abandonment, that "self-shattering ecstasy" Leo Bersani (see 1995, p. 101) associates with the sexualized dissolution of the ego's boundaries. It may be less the specific sex act—for Bersani, male-male anal sex shatters the self—than the prostitute's destitute social position. Being with Bozena, Musil tells us, was for Torless a "cruel rite" of "self-sacrifice," breaking the "bounds" of his "ordinary" life, suspending his "privileged position," those ideas and feelings with which he had been "injected" (p. 37). There is a drug-like element to the notion of "injection." As in the movie *Ricochet*, it is an eroticized penetration (see Pinar 2006a, chapter 5).

Not only the village enables Torless to "break the bounds" of his everyday life. He is able to do so on campus, in the school building itself, in an out-of-the-way room upstairs. Like the painter's apartment described in Kafka's *The Trial*, the room seems suffocating: a "narrow" room with a low ceiling, built, perhaps, for the storage of tools (see p. 49). It looked "fantastic" in the light of the small, flickering oil-lamp Beineberg illumines (p. 49). So low that one is unable to stand upright like a civilized man, one must bend over, and the tools in the room ... well, they would seem to be psycho-sexual ones.

There is a phallic symbol - a "loaded revolver" (p. 50)—present. It foreshadows the peculiarly masculine rites that would take place there. The room's "constriction" and "isolation" appeal to Torless; it felt to him like being buried "inside" a mountain, and the "smell" produced "vague sensations" in him (p. 50). Its "fantastic" quality appeals to him, enabling him to still feel the "excitements" of "solitude" and the "hallucinations" of darkness after he has returned to the daylight and life among the other boys (p. 51). The darkness of solitude illumines the underside of sociality.

This room is away from the everyday, the official, the taken-for-granted, where desire can be enacted. Is it because everyday life forbids desire that its enactment becomes destructive? Torless is, we are told, "torn" between the two worlds, the one the "solid," and "everyday world" of "respectable" citizens, in which social life was "regulated" and "rational," a world he associated with home. The other Musil describes as a world of "adventure," full of "darkness, mystery, blood, and undreamt-of surprises" (quoted passages on p. 53).

Like the cultural-historical crisis he personifies, Torless will be shaken by external events, by the aggression of his classmates. At the time of the novel's publication, we are still eight years away from the catastrophic devastation of World War I, but in this narrow corner of a prestigious residential school, violence, too, erupts. Musil is suggesting that "external events" erupted from a cultural cauldron of contradictory and conflicting currents. The geological metaphor has limited legitimacy, as in the human world individual action is required to enable eruption.

Our "change agent"—as school reform advocates used to imagine themselves— is no member of the ruling elite. Reiting is just a student, but one "quite capable" of putting his ideas into "practice," if, for the present, on a "small scale." As Jacques Daignault (1992) has observed, forcing theory into practice is one form of terrorism. Reiting, Musil tells us, was a "tyrant," indeed "inexorable" in his treatment of those who contested him (p. 52).

Terrorism is an apt term to depict Reiting's treatment of Basini. Reiting discovers that Basini has been stealing their classmates' money, petty crime in the service of Basini's social pretensions. It is evident by his name that Basini is not German. Nor, in Reiting's eyes, is Basini a "man." In this conflation of gender and nationality, Reiting acts. Does Reiting turn over Basini to the school authorities? Does he insist that he return what he has stolen? No, Reiting exploits Basini's vulnerability by black-mailing him. It is not money Reiting wants, however. He wants Basini's submission (see p. 55).

The southern European boy is, presumably, not as smart as his northern counterparts. He is, presumably, not as muscular as the Aryans he learns to fear. In his recognition of his interpellated inferiority, Basini compensates by being agreeable, becoming a version of the colonial subject, using his smile to ward off the violence initiated by the "superior," colonizing race (see Fanon, 1967). The gendering of this power becomes clear in Musil's characterization of the boy, described as "slight" in build, with "slack, indolent movements" and "effeminate features," including "rather coquettish" manner of making himself "agreeable" (p. 68). It is not a tactic that succeeds.

Basini's pretensions are not only social (propped up by stolen money), but sexual. He visits the prostitute, but, Musil tells us, only because he wanted to "play the man" (p. 68). Basini is effeminate, perhaps today he would even claim to be queer, but in this less identity-polarized time he simply is a target for the more masculinized Reiting and Beineberg. Because he is (perhaps) Italian, presumably darker in complexion than the German boys, there is a racial element in his subjugation.

At first Basini denies his transgression, his "criminality." But under the interrogation, Basini begins to break, "suddenly" turning "white." Mason Stokes (2001) argues that black is the color of sex; is white the color of accusation and guilt? Reiting tells Beineberg and Torless he had seen something similar only once before, while he was walking in the street and police were arresting a murderer. It was an act, Reiting makes clear, of interpellation (see pp. 58-59). Basini is not a murderer, only a petty thief, but Reiting will exploit the occasion to name him, to make him what he wants him to be.[5] Reiting asks his listeners, "what ... we should do with him?" (p. 59)

Now that Basini has been renamed, repositioned from "fellow-cadet" to "other," the question becomes "what should *we* do with *him*?" What is underneath the social surface of school, what is psychologically provocative, now calls to Torless: "All that was stirring within him still lay in darkness, and yet he already felt a desire to gaze into this darkness" (p. 68). This racialized darkness of desire is contrasted with the light of the law, including that "law" taken into one's own hands (as it were).

The law is a system of desire, Guy Hocquenghem (1978) asserted. In this novel, the law, the social code, the rules of the school, represent codifications of a masculinized sexualized sadomasochism. The triumvirate (although Torless is at first a reluctant and unwilling member) decides to take action; Basini will be placed under "surveillance." The action was taken, Musil tells us, "without ceremony," after

Reiting delivered a "speech," during which, Basini remained "very pale" and speechless. Torless found the scene both tasteless and significant (see p. 67).

The scene is significant not only because Basini is repositioned within the all-male school society of equals, the members of the self-appointed tribunal are repositioned as well. They have relocated themselves as the moral agents of society, the enforcers of "law and order," conferring upon themselves legitimacy, justification, the righteousness of authority.

Those who usurp power are compelled to protect it. In order to nullify any possible opposition, any collectivization within the tribunal that might threaten his position, Beineberg works to divide Torless and Reiting. He tells Torless that Reiting is double-crossing them, giving Basini money so that Basini will remain in Reiting's debt (see p. 73).

The debt accrues interest. The currency of Basini's "repayment" becomes clear soon enough. Reiting tries to explain the scheme to Torless, but at first he doesn't get it. Reiting makes his point by relating another incident, one that happened a few years ago at the same school, thanks to a "pretty boy" to whom the other students were attracted. Things went "too far," and "that's what Reiting's doing with Basini!" (p. 75)

Torless can't believe it; he would never dream "that" of Reiting. Still trying to make sense of what he has been told, he asks if he is in love with him, but Beineberg assures him Reiting is no "fool," that sex with the boy is only an amusement: "he gets some sort of excitement out of it" (p. 75). Evidently, he "gets" something in addition to excitement, or that is a straight boy's rationalization for homosexual exploitation? Finally, Torless asks about Basini. Beineberg exclaims: "Oh, him! Hasn't it struck you how uppish he's become recently?" (p. 75)

That word, of course, conveys the classic characterization of African Americans by whites determined to maintain the racial caste system. And not unlike that system's provision for those blacks who stayed in their place, Basini, too, will be taken care of, as Beineberg tells Torless that Reiting has promised to "look after" Basini as long as Basini does what he is told (p. 75). In this exchange we discern the relations among surveillance, sexuality, and subjugation. The three are now rationalized in educational terms, as Beineberg claims he wants Basini for himself, "as something to learn from" (p. 80).

Torless protests: they should simply turn him into the school authorities. But Beineberg has "something different" in mind, "let's call it tormenting him" (p. 81). Moreover, he tells Torless, Reiting is not about to back off either, as he finds a "special value" in Basini's subjugation: "he can use him for the purpose of training himself, learning to handle him like a tool" (p. 81).

As his National Socialist successors would declare thirty years later, Beineberg announces: "being human means nothing " (p. 82). And like the professional classes in Weimar Germany who later allowed Hitler to seize power, Torless seems powerless to respond, unable to act. By the end of the speech, Torless is "dreaming" rather than "thinking" (p. 85), incapable of distinguishing his own inner complexity from Beineberg's maniacal fantasies. He feels his throat constrict; nothing more was said between them.

Beineberg rationalizes his sexual engagement with Basini in terms of experimentation. Reiting underscores Basini's unworthiness, his location at the bottom of their Chain of Being. Speaking of Basini to Torless, Reiting calls Basini a "skunk" (p 94), a mild epithet given terms common today. Torless protests, somewhat awkwardly we're told, as if he is ashamed he is not being more indignant with Reiting. Reiting is unmoved (see p. 94).

In the upstairs room, where the "experiments" occur (access to it is only through "darkness"), the air is "warm" and "stale" (p. 97). There, Basini's "trial" begins, with Beineberg reciting the list of Basini's crimes, "monotonously," his voice "hoarse." Finally the question: "So you're not ashamed at all?" (quoted passages on p. 99) Basini turns to Reiting, as if to say, can you help me? Reiting hits him in the face. Basini falls back, trips over a beam, and falls onto the floor. Beineberg and Reiting attack.

In the scuffle the lamp is knocked over, its light now illuminating the scene only in shadows. But even if the half-light Torless can tell that they strip Basini of his clothes, then whip him, Basini "whimpering" and crying in pain, pleading for mercy. Finally there is only a "groaning," a "suppressed howling" as Beineberg curses in a "low" voice punctuated by his "heavy, excited breathing" (quoted passages on p. 99). This is not experimentation; this is not punishment: this is rape.

It is homosexual rape rationalized as retribution for theft. The original crime is lost in the dark, in its conversion into rationale for righteousness, in the boys' pretense that experimentation and social order legitimate violence, including sexual assault. While it is homosexual rape, it is not the act of homosexuals. What we have here are straight boys raping another boy, not, it turns out, not a rare phenomenon (see Scarce, 1997). Basini is a criminal, he is effeminate, he is not Aryan. Is the alterity of the other always sexualized? (see Pinar, 2006b)

By definition, sexual subjugation is violent. In the present instance, the boys must express their disavowal of homosexual desire while performing that desire. Through whipping, beating, through psychological torture they enact the inner self-structure of homosexual desire denied as they get off. They project onto Basini their own negated selves, now relocated and, once again, subjugated, whipped and beaten into submission, sexual submission.

What about young Torless, our secular, sensitive young intellectual, the generational personification of the new world order? Does he intervene to save Basini? Torless discovers not only does he not intervene, he discovers that he cannot even just watch, pretending to be a neutral observer. Listening to Basini whimper, Torless was "disconcerted" to discover himself in a state of "sexual excitement" (p. 100).

Lyrically, Musil links Torless present excitement to the "innocence" of childhood, a time when that "peculiar" excitement led "to press himself against the floor." Having had their way with Basini, Beineberg and Reiting grope their way back, sitting now in satiated silence. Beineberg stares at the lamp as Torless stares at his childhood sexuality, understanding that it was "the same!" (p. 101) Now Torless is ready to participate; he demands that Basini acknowledge he is a thief. Startled, Basini hesitates; Beineberg strikes him in the ribs as he orders him to comply.

There is a pause, then quietly, Basini murmurs: "I'm a thief" (p. 103). In this scene is the cop's self-excitation with his power, a masturbatory scene in which only his pleasure counts, the others fantasy objects in a "hall of justice."

Here, however, the scene is not sublimated. Here, sex is not converted into the exhibitionism of the lawyers, the voyeurism of juries, staring at the defendant's vulnerability, all governed by the gaze of Judge. In this novel the courtroom is a room of rape. To Basini the "prosecutor" demands that he confess that he is "*your* pilfering, dishonest, filthy beast" (p. 104). Basini complies.

Like "honor" in the American South (see Pinar, 2001, p. 979), ritualized respect may be another form of sublimated sexuality, specifically a defensive and compensatory recoding of the incest taboo (see, also, Pinar, 2006b), as is suggested in a passage describing Torless' visit to his mathematics teacher's chambers. The awe of this early twentieth-century schoolboy expresses his fantasy of the world that the older man carries inside him but supposes to exist all around them. Within this awe, this curiosity, is a vulnerability, not that associated with chronic psychological insecurity, but with the titillation of being in the presence of one-who-knows (p. 108).

The student-teacher relationship is not the only eroticized one, however. The teacher's relationship to his "discipline" exhibits a certain erotic content as well; it is described as a "daily cohabitation" with mathematics. His room – wherein this "cohabitation" takes place—is filled with the smell of "cheap tobacco-smoke" (p. 109).

Early on, the encounter between the older and younger man becomes awkward, as Musil tells us that there is an "atmosphere" of "misunderstanding" between the two. Torless feels as if he were talking through a "dense" and "gloomy fog," that his best words had disappeared inside in his throat (p. 110). After listening to Torless stumble over the presence of the irrational in the rational universe of mathematics, the teacher acknowledges, awkwardly, with hesitation, that there are, yes, "*transcendent* factors ... beyond the strict limits of reason" (p. 111). Imprisoned in his professional role, wrapped in reason, the mathematics teacher is unclear how to incorporate the transcendent in his midst, personified in the handsome young Torless. The boy never gets inside him, either; the teacher remains insulated inside his cell.

## THE INTIMATE OTHER

What does it mean ... when a social or political relationship is sexualized?

Eve Kosofsky Sedgwick (1985, p. 5)

Outside the teacher's apartment, in the social sphere of the school, it is Basini who represents the non-rational, that which lies beyond comprehension, the "other." It is his very distance from convention, from the everyday reality of school life, his position as humiliated, as contemptible, as barely human (indeed, a "beast") that makes him, well, interesting. Not yet asleep Torless listens for the sound of Basini breathing (p. 139). Musil makes this relationship between "otherness" and sexual excitation explicit:

> It seemed then that some physical influence emanated from Basini, a fascination such as comes from sleeping near a woman and knowing one can at any instant pull the covers off her body. (p. 140)

Moreover, what seems to exist as allure *in* the other now is converted into desire *for* the other. Musil tells us that at night Torless filled with a "murderous lust" (p. 145). He falls asleep "just in time" (p. 145).

Is Torless' passion—a passion unfelt before his participation in the "othering" of Basini—unrequited? Quietly, in the dark, suffering an "uneasy, feverishly hot half-sleep," Torless listens for Basini. Finally, he hears him "undressing." Torless holds his breath; he hears nothing. Even so, he feels Basini lying wide awake, also "straining" to hear through the darkness, "just like himself" (p. 145). Is Basini listening for him? Or is Torless projecting his desire onto Basini, imagining that the savage desires the civilized?

As Torless lies there, tormented, struggling with himself, Basini slips out of his bed, looks at him, and begins to walk in the direction of the secret room. This must have happened to Basini many times before, Torless realizes, as he follows the boy upstairs. Once inside, Torless turns toward him: Basini is already naked. He is, Musil tells us, "beautifully built ... like ... a young girl" (p. 148). Torless almost succumbs to this beauty, but, at the last minute, his inner resistance surfaces. In his shame he acts shocked and surprised, demanding Basini why he is naked, demanding that he clothe himself. Now it is Basini who is shocked.

His desire blocked, Torless slips from id to superego, demanding that Basini go to the authorities to confess, not the crime of the triumvirate, but his own petty theft. Basini's sexualized degradation seems to him the less horrible fate, and he begs Torless not to force him to confess. Basini blurts out that it's not the beatings he fears; it's the sex (p. 150). And it's the sex that makes Basini interesting to Torless, that Basini's body is no longer only Basini's body, no longer "private property" but public currency, passed from boy to boy.

Due to the incest taboo, the desire of and for the mother is repressed. Not only must its expression be blocked, its very existence must be denied, and by both mother and child. Is it his father's sexual possession of his mother that renders her body appealing to the son? Torless' mother is replaced by the public bodies of Bozena (Webber, 1990, p. 108) and Basini. The already-possessed "public" character of these bodies seems to be a source of stimulation. Men understand that prostitutes have experienced the bodies of hundreds of men.

Is this what Foucault liked about the gay bath houses? There, a man's body is a public body, not private, not his alone, but, in the dark public spaces of the "common" rooms, belongs to whomsoever takes it. Are not Reiting and Beineberg saying to Basini, in a kind of inverted spiritual possession: "You are in that body, but that body belongs to me." I possess you. Is this not the homoerotic of slavery? (Hartman, 1997)

It is Basini's public body that is the shared site of the boys' indirect sexual encounter with each other. Torless demands to know what Beineberg and Reiting do with him, but Basini balks. Summoning Foucault's confession in the service of surveillance, Torless demands that Basini tell him everything, but Basini tells him what he already knows: "They make me undress." Torless wants details, but Basini is reticent. Torless demands of him:

"So you're their-mi-mistress?"

"Oh no, I'm their friend!" (p. 151)

Is Basini playing with Torless? Does Basini rationalize his sexual servitude as a form of voluntary friendship? Torless is unconvinced (p. 151).

The sexual structure of the boys' sadomasochistic ritual reproduces, in sexualized form, the gendered social structure of the school. As Teresa De Lauretis (1994, p. 303) points out, "individual sexual structuring is both an effect and a condition of the social construction of sexuality." Reciprocal relations among sadomasochism, militarism, and disavowed homosexual desire (see, for instance, Mosse, 1985) structure Basini's submission. He confesses that Reiting makes him undress, then makes him read from military history, during which time he is "affectionate." "Afterwards," Reiting beats Basini. "After what?" Torless asks. "Oh, I see" (p. 152).

Like those assaults younger men endure in coming-of-age rituals worldwide (see Gilmore, 1990), Basini, too, suffers masculine conflations of desire and violence, rage and tenderness, power and vulnerability. He tells Torless that Reiting says he beats because if he didn't, "he couldn't let himself be so soft and affectionate to me.... I'm his chattel[6], and so then he doesn't mind" (p. 152). The possession of another person is not only economic. Nor does it affect only the minds of those possessed.

From the sadomasochism of the school we move to the sadomaschism of the church. Torless asks about Beineberg. Basini's first response is to complain about his breath, revealing their physical intimacy. Experiencing the complaint as a wedge their solidarity, Torless tells him to shut up, demands again that he tell him what Beineberg does with him. Basini begins by admitting that both boys beat and rape him, but he interrupts himself by asking Torless not to yell at him again. Basini has feelings for Torless. "Get on with it," Torless demands, distancing himself. Basini allows that Beineberg "goes about it differently. First of all he gives me long talks about my soul" (p. 152). We are reminded of Beineberg's interest in India, but we are also reminded of numerous scandals involving sexual assault in Christian churches. Reiting plays school; Beineberg prefers to play church: are the institutions two sides of the same coin?

As Foucault appreciated, Christians exploit confession to control the minds of the vulnerable. In this novel, it is clear that the penetration of the soul is sexualized. Basini reports that Beineberg tells him to let "my soul go to sleep and become powerless." Then, Basini reports, Beineberg claims he can have "intercourse with my soul" (p. 153). Torless is dumfounded, and asks Basini to explain. It seems that

Beineberg is not only a priest but a social scientist, as Basini allows that the penetration of his soul is, Beineberg tells him, an "experiment" still underway. Beineberg requires Basini to lie on the ground so that he can put his feet on him, demanding he stare into a glass, presumably to make him drowsy. He orders Basini to bark like a dog, instructing him "exactly" how to do it, followed by grunting like a pig, all the while telling Basini that he is, in fact, a pig (p. 153).

For the time being, Torless' desire remains expressed as curiosity. He continues to ply Basini with questions, demanding to know Basini's experience of torture. Basini tells him: "Oh, I didn't like it, of course. Because it had to be done just like that, being ordered to.... I dare say it's not so bad then" (p. 155). Suddenly Torless abandons the vicarious position; he orders Basini to strip. Basini smiles; Torless rebukes him for this familiarity. Once naked on the floor, Torless points out to him that he could spit on him if he wanted, make him bark like a dog, eat dust like a pig. At that Basini breaks down, and begins to weep: "You're tormenting me." Undaunted, Torless becomes the social scientist: "What happens inside you? Doesn't the picture you've made of yourself go out like a candle?" (pp. 156-157) Torless is demanding to know the experience of what Leo Bersani (1995, p. 99) characterizes as the "nonsuicidal disappearance of the subject." It is what Musil (1995) was later to portray as a "man without qualities."

The night's encounter is over. The two boys return to the dormitory, departing that space where the "other" is present. More than once in the novel this upper room is contrasted to the everyday social field, i.e., the classroom, the school. These are flat, superficial, appropriate, official, and unreal. Reality resides elsewhere, upstairs. It even seems to exist in another time; Musil describes the room as a "lair," and likens it to "some forgotten scrap" from the Middle Ages, ever so "remote" from the "warm, bright-lit life of the class-rooms." In the upper room, Beineberg and Reiting are no longer the people they are "down there." In the upper room, they become "something else, something sinister, blood-thirsty, figures in some quite different sort of life" (quoted passages on p. 158). One night these two worlds collide, or, I should say, embrace.

## THE LOVE THAT DARE NOT SPEAK ITS NAME

There is no necessary reason for identification to oppose desire, or for desire to be fueled by repudiation.

Judith Butler (1997, p. 149)

Torless is trying to fall asleep, but the memory of Basini, of his "bare" and "glimmering" skin, left a fragrance, like lilac, in that "twilight" of "sensations" preceding sleep. Even the "moral revulsion" has faded away, Musil tells us, as Torless falls asleep. He is awakened by Basini, who has crawled into bed with him (p. 161). Shocked, Torless pushes Basini away.

Basini responds by begging him not to reject him. You're different than Beineberg and Reiting, he tells Torless, begging him not to treat him as they do. Basini confides: "I love you." Torless is dumbfounded. He tries to set things straight,

PINAR

claiming not to know what Basini is saying. Torless pushes Basini away, but the "hot proximity" of Basini's "soft skin … haunted" him. Basini feels Torless' resistance weaken, and he whispers to him: "Oh yes...please, I should so gladly do whatever you want!" (quoted passages on p. 162)

Again, Torless pushes Basini away. His arms, however, become "heavy" and "warm," the muscles in them slacken, and suddenly, he discovers that, as if in a "dream," he has drawn Basini "closer" (p. 162). Torless has succumbed to the pretty boy, once a thief, once safely located a million identity miles away. Now, suddenly, that the thief is a beautiful boy in bed with him. Without mind or muscle in its way, desire proceeds. In the midst of love-making, Torless tries to reassure himself that this is not who he is, that tomorrow he will be different (p. 163).

Tomorrow arrives, but Torless is not restored to his prior fantasy of himself. He finds himself "ashamed," not due to the sex— "for that," Musil tells us, "was nothing so very rare at boarding-school"—but because he was now split into two, feeling both "tenderness" (p. 164) for Basini, and contempt.

Ambivalence does not deter Torless, however, and the two become lovers, meeting "quite often" (p. 164). Torless even becomes jealous of Beineberg and Reiting, but the two, Musil tells us, are "aloof," perhaps already bored with Basini (p. 164). This is no fling; Musil tells us that the "desire" Basini had "aroused" in Torless was a desire "thorough-going" and "real" (p. 165). But Basini turns out to be what Winnicott (1990, p. 9) would later characterize as a "transitional object," what Musil describes as a "substitute," a "provisional object" of a deeper "longing." So sex is the substitute? Yes, Musil is saying so (p. 165).

Whatever drew Torless to Basini, it was not, presumably, homosexual desire. Musil allows that—"at first"—it had been the "nakedness" of the boy's "slim" body that drew him, but that what he felt would have been no different had he been confronted with the naked body of a "little girl," a body, he tells us, that is "utterly sexless, merely beautiful" (p. 165). An "utterly sexless" body (is there such at thing?) would seem to stimulate snuggling, not sex, not assault, not shame.

Musil's resistance to his main character being homosexual aside, there are other "motives" at work. Musil understands that desire, especially for the young, can be, in clinical terms, object non-specific, diffuse, on occasion everywhere, not just bisexual, but pansexual. Lyrically, Musil describes such desire as the "secret, aimless, melancholy sexuality of adolescence," a "sensuality" attached to no one person (p. 166). It seems attached to Basini not, for example, to Bozena.

Indeed, Musil characterizes his experience with the prostitute as "blighted" and squalid (p. 166). Whether that experience was specific to Bozena, or a function of classism (as Musil's earlier description hints), the fact of the matter is that it is Basini's body, a male body, wherein the young Torless "encountered something warm, something that breathed and was fragrant, was flesh" (p. 166).

Torless flees the experience. While they are lovers at night, during the day they are trapped in the homophobic world of the school. Were Basini a girl, and the school a public and co-educational one, they could testify to their sexual involvement with each other. But Basini is a boy, and Torless seems thoroughly identified with the homophobic regime; he avoids Basini whenever possible. When he can-

362

not, he feels disgusted, and his former desire for him seems "unspeakably senseless and repulsive" (p. 167). Not for long, however.

Indeed, Musil makes clear that this revulsion is only the undercurrent of desire, that what Torless loathes is what he wants. At some point in the sequence of avoidance and disgust, Torless would weaken, "then he knew that he *would* debase himself" (p. 168). Torless could not name his emotions, we are told, nor did he know what they portended. It was in this "intoxicating" self-same alterity wherein he no longer knew himself and from which his desire became a "wild, contemptuous debauchery" (p. 169).

Now Musil moves us ahead of events: intoxication is replaced with sobriety, self-abandon becomes self-control, the mask is removed and it's one's own naked face at which one stares in the mirror.[7] From this imaginary moment in the future, Musil asks if the episode was a disaster for our young hero. Not so, he tells us, as the affair with Basini left "something behind" (p. 170). Soundly alchemical or, perhaps, homeopathic, Musil describes this "something" as a "small admixture of a toxic substance" (p. 171), saving the soul from over-confidence and complacency. Despite the evasion of sexual identity, the statement is a precise description of "biographic function," of how events function in the evolving life history of the individual (Pinar, 2004). The experience would remain with him, we are told, like a "deep note resounding from afar" (pp. 171-172).

Assured that our hero will not be ruined by the affair, we return to the time-line. We watch as the matter moves toward its conclusion. Reiting acts first, informing Torless that he and Beineberg have concluded that "things can't go on." Is it because they're bored with him? Perhaps, but what Reiting says is that they must act because Basini has grown accustomed to his subjugation. Not only does his sexual slavery no longer make him "miserable," he has become as "impudently familiar as a servant." He and Beineberg conclude they must take things "a step further," they must "humiliate" him "completely" in order to determine "how far it can go" (quoted passages on p. 174).

Any prospect of mercy disappears. Indeed, we learn that the only question is how to accomplish Basini's complete collapse. Unsurprisingly, Reiting has already been reflecting on the problem, and offers the following suggestions: 1) make Basini sing psalms of thanksgiving as they flog him, 2) make him bring to them the "filthiest" items in his mouth, like a "dog," 3) take him to Bozena's where they force him to read aloud letters from his mother, punctuated by Bozena's jokes. Reiting has thought of involving other classmates in the procedure, acknowledging that he has preference for these "mass movements" (quoted passages on pp. 174-175). We know.

Like Foucault's passion (see Miller 1993), sex is, for Beineberg, the medium of research and experimentation, a passageway through which the effects of power flow. Beineberg tells Torless that he regards sex as an "experiment" (p. 176). Unlike Foucault, for Reiting and Beineberg sex is an experimental weapon.

Like the comment about mass movements (who cannot but think of the Nazis' Nuremberg rallies?), another prescient comment, this time from Beineberg, slides into the text. In contrast to the school authorities, he says, "we are young, we are a generation later, and perhaps things are destined for us that they never dreamt of in all their lives" (p. 178). As a German whose generation is responsible for World War II and the Holocaust, he is, of course, nightmarishly right.

The final scene unfolds, again in the "lair." It also cannot be read without Nazi Germany in mind. Torless and Reiting, we are told, "tense" with "expectation" as they arrive, discovering that Beineberg was already there with Basini. Again Musil describes the room as dark, filled with "stale air," creating a feeling of "drowsiness," a "weary, sluggish indolence." Beineberg commands Basini to undress. In the shadowy light, Basini's naked skin seemed "bluish" and "moldy." There was, Musil tells us, nothing "provocative" about Basini's body tonight (quoted passages on p. 182).

Suddenly Beineberg takes a gun out of his pocket and aims it at Basini. Not even Reiting is prepared for this move; he leans forward, as if to move between the two of them. Even for Reiting, Beineberg has, this time, gone too far. Beineberg is pleased; he smiles as Basini drops to knees, as if "paralyzed," mesmerized by the gun, his eyes "wide with fear." Beineberg assures him that if he does exactly what he's told to do, he will come to no harm (p. 182). Like the "good" German, Torless watches (p. 183).

Beineberg and Reiting now engage in some form of quasi-hypnosis, again anticipating the Nazis' pseudo-science some thirty years later. "Turn sideways," Beineberg ordered. "What obeys now is only the brain," he murmurs. "Bend forward, Basini—that's right—slowly, slowly.... Bend forward" (p. 185). Basini loses his balance and crashes to the floor at Beineberg's feet. He screams in pain.

Beineberg becomes enraged, takes hold of Basini's hair and begins to beat him with his belt. Basini howls in pain, like a dog (pp. 185-186), a reoccurring image. During the beating, Torless departs, quietly. Beineberg continues to beat Basini; he would continue, we are told, until he can beat him no longer (see p. 186). Torless' horrified fascination with the situation is now over (p. 187). Basini begs for his lover to help him, but Torless refuses.

Reminiscent of Stanley Elkins' (1959) analysis of enslavement, Basini has been shredded. What is left of him? He had been beaten so savagely, we are told that "every trace of personality seemed to have gone out of him; only in his eyes there was still a little residue of it, and it peered out shakily, imploringly, as though clutching at Torless" (p. 188). Free of his fascination with the "experiment" in which Reiting and Beineberg had engaged, Torless tells Basini that he doesn't "arouse" in him the "slightest feeling" (p. 189). He turns to go.

Basini strips and throws himself against Torless, who is disgusted (p. 190) by the welts covering Basini's body. "Nauseated" (p. 190), Torless pushes him away and departs. He encounters Reiting, who demands to know if Torless has been seeing Basini secretly. He demands to know what Basini wants; protection, offers. Finally, too late, Torless manages to express his contempt for his comrades, telling Reiting how "vulgar" and "brutal" they are. Reiting tries to reestablish solidarity by focusing on Basini, but Torless tells him the matter is no longer of any interest to him. In reply to Reiting's exclamation that the matter "certainly used to" be of interest to him, Torless replies that his only interest in Basini was intellectual, because Basini was a "riddle" to him. He says he has learned nothing from the experience, only that "things just happen (p. 191). Here Torless sounds like Roquentin in Sartre's *Nausea*.

Unlike Roquentin, Torless expresses a moment of triumphant disaffiliation and self-righteousness. In a subsequent scene, he tells Beineberg that their conduct amounts to nothing less than the "brainless, senseless, disgusting torture of someone weaker" (p. 191) Beineberg is not chastened; Torless' defection becomes yet another opportunity to assault Basini (p. 193). Beineberg tells him to meet them afterward; Torless refuses (see p. 194). Beineberg draws a "deep breath," as if he were concentrating "all the venom he had in him," and then he confronts Torless: "Do you think we don't know how far you've gone with Basini?" Torless becomes angry: "I don't care what you know, I don't want to have any more to do with your filthy goings-on!" To which Beineberg replies: "Oh, so you're getting impertinent again!" Torless is not intimidated: "You two make me sick! Your beastliness is utterly senseless! That's what's so revolting about you" (quoted passages on pp. 193-194). Beineberg threatens Torless with the same fate Basini has suffered. Unless he cooperates, Torless too shall become a sexual slave. Torless doesn't buckle.

Defeated by this break in German solidarity, Beineberg and Reiting tell everyone, that is, tell everyone what it is they want them to know. Among their fellow cadets, "excitement grew," their faces at first animated by grins, then filled with "hostile glances" cast toward Basini, and, finally, "dense with a silence that was charged with tension, with dark, hot, sinister urges" (p. 198). Gang rape seems possible (see p. 199). But the entire matter shifts from the boys to the school authorities. Of course, the boys blame Basini (p. 204).

Torless attempts to describe to the school authorities what had happened. What is going on in this speech, several critics suggest, has everything to do with the fissures between language and reality, between what is visible, and what is not (see, for example, Janik & Toulmin, 1973). What is going on, as a post-Stonewall queer might say, has everything to do with being in or out of the closet. "There's something dark in me," Torless tells the astonished school officials, "deep under all my thoughts, something I can't measure out with thoughts, a sort of life that can't be expressed in words and which is my life, all the same." That "silent life" haunted him, demanding that he "stare at it." He felt tormented by the prospect that his whole life might be likewise, that he was condemned to see "sometimes with the eyes of reason, and sometimes with those other eyes" (quoted passages on pp. 211-212).

Is what is missing in modern life homosexual desire, now safely bifurcated and segregated as an identity? Is homosexual desire the "other" life for which Musil himself searched, the life Musil—metaphorically and literally (he marries after writing this novel)—left behind when, through his narrative of the novel, he disclaimed Torless' desire for Basini?

Banished from daylight, homosexual desire circulates at night, not in the classroom, but upstairs, in the attic room the authorities have forgotten is even there. Like a vampire, it disappears at dawn. In daylight Torless is straight, which is not to say his homosexual desire has disappeared; it only lies in the coffin, waiting for the light of compulsory heterosexuality to fade.

Basini is now only a memory; he has been "expelled." In his expulsion, we are told, the school loses something (p. 215). Torless, too, decides to leave. His mother reclaims her son. On the way to the railway station, they passed, on the right, the woods where Bozena lived. He glances at his mother.

"What is it, my dear boy?"

"Nothing, Mamma. I was just thinking."

And, drawing a deep breath, he considered the faint whiff of scent that rose from his mother's corseted waist. (p. 217)

Basini had replaced Bozena, and his mother's bourgeois scent replaces the smell of the beautiful boy. Torless is, presumably, no longer confused; he is going home.

## MORE THAN A SCHOOL STORY

We do not have too much intellect and too little soul, but too little intellect in matters of the soul.

Robert Musil (1990, frontispiece)

*The Confusions Of Young Torless*, Frederick Peters asserts, is essentially a novel of ideas. The plot functions as a framework for the exploration of perennially important ideas in Western Europe: the nature of reality, the limitations of reason, the character of sexuality, and the emptiness of conventional moral codes. For J. M. Coetzee (2001, p. xiii), the "master metaphor" of the novel is that there are no foundations of the real, everyday world. While an ontological assertion (and, thus, a "perennial" idea), it is also historical.

It is at the close of the nineteenth century, Foucault argues, that the concept of "adolescence" appears, a concept created to describe and control those increasing numbers of young adults, specifically young men, required to remain in institutions (especially schools) rather than seeking their fortunes in the world. For Musil, adolescence was less about the disciplinary society than about the architecture of self.

For Musil, adolescence was that period just before the individual constructs the fiction of character, of ego, of the "adult" he or she wishes to be. For Musil, there is an inner void that must be concealed if "character" is to be constructed. Once the formation of character has been accomplished, it serves as a permanent if opaque "floor" over a forgotten inner void. Musil believed that schools functioned in two ways to conceal the inner void during this dangerous time. First, the student is encouraged to read literature, especially that deemed by educators as edifying. Literary study represents a narrative means of strengthening the "floor" of character. Second, the student is encouraged to take up sports. Musil believed that sports keep the adolescent boy in a constant state of exhaustion, leaving him neither the time nor the energy for excessive introspection during which time he might discover the void (Peters 1978; Simpson 1994). In other words, symbolizing and exhausted young men might reroute the intense homosexual desire of the adolescent period into sublimated forms of intellectual expression and homosocial physicality (Young-Bruehl,1996).

Surely Musil's "theories" of character formation, of *Bildung*, are self-referential. Maybe Torless represents Musil when he himself was a cadet, despite his disclaimers. If so, it would appear, Peters (1978) suggests, that Musil found himself in the dilemma of being at once too intellectually inclined for sports but also uninterested in literature, creating a vacuum the Basini affair filled.

Character is a conceptual synthesis, Musil thought. He defined the word "character" as an abbreviated formula for that mechanism of simplification that limits the individual to a single perspective (or sexual orientation, I'd add). If strength of character follows from a restriction of perspectives, and a consequent lack of ambivalence, then strong character is indicative of machismo.[8] Because Torless is a "weak" character, his intellect remains somewhat complex. He is able to regard his experience from many multiple perspectives (Peters, 1978).

The void beneath character is laced with sexuality. Peters (1978) points out that any transgressive experience of the bourgeois codes of his parents is sexualized for Torless. Certain sexualities become occasions for the dissolution of character structures. (For Foucault, this will become an opportunity, not a threat: [see Miller 1993]). Torless' affair with Basini destabilizes Torless, enabling new (if very uncomfortable) experience and character building. Torless has trouble articulating this educational experience, at least to those figures of authority and reason—the school officials—whose bourgeois codes he has violated.

In Musil's view, it is only during early (male?) adolescence that the trap door is likely to open in the "floor" of character. As the individual ages, this "floor" is likely thickened or hardened by prejudices and other forms of self-deception. In his diaries Musil associates this void with mysticism, a Dionysian mysticism in which the self is absorbed, sometimes even extinguished, a state reminiscent of, if not identical to, Bersani's (1995) self-shattering ecstasy.

Because Torless' concept of himself is so fragile, Peters suggests, such states are distressing and threatening. In this sense, Peters (1978) concludes, the novel is a literary experiment in which Musil explores what happens when bourgeois gender codes are rejected, and sexual fantasies become the primary reality. What arouses Torless' desire for Basini is Basini's status as a criminal (thug?), as other, as a public body, rendering that body exotic and sexualized. Musil also tells us, simply, that Basini is beautiful. Like other critics, Peters (1978) ignores this clue, and focuses on non-sexual motives to explain Torless' sexual involvement. He suggests that Torless is intrigued by Basini's fall because it means that he too could fall. The issue for Peters is less a sexual than epistemological question: how does one know who one is or can be?

Before Basini, Torless had been able to keep the two worlds—the everyday, respectable bourgeois world around him and the borderless sexual world within him—segregated by associating the Dionysian realm with a socially inferior class. They become integrated in the upper-class thief: Basini. With the revelation that a fellow cadet could be a criminal, the floor of Torless' naive perception of himself begins to collapse (Peters, 1978). I ask: how can the epistemological be separated from the sexual? (Pinar,2006b)

To flee the sexual, Torless focuses on the epistemological. He displaces his own crisis of self-identity and gender affiliation onto mathematics, and, specifically, to the problem of irrational numbers. To traverse the inner void by means of mathematics is, therefore, an intellectual replacement for the crumbling floor of his character. If he can fully comprehend the nature of irrational numbers in mathematics, he can comprehend the irrational elements in Basini's soul, as well as those irrational elements in himself and his "friends" that have precipitated his fall into the void.

His teacher tells him that the problem of irrational numbers and their relationship to everyday life involves a controversial question: the presence of "transcendent factors" (p. 94) in daily existence. He tells Torless he does not consider himself sufficiently qualified to speak on this subject. His teacher seems unwilling to discuss any subject that could conceivably lead to controversy between himself and his colleagues, including the school chaplain (Peters, 1978). Musil is having his fun here.

Torless comes to regard reason as a form of self-protection. Reason is not a means of exploring the depths of being which, like irrational numbers, are somehow split off from the rational universe. Torless' self-shattering experience functions first to increase the distance between himself and the adult world of reason, and, second, to extend this estrangement to include education itself, which he then comes to regard as superficial and disengaging. Torless now sees passion as the primary reality. In contrast, the everyday world of teachers, parents and the school seems stupid, boring, pointless (Peters, 1978).

Unable to find his way in the sublimated world of mathematics and the school, Torless is drawn to the outcast Basini. He decides to question Basini to discover what it is like to live within the sphere of the "other." Torless demands that Basini tell him what happens inside himself when he steals or is raped by Reiting and Beineberg. Basini hasn't a clue what Torless is talking about (Peters, 1978). He experiences Torless' questioning as another form of assault, let us say, epistemological assault.

Torless recognizes that within himself exist realms of experience more complex and powerful than the academic world of reason. He is unclear how to respond to this revelation. Musil says simply that Torless has come to understand that he has an inner life, a developmental accomplishment given the view among many fin-de-siecle and twentieth-century intellectuals that subjective experience itself became a casualty of industrial capitalism, mass society, and war (Jay, 2005).

In *Young Torless*, there is a portrait of pedagogy as social engineering, instruction as unapologetically manipulative. (The Bush Administration would be pleased: evidence-based practice is legislated by these present-day fascists.) Our experimental pedagogue is Reiting, who investigates Basini's psychological reactions to his torture and sexual assault in order to discover how others might be likewise manipulated. In one experiment Beineberg tries to induce in Basini a semi-mystical trance. In erasing the sensation of being in a body, in stripping away the physical experience of flesh, Beineberg speculates that he might then be able to engage in direct intercourse with Basini's soul. Like Torless, Beineberg recognizes the inadequacy of reason to the project of comprehending the "void." Beineberg believes in character. For him, character is not an illusion created by the call of the other, but rather an index of strength and power (Peters, 1978). For Beineberg, character is a matter of manhood.

Torless is in the pedagogical experimentation game too, demanding to know, via interviews that fail, how Basini experiences the "other side." It is their love affair that refocuses Torless' desire to experiment. Musil, and many critics, seem quick to concede that the affair with Basini was degrading. The affair becomes justified, Musil suggests, because it eventually leads Torless to greater knowledge, especially of himself, but of others and the world as well. To put the matter differently: for Musil, health and illness are concepts specific to the existing individual. There are individuals who may require illness in order to evolve. Before a moral judgment can be made concerning an illness (or any event or action), it is first necessary to understand the individual's spiritual, intellectual, and emotional situation, as well as of those ideas that frame his or her choices (Peters, 1978). Of course, AIDS is AIDS, but its biographic effect on the sufferer's soul would be, for Musil, not self-evident.

What effect has this episode had upon Basini's soul? Musil does not comment on this point. Clearly his interest is Torless, and, evidently, Basini's meaning *is* his contribution to Torless' self-knowledge and spiritual growth (Peters, 1978). We would seem to have here is an instance of the narcissism that accompanies hegemonic forms of masculinity, a self-absorption that allows others to become "others," useful as they hold significance for oneself, then expendable. Within such character structure, the abject are disavowed. The abject is the other side of the same coin that is the narcissistic self. Other critics have noted that Basini is Torless' double (Webber, 1990).

For Hannah Hickman, Torless' fundamental dilemma is not his involvement in ongoing sadistic sexual assault and torture. Nor is it his discovery of his own homosexual desire and capacity to love a boy. Instead, Torless' dilemma is his incapacity to express these experiences in words. Complicating and intensifying his frustration is the fact that his parents, teachers and even his fellow cadets do not appear to notice anything that he sees. He wonders if he is going mad; his friends and those around him appear completely sane (Hickman, 1984).

It may be true that Musil was not very interested in the events themselves, but, rather, in problems of perception and expression, specifically in the relationship between intellect and emotion. However, it is also true that Musil chose *these* events and characters in order to concentrate on these problems. The problems of intellect and emotion are not necessarily associated with homosexual desire in a heterosexist regime of reason, but certainly they can be linked. The suppression of homosexual desire creates an "inner" and "outer" world, a world of felt emotion and an outer world of appearances. Hickman (1984) puts in the matter this way:

[Torless'] original interests reasserted themselves, leaving him each time with the feeling of constant conflict between his private inclinations and the rationalist and utilitarian ethos of the adult world which resulted in his insecurity and lack of confidence. (p. 35)

This is the conflict, the apparent contradiction, between felt reality and the "world." This "gap" is possible only for the outsider, in Torless' case, a marginality created first by his unusual sensitivity (e.g., "homosexuality") and indeed his participation in the sadomasochistic "experiments" Beineberg and Reiting undertake. Hickman is right not to confine the novel to "adolescence." Like Peters, she notes: "The confusions of Torless may therefore be described as mainly epistemological, but also social. The problems of adolescence add to his difficulties, but it is not helpful to take them as central" (Hickman, 1984, p. 37). In this novel, the epistemological, the social, and gender are intertwined.

The problem of the "epistemological" becomes most vivid toward the end of the novel when Torless attempts to tell his story. Baffled by his vague account, the teachers rework his account into a conventional social or religious narrative, but Torless insists that his interpretation is accurate. Hickman (1984) notes that Torless' stance is not unlike Wittgenstein's: "There are, indeed, things that cannot be put into words. They make themselves manifest. They are what is mystical" (quoted in Hickman, 1974, p. 41).

Torless believes words will come, only if he waits for them. Torless, and Musil, seem to be asserting that words can be fashioned which represent one's "state of mind." This is the "expressivist paradigm" of subjectivity, Stefan Jonsson (2000, p. 38) suggests. This paradigm structured aesthetic and intellectual activity in Europe (especially in Germany and Austria) for almost a century and a half. It ended, Jonsson asserts, with the publication of Musil's *Torless* in 1906:

For if the development of bourgeois society entailed the constitution of a subject split between inwardness and outward activity, it also produced a field of compensatory ideas, a topography of symbols allowing the subject to imagine an expressive relationship to the world by which the division could be healed. (p. 38)

Torless so imagines.

Gert Mattenklott (1973, in Rogowski, 1994)[9] regards Torless as a representation of the disoriented intellectual at the end of the nineteenth century. As a function of this disorientation, local and specific conditions are imagined as global. Just as bourgeoisie obfuscate their own class interests by misrepresenting their problems as expressions of an allegedly universal human condition, Torless too experiences his predicament as an ontological problem. In Mattenklott's reading, Torless' sexual, ethical, and existential crisis reformulates the specific social and political problems of those segments of the middle class that had become marginal in capitalism's movement toward increased monopolization.

The narrative perspective in the novel is complex and volatile, Huber and White (1982) point out. This sophistication is not gratuitous. The narrative perspective is the aesthetic correlative of the complexity and volatility of Torless' experience and development. All that Torless undergoes functions to open a door (for Elizabeth Stopp [in Rogowski 1994], this is a key metaphor) into a world that is beyond—but still implicated in—the everyday world of the knowable and the sayable. Witnessing and participating in the torturing of Basini admits Torless into a world of sado-masochism, of unchartered sexual realms. The discovery of irrational numbers in mathematics prompts Torless to notice that even within the spheres of rigorous logic and quantification, the irrational is evidently necessary in order for practical calculations to work. When Torless gazes at the sky he is reminded that this every-day life is surrounded by and drenched in the infinite, the mysterious (Swales, 1982).

Swales (1982) suggests that Torless develops to the point where his voice, his perceptions, his formulations merge with the voice, perceptions, the formulations of the omniscient narrative voice telling the story. If Torless' development, then, can be seen, as Swales (1982) argues, as an assimilation to the narrative perspective, then this explains perhaps why the narrative voice is so insistent, so fore-grounded. It may recapitulate Musil's own move to heterosexual marriage and "re-spectability," his assimilation to a patriarchal position. Despite Musil's move, his assimilation always remains, like the narrative structure of the novel, complex and volatile.

Margret Rothe-Buddensieg (1974, in Rogowski, 1994) insists on the importance of the sexual theme. Musil's text primarily provides an example of a problematic quest for male identity. She positions the attic as demonic and clandestine counter-idyll to the repressive social reality that is the school. Here, removed from every-day institutional life, Torless is confronted with the sadistic potential of his own sexual desire. His narcissistic crisis—in which both Torless and Basini are impli-cated as subject and object of mutual sexual repression—replicates the patriarchal social structures around them. Rogowski (1994) tells us that Rothe-Buddensieg is the first critic to raise the issue of gender in Musil criticism, pointing to Torless's crisis as a specifically male predicament rather than a gender-neutral, indeed, onto-logical one (Rogowski, 1994).

Also pointing to sexual aspects of Musil's novel and their political and moral implications, David Turner (1974, in Rogowski, 1994) characterizes Torless as an a-moral decadent. His development deviates sharply from the wholesome path of self-cultivation -- *Bildung*, in Goethe's sense -- and instead culminates in a politi-cally dangerous form of aestheticism. Turner's moral indignation with Musil's hero is most apparent when he suggests that Torless belongs to that class of intellectuals who would later opt for political appeasement, accommodating themselves to in-tolerable political conditions via an *inner emigration*, a withdrawal to the ostensi-bly apolitical private sphere (Rogowski, 1994). Likewise, Volker Knüfermann (1986, in Rogowski 1994) argues that Torless survives his crisis by assuming the position of the detached aesthete. Knüfermann concludes that Torless' role-playing allows him to form a self-sufficient identity through aesthetic self-creation (Rogowski, 1994).

Critics make too much of Torless' detachment, I believe. What enables him to survive the crisis—and it is by no means just his but Basini's and the school's as well—is that he falls in love with Basini. Their shared love allows Torless to feel another side of the abusive rituals in the attic. It allows Basini feelings of acceptance, of recognition. Beineberg and Reiting break the scandal, requiring an institutional ending to the episode, but emotionally, in terms of identity, it is Torless' ability to love that enables him some degree of detachment, enabling him to move through the emotionally fraught episode. Interestingly, his "detachment" at the end of the novel is marked by his mother's taking him away, an apparent return to the pre-pubescent quasi-symbiotic relationship of late childhood, i.e., latency. In terms of Grumet's (1988) construal of school curriculum as "bitter milk," it is a matriarchal theft of the boy from patriarchy.

The school had been a kind of double patriarchy: itself run by men for boys preparing for military service. The all-male rape ring, Hans-Georg Pott (1984, in Rogowski, 1994) argues, represents an attempt to structure social (specifically sexual) tendencies excluded from school discourse, from the symbolic order maintained via institutionalized rules of speech and conduct. In its violent aspects, this violent structuration recalls the formation of the "authoritarian personality" formulated by Horkheimer and Adorno (for a review, see Young-Bruehl, 1996).

Like Peters and Hickman, Pott argues that how one thinks and speaks about the world, i.e., discourse, seems to be more important than the characters' actions themselves. Torless is removed from school, Pott suggests, not because he has participated in unsavory activities but because, in his efforts to communicate his disturbing experience, he violated the rules of acceptable speech. It is his poetic mode of speaking, for Potts a deviant discourse that resists assimilation into acceptable speech, that brings Torless into irresolvable conflict with those representatives of the social symbolic order, e.g., the school authorities.

In his participation in homosexual sado-masochism, Torless has encountered— Pott insists—not something beyond the social order, something that might threaten it from the outside. Rather, Pott continues, Torless has encountered something that comprises the very textual center of that social order: the sutures within Western rationality itself. Pott's essay represents, Rogowski's (1994) judgment, a major effort at combining German intellectual traditions (Freud, the Frankfurt School) with French theory (Lacan, Foucault) in the study of *Young Torless*.

As we have seen English-language critics do, Aldo G. Gargani (1984, in Rogowski, 1994) associates Musil's novel with the overall cultural crisis of the period. In a crisis characterized by a complex mix of childhood memories, sensual longings, ecstatic experiences, and a rational quest frustrated by the ineffable and non-rational, Torless slips into the space unarticulated by conventional rationality. He attempts to discover a "new logic," a search characteristic of turn-of-the-century Viennese intellectuals. Like others in the Vienna circle, Torless realizes that these apparently contradictory spheres of existence cannot be isolated but must be regarded as intertwined (Janik and Toulmin, 1973).

Such a realization represents, as Joseph Vogl (1987 in Rogowski, 1994) appreciates, a comprehensive critique of European civilization. Vogl argues that one major motif in the novel is that of the searching gaze that finds no reciprocity. In this respect the novel questions the European idea—an idea structuring the key concept of *Bildung*—that a self is formed in a process of interaction between a subject and an objective world (see Westbury, Hopmann & Riquarts, 2000). Torless seeks affirmation through the transgression of the limits of permissible experience. This apocalyptic interplay of mystery and revelation yields an awareness that the destination of the quest resides outside the spheres of cognition and language.

This antimetaphysical element of *Young Torless* represents, for Vogl, a radicalization of the Enlightenment project of the demystification of belief systems, i.e., the disenchantment of the world in its rationalization. Like Nietzsche before him and Foucault after him (I would add Deleuze to that list), Vogl suggests, Musil is engaged in an effort to establish a new anthropology, an image of human nature and experience grounded in immanence rather than transcendence.

Also taking his cues from critiques of Western rationality by Nietzsche and Foucault, Lucas Cejpek (1984, in Rogowski, 1994) describes Musil's novel as a tension between "reason" and "madness" in European bourgeois civilization. Cejpek defines the historical field in which Musil's novel originates as the pre-War sphere (referring to both World Wars as one connected if separated event) to distinguish it from his own context, that of a post-War perspective. Cejpek argues that war is not an unfortunate aberration from the true nature of European rationalistic civilization but an inevitable consequence of it. Cejpek credits Musil with understanding the madness at the core (or, in Pott's metaphor, the sutures) of Western rationality, one key consequence of the marginalization of what cannot be integrated by "reason." Cejpek suggests that all utopian models remain confined within the destructive logic of European culture and therefore cannot be viewed as real or desirable (quoted phrases in Rogowski 1994, p. 165). Confining her critique to Christian culture, Marla Morris (2001) makes the same point.

CONCLUSION

The unconscious is this: that persistence on another scene, contrary to our clear and distinct reflections, of a link which can no longer be conceptualized.

Jean-Joseph Goux (1992, p. 52)

Literary educational research enables us to see not only visible political, historical and institutional structures (such as the school), it enables us to study our inner experience of such structures. In *Young Torless*, we gain a glimpse of the historical situation faced by Europeans living at the end of nineteenth and the beginning of the twentieth century, what will turn out to be the bloodiest century in recorded human history. This pungent and corrosive moment—the end of the Hapsburg Empire—had not yet devolved into an irreparable political crisis, but it was a cultural crisis[10] in which various artists and intellectuals—Musil and Freud among them—labored to articulate their lived experience of the sutures linking and the ruptures separating reason and passion, sexual desire and respectability, ethics and experimentation.

For students of education, the novel underscores the dangers of a school curriculum estranged from the lived experience of students (see Pope, 2001). While one cannot characterize the sexual assaults on Basini as a consequence of the school curriculum (its inability, metaphorically, to incorporate non-rational numbers), we cannot understand the event apart from it either, as the literary scholarship we have just glimpsed makes clear. In our time, I link the curriculum taught to standardized examinations (rather than directed to the inner experience of students) to an intensification of bullying and other forms violent alienation, such as substance abuse. There is no simple cause-effect relationship, of course, but the latter cannot be comprehended apart from the former. While the school curriculum cannot be organized only around students' experience and interests, it is, I submit, educationally and cultural catastrophic to sever it from them (see Pinar, 2004).

After Pott, we can understand bullying—like the activities of the triumvirate in *Young Torless*—as an effort to structure the social estrangement the school ignores or, through its institutionalization of "reason," is unable to acknowledge in the curriculum. More specifically, bullying structures the disavowal of homosexual desire all men—but, apparently, especially adolescent boys—experience but are prohibited from exploring. This specific authoritarian structuration of disavowed homosexual desire expressed a European crisis of masculinity discussed extensively by historians and cultural critics (see Pinar 2006b, chapter 5). While the nightmarish events of the twentieth century cannot be understood only in gendered terms, they cannot be grasped apart from them, either.

While a contested term (see Pinar 2001, chapter 6), the crisis of masculinity was not limited to fin-de-siecle Europe; it was, at the same time, pandemic in America (see Pinar, 2001). Nor is it limited to the West. Boys who do not demonstrate the toughness almost universally associated with manhood (Gilmore, 1990) can be targets for those whose inner ambivalence can admit of no external threats. "Beating a homosexual," Elisabeth Young-Bruehl (1996, p. 317) points out, "is like beating down a possibility in the self, from the past." For many, this process requires exclusion of sexual complexity or, as Musil would have it, "confusion." But bullying accomplishes more, as Scott S. Derrick (1997, p. 81) observes,

> Violence sublimates same-sex desire and reinforces paranoid distances between men. At the same time, it terrorizes and subjugates women who are necessary to establish the heterosexuality of the masculine order.

Like the Hapsburg Empire, it is an order best located in the past.

ACKNOWLEDGEMENT

My thanks to Peter Taubman for introducing me to Musil and to Alan Block for engaging my questions regarding *Young Torless*.

## NOTES

[1]. "Adolescence" is culturally constructed (see Lesko, 2001).

[2]. While hardly alone, probably no scholar has more famously employed fiction and literary theory to study education than Maxine Greene.

[3]. All references are to the 1955 edition.

[4]. Musil is not being theological; he associates soul with a person's "inner contour," what is an "ulti-mate" and "immovable background" (pp. 10-11).

[5]. When Adrian LeDuc (played by Colin Firth) confronts his handsome roommate Jack Carney (played by Hart Bochner) in the film "Apartment Zero," demanding to know who he is, Bochner's character replies, seductively, "whoever you want me to be."

[6]. With that word, of course, U.S. readers are back in the ante-bellum South; no one expresses its psy-cho-sexual scenes of subjugation more insightfully than Saidiya Hartman (1997).

[7]. Burroughs (1992 [1959]) comes to mind, of course, as does the psychoanalytic and specifically La-canian idea that one's reflection in the mirror guarantees self-misrecognition (see, for instance, Silverman 1988).

[8]. This is a point, may I say, I made more than twenty years ago in regarding to the production of mascu-linity (Pinar, 1983).

[9]. Much Musil criticism has not been translated into English; Rogowski reports some of it.

[10]. The European cultural crisis of the late nineteenth century is resonate, I suggest, with the contempo-rary crisis of European culture in America (see Pinar 2002).

## REFERENCES

Aoki, T. T. (2005 [1985/1991]). Signs of vitality in curriculum scholarship. In William F. Pinar and Rita L. Irwin (Eds.), *Curriculum in a New Key* (pp. 229-233). Mahwah, NJ: Lawrence Erlbaum.

*Apartment Zero* (1988). Summit Company. Produced by Stephen Cole. Directed by Martin Donovan. Starring Colin Firth, Hart Bochner.

Baker, B. M. (2001). *In perpetual motion: Theories of power, educational history, and the child.* New York: Peter Lang.

Bersani, L. (1995). *Homos.* Cambridge, MA: Harvard University Press.

Burroughs, W. S. (1992 [1959]). *Naked lunch.* New York: Grove Press.

Butler, J. (1997). *The psychic life of power: Theories in subjection.* Stanford, CA: Stanford University Press.

Chodorow, N. (1978). *The reproduction of mothering.* Berkeley, CA: University of California Press.

Coetzee, J. M. (2001). Introduction to Robert Musil's *The Confusions of Young Torless.* New York: Penguin.

de Lauretis, T. (1994). Habit changes. *Differences, 6,* 296-313.

Derrick, S. S. (1997). *Monumental anxieties: Homoerotic desire and feminine influence in nineteenth-century U.S. literature.* New Brunswick, NJ: Rutgers University Press.

Doty, Al. (1993). *Making things perfectly queer.* Minneapolis, MN: University of Minnesota Press.

Elkins, S. M. (1959). *Slavery: A problem in American institutional and intellectual life.* Chicago: Uni-versity of Chicago Press.

Fanon, F. (1967). *Black skin, white masks.* [Trans. by Charles Lam Markmann.] New York: Grove Weidenfeld. [Originally published in French under the title *Peau Noire, Masques Blancs*, copyright 1952 by Editions du Seuil, Paris.]

Gilmore, D. (1990). *Manhood in the making.* New Haven: Yale University Press.

Goux, J.-J. (1992). The phallus: Masculine identity and the "exchange of women." [Trans. by Maria Amuchastegui, Caroline Benforado, Amy Hendrix, and Eleanor Kaufman. *Differences, 4,* 40-75.

Grumet, M. R. (1988). *Bitter milk: Women and teaching.* Amherst: University of Massachusetts Press.

Hartman, S. V. (1997). *Scenes of subjection: Terror, slavery, and self-making in nineteenth century America.* New York: Oxford University Press.

Hickman, H. (1984). *Robert Musil and the culture of Vienna.* London: Croom Helm.

Hocquenghem, G. (1978). *Homosexual desire.* London: Allison & Busby.

Huebner, D. E. (1999). *The lure of the transcendent.* Mahwah, NJ: Lawrence Erlbaum.

Jay, M. (2005). *Songs of experience: Modern American and European variations on a universal theme.* Berkeley: University of California Press.

Jonsson, S. (2000). *Subject without nation: Robert Musil and the history of modern identity.* Durham, NC: Duke University Press.

Lesko, N. (2001). Act your age! A cultural construction of adolescence. New York: Routledge/Falmer.

Miller, J. E. (1993). *The passion of Michel Foucault.* New York: Simon & Schuster.

Morris, M. (2001). *Holocaust and curriculum.* Mahwah, NJ: Lawrence Erlbaum.

Mosse, G. L. (1985). *Nationalism and sexuality: Respectability and abnormal sexuality in modern Europe.* New York: Howard Fertig.

Mosse, G. L. (1996). *The image of man: The creation of modern masculinity.* New York: Oxford University Press.

Musil, R. (1955 [1906]). *Young Torless.* [Preface by Alan Pryce-Jones.] New York: Pantheon Books Inc.

Musil, R. (1990). *Precision and soul: Essays and addresses.* [Edited and translated by B. Pike & D. S. Luft.] Chicago and London: University of Chicago Press.

Musil, R. (1995). *The Man Without Qualities.* [Trans. by S. Perkins & B. Pike.] New York: Knopf.

Peters, F. G. (1978) *Robert Musil: Master of the hovering life.* New York: Columbia University Press.

Pike, B. (1961). *Robert Musil: An introduction to his work.* Ithaca, New York: Cornell University Press.

Pinar, W. F. (1983). Curriculum as gender text: Notes on reproduction, resistance, and male-male relations. *JCT, 5,* 26-52. Reprinted in *Autobiography, politics, and sexuality: Essays in curriculum theory 1972-1992* (1994, Peter Lang.)

Pinar, W. F. (1988). Autobiography and the architecture of self. *JCT, 8,* 7-36. Reprinted in *Autobiography, politics, and sexuality: Essays in curriculum theory 1972-1992* (1994, Peter Lang).

Pinar, W. F. (2001). *The gender of racial politics and violence in America: Lynching, prison rape, and the crisis of masculinity.* New York: Peter Lang.

Pinar, W. F. (2002). Robert Musil and the Crisis of European Culture in America. In William E. Doll, Jr. and Noel Gough (eds.), *Curriculum Visions* (pp. 102-110). New York: Peter Lang.

Pinar, W. F. (2004). *What is curriculum theory?* Mahwah, NJ: Lawrence Erlbaum.

Pinar, W. F. (2006a). *The synoptic text today and other essays: Curriculum development after the Reconceptualization.* New York: Peter Lang.

Pinar, W. F. (2006b). *Race, religion, and a curriculum of reparation.* New York: Palgrave Macmillan.

Pope, D. C. (2001). *Doing school: How we are creating a generation of stressed out, materialistic, and miseducated students.* New Haven: Yale University Press.

Rogowski, C. (1994). *Distinguished outsider: Robert Musil and his critics.* Columbia, SC: Camden House.

Said, E. W. (1979). *Orientalism.* New York: Vintage.

Sartre, J.-P. (1964). *Nausea.* New York: New Directions.

Scarce, M. (1997). *Male on male rape.* New York: Insight Books/Plenum Publishing Corporation.

Silverman, K. (1988). *The acoustic mirror: The female voice in psychoanalysis and cinema.* Bloomington: Indiana University Press.

Silverman, K. (2000). *World spectators.* Stanford, CA: Stanford University Press.

Simpson, M. (1994). *Male impersonators: Men performing masculinity.* [Foreword by Alan Sinfield.] New York: Routledge.

Stokes, M. (2001). *The color of sex: Whiteness, heterosexuality, & the fictions of white supremacy.* Durham, NC: Duke University Press.

Stoler, A. L. (1995). *Race and the education of desire: Foucault's history of sexuality and the colonial order of things*. Durham, NC: Duke University Press.

Taubman, P. (1992). Personal correspondence.

Webber, A. (1990). *Sexuality and the sense of self in the works of George Trakl and Robert Musil*. London: The Modern Humanities Research Association for the Institute of Germanic Studies, University of London.

Westbury, I., Hopmann, S., & Riquarts, K. (Eds.) (2000). *Teaching as reflective practice: The German didaktik tradition*. Mahweh, New Jersey: Lawrence Erlbaum Associates, Publishers.

Winnicott, D. W. (1990) *Playing and reality*. New York: Routledge.

Young-Bruehl, E. (1996). *The anatomy of prejudices*. Cambridge, MA: Harvard University Press.

Zizek, S. (1991). Looking awry: An introduction to Jacques Lacan to popular culture. Cambridge, MA: The MIT Press.

ALICE J. PITT AND DEBORAH P. BRITZMAN

# 15. SPECULATIONS ON QUALITIES OF DIFFICULT KNOWLEDGE IN TEACHING AND LEARNING

*An Experiment in Psychoanalytic Research*

Our research project wavers between two questions and the theoretical issues prompted by each: What makes knowledge difficult, and what is it to represent and narrate "difficult knowledge"? Whereas the first question resides in the content of knowledge, the second foregrounds issues of encountering the self through the otherness of knowledge. Moreover, if the first question takes its inspiration from psychoanalytic theories of trauma, it is the second question that moves us un-equivocally into the more general realm of the psychical dynamics that animate teaching and learning. These questions and the oscillations between them charac-terize what Britzman (1998) has called "difficult knowledge," a concept meant to signify both representations of social traumas in curriculum and the individual's encounters with them in pedagogy.

Our project centred difficult knowledge as intersecting philosophical, peda-gogical and methodological dilemmas. Philosophically, we were drawn to discus-sions of postmodernity that question the status of knowledge, authority and power in the university (Lyotard, 1987; Code, 1991; Readings, 1996; Martin, 1997). These were brought into tension with pedagogical discussions on what learning means when knowledge references incommensurability, historical trauma, and social breakdowns (Felman & Laub, 1992; Caruth, 1996; Ellsworth, 1997; Britz-man, 1998; Cheng, 2001). Both philosophical and pedagogical views of "difficult knowledge" question the relationship between education and social justice because they assume, albeit differently, a kernel of trauma in the very capacity to know. Contemporary efforts in critical, feminist, and gay-affirmative pedagogies elabo-rate some of these breakdowns in understanding. They focus on understanding the interests of learners to engage critically both with narratives of historical traumas such as genocide, slavery, and forms of social hatred *and* questions of equity, de-mocracy and human rights (McCarthy & Crichlow, 1993; Pinar, 1998; Simon et al, 2000). For pedagogical theorists, "difficult knowledge" also signifies the problem of learning from social breakdowns in ways that might open teachers and students to their present ethical obligations (Britzman, 2000; Pinar, 2001; Todd, 2001).

*K. Tobin & J. Kincheloe, (eds.), Doing Educational Research—A Handbook, 379–401.*

Our second question, what it means to represent and narrate "difficult knowledge," also draws some of its urgency from contemporary methodological discussions in education on the uses of poststructuralism in qualitative research raised by Bloom (1998), Lather (2000; In Press), Laws and Davies (2000), Rhedding-Jones (2000), St. Pierre and Pillow (2000), Talburt (2000), and Yon (2000). Poststructuralist method heightens the problem of the verisimilitude embedded in such foundational concepts in qualitative studies as voice, identity, agency, and experience while still expecting to offer some contingent observations about how individuals – including the researcher– make knowledge in and of the world. This methodology offers a new tension to educational studies by bringing to bear on participant narratives the very problem of narrating experience and by asking what conditions or structures the narrative impulse. This linguistic turn in qualitative research is now known as "the crisis of representation" in that the adequacy of language to capture experience is considered an effect of discourse rather than a reflection of that experience.

Yet if we consider psychical dynamics as influencing and being influenced by encounters with knowledge, there is, working in our research questions, a further problem. If the crisis of representation is made from the logical priority of expression over experience (Volosinov, 1986), psychoanalytic research (Felman & Laub, 1992; Young, 1994; Phillips, 1998; Appel, 1999; Chodorow, 1999) adds another dimension to this crisis, making the sum of our philosophical, pedagogical, and methodological concerns into a complex. Significant psychoanalytic concepts– namely the unconscious, phantasy[1], affect and sexuality– all work to unseat the authorial capabilities of expression to account exhaustively for qualities of experience, to view history as a causal process, and to separate reality from phantasy. In other words, psychoanalytic inquiry begins with the problem of resistance to discourse, and, as Laplanche reminds us, "must take account of the fact that the human subject is a theorizing being and a being that theorizes itself" (1989, p. 10). Socially-sanctioned discourses play a role in self-theorizing activities but do not exhaust the material. Psychoanalytic research posits education as an exemplary site where the crisis of representation that is outside meets the crisis of representation that is inside (Britzman, 1998; Pitt, 2000). Freud (1914a, p. 154) called this unexpected meeting "the playground of transference," where the means of knowing cannot be separated from one's own libidinal history of learning. We have come to believe that traces of this representational crisis, conveyed through the transference, can be theorized from attempts to narrate teaching and learning.

In this chapter we speculate on the various resonances that the crisis of representation leaves in narration by way of three psychoanalytic concepts: deferred action, transference, and symbolization. Because knowledge is lost and found in these psychical dynamics, they leave traces in narratives about knowledge. We are calling these traces "difficult knowledge." We consider constructions of difficulties in teaching and learning from the vantage of psychoanalytic writing and our own attempts to interview university teachers and students on how they think about difficult knowledge.[2] Throughout this paper, we elaborate a constitutive difficulty educational research confronts, namely representing teaching and learning. Thinking about this constitutive difficulty challenges us to rethink what counts as data and what data counts as. Thus, in this chapter, we move from being preoccupied with the content of our inquiry– that is with considering "data" as a property of what participants produce and as the culmination of research– to what we can learn about theory and narrative by working psychoanalytically.

We begin with a conceptual archaeology of our project. This is followed by discussions of three contexts where difficulties are elaborated, each of which is a resource that orients us toward our speculations on the qualities of difficult knowledge in teaching and learning. We first offer some clinical discussion written by psychoanalysts on the difficulties of narrating teaching and learning. We then provide some constructions of difficulty proposed in a "thought experiment" we designed as the basis for interviews with university teachers and students. Finally, we turn to further research constructions of difficulty in our interviews. We conclude with the claim that research cannot be immune from crises of representation in education and that the very design of narrative research enacts the crisis of representing teaching and learning.

## THREE METAPHORS FOR RESEARCH: A CONCEPTUAL ARCHEOLOGY

To understand something about what makes knowledge difficult, our first research question, we turned to Steiner's (1980) essay, "On difficulty," on reading poetry and then to psychoanalytic theories of trauma. We wondered about metaphors of learning that might serve as an index for cataloguing "difficult knowledge." Poetry, the focus of Steiner's study, is a useful metaphor for inquiry in that the evocative qualities that language conveys resist interpretation, and this struggle is an important aspect of experiencing the strange demands of the poem. There is, in the reading of a poem, a felt tension between idea and affect and questions about the very nature of representation and understanding. There is a gap between experiencing the poem and recounting its meaning. Steiner offers four categories for grasping the individual's struggles with the elegiac text: contingent difficulties require homework to fill in the reader's gap of knowledge; modal difficulties concern the problem of constructing relevance; tactical difficulties draw attention to conflicts within the poem between innermost meaning and public statements; and, finally, ontological difficulties are met when the poem calls attention to the very possibility of understanding and communication as we know them (pp. 22-47). Steiner's categories did seem pertinent to relations between text and reader; they did not, however, illuminate for us the pushes and pulls in social relations that also compose the psychical landscape of teaching and learning in classrooms. Nor could Steiner's model address the work of phantasy, a concept to which we return in the next section.

Contemporary uses of psychoanalytic theories of trauma in the humanities (Felman & Laub, 1992; Caruth, 1996) offered a second metaphor for thinking about difficult knowledge as a complex event. The event of trauma is characterized by a quality of significance that resists meaning even as the affective force of the event can be felt. Caruth (1996) uses the term "unclaimed experience" to suggest the paradox of having painful experience but being unable to know just what has happened or why it is important to one's present. Originally, theories of trauma were useful to us because they centre the quagmire of insufficiency of knowledge, primal helplessness, and the incapacity to respond adequately. These dynamics, we believe, characterize one's early experiences in having to learn and later return as anxiety when one faces new knowledge that requires something significant of the learner.[3] And yet, the metaphor of trauma for our inquiry was not so useful in a key way: it occluded our own consideration of what happens when experience is merely conflicted, not elided. We began to wonder if our interest in the relation between historical knowledge that emerges in the wake of profound social traumas and learning from such knowledge foreclosed a curiosity toward the ways in which people do construct, through the transference and from their narratives of teaching and learning, emotional significance.

Our first question, "what makes knowledge difficult in teaching and learning"?, one that emerged from our early work with Steiner's index and with psychoanalytic theories of trauma, transformed into our second question, now refined as follows: How do difficulties interfere with the coherence of narrative construction as part of the complex of difficult knowledge alluded to earlier? Now we are able to consider, not only our own experiences of difficulty in writing this chapter, but, more generally, what our psychoanalytic research has come to be about: tracing the difficulties of representing teaching and learning in research itself.

Our research story, then, is told in the strange time of deferred action, a psychoanalytic concept that heightens the problem of how emotional significance and new ideas are made from past and present experiences. The supposition is that settling on significance is delayed for two reasons: the force of an event is felt before it can be understood, and a current event may take its force and revisions from an earlier scene. While the notion of deferred action is closely tied to Freud's theory of trauma, it can also signal more ordinary phenomena and therefore be used as a bridging concept between traumatic crises and thinking about them. In the time of deferred action, old experiences can be revised, and new psychical significance to current and past events can be constructed (Laplanche & Pontalis, 1973, p. 111). The new event, however, bears the traces of the dynamics of earlier experience even as the earlier experience can be revised. Conceptualizing the strange time of deferred action brings us to the intimacy of the psychoanalytic dialogue and the third metaphor for our inquiry: clinical experience. Such experience serves, not only as the grounds of therapy, but also as the laboratory for psychoanalytic research into its own theories and practices.

While we will suggest, over the course of this paper, what it means for us to do psychoanalytically-informed research, here we want to provide a brief sketch of some qualities that distinguish this approach. As we have just suggested, emotional significance is constituted in the time of deferred action (Bollas, 1999). Understanding, then, is not a feature of experience but a problem of symbolization. This leads to another quality of psychoanalytic research: the strange and conflictive interplay between data and theory. Both are narratives, yet neither is beholden to empirical claims nor confirmed through observation (Freud, 1900; Green, 2000).

They gain their currency through speculation and belief because narratives are not the culmination of experience but constructions made from both conscious and unconscious dynamics. Data and theory, therefore, are like dreams in that they work at two levels, the manifest and the latent (Kohon, 1999; Kristeva, 2000a). While a narrative is made from a specific context, the affective force of what precisely is represented in narrative may derive from other scenes and from unresolved psychical conflicts. This is the dynamic of transference where one makes sense of new situations through the imperatives of older conflicts. In this view, representation is a compromise, an attempt to ward off crisis, because constructions are made from an argument between the wish for coherence and the anxiety over what coherence excludes (Little, 1990; Kristeva, 2000b; Bass, 2001; Kristeva, 2000b). All of these qualities suggest an interpretive paradox at the heart of psychoanalytic inquiry: interpretation makes narrative, but there is also something within narrative that resists its own interpretation. There can be no original moment in research that gives birth to interpretation even as we must use narratives as the force of interpretive research. The next section illustrates this dilemma.

## SOME CLINICAL EXAMPLES OF DIFFICULTY IN NARRATING TEACHING AND LEARNING

In the clinical setting something of the intimacies of narrative in terms of its surprising associations, or the things furthest from one's mind, are reconstructed through the analytic dialogue by means of the push and pull of interpretations. This is slow work. Freud (1937, p. 261) named any encounter with interpretation "a preliminary labour performed by constructions" because narrative for Freud is inaugurated by a confusion of time, and this makes reasoned persuasion futile. Indeed, because both agreement and disagreement are also constructions, for any construction to matter, it must bear the cumulative weight of an event's emotional significance. When presentation and representation meet, symbolization emerges. But emotional significance is not something one makes once and for all because of the confusion of time that is narration. Where does one situate the event that is experience, in the past that is narrated or in the presence of its interpretation? For Freud both positions of time are embodied in the transference. We believe that construction as a problem of time and place opens a new question for the work of representing teaching and learning: how does one distinguish between obstacles to teaching and learning and obstacles to representing teaching and learning? As we will see, there is something utterly difficult about our recollections in terms of our capacity to locate them in the past and understand what they can mean for the present. What makes recollections of our educational history a form of difficult knowledge is that obstacles to learning become entangled with obstacles to representing learning.

Freud's (1914b, p. 241) efforts to recollect his own schoolboy days suggests this difficulty:

It gives you a queer feeling if, late in life, you are ordered once again to write a school essay. But you obey automatically, like the old solider who, at the word 'Attention!', cannot help dropping whatever he may have had in his hands and who finds his little fingers pressed along the seams of his trousers. It is strange how readily you obey the orders, as though nothing in particular had happened in the last half century.

Originally written for a celebration of the 50th anniversary of a school Freud attended as an adolescent, today "Some reflections on schoolboy psychology" is read less as an affirmation than as a reminder of the difficulties one confronts when trying to reflect upon and remember experiences of learning and teaching. One key difficulty is that school memories invoke not just relations with authority but also repeat one's own childhood helplessness, dependency, and desire to please. This strange combination means that reflecting on one's learning seems necessarily to pass through these unbidden repetitions of love, hate and ambivalence that make the transference, reminding us of the very earliest scenes of education, learning for love, even as we encounter ideas and selves that seem far removed in time.

But an earlier problem is also significant here. What happens when school experience cannot be recollected? Psychoanalyst Milner (1993) offers a description of her work with an eleven-year-old boy who was "suffering from a loss of talent for school work" (p. 18). She explores the force of these conflicts prior to their symbolization and narrates one game the boy devised for her in the analytic setting:

> [H]e himself became the sadistic punishing schoolmaster, and I had to be the bad pupil. For days, and sometimes weeks, I had to play the role of the persecuted schoolboy: I was set long monotonous tasks, my efforts were treated with scorn, I was forbidden to talk and made to write out "lines" if I did; and if I did not comply with these demands, then he wanted to cane me. (p. 21)

Milner assures us that the boy knew that he had never been treated as badly as he was treating his analyst. Even though the school made efforts to "adapt to his difficulties" (p. 21), she also suggests that memories of learning are closely tied to phantasies of refusing to learn, an insight that helped us think about the paradox of research discussed in our introduction. Phantasies of refusing to learn can take the form of reversing positions where the helpless learner becomes the demanding teacher. Then, not learning is symbolically equated with having to be punished. This little boy's distress was impervious to the demands of reason, and Milner's sense of frustration in her role as powerless schoolboy testifies eloquently to the boy's emotional reality. The boy's transference of an imagined education onto his present conflicts represents, for Milner, "difficulties in establishing the relation to external reality as such" (p. 21). As the boy's capacity to play creatively with the toys provided by the analyst increased, so too did his ability to symbolize his school experience with greater fluency, less as an equation where the symbol becomes collapsed with the object it represents, and more as construction (see also Segal, 1997). He began to tolerate the inevitable frustrations of learning while also being able to enjoy his engagements with knowledge. If transference is an obstacle to representing learning in the present, symbolization allows one to return the obstacles to the archaic conflicts they represent.

The work of symbolization, clearly at stake in both producing knowledge and reflecting upon learning, provides a route out of the tensions of childhood helplessness alluded to in Freud's narrative and enacted in the game Milner must play. Milner speculates that symbolization cannot be confined to the developmental task of adapting to external reality. For adapting to reality, at least in psychoanalytic views, may be akin to closing the gap between the symbol and that to which it refers. This is compliance, and it is justifiably experienced as coercion. Symbolization, she suggests, does not merely name the world and its objects; it also reflects the capacity to express emotional significance within a symbolic language (see also Mannoni, 1999). That is, in symbolization, the idea and the affect influence one another. This relation is, for Milner, the grounds of creative thought. But because symbolization flows from the oscillations between the necessity to search for substitutes for original objects and "the emotional experience of finding the substitute" (p. 17), its rational quota can become undone by an excess of affect. Here too, between the agony of losing beloved (though also often feared) objects and the ecstasy of finding beautiful substitutes, questions of knowledge are made and broken.

These two stories of clinical experience, one from the vantage of maturity and the other more firmly anchored in the time of dependence, testify to the difficulties of representing our most meaningful encounters with knowledge and learning. This brings us to an intimate problem: learning is uncannily organized by repetition of past investments and conflicts–or, in short hand, new editions of old conflicts– projected onto present experiences, people, and events. Transference poses intimate problems for representing learning (Britzman & Pitt, 1996; 2004) because presentations of learning are still imbued with phantasies and are not yet representations. Our focus on the transferential qualities of learning works against the idea that the grounds of knowledge are made rationally and that rationality will somehow win out, provided that the knowledge is persuasive enough, that the teacher creates sufficient scaffolding, and that the learner is able to use what is provided[4]. Instead, the transference represents both the obstacles and promise made from emotional ties consisting of love, hate, and ambivalence toward both new and old events. Transference is the signature we make upon histories of learning, but it writes in invisible ink. If learning begins with efforts to sustain one's continuity– through familiarity– the transference represents something of one's unresolved conflicts that remain obscured until acknowledgement of the emotional experience of knowledge itself can be symbolized. These are the problems that our protocol invoked both for the participants and for us.

## SOME RESEARCH CONSTRUCTIONS OF DIFFICULTY

We created a "thought experiment" to help university teachers and students talk about the emotional significance of their encounters with "difficult knowledge." The document (see Appendix A) did become the basis of conversation, and at first we thought of the interviews as our "research data." This formulation and the chronology it assumes are, however, at odd with our theory. Our "thought experiment" is already both interpretation and data, and we asked participants to make a relationship to it. But here is precisely where narrative loses its referent: just as there is no original moment to interpretation, there is no original thing as "data." While we had hoped that participants could make coherent narratives of teaching and learning, one inaugural difficulty that we failed to appreciate is just how utterly difficult it is to represent teaching and learning. What we came to understand, long after the interviews were over, was that our research document became, for our participants, a metaphor for difficult knowledge.

The document lists affective experiences in constructing knowledge and therefore invites reflections on how individuals conceptualize knowledge when meaning breaks down and when they attempt some sort of repair, with what comes to count as difficult for them in teaching and learning, with how they describe the qualities of knowledge in difficulty, and with how they characterize and perhaps work through problems of emotional significance in pedagogical encounters with others or with texts. Divided into fifteen topics, all of which begin with the heading "Thinking About," the document asks for discussion on the following kinds of experience: breakdowns with others, fights with knowledge, experiences of influence, aloneness, hostility, anxiety, and confusion in teaching and learning, encounters with authority, insufficient knowledge, and promises of knowledge, desires for relevance, privacy, and hiding, and views on obstacles to learning, writing, and speaking. Our "thought experiment" is rich in negativity, in the insistence that conflict provokes learning, and in the view that acquiring knowledge is a transferential relation characterized through the dynamic of resistance– an odd combination of new editions of old conflicts, of relations and fights with new and old forms of authority, as ambivalent and partial, and as charged by tonalities of love and hate.

Participants received the document a few days prior to the hour-long interview so that they could consider the project's interests as they reflected on their own experiences. Their thoughts on what they had read structured the discussion, and individuals were invited to comment upon, in any order, whatever aspects of the document they found interesting, and including the structure and contents of the "thought experiment." Only now do we understand this difficulty. While we had hoped to move people from discussing obstacles to teaching and learning to discussing obstacles to representing teaching and learning, the experiment was also, for everyone involved, an experience[5] that presented two kinds of obstacles: it was an obstacle to interpret and an obstacle to interpretation.

We asked participants to set their emotions and intellect side by side as they considered experiences of difficulty in knowledge. What they produced was a blend of plot-driven narratives and something akin to what Julia Kristeva (2000b, p. 3) calls 'pre-narrative envelopes': "This pre-narrative envelope amounts to an emotional experience, both physical and subjective based on the drives in an interpersonal context. In other words, it is a mental construct that emerges from the real world: an 'emerging property' of thought." Individuals tried to grapple with emotions that came first on their way to knowledge, but they were caught as well in trying to articulate this coherently. They often met an obstacle made from a collision between the force of their affect and the insistence of the idea itself. Frequently, talk about affective attachment to knowledge could not create enough distance for this knowledge to have an existence outside of the force of the emotional response. While knowledge did not cause their affective response, it surely became entangled in it. We attribute this to a constitutive difficulty of that other scene: what it means to create a narrative and consider narrative as both construction and as resistance to construction.

If the crisis of representation plays out during our efforts to narrate teaching and learning, our research on how difficult knowledge is encountered and made significant continues this dilemma. In reading our interview transcripts, we at first wondered who and what are represented in these stories. At the manifest level, individuals were offering stories of their identity and experience. And yet many of the narratives resisted the coherence brought by their identity claims because, in stories of breakdown, the ideal self cannot be represented. That is, while the content of the story tried to settle the meaning, the structure and dynamics of the story hinted at the intrusion of another time: when meaning had lost its valency and when phantasy both propelled and impeded the construction of knowledge. Here, language becomes implicated in the communicative performance: there may be no words or too many words. Kristeva's notion of the pre-narrative envelope suggests this dilemma: the force of conflict bothers the narrative's attempt to make closure.

When individuals narrate experience, they also express their affective investments in knowing and being known, in new editions of old educational conflicts, and in their fragile work of reconsidering what shall count as worthy and worthless in teaching and learning. These dynamics, as we have tried to show, also transformed and refined our research questions. We now offer fragments from five interviews and ask the following question: What can we learn about the crisis of representing teaching and learning from reading conflicted stories about encounters with knowledge?

## PARTICIPANTS' CONSTRUCTIONS OF DIFFICULTY MADE FROM THE PROTOCOL

An undergraduate student expresses strong feelings in all of her narratives. Her relations to knowledge are described as marked by a strange combination of fear, hostility, and excitement. Early on in the interview, she offers an example of how she understands the transformative force of knowledge as a danger to the self:

> there's a lot of books I'm afraid to pick up because I am afraid it's going to shake my entire foundation. . . . I believe in evolution . . . and Darwin's theory of natural selection, and there's a book now which is called Darwin's Black Box, and it's in direct conflict with you know, and I'm afraid to pick it up cause now where's that going to leave me? . . . A lot of things would just fall out from under me . . . where would I be?

Conflict, in the stories this student tells about knowledge, is a vibrant force that animates her interest in learning and her ambivalence toward the power of knowledge to influence. Even though several of her stories take up knowledge as something to be warded off or something that might be pulled out from under her, she also expresses anger at those who withhold knowledge that she has come to deem important (such as knowledge about the cruel treatment of animals that we use for food). She recounts times when her own impatience and anger interfered with her capacity to make use of knowledge and classroom experience. She worries about using her knowledge to create crises of belief in others while at the same time remaining convinced that others need access to her point of view. Knowledge seems propelled by two phantasies. It might be a magical weapon that bestows control and power upon her when she is the one who possesses it. At the same time, being in possession of knowledge can leave her vulnerable: others might steal it away. If knowledge seems almost magical in its capacity to transform the self, it may be because knowledge returns to the self as belief that threatens to crumble. Belief may locate the self, but knowledge can make it disappear. Influence rests uneasily between knowledge and belief, threatening both.

Some of these dynamics repeat with another undergraduate student who begins to discuss "Times when an idea or a viewpoint prompted you to reconsider previous views." In creating this prompt, we had assumed that individuals would already be in a position of having worked through initial difficulties with contradictory ideas. But this narrative suggests the difficulties of trying to settle, once and for all, the place new knowledge occupies when old beliefs persist. This psychology major enrolled in a feminist course on mothering and motherhood and was surprised to encounter perspectives that called into question her previous theories of child development. Her old theories had not addressed the possibility that the child makes the parent: "... a lot of theories . . . in psychology always tend to, well, how it's affecting the child, but little is there ever talked about how the parent is affected by the child." She came to value a feminist perspective but worried about what that would do to her old knowledge of psychology.

This student articulates two kinds of worries, both of which continue her anxiety over influencing others or being influenced. She has the impression that she would have to abandon all psychoanalytic theory, which she enjoys, in order to pursue new lines of inquiry made from feminist critique. While she views feminism as holding great relevance for her life and thought, she also finds value in the Freudian concept of the unconscious. She answers her unspoken question, "Must I choose?", with an anxiety that anticipates the consequences of fighting openly with the traditions of psychology. Is it the case that one can revise received ideas without also running into the received self?

> I'm beginning to think perhaps . . . my imagination I know could run wild but just maybe little things like not, well not little things, but not getting grants for particular research . . . . "no, no, sorry, we can't . . . give you money for that research or it's not going to be easy to publish." Even if I did get the money, it may not be published or received very well, and even though I

know that I shouldn't really necessarily care what others think, I could see that opening me to a lot of scrutiny.

At the level of manifest content, we see an undergraduate quite puzzled about the daily work of academics. In a certain way her over-populated phantasy does contain what Freud (1937) observed as "a kernel of historical truth" with punishing institutions and arbitrary decisions. If at the manifest level, she may be intimating the dilemma between theoretical integrity and institutional recognition, at the latent level, the workings of knowledge are not easily discerned. As the conversation proceeds, her struggles with knowledge become ever more difficult to untangle from obstacles to learning. Just as the boy in Milner's story became the punishing teacher in order to deflect his own feelings of being misunderstood, this student rehearses the punishments of having to learn by insisting that her intuition is devalued; that if texts are difficult, they hold no meaning; and teachers bore her with their knowledge. At first glance, the influence of others is refused in all of these turns, yet her statement," I know that I shouldn't necessarily care what others think" may be a negation of the conflict. For if the thoughts of others mattered, what would happen to hers?

When she discussed her strategies for working through dense texts, the difference between obstacles to learning and obstacles to representing learning collapses:

> Don't give me that schmancy fancy kind of stuff. Give me, just give me the idea. And from there I like to work with a method. I don't like working with ideas.

As each kernel of her narrative suggests, one never just gets the idea at two levels: ideas are not transmitted, nor are they immediately available for use. But there is something more, and this returns us to what the protocol was asking. While the notion of influence appears throughout the protocol, we are beginning to appreciate just what a pervasive and threatening force it is to imagine the self as influenced by knowledge. Just as there is no original moment to interpretation, there is no original moment of influence. This student tries to divide knowledge as a means to control the force of influence. Perhaps if knowledge cannot be put in its proper place, it can return as a threat that divides the learner.

A professor of religious studies at the end of her career speaks eloquently of her own strategies for managing conflict and ambivalence made from influencing others and being influenced. While the professor began the interview by noting that many of the conflicts articulated in the protocol were once preoccupations for her as a beginning teacher and wondered if she anything to offer our project, her use of the protocol moved from viewing the items as concrete events to recount to speculating on the difference between her and her students and her own self-difference as a scholar.

Towards the end of the interview she began to muse on her pedagogical strategies with students:

I've been dealing with the Bible for a long time, and I do say to them, right at the beginning, in the introductory lectures, that I'm not dealing with this as a foundation of belief. I'm not dealing with it as the word of God at all. I'm dealing with it as a document that can be analysed from a mythic point of view, an anthropological point of view, a literary point of view, or whatever. And the fact that we analyse it in this way doesn't undermine it as a document that can underpin belief.

In this pedagogical encounter, the use of knowledge can temper and draw attention to the force of influence. She went on to define religious belief as "absolute knowledge" but qualified her scholarship as "relative," as "always in question." This allowance is made from her own revisions of herself in knowledge:

I find it's hard when you've got this lovely theory and you have to give it up. I mean, I have been working through, and I do it all the time, slowly, slowly, on coming to a conclusion that something I wanted to prove very much, and I'm using the word believe, as a feminist I can no longer believe. I had to abandon, for instance, my idea, when I first started, [that] goddess stuff was the original. In the Palaeolithic times, there was once an original great goddess who was all over the place. Now I certainly abandoned that one, but it took me a long time, and now I'm coming to the conclusion that actually most religion is based in male/female complementarity. I'd have preferred not to have that either.

If we make a division between "lovely knowledge" and giving that up, and if we can hold in tension our preferences for what we want with what we find, we also see that a working distinction between belief and knowledge opens one to accept the losses that compose the force of learning. This professor brings us close to Milner's (1993, p. 16-18) observations that scholarly creativity requires times when what is real and what are phantasies are allowed to mingle. The risk of siding with one to the exclusion of the other, as we saw in the previous interview, is to forget that both phantasy and reality organize our relation to knowledge and thus allow knowledge its affective force. In this narrative, difficult knowledge is what one makes from the ruins of one's lovely knowledge.

If lovely knowledge is knowledge that one loves, what does one love when lovely knowledge is lost? A recently-graduated PhD, about to begin her first university post, came to the interview with the protocol well underlined. She wanted to discuss her breakdowns in meaning experienced while constructing knowledge. These breakdowns concerned her thesis topic, her theoretical framework, and her relations with people in and outside the academy. As the narratives unfolded, distinctions between scholarship and people could not be maintained. This, in fact, is a feature we have noticed across the interviews. Part of their blurring had to do with questions of love. Her dissertation was an oral history with female members of a political and military separatist organization in Europe that has been fighting actively for territory and political autonomy for many years. Originally conceived as a feminist inquiry into women's experiences of civil war, the longer she interviewed for her dissertation project, the more she questioned the veracity of the study's framework:

I guess if you want to think about people, in a way – how they were forcing me to re-evaluate constantly what I considered to be my own, the knowledge that I was coming with to the project – in a way that was constantly challenging. And I often asked myself what my theoretical framework and indeed what my kind of background as a academic, how that was relevant to the topic. One example, quite early on, maybe it was about a year into it actually, was a woman who said, "I don't think we're ready to listen to women's stories because men's stories haven't been told yet." And I thought, well, there are lots of books talking about men's experiences in this organization. . . . And she said, "no, I've never, I haven't read anything really that talks about my husband's experience, for example." Her husband had been killed by [state] authorities. And I really kind of got into a little exchange with her about her being an insider and me being an outsider, but it wasn't in any way an accusation at all. She just said straight out, "Well, you have an outside perspective and that's good, and I have an inside perspective and *that*'s good." But she was one of the few people who put that in a way, but not in a way that was about being politically correct, or me having to lay out my identity, but just a kind of way of saying, 'we have different perspectives, my knowledge is inside knowledge, and you are coming from the outside, and we need that, too.' And so I feel that my own idea about what had been written previously and whose voices need to be heard was actually being questioned by the very people I was interviewing who were not only saying, "Yes, we want our voices heard." They were also saying, "We actually want the men's voices heard too, and somebody's got to do that." It really hadn't actually occurred to me before I started talking to the women– because in most cases, they were very close to the men. They were.

This historian was surprised to confront the wishes of her (lovely) knowledge and its adequacy to bridge what these women had to say with what she imagined they should say. This confusion between wish and external reality, we are suggesting, is also a dilemma for our own research and may well be a constitutive feature of any research project. What is uncommon is not the observation but how one elaborates its specificity.

Our historian could appreciate the fact of difference in whose voice needs to be heard, but, as we shall see, voice is never monolithic and is only represented as such if it can be reduced to the difference that is standpoint. Left over when perspectives are exchanged, and what makes one voice more than it can say, is the residue of sexuality. Self-difference, that is, the difference within made from sexuality, is neither easily exchanged nor stabilized through standpoint:

When I wanted to talk about prison experiences and [the women's] relationships [when they were] in prison, I thought, do I now come out? Is that a good thing to do? Is that relevant to the interview? Will that help draw something out of someone that maybe they wouldn't normally want to admit that they'd had sexual relationships with other women in prison. . . . I do remember a couple of times thinking, Is this a strategy? . . . And then of course this repeats itself when I'm teaching often.

In trying to speak about women in prison, our narrator presents her own phantasy of being in prison. The phantasy is erotic, but she disrupts it through her question, "Is this a strategy?" In the previous excerpt, the women forced her to rethink; in this excerpt, her phantasy provoked the thought of the otherness of the women. If research returns to the researcher the startling question of how to use one's own subjectivity– even as the method claims intersubjectivity– part of that work requires confronting the phantasies that render one's own knowledge so lovely and so demanding. The question that shadows her narratives might go something like this: what good is my knowledge here, to you? Differences in perspective may not turn the researcher away from lovely knowledge toward difficult knowledge. It takes a move from presentation to symbolization to allow the first question its affective force: As to my difference, if my knowledge is no good to me, what good am I to you? Difficult knowledge is made from the ruins of erotic ties.

We conclude our discussion of participants' construction of difficult knowledge with one interviewee's comments about the protocol. For this advanced doctoral student, there is something quite wrong with the distinction we have made between knowledge and teachers: she believes that the most important experience in learning is the relationship one has with the teacher and not with the knowledge. At first glance, her insistence seems close to Freud's (1914b, p. 242) question as to whether he was affected more by "a concern with the sciences that we were taught or with the personalities of the teachers."

Part of what I noticed when I was reading [the protocol] was what prompts or what questions were particularly evocative of emotional responses and questions. Like number 12, 'Times when an encounter with knowledge made you feel ashamed, or guilty or fearful', it is like or, 'when knowledge betrayed'. It is like part of what is at stake in the construction of knowledge is a kind of authority that is not always a positive authority. So that knowledge will betray you, that knowledge will make you feel bad about yourself or knowledge will make you feel alone. Or like the stranger in the classroom, or whatever. Just that, you know, they struck me as interesting frames, interesting ways of setting up knowledge as, at the same time, something outside the individual, outside of the subject, outside of the person. But also completely not outside of that either. So, infused with or over determined by the people who actually participate in knowledge, therefore figure as teachers.

A bit later on, she tried to clarify for the interviewer her interest in what actually happens in classrooms, particularly English literature classrooms:

We all supposedly read the book, and now we are going to talk about the relationship between all of those things and why the book is in the course and what is actually in the text that relates back to the sort of structuring mechanism of the course . . . the sort of purpose that we are all there for. But that is separate from what . . . actually happens. And so I would want arbitrarily and strategically to set those two processes up as quite different and bring the teacher back in, which . . . the [protocol] questions don't do. They sort of reify knowledge and separate it from an individual or subjects in a classroom. And yet personify that at the same time, which I thought is a kind of interesting contradiction.

We read this narrative with Kristeva's (2000b) theme of the "pre-narrative envelope." Perhaps it cannot be otherwise because representing learning returns one's own ambivalence in learning. This individual returns to the protocol its own questions. Where does authority come from in learning? Is authority found in the epistemological framework of the course or the teacher who represents the framework for students? There is also a question about symbolization: Should knowledge be personified and accorded with such casual force? Does knowledge stand on its own, creating its own effects on students? Or, does the teacher personify both knowledge and pedagogy?

These questions, as we have tried to show in our interview extracts, represent something of the difficulty of trying to determine the difference between obstacles to learning and obstacles to representing learning. If obstacles to learning are made from all that impedes from the outside, obstacles to representing learning return us to the inside. Conflicted stories about learning enact this distinction on their way to becoming stories about conflict, desire and ambivalence in learning. The detour, as we have tried to suggest, is in the movement from presentation to symbolization.

## RESEARCH AS PRELIMINARY LABOUR

Laplanche and Pontalis's (1973, p. 112) entry on 'deferred actions' notes three characteristics: an experience that cannot be assimilated into lived experience; a revision of the first event because of a second event; and uneven development. The term suggests a revision and a repetition of time because of a quality of experience itself: events are not and cannot be immediately assimilated into meaning, and this aspect disrupts the possibility that the meaning of an event is set by its chronological order. Indeed, chronology is lost and found through an affective logic, and experience may emerge from a kernel of incomprehensibility. Caruth (1996, p. 11) suggests that 'unclaimed experience', can only be reclaimed via a confrontation "with the possibility of a history that is no longer straightforwardly referential (that is, no longer based on simple models of experience and reference)." We bring this insight to our research project to suggest that narratives and data work in a similar fashion. From the vantage of deferred action, we might also begin to reconsider the problem of how experiences or practices in the human sciences become the "preliminary labour" for both insight and blindness.

Indeed, as researchers we learn something of our own knowledge when we stumble in the face of our own persistent blind spots, and we collude with interviewees in their production of satisfying narratives that dance around the surprise of self-implication. We are reminded of the various ways in which Freud conceptualized resistance in his work with his early patients. Over time, he became dissatisfied with his earliest formulations that resistance to his treatment emanated from the unconscious, thus preserving intact repressed material. Instead, he began to understand resistance as a defence mounted by the ego so that the ego might continue to enjoy its carefully crafted and, in many ways, useful symptoms. He learned that treatment itself provoked resistance. We bring this clinical insight to the problem of representing research. Fink (1997, p. 9), a Lacanian analyst, names the stakes of learning in analysis when he argues that "in therapy, the analyst sidesteps the patient's demands, frustrates them, and ultimately tries to direct the patient to something he or she has never asked for." On this view, we might consider the time of our research as organized by the pull of mastery against the threat of fragmentation and the push to destabilize old forms of mastery and allow new thought. But for this to occur, research must be understood as provoking, not representing, knowledge. We have called this provocation "symbolization," itself a quality of difficult knowledge.

Our "thought experiment" may indeed ask everyone involved what no-one can be prepared to offer. Our efforts to frustrate the linear, cohesive narrative are paradoxically familiar and strange, desired and unasked for. But if the crisis of representation is to become a central dynamic in any research endeavour, then the argument over the difference between obstacles to research and obstacles to representing research becomes part of the preliminary labour of constructions in research, a labour that is also a symptom of the crisis in representation. The paradoxical qualities of obstacles ushered into play by our "thought experiment" and the difficulty of deciding what shall count as an obstacle to experience and what might be better described as an obstacle to narration have also had a curious effect on this chapter. The metaphor of trauma turns out to be very difficult to hold in abeyance notwithstanding our earlier efforts to abandon it. Trauma returns, however, with a difference. The kernel of trauma that we have encountered in our theoretical investments, our stories of clinical experience, our protocol, and our interviews is not tied to models of pathology. Rather it emerges as a metaphor for the pushes and pulls between knowing and being known, between phantasy and reality, between one's early history of learning and one's haunted present of learning, and between experience and its narration. Our three psychoanalytic concepts– deferred action, transference, and symbolization– have helped us symbolize the experience and event of our research in ways that exceed identity as they move us towards these new kinds of relations to characterize this more ordinary yet ubiquitous trauma of having to learn.

## NOTES

[1] We adhere to a spelling of fantasy that is close to its German origins in 'Phantasie' to signal the range of modes of fantasy that are worked with in psychoanalysis and that exceed the associations common to the English 'fantasy'. See Laplanche and Pontalis (1973, p. 314-319) for a discussion of the distinctions among "conscious phantasies or daydreams, unconscious phantasies like those re-

covered by analysis as the structures underlying a manifest content, and primal phantasies" (p. 314). It is with the second mode we are primarily concerned in this essay.

[2]  We conducted, with graduate students associated with our project, fifty in-depth interviews with faculty and students.

[3].  Herrnstein Smith's (1997) model of cognitive dissonance comes close to describing the disorganizing features of encounters with new knowledge we are suggesting here:

an impression of inescapable noise or acute disorder, a rush of adrenalin, sensations of alarm, a sense of unbalance or chaos, residual feelings of nausea and anxiety. These are the forms of bodily distress that occur when one's imagined, taken-for-granted sense of how certain things are– and thus presumably will be and in some sense *should* be– is suddenly or insistently confronted by something very much at odds with it. Perceptually, it is the wave of vertigo one may experience at an unexpected sight. (p. xiv)

Where we depart from this model of cognitive dissonance is in highlighting uncanny qualities, when one attempts to make sense, not just of the unexpected, but what was, in fact, anticipated through the lens of anxiety. In bringing the concept of the uncanny to cognitive dissonance, we can begin to consider how even the familiar can become a source of difficulty. For some other approaches to emotional conflict in learning, see also Bogdan et al, 2000 and Sedgwick & Frank's (1995) introduction to the psychological theories of Sylvan Tomkins.

[4]  If transference organizes and disorganizes experience at the same time, Gallop's (1997) discussion of how she came to be accused of sexual harassment suggests the difficulty of institutional efforts to make sense of it. Gallop, too, has trouble because her story can only be narrated in the time of deferred action: "But I won't be telling what happened chronologically; the story will appear broken into pieces and out of order" (p. 6). One piece of her story concerned whether there can be pedagogical uses of the transference. Gallop's argument to university officials is that the transference is a central quality of her pedagogical relation to students, but their response to her has no sympathy: "In the official report on my case, the university recommends that in the future I should stop working with any student who has such a transference unto me. Which means I would not work with any student who really believed I had something important to teach her" (p. 56).

[5]  Laplanche, in his discussion of the human being as a self-theorizing or self-symbolizing being, argues that "all real theorizing is an experiment and an experience which necessarily involves the researcher" (1989, p. 12-13). He is thinking here of Freud's use of his own dreams and observations as the basis from which to develop psychoanalytic theory. We had not anticipated the ways in which our experiment not only inquired into experience; it also constituted its own experience.

## REFERENCES

Appel, S. (Ed.) (1999). *Psychoanalysis and pedagogy.* Westport, CT: Bergin & Garvey.

Bass, A. (2001). *Difference and disavowal: the trauma of eros.* Stanford, CA: Stanford University Press.

Bloom, L. (1998). *Under the sign of hope: Feminist methodology and narrative interpretation.* Albany, NY: State University of New York Press.

Bogdan, D., Cunningham J.E. & Davis, H.E. (2000). Reintegrating sensibility: Situated knowledges and embodied readers. *New Literary History: Philosophical and Rhetorical Inquiries, 31,* 476-507.

Bollas, C. (1999). *The Mystery of things.* London: Routledge.

Britzman, D. P. (1998). *Lost subjects, contested objects: toward a psychoanalytic inquiry of learning.* Albany, NY: State University of New York Press.

Britzman, D.P. (2000). If the story cannot end: deferred action, ambivalence and difficult knowledge. In R. I. Simon, S. Rosenberg & C. Eppert (Eds.), *Between hope and despair: Pedagogy and the remembrance of historical trauma* (pp. 27-56). Lanham, MD: Rowman & Littlefield .

Britzman, D.P. &Pitt, A. (2004). Pedagogy and clinical knowledge: Some psychoanalytic observations on losing and refinding significance. *JAC: A Quarterly Journal for The Interdisciplinary Study of Rhetoric, Writing, Multiple Literacies And Politics, 24,* 353-374.

Britzman, D. P. & Pitt, A. J. (1996). Pedagogy and transference: Casting the past of learning into the presence of teaching. *Theory Into Practice, 2,* 117-123.

Caruth, C. (1996). *Unclaimed experience, trauma, narrative, and history.* Baltimore & London: John Hopkins University Press.

Cheng, A. A. (2001). *The melancholy of race: Psychoanalysis, assimilation, and hidden grief.* Oxford: Oxford University Press.

Chodorow, N. J. (1999). *Power of feelings: Personal meaning in psychoanalysis, gender and culture.* New Haven: Yale University Press.

Code, L. (1991). *What can she know?: Femininity in the construction of knowledge.* Ithaca, NY: Cornell University Press.

Ellsworth, E; (1997). *Teaching positions: Difference, pedagogy and the power of address.* New York & London: Teachers College Press.

Felman, S. (1992). Education and crisis, or the vicissitudes of teaching. In S. Felman & D. Laub (Eds.), *Testimony: Crises of witnessing in literature, psychoanalysis, and history* (pp. 1-56). New York: Routledge.

Felman, S. & Laub, D. (Eds.), (1992). *Testimony: Crises of witnessing in literature, psychoanalysis, and history.* New York: Routledge.

Fink, B. (1997). *A clinical introduction to Lacanian psychoanalysis: Theory and technique.* Cambridge, MA & London: Harvard University Press.

Freud, S. 1953-1974. *The standard edition of the complete psychological works of Sigmund Freud.* J. Strachey in collaboration with A. Freud , assisted by A.Strachey & Alan Tyson, (Eds.& Trans). 24 vols. London: Hogarth Press & Institute for Psychoanalysis.

Freud, S.(1900). Interpretation of Dreams. 2$^{nd}$ part. *Standard edition, 5,* 339-610.

Freud, S. (1914a). Remembering, repeating and working through (Further recommendations on the technique of psycho-analysis II. *Standard edition, 12,* 145-156.

Freud, S. (1914b). Some reflections on schoolboy psychology. *Standard edition, 13,* 241-244.

Freud, S. (1937). Constructions in analysis. *Standard edition, 23,* 255-269.

Gallop, J. (1997). *Feminist accused of sexual harassment.* Durham: Duke University Press.

Green A. (2000). *Chains of eros: The sexual in psychoanalysis.* L. Thurston (Trans.). London: Rebus Press.

Herrnstein Smith, B. (1997). *Belief and resistance: dynamics of contemporary intellectual controversy.* Cambridge: Harvard University Press.

Kohon, G. (1999). *No lost certainties to be recovered.* London: Karnac Books.

Kristeva, J. (2000a). *The sense and non-sense of revolt: The powers and limits of psychoanalysis.* J. Herman (Trans.). New York: Columbia Press.

Kristeva, J. (2000b). From symbols to flesh: The polymorphous destiny of narration. *The International Journal of Psychoanalysis, 81,* 771.

Laplanche, J. (1989). *New foundations for psychoanalysis.* D. Macey (Trans.). Oxford: Basil Blackwell.

Laplanche, J. & Pontalis, J.-B (1973.) *The language of psycho-analysis.* D.Nicholson-Smith (Trans.). New York: Norton.

Lather, P. (2000). Drawing the line at angels: Working the ruins of feminist ethnography. In E. St. Pierre & W. Pillow (Eds.), *Working the ruins: Feminist poststructural theory and methods in education,* (pp. 284-311). New York: Routledge.

Lather, P. (In Press). Postbook: working the ruins of feminist ethnography. *Signs, 27.*

Laws, C. & Davies, B. (2000). Poststructuralist theory in practice: working with "behaviorally disturbed" children. *International Journal of Qualitative Studies in Education, 13,* 205-221.

Little, M. I. (1990). *Psychotic anxieties and containment: a personal record of an analysis with winnicott.* Northgate, NJ: Jason Aronson Inc.

Lyotard, J.-F. (1987). *The postmodern condition: A report on knowledge.* G. Bennington & B. Masami (Trans.). Manchester: Manchester University Press.

Mannoni, M. (1999). *Separation and creativity: Refinding the lost language of childhood.* S. Fairfield (Trans.) New York: The Other Press, 1999.

Martin, B. (1997). Success and its failures. *Differences: A Journal of Feminist Cultural Studies, 9*: 102-131.

McCarthy, C. & Crichlow, W. (Eds.). (1993). *Race, identity and representation in education.* New York: Routledge.

Milner, M. (1993). The role of illusion in symbol formation. In Peter L. Rudnytsky (Ed.), *Transitional bjects and potential spaces: Literary uses of D.W. Winnicott,* (pp. 13-39). New York: Columbia University Press.

Phillips, J. (1998). The fissure of authority: violence in the acquisition of knowledge. In. L. Stonebridge and J. Phillips (Eds.), *Reading Melanie Klein,* (pp. 160-178). London & New York: Routledge.

Pinar, W. (Ed.). (1998). *Queer theory in education.* Mahwah, NJ: Lawrence Erlbaum Associates.

Pinar, W. (Ed.) (2001). *The gender of racial politics and violence in America: Lynching, prison rape, and the crisis of masculinity.* New York: Peter Lang.

Pitt, A.J. (2000). Hide and seek: The play of the personal in education. *Changing English: Studies in Reading and Culture, 7*: 65-74.

Readings, B. (1996). *The university in ruins.* Cambridge: Harvard University Press.

Rhedding-Jones, J. (2000). The other girls: culture, psychoanalytic theories and writing. *International Journal of Qualitative Studies in Education, 13,* 263-279.

Segal, H. (1997). On symbolism.In *Psychoanalysis, literature and war: Papers 1972-1995,* 41-63. London & New York: Routledge.

Segwick, E & Frank, A. (Eds.). (1995). *Shame and its sisters: A Silvan Tomkins reader.* Durham & London: Duke University Press.

Simon, R., Rosenberg, S. & Eppert, C. (Eds.) (2000). *Between hope and despair: Pedagogy and the remembrance of historical trauma.* Lanham, NJ: Rowman & Littlefield.

St. Pierre, E. & Pillow, W.(Eds.) (2000). *Working the ruins: Feminist poststructural theory and methods in education.* New York: Routledge.

Steiner, G. (1980). On difficulty (1978). In *On difficulty and other essays,* (pp. 18-47). Oxford: Oxford University Press.

Talburt, S. (2000). *Subject to identity: Knowledge, sexuality, and academic practices in higher education.* Albany: State University of New York Press.

Todd, S. (2001). Bringing more than I contain: Ethics, curriculum, and the pedagogical demand for altered egos. *Journal of Curriculum Studies, 33,* 431-450.

Volosinov, V. N. (1986). *Marxism and the philosophy of language.* L. Matejka & I.R. Titnuk (Trans.). Cambridge: Harvard University Press.

Winnicott, D. W. (1972). *Playing and reality.* London & New York: Routledge.

Yon, D. (2000). *Elusive culture: Schooling, race, and identity in global times.* Albany, NY: SUNY.

Young, R. M. (1994). *Mental space.* London: Process Press.

APPENDIX A: INTERVIEW PROTOCOL: DIFFICULT KNOWLEDGE PROJECT

DESIGNED BY PROFESSORS DEBORAH BRITZMAN AND ALICE PITT, FACULTY
OF EDUCATION, YORK UNIVERSITY

As described in the letter of informed consent, we are providing you, prior to the actual interview, a copy of our interview protocol. Our purpose is doing so is to familiarize you with the conceptual geography of the project and to allow you to think about your learning and teaching prior to the actual interview. At the time of the interview, you will be asked to describe yourself in any way you choose and then begin by discussing any of the "thought prompts" discussed below.

This interview is organized around the large question, what sorts of knowledge and what kinds of experiences are difficult in teaching and learning in university class-rooms. We are also interested in times when learning is rehearsed in preparing for the classroom and times when knowledge is reflected upon after classroom en-counters. We are interested in how people currently involved in university settings describe and narrate their difficulties with knowledge. Most generally, what counts for you as difficult knowledge? What happens to knowledge in times of difficul-ties? We are also exploring the question, what makes knowledge difficult in teach-ing and learning. We are interested in having you explore times in your university studies or teaching where you noticed difficulties for yourself. We are also inter-ested in your narratives of times when meanings have broken down in learning and teaching and times where you attempt some sort of repair in making meanings.

To help you consider the sorts of experiences we are interested in, we offer the following "prompts" for you to think about prior to the interview. During the inter-view we will ask you to select and speak to whatever prompt that allows you to narrate experiences on difficult knowledge for you. At the end of the interview, we will also ask for your thoughts about the prompts for your experiences.

**1. Thinking about breakdowns in encounters with others:**
Times when you felt misunderstood in the classroom
Times when you felt let down or disappointed by others
Times when someone's response felt disappointing
Times when you tried to persuade others and were not successful

**2. Thinking about fighting with knowledge:**
Times when you encountered ideas that initially and perhaps still bother you
Times when you worried about knowledge
Times when your ideas and your feelings were at odds with each other
Times when you could not separate the good from the bad in knowledge

**3. Thinking about reconsidering knowledge:**
Times when an idea or viewpoint prompted you to reconsider previous views
Times when you questioned the ways you were seeing things

Times when you fell out of love with an idea or theory
Times when your identity as a teacher or student became irrelevant
Times when you created new conditions for learning and teaching

## 4. Thinking about experiences of influence:
Times when you misunderstood others
Times when empathy was tried and failed
Times when the advice of others felt meaningless
Times when you decided you needed to ask for help
Times where you wanted to explain something but words failed you or when you could not find the right words
Times when you received criticism that was difficult to listen to
Times when you felt overly susceptible to the influences of others
Times when you tried to help others
Times when your intuitive response failed
Times when the help you gave proved unhelpful

## 5. Thinking about experiences of aloneness with others:
Times you felt alienated in the classroom
Times when you needed help but could not ask
Times when you felt lonely in the classroom or in learning
Times when you felt like a stranger in the classroom

## 6. Thinking about experiences of confusion:
Times when you realized you were mistaken but could not turn back
Times when you felt lost or were falling behind
Times when learning about the world seemed to ask a great deal from you
?Times when you worked through confusion
Times when you felt you were on the wrong track
Times when knowledge felt too exciting
Times when you felt ambivalent about knowledge
Times when knowledge overwhelmed you

## 7 Thinking about encounters with insufficient knowledge:
Times when knowledge felt insufficient
Times when knowledge seemed suspicious
Times when knowledge seemed absurd
Times when knowledge betrayed you
Times when knowledge felt empty
Times when knowledge did not seem to count
Times when the purposes of your knowledge lost focus
Times when you had difficulty using knowledge
Times when an idea felt threatening or incomprehensible
Times when you were bored by knowledge

## 8. Thinking about encounters with the promise of knowledge:
Times when your returned to read a book and found something unexpected in the second reading
Times when you fell in love with an idea or theory
Times when knowledge felt promising
Times when you felt represented in learning and teaching
Times when you did not care whether you were represented
Times when you discovered you were deceiving yourself
Times when you have been asked a question that surprised you and pushed you to consider something about yourself that you had not previously considered

## 9. Thinking about encounters with the promise of learning:
Times when difficulties could be tolerated and learned from
Times when you were excited in the classroom
Times when you felt the force of surprise in learning or teaching
Times when you dramatically changed your mind
Times when your practices of learning dramatically changed
Times when you rethought your own self knowledge

## 10. Thinking about experiences of hostility:
Times when you felt attacked or when you wished you could express hostility
Times when you used knowledge to shock others
Times when you refused to read a particular text or participate in a particular discussion
Times when you wished for the teacher's or student's removal
Times when the present felt repetitious
Times when you could not attach to ideas
Times when books made you angry
Times when you became defensive toward ideas or others
Times when you had nothing to say

## 11. Thinking about encounters with authority:
Times when you recognized the constraints of the institution upon your learning and teaching
Times when you became aware of the history of your learning practices
Times when your identity as student and or teacher became irrelevant
Times when authority could not be located
Times when you questioned authority
Times when your own authority was questioned by others
Times when evaluation felt meaningless or inadequate

## 12. Thinking about encounters with anxiety:
Times when you felt remorse in teaching and learning
Times when you disappointed yourself
Times when knowledge embarrassed you

Times when an encounter with knowledge made you feel ashamed
Times when an encounter with knowledge made you feel guilty
Times when an encounter with knowledge made you feel fearful

## 13. Thinking about encounters with relevance:
Times when it was difficult to distinguish the important from the unimportant
Times when theory and practice seemed in profound conflict
Times when you noticed that your ideas were irrelevant
Times when what you thought was important was considered trivial
Times when something you learned altered other knowledge you held
Times when you discovered you had been deceived by the absence of knowledge
Times when you became dissatisfied with school knowledge

## 14. Thinking about experiences of time in learning and teaching:
Times when you felt as if your response in the present was really about something that happened in the past
Times when your learning occurred much later than the lesson
Times when your fantasies or rehearsals about teaching or learning failed you
Times when you began to question what you were learning
Times when you began to question why you were learning
Times when teaching or learning felt fragmented

## 15. Thinking about encounters with obstacles:
Times when your writing was blocked
Times when your reading was blocked
Times when your speaking with others was blocked
Times when you lost your interest
A different kind of question: Thinking about your story, how would you describe the qualities of knowledge and where would you put the difficulty?

# III REFLECTIONS: AFTER DOING THE RESEARCH

PHIL FRANCIS CARSPECKEN

# 16. LIMITS OF KNOWLEDGE IN THE PHYSICAL SCIENCES

INTRODUCTION

This chapter is an excerpt from a longer essay I have written on the limits of knowledge in both the physical and human sciences (Carspecken, forthcoming). The longer essay itself is a preliminary articulation of findings from what is a large on-going project. What the reader will find here is my initial investigation of physical science, oriented specifically toward revealing conditions that simultaneously make physical science *possible* and *limit* the type of knowledge it can produce.

The arguments developed and the conclusions made in this excerpt are further expanded within the larger essay. We will find, by the end of this excerpt, that transcendental argumentation and the concept of reflection are of interest to us. But we will not have fully explored what these two related things are. That exploration occurs in the next major portion of the larger work. Reflection and the transcendental inference turn out to be features of the conditions within which *human* sciences operate. They are features of intersubjectivity, in my developing a theory of that. Yet another section of the larger work explores intersubjectivity itself more fully. Kantian insights that one will find in use within this excerpt are there explained in ways that differ very much from Kantian philosophy. The exploration of intersubjectivity reveals conditions that enable and yet constrain *human* sciences in ways analogous to the enabling and limiting conditions discussed in this excerpt. But the limiting and enabling conditions of the human sciences have a different ontological and epistemological status from those in play with physical science. Finally, the longer essay concludes with a section on "what lies beyond the narrative horizon": a look at the implications that limits to knowledge in both physical and human science entail. Once the full essay has been read various points and arguments made in its different sections, including this section on physical science, take on additional significance and meaning. Obviously that circling / spiralling feature of the full essay's structure is lost with the publication of one section in isolation.

The exploration of limits to knowledge in the physical sciences that we have below stands on its own in many respects. Its relevance to today resides in the recent growth of a particularly virulent form of scientistic ideology. Scientism is the belief that all knowledge must take the form it has in the physical sciences if it is to be knowledge at all. This ideology has been around for a long time, but for ap-

K. Tobin & J. Kincheloe, (eds.), Doing Educational Research—A Handbook, 405–437.

proximately eight years now, in the United States and other nations as well, we have seen new and growing efforts to suspend funding for any social research that does not use experimental methods. The argument is that only experimental methods can determine "what works," and thus only this sort of research produces genuine "knowledge." An examination of the limits to knowledge in physical science should be at least helpful in the battle against scientism. In my longer work the critique of physical science to be found below leads directly into an elucidation of what is distinctive about inquiry in the social sciences—including what it can tell us that scientistic methods cannot.

## THE "THEORY OF EVERYTHING"

A special issue of *Scientific American*, published in September of 2004, had on its cover:

### Beyond Einstein
*Toward a theory of everything*
*Energy that expands the cosmos*
*Different physics, infinite universes*
*And more ...*

It is the blurb, "toward a theory of everything," that most captures the concerns of this chapter. The theory of everything, or T.O.E., has acquired slogan status in recent writings and television programs on string theory, oriented to the general public. It is used frequently by Brian Green in his three-part Nova program on strings, and crops up many times as well in his very popular book, *The Elegant Universe* (Green, 2003). T.O.E. has been referred to by physicists and other scientists in their more technical publications for about twenty years (e.g., see Davies, 2004, p. 17, and Ellis, 2004, p. 632). Now it is a phrase known to many outside the physics community as well. Brian Green writes:

> For the first time in the history of physics we ... have a framework with the capacity to explain every fundamental feature upon which the universe is constructed. For this reason string theory is sometimes described as possibly being the "theory of everything" (T.O.E.) or the "ultimate" or "final" theory. These grandiose descriptive terms are meant to signify the deepest possible theory of physics—a theory that underlies all others, one that does not require or even allow for a deeper explanatory base. (2003, p. 16)

### Methodological Naturalism and Reductionism

If a theory of everything really could explain *everything*, then could it explain its own production as a theory? In other words, would it form the basis at least of a theory of knowledge? An answer of "yes" would commit one to the philosophical stance of methodological naturalism which is the idea that the methods and logic of physical science exhaust all methods and logic for attaining knowledge of any kind. Knowledge of any type will be fundamentally the same with respect to how it is gained or produced, with respect to its basic form, its principles of acquisition, and its principles of verification. An answer of "yes" would also entail a commitment to reductionism whereby sociology, psychology, ethics, and other domains of inquiry into human phenomena would be proved reducible to biology, biochemistry, chemistry and finally physics. An answer of "no," on the other hand, would entail challenges to the concept of knowledge that we find in methodological naturalism, and put reductionism into doubt.

This question of whether a physical theory of everything could explain itself has much relevance to the so-called human sciences: social and cultural inquiry, and psychology. If a theory of everything, which is from start to finish a physical theory, could explain itself then methodological naturalism would be vindicated and social science really should go in the direction that many funding and government agencies are currently trying to push it (see Delandshere, 2002, 2005). Experimental methods should then indeed be the "gold standard" for social and psychological science (Delandshere, 2005). Research should be focused solely on "what works," or at least on what can be predicted given certain measurable initial conditions and a measurable intervention. Qualitative social research would no doubt have a place in the picture but as something to use in exploratory and descriptive ways. Qualitative research would ask questions, collect data, and suggest answers in a way that could in principle always be translated into the vocabulary of measurable initial conditions, treatments, and outcomes. Values, morals, states of awareness, intentions and the like would become things to study in forms analogous to physical systems, once they are objectivated in observational terms. They would take their place within the language of inquiry solely in the position of references rather than as terms intimately bound up with forms of inference and reasoning distinguished from those used in the natural sciences.

## Scientism

Of course, there is some tongue-in-cheek at play when physicists speak or write about the T.O.E. However, the mild sense of facetiousness we find in uses of the phrase do *not* allude to doubts about methodological naturalism and reductionism. What is alluded to is rather such things as the question of whether any physical theory could provide its own initial conditions—a question that could eventually be answered "yes" or "no" solely *within* the framework of inquiry used by natural science. And when it comes to popular works on science for the "lay person" there isn't even this slight sense of the facetious. Most practicing scientists who write for the general public today appear to believe in methodological naturalism and the possibility of reducing all the sciences, level by level, to the principles of physics. The philosophical stances of naturalism and reductionism are ideologies when they are simply assumed to be true. Taken together we have the belief that all knowledge must have the form of knowledge it has in the physical sciences. Anything else will not be knowledge at all. This belief has often been called "scientism" and it pervades our culture today with potentially dire consequences for the social sciences (see for example, Schwandt, 2002).

## LIMITS TO EMPIRICAL KNOWLEDGE

There are many good reasons for doubt when it comes to a scientific theory of everything and the most significant of these reasons have to do with the idea of *necessary* limits to types of knowledge. These are limits that work in two ways: 1) they *enable* a method of inquiry with respect to an associated domain of phenomena; 2) they set aside other domains of phenomena which they *depend upon* and yet which cannot be studied with the method of inquiry they enable. In other words, limits of this type simultaneously make a domain of inquiry *possible* and *prohibit* it from accessing other domains.

This understanding of limits to knowledge, as both enabling and constraining conditions, is apparently lost on most physicists and other scientists writing about their field for the general public. The physicist and Nobel Laureate Steven Weinberg has given lectures and written articles about the limits to scientific knowledge which will be helpful to our explorations in this essay. His book of 2001, *Facing Up; Science and its Cultural Adversaries,* is a collection of such essays, many of them originally published in the *New York Review of Books* to answer challenges made by postmodern and critical theorists to the ideology of scientism. His article on the Sokal Hoax is probably well known to many readers of this paper [for the hoax, see (Sokal, 1996a) and (Sokal, 1996b)]. Weinberg's articles have served an excellent purpose by correcting a number of misunderstandings of contemporary physics, and invalid inferences that have been made from contemporary physics to the social sciences, by people working in our own field of social and methodological theory.

Reading Weinberg is illuminating both for an initial grasp of where limits to knowledge present themselves in theoretical physics and for gleaning an idea of how the scientific community (in so far as Weinberg is representative) tends to understand "limits." I have found three categories of limit within Weinberg's writings. One is a large category that has already been mentioned; a category pertaining to initial conditions for the theory of the expansion of the universe. Another category concerns the question of whether a physical theory could explain consciousness. And a third category concerns the observer-observed relation as this manifests in quantum physics. All three categories are related to the question of whether a theory of everything could explain itself. I will take them one at a time in an effort to find what they may tell us about limits to knowledge.

### 1. Could Initial Conditions Be Derived From a Fundamental Theory of Physics?

The problem of initial conditions is of interest to us here only because it illuminates more general issues about physical theories. First let's understand the problem. Certain initial quantities and ratios between quantities in our universe must be as they are or our universe would be radically different. The ratio of matter to antimatter soon after the big bang is an example. In big bang theory, at about $10^{-12}$ second after the "nominal moment of infinite temperature":

The temperature of the universe had dropped by then to about $10^{15}$ degrees, cool enough for us to apply our present physical theories. At these temperatures the universe would have been filled with a gas consisting of all the types of particles known to higher energy nuclear physics, together with their antiparticles, continually being annihilated and created in their collisions. As the universe continued to expand and cool, creation became slower than annihilation, and almost all the particles and antiparticles disappeared. If there had not been a small excess of electrons over antielectrons, and quarks over antiquarks, then ordinary particles like electrons and quarks would be virtually absent in the universe today. It is this early excess of matter over antimatter, estimated as one part in about $10^{10}$, that survived to form light atomic nuclei three minutes later, then after a million years to form atoms and later to be cooked to heavier elements in stars, ultimately to provide the material out of which life would arise." (Weinberg, 2001, pp. 72-73)

There are other quantities and other initial conditions and "input parameters" (Green, 2003, p. 143) to proposed fundamental theories of physics that are hard to explain though they are essential for the existence of the universe as we find it. Most can be calculated but not *derived* from the standard model of particle physics and other scientific theories. String theory is considered a strong possible candidate for the Theory of Everything because many of these initial conditions and quantities *can* be derived from it. And in addition, string theory seems capable of combining general relativity theory and quantum theory which is something that the standard model in particle physics cannot do. Brian Green, in his book *The Elegant Universe*, explains that string theory already makes deductively derivable many constants that the standard model of particle physics had to simply use as inputs. In terms of a full cosmological theory Green admits:

We don't know whether the question of determining the initial conditions is one that is even sensible to ask or whether—like asking general relativity to give insight into how hard you happened to toss a ball in the air—it is a question that lies forever beyond the grasp of any theory. Valiant attempts by physicists such as Hawking and James Hartle of the University of California at Santa Barbara have tried to bring the question of cosmological initial conditions within the umbrella of physical theory, but all such attempts remain inconclusive. … our cosmological understanding is, at present, just too primitive to determine whether our candidate 'theory of everything' truly lives up to its name and determines its own cosmological initial conditions, thereby elevating them to the status of physical law. (2003, p. 366)

As string theory is further developed it *could* perhaps become the Theory of Everything such that it does explain all initial quantities and conditions we find in the universe and, as we see, there is work being done at this time toward this end. What is philosophically of interest is the *idea* of a theory of everything—of what would have to be accomplished to arrive at one and what such a theory would look like in general terms.

*The quest for ultimate substance: Scientific models and transcendent postulates*
Now let's look a little closer at what this idea of a final theory could mean. The standard model of particle physics has to use specific quantities, such as the mass of twelve fundamental particles (see Green, 2003, p. 9) as in-puts that come from outside the model itself. Part of the impetus to develop string theory is to reduce twelve to one:

> String theory alters this picture radically by declaring that the 'stuff' of all matter and forces is the *same*. Each elementary particle is composed of a single string—that is, each particle *is* a single string—and all strings are absolutely identical. Differences between the particles arise because their respective strings undergo different resonant vibrational patterns. What appear to be different elementary particles are actually different 'notes' on a fundamental string. The universe—being composed of an enormous number of these vibrating strings—is akin to a cosmic symphony. (Green, 2003, p. 146)

Strings can be thought of as the ultimate "stuff" from which everything else comes and to which everything else can be reduced for explanatory purposes. It is the idea of an ultimate *substance*, despite modifications made to everyday notions of "stuff" in scientific models. One way to have a theory of everything would be to provide evidence for the claim that all things are really just different forms and states of a single substance that underlies them. There must then also be a way to explain different forms and states as well as changes between them. String theory in fact conforms well to the basic idea of the substance/accident or substance/property distinction that has long been discussed in philosophy. Strings occupy the position of substance and the 12 fundamental particles of the standard model occupy the position of the most basic sorts of properties, because these 12 fundamental particles are interpreted in terms of different resonances of the same material: strings.

What is significant about this? Well, is it possible to produce an ultimate theory, a fundamental theory of physics that could explain its own initial conditions (and also in some way explain itself, through reductionism as explored below) *without* invoking a concept of substance? "Substance" is a metaphor that is extended and abstracted from in physics to produce such concepts as matter, fields, energy, and elementary particles. The *sense* these concepts have to us intuitively depend upon a concept of substance, even though it has undergone various refinements and extensions to guide the formulation of mathematical models. Substance is something like a conceptually necessary concept for trying to produce a theory about anything objective.

We really don't have to emphasize "substance" too much because there are other basic concepts at work in the very idea of a fundamental theory. There is the concept of "sameness" and the concept of "difference," for example. There is of course "space" and "time" which seem to be conceptually necessary for any physical theory even though they can be altered from traditional conceptualizations to a great extent as has happened with general relativity theory (I discuss this more in the longer essay).

But let's take substance as our example here because strings certainly suggest it. Now, some readers may already be thinking that the concept of "string" in physics is not tied to its metaphor of origin because all that physicists are really interested in are the mathematical models that represent strings and the measurements and predictions they make possible. But I will soon argue against this objection in the section on realism versus positivism. Meanwhile, where did the idea of "substance" come from? "Substance" underlies concepts that are postulated as *transcendent entities* in scientific models. We cannot perceive strings, quarks, fields and the like but we conceive of them as small bits of substance (strings) or particles of substance (quarks) or as something that has spatial spread without having material (fields: an abstraction from "substance") and in each case we have concepts whose sense in some way depends upon one basic idea: substance.

The case of the concept of "field" is particularly illuminating here. It was first used very consciously as a metaphor for magnetic and electrical phenomena. When magnetically active substances were placed in proximity to each other it was apparent that attractive and repulsive forces were in play, following an inverse square law similar to that of gravitational force. The "lines of force" studied form in a shape that resembles a "field." But physicists believed that the phenomena were analogous to Newton's theory of gravity whereby forces form only when the entities that so interact are placed in proximity. "Field" was used consciously as a metaphor to help with keeping track of where objects would align but not as something that "really existed." Then Maxwell's work, building on work of Faraday, suggested that fields did have a physical reality to them such that one field could sort of "push" another field into being—that is what led to the idea of light being an electromagnetic wave requiring no other medium than the fields that propagate by creating new fields progressively in one direction, in a vacuum. A concept that began as simply a model to help with record keeping ended up being a full transcendental postulate. Fields were thought of as a sort of "substance" as soon as they were accorded physical reality (see Penrose, 1989, p. 184-5). Prior to that, substance was an implicit metaphor underlying that of "field," but "field" was employed consciously as only a metaphor to aid in producing mathematical models.

Kant's idea of *a priori* concepts could be involved in this situation [by drawing attention to metaphors in my analysis I will depart from Kant in some important ways. For Kant on substance see (Kant, 1965, p. 113, A 80 / B 106)]. Where did the idea of substance come from, and could it be something like an *a priori* category, which is to say a category that is necessary for experience but not given through experience?

Initially we would not be too attracted by an *a priori* category in the case of substance because "substance" has a *history* in philosophy that we can trace back to Plato and Aristotle and follow forward through Locke, Berkeley, Spinoza, and Kant. When examining the history of the concept its basis in metaphor seems clear. For Aristotle, substance (*ousia*) referred to things that exist in themselves: particular beings. This is related to the notion of *persistence*. After Aristotle substance acquired the meaning of that which exists and persists behind appearances (Hamlyn, 1984, p. 60). The Latin etymology of the word suggests something existing behind the properties and accidents that appear in perception. This was the sense that Locke gave to the term: it is more like external being-in-general than particular being; that which stands beneath the properties of particular things that we experience. We are used to thinking of the *a priori* as concepts and conditions that are prior to experience and hence a history that displays the evolving metaphorical basis for a concept would seem to run counter to the idea of *a priori* concepts. What is suggested is perhaps that experience is simply always interpreted and in the course of time certain interpretative metaphors become sedimented as features of common sense.

Yet, Kantian insights are in fact relevant here. Kant distinguished between the transcendental, as in "transcendental logic," and the transcendent. The latter are postulated supersensible entities and processes that Kant found illegitimate in the quest for valid knowledge. Knowledge must be based on experience, both Kant and the empiricists agreed on this. Transcendent entities are never items within experience and yet, he believed, they are constructed with categories that *are* applied to experience legitimately. Hence transcendent metaphysics for Kant was the result of improperly employing categories of the human understanding; using them without sensory input. These categories were *a priori* for Kant, but with a careful appropriation of Kantian insights we could argue that certain concepts are unavoidable in efforts to model objective reality *and* many of them have metaphorical roots. The full significance of that idea will gradually unfold.

In Kant's account the transcendental, as opposed to the transcendent, consists of conditions and concepts that can be found to be necessary for experience in general to be possible. These can be discovered by reflecting upon something certain, like "there is experience," in order to find out what would have to be the case *for* this certainty to be. It is a form of reflective inference. Kant illustrates this form of making inferences when he discusses the idea of *a priori* concepts in *The Critique of Pure Reason*:

> If we remove from our empirical concept of a body, one by one, every feature in it which is empirical, the colour, the hardness or softness, the weight, there still remains the space which the body (now entirely vanished) occupied, and this cannot be removed. Again, if we remove from our empirical concept of any object, corporeal or incorporeal, all properties which experience has taught us, we yet cannot take away that property through which the object is thought as substance or as inhering in a substance (although this concept of substance is more determinate than that of an object in general). Owing, therefore, to the necessity with which this concept of substance forces itself upon us, we have no option save to admit that it has its seat in our faculty of *a priori* knowledge. (Kant 1965, p. 45, B 6)

Contemporary versions of transcendental argumentation and modified understandings of what *a priori* can mean are discussed in my longer essay, not here. What captures our interest now is the question of whether fundamental concepts and categories can be found to be already presupposed and in play when we engage in scientific research. Scientific research on the physical world has to begin with ideas about objects and events in general. These ideas have then become refined as research has progressed, but those processes of refinement, further abstraction, could be limited with respect to how far they may proceed. "String" is a highly refined concept but one that still has something like a concept of substance behind it, which makes it intelligible. "Substance" in turn has something about "objectivity-in-general" behind it, which makes *it* intelligible. Perhaps the explicit concepts used to produce the transcendent postulates used in scientific models all are foregrounded notions that depend upon backgrounded and implicit concepts; horizons of intelligibility. The conceptual relations here are ones of implication: foregrounded concepts *implicate* backgrounded ones in that the foregrounded concepts are not intelligible – have no sense – without the backgrounded concepts implicitly understood along with them. Perhaps these backgrounded concepts recede toward a limit, a limit of what *objectivity* is in general. Transcendental forms of thinking could help in an investigation of this possibility because reflection is a process that helps to reveal what was already presupposed. Peter Strawson (Strawson, 1966) expresses the basic idea here in terms of the questions that a transcendental-style investigation would seek to answer:

> How in general must we conceive of objects if are to make empirical judgements, determinable as true or false, in which we predicate concepts of identified objects of reference? Or: What in general must be true of a world of objects of which we make such judgements? (1966, p. 82)

If it is the case that general concepts associated with the very notion of objectivity, of objects that can be perceived, measured and manipulated—are unavoidable then we must ask whether these general concepts could still somehow be explained with the methods of physical science. If we could show that there *are* fundamental concepts that do tell us what has to be true of a world of objects and events and yet cannot be studied with the methods of physical science (because they must be already presupposed as true as soon as one begins a scientific investigation), then we might still be able to explain them in a more roundabout way by trying to explain consciousness and thought empirically. Or we might be forced to conclude that the nature of the concepts must be studied in some way other than through the use of the methods of physical science.

For example, we might be able to show through conceptual argumentation alone that *in some manner* space and time will have to be included in any physical theory simply because the general domain explored in all possible physical theories *must* have spatial and temporal structure. Well, then maybe these structures, space and time in this case, perhaps substance and accident as well, have to be studied and explained in some other way than through physical models. Or maybe these categories and structures we find through transcendental forms of thinking can indeed be explained empirically but in a sort of circular way. This circularity would amount to being able to produce a fundamental physical theory to which all other sciences can be reduced: from philosophy to neuropsychology to biochemistry right down to physics.

So let's begin with the idea of categories or concepts or structures or conditions that cannot be grounded as valid for knowledge through measurements and predictions but that can be shown to be necessary for having physical knowledge. In the transcendent postulates of scientific models is there a framework that limits the direction in which all possible models can go? Do the entities postulated in the models presuppose something that applies for all possible physical models and that cannot itself be modelled?

We will actually make progress in exploring this issue by considering an objection to it from the start. That objection is the argument that scientific models do nothing more than guide measurements and make predictions. They are bookkeeping devices, not ontological representations. It does not matter whether the models depend upon metaphors or anything else because metaphors are simply metaphors and not to be taken literally. The meaning of "string" in string theory is not its *sense* but its *reference*. Let's examine this idea through the realism versus positivism debate in the philosophy of science.

*Realism Versus Positivism*
The relation between theory and measurement becomes important here. On the side of theory in fundamental physics we find postulated transcendent entities and events—things that are supersensible, that exceed direct sense experience but that are postulated as existing "behind" sense experience such that they provide correct predictions of what does come directly through the senses, usually as mediated by instruments. The validity of such models pertains to the measurements they direct and the predictions they provide. Thus one philosophical question that arises immediately when considering the role played by models in scientific explanations is whether the entities referred to in the models really exist or not. A number of practicing scientists argue that this is basically not an interesting question. Measurements are the heart and soul of science. So long as a model gives accurate predictions we have the knowledge we seek, and we cannot expect to have any more knowledge than this. Steven Hawking (Hawking, 2001) writes:

> Any sound scientific theory, whether of time or of any other concept, should in my opinion be based on the most workable philosophy of science: the positivist approach put forth by Karl Popper and others. According to this way of thinking, a scientific theory is a mathematical model that describes and codifies the observations we make. A good theory will describe a large range of phenomena on the basis of a few simple postulates and will make definite predictions that can be tested. If the predictions agree with the observations, the theory survives that test, though it can never be proved to be correct. On the other hand, if the observations disagree with the predictions, one has to discard or modify the theory. (At least, that is what is supposed to happen. In practice people often question the accuracy of the observations and the reliability and moral character of those making the observations.) If one takes the positivist position, as I do, one cannot say what time actually is. All one can do is describe what has been found to be a very good mathematical model for time and say what predictions its makes. (2001, p. 31)

Hawking does not have things quite right here in that Karl Popper was *not* a positivist and even regarded his philosophy of science to be a refutation of positivism, particularly in its logical-positivist form. Use of the term "positivism" by Hawking and Green should be understood to refer to a very strict form of empiricism with all realist claims bracketed out of the picture and endorsing Popper's critique of verificationalism. But because Hawking and Green write primarily in realist terms, as if all the supersensible entities and geometries of space-time *exist*, and then appeal to "positivism" when some of the models do raise problems for realism, the expression "quasi-positivism" seems appropriately applied to them.

Here then, is another exemplary passage from Hawking regarding his quasi-positivist position:

> From the viewpoint of positivist philosophy, however, one cannot determine what is real. All one can do is find which mathematical models describe the universe we live in. (2001, p. 59)

And one more:

> From a positivist viewpoint, one is free to use whatever picture is most useful for the problem in question. (Hawking, 2001, p. 118)

Brian Green, whose philosophical position is actually not precisely clear from what he writes in *The Elegant Universe*, makes an appeal to positivism at least with respect to one particularly important issue. One of the difficulties that string theory seems able to solve has been the relation between general relativity theory and quantum theory. According to general relativity theory, space is a continuum—it is smooth though it will bend with gravity. According to quantum physics at very small distances space is not continuous. It is rather characterized by "quantum foam." But strings have a size that is larger than the distances at which quantum foam effects occur. That means that *measurements* would in principle be impossible to make when the distances between whatever it is we wish to measure are smaller than the size of a string. Positivism therefore seems to make certain problems simply vanish because the nature of these problems cannot be formulated in measurement terms:

> In a universe governed by the laws of string theory, the conventional notion that we can always dissect nature on ever smaller distances, without limit, is not true. There *is* a limit, and it comes into play before we encounter the devastating quantum foam. Therefore, ... one can even say that the supposed tempestuous sub-Planckian quantum undulations *do not exist*. A positivist would say that something exists only if it can—at least in principle—be probed and measured. Since the string is supposed to be the most elementary object in the universe and since it is too large to be affected by the violent sub-Planck-length undulations of the spatial fabric, these fluctuations cannot be measured and hence, according to string theory, do not actually arise. (2003, p. 156-157)

The quasi-positivist position that Green and Hawking appeal to from time to time seems to be motivated only when transcendent postulates become too counter-intuitive or even raise contradictions if taken as real. Otherwise their writings on science definitely take the form of claims about what the universe is "really like," what actually exists and so on. It is basically extremely difficult to actually *practice* science, believing all the time that one is simply coming up with useful fictions that for some reason produce accurate predictions. The tendency is to think in terms of *what really exists* outside sense experience, but measurable with instruments or having effects that can be measured by instruments.

In the philosophy of science efforts to *completely* reduce scientific theories to measurements and predictions of measurements, a project that logical positivism deemed possible, produced such things as a tight distinction between the "observation language" and the "theory language" of scientific discourse. The observation language was the language in which all terms are defined by measurements. The grounding of all claims made with theoretical language had to reside in the translation of its terms to the observation language. This effort did not succeed in winning broad consent for very long. "Semantic realism" currently has won wide consensus in the philosophy of science. This is a more modest form of realism than "metaphysical realism" because it focuses on language as it is used in science and argues that such language use will always exceed strictly measurement terms. Psillos (Psillos, 2003) writes of semantic realism as follows:

> Semantic realism is no longer contested. Theoretical discourse is taken to be irreducible and assertoric (contentful) by all sides of the debate. Making semantic realism the object of philosophical consensus was by no means an easy feat, since it involved two highly non-trivial philosophical moves: *first*, the liberalization of empiricism, and the concomitant admission that theoretical discourse has 'excess content', that is, content which cannot be fully captured by means of paraphrase into observational discourse; and *second*, a battery of indispensability arguments which suggested that theoretical terms are indispensable for any attempt to arrive, in Carnap's words, at 'a powerful and efficacious system of laws' and to establish an inductive systematization of empirical laws. (Psillos, 2003, p. 61)

We can say that the tension between the quasi-positivist perspective and the realist perspective is simply that: a *tension* that science works within. Semantic realism shows us that scientific language cannot be reduced purely to measurements. It has "excess content" of a realist nature; references to objects and object-like entities that are not completely captured by measurements and use of language-embedded categories that make induction possible (but cannot themselves be induced). Metaphors are a case in point. But at the same time, the use of metaphors and other terms with objective referents in scientific models is under great pressure to strip down towards measurements and observations. Operational definitions and "coordinate definitions" (Reichenbach, 1991) strip linguistic references down toward observations and instrument readings. This direction is an important enabling condition for progressive research in the physical sciences. The limit case presupposed by this direction is that of a language in which only human-to-physical-world relations become represented. The operational definition is a definition in which the only meaning to be taken seriously for a term is the *act* of taking a measurement. Measurements in turn use a vocabulary ("length," "velocity," etc.) that are defined through "coordinate definitions":

> Defining usually means reducing a concept to other concepts. In physics, as in all other fields of inquiry, wide use is made of this procedure. There is a second kind of definition, however, which is also employed and which derives from the fact that physics, in contradistinction to mathematics, deals with real objects. Physical knowledge is characterized by the fact that concepts are not only defined by other concepts, but are also coordinated to real objects. This coordination cannot be replaced by an explanation of meanings, it simply states that *this* concept is coordinated to *this particular thing*. (Reichenbach, 1991, p. 473)

Thus, argues Reichenbach, terms used as part of measurement practice take on coordinate definitions that refer to physical objects paradigmatic for certain measurement concepts: e.g., "length" is coordinated with "measuring rod." Whatever there is about language that deals specifically with human-to-human relations, the social world, as well as human-to-self relations would be absent in scientific language were its limit case to ever be reached. Semantic realism, however, draws attention to the fact that language is essentially a human-to-human medium. It will have "excess content" both in its use of terms for scientific models (giving us an unavoidable realist presupposition) and its use in communications between members of a scientific community.

When the excess content of scientific language starts to challenge intuition too far (e.g., a two dimensional model of time with imaginary numbers on one of its axes: see just below) or suggest contradictions (e.g., the wave *and* particle nature of elementary particles in quantum mechanics, the concept of space as a continuum *and* as something with discrete units) one can always appeal to quasi-positivism so as to ignore the philosophical issue. Thus Hawking writes of the two-dimensional model of time, having an imaginary axis as well as a real-number axis, and also of models of time in which there is a minimum or maximum value *without* it being intelligible to ask what happened "before" or "after" them (just as with respect to the surface of the earth—curved two-dimensional surface—it does not make sense to ask what is "north of north"). He then explains that the apparent conceptual difficulties of such models are resolved when one defines concepts in terms of measurements:

> In general relativity, on the other hand, time and space do not exist independently of the universe or of each other. They are defined by measurements within the universe, such as the number of vibrations of a quartz crystal in a clock of the length of a ruler. (2001, p. 35)

The debates between realist and "positivist" interpretations of scientific theories leave us with more clarity on the nature of scientific models. They are dependent on a language that *exceeds* measurements but scientific language has moved in the direction of defining terms as exclusively as possible as acts of measurement, and will no doubt continue to do so without ever being able to fully subsume language to measurement. It is this dependency on language with its "excess content" that is important in the quest for limits on scientific knowledge.

*Restrictions on language, practice and experience*
As Reichenbach says, definitions of concepts in scientific language use both other concepts and measurements which are themselves coordinated with physical objects. It is the fact that *other concepts* are still part of the picture that is important, and that the language in general retains excess content. Excess content enters into scientific language at least partially through the processes of metaphorical extension and abstraction. Even a strictly empiricist interpretation of string theory would acknowledge that the metaphor of "string" serves the function of a *guide* to the construction of mathematical models.

There are some qualifications to be here in so far as the foregoing might imply that scientific language uses metaphors rather simply. It doesn't. There is a lack of intuitively available metaphors to represent some phenomena in particle physics—for example, the wave *and* particle characteristics we find within the domain of the very small. There is also the constructive process in mathematical knowledge, the expansion of the idea of dimensions so that spaces can have any number of them, the introduction of imaginary numbers with physical interpretations, and so on. But it seems that incompatible metaphors are juxtaposed when a single one will not capture what is meant to be modelled (wave *and* particle; continuity *and* discreteness), and new ideas developed by abstracting yet more from common metaphors ("quantum superposition" instead of just "position").

Either with a realist claim that strings really *are* existing ultimate substance or a quasi-positivist claim that this idea of "string" is to be taken as a metaphorical guide to the production of mathematical models, or something in-between, we have a philosophical issue of immense importance. A "string" is a kind of *object* in its sense, either in aiding record-keeping or as a postulated real entity, and like all objects it cannot be understood entirely on its own. Now, it is true that modern physics *abstracts* from ideas we find used commonly in ordinary language to produce counter-intuitive results, mathematical models that do not conform to ordinary ideas about objects and events. But the process of abstraction is limited by the material upon which it is worked. We can add greater dimensionality to the concept of object so as to have objects of more than three dimensions. We can model objects (containers) that have finite volumes but infinite surfaces and perhaps get accurate predictions of measurement from such things. The concept of "object," is connected to the concepts of space and time but the normal way we intuit this relationship can be surprisingly altered as in relativity theory. But each of these modifications is worked upon a background of concepts possessing excess content. These feats in modern physics are feats in taking the concept of objectivity as we find it in normal everyday communication and then, through abstractions and extensions, producing new counter-intuitive or just plain surprising models *without ever being able to escape the framework of objectivity-in-general.*

Scientific language has grown in this direction of greater objectivity through restricting attention to other referential functions of ordinary language and making the act of measurement more fundamental to the referents of key concepts. Everyday language use is essential for the metaphors, coordinate-definitions, and operational definitions of scientific models. Ordinary language is never completely abandoned in this process but rather accounts for the excess content we find in scientific discourse. Scientific discourse would not be possible without ordinary language.

The strict operationalization of meaning for the use of these models, such that a limit case is approached whereby the meaning of all referential terms in a scientific language would be entirely absorbed in the practice of measurement, suggests another restriction, this time placed on the large range of actual human *actions* or practices. Measurement is a subset of one kind of human action, instrumental action, which itself is a subset of human action in general. In each case, that of restricted language use and that of restricted practice, explicit rules have been generated to formalize both language use and action. Neither this explicitly restricted use of language nor this explicitly restricted form of practice could exist without something upon which the restrictions were made: the full range of human practices and the complete use of language as occurs in everyday life.

Restrictions on language use and practice correlate with restrictions on human experience. Third person, observational or perceptual experience becomes paradigmatic for experience in general. The restriction on experience is discussed more in the next section.

One more point needs to be made. The specialized language of scientific inquiry cannot, in an important sense, *itself* be a feature of the object domain to be studied. Language and measurement are *externally* related, such that language *use* can never be examined internally as a part of scientific method. The sorts of semantic investigations that semantic realism is based on are *not* investigations using the methods of physical science. If language use were to be studied with scientific method, then it would be objectivated into something that can be *observed* (measured) and a new specialized and restricted language, with "excess content," will be formed to produce models of it (as is done in empiricist linguistics). In the empirical sciences like physical science (and like empirical-only investigations of social life) the language of theory always comes from the *outside* in order to model observations.

In summary, we can make a preliminary statement about scientific models with figure 16.1.

The idea that concepts might be presupposed as soon as a project to take measurements begins, concepts that cannot themselves be grounded in their validity in terms of measurements, has led us to notice a set of restrictions that characterize scientific explanations. It is possible to explore more in the direction indicated by Strawson to try to find, "what in general must be true of a world of objects," but doing so would require a close look at *what has been restricted* to produce scientific explanations and practice: ordinary language use, the full range of human practices, the full range of human experiences. From *within* this restored position we would then need to investigate communicative structures in ordinary language for how objective references are related to other types of references and how instrumental actions are related to other types of actions. This would aid us in seeking specific internal limits or boundaries to the process of specializing in the study of objectivity.

### Scientific Models Involve:
1. A restriction on human experience to make experiences of objects and sense-experiences in general epistemologically primitive and exclusive,
2. Postulated transcendent entities interpreted in either a realist or quasi-positivist manner,
3. Explicit rules to restrict language use,
4. Explicit rules to restrict practice, or human action,
5. An external relation between language and practice, theory and action.

*Fig. 16.1: Scientific models.*

To seek specific limits in this way would actually be a large project. Kant basically took the first person position associated with observation and perception in order to discover transcendental conditions. We would have to examine first, second and third person positions together to explore the nature of internal limits that arise conceptually, when only the first person plural position is allowed. In sections below a very small part of this work is begun, but it isn't necessary to go further with such a project to demonstrate limits to knowledge in the physical sciences. The discovery of restrictions alone provides evidence for such limits but raises new questions which are to be investigated next.

*Section summary*
The question of whether a theory of everything can explain initial conditions and quantities for the universe as we find it has been interesting by guiding our explorations toward the nature of scientific explanations—modelling reality with an emphasis on measurements and predictions. Categories and concepts, like substance, space, and time are encountered that seem to pertain to the notion of objectivity-in-general necessarily and in way that removes them from being possible objects of measurement themselves. A theory of everything might one day be produced in the sense that initial conditions and quantities can be derived from it, but we have found that such a theory would seem to depend upon a set of restrictions already introduced, at the start, on full human experience, language use, and practice. Core concepts involved in *any* such model can be found through reflective thinking.

Now our second two questions become foregrounded because we can ask whether or not these reflective inferences and the fundamental conceptual-metaphorical nexus underlying scientific models in general can be explained empirically in other ways. Can we start with a totalizing physical theory, for example, and then wrap it around, so to speak, to explain the process of producing theories? That would require a physical theory of consciousness. Or can we examine the relation between consciousness and the process of observation (taking measurements) more directly so as to somehow include consciousness in our theory of everything? Problems in interpreting quantum physics at the level of the measurement/measured relation are suggestive for this question. Both issues are entailed in another point made by Steven Weinberg in his exploration of the boundaries of knowledge:

> Much as we would like to take a unified view of nature, we keep encountering a stubborn duality in the role of intelligent life in the universe, as both the observer of nature and part of what is observed. (2001, p. 77)

## 2. Can a Theory of Everything Explain Consciousness?

### Reductionism

Despite Weinberg's admission that we have a "stubborn" duality when it comes to a universe containing observers that are both the subject and part of the object of knowledge, he fully believes the duality can eventually be resolved through the success of a project of reduction:

> There are well-known problems in the description of consciousness in terms of the working of the brain. They arise because we each have special knowledge of our own consciousness that does not come to us from the senses. But I don't think that this means that consciousness will never be explained. The fundamental difficulties in understanding consciousness do not stand in the way of explaining the *behavior* of other people in terms of neurology and physiology and, ultimately, in terms of physics and history. When we have succeeded in this task, we will doubtless find that part of the explanation of behavior is a program of neural activity, that we will recognize as corresponding to our own consciousness. (2001, p. 76)

Weinberg and many others express confidence that one day consciousness will indeed be explained with a physical theory through reducing the phenomena studied by all the various scientific disciplines right to the most fundamental level of particle physics. If full reductionism were possible, then all phenomena could be ordered hierarchically in terms of its level of complexity. Ellis (2004, p. 608) presents a traditionally conceived form of reductionism in one hierarchical list, all disciplines being reducible to the discipline below it because all of the phenomena studied in one discipline will be reducible to the phenomena studied by those underneath. I reproduce this in figure 16.2.

- Sociology/Economics/Politics
- Psychology
- Physiology
- Cell biology
- Biochemistry
- Chemistry
- Physics
- Particle Physics

*Figure 16.2. Traditional version of reductionism.*

*Subtle methodological naturalism: Emergence*

The theory of emergent properties has been touted as an alternative to pure reductionism that yet preserves methodological naturalism. There are many positive and promising features of emergence theory but also large problems when it comes to trying to explain subjectivity as an emergent property. Since the problems we can identify with emergence theory as used in arguments to support methodological naturalism are *also* problems with versions of traditional reductionism, and since the converse is not immediately obvious, I will regard emergence theory as the best candidate for an effort to explain consciousness with a physical theory, seeking to cast doubt on methodological naturalism as a whole in the process.

The basic idea here is the familiar one that a whole can be greater than the sum of its parts. John Wheeler explains the idea simply as follows:

> When you put enough elementary units together, you get something that is more than the sum of these units. A substance made of a great number of molecules, for instance, has properties such as pressure and temperature that no one molecule possesses. It may be a solid or a liquid or a gas, although no single molecule is solid or liquid or gas. (Wheeler, 1998, p. 341)

Perhaps phenomena that we study in the human sciences—like meaning and values and morality and subjective states—cannot be strictly reduced to physics because as we ascend from one level of complexity to the next we must introduce new properties, new causal entities, new processes with their own laws and so on and so forth. The laws of physics cannot be used, if this were the case, to *deduce* laws that operate on higher levels. This would still be a version of reductionism because we would wish to find "laws" to explain the emergence of new properties, entities and processes. And the ontological status of these laws would have to be retained within the basic framework of physical science. Ellis presents a modified version of reductionism which includes emergence. I reproduce it in figure 16.3.

The upper column on the right involves phenomena with emergent properties. The reference to metaphysics at the very bottom and at the top left column will not be discussed here. But readers should note that use of this term in both places is relevant to arguments I will soon make regarding Strawson's conceptualization of non-transcendent metaphysics—in ways that Ellis does not consider.

| | |
|---|---|
| Metaphysics | Ethic |
| Cosmology | Sociology |
| Astronomy | Psychology |
| Geology | Physiology |
| Materials | Biochemistry |

Chemistry
Physics
Particle Physics
"Theory of Everything"
Metaphysics

*(Ellis 2004: 634)*

*Figure 16.3. Reductionism with emergence taken into account*

Emergence theory is currently under much debate. Critics of emergence theory argue that "emergence" is simply shorthand for a group or cluster of discrete phenomena. The concepts of solid, liquid and gas, for example, could easily be understood this way, and so could the fact that temperature and pressure do not apply to a single molecule but rather to the behavior of a collection of them. These critics argue against emergence theory to favor a traditional version of reductionism.

A further problem for emergence theory at this time concerns all the different versions of emergence we can consider. Given a fairly large list of types of emergence we must wonder which might be grouped together into a single type, which are valid forms of emergence and which are not. Clayton summarizes these versions of emergence as follows:

- temporal or spatial emergence
- emergence in the progression from simple to complex
- emergence in increasingly complex levels of information processing
- the emergence of new properties (e.g., physical, biological, psychological)
- the emergence of new causal entities (atoms, molecules, cells, central nervous system)
- the emergence of new organizing principles or degrees of inner organization (feedback loops, autocatalysis, 'autopoiesis')
- emergence in the development of 'subjectivity' (Clayton, 2004, p. 597)

Of course, it is the last type of emergence that we are most interested in here. Can subjectivity and consciousness be regarded, explained even, as forms of emergence? This type of emergence is the one regarded as most problematical by Clayton and other writers on emergence. I think there is a very good reason why this last type of emergence, emergence of consciousness or subjectivity, has posed the greatest challenge. The reason is that emergence theory, as it is currently being explored and expounded, is located firmly within the framework of a physical scientific theory. Clayton's list of strictures for the study of emergence is very revealing and worth quoting in this regard. I present three of his strictures below:

1. Emergence studies will be scientific only if emergence can be explicated in terms that the relevant sciences can study, check, and incorporate into actual theories.
2. Explanations concerning such phenomena must thus be given in terms of the structures and functions of stuff in the world. As Christopher Southgate writes, 'An emergent property is one describing a higher level of organization of matter, where the description is not epistemologically reducible to lower-level concepts' (Southgate, 1999, p. 158).
3. It also follows that all forms of dualism are disfavored. For example, only those research programs count as emergentist which refuse to accept an absolute break between neurophysiological properties and mental properties. 'Substance dualisms,' such as the Cartesian delineation of reality into 'matter' and 'mind,' are generally avoided. (Clayton, 2004, pp. 579-80)

What we see here are the boundaries of natural science articulated acutely about the concept of "substance" once more. If subjectivity is to be understood as an emergent property in this way, then it is to be understood as a type of "stuff"—substance (point #2 in the quotation). Not only is subjectivity to be a type of stuff, but rather a form of the *same* stuff that ontologically is believed to underlie everything from the perspective of this realist version of scientism. Now, there are good reasons for the claim here that Cartesian dualism is something to avoid when trying to understand subjectivity (point #3). But the emergence theorists we find here (Clayton and Southgate) seek to avoid the problems of dualism by appeal to a single substance rather than two radically different substances. The main problem with Cartesian dualism is *not* that two substances were proposed by Descartes, but rather that *subjectivity was regarded as a substance in the first place*.

*Can subjectivity be modelled?*
From a roughly Kantian perspective we can say that the effort to think of subjectivity as a form of emergence in the sense given above makes the mistake of using a category of understanding employed (necessarily, for Kant) when we experience something through the senses – the category of "substance" in this case – to trying to understand something that we do *not* have access to through the senses. Subjectivity is ultimately not a sense phenomenon at all, but is rather presupposed whenever we experience something. Hence subjectivity cannot be modelled in the same way that objectivity can. In the case of objectivity, all models have the conceptual *possibility* of representing something physical, such that terms in the model do not differ by conceptual type from what they represent, even though what they repre-

424

sent escapes experience. In the case of subjectivity, no model could actually be constructed with this congruency between conceptual types. It is true that models of subjectivity can and have been produced to predict behaviors under certain conditions, but in this case subjectivity *itself* has been dislocated to the interpretive processes of the model-maker and to the subject modelled in so far as she will be able to change her behavior as soon as she learns of the model that supposedly predicts it. A model of, for example, the relation between an "attitude" and behavior in certain situations treats "attitude" like a physical object by calling it a "variable" and locating it within a set of external relations (correlational or causal relations between attitude, measurably defined situation and behaviour). An "attitude," however, is ontologically not a discrete entity. Nor is it a shorthand term for a behaviour pattern—few people are still convinced by behaviorist doctrines and for good reasons.

Now, there are different layers of subjectivity that have to be taken into account when making an argument like this. Subjectivity pertains to what Kant called the phenomena of "inner sense" as distinguished from the phenomena of "outer sense." And in addition, subjectivity has to do with the "I" – the ultimate *subject* of both kinds of experience ("inner," and "outer").

### The inner/outer distinction

On the inner-sense / outer-sense distinction, we have experiences of trees, rocks and air as things somehow outside ourselves and we experience emotions, desires and thoughts as somehow inside. Kant pointed out that all objects of outer experience are framed both spatially and temporally but all objects of inner experience are framed only temporally, not spatially. An emotion has no spatial position, only a position in the temporal flow of experience (as in, I feel happy now but did not feel happy ten minutes ago). Recognizing an experience as one of the inner variety will *not* employ a category like that of "substance" whereas recognizing an experience as one of an object "outside" the self will require a category like substance. Hence if there is anything right about Kant's phenomenological description of the inner / outer distinction, subjectivity cannot be modelled in any way that involves the concept of "stuff." This is one argument to make against reductionism. Its full force is only grasped when we understand that to locate some objects of experience within space *and* time depends upon the possibility of having experiences of states and events that are *not* in any way possible to locate in space, and vice versa. In fact, the temporal orders of the objects of inner sense and outer sense themselves have to be distinct for any intelligible concept of experience-in-general (this is expanded in the longer essay). That means that to model subjectivity as a kind of "stuff" existing in some sort of special organization is to actually introduce an implicit contradiction to the situation. Let's examine this a little more carefully.

Wilhelm Dilthey modified Kantian arguments in his efforts to distinguish the sciences of nature (*Naturwissenschaften*) from the human sciences (*Geisteswissenschaften*). His argument was that the categories of understanding used for studying objects in the physical world are produced by a truncation of experience through the process of objectivation. Human experience is very multifaceted and does not consist primordially of mere experiences of objects in a physical world, mere perceptions of the outer-sense variety. But natural science has progressed by restricting full human experience to that which is most objective, most stripped of any subjectivity. Dilthey thus modifies Kant to argue that the categories he considered to be transcendental categories of consciousness, necessary for *all experience*, are actually categories produced by a truncation of experience (at least in many cases—this need not be true in all cases of the Kantian categories as I show in the longer essay).

> …this idea of the world based on spatial extension is the original source of all knowledge of uniformities, and we are advised from the start to reckon with them. We gain control of this physical world by the study of its laws. These laws can only be discovered insofar as the lived character of our impressions of nature, the connection we have with nature to the extent that we are ourselves part of it, and the lively feeling in which we enjoy it recede ever more behind the abstract comprehension of it according to the relations of time, space, mass, and motion. All these moments work together to ensure that man effaces himself in order to construct—on the basis of his impressions—this great object, nature, as an order governed by laws. It then becomes the center of reality for man. (Dilthey, 2002, p. 104)

From the "lived character" of holistic full experience we obtain the objective world studied by natural science through a sort of self-effacement. There are two senses to this idea of a self-effacement: one is the reduction of experience to observational experience, the other is something I will discuss shortly—the "I" of experience becomes set aside and presupposed as a purely anonymous subject without any properties whatsoever. In terms of the first sense of self-effacement, we construct an objective world by giving meaning only to the *most* objective portions of experience. This means, among many other things, that what Kant called "outer-sense" experiences now are taken to be the paradigm for *all* experiences. This world we access through outer-sense prioritizes the third person position over the first person position. It results in *abstractions* used to explain the physical world in the form of those transcendent postulates we have discussed already, which are brought to *explain* regularities in experience *from outside experience itself*. Hence Dilthey called these transcendent postulates that characterize scientific models "auxiliary constructions":

> The formation of the natural sciences is determined by the way in which their object, nature, is given. Images emerge from a continual flux, they are referred to objects, these objects fill and occupy empirical consciousness, and they form the object of descriptive natural science. But even empirical consciousness notices that the sensory qualities exhibited in images are dependent upon the standpoint of observation, upon distance, and upon illumination. Physics and physiology show ever more clearly the phenomenality of these sensory qualities. Thus the task arises of thinking of objects in such a way that both their phenomenal changes and the uniformities emerging ever more clearly amidst these changes become intelligible. The concepts through

which this happens are auxiliary constructions that thought creates for this purpose. Thus nature as foreign to us, transcending the apprehending subject, is elaborated by auxiliary constructions based on the phenomenally given. (Dilthey, 2002, p. 111)

The role of metaphors in scientific models that we discussed earlier is hence further clarified here. Auxiliary constructions are *based* on the phenomenally given, in all its richness, but metaphorical extensions and abstractions from full experience produce transcendent entities that we do not and cannot experience. Natural use of language not only references more than objectivity, not only references everything within lived full human experience, but is a *part* of this experience. So we see once again, from a slightly new perspective here, that the formal languages of science are another domain in which we can find the employment of restrictions to enable the workings of physical science.

There is nothing wrong about this feature of the physical sciences *unless* the metaphors used to make sense of the physical world, metaphors that originated through a process that had to pull meaning away from a context of full lived experience toward only the objective side, are *next* used to try to explain subjectivity. Refinements introduced on third person experience already presuppose a dependence on, and distinction from, first person experience. First and third person modes of experience are in fact mutually dependent. Neither differentiated domain of experience can produce the conceptual basis for explaining the other.

Hence at this point we can argue that inner experience cannot be modelled at least in the way that outer experience can be. Clayton, in his fine discussion of emergence theory, expresses strong doubts about the possibility of explaining consciousness in terms of emergence for similar reasons. He quotes the consciousness theorist Chalmers:

The really hard problem of consciousness is the problem of experience. When we think and perceive, there is a whir of information-processing, but there is also a subjective aspect. As Nagel has put it, there is something it is like to be a conscious organism. This subjective aspect is experience. When we see, for example, we experience visual sensations: the felt quality of redness, the experience of dark and light, the quality of depth in a visual field. Other experiences go along with perception in different modalities: the sound of a clarinet, the smell of mothballs. Then there are bodily sensations, from pains to orgasms; mental images that are conjured up internally; the felt quality of emotion, and the experience of a stream of conscious thought. What unites all of these states is that there is something it is like to be in them. All of them are states of experience." (Chalmers, 1995, p. 201, in Clayton, 2004, p. 601)

Chalmers' point is better expressed by the quotations I have supplied from Dilthey in this section, but Chalmers' insight is precisely where Dilthey's was. Reductionism, using emergence or not, will not work when it comes to subjectivity, in part because a whole category of phenomena, with its own ontological significance, is shaved from experience. Neural science and its sister disciplines can be expected to produce *correlations* between first person experience and third person observations of neural activity. But reductionism would have it that the relation between the objective and subjective sides of such correlations is one of identity (e.g., thoughts simply *are* the neuro-physiological states they correlate with). And that proposition is in the end contradictory.

### Subjectivity as the "I"

The second sense in which a type of self-effacement occurs in the enabling of physical science is linked to Kant's theory of the "I." Kant provides us with a great insight here that is progressively referred to, developed and finally modified within the longer essay. Kant argued that an "I think" (potentially, to be more accurate) accompanies all experiences and we are invited to notice this in the fact that all experiences can in principle be understood as "my" experiences. In section III of the longer essay I take a closer look at this idea of an "I" that accompanies all experiences but that is not itself an object of experience, because in this notion we find not only a precondition for natural science that cannot be studied by natural science, but also a special type of effacement that depends upon a fuller sense of the self, one which is deeply and essentially non-empirical but that includes more than the effaced "I." The distinction between inner-sense and outer-sense is worthy of attention but requires refinements when examined carefully because it is a distinction that is *produced* through intersubjectivity and can vary culturally in its specifics. It is not precisely as Kant would have it. But the "I" is something that can be argued for quite rigorously, as a type of *a priori* condition which cannot be explained empirically.

However, here we are simply exploring objections to the project of reductionism. And all we need to note is that experience includes an "I" that is yet not an object of experience. No experience could be possible if *some* experiences didn't have the accompaniment of the "I" within them. Experiences are always experiences *of* something. With the "I" in this most primordial and effaced sense we do not have something that is ever the "of" in an experience, but rather its counterpart: that which makes use of the term "of" intelligible when we say we have an experience of this or that. In Hegelian terminology we have the negative, or negation, in experience with the "I." The "I" is there whenever we find ourselves aware of something as something *else*, something other to us. The "I" is at first the *elseness* of any object of experience (whether an inner or an outer experience). The *elseness* of the object of experience is rather like finding a mirror in the object without finding what it reflects. It is in this sense the negative.

This is a more profound reason for rejecting reductionism in all its forms. The "I" of experience, we shall soon see (but only in the longer essay), is implicated by the distinction between inner and outer, by the concept of an objective world as well as a subjective world. The "I" will form a bridge for us to arrive at the full self and land firmly with the framework of the human sciences as those that study a domain presupposed and yet barred by the physical ones precisely through such things as this "I."

*Emergence and reductionism do not work*

It is for these reasons that the reductionistic project cannot work. Emergence theory is primarily an effort to shore-up the traditional version of reductionism and present a new argument in favor of methodological naturalism. Many things in emergence theory are exciting and will no doubt be fruitful. But the theory has so far been confined to the framework of physical science, as we see in the strictures that Clayton applies to it. Physical science has been enabled through a series of restrictions made on full human experience and full natural language use. Everything left out in this process of restricting cannot be explained by the resulting methodology. Emergence theory tries to keep everything within the boundaries of causal relations between entities, with entities conceptualized just in the way Dilthey elucidates: a process of abstraction that is bounded by basic concepts of objectivity-in-general. For example, Clayton writes about emergence theory as applied to the concept of subjectivity by casting the problem in terms of the "mind" and "brain" distinction:

> ...research programs in emergence tend to combine sustained research into (in this case) the connections between brain and 'mind,' on the one hand, with the expectation that emergent phenomena will not be fully explainable in terms of underlying causes on the other. (Clayton, 2004, p. 580)

*Causation* remains the fundamental category. But within the domains of meaning, culture, inner experience and understanding another human subject we do not find causal relations. We find other sorts of relations such as logical relations, semantic relations, illocutionary relations and much else. We must reject reductionism and emergence theory when the line is crossed from physical phenomena to those phenomena that were set aside in order to give the clearest most precise access possible to physical phenomena. Once that line is crossed we find entirely new categories within which to pursue inquiry. We must agree with Dilthey when he says:

> No real category can claim the validity it has in the natural sciences for the human sciences as well. If the abstract procedure expressed in a natural science category is transferred to the human sciences, then the natural sciences transgress their limits." (2002, p. 219)

## 3. The Observer-Observed Relation as it Arises in Quantum Mechanics

Reductionism and emergence are not viable ways for a theory of everything to explain consciousness, subjectivity and other things that are definitive for the human sciences (meaning, culture, etc.) because these things cannot be made objects of study. They are non-objective, yet necessary conditions for objectivity itself.

But perhaps consciousness could be included within a physical theory of everything in some other way. Anything objective is something that can be measured. What if the subject/object distinction were brought into play within the concept of a measurement such that they could be understood as dependent upon one another ontologically and not just epistemologically? This would change the traditional distinction made between ontology and epistemology, putting them together in some way `as yet to be elucidated. It would remove the notion of ontology from dependence on a backgrounded concept of the purely objective, like "substance." In philosophy we already have had proposals to change our understanding of ontology in ways like this. Hegel famously claimed that "substance is subject," and he developed an ontology which consists of the dialectic between forms of knowledge and the sorts of subjectivity related to each form, the whole process of which is explained as a movement of something (*Geist*) to know itself, importantly involving reflection. Heidegger included the hermeneutic circle (something that is most readily grasped as an epistemological process) into his *ontology* of human-being, and altered traditional notions of being as substance. Both Heidegger and Hegel, whose philosophies nevertheless differ very importantly from each other, alter our common sense understandings of time in the course of their work with ontology. They show us that there are *possibilities* for understanding substance, subject, existence, being, time and so on that differ from the more commonsense ways in which these concepts are understood.

*Measurements in quantum mechanics*
In physical science, quantum mechanics has forced philosophical issues similar to these, hovering about the relation between epistemology and ontology. There are experimentally demonstrated problems in the relation between measurement and what is measured when it comes to very small entities like photons and electrons. Quantum mechanics is a formal mathematical system that provides extremely accurate predictions between measurements of initial states and final states of physical systems following an intervention. There are no problems with its uses for making predictions. But there are very large problems when it comes to providing a physical interpretation of quantum mechanics. Weinberg summarizes the situation as follows:

> In quantum mechanics the state of any system is described by a mathematical object known as the wave function. According to the interpretation of quantum mechanics worked out in Copenhagen in the early 1930s, the rules for calculating the wave function are of a very different character from the principles used to interpret it. On the one hand, there is the Schrodinger equation [the wave function], which describes in a perfectly deterministic way how the wave function of any system changes with time. Then, quite separate, there is a set of principles that tells how to use the wave function to calculate the probabilities of various possible outcomes when someone makes a measurement. ...

> ... before a measurement the wave function of a spinning electron is generally a sum of terms corresponding to different directions of the electron's spin; with such a wave function the electron cannot be said to be spinning clockwise or counterclockwise around some axis, however, [when taking a measurement] we somehow change the electron's wave

function so that the electron is definitely spinning one way or the other. Measurement is thus regarded as something intrinsically different from anything else in nature. And although opinions differ, it is hard to identify anything special that qualifies some process to be called a measurement, except its effect on a conscious mind. (2001, p. 77)

This is one of a number of things about quantum mechanics that has captured the imagination of the public and has resulted in the play, *Copenhagen*, by Michael Frayn. Is physical reality dependent, *ontologically*, on having an observer? In the famous two-slit experiment we have hard core data that is extremely hard to interpret with any ontology of the physical world. Roger Penrose's summary of the two-slit experiment is concise and clear:

Here we have a source of particles and a detector screen, where there is a barrier with a pair of narrowly separated parallel slits in it, situated between source and screen. We suppose that one particle at a time is emitted, aimed at the screen. If we start with one slit open and the other closed, then a haphazard pattern of dots will appear at the screen, forming one at a time as individual particles from the source hit it. The intensity of the pattern (in the sense of the greatest density of dots) is most extreme in a central strip close to the plane connecting source to slit, as is to be expected, and it falls off uniformly in both directions from this central strip. This pattern is effectively the same if the experiment is repeated with the other slit being the open one. No puzzle here. But if the experiment is run once more when both slits are now open, then something extraordinary happens. The particles still make dots on the screen one at a time, but now there is a wavy *interference* pattern of parallel bands of intensity, where we even find that there are regions on the screen that are never reached by particles from the source, despite the fact that when just one or the other of the slits was open, then particles could reach those regions perfectly happily! Although the spots appear at the screen one at a time at localized positions, and although each occurrence of a particle meeting the screen can be identified with a particular particle-emission event at the source, the behaviour of the particle *between* source and screen, including its ambiguous encounter with the two slits in the barrier, is like a wave, where the wave/particle feels out both slits during this encounter.

If the particles (e.g., photons or electrons) were indeed particles, then having both slits open would simply result in a pattern on the screen that would be the sum of the two patterns obtained with first having one slit open, then closing it and opening the other. Instead we get a new pattern, a wave-interference pattern, that would be expected if the emissions were waves rather than particles. Yet experimenters see particle-like impacts on the destination screen *one at a time* with both slits open. If we really had waves we would see several places on the destination screen record an impact at once!

That is odd, but it gets even odder! If one tries to get more information about this puzzling result by placing another photographic plate at the side of the barrier when both slits are open in it, in order to sort of "see" (by recording) what happens when the particles reach the two slits, then the interference pattern on the original photographic plate (the destination screen) completely washes out and what one finds at the screen is what one would expect if the particles were truly and unambiguously particles. It is as if the particles (e.g., photons or electrons) "know" that we have tried to catch them as something between waves and particles, and change their behavior accordingly.

Here is a case in which no single transcendent postulate based on metaphors ("particle," "wave") can account for measured physical phenomena. Moreover, the act of taking a measurement appears to be in some way connected with what *exists* and even what *existed* in the past. Davies writes: "…the experimenter not only can participate in the nature of physical reality that is, but also in the nature of physical reality that *was*." (2005, p. 9) It is therefore extremely difficult to provide a physical interpretation for the formal mathematical model of quantum mechanics.

The concept of a "physical state" in classical physics is such that a state will be described through specifying the values of its variables. In quantum mechanics the term "state" was given a different meaning. The state of a physical system in this case is defined with the wave function $\Psi$ which changes deterministically with time. From $\Psi$ we can calculate the probability of getting various values for the variables of the system at a certain time if a measurement is taken. Once a measurement has been taken the value of the state, $\Psi$, changes in a way that can be calculated by taking the measurement value into account. But this change in $\Psi$ is "sudden." It is non-continuous, and it is very difficult to understand such changes ontologically.

The values of variables in a physical system are not given an ontological status prior to the taking of a measurement. The position of a particle, for example, can be thought to "exist" simultaneously with different values (normally a contradiction) and hence the term "quantum superposition" is used. Position is, so to speak, "spread out" over a range. A measurement "collapses the wave function" so that a single value manifests. This is not a matter of simply "not knowing" which real value a variable has at any one time, it is a matter of there *being* no single existing value to the variable when measurements are not made.

Some have consequently argued for a new understanding of the universe that makes it dependent upon consciousness in some way. But this is a large leap to make from the puzzles of quantum mechanics which are at first appearance a matter of *measurements* in relation to the question of *what is measured*. It is not at first obvious that the measurer need be conscious. What is really involved, at first appearances, is the relation between a micro physical system (the particles) and a macro physical device that responds to it. Hence there have been efforts to argue for *observer*-independent interpretations / explanations of quantum mechanics (e.g., see *Physics Today*, March 1998, March 2000, September 2000 for some fairly technical arguments).

In the relational theory of quantum mechanics, the wave function is regarded as a sort of bookkeeping system rather than an ontological representation and the actual measurements taken are regarded as "real." This resolves the difficulty of trying to think of reality in terms of multiple but incompatible values of variables existing all at once: a particle spread out in a discontinuous way, for example. Thus in this interpretation there is simply no meaning to the idea of the variable having any sort of value when a measurement is not taken. But it raises a new problem which becomes apparent when we notice that the instrument used to measure a physical system is another physical system, and the measurement is an interaction within a larger physical system containing the original system of interest and the observation system (instrument). Once this is noticed then the meaning of a value obtained through a measurement becomes "relational":

> The core idea is to read the theory as a theoretical account of the way distinct physical systems *affect each other* when they interact (and not of the way physical systems 'are'), and the idea that this account exhausts all that can be said about the physical world. (Laudiser, 2005, p. 2)

But then we can have a measurement of the original physical system of interest made by the initial observation system that produces a value for the original physical system (from the perspective of this measurement system) *and* have an interpretation of the observer-observed system from the perspective of another measurement system that does not yield this value but only a correlation between the physical system and the original observation system—a correlation without any outcome. Those who argue for relational quantum theory have relativized core concepts of "event," "position," "spin" and so on to having meaning only in terms of correlations—taking an observing apparatus into account and defining fundamental terms relationally.

However, a total physical system inclusive of all possible interactions with measuring systems would have to measure *itself* and this is not possible. Weinberg writes:

> At present, we do not understand even in principle how to calculate or interpret the wave function of the universe, and we cannot resolve these problems by requiring that all experiments give sensible results, because by definition there is no observer outside the universe who can experiment on it. (2001, p. 79)

What seems to be endemic to the situation is the inevitable transcendence of the "final" observer from all possible descriptions of physical systems. Marisa Dalla Chiara has related the debates over the significance of the observer in quantum mechanics to the self-reference issue in logic, first brought to the attention of the world by Godel with his incompleteness theorems. Chiara writes:

> If the apparatus observer $O$ is an object of the theory, then $O$ cannot realize the reduction of the wave function. This is possible only to another $O'$, which is 'external' with respect to the universe of the theory. In other words, any apparatus, as a particular physical system, can be an object of the theory. Nevertheless, *any apparatus which realizes the reduction of the wave*

*function is necessarily only a metatheoretical object* . (Dalla Chiara, 1977, p. 340).

When a system to be studied includes *both* a physical system and an observer (another physical system) of it, quantum equations *can* describe the resulting complex system entirely, but only from the point of view of a new observer taking measurements—an observer who transcends what is described.

Similarly, Thomas Breuer published an independent proof for the impossibility of any physical system, whether conceptualized in quantum *or* classical terms, to measure itself (Breuer, 1993). Hence:

> If one is interested in the quantum theory of the entire universe, then, by definition, an external observer is not available. Breuer's theorem shows then that a quantum state of the universe, containing all correlations between all subsystems, expresses information that is not available, not even in principle, to any observer. In order to write a meaningful quantum state ... we have to divide the universe in two components and consider the relative quantum state predicting the outcomes of the observations that one component can make on the other. (Laudisa, 2005, p. 6)

In terms of conceptualizing knowledge of the universe, then, one can include observer positions by taking a third person position with respect to them. Any description of the whole universe has to make at least one division of it to produce an observation system and the physical system that remains. The universe is then relativized to a "second observer" position not included in the resulting description: the position from which choice of the division is made.

Quantum mechanics, like relativity theory, has pushed physical science forward by relativizing yet another set of terms that were thought to be absolute and unproblematical. In this case the terms are extremely basic—going right to the concept of "existence." The resemblance of the results of this work to the classical problem in philosophy that was raised to awareness most markedly by Kant is remarkable—the presupposition of subjectivity in all objective claims, with subjectivity presupposed in such a way to make it impossible for it to ever become an object of experience. We can choose observational systems conceptualized in purely physical terms and produce correlations between them and the rest of the universe, but *doing* this presupposes a second observer position that is not captured in physical terms and cannot be without presupposing yet another observer position.

Of course, many discussions of this topic do not refer to "consciousness," subjectivity or the "I," but rather to "observer" and mean by this a physical system that correlates with the physical system "observed." However, the bottom line seems to me and others who have contributed to discussions in this area that for a physical system to be an instrument-observer makes sense only through the fact that it is *read*. It delivers meaning. Hence some scientists have been toying with the idea of information theory in order to suggest a new ontological picture. The "it" of the universe is dependent on the "bit" – the unit of information that must have meaning, must not be strictly formal like a physical object or process but have semantic properties.

John Wheeler urged investigations into the question of whether or not we live in an "it from bit" universe, referring to the origins of the "bit" concept in computing:

> In the universe ... chance plays a dominant role. The laws of physics tell us only what *may* happen. Actual measurement tells us what *is* happening (or what *did* happen). Despite this difference [between computers and the universe], it is not unreasonable to imagine that information sits at the core of physics, just as it sits at the core of a computer.

> Trying to wrap my brain around this idea of information theory as the basis of existence, I came up with the phrase "it from bit." The universe and all that it contains ("it") may arise from the myriad yes-no choices of measurement (the "bits"). Niels Bohr wrestled for most of his life with the question of how acts of measurement (or "registration") may affect reality. It is registration—whether by a person or a device or a piece of mica (anything that can preserve a record)—that changes potentiality into actuality. I build only a little on the structure of Bohr's thinking when I suggest that we may never understand this strange thing, the quantum, until we understand how information may underlie reality. Information may not be just what we *learn* about the world. It may be what *makes* the world (Wheeler, 1998, pp. 340-341).

## Two options?

I will not speculate more on this fascinating intersection of philosophy with physics. Let us end this chapter by noting that we *seem* to have two options facing us here, both of which emphasize necessary limits to physical knowledge.

One option is to acknowledge that we find ourselves within a universe in which everything is relational right down to the most core of all our fundamental concepts for acquiring knowledge of it, such that "a theory of everything" is really not possible because it runs into the idea of a whole universe without an observer.

The other option is to work the "it from bit" hypothesis towards an ontology that finds subject-object fusion at the heart of our most fundamental concepts: concepts of being, existence and so on. In this latter case we might have something like a dialectical concept at the far reaches of purely objectifying exploration. We might have a universe that contains "loops of meaning" as Wheeler expressed it. Meaning is something that cannot be reduced to physical states unless reductionism was possible, which I have argued is not the case.

Of relevance to both options is a now famous picture drawn by John Wheeler. This consists of a "U" standing for "universe" with an eye at the top of one of its columns, staring at the other column. The universe, he was suggesting, consists of both what is observed and the observer. A good reproduction of the diagram is given in Clayton's article (2004). Lucien Hardy modified Wheeler's drawing by adding a hand to the eye, a hand touching what the eye gazes at (Hardy, 2004, p. 45). Measurement is not a passive affair, it is active and its central concepts have developed in relation to human action, or rather one subset of it: actions orientated toward the physical world in expectation of consequences.

The enabling conditions for the physical sciences limit the knowledge it can produce in ways that can easily be forgotten, unnoticed, hidden from view. They are restrictions on something else that physical science cannot itself study directly nor completely because its acts of measurement, its formalization of language and its restrictions on human experience only have the meaning they possess by already presupposing this other domain. This other domain can only be accessed in ways prohibited by the methodology of physical science. It is the core domain of the human sciences even though scientistic ideology has hidden this from even many social scientists. It is the subject of the next sections in the longer essay where its own key enabling conditions are explored and a new set of limits to knowledge uncovered.

## REFERENCES

Breuer, T. (1993). The impossibility of accurate state self-measurements. *Philosophy of Science, 62*, 197-214.

Carspecken, P. F. (forthcoming). *Can a Theory of Everything Explain Itself? An essay on limits to knowledge in the physical and social sciences.* Rotterdam: Sense Publishers.

Chalmers, D. (1995). Facing up to the problem of Consciousness. *Journal of Consciousness Studies, 2*(200).

Clayton, P. D. (2004). Emergence: us from it. In J. D. D. Barrow, C. W. Paul & C. Harper, Jr. (Eds.), *Science and Ultimate Reality* (pp. 577-606). Cambridge: Cambridge University Press.

Dalla Chiara, M. L. (1977). Logical self-reference, set theoretical paradoxes and the measurement problem in quantum mechanics. *Journal of Philosophical Logic, 6*, 331-347.

Davies, P. C. W. (2004). John Archibald Wheeler and the clash of ideas. In J. D. D. Barrow, C. W. Paul & C. Harper, Jr. (Eds.), *Science and Ultimate Reality* (pp. 3-26). Cambridge: Cambridge University Press.

Delandshere, G. (2002). Assessment as inquiry. *Teachers College Record, 104*, 1461-1484.

Delandshere, G. (2005). "Scientific" research in disguise and the threat to a spirit of inquiry. In B. H. Doecke, M.; Sawyer, W. (Eds.), *'Only connect': English teaching and democracy.* Kent Town, Australia: Wakefield Press.

Dilthey, W. (2002). *Selected works, volume III; The formation of the historical world in the human cciences* (Vol. 3). Princeton and Oxford: Princeton University Press.

Ellis, G. F. R. (2004). True complexity and its associated ontology. In J. D. D. Barrow, Paul C. W.; Harper, Charles Jr. (Eds.), *Science and ultimate reality* (pp. 607-636). Cambridge: Cambridge University Press.

Green, B. (2003). *The elegant universe; superstrings, hidden dimensions, and the quest for the ultimate theory.* New York: Vintage Books.

Hamlyn, D. (1984). *Metaphysics.* Cambridge: Cambridge University Press.

Hardy, L. (2004). Why is nature described by quantum theory? In J. D. D. Barrow, Paul C. W.; Harper, Charles Jr. (Eds.), *Science and ultimate reality* (pp. 45-71). Cambridge: Cambridge University Press.

Hawking, S. (2001). *The universe in a nutshell.* New York: Bantam Books.

Kant, I. (1965). *Critique of pure reason* (N. K. Smith, Trans. Unabridged ed.). Boston; New York: Bedford/St. Martin's.

Laudisa, F. a. R., Carlo. (2005). Relational quantum mechanics. In E. N. Zalta (Ed.), *The Standford Encyclopedia of Philosophy.*

Penrose, R. (1989). *The emporor's new mind; Concerning computers, minds, and the laws of physics.* New York: Penguin Books.

Penrose, R. (2005). *The road to reality; A complete guide to the laws of the universe.* New York: Alfred A. Knopf.

Psillos, S. (2003). The present state of the scientific realism debate. In P. C. a. K. Hawley (Ed.), *Philosophy of Science Today* (pp. 59-82). Oxford: Clarendon Press.

Reichenbach, H. (1991). The philosophy of space and time; Selections. In R. G. Boyd, Philip; and Trout, J.D. (Eds.), *The Philosophy of Science* (pp. 473-484). Cambridge, MA: MIT Press.

Schwandt, T. (2002). *Evaluation practice reconsidered.* New York: Peter Lang.

Sokal, A. D. (1996a). A physicist experiments with cultural studies. *Lingua Franca, May/June 1996,* 62-64.

Sokal, A. D. (1996b). Transgressing the Boundaries; Toward a transformative hermeneutics of quantum gravity". *Social Text, Spring / Summer 1996,* 217-252.

Southgate, C. e. a. (1999). *God, humanity, and the cosmos: A textbook in science and religion.* Harrisburg, PA: Trinity Press.

Strawson, P. F. (1966). *The bounds of sense; An essay on Kant's Critique of Pure Reason.* London and New York: Routledge.

Weinberg, S. (2001). *Facing up; Science and its cultural adversaries.* Cambridge, MA; London: Harvard University Press.

Wheeler, J. A. w. K. F. (1998). *Geons, black holes and quantum foam; A life in physics.* New York, London: W. W. Norton and Company.

JOHN WILLINSKY

# 17. WHEN THE RESEARCH'S OVER, DON'T TURN OUT THE LIGHTS

To speak of *doing research*, as this handbook does, suggests being caught up in the midst of researching. It invokes a sense of being out there in the field, lost in the archives, sitting on a classroom floor with children, or in a café recording an interview.[1] Doing research calls forth ideas of methods and processes, systematically executed, painstakingly recorded with flawless precision and rigorous attention to detail. But surely the field-work-in-rubber-boots is only part of what it means to *do research*. I can say that because it is obvious that the research is not *done*, if after all the data are collected and carefully analyzed, the work then sits in an file on one's computer and goes no farther. The responsibilities of the researcher extend beyond the immediate design, conduct, and supervision of the research. Those additional responsibilities have both epistemological and ethical implications for what it means to do work that goes by the name of *research*, and those implications have to do with how the research is circulated and shared.

My theme with this chapter, then, is that the research is not done or complete, until it has been made available to others, and how it is made available carries with it a new set of epistemological and ethical responsibilities that are the result of changes in how scholarly work is now being published. Research worthy of the name has always had to appear in some publicly accessible form. It may be filed in a university library as a dissertation, submitted to a client as a report, read at the annual meeting of a local society, or published in a journal or book. When it comes to talking about the contribution that research makes to the common stock of knowledge, the way in which the work has been circulated and the way in which it is open to review serve to warrant its claims to be *research*. Just how much of the research that is made public is critical to its claims. The research must identify the sources in great detail on which it has drawn; it must justify the design and method deployed; it must share some portion of the data; it must demonstrate how the conclusions were arrived at, while accounting for counter-examples; and finally, it must situate the findings within the larger picture, in ways that speak to immediate implications and future directions.

The critical elements of the well-formed research article have emerged out of a publishing tradition that goes back to the very public scrutiny of Isaac Newton's one and only published article, which was on optics, in the January 3, 1671 edition of the *Philosophical Transactions*, during the first decade of the new genre that has come to be known as the scientific journal (Willinsky, 2006, pp. 234-244). The critical questions raised by readers of this article in letters to the *Transactions*

*K. Tobin & J. Kincheloe, (eds.), Doing Educational Research—A Handbook, 439–456.*

forced Newton to further clarify his research design and method, as well as the scope of his results. The back and forth between Newton and his critics in the pages of the *Transactions* until, after four years, Newton said, "No more," to the journal's earnest editor, Henry Oldenburg, amounted to the setting of a standard for making research public, a standard that placed the reader in a position not only to replicate the experiment, but to check the sources, scrutinize the analysis, and challenge the conclusions (Kuhn, 1978).

Which is only to say that the researcher's responsibilities for opening a work to the widest possible public scrutiny is no less important to its standing as research than all of the thought and care that she originally invested in the designing and carrying out of the research. In terms of epistemology, we would say that one requisite for believing that a study's conclusions are true, and not mistaken or misguided, is that the study has been subject to critical scrutiny. Sometimes we make that call ourselves, but more often we leave it up to the editorial and peer-review process, which represents the great contribution of the journal system for scholarly publication. Here, the normally opposed reprobate postmodernist and recalcitrant positivist share a point of common understanding: If you will not allow us to see your work, your claims to having been *doing research* on a topic is just so much cant. This is otherwise known as, "put up or shut up."

Yet if that is the epistemological side of the coin we would forge in the act of completing the research study, then there is also the ethical side of going public to consider. While most of the talk on research ethics is concerned with protecting the rights of research subjects to informed consent and the right to withdraw it at any point, the ethics involved in publishing the research are no less compelling. The researcher has an ethical responsibility to see work that has arrived at some warranted conclusions enter the public domain by some means. The work was undertaken, after all, in good faith that it had a contribution to make to our understanding.

A recent instance of the ethics at stake in publishing is found in the tendency of certain corporate sponsors of clinical trials research in the life sciences to leave unpublished or suppress the publication of studies that conclude a given treatment is not helpful, or worse. The situation had become so alarming that the International Committee of Medical Journal Editors recently declared that it would only publish studies that had been previously registered "at or before the onset of patient enrollment" with that registration taking place at a publicly accessible site, such as Clinicaltrials.gov run by the U.S. National Library of Medicine (De Angelis et al., 2004).[2] This meant that no study could escape scrutiny, unless its corporate sponsors wanted to risk not being able to publish the results at all.

The more general ethical principle at stake with the publishing of research has to do with conceptions of public trust and public good. The warrant for conducting research is that such work will contribute to knowledge, which is regarded as a matter of public good. The support of salaries, grants and facilities, especially as these involve public or non-profit institutions, only adds to the weight of public trust at issue in doing research. Thus, the ethical compulsion to do the research well, and to make the resulting knowledge publicly available, ideally through some form of publication that, through its review process, ensures that the work has some initial claim to being research, notwithstanding the further scrutiny it will undergo as a public document.

That is all well and good, you might interrupt at this point, but surely the importance of publishing research goes without saying. The reason for that, I would counter, is largely because publication is about other things besides epistemology and ethics. Publishing well is a necessary aspect to being recognized as a researcher and a scholar. The very right to continue conducting research depends on the publication of previous work, even as the blind review process ensures that attention is paid to the merits of the current piece of research, rather than judging it on the author's established reputation. Yet the current and intense focus on publishing turns out to have little to do with the open circulation of the work. Getting research into a peer-reviewed journal or an edited book becomes an end in itself for the majority of scholars. There is a small group of academic stars whose work thrives on widespread readership and citation, but for most, publish and perish has become the mark of an academic life.

However, a historic moment may well be upon us, one that gives new meaning to the epistemological and ethical issues entailed in the circulation of research. In the course of little more than a decade, the Internet has proven itself a powerful, global publishing medium for research and scholarship, especially at the level of the article. The researcher has now to reconsider what it takes to do research in a responsible manner, when the public presence of that work has the potential to be—and in many cases has already been—radically expanded. It may look like business as usual within the journal system that dominates scholarly publishing. The vast majority of journals simply moved online without changing how they look or publish (much as Gutenberg's printing of the Bible, with its cursive font and illuminated first letters, created a book that resembled the medieval manuscripts, which the printing press was about to put an end to as a publishing form). Yet the Internet has opened a new world of access to the forms of knowledge that are recorded in journals, if far less so with scholarly books at this point.[3]

You can now walk into a public library or a high school, sit down at a computer station, and tap into a small, but substantial portion of the scholarly work and scientific research that is being currently published; you can explore historical documents and archives, as well as vast sets of data, including the human genome.[4] This work has not just been published within a limited community of subscribing institutions, but has also been made open to readers wherever there is Internet access. This access represents a great increase in the ability to tap into the storehouses of knowledge, but when it comes to the scholarly literature, a very small proportion, perhaps amounting to 15-20 percent of the annual output, is made freely available to readers. This public access has been afforded by a new breed of scholarly journal (some having grown out of long-standing print titles, such as the *New England Journal of Medicine*), which makes their contents freely available to readers online, whether immediately on publication or some months after the issue is released (to give subscribers an incentive to keep subscribing). Yet while journals that offer open access provide one important source of a new global access, a greater part of that 15-20 percent of scholarly work that is now open comes from those authors who, having published in a journal that is restricted to subscribers, have taken advantage of that journal's self-archiving policy to post their published work to an open access institutional repository run by their library or to their own website.[5] This is not just a hypothetical increase in access, as there are now a good number of studies that make it clear that studies which are made available through open access journals or institutional repositories are read and cited by more people than those that are not.[6]

Suddenly, *doing research* raises a new set of responsibilities for how that research is allowed to circulate, given that there are a whole new range of options for opening it to critical scrutiny and having it enter the public sphere. When print was the only means of publication, the idea of printing a limited number of copies of a journal—determined by the number of subscribers who covered the costs and to whom it was then exclusively delivered—made perfect sense, with a little photocopying and off-print circulation on the side. This is the time, I am proposing, for reviewing the researcher's epistemological and ethical responsibilities in light of the *open access* option, an option which some journals are actively pursuing, and which the majority of journals, that are not going this way, have at least recognized as falling within the rights of their authors (as they permit authors to self-archive the work the journal has published).

In what follows, I want to make clear where this access principle fits in doing research by examining its (missing) place in one of the most important statements on education research to be published in some time, *Scientific Research in Education*, the National Research Council's report on how to foster a scientific culture within a federal education research agency (Shavelson & Towne, 2002). In the process, I am also *doing research* that will demonstrate a method of close reading or textual analysis that has grown out of my own training in literature and the history of ideas.[7]

The executive summary of *Scientific Research in Education* features six "scientific principles" said to "underlie all scientific inquiry, including education research" (Shavelson & Towne, 2002, p. 2). The first thing to note about this report, however, is that these are not so much principles as prescriptions, written in the imperative, numbered in the order to be followed, and directed at researchers ("1. Pose significant questions that can be answered empirically; 2. Link research to relevant theory... 5. Replicate and Generalize Across Studies..."). The scientific principles are followed by six "design principles," which take a similar approach to directing those responsible for setting up the U.S. Department of Education's Institute of Education Sciences.[8]

To appreciate why the National Academy of Education committee behind the report took this prescriptive approach to promoting scientific research in education, it helps to consult the foreword to the report written by Bruce Alberts, president of the National Academy. Alberts points out that the National Academies more typically issue reports devoted to "bringing science to bear on pressing problems" that confront the United States, while *Scientific Research in Education* is something of an exception, as it tries "to comment on the nature of the scientific enterprise itself" (p. vii). Yet it does not appear to be the exception insofar as a National Academy might tend to pronounce on a pressing problem in this pointedly prescriptive and authoritative way. And as for the pressing problem, the report goes on to explain, the National Academies felt the need to weigh in on the scientific quality of education research, given what the authors describe as a widespread skepticism over the cumulative value of education research, a skepticism which has led, in their estimation, to explicit requirements for "scientifically based research" in the No Child Left Behind Act of 2001 (p. 1).

Without presenting any evidence one way or the other on the current quality of education research, the authors of the report appear to have bought into this skepticism. For they interpreted their original mandate— "review and synthesize recent literature on the science and practice of scientific educational research and consider how to support high quality science in a federal education research agency" (p. 1)—as best handled by providing education researchers with a six-step plan for properly setting their work back on a scientific track. Setting out the principles in this way is bound to suggest to some that a significant number of researchers is not posing significant questions, is not linking its work to the relevant theory, and so the implications of the report appear to run. These researchers would thus benefit from following such succinctly stated advice in bringing their work under the rubric of *scientific*.

In this way, the report's six scientific principles also suggest a divide exists between *scientific* research and research that falls short of this scientific standard. Others have considered the shortcomings of the six scientific principles as a whole, while my focus here is on the sixth and final principle, the one that deals with the dissemination of research.[9] The work—dare I call it scientific research—that I have been doing over the last few years on how research and scholarship can contribute more to what might be called, after John Dewey, the democratic quality of our lives, leads me to declare that the National Research Council report's perspective on research dissemination is an important statement on scientific processes and yet unduly constrained in ways that neither serve science nor society.

Scientific Principle 6 reads, in full, "Disclose research to encourage professional scrutiny and critique" (p. 5). The principle is accompanied by an explanation that refers to the need for wide dissemination of education research, followed by "ongoing, collaborative public critique" (*ibid.*). I could not agree more with the importance of such an approach to ensuring the quality of knowledge and the healthy state of science. Reference is made in the explanation, as well, to adhering to "publicly enforced norms," even as the report reasserts that the audience that matters is made up of "professional peers" and "the community of scientists" (Shavelson & Towne, 2002, p. 5). The National Research Council report is concerned that the professional scrutiny of research is an open process within the education research community, and as such the review of research should not be entrusted to a single authority or body. The report allows for both peer review and continuing critical scrutiny that might, for example, entail a reanalysis of the data or further research of the problem at issue. This sixth principle of disclosure might, then, be thought of as simply a final step in ensuring that education research falls within long established norms for the republic of science. Again, no evidence is presented on whether an adequate level of professional scrutiny and critique is being applied to education research, whether through the countless peer-reviewed journals and grant competitions, as well as, if to a lesser degree, with edited volumes and books in the field. And just as troubling, the principle of dissemination and distribution of research stops there, with professional scrutiny and critique.

This last scientific principle on the dissemination of research does not address this particular science's place within the larger republic. It does not consider the particular place of research in a democracy, especially as that research bears on an aspect of life as critical to democracy as education clearly is, and as it is directly related to a federal education research agency. Certainly, it falls within the mandate of the National Academies to, Alberts says, "comment on the nature of the scientific enterprise itself," but they are first and foremost "advisors to the nation," as the slogan on their website and elsewhere puts it. Thus it would seem worthwhile to give some thought to how this public responsibility can be more fully integrated into the scientific principles that are intended to guide researchers, rather than suggesting that scientific research—in an area of such pressing public concern as education—operates apart from the world that it observes and pronounces on. If the point is lost in the report's scientific principles, it turns up, to the credit of the National Research Council committee, later in the report with the insistence that "research results must be brought into the professional and public domain if they are to be understood, debated, and eventually become known to those who could fruitfully use them" (Shavelson & Towne, 2002, p. 73). How this public access and engagement will be achieved, when it does not figure in the basic principles of scientific research, becomes for me a call to assist the National Research Council in articulating both the means, as well as the scientific and public value, of making greater access to research a goal of the federal education research agencies.

The very sense that research is something that is *disclosed* gets things off on the wrong foot in the sixth scientific principle—"Disclose research to encourage professional scrutiny and critique"—and this sense of restricted disclosure is all the more inappropriate for education research. It is as if such research were indeed a professional secret, one that should only be disclosed to those who can be trusted with it. Against such a notion, I would argue that the final step in any research project should be about ensuring the circulation and exchange of knowledge in as wide a fashion as is feasible. I use the word *feasible* because I recognize that there is a whole range of limits to the circulation of knowledge, from economic to educational.

However, it also needs to be noted that the possible global and public scope for the circulation of research has recently and rather radically changed with the introduction of new information technologies in relation to the Internet. The overwhelming majority of scientific journals have moved to the Internet over the last ten years. This enables a level of global and public distribution of knowledge that far exceeds what was possible with print technologies. What researchers then need to consider, in the midst of this great migration, is how this new publishing medium can be used to improve both the scientific and public value and impact of research, not just as a source of scientific information, but as a source of public knowledge. The viability of this greater distribution and greater integration of research into public life has been demonstrated by a small but important number of journals that are offering their contents free to the reader.

In education, for example, there are close to 200 journals that make all or some portion of their content free to read online, among them *Educational Researcher, Teachers College Record, Educational Policy Analysis Archives*, and *Current Issues in Education*.[10] This manner of "open access" publishing is being implemented through a number of different economic models that include using entirely volunteer labor and publishing online only, relying on author fees (largely used in the well-funded sciences), providing open access after a period of subscription-only access, or offering open access to developing countries. In addition, a number of the major publishers of education journals, such as AERA, Sage, Blackwell, and Taylor and Francis, have policies in place that permit authors to post their work in their libraries' institutional repositories.[11]

The road that scholarly publishing had been heading down, prior to this open access movement, and continues to head down in the face of this new development, is one of increasing corporate concentration, with publisher mergers and acquisitions (as well as the corporate acquisition of scholarly society journals). The resulting price increases driven by opportunity as much as anything has been leading over the last two decades to a declining state of access to research, judging by the journal cancellations that have trimmed collections at the best university libraries, while decimating those of less privileged institutions (ARL, 2002). The introduction of open access models through online publishing appears to offer the universities another direction in which to take the circulation of knowledge. Scholarly associations, journal editors and university libraries need to carefully weigh the dissemination of research in terms of this juncture, especially as it bears on the scientific principle of seeking the widest possible circulation, exchange, and scrutiny for knowledge.

Open access publishing serves scholar and public alike, by providing a much wider readership than is afforded by subscription-fee journals (online or on paper). The open access model not only opens the research work to more thorough "professional scrutiny and critique," as per the National Research Council's sixth scientific principle, it also provides greater *accountability* and *visibility* for education research (to draw on the American Educational Research Association conference themes for 2003 and 2004). Up to this point, American Educational Research Association, ERIC, and other organizations have approached this public side of science by providing a form of research digest and "translation" on selected topics.[12] While representing a commendable effort, this is obviously a costly process that can provide at best a limited coverage of the literature. It could be greatly extended, I am suggesting, by integrating much more open access to this literature into the very systems for circulating that knowledge.

Now, in invoking the role of research in a democratic culture, I realize that public access to *what is known* through scholarly inquiry, as well as to the debates and controversies that arise through that inquiry, is but one small aspect of what should contribute to the quality of contemporary democracies.[13] It may be a small aspect, but it is precisely the aspect over which education researchers have control. It is the very point of their professional contribution, as scholars and educators. Now, I also realize that the very act of providing broad and open access to the full range of education research activities may strike some among us as likely to only further undermine public confidence and feed the skepticism that inspired, in part, the National Research Council report at issue here. The skepticism point has been elaborated by Michael Feuer, Lisa Towne, and Richard Shavelson elsewhere, as they speak of the National Research Council report arising out of a context in which education research "is perceived to be of low quality" and does not inspire "confidence" in lawmakers or others (2002, p. 5). For their part, they believe that "the conventional wisdom about weaknesses of scientific educational research relative to other sciences is exaggerated"—which is not to say that it is untrue (p. 5.).[14] In the face of this lack of confidence in education research, however exaggerated, it would have made as much sense for the National Research Council report to call for improving the visibility of research, making it more readily a part of the public and professional discourse, by providing, in the first instance, much better access to it through the coordinated efforts of ERIC and journals in this field of study. Yet what would the public think of the differences in research findings, of variations in research methods, of theoretical and philosophical studies, of semiotic or hermeneutical inquiries?

At one level, this possibility that some of the public might think less of our work, in all of its diversity and differences, is no defense for keeping it from public view. At another level, greater access to the whole of the research enterprise is bound to be educational for researchers and public. But more than that, in the social sciences above all, maximizing access to research, access for policymakers, administrators, educators, the media, and the public, access for those who have been studied and those who would feel the impact of studies, access for those who have a stake in the funding of the research, is integral to what is scientific and scholarly about research in education. It has everything to do with sustaining a culture of "professional scrutiny and critique," to quote Scientific Principle 6, once more, scrutiny and critique from those whose professional and public lives are both the object of and subject to this knowledge.

Now, the National Research Council report, *Scientific Research in Education*, does speak to how education research can serve as a guide for policymakers who are working on issues related to schooling, just as the report refers to how researchers need to collaborate with educators in conducting their research (Shavelson & Towne, 2002, pp. 155-156). But guiding policymakers and collaborating with teachers is not necessarily the same thing as fostering a more democratic approach that might better inform public deliberations over educational matters. As I have pointed out in earlier work, there is nothing inherently democratic about policymakers following research evidence in arriving at the most effective strategies for implementing specific policy goals (2001a). And the capacity for self-governance among a people, as well as the capacity for educational leadership among the teaching profession, are not necessarily furthered when teachers partner with researchers to produce research designed, for example, to improve policy-mandated practices in schools.

What is needed, I have suggested before, is a considerable extension of the dissemination principle of scientific research and design, one that recognizes the role of science, especially the social sciences, in a democracy. This principle would constitute education research as a vital part of a larger democratic process, one that situates the study of learning and teaching in classrooms, communities and states, one that recognizes research's contribution to the educational and democratic qualities of this society. From this perspective, the National Research Council's sixth scientific principle—"Disclose research to encourage professional scrutiny and critique"—seems contrary to our democratic responsibilities, as education researchers. Our responsibility is not concerned with *disclosure* (except in conflict of interest cases between our private and public interests), but about encouraging as open a flow and exchange of information as is possible. As this dissemination principle now stands, it may seem to bolster education research's commitment to scientific research, but in fact does little to address concerns felt by various stakeholders about the cumulative value of this body of research which would seem to be facilitated by enabling people to consult and connect the work that has been done, even when, as is most often the case, it does not add up to a neat and tidy research finding.

Without taking anything from the importance of discussing scientific standards, norms, and training, I am also asking that something more be done by this research community to address public concerns with education research. Within the American context, organizations such as the new federal Institute of Education Science, National Library of Education, the National Academy of Education, and scholarly associations like AERA, all have the opportunity to do much more in fostering the utilization of and support for research in education by placing this research within the scope of *public culture*. They need to recognize that new information technologies can greatly improve the linkages among this research, as well as provide far greater public access to this research. They need to see the value of building this research more fully into the fabric of public discourse. Exploring and testing feasible models for providing open access to the journal literature, as well as developing greater linkages among the databases, is what I am recommending as the first step in increasing the public value of education research. This greater public engagement is bound to have an influence on how the research is conducted and how it is written up.

While *Scientific Research in Education* expresses a concern with research ethics, it is focused on respecting the rights of individuals who participate in research. It does not, for example, acknowledge a corresponding right among the public to consult the resulting knowledge. Obtaining the *informed consent* of the research subject seems only half the story to me, given the assumption that the research being conducted will constitute a public good held to be of interest to the welfare of the larger society. What then of the researcher's responsibilities, or rather the research community's responsibilities, to establish public norms that support *informed participation* in this democracy not just among the immediate participants, but also among the larger community? That the research must be disclosed to professional scrutiny is a safeguard or check on its quality. To see that it is open to wide circulation and easy access is what ensures that the research falls within a democratically informed public sphere.

Now, many education researchers are tired of sibling comparisons between education and medical research. Still, the National Research Council report jumps on the medical research analogy in its opening sentence.[15] And from my perspective, medical research has succeeded in making itself part of public culture over the last decade, with its breakthroughs, controversies, reversals, indeterminate results, and all. The lessons that education research has to learn from the life sciences are not about the value of meta-analysis (for which they owe education's own Gene Glass a great debt) or their authoritative and definitive findings; the lessons education research need to learn from this work concerns how the scientific culture of medical research is unmistakably part of the public culture of daily talk and dinner tables, of politicians and media pundits.

The expanded coverage of health information in the media, under the rubric of news-you-can-use, is easy to track in newspapers, on television, and the Internet. During the week that I began to compose this review of the National Research Council report, the *New York Times Magazine* devoted its entire issue to the theme "Half of What Doctors Know is Wrong" (March 16, 2003). It featured articles with titles such as "Medicine's Progress, One Setback at a Time" and those articles thought nothing of describing the details of sample sizes, risk probabilities, and research design flaws of studies published in the *British Medical Journal* and elsewhere. The magazine makes the dynamics of research present: the tentative search for an answer, the challenges and revisions, the study released last week, the reversed position. True, it is the *Times*, which is not everyone's daily newspaper, but this public exposure of medical research's reversals (hormone therapy) and design flaws (mammograms) has appeared, with less detail, on the television nightly news and the tabloid press. And it has not reduced public support for medical research; it has arguably fed support for it, creating a public appetite and expectation of a right to know as a function of the democratic state to support and make available.

The education research community would do well to consider how this knowledge is now working as part of a public culture, adding to that culture's democratic, and intellectual, quality. That is, this increase in access to health information has changed the relationship of medical research to the public body, changed it in a way that I am tempted to describe as reducing the tyranny of expertise. From the physicians' perspective, having patients and their families arriving at their office with medical research and other health information in hand has led to a "new method of care," a method which has been encouragingly labeled "shared decision making" (Brownlee, 2003, p. 54). I hardly need add that *shared decision making* sounds a lot like democracy in action, whether one thinks of a doctor's office, a community school, a nation. This particular form of sharing has only been made possible by increases in medical research's presence in public culture, and I would offer as one indication of that National Institute of Health estimate that six million

Americans go online each day in search of information about health and disease (NIH, 2003)—although only a small percentage may be consulting research—as well as the NIH's commitment to seeing all of the research that it sponsors publicly available through institutional repositories or open access journals (Suber, 2005).

In an effort to feed this hunger for information, as well as address the right to know, doctors in the state of Georgia are experimenting with a "health information prescription" (Brownlee 2003, p. 54). The prescription will guide patients to reliable sources including the National Library of Medicine's MedlinePlus, which includes a layperson's guide to symptoms, diagnosis, and treatment. MedlinePlus, however, also provides patients with direct access to the latest medical research, through the NLM's PubMed database, although most of the 11 million articles in it are not available to the public beyond their abstracts, because of the small, but growing, proportion of the articles that have been made open access and thus publicly available.

As the conversation between physician and patient takes on this more informed quality, concerned as it is about both risk and quality of life factors, the educational quality of that exchange goes up for both parties. Clearly, physicians are also beneficiaries of this increased access to research. Doctors speak of having the "newest and best in medical research right at our own desks," if only to discover that "leeches, for example, are now used on some patients to treat the pain of arthritis" (Sanders, 2003, p. 29). Patients make informed decisions based on their own value systems: "For me, it's a trade-off," as one woman said in deciding to stay with menopause hormone therapy for the mental agility it provided her against the recently established increased health risks of such therapy (Kolata, 2003).

What has changed with medical research, and what needs greater recognition by both the Institute of Education Sciences, and by everyone doing education research, is how productive this new emphasis on public access to research is for professionals. To go a little farther with the medical research access analogy, the perfect example of this democratic and public engagement with research is ClinicalTrials.gov, a website sponsored by the National Institutes of Health, other Federal agencies, and the pharmaceutical industry. The site was launched in February 2000 and as of December 2005 lists 23,500 clinical studies, which are inviting participation from qualified subjects, as well as informing the public about ongoing investigations. The site is global, involving studies in about 120 countries, although most are in the United States and Canada, and it receives approximately 20,000 visitors a day.

Think of what it would mean to have a comparable system for alerting people to what studies are underway, what ideas are currently being explored and tested, in education research on a global basis. It would not need to be, and in fact should not be, restricted to clinical trials or large-scale studies. A research registry for education could offer a far more methodologically diverse invitation from researchers to educators and others to participate in proposed or ongoing research. An education research site devoted to recruiting participants in both large and small scale studies would support the desired expansion of clinical trials in schools, as well as provide opportunities to conduct more wide ranging qualitative studies. Educators would be in a far better position to participate in a dialogue over research agendas, by virtue of the studies they signed up for, while learning far more about the nature and scope of education research by reviewing their options. It may well lead to parents and educators discussing what they want to achieve and what they want to learn more about, as they review the current field of studies underway. A research-opportunities and research-underway database could well fall within the National Research Council report's call for "infrastructure that promoted ongoing collaborations among researchers, practitioners, and policymakers," as part of its sixth design principle (Shavelson & Towne, 2002, pp. 155-156).

Medical research is increasing its public presence and is becoming an integral part of its scientific culture, in large part through the government's life sciences indexing services PubMed. We are left to wonder why education research has not had a greater boost from its own open access research indexing database, through the Nation Library of Education's ERIC (Education Resources Information Center).[16] ERIC currently has 1.1 million citations with over 100,000 "full-text nonjournal" documents that are freely available. Yet ERIC has only begun to take full advantage of the open access already available in the journal literature. At this point, ERIC's index entries for articles in the open access journal, *Australian Educational Researcher,* provides links to the full-text articles online, but this is not yet the case for other open access journals, such as *Education Policy Analysis Archives* and *Education Researcher.*

The issue in education is awareness and expectation, as professional and public interest in this *right to know* is not yet operating at the level it is in medicine. Clearly, the personal urgency of health issues for people leads to greater attention paid to medical research, but the growing public presence of medical research is also influenced by a combination of readily available technologies of access to this knowledge and an emerging culture of expectation that has grown up around the right to know what is known about our health. The schooling of the young, the state of the teaching profession, and the general state of education are only somewhat less of a concern to people, and it takes little to imagine this *right to know* contributing to education to what has happened with medical information, in what the Pew Charitable Trusts has called the "online health care revolution" (Fox & Rainie, 2000). The current state of open access within ERIC is only part of the story on education research's public role, a story that also involves, to reiterate, education researchers depositing work that they publish in the institutional repositories managed by their libraries, if the work has not been published in an open access journal. My perhaps naïve hope is that those doing education research will take the lead in establishing greater public access to this work, out of a growing awareness among them of the epistemological and ethical responsibilities posed by the possibilities of this new medium.

However, where this increased attention paid to health research has had an impact on other area of public interest has with the rise of "evidence-based" policy initiatives (Willinsky, 2001b). In education, the evidence-based approach to research shows up in the No Child Left Behind Act of 2001. As the National Research Council report observes, No Child Left Behind has legislated a new emphasis specifically on "scientifically based research," with no less than 111 references to this term in the No Child Left Behind (as noted by Feurer, Towne, & Shavelson, 2002, p. 4). Suddenly, the federal government's support for state education initiatives is dependent on the state's ability to make use of the relevant research. The new legislative attention being paid to education research strikes me as offering its own call for greater accessibility to education research. No Child Left Behind makes it imperative for education authorities to consult the relevant research as part of the process of deciding matters of program and policy for the schools.[17] I might even go so far as to suggest that greater access to education research is a basic requirement for compliance with the law. Are we doing enough, then, to support people's need to consult education research, to support their right to know what has been learned at public expense? If we want to improve people's appreciation of education research, largely by fostering an appreciation of our scientific and scholarly culture, and if we want to aid people's ability to not only comply with the law but more actively participate in the design of informed policies and programs, we need to pay more attention to how we circulate this knowledge, beginning with providing more open access to it.

Yet these legislative measures also raise issues around the politics of research that should provide education researchers with a further reason to become champions of open access to education research. After all, what is meant by scientifically based research, in terms of the U.S. Department of Education, has everything to do with, according to the legislation that led to the formation of the Institute of Education Sciences, the Education Sciences Reform Act (2002), "employing systematic, empirical methods that draw on observation or experiment"; "relying on measurements or observational methods that provide reliable data"; and "making claims of causal relationships only in random assignment experiments or other designs."[18] The Institute is further supported by the U.S. Department of Education's What Works Clearinghouse, another evidence-based policy initiative which "collects, screens, and identifies studies of the effectiveness of educational interventions (programs, products, practices, and policies)," based again on the findings of "scientifically based research."[19]

The privileging of one form of research can only end up obscuring the contribution, as well as diminish the funding and support, for other kinds of research. What then, one wants to ask, of critical pedagogy (e.g., Kincheloe & Steinberg, 2006) to name one of so many different ways of doing education research, which help us to make sense of schooling through no less an application of rigorous and systematic methods, apart from the methods celebrated under the rubric of "scientifically based research." Surely, the full spectrum of research needs to be made freely available to teachers, administrators, parents, the press, and the public through open access, so that it can demonstrate its value to education, so that it can easily play a part in decision-making and deliberation over the quality of the child's educational experience, in the nature of the lessons learned, in the democratic contribution of schooling, in the shaping of the curriculum.

If access to this body of research is going to remain restricted to research libraries, because education researchers are focused entirely on getting their research published rather than read, then only this narrowly defined range of scientifically based research is going to play a public and legislated part in education. Again, I would say that researchers have a responsibility to see that their work receives the largest possible play in the public arena, insofar as they believe they have something valuable to contribute to the state of education and the well-being of those involved in it. On the one hand, the very future of their research approach or method, at least in terms of official government recognition and support, might be said to depend on the increased public and professional presence of this research that open access can bring, while on the other hand, the increased access—so readily within reach through open access journals and institutional repositories—can have the fortunate side-effect of advancing researchers' careers, even as they increase their contribution.

The National Research Council report makes passing reference, under its section on infrastructure, to "the emergence of new technologies for data collection, management, and analysis," and these same new technologies can be used to improve the collection, management and analysis of the research literature, enabling readers to gain a sense of the different lenses and methods research offers, as well as the values and perspectives it brings to bear on things educational (Shavelson & Towne, 2002, p. 151). More than that, the potential now exists to create interactive linking between data sets and published articles in ways that will encourage a level of re-analysis and replication studies that will increase the rigor and scientific quality of these studies. In one experimental project on fostering multiliteracies that I have been involved in, we have developed an online site where researchers work alongside of students and teachers, with the researchers assembling their case studies, even as the students use the site for an annotated, sometimes animated, gallery of their multiliterate work, while the teachers set up online demonstrations of how their approaches to teaching in this environment works. This Multiliteracy Project website serves to provide a public account of the learning going on among all three parties to this work, in real time, as the work develops.[20] Of course, there is a long-standing tradition of secrecy and retentiveness among researchers, that I referred to earlier using Newton as my example, and yet the counter-forces of an open science may yet prevail with growing evidence of how this openness augments the scholarship and strengthens the claims of research (Willinsky, 2005).

Given that the education research community is working on improving instructional programs in information literacy, subject domain learning, and hypertext reading, why wouldn't a federal agency devoted to the study of education draw on this expertise to support and build "the research capacity" of practitioners, policy makers and the public? Is there something amiss with education researchers being so intent on finding ways to improve the literacy of citizens, on the one hand, while on the other, they are not interested in making what they learn about education part of the public discourse in the democratic determination of education? The NRC report does call for this federal agency to produce "regular syntheses of research findings" to inform "practitioners and policymakers" (p. 15). And while ERIC has provided excellent research digests in the past—with that service terminated in the recent contracting out of ERIC due to the costliness of the digests—what can now be provided, as demonstrated by open access journals and indexes, are systems that can increase and improve readers' direct access to research, in support of their democratic right to know.

Scholarly associations such as AERA could, for example, take the lead, in conjunction with the current reform of ERIC, to support the adoption of standards for automated journal indexing and linking that would greatly increase the number of articles in ERIC that provide links to the full text of the articles themselves, without adding significantly to the cost of this indexing. The ready ability to connect study to study, to compare results and see ideas challenged and discussed, can only add to the quality of scholarly and public discourse about education. But more than that, our work through the Public Knowledge, at the University of British Columbia, has demonstrated how the Internet can now support systems of "Reading Tools" that can enable readers of a research article to connect the article they are reading not only to related studies, but just as easily to current newspaper articles and government reports on the same topic, to sites with instructional materials for teaching the topic and to online forums where the topic is informally debated.[21] The promise here is of having greater public access to research, combined with greater connectivity among different orders of knowledge (from research to practice and policy), incorporated into the design of scholarly publishing environments in ways that improve the quality of the peer review process (with access to the original data sets) as well as support public accessibility, for example, by providing access to related materials in the media and other public documents.

It is fair enough to raise questions about what this new public presence of research may mean for the integrity of research. Certainly, discomfiting instances are to be found of the political and social corruption of scientific practices. Think of the role that anthropology often played in the service of colonial administrations, or the eugenics movement in the early decades of the twentieth century. Today, with the George W. Bush administration in the United States, issues of political interference in research abound.[22] Yet such abuses, while a source of concern and caution for researchers, hardly argue for isolating or insulating scientific culture from public and democratic culture, especially for a science of education that holds to the importance, as a first principle, of posing *significant* questions. The open and public discussion of those questions seems a critical element in keeping science a principled enterprise in an ethically responsible sense.

Public education has long been about developing and extending the democratic right to know, and the right to act on that knowledge (within the rule of law). Public education has also been about increasing the intellectual quality of public life through its engagement with scientific knowledge. If the United States is entering an age of greater public and professional concern with education research—as attested to by the recent Education Act—then researchers would do well to consider that what is scientific about doing research is not simply the ability of this work to determine the best practices for improving achievement results. What is scientific is far more about the open and free inquiry into these educational phenomena. What is scientific is the systematic and imaginative ways in which education researchers seek to contribute to the very quality of public deliberation over education's ends and means. Rather than think about disclosing education research for the purpose of affording sufficient scrutiny from other researchers, researchers need to consider these new ways of expanding the circulation of this knowledge. Doing research today means testing the potential of new publishing technologies for opening research to greater scrutiny and impact, as well as to greater integration with other forms of knowing. At this moment, as the research literature moves into this new publishing medium, the researcher has indeed assumed a new responsibility, a new level of accountability, over how public access to the research literature can be improved, as both a scientific and design principle that will only serve to strengthen scientific culture within an informed and democratic public realm.

## NOTES

[1] This article was originally published, in a somewhat altered form as "Scientific Research in a Democratic Culture: Or What's a Social Science For?" *Teachers College Record, 107(1)*, 2005, p. 38-51, and builds on arguments presented in Willinsky (2001a; 2002) with the specific context of the National Research Council report, *Scientific Research in Education* (Shavelson & Towne, 2002).

[2] From the statement of the medical journal editors: "Irrespective of their scientific interest, trial results that place financial interests at risk are particularly likely to remain unpublished and hidden from public view. The interests of the sponsor or authors notwithstanding, anyone should be able to learn of any trial's existence and its important characteristics" (De Angelis et al., 2004).

[3] In terms of the *open access* book, the editors of this handbook, Joe Kincheloe and Ken Tobin, are to be commended for selecting as their publisher, Sense Publishers, which makes it a practice to provide free online access to PDF files for all of its books through its website (http://www.sensepublishers.com/). As well, the National Research Council's publications, including *Scientific Research in Education* which is discussed in detail in this chapter, are available in open access on its website, as well as for sale in other formats.

[4] On open access to research data in the sciences, a recent *Nature* editorial refers to how researchers can retain credit and rights over the data sets they contribute to the "global academy" by making it freely available online through the use of a Creative Commons license (http://creativecommons.org.

[5] See the Sherpa Project (http://www.sherpa.ac.uk/), in which a survey of 127 publishers reveals that 75% grant permission for authors to post some version of their published article in an institutional archive or on a personal Website.

[6] See Steven Hitchcock's (2005) running bibliography of studies on the citation impact of open access articles.

[7] For examples of how this has been applied, in my own case, on a more extensive basis in education research, see Willinsky (1991; 1998).

[8] Institute of Education Sciences (http://www.ed.gov/about/offices/list/ies/index.html).

[9] For critical reviews of other aspects of the *Scientific Research in Education* report (Shavelson & Towne, 2002), see Erickson (2005), Gee (2005), Moss (2005), and Walker (2005).

[10] See the American Education Research Association list of open access journals in education maintained by Tirupalavanam Ganesh (http://aera-cr.asu.edu/links.html).

[11] See Willinsky (2006) on different types of open access journal publishing, and to check the current self-archiving policies of publishers and journals see the SHERPA project database (http://www.sherpa.ac.uk/romeo.php).

[12] See, for example, AERA's *Research Points* (http://www.aera.net/publications/?id=314).

[13] The more common philosophical formulation of the relation between science and democracy focuses on the democratic regulation of science, as when Helen Longino asks, "What kind of institutional changes are necessary to sustain the credibility, and hence value, of scientific inquiry while maintaining democratic decision making regarding the cognitive and practical choices the sciences make possible and necessary?" (2002, p. 213). Also see Philip Kitcher (2001) for a similar approach. My argument for improved access to research will, of course, bear on the democratic decision making affecting science.

[14] As far back as the 1960s, when the social sciences were entering a time of considerable government influence, Fritz Marchlup noted the suspicion with which social science research was still regarded: "New knowledge in the natural sciences is always welcomed as 'discovery' and 'progress'; new knowledge in technology is hailed as 'invention' and 'advance'; but new knowledge in the social sciences is suspected, if not decried, as either 'subversive' or 'reactionary' or 'trivial'" (1962, p. 205).

[15] "No one would think of going to the Moon [sic] or of wiping out a disease without research" (Shavelson & Towne, 2002, p. 1).

[16] As a point of comparison, in 2002 the U.S. government allotted $274 million to the National Library of Medicine, which operates PubMed, compared to $12 million to the National Library of Education.

[17] "To provide funding to enable State educational agencies and local educational agencies to implement promising educational reform programs and school improvement programs based on scientifically based research." SEC. 5101.(a) (2), *No Child Left Behind Act of 2001.*

[18] The relevant passages from "Education Sciences Reform Act of 2002" which was used as a basis for establishing the Institute of Education Sciences: "The term 'field-initiated research' means basic research or applied research in which specific questions and methods of study are generated by investigators (including teachers and other practitioners) and that conforms to standards of scientifically valid research" and The term 'scientifically based research standards' means research standards ... (i) employing systematic, empirical methods that draw on observation or experiment; (ii) involving data analyses that are adequate to support the general findings; (iii) relying on measurements or observational methods that provide reliable data; (iv) making claims of causal relationships only in random assignment experiments or other designs (to the extent such designs substantially eliminate plausible competing explanations for the obtained results)..."

[19] What Works Clearinghouse is "administered by the U.S. Department of Education through a contract to a joint venture of the American Institutes for Research and the Campbell Collaboration" (http://www.whatworks.ed.gov/).

[20] See the Multiliteracy Project website (http://www.multiliteracies.ca) and Early and Potts (2005).

[21] See the Public Knowledge Project website for demonstrations of a Reading Tool that is included in the project's journal and conference publishing systems, and is designed to integrate research more fully into other forms of knowledge (http://pkp.sfu.ca/ojs).

[22] See the Union of Concerned Scientists, who document the degree to which "an unprecedented level of political interference threatens the integrity of government science" (http://www.ucsusa.org/scientific_integrity/).

## REFERENCES

Brownless, S. (2003, March 18). The perils of prevention. *New York Times Magazine*, 52-55.

De Angelis, C. Drazen, J. M., Frizelle, F. A., Haug, C., Hoey, J., Horton, R., Kotzin, S., Laine, C., Marusic, A., John A., Overbeke. P. M., Schroeder, T. V., Sox, H. C., & Van Der Weyden, M. B. (2004). Clinical trial registration: A statement from the International Committee of Medical Journal Editors. *New England Journal of Medicine, 351,* 1250-1251. Retrieved December 12, 2005, from http://content.nejm.org/cgi/content/full/NEJMe048225

Early, M. & Potts, D. (2005, November). Hard work, good learning: Multiliterate pedagogies and possibilities. *BC Educational Leadership Research, 2.* Retrieved December 12, 2005, from http://slc.educ.ubc.ca/eJournal/Issue2/Early_Potts.pdf

Education Sciences Reform Act of 2002. H. R. 3801. Retrieved December 12, 2005, from http://www.ed.gov/policy/rschstat/leg/PL107-279.pdf

Erickson, F.(2005). Arts, humanities, and sciences in educational research and social engineering in federal education policy, *Teacher's College Record, 107,* 4-9.

Feuer, M. J., Towne, L., & Shavelson, R. J. (2002). Scientific culture and educational research. *Educational Researcher, 31,* 4-14.

Fox, S., & Rainie, L. (2000). *The online health care revolution: How the web helps Americans take better care of themselves.* Washington, DC: Pew Internet and American Life Project.

Gee, J. (2005). It's theories all the way down: A response to scientific research in education, *Teacher's College Record, 107*, 10-18.

Kincheloe, J. & Steinberg, S. (Eds.) (2006). *Cutting class: Social Class and education*. Lanham, MD: Rowman and Littlefield.

Kitcher, P. (2001). *Science, truth, and democracy*. Oxford, UK: Oxford University Press.

Kolata, G. (2003, March 18). Hormone therapy, already found to have risks, is now said to lack benefits. *New York Times*, A26.

Kuhn, T. S. (1978). Newton's optical papers. In I. Bernard Cohen (Ed), *Isaac Newton's papers and letters on natural philosophy and related documents* (pp. 27-45). Cambridge, MA: Harvard University Press.

Let data speak to data. (2005), *Nature, 438* (531), doi:10.1038/438531a.

Longino, H. (2002). *The fate of knowledge*. Princeton, NJ: Princeton University Press.

Machlup, F. (1962). *The production and distribution of knowledge in the United States*. Princeton, NJ: Princeton University Press.

Moss, P. (2005). Toward "epistemic reflexivity" in educational research: A response to scientific research in education, *Teacher's College Record, 107*, 19-29.

National Institutes of Health (NIH). (2003, March 18). *The health information prescription*. Washington: National Library of Medicine. Retrieved December 12, 2005, from http://www.nlm.nih.gov/news/press_releases/GAhealthRX03.html.

Sanders, L. (2003, March 16). Medicine's progress, one setback at a time. *New York Times Magazine*, 29-31.

Shavelson, R. J. & Towne, L. Eds. (2002). *Scientific research in education*. Washington, DC: National Academy Press.

Suber, P. (2005). Strengthening NIH policy. *SPARC Open Access Newsletter, 92*. Retrieved December 12, 2005, from http://www.earlham.edu/~peters/fos/newsletter/12-02-05.htm

Walker, V (2005). After methods, then what? A researcher's response to the Report of the National Research Council. *Teacher's College Record, 107*, 30-37.

Willinsky, J. (2006). *The access principle: The case for open access to research and scholarship*. Cambridge MA: MIT Press.

Willinsky, J. (2005). The unacknowledged convergence of open source, open access, and open science. *First Monday, 10*(8). Retrieved December 12, 2005, from http://firstmonday.org/issues/issue10_8/willinsky/index.html

Willinsky, J. (2002). Education and democracy: The missing link may be ours. *Harvard Educational Review, 72*, 367-392.

Willinsky, J. (2001a). The Strategic Education Research Program and the public value of research. *Educational Researcher, 30*, 5-14.

Willinsky, J. (2001b). Extending the prospects of evidence-based education. *IN>>SIGHT, 1*, 23-41.

Willinsky, J. (1998). *Learning to divide the world: Education at empire's end*. Minneapolis, MN: University of Minnesota Press.

Willinsky, J. (1991). *The triumph of Literature: The fate of literacy*. New York: Teachers College Press.

# CONTRIBUTORS

*Kathleen Berry* is Professor of Education at the University of New Brunswick in Frederickton, New Brunswick. She has published extensively in the field of critical studies, drama education, and social justice. She has received the Allan P. Stuart Award for Excellence in Teaching.

*Deborah P. Britzman* is Professor of Education at York University and the author of numerous books and articles on curriculum, teacher education, and psychoanalysis and education.

*Phil Francis Carspecken* is Professor of Education at Indiana University and author of numerous books and articles about social theory and research.

*Aaron David Gresson* is Professor of Education and Human Development at Penn State University. He is recognized internationally as a leading social psychologist of racism in education.

*Jaime Grinberg* is Professor of Education at Montclair State University. He has published numerous books and articles in educational foundations, critical social theory, history of education, curriculum, and English as a second language education.

*David W. Jardine* is Professor of Education at the University of Calgary. He is the author of numerous books and articles on hermeneutics and education, curriculum theory, and teaching.

*Pam Joyce* is a teacher in the New Jersey public schools and a doctoral student at the City University of New York Graduate Center where she focuses on the analysis of race and education.

*Joe L. Kincheloe* is Canada Research Chair in the Faculty of Education at McGill University and is the author of numerous books and articles on critical pedagogy, the politics of knowledge, and research.

*Frances Helyar* is a doctoral student in education at McGill University. Her primary focus is history of education, in particular the history of textbooks.

*lisahunter* is currently teaching at Griffith University, Gold Coast, Australia where she studies youth lifestyle cultures, subjectivities, teachers and students as activists, girls in board sports, and socially just teacher education.

*Christine A. Lemesianou* is Assistant Professor of Speech Communications at Montclair State University. Her scholarly work addresses issues of globalization, identity, and new technologies.

*Rebecca Lloyd* recently completed her Ph.D. in Education at Simon Fraser University. She is presently researching physical education pedagogy and serves as a consultant and motivator for fitness professionals and figure skaters.

*Peter McLaren* is Professor of Education at UCLA. He is recognized as one of the leading architects of critical pedagogy worldwide.

*Gregory Martin* is a Lecturer in the School of Education and Professional Studies at Griffith University, Gold Coast Campus. His research interests include adult education, critical pedagogy, and socially critical action research.

*Diana Moyer* is Assistant Professor of Education in Instructional Technology and Educational Studies at the University of Tennessee. Her scholarship has focused on women and education.

*William F. Pinar* is Canada Research Chair at the University of British Columbia. He is a central figure in the global transformation of curriculum studies over the last three decades. He is also a scholar of racism, homophobia, and research methods.

*Alice J. Pitt* is Associate Dean of the Faculty of Education at York University. Her publications focus on the implications of psychoanalytic theory for teaching and learning in feminist classrooms and in teacher education, curriculum theory, and educational research.

*Wolff-Michael Roth* is Lansdowne Professor of Applied Cognitive Science at the University of Victoria. His interests include science education in a variety of settings, autobiographical inquiry, and innovative research practices.

*Stephen J. Smith* is Associate Professor of Education at Simon Fraser University. His research and publications are concerned with curricular and instructional issues in physical education and educational research, phenomenology in particular.

*Shirley R. Steinberg* is Associate Professor of Education in the Faculty of Education at McGill University and the author of numerous books and articles on popular culture, cultural studies, research, and issues of race, class, gender, and sexuality.

*Barbara Thayer-Bacon* is Associate Professor of Education at the University of Tennessee, Knoxville in the Department of Educational Leadership and Cultural Studies. She has published numerous books on the philosophy of education, critical thinking, epistemology, feminist theory, and educational reform.

*Kenneth Tobin* is Presidential Professor at the City University of New York Graduate Center and is the author of numerous books and articles on science education, urban education, and research.

*Joelle Tutula* is a teacher in the New Jersey public schools and a doctoral student at the City University of New York Graduate Center where she is interested in social studies education and anti-racist, anti-sexist education.

*Leila E. Villaverde* is Assistant Professor of Education at the University of North Carolina at Greensboro. Her research and publications involve anti-racist and anti-sexist education, whiteness studies, art education, and creativity and cognition.

*John Willinsky* is Pacific Press Professor of Education at the University of British Columbia. He is the Director of the Public Knowledge Project and has published extensively in the areas of language, literacy, and literature, anti-racism, postcolonialism, curriculum history and theory, and technology and education.

Photo: Joe Kincheloe (r) and Kenneth Tobin .

# INDEX

## A

absolute truth ............................. 100
accent ............. 40, 61, 302, 307, 308
  agogic ............. 301, 302, 307, 308
accountability ............................. 155
achievement gap.... 71-73, 75, 76, 78
acting white .................................. 34
action research 92, 93, 103, 157-159,
  163-166, 169, 173-177, 180, 183,
  187-190, 222, 230, 232, 459
activity .... 10, 24, 31, 38, 42, 80, 87,
  97, 98, 100, 104-106, 111, 112,
  131, 169, 180, 193, 214, 239, 240,
  250, 254, 260, 289, 291, 293, 294,
  296, 298, 306, 307, 320, 370, 421,
  428
  physical .... 4, 6, 7, 9, 66, 112, 114,
    180, 254, 261, 290-292, 296,
    297, 299-302, 306, 307, 309,
    316, 338, 350, 359, 360, 369,
    386, 405-414, 416-436, 459
  running ... 290, 291, 293, 298, 299,
    300, 307, 334, 388, 454
  swimming ....... 290, 293, 296, 298,
    305, 307
Adelman, Clem ........................... 174
adjacency pairs ........................... 242
adolescence ...... 347, 362, 366, 367,
  370, 376
aesthetic experience ............ 270, 271
affirmative presentism 326-329, 341
African American scholars .......... 320
agency .... 7, 8, 13, 23, 27, 28, 29, 34,
  40, 43, 44, 46, 49, 50, 54, 57, 71,
  78, 81, 93, 100, 103, 105, 158,
  159, 164, 165, 168, 171, 176, 177,
  184, 189, 190, 191, 193, 194, 195,
  202, 203, 206, 207, 229, 312, 318,
  321, 380, 442, 443, 444, 452

agency|structure ..................... 29, 44
agents of change .......................... 63
Akhtar, S. ........................... 193, 207
Alberts, Bruce .................... 442, 444
alethia ............................... 282, 284
alignment ............................ 51, 251
Alridge, Derrick ...... 191, 193, 207,
  320, 327, 328, 342
alternative rationality ................. 320
amplitude .............................. 24, 51
analytic memoranda ............... 30, 54
analytic philosophers .................. 144
anti-colonialism ......................... 171
Aquinas, Thomas ....................... 274
archeological genealogy . 93, 98, 106
archival manuscripts ................... 321
Arendt, Hannah .. 224, 231, 270, 275,
  285, 286
Aristotle ............. 143, 225, 291, 411
assent ................... 17, 18, 19, 20, 21
assimilate ................................. 100
audiencing ................................. 121
Austen, Jane .............................. 149
Australian Educational Researcher
  .............................................. 450
authenticity criteria ... 16, 27, 28, 38,
  55
authority ..... 62, 89, 96, 99, 114, 119,
  127, 130, 142, 160, 161, 162, 164,
  169, 174, 184, 226, 230, 303, 350,
  352, 356, 367, 379, 384, 386, 392,
  393, 397, 400, 443
auto/biography ............................. 16
auto/ethnography ............. 16, 26, 39
autobiography ...... 41, 43, 204, 213,
  221, 228
autonomy .. 18, 44, 48, 110, 175, 390

B

Baehr, Alan. ........................ 192, 207
behaviorism ................................ 337
Belmont Report ...................... 18, 56
beneficence ................................. 18
benefits... 3, 4, 8, 18, 23, 25, 68, 146,
    158, 171, 180, 214, 222, 226, 230,
    332, 340, 456
Berger, Peter ...... 117, 118, 132, 133,
    135, 136, 193, 207
Berry, Kathleen .. v, 6, 13, 87, 88, 89,
    98, 101, 102, 114, 120, 137, 323,
    327, 344, 458
Bersani, Leo ........ 354, 361, 367, 375
bifurcations ........................... 89, 97
Bildung ................ 281, 367, 371, 373
binarisms ................................... 104
Block, Alan ................................ 374
blurred genres.... 91, 92, 97, 103, 113
body movement ....... 24, 44, 51, 253,
    260, 262, 267
Bond, Horace Mann .................... 320
bricolage ..... 6, 13, 79, 83, 87, 88, 89,
    90, 93-95, 97-99, 101-114, 117,
    119, 120, 122, 124-128, 137, 221,
    323, 327, 329, 334, 338, 340, 343,
    344
bricoleur ...... 87, 90, 93, 94, 99, 101-
    108, 112, 119, 120, 125, 329
British Medical Journal .............. 448
Brownless, S. .............................. 455
Burke, Edmund ........................... 316
Bush, George W .. 332, 347, 368, 453

C

canonical knowledge ...................... 48
capitalism ... 114, 171, 172, 173, 175,
    189, 224, 318, 368, 370
Capitalism ................................. 231
Carr, E. H. ... 151, 155, 169, 174, 175,
    187
Caruth, Cathy ...... 379, 381, 393, 396
case studies ....... ii, 24, 183, 213, 221,
    272, 452

causal explanations .................... 240
causal relationships ..... 13, 200, 451,
    455
causality ............................... 11, 313
Cejpek, Lucas ............................. 373
Channel One .............................. 339
chaos and complexity ........... 89, 113
character ................................... 367
Chaudhry .................... 191, 195, 207
chronology .......... 312, 313, 386, 393
Clapp, Elsie Ripley ..... 150, 152, 153
class 4, 6, 7, 9, 15, 17, 19-22, 24, 25,
    28, 29, 30-32, 34, 36-38, 40, 41,
    43, 45, 50-53, 55, 56, 61, 62, 64,
    65-67, 69, 70, 73, 74, 78, 80, 90,
    97, 100, 101, 105, 107, 108, 110,
    111, 112, 114, 119, 120, 121, 125,
    126, 127, 132, 134, 135, 149, 152,
    158, 159, 164, 165, 166, 167, 168,
    171, 184, 186, 191, 193, 194, 196,
    197, 211, 212, 214, 216, 217, 219,
    222, 229, 252, 295, 319, 322, 324,
    325, 328, 330, 332, 335, 336, 337,
    342, 343, 350, 352, 361, 367, 370,
    371, 456, 459
clinical trials ...................... 440, 450
coding ..... 73, 74, 194, 200, 201, 202
Coetzee, J. M. ..................... 366, 375
cogenerative dialogues ... 19, 24, 32,
    39
cognitive abilities ......................... 11
coherence. 22, 25, 26, 27, 30, 32, 33,
    54, 55, 147, 151, 382, 383, 387
collectivity ................................. 235
Collins ... 43, 56, 136, 216, 218, 231,
    252
colonialism ................. 114, 231, 343
commitment... 31, 65, 159, 164, 173,
    174, 177, 191, 192, 193, 194, 195,
    196, 197, 198, 199, 200, 201, 202,
    203, 204, 205, 208, 214, 228, 250,
    289, 407, 447, 449
    theory .................................... 202
commodification .......................... 218
common sense ..... 98, 107, 109, 223,
    225, 226, 227, 239, 412, 430

complexity.. 4-11, 13, 63, 66, 78, 80, 81, 87, 88, 91, 95, 97, 100, 101, 102, 103, 105, 106, 108, 109, 111, 113, 114, 128, 129, 137, 168, 185, 220, 322, 323, 324, 326, 327, 330, 332, 333, 344, 356, 371, 374, 421, 422, 436

conceptual analysis .....................315

conceptual archaeology...............381

conceptual history ...............312, 344

conditional relevance .................242

consciousness...3, 5, 8, 71, 119, 127, 129, 135, 136, 170, 177, 224, 281, 290, 292, 294, 295, 296, 302, 305, 307, 312, 316, 319, 320, 321, 329, 408, 413, 421, 422, 424, 426, 427, 429, 430, 432, 434

   animate....................302, 307, 379

   kinaeshetic.......293, 299, 301, 304

consent .............17-22, 214, 257, 416

constraints ....60, 170, 172, 235, 266, 400

constructivism ....8, 13, 66, 187, 193, 271, 287

constructivist..8, 9, 68, 69, 123, 255, 313

content analysis...............ii, 119, 122

context . ii, 4, 5, 7-12, 15, 21, 38, 39, 42, 55, 59, 64, 70, 71, 72, 75, 76, 79, 80, 82, 87, 89, 105, 106, 109, 118-123, 126-135, 142, 144, 152, 154, 157, 163, 164, 167, 179, 181, 185, 186, 191, 196, 198, 199, 200, 201, 203, 205-207, 213, 215, 217, 218, 221-224, 229, 240, 260, 274, 277, 315, 316, 318-321, 324, 325, 327-329, 341-343, 346, 373, 383, 386, 427, 446, 447, 454

contextual embeddedness................7

contextual issues ........................222

contextualization ....10, 90, 105, 107, 120, 131, 346

contingent.......17, 97, 128, 215, 217, 218, 221, 222, 237, 240, 263, 315, 380, 381

contradictions   22-28, 30, 32-34, 39, 42, 44, 54, 55, 60, 100, 101, 102, 104, 111, 121, 129, 161, 164, 171, 172, 175, 187, 191, 192, 194, 202, 217, 231, 233, 276, 416, 417

conversation analysis......   235, 240, 241, 243, 253, 262, 264, 265, 266, 267

coordinate definitions .........416, 417

Corey, Stephen ...................173, 174

corporatization........................3, 229

coteaching. 17, 19, 29, 30, 38, 39, 42

coursework .................. 12, 68, 72, 75

credibility.............. 16, 184, 203, 455

credible voice................................69

crisis of representation. 92, 114, 380, 387, 394

critical bricoleurs ..........................89

critical consciousness .... 62, 71, 75, 77, 78, 134, 174, 311, 316

critical discourse.. 34, 106, 203, 224, 341

critical discourse analysis ...........106

critical epistemologies........211, 212

critical epistemology...................329

critical ethnography .. 16, 43, 44, 126

critical hermeneutics.... 79, 119, 125, 126, 131, 133-136

critical history.............................320

critical history of education ........320

critical interpretation........... 196, 314

critical meta-analysis ..................319

critical paradigm.................211, 212

critical pedagogy . 59, 134, 165, 182, 189, 451, 458, 459

critical reflection........................219

critical reflexivity ......................219

critical research.... 5, 7, 81, 119, 120, 130, 136, 169, 191

critical theorist...... 94, 122, 129, 408

critical theory...... 56, 77, 78, 79, 83, 120, 131, 137, 166, 169, 174, 175, 183, 184, 185, 188, 208, 211, 215, 232, 264, 318, 319, 320, 343

critical tradition ...... 4, 135, 169, 177

criticality ...... 77, 80, 113, 222, 226, 227, 318, 323
Cross .................................203, 207
Cuban, Larry ...... 154, 156, 229, 332, 334, 343
cultural misunderstandings.............11
cultural pedagogy........117, 119, 135
cultural pluralism .........................60
cultural production .26, 55, 129, 135, 164, 233
cultural reproduction .....................26
cultural studies ...ii, 4, 117, 118, 119, 131, 136, 140, 141, 152, 181, 228, 437, 459
culturally responsive teaching.60, 82
culture ..9, 11, 23, 26, 28, 30, 34, 40, 43, 51, 55, 57, 64, 67, 71, 82, 92, 95, 96, 103, 107, 110, 113, 114, 117-121, 123, 126, 128, 131-135, 137, 146, 152, 188, 189, 190, 194, 196, 202, 232, 233, 247, 256, 260, 283, 287, 288, 317, 318, 319, 336, 343, 344, 373, 375, 376, 377, 396, 397, 407, 429, 430, 442, 446, 447, 448, 450, 451, 453, 454, 456, 459
curriculum .....ii, 7, 8, 10, 40, 41, 61, 81, 104, 109, 119, 120, 128, 132-135, 139, 140, 155, 159, 165, 166, 167, 173, 174, 180, 181, 183-187, 224, 240, 266, 270, 287, 291, 309, 323, 327, 333, 338, 347, 348, 352, 353, 372, 374-376, 379, 397, 452, 458, 459, 460
cyberspace......................11, 12, 188

D

Daignault, Jacques .....................354
Dalton School.............................334
Darwin, Charles .................215, 387
data analysis ..........................30, 206
De Angelis, C..............440, 454, 455
De Lauretis, Teresa .....................360
Deakin University .....175, 187, 188, 189
decentering..................107, 108, 112

decontextualized ...... 5, 9, 10, 11, 92, 130, 324
decontextualized knowledge.........92
deferred action ... 380, 382, 393, 394, 395
deficit perspectives ... 10, 39, 75, 192
deictic .........................................253
democracy.... 60, 128, 134, 146, 148, 183, 187, 231, 319, 329, 330, 335, 336, 339-341, 347, 379, 436, 444, 447, 448, 449, 455, 456
democratic reconceptualization .... 63
Derrida, Jacques .... 6, 87, 152, 260, 265
Descartes, Rene ..... 5, 272, 274, 276, 280, 287, 424
descriptive observation .................91
deskilling practices .......................63
Dewey, John ...... 132, 144, 145, 150, 334, 443
dialectic .............. 119, 265, 322, 430
dialectical relationship..... 15, 171, 254
dialectically........... 28, 30, 55, 184
dialectics ................. 192, 200, 208
dialogue ...... 24, 59, 63, 65, 97, 115, 121, 124, 128, 159, 164, 165, 181, 182, 194, 226, 318, 324, 382, 383, 450
difficult knowledge.....379-383, 385, 387, 390, 392, 394, 395, 398
digital technologies................. 88, 95
discourse analysis ...... 24, 107, 213, 221, 228, 315, 346
discourse of possibility ...............319
discourses of emancipation...........88
discursive formation ...................217
disposition .. 175, 290, 292, 301, 311
dispositions....... 9, 43, 172, 219, 302
diversity . 62, 69, 88, 90, 94, 95, 100, 101, 120, 128, 179, 186, 203, 207, 216, 326, 340, 446
dominant ideology .............. 161, 172
domination. 118, 119, 127, 128, 134, 213, 351
Donne, John ...............................331

Drazen, J. M. ............................455
dualisms .................... 144, 216, 424
Duberley, J. .........................191, 208
DuBois, W.E. B. .204, 209, 318, 320
Dussell, Enrique .........................320

E

Early, Margaret ....61, 272, 350, 358,
    387, 455, 456
Edison Schools....................339, 342
Education Sciences Reform Act
    (2002)......................................451
educational psychology.......220, 329
Educational Researcher......155, 207,
    211, 227, 231, 233, 445, 456
educative authenticity ..................27
eidetic..................................106, 112
Eisenstein, Zillah R. ............203, 207
Eliade, Mircea.............279, 281, 287
Elkins, Stanley ....................364, 375
Elliot, John ..174, 175, 177, 179, 187
emancipation..... 131, 134, 135, 184,
    204
emancipatory....... 80, 136, 163, 165,
    170, 182, 184, 187, 204, 214, 220,
    320, 328, 340, 342
emancipatory practices................220
emergence theory 422-424, 427, 429
emotions
    emotion ..127, 252, 297, 300, 301,
        320, 369, 425, 427
    emotional....48, 66, 127, 133, 136,
        157, 183, 214, 250, 305, 317,
        349, 369, 382, 383, 384, 385,
        386, 392, 395
    emotional energy......................48
    emotional experience of
        knowledge...........................385
    emotional state .......................250
empathy..52, 63, 127, 177, 251, 323,
    399
empirical science....................6, 419
epistemic ....................141, 217, 456
epistemology ......4, 8, 9, 13, 97, 102,
    170, 176, 178, 192, 196, 208, 214,

215, 216, 217, 227, 232, 313, 430,
440, 441, 460
epistemological. 3-5, 8, 10, 23, 82,
    128, 133, 134, 152, 170, 177,
    185, 187, 193, 212, 214, 223,
    227, 230, 323, 324, 325, 340,
    341, 342, 346, 353, 367, 368,
    370, 393, 405, 430, 439-442,
    451
epistemological assumptions ... 10,
    170, 214, 324
equity ..... 15, 27, 59, 60, 61, 65, 103,
    109, 224, 317, 379
ERIC................... 445, 446, 450, 453
Erickson, Frederick............. 455, 456
essence..... 20, 71, 77, 133, 206, 302,
    307, 315
    essencing...... 294, 300, 301, 302,
        304, 307
essentialism............................... 203
essentializing ..................... 100, 228
ethics.......................................... 397
ethnocentrism ........................... 219
ethnography ....23-26, 35, 36, 39, 92,
    96, 98, 101, 114, 120, 121, 124,
    128, 136, 139, 152, 191, 194-196,
    199, 231, 287, 329, 396
    ethnographic research......... 29, 93
    ethnographic work .. 198, 219, 239
ethnomethodology ..... 241, 263, 265,
    266, 267
Eurocentrism.............................. 325
evaluation .. 8, 56, 99, 105, 117, 129,
    147, 160, 163, 173, 213, 400
evidence-based research ................ 7
exclusion.... 104, 146, 213, 215, 335,
    337, 374, 390
exercise...... 18, 101, 223, 290, 294,
    301, 303, 304, 306, 307, 308, 314
experience
    living.. 11, 76, 100, 106, 107, 121,
        129, 165, 191, 198, 206, 269,
        274, 277, 280, 282, 283, 286,
        289, 291, 292, 293, 297, 298,
        302, 306, 307, 311, 320, 326,
        333, 344, 373

reflection on .................... 191, 342
extraneous perturbations ................ 6

F

far-from-equilibrium conditions ... 89, 98
fecundity ..................................... 286
feedback looping ..................... 89, 97
feminism .. 59, 65, 93, 120, 126, 127, 128, 171, 174, 207, 341, 388
feminist research ...... 126, 127, 176, 193, 207
feminist theory ........................... 232
Feuer, Michael J. ................ 446, 456
Fine, Michelle ..................... 195, 208
Fink, Bruce ......................... 394, 396
Fishbane, M.D. .................... 196, 208
fitness ................. 290, 298, 305, 459
focus groups ... 92, 93, 162, 181, 182, 183
Ford Teaching Project ................ 174
Foucault, Michel .... 93, 99, 106, 152, 162, 187, 217, 223-226, 230-232, 359, 360, 363, 366, 367, 372, 373, 376, 377
Fox, S. ................. 275, 287, 450, 456
Frankfurt School ...... 122, 128, 131, 174, 311, 318, 346, 372
Franklin, V.P. ............................. 320
Freire, Paulo ....... 59, 65, 67, 83, 134, 137, 165, 174-176, 188, 219, 232, 320, 342
Freud, Sigmund .. 306, 372, 373, 380, 382-385, 389, 392, 394-396
Frizelle, F. A., ............................ 455

G

Gabriano, James ............................ 66
Gadamer, Hans-Georg ...... 132, 269, 270-275, 278, 279-288, 353
Ganesh, Tirupalavanam ............... 455
Gary Plan ................................... 333
Gee, James .......................... 455, 456

gender .... 4, 6, 7, 24, 25, 47, 65, 78, 90, 100, 105, 107, 114, 119, 126, 135, 152, 156, 164, 171, 173, 191, 193, 214, 216, 217, 219, 222, 228, 319, 321, 322, 324, 328, 330, 342, 355, 367, 368, 370, 371, 376, 396, 397, 459
genealogy ............ 221, 224, 228, 233
generalizability ............................. 16
generalize ................... 100, 222, 318
genre ... 100, 120, 125, 126, 137, 439
geographical place ................. 6, 119
gesture ..... 24, 52, 56, 237, 253, 254, 255, 266, 295, 296, 297, 301, 303, 304, 308
Gilligan, Carol ....................... 64, 83
Giroux, Henry .... 137, 162, 165, 187, 188, 213, 232, 317
Glaser, B. .................... 199, 206, 208
Goffman, Erving.    172, 188, 193, 208, 241
Google ...................................... 330
grain size ............................... 16, 54
Gramsci, Antonio ...... 140, 145, 155, 214, 223, 232, 330
Gresson, Aaron D.. v, 122, 137, 191, 193, 194, 196, 198, 202, 203, 206-208, 328, 343, 344, 458
grounded theory . 195, 196, 199, 201, 205, 206, 207, 208
Grumet, Madeleine ............. 372, 375
Gurin, Gerald ...................... 194, 208
Gutenberg, Johann ..................... 441
Guthrie, Robert V. .............. 192, 208

H

habitus ........................ 41, 42, 219
hand gestures ............................ 254
Hapsburg Empire ........ 348, 373, 374
Harding, Sandra . 213, 216, 217, 232, 340, 343
Hartsock, Nancy 171, 176, 178, 188, 213, 216, 232
Haug, C. ..................................... 455
Hegel, Georg .............. 153, 316, 430

hegemony...117, 140, 141, 142, 145, 149, 223, 225, 321, 330

Hegemony hegemonic......132, 140, 141, 184, 214, 321, 369

Helyar, Frances.....vi, 311, 329, 341, 458

Henry Oldenburg..........................440

hermeneutic phenomenology.........92

hermeneutics..v, 129, 130, 133, 135, 137, 269, 271, 272, 273, 274, 278, 280, 281, 282, 346

Herrnstein, Richard....334, 335, 343, 395, 396

Hickman, Hannah.......348, 369, 370, 372, 376

Himmelfarb, Gertrude.151, 152, 155

Hirsch, E.D..........330, 334, 335, 343

historical knowledge...152, 227, 382

historical moments90, 92, 93, 94, 97, 104, 327

historical research......60, 103, 139, 148, 150-152, 229, 317-327, 329, 333, 336, 340, 344

historiography....151, 152, 155, 221, 311-315, 317, 318, 319, 320, 322, 323, 324-326, 328, 330, 340, 341, 342, 346

Hocquenghem, Guy............355, 376

Hoey, J. ........................................455

holocaust..............................364, 376

homosexuality.....................110, 370

Horton, Myles...........59, 65, 83, 455

Hull, Gloria T......................193, 208

human subjects.............16, 18, 25, 56

Hurston, Zora Neale.....................204

Husserl, Edmund.........281, 287, 288

Hutchinson, S. A. ........193, 199, 208

hyperreality/hyperrationalism .. 5, 7, 8, 117, 123, 133, 327

hypertexting .................................89

I

iChat..................................33, 40, 56

ideology...... 4, 7, 10, 103, 117, 120, 121, 123, 125, 126, 127, 132, 133, 134, 159, 162, 164, 171, 172, 175-177, 183, 188, 192, 195, 203, 223, 224, 263, 311, 312, 314, 315, 319, 320, 321, 339, 340, 342, 346, 405, 408, 436

critique........................... 159, 164

imagination...... 135, 143, 145, 269, 272, 287, 290, 296, 316, 318, 322, 341, 388, 431

iMovie 32, 36, 44, 51, 123, 124, 262

inclusiveness............. 88, 90, 94, 100

index card notations.....................73

individual case ........................... 286

inequity.............................27, 34, 60

informed consent . 16, 18, 21, 22, 23, 25, 398, 440, 447

Institute of Education Sciences.. 442, 449, 451, 454, 455

institutional repository................ 442

Institutional Review Board (IRB). 16

intentionality.......................295, 303

interaction...... 6, 18, 24, 48, 49, 53, 118, 120, 121, 126, 132, 171, 177, 205, 213, 218, 239, 240, 241, 245, 247, 250, 253-257, 261, 263, 265, 301, 305, 306, 322, 328, 373, 433

interaction analysis .....................213

interconnectivity ......................... 101

interculturalism........................... 325

interdisciplinary studies.......... 91, 95

International Committee of Medical Journal Editors................ 440, 456

internet... 12, 41, 45, 95, 98, 99, 113, 441, 444, 448, 453, 456

interpretation.. 7, 35, 49, 80, 91, 101, 104, 106, 107, 120, 122-125, 129-133, 135-137, 150, 151, 160, 177, 182, 195, 198, 204, 206, 212, 218, 232, 238, 242, 244, 249, 261, 272, 280-282, 287, 289, 312, 314-317, 321, 323, 328, 335, 341, 346, 370, 381, 383, 386, 389, 395, 418, 430, 432, 433

interpretive bricolage...................98

interpretive research...... 22, 30, 176, 383

interracialism........................325, 341

intersubjective ....239, 242, 255, 392, 405, 428

interview ..19, 22, 33, 34, 35, 70, 91, 106, 110, 121, 144, 162, 167, 197, 198, 202, 205, 212, 239, 243, 250, 253, 263, 380, 386, 387, 389, 390, 391, 393, 398, 439

intuition. 70, 124, 143, 145, 389, 417

iPod .................................................29

iTalk ..................................................29

J

Jackson, James ...111, 170, 188, 194, 198, 200, 208, 295, 304, 308

John, A..vi, 120, 121, 125, 132, 137, 150, 174, 309, 331, 334, 396, 422, 435, 436, 439, 443, 455, 460

Johnson, P..174, 188, 191, 208, 271, 287, 308

Jones, Susan R. ...349, 376, 380, 397

Jonsson, Stefan....................370, 376

journal ...62, 70-72, 77, 80, 150, 167, 181, 182, 211, 227, 228, 265, 289, 296, 298, 299, 439-442, 445, 447, 450, 453-455

justice ..... 7, 18, 65, 78, 94, 113, 120, 129, 134, 157, 165, 169, 180, 183, 224, 273, 319, 324, 341, 358

K

Kant, Immanuel..292, 316, 411, 412, 420, 424-426, 428, 434, 437

Kanter, Rosabeth Moss ..... 194, 200, 208

Kemmis, Stephen ...... 159, 169, 171, 174, 175, 179, 181, 184, 187, 188, 189

Kincheloe, Joe L. ii, iii, v, vi, 3, 6, 8, 13, 27, 56, 62, 63, 78, 79, 82, 83, 88, 89, 93, 98, 100-102, 113, 114, 120, 127-135, 137, 159, 165, 173,

177, 188, 191, 198, 208, 215, 221, 222, 232, 233, 311, 315, 318, 319, 323, 335, 340, 343, 344, 345, 451, 454, 456, 458

Kitcher, Philip..................... 455, 456

knowledge....... vi, 93, 96, 115, 152, 215, 216, 265, 379, 388, 397, 398, 405, 406, 408, 412, 453, 455, 460

Knüfermann, Volker.................. 371

Kolata, Gina....................... 449, 456

Koselleck, Reinhart ... 312, 313, 314, 344

Kotzin, S. ................................... 455

Kramer, S........................... 193, 207

Kristeva, Julia.... 108, 383, 386, 387, 393, 396

Kuhn, Thomas ..... 89, 114, 319, 440, 456

L

Labaree, David ... 221, 233, 339, 344

Lacan, Jacques............ 353, 372, 377

Ladner, Joyce..... 191, 192, 195, 196, 203, 206, 208

Laine, C. ..................................... 455

language. 7, 25, 61, 87, 93, 114, 117, 122, 134, 144, 165, 174, 215, 218, 221, 226, 247, 256, 260, 269, 296, 297, 308, 311, 312, 314-316, 335, 337, 339, 342, 348, 351, 352, 353, 365, 372, 373, 380, 381, 385, 387, 396, 397, 407, 416-421, 427, 429, 436, 458, 460

Laplanche, Jean . 380, 382, 393, 394, 395, 396

Lather, Patti ... 27, 56, 155, 156, 176, 184, 188, 189, 204, 208, 380, 396

learning environments  15, 16, 17, 24, 26, 28, 40, 43, 44

Leben ......................................... 282

legitimization........................... 123

legitimized research..................... 99

Lethe ......................................... 285

Levis-Strauss, Claude .................. 87

Lewin, Kurt................ 173, 175, 189

liberal democracy ................ 146, 156
liberation ..... 65, 137, 170, 232, 320, 323
Liberty Bell ..... 330, 331, 334, 335, 337
liminal period ..................... 279, 288
listening.... 36, 49, 64, 247, 260, 261, 281, 358, 359
literal method of interpretation.... 123
literature review .. 75, 76, 89, 94, 109
local knowledge ......................... 218
Locke, John ......... 143, 146, 156, 411
Longino, Helen ................. 455, 456
Lorde, Audre ....... 194, 200, 202, 206
Luckmann, Thomas ............. 193, 207

M

Macedo, Donaldo ................ 232, 317
Malcolm X ................................. 204
Marchlup, Fritz ........................... 455
marginalization .... 96, 167, 177, 213, 373
   marginalized groups ...... 212, 216, 217
   marginalized individuals . 320, 324
   marginalized voices .................. 64
Marusic, A. ................................. 455
Marxism .............. 171, 265, 346, 397
masculine epistemologies ............ 216
mass culture ...................... 118, 137
Mattenklott, Gert ......................... 370
McCullough, W. .................. 194, 208
McLaren, Peter ... ii, v, 27, 56, 78, 83, 137, 157, 158, 159, 162, 164, 165, 169, 176, 177, 180, 182, 184, 188, 189, 191, 208, 215, 221, 232, 459
Mehra, B. ............................ 195, 208
member checking ..................... 32
mentor ...................................... 70, 205
Menzies, Charles R. ... 191, 195, 199, 208
Merchant, Betty M. ..... 193, 204, 207, 208
meta-analysis ....... 314, 343, 346, 448

metaphor .. 54, 55, 89, 102, 132, 195, 206, 215, 279, 298, 330, 331, 340, 354, 366, 371, 373, 381, 382, 386, 394, 410, 411, 414, 416, 418, 419, 427, 432
Mexican Americans ............ 146, 231
Milner, Marion .. 384, 385, 389, 390, 397
Morgan, Bill ....... 142, 213, 214, 231
Morland, Catherine ..................... 149
Morris, Marla ............. 153, 373, 376
Moss, Pam .................. 194, 455, 456
Mostern, Kenneth ............... 204, 209
Motley Crüe ............................... 331
multiculturalism .......... 137, 189, 323
multiliteracy ...................... 452, 455
multilogicality ................... 318, 340
multiperspectival ................... 8, 327
multiple theories ....... 90, 93, 98, 102
Murdoch University .... 158, 181, 190
Murray, Charles ......... 334, 335, 343
Musil, Robert ....... 347-355, 357-359, 361-377
Myers, Lena Wright .... 194, 203, 209

N

National Institute of Health ........ 449
National Research Council 154, 442, 443, 444, 445, 446, 447, 448, 450, 451, 452, 454, 456
native ................... 60, 146, 188, 208
Native Americans ....................... 146
Nazi Germany ............. 173, 349, 364
New England Journal of Medicine ...................................... 441, 456
New York Times Magazine 448, 455, 456
Newton, Isaac .... 102, 411, 439, 452, 456
Nietzsche, Friedrich ................... 373
No Child Left Behind 331, 332, 347, 443, 451, 455
Nussbaum, Martha ............. 145, 156

## O

ontology ..... 13, 26, 77, 97, 170, 171, 177, 214, 215, 314, 430, 431, 435, 436
   ontological..... 4, 5, 23, 26, 27, 42, 81, 134, 154, 187, 188, 193, 213, 276, 279, 323, 325, 340, 366, 370, 371, 381, 405, 414, 422, 428, 432, 433, 435
   ontological assumptions..........276
   ontological authenticity.23, 26, 27
   ontologies...................26, 157, 171
open access....... 442, 445, 446, 447, 449-456
operational definitions.................419
oppression ...... 8, 27, 126, 127, 135, 159, 164, 176, 177, 180, 187, 191, 192, 198, 201, 202, 204, 214, 224, 228, 318, 322, 324, 342
oral history ...................228, 325, 390
Overbeke. P. M. ...........................455
overlapping speech......49, 50, 52, 53

## P

paradigms...102, 187, 204, 212, 216, 218, 221, 231
Parkhurst, Helen...........................334
participant observation................196
part-whole dichotomies.................15
pathologize...........................100, 224
pedagogical
   attentiveness.............290, 298, 299
pedagogy....10, 59, 60, 77, 115, 117-120, 123, 131, 132, 136, 176, 188, 189, 190, 208, 231, 286, 288, 290, 294, 301, 304, 306, 307, 308, 309, 319, 320, 334, 341, 342, 343, 345, 368, 379, 393, 395, 396, 459
peer debriefing .............32, 33, 40, 42
peer-review .................440, 441, 444
Pena, Ezequiel.............................193
personal narratives ................59, 107
Peters, Frederick...83, 134, 137, 366-370, 372, 376

Pew Charitable Trusts................. 450
phenomenological
   essences .......................... 294, 307
   reflection...... 63, 65, 78, 168, 183, 191, 202, 213, 219, 233, 250, 277, 293, 295, 296, 300, 301, 313, 315, 342, 375, 380, 405, 413, 430
Piaget, Jean ......................... 272, 287
Pike, Purton ........ 347, 348, 349, 376
Pinderhughes, Elaine .......... 193, 195
Pini, Monica ...................... 339, 344
Pinkola-Estes, Clarissa ............... 284
pitch ..... 19, 51, 52, 53, 56, 237, 244, 247, 250, 251, 252, 261, 265, 267, 308
Plato.................... 143, 145, 156, 411
plurality ..... 88, 90, 94, 95, 100, 101, 103, 109, 183, 217
pointing.. 23, 52, 162, 236, 246, 248, 253, 255, 270, 274, 303, 371
positionality ... 4, 100, 101, 125, 169, 225, 227, 230, 319, 341
positivism .. 13, 78, 91, 94, 104, 107, 108, 112-114, 173, 177, 187, 188, 212, 214, 216, 220, 221, 411, 414, 415, 416, 417
post discourses.... 56, 87, 88, 89, 93, 94, 95, 98, 102, 113, 114, 120, 121, 123, 127, 130, 133, 134, 135, 136, 137, 151, 152, 155, 170, 188, 189, 213, 216, 217, 231, 315, 320, 323, 343, 344, 345, 379, 380, 396, 397, 408, 440, 460
Pott, Hans-Georg ........ 372, 373, 374
Potts, Diane................. 372, 455, 456
power. 3, 4, 6, 7, 8, 9, 11, 12, 34, 36, 62, 67, 68, 76, 77, 78, 80, 82, 93, 98, 102, 103, 105, 113, 114, 117, 119, 121, 126, 129, 134, 137, 141, 150, 151, 152, 153, 156, 161, 164, 165, 169, 172, 174, 176, 177, 178, 180, 183-189, 199, 211, 212, 214, 216, 218-228, 230-233, 257, 258, 263, 271, 279, 296, 298, 315, 317-324, 337, 339-342, 348, 349, 355,

356, 358, 360, 363, 369, 375, 379, 388, 396

power blocs ............................ 324

power relations ..... 9, 94, 134, 165, 176, 178, 211, 214, 216, 218, 228, 319, 321

PRAAT ... 24, 51, 261, 263, 265, 267

practices|schema ........................... 29

praxis ...... 6, 29, 42, 65, 92, 164, 170, 171, 178, 179, 187, 189, 208, 240, 241, 311, 317

progressive education .......... 152, 156

proof ................ 89, 94, 129, 313, 434

prosody ................ 247, 252, 262, 267

PubMed ...................... 449, 450, 455

## Q

quasi-experiments ........................ 15

QuickTime ................. 32, 36, 44, 51

## R

race ... 4, 7, 15, 25, 64, 65, 72, 78, 83, 90, 96, 100, 105, 107, 114, 119, 126, 135, 152, 170, 173, 192, 193, 200, 203, 206, 208, 214, 216, 217, 222, 319, 320, 322, 324, 330, 336, 342, 355, 396, 397, 458, 459

Rainie, L. .................................... 456

randomness ........................... 89, 97

rationalism 5, 6, 8, 10, 11, 89, 91, 94, 102, 108, 109, 112, 113, 114, 119, 133, 161, 172, 349, 372, 373, 385

realism 136, 157, 411, 414, 415, 416, 419, 437

reductionism ....... 4, 6, 10, 12, 15, 95, 109, 113, 114, 117, 324, 325, 328, 407, 410, 421-423, 425, 428, 429, 435

Reese, William ... 329, 330, 331, 336, 339, 344

reflection .. 63, 65, 78, 168, 183, 191, 202, 213, 219, 233, 250, 277, 293, 295, 296, 300, 301, 313, 315, 342, 375, 380, 405, 413, 430

reflexivity .. 151, 176, 183, 186, 191, 219, 314, 456

relationality. 106, 109, 111, 113, 300

repair .. 241, 243, 244, 246, 266, 333, 386, 398

representation 76, 176, 177, 185, 215, 220, 221, 230, 259, 312, 345, 370, 380, 381, 383, 394, 397, 433

repression ........................... 127, 371

resistance ..... 5, 35, 37, 93, 104, 128, 134, 158, 159, 164, 181, 182, 189, 190, 225, 226, 253, 312, 359, 362, 376, 380, 386, 387, 394, 396

right-wing religious conservatives ............................................. 327

rigor 13, 94, 105, 109, 123, 202, 214, 219, 220, 221, 323, 343, 452

Rilke, Rainer Marie ........... 271, 274

Rogowski, Christian .. 347, 370, 371, 372, 373, 375, 376

Rothe-Buddensieg, Margret ........ 371

Rousmaniere, Kate ............. 152, 156

Rousseau, Jean Jacques ..... 146, 156, 292

## S

Salinger, J.D. ............................. 347

sampling, methods of
theoretical sampling 196, 198, 201, 202, 206

Santayana, George ............. 149, 153

Sartre, Jean-Paul . 282, 288, 365, 376

schema ............................ 29, 30, 54

Schroeder, T. V. ......................... 455

scientific research in education .. 154, 442, 443, 446, 447, 454, 455

Scott, Bell Patricia ..... 151, 152, 155, 156, 193, 208, 374

Scott, Joan .. 151, 152, 155, 156, 193, 208, 374

secondary source ....................... 314

Sedgwick, Eve Kosofsky .... 358, 395

Seeman, Melvin ................. 201, 209

self-organization .................... 89, 98

semantic realism ................ 416, 417

semiotics ...... 93, 101, 119, 122, 126, 128, 221, 228, 327, 329, 346

sex .. 23, 46, 212, 232, 350, 353, 354, 355, 356, 358, 359, 362, 363, 374, 376

sexual ...... 6, 23, 215, 217, 297, 322, 324, 349, 352-355, 357, 359, 360, 362, 363, 365, 367-372, 374, 375, 392, 395, 396

Shavelson, Richard J.. 442-444, 446, 450-452, 454-456

Simpsons, The .............................. 145

situated action ............................. 240

situatedness ......................... 169, 318

situating ............... 107, 108, 132, 133

Smith, Barbara ...... vi, 99, 113, 115, 128, 137, 155, 156, 174, 190, 193, 208, 219, 232, 233, 264, 266, 272, 273, 288, 289, 291, 294, 297, 306, 308, 309, 336, 345, 395, 396, 437, 459

social change ...... 83, 159, 169, 170, 171, 177, 190, 214, 231, 311, 314, 315, 319, 346

social justice ... 59, 60, 82, 88, 90, 94, 100-103, 105, 109, 157, 159, 164, 169, 180, 181, 188, 232, 339, 379, 458

social life ...... 15, 26, 44, 54, 55, 169, 172, 235, 238, 264, 354, 419

social organization .............. 235, 240

social relations ... 159, 169, 173, 177, 235, 240, 260, 263, 381

social reproduction ................ 31, 175

social structure ... 214, 217, 235, 240, 241, 244, 260, 311, 360, 371

social theory ..... 8, 78, 128, 132, 170, 182, 321, 458

sociocultural theory ..... 15, 16, 42, 43

sociology ..... 57, 114, 188, 191, 196, 266

solidarity ...... 52, 53, 170, 225, 233, 251, 325, 349, 360, 364, 365

South Park .................................... 145

Southern Illinois University ...... 150, 153

Sox, H. C. .................................... 455

speech intensity .......... 247, 251, 265

spontaneity .............................. 89, 97

standpoint theory ................ 216, 217

Steinberg, Shirley ...... v, 7, 8, 13, 93, 117, 127, 131, 137, 221, 222, 233, 315, 335, 344, 345, 451, 456, 459

Steiner, George ........... 381, 382, 397

Stenhouse, Lawrence ................. 174

Stewart, James .................... 195, 209

Stokes, Mason ..................... 355, 376

Stopp, Elizabeth ......................... 371

Strauss, Anselm ...... 6, 88, 114, 119, 137, 199, 206, 208

structure ... 27, 29, 35, 43, 49, 50, 52, 57, 89, 95, 98, 102, 114, 127, 145, 147, 162, 169, 177, 181, 184, 216, 223, 237, 238, 240, 248, 249, 263, 298, 306, 314, 322, 335, 343, 357, 360, 369, 371, 372, 374, 386, 387, 405, 413, 435

structural history ..................... 312

student researchers.... 33, 34, 35, 36, 37, 38, 39, 52

Suber, Peter ......................... 449, 456

subjective ... 7, 91, 93, 107, 109, 128, 135, 137, 150, 151, 177, 193, 198, 200, 203, 206, 225, 271, 274, 276, 281, 282, 301, 314, 319, 322, 323, 326, 348, 368, 370, 386, 392, 422, 423, 424, 425, 426, 427, 428, 429, 430, 434

subjugation 126, 214, 223, 355, 356, 357, 363, 375

subordination ...................... 213, 225

symbolization .... 132, 349, 380, 382, 383, 384, 385, 392, 393, 394

synchrony ................. 24, 46, 49, 290

T

Taubman, Peter .. 294, 309, 347, 374, 377

teacher research .. 24, 34, 63, 70, 187

Teachers College Record ... 436, 445, 454

technology...... 12, 30, 112, 139, 140, 153, 172, 188, 223, 241, 262, 332, 339, 455, 460

teleology......................................313

temporal issues...219, 247, 249, 253, 302, 307, 312, 313, 315, 327, 352, 413, 423, 425

theoretical bricolage...... 94, 98, 101, 108

theoretical framework .... 32, 43, 54, 55, 59, 66, 75, 77, 79, 128, 151, 195, 317, 390, 391

theoretical tools...............................8

thick description.......42, 54, 55, 130, 218, 315

thin coherence..............26, 30, 54, 55

think aloud ...............................250

Thomson, Pat ......................157, 190

Thorndike, Edward..............335, 337

Tobin, Kenneth .... ii, iii, v, 3, 19, 21, 33, 44, 56, 57, 240, 266, 454, 460

totalizing frameworks ..................89

Towne, Lisa ..... 442-444, 446, 450-452, 454-456

transcription conventions .....56, 236, 259

transdisciplinary................4, 61, 184

transference...... 380, 382, 383, 384, 385, 394, 395, 396

triangulation ...............162, 163, 182

triple quandary .......................43, 56

Tripp, David....... 160-163, 165, 181, 183, 190

truth......4, 8, 47, 100, 103, 114, 127, 133, 150, 155, 170, 215, 216, 217, 226, 229, 230, 269, 271, 278, 280, 282, 283, 285, 286, 319, 324, 346, 389, 456

Turner, David..............279, 288, 371

U

unconscious..26, 219, 373, 380, 383, 388, 394

underachievement  69, 71-73, 75-81

Union of Concerned Scientists....455

universalize........................ 100, 318

University of Tennessee ..... 142, 459

urban education ... 33, 39, 41, 59, 66, 69, 78, 460

utterance ..... 49, 56, 242, 244, 246, 247, 248, 250, 254, 264

V

validity..... 9, 56, 132, 147, 148, 154, 164, 183, 184, 188, 191, 220, 222, 223, 226, 230, 346, 412, 414, 420, 423, 429, 455

Van Der Weyden, M. B............. 455

Vico, Giambattista.............. 272, 279

Villaverde, Leila... vi, 311, 316, 345, 460

Vogl, Joseph ...................... 372, 373

Voltaire...................................... 149

von Ranke, Leopold................... 150

W

Walker, Alice..... 194, 200, 206, 455, 456

Walker, V. .. 194, 200, 206, 455, 456

Washington, Mary Helen..... 56, 194, 200, 206, 332, 456

ways of seeing the world . 3, 97, 128, 328

Wehler, Hans-Ulrich.................. 311

What Works Clearinghouse..... 451, 455

White, Hayden..... 56, 100, 137, 189, 191, 193, 196, 197, 198, 200, 203, 204, 315, 316, 317, 344, 345, 370

Whitehead, Albert North ............ 275

Whittle, Christopher ... 339, 342, 345

Willinsky, J... vi, 439, 451, 452, 454, 455, 456, 457, 460

Willis, Arlette Ingram 193, 204, 207, 208

Woodson, Carter........................ 320

## Z

Zeitgeist...........................3, 326, 346

Zinn, Howard.............................. 149
zooming.................................. 18, 55

Printed in the United States
101420LV00001B/60/A